'The Greatest Squadron
of Them All'

'The Greatest Squadron of Them All'

The Definitive History of
603 (City of Edinburgh) Squadron,
RAauxAF

David Ross
Bruce Blanche & Bill Simpson

Volume I
Formation to the end of 1940

GRUB STREET · LONDON

Published by
Grub Street
The Basement
10 Chivalry Road
London SW11 1HT

British Library Cataloguing in Publication Data
The greatest squadron of them all: the definitive history of 603
 (City of Edinburgh) Squadron, RauxAF
 Vol. 1: formation to 1940
 1. Great Britain. Royal Auxiliary Air Force. Squadron, 603 – History
 2. Bombers – Great Britain – History 3. Fighter planes – Great Britain –
 History 4. World War, 1939-1945 – Aerial operations, British.
 I. Ross, David (David M. S.), 1958– II. Blanche, J. Bruce
 III. Simpson, William
 358.4'00941

ISBN 1 904010 49 0

Typeset by Pearl Graphics, Hemel Hempstead

Printed and bound in Great Britain by
Biddles Ltd, Guildford and King's Lynn

Editor's Note
**The material appearing in this book which has been quoted from letters,
reports, communications and the like has been deliberately left in the style of the
original to preserve their authenticity.**

CONTENTS

Acknowledgements   vii

Foreword   Lord Selkirk of Douglas, Air Commodore Lord   ix
James Douglas-Hamilton. Honorary Air Commodore
No.603 (City of Edinburgh) Squadron RAuxAF

Preface   Wing Commander Alasdair Beaton, Officer   xi
Commanding No.603 (City of Edinburgh) Squadron

Introduction   xiii

Equivalent Ranks   xv

Chapter 1   Formation and the Early Years   1
Chapter 2   From Bomber to Fighter Squadron   16
Chapter 3   To War with Spitfires!   43
Chapter 4   'First Blood the Auxiliaries'   55
Chapter 5   Early Encounters/The Phoney War   93
Chapter 6   The Battle of Britain   136
Chapter 7   The Squadron's First Battle of Britain Casualty   166
Chapter 8   Out of the Flying Pan…. South to 11 Group   174
Chapter 9   'Gin Ye Daur'   184
Chapter 10   Success… but at a Price   205
Chapter 11   Battle of Britain Day   251
Chapter 12   The Many and the Few   256
Chapter 13   After the Battle   293
Chapter 14   Back to Scotland   303

Appendices

1.   The Conception of the Auxiliary Air Force   308
2.   Air Force List for August 1938   311
3.   Nominal Roll of Officers 3 September 1939   312
4.   Nominal Roll 3 September 1939   313

5.	Squadron Badge	315
6.	Honours and Awards	316
7.	Roll of Honour	317
8.	603 Squadron Chronology	318
9.	The Esher Trophy	318
10.	DFC, *London Gazette* Entries	319
11.	Honorary Air Commodores	320
12.	Commanding Officers	321
13.	Squadron Bases	322
14.	Summer Camps	322
15.	Markings and Codes	323
16.	Aircraft Flown 1925-41	323
17.	Gifted Spitfires	332
18.	Battle of Britain Survivor	333
19.	AuxAF in the Battle of Britain	335
20.	Ground Crew Movements	336
21.	Selected Pen-portraits of Commanding Officers	337
22.	Combat Claims During the Battle of Britain	342
23.	Life After 603	344
24.	The Saga of Rusty's Grave	357
25.	The Mystery of the Third Ju88 Lost on 16 October 1939	362
26.	The 603 Battle of Britain Class *603 Squadron* Locomotive	364
27.	Battle of Britain Class Locomotives	366
28.	Readiness at Dawn	366
29.	The Edinburgh RAFVR Centre	368
30.	Dowding and Gun Harmonisation	372
Notes		373
Maps		375
Bibliography		377
Index		379

ACKNOWLEDGEMENTS

A work of this size has taken many years to produce and we are indebted to a great many people for their commitment to helping us. In addition to the RAF and Squadron records, flying log books, personal diaries and letters, first-hand anecdote and testimony have been put at our disposal as well as selected photographs from a unique accumulation of over 1,000 from the authors' collections/603 archive. The faith, support and trust of many Squadron veterans and their families, as well as the family members of those who did not survive, has also been a major factor. Their input has been vital and we therefore hope they share our pleasure at seeing this work come to fruition. The history of 603 Squadron is on-going and therefore we look forward to hearing from anyone with information for the 603 archive.

The authors would like to express their gratitude to the following and apologise in advance to anyone who may have inadvertently been omitted:

Lord Selkirk of Douglas, Honorary Air Commodore, 603 Squadron, for his unceasing support of this project and his own expertise on the history of the Edinburgh Squadron.

Mr C.J. Burnett (ret), Allan Carswell and Edith Philip of the National War Museum of Scotland, Edinburgh Castle, for access to Squadron historic documents; Dr Ann Matheson, Keeper and Mrs Hegarty, National Library of Scotland; Mr Peter J.V. Elliott, Senior Keeper, Joanne Ratcliffe and Anna McIlwaine of the Department of Research/Information Services, Royal Air Force Museum, Hendon; Mike Hatch, Alan Thomas, Russell Smith, Susan Dickinson and Flight Lieutenant Mary Hudson at Air Historical Branch (AHB), RAF; staff at the Public Records Office (PRO) at Kew; staff at the Imperial War Museum Library; the Commonwealth War Graves Commission, Maidenhead; Mr George West (researcher) *Scotsman,* (*Edinburgh Evening News*, Bulletin 1925-57); *Kent Messenger*, Robert Vacha of the *Edinburgh Evening Despatch*; Adam Smith, Dawn Kemp and Colin Hendry at the Museum of Flight, East Fortune; Geoff Nutkins and the Shoreham Aircraft Museum; researchers, Martin Cutler, Andrew Davies, Patricia Hammond, Jean Liddicoat, Ted McManus, 'Pat' Patterson, Lynne Robinson, Ted Sergison, Colin Stevens, Barney Travers, Dr Mark Whitnall, Muriel 'Pop' Wilde and Colin and Rose Smith of Vector Fine Art.

The 603 Veterans
The late: AVM J. Berry; Air Commodore Ronald Berry OBE, DSO, DFC and Bar; Flight Lieutenant Bill Caister DFM; Group Captain George Denholm DFC, AE; Air Commodore George Gilroy DSO, DFC and Bar, DFC (US), AE; Group Captain Ivone Kirkpatrick; D.M.T Macdonald CB; Air Commodore Brian Macnamara CBE, DSO; Flight Lieutenant Bill Read AFC; Squadron Leader Jack Stokoe DFC; Sir Hugh Walmsley; Flight Lieutenant Keith Lawrence DFC; Group Captain Barrington Mason; Squadron Leader Graham Hunter; Flight Lieutenant Ludwik Martel; Squadron Leader B.G. Stapleton DFC, DFC (Dutch); Air Commodore Sir Archie Winskill KCVO, CBE, DFC*, RAF (Ret'd); and Wing Commander Geoffrey T. Wynne-Powell DFC, AE.

The late Chairman, John Mackenzie, members and non-members of the 603 (City of Edinburgh) Squadron Association, in particular: S. Archer (via D. Archer), E.P. Belford, James Bell BEM, C.D.P. Black, Duncan Brown, Arthur Carroll, Charles Cessford, Reg Cockell, W.G. Darling, T.F. Dickson, A. Deas, Charles Dorward, A. Duff, Cecil Gibson, Joseph Hunter, John Inkster, D.K. Kelly, George Knox, the late S. Liddle, Alec Mackenzie, W. Marr, J. Marshall, I. Miller, George Mullay Jnr, Robin Murray-Philipson, the late Jim Newhall, P. Oliver, Bertie Pringle, the late Philip

Reilly, John Rendall, Jim Renwick, W. Ritchie, J.M. Robertson, Harry J. Ross, Jim Skinner, Bill Smith, James Somerville, H. Spencer, Moray Wallace, Bob Wilson, Willie H. Young, and R.B. Young.

Jean Blades (neé Waterston), Desmond W. Carbury, Jean Cunningham, Lyn Deans, Betty and Paul Denholm, P. Gilroy, Patricia Hirst, Margaret Iggulden, Joan Merton-Jones (neé Palmer), the late Mardi Morton, Roderick Morton, Molly Ritchie, Wendy Roberts, Caroline Stanley, Bill Strawson, and Mary Wale.

Squadron Leader Peter Brown AFC, RAF (Ret'd); Squadron Leader Paul Day OBE, AFC, RAF, Officer Commanding, Battle of Britain Memorial Flight; Group Captain Bob Kemp QVRM, AE, ADC, FRIN, Inspector RAuxAF; Helmut Rau; Malcolm Smith Hon. Sec. of the Battle of Britain Fighter Association; and Wing Commander John Young AFC, RAF (Ret'd), Official Historian for the Battle of Britain Fighter Association.

Members of 603 (City of Edinburgh) Squadron, RAuxAF, 2003, including: Wing Commander Alasdair Beaton, Officer Commanding 603 Squadron; Squadron Leaders Barry Greenhalgh and Derek Morrison RAuxAF; Flight Lieutenants Graeme Lyall AE and Barbara Murray AE RAuxAF and Flight Lieutenant Rachel Newton RAF.

The historians: Henry Boot, M.J.F. Bower, Chaz Bowyer, Henry Buckton, John Coleman, Ken Delve, Jack Foreman, Norman Franks, Chris Goss, Peter Green, James J Halley OBE, Mike Hooks, Leslie Hunt MBE, AE; Andrew Jeffrey, The Rev J.D.R. Rawlings, Bruce Robertson, Andy Saunders, Chris Shores, Richard C. Smith, and Squadron Leader Andy Thomas.

Squadron Leader Bruce Blanche would like sincerely to thank Wing Commander A.E. Ross DFC, AE, for his support and assistance in contributing to the history of this prestigious Edinburgh Squadron, particularly for his permission to have full access to and to quote freely from his history 'The Queen's Squadron' published privately in 1989.

John Davies, Anne Dolamore, Louise King and Luke Norsworthy at Grub Street Publishing for your support and hard work.

Finally to our families who tolerate us. For your love and support: Squadron Leader Cliff Ross RAF (Ret'd), Maureen Ross, Kerry and George Cathro, Alison Bellew; Jean Blanche and Marion Simpson.

Photographic acknowledgements
Photographs in this book collected over many years belong to David Ross and Bruce Blanche with due acknowledgement to the many kind contributors, including: Air Commodore Rt. Hon. Lord Selkirk of Douglas QC, MA, MSP; Air Commodore Hugh Chater DFC, John Coleman, Martin Cutler, Andrew Davies, Lyn Deans, Betty Denholm, Patricia Hirst, Margaret Iggulden, J.A.C. Kirke, George Knox, Flight Lieutenant Keith Lawrence DFC, the late Mardi Morton and the Morton family, and John Rendall, B. Richardson, Wendy Roberts, Andy Saunders, Mrs M. Simpson, Squadron Leader B.G. Stapleton DFC, DFC (Dutch), Bill Strawson, Mark Whitnall, and numerous members of 603 Squadron Association.

Maps were provided by David Martin and Kerry Cathro.

FOREWORD

No.603 (City of Edinburgh) Squadron chose as its motto the Doric words 'Gin ye Daur', or 'If you dare'. Anyone who joined the Squadron did so in the knowledge that he might have to face immense challenges and 603 pilots were involved from the very outset in the first enemy action over British soil of the Second World War on 16 October 1939 when Luftwaffe bombers attempted to bomb naval units in the Firth of Forth. Also in action with 603 Squadron were 602 (City of Glasgow) Squadron, and each unit shot an enemy bomber into the sea as part of the same action.

On 28 October, 603 and 602 Squadrons were again tested, shooting down the first enemy bomber onto British soil in the Lammermuirs, but the greatest threat of all would come in the Battle of Britain.

The fortunes of war propelled 603 into the very eye of the storm. Sent to Hornchurch in South East London, the pilots were hopelessly outnumbered in confronting the massed bombing formations of the Luftwaffe, accompanied by huge numbers of fighter aircraft.

603 sustained heavy losses in the unrelenting duel high up in the sky, but after each casualty another volunteer came forward, and their morale held. By the end of the Battle of Britain they had emerged as the top scoring squadron in the whole of the Royal Air Force and Auxiliary Air Force.

Their actions and those of all fighter pilots were immortalised by the wonderful writing in his book *The Last Enemy* by Richard Hillary, a young 603 pilot, who after a number of successful battles had sustained terrible burns in the Battle of Britain. He conveyed the message that under the shining gleam of medals lies a shadow. Accompanying the courage and heroism, there is also the suffering and sacrifice.

It was not the only great battle or campaign in which 603 would be involved. Throughout the war their pilots were in the thick of the fighting. Indeed on 10 May 1942, 603, along with other squadrons, won a decisive victory over the Luftwaffe in the air battle for Malta. The victory that day represented the turning point in the struggle for the Mediterranean, North Africa and the Middle East.

So, who were the young men of valour who had joined 603 Squadron? Group Captain Cecil Bouchier, Officer Commanding RAF Hornchurch during the Battle of Britain wrote:

> 603 was composed of a collection of quiet and serious young men; men from the city desks of Edinburgh and the fields of the Lothians, led by one whose quiet personality wrapped his Squadron round as with a cloak and made of them by his concern for them and by his leadership example a great and valiant Squadron.

Today 603 is made up of young women as well as young men, and with the onward march of technology they now have much greater technical expertise. Even so the qualities of fortitude, determination, dedication and professionalism which had been shown by their predecessors are every bit as evident today.

At all times both in the past and in the present 603 (City of Edinburgh) Squadron has retained the closest links with the people of Edinburgh and Scotland. They are entitled to be deeply thankful to those who have served and are serving their country so well.

The authors have made a very significant contribution to the history of the Royal Air Force and the Royal Auxiliary Air Force by telling the fascinating, colourful and heroic story of what came to be known as the 'Queen's Squadron'.

Signed

James Douglas-Hamilton
Lord Selkirk of Douglas

Her Majesty The Queen has been graciously pleased to accept the title of Honorary Air Commodore of 603 (City of Edinburgh) Squadron, Royal Auxiliary Air Force to be effective from 11 December 2000.

NB: Noting Lord Selkirk's unique and important family associations with 603 Squadron, and his most distinguished, effective and loyal performance as Honorary Air Commodore of both 2 (City of Edinburgh) Maritime Headquarters Unit and 603 (City of Edinburgh) Squadron, Her Majesty expressed her wish that Lord Selkirk continue to act as Honorary Air Commodore on her behalf. Thus 603 (City of Edinburgh) Squadron has the unique distinction of having Her Majesty Queen Elizabeth II as its Honorary Air Commodore with Lord Selkirk of Douglas representing her on a day-to-day basis.

PREFACE

On 10th March 2000, it was with deep pride as an Edinburgh boy that I was privileged to lead 603 back again, along Princes Street, on our Squadron's Reformation Parade. We marched, exactly on the 43rd anniversary of 603's post World War Two disbandment. Service and civilian dignitaries, current and former members of the Squadron, families and citizens and visitors to Edinburgh proudly witnessed the march-past as Air Chief Marshal Sir Peter Squire, C-in-C RAF Strike Command and Mrs Marion Morton, Deputy Lord Provost of the City of Edinburgh, jointly took the salute. Overhead formations of Nimrod and Tornados from Scotland's RAF stations flew past, in what was a very deep mark of respect and affection for the return of Edinburgh's own and most famous Royal Auxiliary Air Force Squadron.

Our nation's traditions in peace and war over the last 75 years have been epitomised by the young men and women of the Royal Auxiliary Air Force, and in particular those who served as volunteer members of 603 (City of Edinburgh) Squadron, since the formation in 1925 at RAF Turnhouse to disbandment on 10 March 1957.

In the early years of our history, 603 was directly involved in flying the aircraft of the day. Their expertise, valour and sacrifices are legendary and are now recorded in history together with the names of the many who paid most dearly with their lives. In war they earned the greatest accolade any squadron could achieve within the Royal Air Force – the highest praise and respect of their service chiefs together with that of their fellow airmen. In today's RAF and now looking towards the future, the development and complexity of modern fighting aircraft has required the auxiliary to focus his or her voluntary assistance through ground operational and defensive support roles, leaving the actual operational flying to today's generation of highly skilled young men and women.

But the spirit that grows from being a member of a squadron, in either the Royal Air Force or the Royal Auxiliary Air Force, builds a strength, camaraderie and sense of fun and belonging from which the tackling of any task, however serious, becomes achievable. 603 always had such a spirit. It was very much a 'can-do' squadron as most volunteer organisations are and certainly will be again in the future.

And so, in recommending to Her Majesty Queen Elizabeth II that today's Auxiliaries of Edinburgh and throughout Scotland be given the reformed title of 603 (City of Edinburgh) Squadron, Royal Auxiliary Air Force, the Air Force Board of the Royal Air Force not only acknowledged 603's most vital contribution to our nation's past, they also made preparations for our new operational future. They gave today's Auxiliaries of Auld Reekie a squadron spirit, and a most honourable foundation upon which to build a new operational future to meet the diverse needs of a modern expeditionary Royal Air Force.

If you were or are a Squadron member, your journey towards the later pages of these volumes will, I hope, bring back fond memories. Alternatively, if you have no previous links with Edinburgh's Auxiliaries, then I am sure that you will find in your reading, the substance from which RAF tradition and respect for such a fine spirit and reputation was born. In discovering or renewing your interest in the story of 603, enjoy stepping back into military aviation history and in so doing acknowledge the humble bravery of the men in wartime, both pilots and ground crews, whose contributions and sacrifices built the foundations for the deep pride and gratitude which is the new 603's inheritance.

Edinburgh's own Royal Auxiliary Air Force Squadron, 603, is back home again.

Gin Ye Daur

Signed

Alasdair J. Beaton

INTRODUCTION

The authors would like to point out that the title for this book was taken from a quote by Air Commodore Cecil 'Boy' Bouchier CBE, DFC, who, as a Group Captain, commanded RAF Hornchurch from December 1939 until December 1940, during the entire Battle of Britain. It is in no way an attempt to place 603 Squadron any higher in the reckoning than other squadrons. Air Commodore Bouchier's initial assessment of the men of 603 when they arrived at his station followed later by a review of those first impressions appear in this book. His quote is as follows:

> ...As I write, memories come crowding in upon me, and from their store I give you this of 603. They were, I think, the greatest Squadron of them all.

* * *

On 14 October 1925, 603 (City of Edinburgh) Bomber Squadron, Auxiliary Air Force, was formed, so beginning a long and unbroken 78-year link of the Royal Auxiliary Air Force with the city and people of Edinburgh – an association which continues to this day.

The Squadron served with distinction for 32 years before, during and after World War Two, claiming the first enemy aircraft shot down over British soil and the honour of highest scoring squadron in the Battle of Britain. As 603 Squadron is best known for the part it played in the Battle of Britain, a day-by-day account of its time with 11 Group is included in this book with the story of the pilots and ground crew embellished by letters and diary extracts passed on to us by families and colleagues. Whilst researching the deaths of the 603 pilots one cannot but marvel at their courage. Although there were those who lived to appreciate the time given to them, their colleagues may have suffered instantaneous death by gun or cannon fire or a long slow, painful demise alone with nobody bearing witness to their torrid last few moments on earth. Such stories feature in this history and help us to understand the men's commitment and sacrifice. It is with them in mind that this book was written. In the words of Joseph Conrad:

> A man who is good enough to shed his blood for his country is good enough to be given a square deal afterwards. More than that no man is entitled to, and less than that no man shall have.

However, the events which occurred in the skies over southern England during the summer of 1940 form just part of the Squadron's history. By the end of 1940 the pilots believed the battle had been won but the war had not and great success continued to be achieved in other theatres both home and abroad featuring many more fine pilots and leaders who wore the mantle of those who had served and fallen before them. Flying 15 different types of aircraft and taking part in eight separate campaigns during the Second World War, the Squadron was disbanded on 10 March 1957, back at the airfield where it had been originally formed, Edinburgh's RAF Turnhouse. Two years later on 1 November 1959, 3603 (City of Edinburgh) Fighter Control Unit (FCU), RAuxAF, a unit which had been set up in 1948 to support 603 Squadron, was also disbanded. On the same day, however, 2 (City of Edinburgh) Maritime Headquarters Unit (MHU), RAuxAF was formed – initially manned by the men and women of the former 3603 FCU. The auxiliaries of 2 MHU thus began a period of

Maritime Operational Support to the RAF – a role which it continued for nearly 40 years.

On 1 October 1999, 2 MHU was re-roled to take on the primary task of Survive to Operate (STO) or Force Protection with the additional role of Mission Support continuing its maritime links, directly in support of RAF Kinloss. With the new re-roling also came the award and return of the prestigious 603 (City of Edinburgh) Squadron, RAuxAF number plate.

Today, the members of 603 Squadron are justifiably proud of their heritage and in the 603 Headquarters, practically unchanged since its acquisition in 1926, they rub shoulders with the ghosts of the previous generations who served the unit so proudly. Their spirit is all pervading.

David Ross, Bruce Blanche, Bill Simpson.
January 2003

This History is dedicated to all members of 603
(City of Edinburgh) Squadron, Royal Auxiliary Air Force,
who gave their lives in peace and war.

EQUIVALENT RANKS

Royal Air Force/Luftwaffe
(With style of abbreviation used in this book in brackets)

Marshal of the Royal Air Force	*Generalfeldmarschall*
Air Chief Marshal (ACM)	*Generaloberst*
Air Marshal (AM)	*General*
Air Vice-Marshal (AVM)	*Generalleutnant*
Air Commodore (AC)	*Generalmajor*
Group Captain (G/C)	*Oberst*
Wing Commander (W/C)	*Oberstleutnant*
Squadron Leader (S/L)	*Major*
Flight Lieutenant (F/L)	*Hauptmann*
Flying Officer (F/O)	*Oberleutnant*
Pilot Officer (P/O)	*Leutnant*
Warrant Officer (W/O)	*Stabsfeldwebel*
Flight Sergeant (F/Sgt)	*Oberfeldwebel*
Sergeant (Sgt)	*Feldwebel*
Corporal (Cpl)	*Unteroffizier*
Leading Aircraftman (LAC)	*Obergefreiter*
Aircraftman First Class (AC1)	*Gefreiter*
Aircraftman Second Class (AC2)	*Flieger*

Although the official style for abbreviating RAF ranks had changed by the reformation of 603 in 1999 (ie: Plt Off) the 'old style' (ie: P/O) has been retained throughout both volumes to maintain continuity.

Times
In this book, many of the accounts of actions and events which took place in the UK during the Second World War are based on official documents such as Squadron and Station Operations Record Books (ORBs), Combat Reports, aircrew log books etc. It is worth noting that during the war, Britain operated a system of British Summer Time (BST) and British Double Summer Time (BDST). BST was one hour ahead of Greenwich Mean Time (GMT) and BDST was two hours ahead of GMT. This was to make best use of the hours of daylight. No clear instructions were given to those who compiled the official records as to which regime was to be used and so there is always doubt as to whether times quoted are GMT or one of the British summer times. (Navigators' logs, however, tended to use GMT.) It is generally accepted that times quoted in the ORBs etc were 'local' time – i.e. either BST or BDST – not GMT. Similarly, the Germans and Italians used Central European Time (CET), which was one hour ahead of GMT and German Summer Time (GST) which was two hours ahead of GMT. Unless otherwise indicated, the times quoted in this book are those recorded in the ORBs etc which are almost certainly 'local' time. For the record, the times used in Britain during the war were:

From 02.00 hrs	Sunday	16 April 1939	BST
From 02.00 hrs	Sunday	19 November 1939	GMT
From 02.00 hrs	Sunday	25 February 1940	BST
From 02.00 hrs	Sunday	4 May 1941	BDST
From 02.00 hrs	Sunday	10 August 1941	BST

The flock of Lapwings swooped over the field, changing direction with impressive agility, immediacy and dynamic control. The dew clung to the long grass which provided suitable cover for any remaining birds on the ground. At the edge of the meadow stood two well attired gentlemen. As they moved into the field, water from the sodden ground quickly found its way into their shoes. Despite the discomfort of the icy cold water the men were too preoccupied to be bothered. There was an air of excitement, of expectation, about them. 'This will be our aerodrome' said the one in charge and, pointing at the flock of lapwings still cutting about the sky, he spoke again 'If we can fly half as good as those chaps over there, and hunt as efficiently as that chap over there' picking out a falcon with his swagger stick as it hovered, looking for prey, '...then we shall be a fine squadron.'

Later, back in the city, the two men were greeted at the front door of a large, beautifully decorated house in one of the most opulent parts of the New Town. As they moved into the hallway and on to the other ground floor rooms the one in charge turned to his colleague and said '...and this will be our town headquarters.'

CHAPTER ONE

FORMATION AND THE EARLY YEARS
1925 – 1938

On October 1925, the first squadrons were formed under the auspices of County or Auxiliary Air Force Associations, one of which was 603 (City of Edinburgh) Bomber Squadron. On 12 October 1925, the Air Ministry issued the following order (Air Order 1611 dated 12 October 1925):

It is notified for information and necessary action by all concerned that an Auxiliary Air Force, No.603 City of Edinburgh (Bombing) Squadron is to commence to form at Turnhouse on 14th October 1925, in accordance with Establishment No.AAF /501.

The Squadron is ultimately to be provided with aircraft to the establishment of a regular single-engined bombing squadron, but it has been decided that on formation the Squadron will have a reduced establishment of aeroplanes to consist of :
4 Avros 6 DH9A's 2 Dual DH9A's

The approved personnel establishment was 23 officers and 158 airmen.

The Squadron was formed under the command of Squadron Leader J.A. 'Jimmy'

Turnhouse c.1932. The aircraft is a Westland Wapiti.

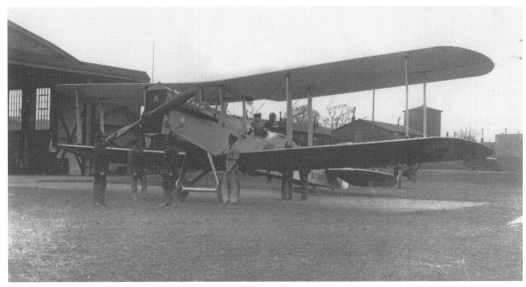

DH9A, Turnhouse, c.1928. The groundcrew are about to swing the prop.

1

McKelvie AFC, a veteran of the Royal Flying Corps, who flew Bristol Fighters with 22 Squadron during WWI and attained the rank of major. In 1941 McKelvie's son, Kenneth, was killed whilst serving as a pilot officer with 603. His story features later. S/L McKelvie's adjutant was Flight Lieutenant Charles R. Keary, RAF, and recruiting began in November 1925. Mr A. Scott Kennedy, Air Correspondent of *The Scotsman* reported on 25 October 1925:

> Major 'Jimmy' McKelvie… is to command the new Edinburgh Bomber Squadron – No 603, Auxiliary Air Force. An excellent choice. I have known him for a long time in and out of the Service. The aircraft at Turnhouse, he tells me, are two Avro 504Ks and one DH9A. I fancy it won't be long before his 'stable' is bigger. I am glad he has invited me to help him with recruiting.

This was to be the start of a long and very productive association in terms of press reporting of the Squadron's activities by Scott Kennedy.*

The initial influx of officers into the Squadron consisted of professional businessmen from Edinburgh and the surrounding districts, and the airmen were of various trades and callings, from corporation employees, and civilian industry, to students from the university.

The Squadron occupied its splendid Town Headquarters at 25 Learmonth Terrace on 19 January 1926. That same month, the pilots flew to Leuchars for their initial training camp, equipped with two DH 9As and three Avro 504Ks. Three officers and 55 airmen attended the camp. Later that year, one of the Avro 504Ks was replaced by a radial-engined Lynx 504N.

25 Learmonth Terrace, Edinburgh, the 603 town HQ.

Their headquarters building had been designed by the Leith architect, James Simpson in 1891 as a home for Arthur Sanderson, a well-known wine merchant and whisky distiller, who had acquired a large and important collection of paintings, antiques, period furniture, porcelain and contemporary sculpture. Following Sanderson's death, it was not until 1925 that it was sold to the Edinburgh Territorial Auxiliary Association for £4,500. Since that date the house has been in continuous occupation by one or another of the City of Edinburgh Royal Auxiliary Air Force units, apart from a period during the war when it was used by the Air Training Corps, 603 Squadron of course having then been mobilised.

Growth and Expansion 1926 – 1935

Aviation was the craze of the 1920s and 1930s and the Auxiliary Air Force did not find itself short of volunteers. Right from its inception 'home defence' was very much its raison d'être. Home defence meant flying and the weekend fliers loved it! On 3 April 1933, Squadron Leader the Marquis of Douglas and Clydesdale and Flight Lieutenant D.F. McIntyre, the officer commanding and flight commander respectively of 602 (City of Glasgow) Squadron, undertook the first manned flight over Mount Everest at 31,000 feet in a modified Westland Wallace (G-ACBR) and a Westland PV.3 (G-ACAZ) as part of the Lady Houston Expedition. They were subsequently awarded the Air Force Cross. The auxiliary squadrons caught the public eye and delighted the crowds in the Empire Air Day displays and Hendon Air Pageants of the late 1920s and early 1930s and the 1935 Silver Jubilee Review at Mildenhall, with their airmanship, skill and colourful squadron markings.

On 10 April 1926, 603 Squadron was inspected by the 'Father' of the Auxiliary Air Force, Air Chief Marshal Sir Hugh Trenchard, Chief of the Air Staff. By December, S/L McKelvie AFC

---

*Jimmy McKelvie and Scott Kennedy feature in the reconstruction at the beginning of this book when the CO took his journalist friend to inspect Turnhouse as a potential base for the Squadron.

Avro 504N, training flight, Turnhouse, c.1928.

reported that 64 airmen had been recruited by 603 and that 61 of these had attended the annual training camp at Leuchars that year. In addition, four officers had been gazetted. This represented attaining 40% of the Squadron's establishment.

In July 1927, the Squadron once more undertook annual training at Leuchars, the Avro 504Ks having been replaced by radial-engined Lynx 504Ns. Inspection during the camp was again carried out by Sir Hugh Trenchard.

Aircraftman James Newhall joined in 1925 on formation and trained as a wireless operator. He recalled the rivalry between all the new auxiliary squadrons at camp, especially as to which would be the first to carry out air to ground radio signalling. Jim Newhall was to achieve this during the Trenchard visit but not without problems. On the appointed day one of the pilots, Flight Lieutenant Winkler, had been stunting in the DH9A and damaged the aircraft resulting in a 24-hour postponement of the event while the aircraft was repaired. The incident was reported in *The Scotsman*:

Air Signaller James Newhall (803045) in walking out dress. He joined the Squadron in 1925 – one of the first to do so.

Plane Crash at Leuchars – Edinburgh Officer's Lucky Escape
Leuchars aerodrome was the scene of a remarkable accident yesterday when a machine piloted by an officer of the Auxiliary Force Flight, with headquarters in Edinburgh, crashed into one of the base offices, causing injuries to two officers inside the office and also to the officers who were in the machine.

The smash occurred about 11 o/c. A short time previously Air Marshal Sir Hugh Trenchard had inspected the Leuchars force, and thereafter some flying practice took place. One of the planes, a DH9, was in the charge of Flight Lieutenant Winkler, who arrived with the Territorial Force Flight about a week ago. He flew around St Andrews and the neighbourhood, accompanied by Pilot Officer Jack, and it was on the return journey to the aerodrome that the smash occurred. There seemed nothing unusual in the flight of the machine.

The smash occurred over the main road between Newport and St Andrews. The machine was on the point of landing, when it struck one of the telephone poles, was entangled in the wires and turned into the end of the accounts section of the base offices. At the moment of the smash, Flight Lieutenant Money, pay officer and Flight Lieutenant Brownlie, medical officer, were in the hut, the wall of which smashed in upon them and the nose of the plane penetrated into the office.

Embedded in Brickwork

Flight Lieutenant Money and Dr Brownlie were rendered unconscious, and a number of the officers who had just been paid and were still in the office ran to safety. The nose of the machine was embedded in the wrecked brickwork, and the end of the office was practically demolished. A rescue party was quickly on the scene, and Flight Lieutenant Winkler and his passenger were extricated with difficulty, but their injuries were not so serious as first thought. Dr Brownlie went to his home in St Andrews, but it was deemed advisable to have Flight Lieutenant Winkler, who was badly cut about the head, removed to Edinburgh. The passenger had a marvellous escape and after a slight treatment returned to the Officers Mess little the worse of his remarkable experience.

The telephone service between Dundee and St Andrews was completely disorganised as a result of the smash, about 30 wires being torn to the ground. It was learnt last night that all the officers involved were making good progress. The wrecked machine was removed after about 3 hours work.

During 1927, both the Special Reserve and Auxiliary Air Force squadrons became 1 Air Defence Group under the command of the Air Officer Commanding, Air Defence of Great Britain. Recruitment was steady and by December 1927, Squadron strength stood at 11 officers and 80 other ranks.

The enthusiasm of the airmen, in particular, was remarkable as their terms of service were by no means generous. Intending recruits had to be between the ages of 18 and 38, physically fit, of pure European descent and the sons of natural born or naturalised British subjects. They were initially engaged for four years and could re-engage for periods of up to four years at a time.

One privilege was given to airmen which was to play a vital part in 603's wartime success. Air Ministry Pamphlet 33, dated November 1927, stated 'When a recruit has been posted to a unit, he cannot be removed and posted to another without his consent.' James Somerville joined 603 in May 1927 for a four-year term:

I was given training as an aero-engine fitter and eventually passed at LAC. My older brother, now deceased, joined the Squadron at the time of its inception in 1925 and became Sergeant carpenter/rigger. He was a World War I soldier having gone right through, in the RAMC, serving in France, Gallipoli and Egypt.

In my time the Squadron was equipped with AVRO 504N training aircraft and De Havilland 9A day bombers. The DH9As had a gun turret behind the pilot and two guns firing forward 'through' the propeller. The engine was a 400 HP American 'Liberty' engine, of V-12 cylinder type, water cooled.

One or two points would possibly be regarded as amusing when comparing with modern aircraft. For instance, the under-carriage of fixed design was given springing by yards of elastic supporting the inner ends of the landing wheel spindles.

This craft tended to be nose-heavy and an instruction plate fitted at the gun turret warned 'Do not fly without passenger or 150 lbs in rear cockpit.' This gave us the impression that, on occasions when we were taken up, our function was that of ballast. However there was never any shortage of volunteers to do this duty. We were sent to the parachute shed and fitted with a parachute. If it was a DH9A the parachute hung in front of the wearer whereas in the Avro it formed a cushion. I think the pilots liked to give us a thrill and the first experience of looping was certainly a bit of a shock.

Starting up the DH9A was normally done by Huck starter, a motorised platform on which was mounted a framework supporting an adjustable shaft, chain driven from the engine. At the front end of the shaft was a cross bar which engaged with a 'dog' on the propeller of the aircraft, much as old cars did with starting handles.

Occasionally, if the Huck was not available, hand starting was resorted to, in which case, three men stand facing alternate directions clasping each others' wrist. No.1 would hold the

603 (B) Squadron, AuxAF at annual camp, Leuchars, July 1928.

propeller blade and at the order the three would pull and run clear of the propeller. The Avro was started by means of a magneto in the cockpit.

Near the end of my four-year term, Westland Wapitis replaced the DH9As and later were in turn replaced by Hawker Hinds or Harts.

In 1927/28/29 annual camp was held at Leuchars. However, in 1930 the Squadron travelled to Manston in Kent for annual camp. I was lucky enough to return to Edinburgh in a DH9A, the pilot being Mr Burton. We started fairly late and stopped for the night at Digby Aerodrome in Lincolnshire. I recall that all went well until we crossed the Cheviots when I suffered from air sickness.

By this time the Squadron had acquired a pipe band whose active 'drum major' was Corporal Fletcher, another World War I soldier.

Major McKelvie, a first class pilot, occasionally gave some excellent displays, performing side slips low over the aerodrome, the falling leaf and other things, tame perhaps by today's standards but to us very impressive.

Auxiliary airmen had to attend a set number of instructional parades and drills each year for which they received no pay or allowances. They had also to carry out annual training of up to 15 days during which they were on the same pay and allowances as regular airmen. If he met all training commitments, an airman was awarded an annual bounty of £2 10s 0d (£2.50). He also received one shilling (5p) for each instructional parade he had attended over and above the minimum number laid down. The total of this additional bounty could not exceed ten shillings (50p). The City of Edinburgh Territorial Army and Air Force Association paid the airman's fare to annual camp but made only a limited contribution towards any expenses he incurred in attending training during the week or at weekends.

During 1928, 603 appointed its first chaplain, Squadron Leader the Reverend W.B.C. Buchanan, who had himself served as a pilot in the Royal Flying Corps.

Tragedy struck on 7 July when Pilot Officer J.T.L. Shiells was killed in a flying accident whilst going solo in the vicinity of Corstorphine. P/O Shiells had introduced the sport of fencing to 603 and was their established expert. Following his death his parents donated a sum of money to the Squadron and the 'Shiells Trophy' for competition other than fencing was established in his honour.* The remainder went to the fencing club. By the end of 1928 the Squadron was manned by 17 officers and 155 airmen.

Also in 1928, James L. Jack, MC joined the Squadron as an armaments officer. A former officer who was commissioned in the field and commanded a machine-gun company, he later served in the

---

*Twelve friends of P/O Shiells had already made plans to establish the Shiells Fencing Trophy for annual competition in their late colleague's name and were about to present it to the Squadron. The trophy is in the form of a large silver cup surmounted by the figure of a swordsman.

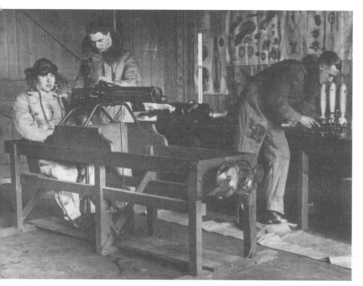

Calibrating a machine gun from a Squadron aircraft.

RAF during the First World War. A banker by profession, he eventually became manager of the Drumsheugh Branch of the Commercial Bank of Scotland. James Jack was a fine officer, a true auxiliary and a tower of strength to the Squadron, not only in the professionalism of his duties but in his interest and concern for his fellow auxiliaries. During the Second World War he served in the RAF as an instructor and by 1979 had compiled a brief history of 603 for which he failed to find a publisher. He eventually produced three copies which were lodged with Buckingham Palace, the Imperial War Museum, and Edinburgh City Chambers.

Edward Belford reflects on the years 1928 to 1931:

At the time of joining 603 (B) Squadron, I was underage but mad keen on flying, and had to lie my way in… at 18 years of age, promising to bring my birth certificate as proof, but it always seemed, somehow, that my memory failed me each week until I was no longer asked for it.

I was enrolled as an aircrafthand (stores account clerk) and employed in the stores at Turnhouse on weekend camps. Turnhouse was just a grass field in those days. At that time we were equipped with Avro 504Ks and DH9As.

F/O Scarlett was our stores officer and I was able to approach him if there was any chance of him taking a plane up and taking me with him. This was successful sometimes and a flip with him was always exciting as I believe he had been a Hendon Pageant pilot. He used to yank the Avro off the deck, put one wing down and race round the field, scaring the grazing sheep out of their wits, to say nothing of what he was doing to me. Even more thrilling when one had stood by for a long time watching the Hucks starter trying manfully to coax a reluctant engine into life.

I have a faint recollection of someone pranging an Avro on top of the pay hut when coming in to land one weekend at Turnhouse and walking away from it with some difficulty. I also flew with S/L McKelvie in both the Avro and DH9, sometimes in formation, which was a thrill. In those days, we flew without parachutes and it wasn't until P/O Shiells was killed in a DH9 crash that we wore chutes.

The annual 14 days training at Leuchars was very enjoyable where we competed against and co-operated with 602 City of Glasgow Squadron.

I served just over two years with 603. Our uniform included breeches and puttees, with the breeches suitably flared to give a macho butterfly effect, with a swagger cane to smack our leg with in the approved manner.

Social occasions at Learmonth Terrace were enhanced by the provision of free beer by P/O Usher of the Edinburgh brewing family which was greatly appreciated by the lads in these hard times. I went on to join the Royal Tank Corps in July 1931.

Would-be pilots had, however, to face preliminary hurdles. If a vacancy occurred, serving officers of the Squadron were asked for recommendations. They were first interviewed by the adjutant. If he felt they were suitable, he sent them to Comiston House, S/L McKelvie's home, to be vetted by the CO and his wife. The survivors then faced the stiffest test of all – a trial flight with the adjutant. In 1929, ten candidates got as far as the test flight, but only one of these, Tom M. McNeil, got through.

Those accepted served for a probationary period before they were commissioned. Officers were initially appointed for five years. Their service could then be extended for further periods of five years.

Training consisted of periodical flying, drills, instructional parades, annual training of up to 15 days, courses in ground gunnery and weekend camps. During the annual camp, on full-time courses and when engaged on flying training, officers received the same pay and allowances as their regular counterparts.

Officers were required to purchase regulation RAF service dress. The uniform allowance was exactly £40. In addition, officers brought mess kit at their own expense. As a mark of distinction, 603 Squadron obtained official permission to wear red silk linings in their tunics and greatcoats, although all auxiliary squadrons eventually adopted this style. The more enthusiastic had their flying helmets made to measure by Gieves.

Avro 504N, Turnhouse. From left to right: P/O Alen Wallace; F/O George Reid; F/O I. D. Shields; P/O J. Somerville; F/O Watts and S/L Rossie Brown.

Although there was no allowance for it in the establishment the 603 adjutant, Flight Lieutenant Walmsley* (later Air Marshal Sir Hugh P. Walmsley KCB, KCIE, CBE, MC, DFC), correctly judged that a pipe band would help focus the enthusiasm of a unit which depended for its efficiency on the keenness of its members. This proposal was warmly supported by S/L McKelvie who persuaded the County Association to grant money for the purchase of the necessary instruments. Those members who played the pipes were at once enrolled and they in turn began to instruct others. The RAF uniform at that time included breeches and puttees and these were not felt appropriate for a pipe band. The Duke of Hamilton agreed to the use of the Grey Douglas tartan and representations were made to the Air Ministry. In 1933, a kilted uniform was approved by HM King George V and uniforms were purchased from Jardines of Forth Street at a total cost of £5.20 per piper for kilt, plaid Balmoral, shoulder plaid brooch, hose tops, spats, sporrans and badges. The 603 pipe band made its first public appearance in 1929 at the annual Territorial church parade and thereafter became an attractive feature of Squadron activities and played at all important parades and at state functions at Holyrood Palace. William H. Young recalls his service during the period in the early 1930s:

> I joined 603 in 1932 and my uniform in those days consisted of puttees and breeches – tunic and cheese cutter hat. A couple of years later, the puttees and breeches were made obsolete, with trousers replacing same. I served as a wireless operator and was fortunate to be on flying duty most weekends. The Squadron was equipped with Wapiti 2-seater bomber aircraft and when detailed for a flight doing wireless communications it

Turnhouse. Shot of ground crew personnel showing uniform of period.

*Walmsley had recently arrived from Halton to take over as adjutant.

F/O Ivone Kirkpatrick drilling the 603 pipe band, 1932.

was very necessary to wear fur lined flying boots, Sid-cot, helmet goggles and gloves. A few years later these aircraft were replaced with Hawker Harts. …we were the first Squadron in the Air Force to have our own pipe band and I was privileged to be one of the founder pipers. My brother, Corporal R.B. Young, was the Squadron's first pipe major.

It's a long time ago but I remember playing the pipes with three other members of the band in the banqueting hall in Holyrood Palace for the Duke of Kent and his wife, then known as Princess Marina. If I recall this took place the week of the General Assembly of the Church of Scotland. That night was the highlight of my piping career. I recall my flight in a Hawker Hart in which I was the observer which made a crash landing at Turnhouse. The pilot was a dear friend of mine, F/O Colper Reid and I was the observer. They took us to the station hospital, nothing serious, slight shock.

Corporal Thomas F. Dickson remembered the pipe band:

I was an older member of 603 (B) Squadron AAF, having joined on 29 February 1932, engaged until 28 February 1937 but re-engaged on 7 May 1939 – in what was then called the Auxiliary Air Force Reserve – and embodied on 23 August 1939. I reported immediately to Turnhouse Aerodrome and from then on confined to barracks when Sunday September 3rd 1939 brought us all bang into war.

I was proud to be a founder member of the Squadron pipe band (being a piper). What a smart bunch of lads we were in our Grey Douglas tartan. I believe we were 16 strong in pipers and drummers.

Joining 603 Squadron of the Auxiliary Air Force in the 1930s was something of a family affair with brother following brother – or teenagers following their old school chums. The late Philip Reilly recalled that, in 1932 when he was a young apprentice lawyer, he joined 603 as a photographer because his brother was already in the squadron: 'I followed suit – and I knew some of my chums from school who were in the photo section so I joined them simply because it sounded interesting.' But aerial photography was in its infancy and required the young Reilly to stand up in the back of an open cockpit:

We used the Westland Wapiti which had a top speed of about 90 mph – and it was damned cold! You were surrounded by all sorts of bits of iron and if you touched the edge the wrong way you could cut your hand. I communicated with the pilot by writing notes. There were no retractable undercarriages and Turnhouse had a grass runway that wasn't level and was very bumpy. These were pioneering days in 1932-33!

Left: RAF Turnhouse May 1931, taken from the south-east. The aircraft types are 9 Westland Wapiti Mk IIas, and 2 Avro 504Ns, all of 603 Squadron. The additional aircraft by the hangar door is the civilian DH 60 Moth of the then CO of the Squadron, Squadron Leader Hylton Ralph Murray-Philipson MP.

Right: Turnhouse 1930. From left to right: P/O Sorel Cameron; ?; S/L J. A. McKelvie AFC; F/O G. A. Reid; F/O A. Wallace; ?; F/O J. E. Glenny; E. H. Stevens; F/L H. S. P. Walmsley MC, DFC; F/O I. E. Chalmers Watson ; P/O T. M. McNeil; P/O A. H. Bruce; ?; F/O J. L. Jack MC.

By November 1928, 603 had 17 officers and 155 airmen, and sufficient pilots were regularly available for it to practice formation flying. Thereafter, this became a standard feature of the flying training. During the period 1926-28, recruiting for the AAF was relatively slow, as the horrific memories of WWI were still vivid in the minds of the general population.

The Squadron also needed to start serious bombing training and began to look for a suitable range. A local landowner, Mr Paton, generously offered land on his estate at Belstane. His gesture was acknowledged by ACM Hugh Trenchard who presented him with a small silver model of a DH9A.

Bombing, map reading and the rear-firing gun were the responsibility of the second member of the crew – the air gunner. Although all auxiliary pilots were commissioned, the air gunners received no special treatment. Until 1934, they were members of the armament section and not attached to flights. Their promotion was not accelerated and some of the air gunners held the lowest rank in the service, Aircraftman Second Class (AC2). Their sole mark of distinction was their proficiency badge. This was awarded only after they had passed bombing and air firing tests, and been examined by the staff armament officer and by a formal board at the Air Armament School, Eastchurch.

In June 1929, the first affiliation exercises were carried out with the fighter aircraft of the regular RAF. A Flight from 23 (Fighter) Squadron stationed at Kenley visited Turnhouse for this purpose. They were equipped with Gloster Gamecocks and were commanded by Squadron Leader Jones-Williams.

603 Squadron continued to enjoy great local support. *The Scotsman* regularly publicised its activities and its aforementioned aeronautical correspondent, A. Scott Kennedy, gave continued help and advice. The Caledonian United Services Club, the second oldest military and naval club in the United Kingdom, offered generous hospitality.

Shortly after annual camp, on 7 September 1929, the adjutant noted 603's first successful airborne tests of wireless telegraphy in DH9A (8805) using different operators on each occasion. Communication was by morse code.

In March 1930, 603 began to convert from DH9As to Westland Wapitis. The prototype Wapiti first flew in 1927. It was planned as a replacement for the DH9A and incorporated as many DH9A parts as possible. The Mk II which 603 received was a two-seat, general-purpose biplane with a fabric-covered metal structure. The advent of a metal-framed aeroplane required the training of metal riggers since up to this time 603's riggers had been carpenters. Their successful conversion was a considerable achievement.

As earlier noted, on 12 July 1930, 603 flew south to annual camp at Manston in Kent. This was the first camp out of Scotland. The journey was made in an assortment of aircraft; DH9As, Avro 504Ks and the new Wapitis, stopping en route at Waddington, Lincolnshire, to refuel. The ground party travelled by train. The Squadron were accommodated in neat rows of tents and thoroughly enjoyed both the training and relaxation. Margate was especially appreciated. During their stay at Manston, 603 were inspected by Air Marshal Sir Edward Ellington, Air Officer Commanding in Chief, Air Defence of Great Britain. The return flight required two stops – Cranwell and Catterick.

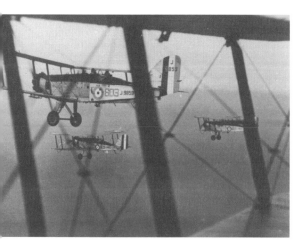

Three Westland Wapiti aircraft of 603 Squadron over the Forth, c. 1931.

The two Squadron padres. W. B. C. Buchanan (left) and James Rossie Brown.

Whilst 603 was away, Pilot Officer Lord Malcolm Douglas-Hamilton took over the duties of assistant adjutant on 15 July 1930. Thus began a family association unique in RAF history. Malcolm was a member of the only family from which all four brothers joined the RAF and all became professional flying instructors and squadron commanders. In due course two of Malcolm's brothers were to command 603.

On 3 August 1930, the Squadron suffered their second fatal accident when the engine in an Avro flown by C flight commander, Flight Lieutenant A.R.H Miller, failed and, contrary to the strict instructions from his adjutant, F/L Walmsley, he tried to turn back to the aerodrome. The aircraft stalled, crashed and Miller was killed. In general, the accident rate was very low. The construction of 603's aeroplanes was such that at the relatively low speeds at which crashes took place, the airframe crumpled and absorbed much of the impact.

Also on 5 August, the Right Honourable The Earl of Stair DSO, DL, JP was appointed first Honorary Air Commodore of 603 Squadron. He had no flying experience and in due course this was to cause comment and prompt appropriate action at a very high level.

The word soon spread around Edinburgh that 603 had been to Margate and this, plus the highly embroidered descriptions of dances and entertainment, encouraged more volunteers.

On 9 November 1930, there was an Armistice Sunday church parade and 603 marched to and from Murrayfield Parish Church led by its pipe band.

As in previous years, large numbers applied for commissions in 603 Squadron. Nineteen of these survived the various hurdles and reached the final stage of a test flight with the adjutant. Only three were successful – E.H. Stevens (later Group Captain Stevens OBE (Military), AE, who eventually became CO of the Squadron), Ivone Kirkpatrick, another future Group Captain, and Iain D. Shields.

With the growth in numbers of airmen, more space was needed for training. Indoor facilities were also required for drill, which could not always be practised outside during the winter months. The Territorial Association therefore sold the land to the west of 25 Learmonth Terrace and used the proceeds to erect a large drill hall at the back of the Town Headquarters (today, the hall is still in use for drill practice).

In January 1931, the Reverend James Rossie Brown MA succeeded Squadron Leader the Rev W.B.C. Buchanan as chaplain. In April, S/L Jimmy McKelvie retired. The Squadron had benefited greatly from the support so generously given by both the CO and his wife. This support was to be continued for many years to come. The new CO was Squadron Leader Hylton Murray-Philipson. 'Hyltie' had learned to fly at Brooklands in 1925, and two years later purchased a Moth which he kept on his estate at Stobo, near Peebles in the Muirfoot Hills. He was an enthusiastic pilot who resolutely disregarded limitations imposed by aircraft and terrain. He constructed a hangar for his Moth at the top of a field sloping down to the River Tweed. Whatever the wind direction, Hyltie

Turnhouse, officers mess gardens, 1932. Standing behind, from left to right: P/O G. H. Gatheral; F/O D. M. T. Macdonald; F/O G. A. Reid and F/O A. Wallace. Front, from left to right: F/O P. Gifford; F/L T. M. McNeil; F/O A. Mitchell; F/O E. H. Stevens; F/O I. D. Shields; F/O C. H. W. Baldero; F/O I. Kirkpatrick; F/L W. Watson; S/L H. R. Murray-Philipson; F/L J. I. Jack and F/L R. J. Legg.

would take off downhill, becoming airborne just before he reached the river. He reversed the procedure for landing and as the Moth had no brakes, relied on the slope to slow him down before he reached the hangar. His wife wisely refused to fly from Stobo with him. He also supplied 603 with a bombing range in his own grounds where he would pitch camp and persuade members of the Territorial Royal Engineers to mark the bombing practice of the Squadron.

Murray-Philipson had no experience of service life and one of the first duties of his adjutant was to teach him to salute before he appeared in uniform before the Squadron. The new Commanding Officer was, however, a brilliant organiser with wide ranging interests and enormous energy. In addition to managing his estate at Stobo with great skill and generosity, he was a magistrate, a county councillor, a commissioner for boy scouts and a leading industrialist. He was several times a parliamentary candidate and in 1932 was elected Member of Parliament for Twickenham. He brought his tireless energy, vision and enthusiasm to 603 and, although a firm disciplinarian, quickly won the admiration, support and affection of all officers and ground staff. He even disconcerted his adjutant on one occasion by demanding to know how much was spent on petrol.

Hyltie was a most generous host and members of 603 were always welcome at Stobo Castle. A highly organised man, he insisted on punctual attendance at dinner. His officers, well aware of this foible, made every effort to make Hyltie himself late. They never succeeded!

When the adjutant, F/L Hugh Walmsley, was invited to Stobo for the first time, he chose an Avro 504N for the journey. He flew around Hyltie's landing strip a number of times before summoning up courage to land. He subsequently made it a firm rule that no officer was to fly to Stobo in a DH9A or a Wapiti. If he felt sufficiently confident in a pilot's flying ability, he would give permission for use of an Avro 504N, feeling that only the Avro was docile enough to meet this stern challenge. On one occasion, this injunction was disregarded and Flying Officer Mitchell overturned his Wapiti on landing. Fortunately, he emerged unscathed.

In May 1931, seven of 603's Wapitis flew over the annual Territorial parade in Edinburgh before the GOC Scottish Command. That year fighter affiliation exercises were undertaken with 19 Squadron.

The Squadron was honoured on 25 June 1931 by an official visit from HRH The Prince of Wales (later King Edward VIII). The Prince was no stranger to Turnhouse and had often landed there on his way to Balmoral or when he was attending official functions in the Edinburgh area. 603 always refuelled and checked his Fox Moth G-ACDD. This was a splendid aircraft with a

Westland Wapiti IIa, Turnhouse.

Sergeant gunner in a Wapiti, Turnhouse. Note the 603 crest.

coupé top and wheel spats. It was painted in the red, blue and white colours of the Guards.

The Prince of Wales was attended at one function by The Earl of Stair, the recently appointed Honorary Air Commodore. On returning by car to Turnhouse, the Prince enquired about the Earl's flying experience and found that he had never flown. Overriding all objections, HRH told his personal pilot, 'Mouse' Fielden, to take the Earl for a demonstration flight, stressing that the object was to convert him to flying, not to put him off. The pair departed for a short flight and were gone nearly an hour. On their return, they explained that after flying over the agricultural show which the Prince had just opened, Fielden had asked his reluctant passenger if he would like to see his estate from the air. Lord Stair agreed and, in a series of gentle banking turns, Fielden displayed the house and its surroundings to the evident delight of 603's HAC.

On 30 June 1931, the second of the Douglas-Hamilton brothers to be associated with 603 joined. Lord George Nigel 'Geordie' Douglas-Hamilton (later Group Captain the Rt. Hon. The Earl of Selkirk KT, GCMG, GBE, AFC, AE, PC, QC) was destined to play a key role in its future development.

On 4 and 5 July, a formation of five Wapitis flew in formation over Edinburgh to mark the arrival and departure of Their Majesties, the King and Queen. During the same month, 603 assembled in strength at Turnhouse for two weeks annual training.

By March 1932, 603 were confident enough to send a formation of ten Wapitis on a cross country formation flight from Turnhouse to Hendon via Grantham. One aircraft developed engine trouble and was forced to land near Grantham but the rest completed their journey successfully.

In April Flying Officer Lord Malcolm Douglas-Hamilton resigned his commission in the RAF and was granted a commission in the Squadron as a flying officer, and Flying Officer D.M.T. Macdonald arrived from 503 (Bomber) Squadron, Waddington, to take over as assistant adjutant.

In May 1932, Mr Paton, the owner of the bombing range at Belstane, died suddenly. He had been a good friend to 603 and had always been keenly interested in their activities but with his passing the Squadron had to find a new range and the CO made one available on his Stobo estate. A. S. Liddle, who joined in 1931 and became an air gunner recalls:

Weather conditions at Stobo were not always favourable for bombing and increasing use was made of the 'camera obscura' recently installed at Turnhouse. This consisted of a lens set in the roof of a small darkened building near one of the hangars. When an aeroplane flew high over the aerodrome its image was projected by the lens on to a chart of the locality. The bomb aimer used the camera obscura building as his target. When he thought he was in the correct position to make a direct hit he pressed the key of his wireless transmitter. The signal was picked up on a receiver in the building and the exact position of the aeroplane was noted on the chart. The probable impact of the bomb was then calculated using the known height and speed of the aeroplane and the estimated wind speed and direction.

Bombing practice could be carried out even when the weather was unsuitable for flying. For this an ingenious apparatus was used in which the bomb aimer was seated on a high platform. A moving picture of the ground as seen from the air was projected on to the floor beneath him. This picture could be made to move at any required speed and in any direction. The picture stopped when the bomb release was pressed and the probable point of impact could then be calculated.

Bombing played an important part in the Esher Trophy contest in which all auxiliary squadrons took part. The trophy, a bronze statuette of Perseus designed by Sir Alfred Gilbert, was presented by the late Viscount Esher in 1925. It was awarded annually to the most efficient auxiliary squadron. In

The annual fixture between the officers of the London and the Scottish squadrons was played on Saturday, 15 April 1933, at Hendon. Sitting, from left to right: F/O Lord M. A. Douglas-Hamilton; F/L R. J. Legg (third) and F/O Lord G. N. Douglas Hamilton (sixth). On ground, from left to right: P/O A. Rintoul (second); F/O D. M. T. Macdonald (fourth); P/O G. H. Gatheral (sixth); F/O P. Gifford (eighth); F/O I. Kirkpatrick (tenth) and F/O A. Wallace (twelfth).

addition to bombing, there were tests of flying efficiency, air firing, air pilotage, wireless communication and photography.

The Wapitis were again on public display on 7 May 1932 when nine flew in formation over the annual ceremonial parade in King's Park. The salute was taken by the GOC-in-C Scottish Command Lieutenant General Sir P. de B. Radcliffe.

Fighter affiliation exercises were held during the first two weeks of June. The visitors were 25 (Fighter) Squadron. The weather was excellent and much valuable experience was gained by operating with a regular squadron.

On 3 June 1932, Air Marshal, HRH Edward Prince of Wales, Duke of Cornwall, was appointed Honorary Air Commodore-in-Chief of the Auxiliary Air Force. On ascending the throne as HM King Edward the VIII on 20 January 1936, the monarch retained the title until his abdication on 10 December 1936.

To the relief of most members of the Squadron, annual camp in July 1932 was again at Manston. During the second week they took part in the Air Defence of Great Britain exercises and were highly commended. Inspection was by the Chief of the Air Staff, Sir John Salmond. Annual camp was made even more enjoyable by the generosity of S/L Murray-Philipson who sent all the airmen over to France from Manston at his own expense.

Wing Commander S.E. Townson recalls an anecdote from 1932, when 19 Squadron were detached to Turnhouse:

I was in B Flight 19 (F) Squadron at Duxford when, in the summer of 1932, we were detached to Turnhouse for three weeks to carry out affiliated/bomber exercises with 603 (City of Edinburgh) Auxiliary Squadron. Because of persistent drizzle during most of our stay, very little flying was possible but our lives were brightened by two notable events.

The Squadron Adjutant Flight Lieutenant Walmsley was promoted to Squadron Leader, on the same day as his wife presented him with a son.

The King's official birthday was also celebrated while we were there and we paraded with the small 'regular' staff of the Squadron. No trumpeter was available but the disciplinary Sergeant-Major – named Ford – was no mean performer on the saxophone. Surely, the only occasion on which the RAF Ensign was hoisted to the General Salute played on such an instrument; and by the senior non-commissioned officer on parade. (The rank of Warrant Officer was not introduced into the RAF until 1934.)

For the second year running fighter/bomber affiliation exercises were held with 25 Squadron, this time commanded by Flight Lieutenant C.R. Hancock DFC. The Caledonian United Service Club, as previously, kindly made all members of the visiting squadron honorary members.

During April 1933 the Commandant of the Central Flying School, Group Captain P.C. Maltby

Squadron Wapitis in formation over Fife, 1933.

DSO, AFC and Flight Lieutenant G.V. Carey tested the flying abilities of all 603's pilots. Weather conditions at the Stobo bombing range did not improve and little practice was possible. F/O 'Count' Stevens offered a site near West Calder and plans were made to move to it in early 1934.

The Inverness Municipal Airport was opened on 17 June 1933 and B Flight under F/L Tom McNeil gave an exhibition of formation flying. On the return journey F/O George A. Reid had engine trouble and was forced to land in a most difficult field near Elgin. It says much for the docility of the Wapiti that it was repaired and flown out of the same field next day. The record notes that great kindness was shown to the pilot by Mr Christie of Blackhill House, Llanbryd.

From 15 to 29 July 1933, annual training was again at Manston. The aircraft flew down direct, whilst the main ground party went by train. The padre, S/L Rossie Brown took command of the ground party for the journey – something which 603 regarded as entirely natural. The Air Ministry was irate, it was most improper for airmen to be under the command of a non-executive officer. Rossie Brown was unrepentant. A fortunate few drove some of the pilot's cars down to Manston so that maximum advantage could be taken of any free time.

Almost immediately after arriving, the Squadron took part in the Air Defence of Great Britain exercises. Five raids were carried out, the targets being Cardington Airship Station, Hatfield Aerodrome and the bridge over the Thames at Henley. Although the Squadron had done no night flying, they landed successfully at dusk after one raid with the aid of ground flares. Whilst at Manston, 603 were inspected by the new Chief of the Air Staff, Air Chief Marshal Sir Edward Ellington, and by the Air Officer Commanding-in-Chief, Air Defence of Great Britain, Air Marshal Sir Robert Brooke-Popham. Holiday makers at Margate greatly appreciated the appearance of the fully kilted pipe band at the local swimming carnival.

The hectic pace continued. In the middle of September a canvas camp sprang into being at Turnhouse. This was to house 33 (Bomber) Squadron who were to take part in the Coast Defence exercises in the Firth of Forth on 22 and 23 September 1933. On the first day of the exercise, 603 dispersed their aeroplanes in fields around Turnhouse. This was quite an easy task given the short distances then required for take-off and landing. On the second day, 603 carried out two raids on capital ships of the attacking force.

One of Murray-Philipson's last actions as CO was to institute an annual magazine. In the introduction to the first issue (December 1933), he wrote:

It was felt that the activities of the Squadron were becoming so numerous and the keenness of all concerned so real, that some permanent record of Squadron events should be made which would be a source of interest and encouragement to everyone in the Squadron as well as those who will join in the future.

He referred to a message from Air Commodore W.F. MacNeece-Foster AOC 1 Air Defence Group, which controlled all auxiliary and reserve squadrons, which states:

The record of 603 Squadron is one of which everyone connected with it may well be proud. I shall not attempt to record the many developments which have given proof of its efficiency and keenness. I will only mention that in July 1933, you as a Squadron created a record for flying untouched by any other Squadron in the Auxiliary Air Force since it has been inaugurated. I realise, almost with embarrassment, the heavy strain under which both officers and airmen were working during the annual camp this year, and I have never lost sight of the fact that this great effort was made during what was for many of you the only holiday of the year.

The CO added:

We are told in that message that we have a record of which one may be proud but we must not be content with that, as we have to strive after greater and greater efficiency. To the outside world 603 Squadron is one of the eight Auxiliary Air Force squadrons, but to the citizens of Edinburgh it is their own Auxiliary Squadron, manned and recruited for 'Auld Reekie'. We, who are in it, are determined to keep the Squadron in the very forefront of the Auxiliary Air Force and show that although there are but two such squadrons in Scotland, we will not yield an inch in keenness or performance to our friendly and more numerous rivals south of the Tweed.

CHAPTER 2

FROM BOMBER TO FIGHTER SQUADRON

In February 1934, five Harts arrived as initial replacements for 603's Wapitis. Conversion was completed the following month.

Ill health finally forced S/L Murray-Philipson to resign and with effect from 1 April 1934 his place was taken by A Flight commander, S/L Lord Geordie Douglas-Hamilton. From his hospital bed, Hyltie wrote to his successor, as reported in the CO's letter in the 1934 Squadron Yearbook:

> It is the Squadron and its well-being that counts – not individuals – they come and go like you and I, but our job is to build up for the future, regardless of anything that anyone may say. I feel it is a privilege to have done just a little to raise the prestige of 603 Squadron.

It was the former CO's last message. He died of cancer on 24 May 1934, aged only 31. A memorial service was held in London on the 28th and the following day Hyltie was buried in the grounds of Stobo. Despite the difficult cross country journey from Edinburgh, all 603's officers and a very large number of auxiliary airmen were present to pay their last respects to a well-loved CO. A Hart circled overhead during what was a very moving ceremony. Not forgetting her close ties with the Squadron, Mrs Murray-Philipson later presented the band with a pipe-major's banner. This now rests in the National War Museum of Scotland at Edinburgh Castle.

At the end of May, 3 (Fighter) Squadron visited Turnhouse for affiliation exercises. On Empire Air Day, 603 opened their aerodrome to the public for the first time and many people came to visit. During the summer two more regular squadrons joined 603 for exercises – 41 (Fighter) and 2 (AC) .

The Squadron were now settling into a smooth, well-organised routine. There were three flights to which all aircraft and pilots were allocated. All pilots

Top: The Douglas-Hamilton brothers during the war. From left to right: Flying Officer Lord David Douglas-Hamilton; Wing Commander The Duke of Hamilton; Lord George Nigel 'Geordie' Douglas-Hamilton and Squadron Leader Lord Malcolm Douglas-Hamilton.

Left: The Wapiti IIa flown by Alen Wallace with George Denholm in the back seat who jumped to the ground. Turnhouse c. 1933. *Above:* Turnhouse c. 1934. Wapiti. Note 'Reception' on hangar and spats on aircraft.

practised instrument flying and several long distance flights were confidently undertaken. Three auxiliary pilots had become fully qualified flying instructors – S/L Lord Geordie Douglas-Hamilton and F/Os Reid and Shields. All three received intensive instruction from Flight Lieutenant George Macpherson throughout the summer prior to attending a course at Central Flying School. One flight almost resulted in tragedy when F/L Macpherson and S/L Douglas-Hamilton experienced a sudden and alarming flash in the immediate proximity of their aircraft. The CO shouted to Macpherson to find out what had happened. 'A high tension cable' was the reply. The pair hurriedly landed back at Turnhouse and, without even stopping the engine, Douglas-Hamilton jumped out to check the aircraft. To his surprise there was no apparent damage. When the propeller was stopped they found a mark on the centre boss – the only place on the aircraft which could possibly have withstood such a impact. In an encounter between plane and high-tension cable, the plane invariably lost. An inch or two higher or lower and 603 might have mourned a second Commanding Officer within the year.

Airmen/gunner crew at Turnhouse.

The Headquarters unit, run by the adjutant, was responsible for such matters as general administration, accounting and discipline. The last was, and would remain for many years, the province of a veteran auxiliary NCO, Sergeant 'Snuffy' Prentice.

The flights were supported by seven specialist sections – armaments, wireless, photographic, parachute, workshops, transport and stores. These sections were supervised by auxiliary officers. Apart from the specialist armament and stores officers, the supervisors were pilots. Their responsibilities were regularly rotated to give them experience of all aspects of the Squadron's activities. The armament section, in addition to maintenance of machine guns, bombs and rifles, was responsible for training air gunners in air firing, bombing and air pilotage. Air gunners were, in 1934, posted to flights to help improve crew co-operation. The armoury looked after the bombing range and the camera obscura.

Wireless handled all communication systems. These were still primitive. Ground/air communication was in morse code. The air gunner had to insert the appropriate coil in his set for the wavelength he was using, lower the trailing aerial and tune carefully to pick up the correct ground signal. This often drifted and had to be found again. The transmitter had also to be tuned. This could take several minutes even with an experienced operator. It was, of course, essential to wind the aerial in before landing. Contact was thus lost in the final stages of any flight. Communication on the ground at Turnhouse was by field telephone. Only sections which worked closely together had direct links. This system was inflexible and inefficient. LAC Harry Ross therefore rewired the entire network so that each extension led directly to a board controlled by the station operator. Any section with a telephone could thus be connected to any other extension.

The photograph section maintained the heavy hand-held cameras and camera guns. It instructed air gunners in the taking of oblique, pinpoint and mosaic photographs.

Accurate map reading was essential for photography. In the Esher Trophy test, eight map references were given to the photographer in a sealed envelope. Each position had to be identified on the map, located from the air and photographed within a total of two hours. The results had then to be developed, printed and forwarded within 48 hours.

Parachutes had long been standard equipment. By October 1919, Colthrop parachutes had been issued to crews of Avro 504Ks and in 1924, just before the formation of 603, the RAF made the Irvin parachute standard equipment. Although no one in the unit had yet used a parachute, the parachute section set a high standard of meticulous packing and maintenance which was maintained for many years and prompted a thoughtful and well intentioned response from the Squadron pilots following the Battle of Britain.

Left: Hawker Harts (from left to right: K3876, K3864 and K3859) of 603 flying over the Bass Rock. Tantallon Castle can be seen in the background.
Right: Hawker Hart I flown by Count Stevens, sometime between 1934 and 1938.

The workshops were nominally responsible for the overhaul, repair and modification of airframes and engines; for maintenance of all Squadron equipment in a serviceable condition and for the manufacture of parts which could not be obtained from a stores depot. In the case of airframes, however, staff in the flights were capable of carrying out all repairs and did not need to call on the central workshops for help.

Transport was responsible for the movement of personnel, stores, fuel, etc. between Turnhouse, Town Headquarters and the bombing range. Journeys were made regardless of weather conditions. The section also provided the ambulance and fire tender.

The stores held and safeguarded adequate stocks of everything needed to maintain aircraft, equipment etc, at maximum efficiency. They re-ordered as necessary to ensure timely arrival. The work was humdrum and unexciting but the administration was complex and the training needed was as exacting as for any other trade.

These activities imposed a heavy strain on the auxiliary airmen. At least two evenings each week were devoted to intensive theoretical instruction in individual trades at Town Headquarters. There was also regular PT and drill. 603 frequently appeared in public in Edinburgh and all ranks were determined that it should be as smart as any unit in Scotland. At annual camp at Manston in 1933, Air Commodore MacNeece-Foster congratulated 603 on carrying out the best piece of drill he had seen by an auxiliary squadron and the following year they performed well in the demanding Scottish military pageant.

There was a scheme for training auxiliary airmen in flight administrative duties. The rank of Leading Aircraftman (LAC) and above attended a class once a month at Turnhouse on the detailed vouchers and paperwork needed to run a flight. Fitters and riggers were sent on short courses to the School of Technical Training at Manston in Kent.

In the past individual instructors had set question papers for their pupils, but from 1933 two examinations each year were organised on the lines of the official Trade Test Boards. The official boards were conducted by the Group Technical Officer and promotion depended on results achieved. Following the introduction of trial examinations there was a marked improvement in the number of passes in official tests.

The Edinburgh trade holidays in July 1934 marked the start of summer camp, again at Manston from 21 July to 4 August. An advance party left to set up tents at the nominated aerodrome. Having seen the aeroplanes off from Turnhouse, the rest of the Squadron assembled at Town Headquarters. Led by the pipe band, they marched through the streets of Edinburgh to the station for a rather uncomfortable 16-hour train journey.

Work at camp started promptly at six each morning. The aerodrome was usually clear for at least two hours and this was helpful for pilots under instruction. The CO's parade was at 09.00 and, after this, work continued until 12.30.

At summer camp, 603 operated as part of the RAF. There were exercises with regular squadrons and these were made as realistic as possible. At Manston in 1934, nine Harts were sent on a triangular course cross-country flight. The leader was told to maintain wireless contact with the ground and the

Left: Hart I, c. 1935. George Denholm at the controls of K3859.
Right: Hart I K3859, over Fidra, Firth of Forth, flown by George Denholm.
Bottom: AAF gathering at Sir Lindsay Everard's estate c.1934. The planes are Wapitis and Harts.

location of targets was given by wireless but only after the formation was airborne. Three machines were detailed for camera-gun practice and these were intercepted and attacked by a fighter. Two aeroplanes were required to make an oblique photograph of targets en route whilst a third took a 'mosaic' of a given area. The remaining aircraft were given targets to bomb.

Ian Millar reflects on his time with 603:

I was brought up at Turnhouse, long before the days of Edinburgh Airport. Apart from golf, football and various other activities I cultivated a great interest in flying. Turnhouse also housed one or two private aircraft of the De Havilland Gypsy Moth vintage. Some of you may know of the young Edinburgh flyer Jim Mollison and his epic flights which brought him many records. These were the days of the flying circuses, and one of the first I saw had as one of its members the selfsame Jim Mollison and his famous Gypsy Moth, G-AAXA, with which he shattered the England to Australia record. I would be about twelve years old at the time and naturally Mollison became my great childhood hero. After all, he came from Edinburgh... and I had actually met him and collected his autograph.

About this time I was lucky enough to have my first flight in a Gypsy Moth, and from that moment I was determined to get into the air again and again. This wasn't possible at that time, although I did manage another flight or two in the Moth.

I soon learned there was a chance of joining the Auxiliary Air Force, but this couldn't be done until I was eighteen. Somehow, I did manage to be accepted, on a provisional basis, about six months before then, but flying was out until I was officially accepted. I knew that only commissioned officers were accepted as pilots, and in the days before the war one simply couldn't obtain a commission without being of private means, but I was quite happy to try to become an observer, if I could. My eyesight wasn't 100%, although I only wore glasses for reading, and although I could have passed the eyesight test I took no chances and sneaked into the medical room one night to memorise the chart. In due course I was officially accepted as AC2 Miller – air observer under training.

Towards the end of 1935, I had my first flight in a Hawker Hart, a two-seater day bomber, and that was me well and truly hooked. All I could think of was to get more and more flying and every weekend saw me at Turnhouse and during summer evenings there was flying on Mondays and Fridays as well. Of course it wasn't all flying and there was a great deal of theory to take up our time. Being an observer meant air gunnery which consisted of a Lewis gun mounted on a Scarff-ring which could be rotated and elevated up or down. One also had to be the bomb-aimer; the Hart could carry eight light bombs, and the bomb sight was

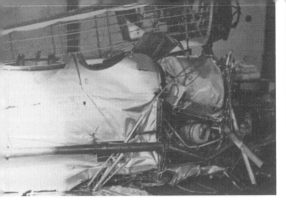
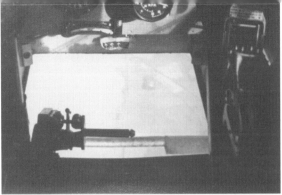

Top left: Crashes were not common and usually the Hart construction protected the crew during minor accidents.
Top right: View through Hart floor used by pilot for bomb aiming.
Bottom: From left to right: Lord G. N. Douglas-Hamilton, two unknown gunners and F/O Stevens. The aircraft is a Hawker Hind. P/O Haig in cockpit.

mounted above a panel in the floor which could be slid back to allow one to lie on the floor and sight the bomb using long hair-wire sights which could be set to allow for height, speed and wind-drift. I was also responsible for the navigation, which was of the dead-reckoning type, using maps and a course and speed calculator. The observer also did photographic work, both vertical, with the camera mounted in the floor, and oblique with a hand-held camera pointing over the side of the aircraft.

These were great days, and I spent many happy afternoons in the air. Communication with the pilot was by speaking tube connected to earphones in the helmets. It wasn't easy, in open cockpits, with a big Rolls-Royce Kestrel engine bellowing away six feet ahead. Later in the Hawker Hinds we enjoyed the luxury of radio-telephone communication, and oxygen equipment.

We did much close formation flying, and I can tell you that a squadron formation take-off consisting of nine machines taking off together was very hairy indeed. It wasn't so bad if you were in the leading machines of the V-formation, but every slight swerve of these leading aircraft made the task of the following ones very dicey indeed. Yet despite flying in really tight formation we had no accidents, and the quality of the piloting was first class. I personally loved photographic work and did a good deal of serious work in this field.

We also dropped bombs – practice bombs fitted with smoke detonation to mark the accuracy. We had two local bombing ranges, one at Fauldhouse in West Lothian, and the other at Dalgety Bay, where we bombed targets towed by the Navy. Undoubtedly my most memorable bombing run was in the summer of 1938 when I went off one Saturday afternoon to drop bombs at Fauldhouse. It was a glorious day, but there was a heat haze over the ground and after one or two passes I decided to return home without dropping the bombs. Coming back just past Bathgate the engine suddenly stopped, and the pilot and I looked at each other with some dismay. We would be flying about five thousand feet up at the time. We both picked on the same field to make a forced dead-engine landing, but as we neared the field at about 80-90 mph we saw it was not exactly level, and looked distinctly bumpy. You don't get another chance in these circumstances, and I knew we were in for trouble. The pilot was strapped in his seat with a full harness, but the poor old observer, who had a lift-up rear-facing seat merely had a harness fastened to his body with a strong steel cable, about three feet in length, attached between the harness and the floor. This was to ensure he was not thrown out of the 'plane during flight, and offered no crash protection. Remembering that one of my colleagues had been killed a few weeks before when his head hit the ground I put up the seat, ducked my head below the rim of the cockpit, and held on tight waiting for the inevitable. As soon as the fixed undercarriage wheels hit the soft ground we somersaulted. The radio shot out from its fixings and there was a great rending and crashing all around. Eventually all was quiet and I realised I was still in one piece. However, I was upside down and when I released myself I finished up in the marsh. The pilot was more fortunate – he fell on to the upside down top wing. Within two or three minutes a crowd had gathered, and I had to enlist the aid of a policeman to keep them from the aircraft, because I still had eight practice bombs on board, and had lost the safety pins in the crash.

The pilot went off to phone Turnhouse and someone flew over at low level and dropped us a bag with safety pins. The bombs secured we were then returned by car. I went into town that evening to find I'd hit the headlines in the late editions of the *News and Dispatch* and when I got back to Turnhouse about 11 pm the wreckage was just arriving at the aerodrome.

I escaped with nothing worse than several hundred tiny cuts and scratches, and was off bombing again at Dalgety Bay the following day. But I can assure you I was listening to every beat of the engine till I got back. After lengthy enquiries it transpired that the aircraft had been flying the previous night, and that the fitter responsible had not refuelled the 'plane but had signed up the documents as 'full' the following day. He was court-martialled, and was sentenced to six months in Aldershot (He was a fulltime member of the RAF.)

By the end of 1934, an aircraft had been allotted to 603 for night flying. The electricians consequently gained valuable experience in fitting and maintaining night flying equipment.

One of the RAF's best fighter squadrons, 19(F), came to Turnhouse in April 1935 for ten days of intensive fighter affiliation exercises. 603 was opposed by Gauntlets, the latest single-seat fighter. There were also a number of co-operative exercises with troops of Scottish Command.

On 4 March 1935, new arrival Pilot Officer Ken Macdonald was commissioned in the AAF. His colleague, Pilot Officer Laurie Cunningham, was commissioned on 6 May. During flying weekends Ken Macdonald shared a room in the officers mess with George Denholm who enjoyed hunting with other Squadron members. Unfortunately, Ken suffered severe asthma attacks triggered by pollen and horses, an affliction which had plagued him since childhood. On returning to his room, George's tweeds were inclined to trigger an attack!

On 11 May, the Duke and Duchess of York drove in procession through the streets of Edinburgh and 603 took part in the parade led by its pipe band. On 25 May the Duke of Kent visited Turnhouse for Empire Air Day – the event was a great success with good weather and an attendance of approximately 4,000 people.

On 6 July 1935 a detachment of six officers and 24 NCOs and men with four aircraft went to RAF Mildenhall for the Royal Air Force Review by His Majesty King George V. There was not one monoplane on the field. Many of the RAF's front line squadrons at this time were equipped with Bristol Bulldogs with a maximum speed of around 170 mph. It is salutary to note that the slowest contemporary Italian bomber was capable of more than 200 mph. The RAF, however, set more store on manoeuvrability than speed.

Annual training in July 1935 was at Tangmere in Sussex from 20 July to 3 August. Three of the Squadron's aircraft managed to do the trip without refuelling. During the AOC's inspection, the band played the slow march 'Mallorca', which had been written by the Prince of Wales. There was a competition for the best-kept aircraft which resulted in a tie between the A Flight Avro, the oldest machine in the unit, and a Hart which had been entirely built by A Flight earlier in the year. This was a striking tribute to the high level of competence attained by fitters and riggers.

Recruiting reopened in September and a large number of men applied for the few vacancies. The Squadron was up to its establishment and well on the way to becoming self sufficient. Nearly all flying instruction was given by auxiliary instructors, and auxiliary airmen did practically all the work at Turnhouse and Town Headquarters, supervised by their own NCOs. The adjutant commented:

> Now this, whilst being very creditable to the Auxiliaries, is equally so to the Regulars. It means that each regular has trained his opposite number, or numbers, among the Auxiliaries to a pitch where he can be trusted to do the job without supervision.

603's aim of self sufficiency was carried further by the appointment of auxiliary accounting and medical officers, Pilot Officer Tommy C. Garden and Flying Officer Iain A.G.L. Dick.

The Forth Bridge, with its massive spans, was a constant temptation to adventurous young pilots, although the RAF sternly discouraged such reckless flying. On one particular occasion a regular officer was court-martialled at Donibristle for the serious crime of flying under the bridge and S/L Lord Geordie Douglas-Hamilton was called as a witness. The CO felt strongly that he could only give accurate evidence if he had first-hand experience so prudently borrowed a civilian aircraft, so that there could be no complaint from the RAF, and flew to Donibristle, passing under the Forth Bridge on his way. He had assumed that the defending officer would ask him if such a feat was dangerous, in which case he could truthfully reply 'Not at all – I flew under it myself on the way here'. Alas, the question was not asked and history does not record what happened to the unlucky pilot.

In addition to keen competition between flights there was also friendly rivalry with 603's sister Scottish squadron – 602 (City of Glasgow). However, both squadrons closed ranks when facing a challenge from south of the border. The late Air Vice-Marshal Sandy Johnstone of 602 recalls an episode when a combined 602/603 rugby team flew south to play English Auxiliaries. It was his first flight in a Hart. Snow started soon after the formation crossed the border. The storm increased and by universal consent, they decided to turn back. Petrol ran low and visibility was almost nil. Having missed the Forth Bridge by luck (they passed between two of the three cantilevers), their fuel ran out. Fortunately Sandy Johnstone and Douglas Farquhar, who later flew from Hornchurch with 603 as part of a wing, managed to land on Portobello beach. The tide was rising but they manhandled their Hart along the sand and up a slipway on to the road. They tied one wing to a lamp-post and the other to a drinking fountain. A passing policeman agreed to stand guard and the intrepid pair took a tramcar to the nearest police station. Another 602 Hart landed on its nose in a field and a 603 aeroplane suffered a similar indignity.

In 1936, the Squadron took delivery of a new training aircraft, the Avro Tutor and F/L James Jack, MC was awarded a well deserved MBE for his work with the armament section.

John Rendall was an apprentice cabinet maker in 1936 when he joined 603 as a rigger and reckoned that he got in because they had wooden planes. In January 1940, John would be the first to be posted from 603 when he was sent to 612 (County of Aberdeen) Squadron, at Dyce. His most painful memory of those early days at Turnhouse was getting a series of injections and then being ordered to fill sandbags with a stiff and very painful arm. According to John, a present-day stalwart of the 603 Association, although everyone in the Squadron was a part-timer in the 1930s, they still had accommodation at Turnhouse:

> I had my own billet in the Auxiliary's barrack block for three years but the moment war broke out I was kicked out and slept for a week on the floor of the hangar before we moved into wooden huts. But it was never like my cushy bed in the barracks.

It came as no surprise to Jim Skinner when he joined in 1938 to find that half the boys with whom he had been at school were already members of 603: 'There were four boys from the same stair [tenement block] in which I lived as well as several others from the same street and we all ended up playing football for the Squadron team.' Jim also recalls that the Squadron had a number of colourful characters including a parachute packer who only worked at night because his hands sweated too much during the day, or the pay clerk who couldn't get up in the morning and regularly wore his pyjamas under his uniform!

During the 1930s Turnhouse was open on Sundays for training and 603 members who turned up for training were given nine-pence a day for their bus fare but this was by no means guaranteed. Later they were to receive more regular payments for their weekends. The highlight for Squadron members was the annual bounty payment which was £5 per year. Phil Reilly recalls: 'When you got the big white five pound note you felt like Andrew Carnagie.' In 1935, Charlie Dorward bumped into a chum from the Boys Brigade:

> He said he was going off to train with 603 so I just went along with him. That was on a Thursday. I had a medical on the Monday – and that was me in. I then discovered I knew a lot of the members of the Squadron Pipe Band who had all been in the Boys Brigade band.

The uniform for the auxiliaries in the 1930s was still a hangover from WWI. According to Charlie 'A swagger stick was issued to everyone and I was never sure if it was there to keep our hands out of our pockets. We wore puttees and breeches, which looked like pantaloons and blew out at the sides.' Charles began as a fitter armourer before eventually becoming an instructor. He left 603 in February 1941, but not before he'd been in the advance party of 30 from the Squadron to take part in the Battle of Britain: 'Within a few days we'd lost three with six injured,' he said. G/C Ivone Kirkpatrick, a pre-war auxiliary pilot, recounted an amusing incident in January 1936:

> It was that month that I was married in the Old Chapel at Turnhouse, a wooden hut at the back of the original officers mess on the other side of the road from the A Flight hangar. It was cold, and dear old Flight Sergeant Champion, then the Squadron NCO in charge of discipline, somehow wangled one bucket of coal, but only one, which I suspect was somewhat illegal! He held it back until the last minute and duly stoked the only means of heating, the old round stove situated in the middle of the hut, and hoped that it would give out sufficient heat to warm the wedding guests, who I must say were somewhat numerous. The ceremony was held by The Rev Rossie Brown, the Squadron Chaplain and my cousin The Rev James Kirkpatrick. Remember, it was a cold winter's day and on leaving the chapel we found F/O Denholm sitting in the driver's seat of the Squadron's firetender – a completely open affair, I think an Albion – and F/Sgt Champion with a blanket (for the bride). We embarked with the four Guards of Honour like myself in full dress uniform, 'porridge bowl' hat and sword, standing on the running board holding on to the mounted equipment and off we drove to the then new officers mess on the far side of the aerodrome – since burnt down.
>
> This performance had some repercussions as it was given much publicity in the press. The Air Ministry wanted to know who gave an officer permission to drive a service vehicle (officers were not allowed to do so), and who authorised the use of service transport? No question was raised as to the bucket of coal !!

In February 1936, Pilot Officer Fred Rushmer's commission was confirmed with effect from 19 October 1935. In April 1936, the CO, S/L Lord Geordie Douglas-Hamilton, requested that the officers of 603 Squadron be allowed to wear the kilt with mess dress. At the same time, his brother, The Marquis of Clydesdale (later to become The Duke of Hamilton), who was the Officer Commanding 602 (City of Glasgow) Squadron, made the same request. On 8 July 1936 HM King Edward VIII approved the wearing of the Grey Douglas tartan with mess dress for both the officers of 602 and 603 Squadrons only, an honour which exists to this day.

The kilt was not to be worn by regular officers. The cost of the new mess dress was very high – Sandy Johnstone recalled that it was about £90 – and 603 reluctantly decided that this was too much and did not avail themselves of the privilege. 602 Squadron studied their various accounts and discovered a contingency fund established early in the Squadron's life for some long forgotten purpose. They felt that the purchase of kilts was certainly a contingency and promptly used the fund accordingly.

The system of training fitters and riggers was again improved. Airmen spent the first three months in a combined class at Town Headquarters. They then split into separate classes for their own trades, at the end of which they took their first Trade Test Board. On passing they went on to advanced classes in their specialised trades. Lectures were typed out and copies given to each pupil to help him with private study.

Training then moved to Turnhouse. The first stage of two to three months consisted of general flight work, handling and care and maintenance of aircraft. Next came preliminary basic training in the workshops. Finally there was advanced work in both flight and workshop. The success of this new system was soon reflected in a higher pass rate in official Trade Test Boards.

Air pilotage now gave way to air navigation on a much more scientific basis. Wireless direction-finding facilities were installed in Scotland and these helped greatly in navigation exercises.

Affiliation with a regular squadron, 43 (Fighter), took place in early May. As usual this was one of the most popular flying exercises of the year and both pilots and air gunners gained valuable experience.

Top: RAF Leuchars Annual Training Camp 1936.
Left: Visit to Turnhouse of King George VI. C/O Lord G. Douglas-Hamilton in black greatcoat, F/L J Jack centre.

On 29 May an ambitious flying programme was arranged at Turnhouse for the Empire Air Day which attracted a magnificent crowd of nearly 8,000 – a clear indication that the citizens of Edinburgh were not just fascinated by the spectacle of flying but were also becoming increasingly proud of 603's activities. The proceeds of £323-3s/11d made up part of a £650 donation to the RAF Benevolent Fund.

On 31 May 1936, 603 flew to Newtownards in Northern Ireland. On arrival they were entertained by the Secretary of State for Air, The Marquis of Londonderry. Among other guests was the German Foreign Minister, Herr von Ribbentrop. He had flown over from Berlin in his Junkers, an aircraft with which the Squadron was to become very familiar in years to come.

For the first time in their history, in 1936 the Squadron went to an armament training camp for their annual summer camp at Leuchars. Despite adverse weather conditions a great deal was done, chiefly air firing and bombing. It was a strenuous time for aircrews and armourers but the work was most interesting. One officer, a keen game shot, was heard to remark that he would rather shoot at the drogue than a rocketing pheasant.

The timetable was changed and the Squadron worked from early morning until late at night. Their efficiency and enthusiasm won high praise from the AOC and the regular staff of the station.

In August, a major change took place at Turnhouse. A regular squadron, No.83, began to form, and with two squadrons it was necessary to establish a station headquarters. S/L Lord Geordie Douglas-Hamilton took charge and the AOC noted: '…the Officer Commanding 603 Squadron has the unique distinction of being the first auxiliary officer to command a station on which regular as well as auxiliary units are under his command.' The change involved considerable work, especially for stores, which now had to meet the requirements of the entire station.

Officer Commanding 83 Squadron was Squadron Leader D.A. Boyle. He had been adjutant to 601 Squadron at Hendon and was well used to the auxiliaries. Relations between 83 and 603 were therefore very cordial. Boyle being a regular officer was appointed CO of Turnhouse in succession to Lord Geordie Douglas-Hamilton. Marshal of the Royal Air Force, Sir Dermot Boyle GCB, KCVO, KBE, AFC, recalled a happy informal arrangement by which he commanded Turnhouse during the week and Lord Douglas-Hamilton took over at the weekend.

Top: Empire Air Day, Turnhouse, 1936.
Above: Tutor K3454 at Turnhouse.
Right: P/O Robin McGregor Waterston, 'Bubble', 3 February 1937.

Unfortunately, 1937 proved to be a less colourful year for 603. In January 1937, Ken Macdonald and Laurie Cunningham received news of their promotion to Flying Officer. Robin 'Bubble' Waterston and 'Hamish' Somerville were commissioned as Pilot Officers in the AuxAF on 3 and 4 February, respectively. All four men were destined to leave an indelible mark on the history of the unit, three of them on the nation. The following entry was made in the Squadron ORB: 'May 12th, Coronation of HM King George VI. Party of 1 Officer and 10 Airmen proceeded to London to act as Street Lining Party. The CO and 3 Officers and 3 Airmen awarded coronation medals.'

F/O Dick, the Squadron Medical Officer, was promoted to Flight Lieutenant and in July, a detachment of five officers and 70 AAF airmen from 603 formed part of the street lining party for the 'State Entry' into Edinburgh of King George VI and Queen Elizabeth.

Also in July, the annual summer camp took place at Hawkinge between the 11th and 25th, attended by 20 officers and 150 airmen. Cross country navigation still held traps for the unwary. In the nine o'clock news one night the BBC broadcast an appeal for information about an aircraft missing on a flight from Edinburgh to Kenley in Surrey. It had last been seen over Welwyn Garden City about lunch time. In the ten o'clock news the BBC reported that one of the first people to respond had been the pilot of the missing aircraft who insisted that he had landed at Kenley at the scheduled time. The airfield and all hangars at Kenley were searched but there was no trace of the aircraft. The Air Ministry eventually found the aircraft at Biggin Hill some seven miles from

Kenley. They explained that F/O Wynne-Powell had landed at Biggin Hill, seen the duty pilot and told him that he was expected and had permission to leave the aircraft until Friday. The duty pilot said he had no instructions but supposed it was all right. Geoff Wynne-Powell then left for London still believing he had landed safely at Kenley, until he heard the radio broadcast!

Unfortunately, the weather for summer camp at Hawkinge was bad. The Squadron were as usual under canvas but a sudden cloud burst in the early hours flooded the tents. The airmen were not displeased. They spent the rest of their stay in the old officers' mess. Nevertheless, by the end of the camp Pilot Officers Hamish Somerville and Bubble Waterston had been awarded the 'flying badge'.

On 12 September the Squadron sports day took place at Turnhouse and involved officers, NCOs and airmen of 603 Squadron and the RAF Station. At that time the 603 personnel included many gifted athletes, including Ken Macdonald, who was a good tennis player and had been an outstanding oarsman at Cambridge, and Pat Gifford, a fine cricketer, squash player and fencer as well as being a good shot – a common skill among the more successful fighter pilots.

At the end of 1937, F/L Frank H. Tyson, the adjutant, wrote in the magazine:

When I was posted to the Squadron in January, I arrived knowing little about the Auxiliary Air Force and less about the working of an auxiliary squadron. From the beginning, I was astounded at the keenness of both officers and airmen, and at the amount of time which they gave up to the work of the Squadron.

I very soon found that the Squadron was a self supporting unit, the ab initio flying training of pupils being undertaken by auxiliary officers, and the inspection and servicing of the aircraft being carried out mainly by the auxiliary airmen.

This was a most satisfactory state of affairs, but I was to be even more impressed when, at annual camp, I found that in almost every department the Squadron could be manned entirely by the auxiliary personnel. The maintenance work in the flights and the specialist work in the sections was of a very high standard and was a great credit to the auxiliary NCOs. It is noteworthy to record that during the period there were no flying accidents or forced landings. It was difficult to find sufficient work for the regular personnel, and it is hoped that it will not be necessary for as many of them to be taken to camp in 1938.

The prospects for the future are particularly good. It seems possible that in the coming year we may be re-equipped.

Left: Ken Macdonald with his older sister Ewen at the family home in Edinburgh 1937. Ken is wearing a black armband following the death of HM King George V.
Right: The 603 pipe band leading the rest of the Squadron, 1937.

The Squadron had played a full part at the Coronation ceremonial in London and during the Royal visit to Edinburgh (of His Majesty King George VI) but there was no event during the year which gave the CO: '…more pleasure than acting as the instrument through which His Majesty presented Coronation medals to officers and airmen of the Squadron in recognition of the value of their services.'

During December 1937, the ORB recorded: 'Two new pupils began ab-initio training: Mr I.S. Ritchie and Mr C.D. Peel.' Ian 'Woolly Bear' Ritchie and Charles Peel became two of the Squadron's most endearing characters with Peel being the first 603 pilot to lose his life during the Battle of Britain.

At town headquarters, 1937. Front, from left to right: F/O Gifford; S/L Lord G Douglas-Hamilton; F/L Jack and P/O Somerville. Middle, from left to right: F/O Denholm; F/O Rushmer; P/O Waterston; F/O Stevens and F/O Wynne-Powell. Back, from left to right: F/L Reid; F/O Watts; F/O Cunningham; F/O Macdonald; F/L Kirkpatrick and F/O Thomson.

In the 1937 Squadron magazine, Air Commodore J.C. Quinnell DFC, Air Officer Commanding 6 (Auxiliary) Group wrote:

> During the past year the Auxiliary Air Force has continued its programme of development, and changes of great importance have taken place.
>
> It had for some time been intended that when the Auxiliary Air Force squadrons became proficient, not only in flying but in their ground organization as well, they should be transferred to the regular groups under which they would operate in the event of war, side by side with the regulars in the defence of the country. The old established auxiliary squadrons were considered to have reached this stage, and foremost amongst the changes during the past year was the decision to carry into effect the policy of transfer to the regular groups. No greater tribute could be paid to the Auxiliary Air Force than this official recognition of its keenness and general efficiency.
>
> At this time 6 (Auxiliary) Group contained all the auxiliary squadrons, totalling 18, and one special reserve unit, and the first units to leave under this new decision were the three fighter squadrons at Hendon. These squadrons were 600, 601, and 604, and they were transferred to 11 Fighter Group in Fighter Command on 1st December 1936, shortly after my message to you last year was written. In February 1937, 602 and 605 Squadrons were transferred to 2 Group in Bomber Command. Later on 607 and 608 Squadrons were placed under the newly-formed 12 Fighter Group in May 1937.
>
> While 603 (City of Edinburgh) Squadron is, I am pleased to say, second to none in efficiency, its transfer to a regular group has been held in abeyance pending a decision as to whether its role is to be changed.
>
> A year ago the total strength of the Auxiliary Air Force was 15 squadrons. Today it stands at 19 squadrons, with one more army co-operation squadron to be formed.
>
> I congratulate all ranks of 603 Squadron on the keenness, energy, and ability they have displayed in promoting the high standard of efficiency which has now been attained by the Squadron: I wish the Squadron the best of luck for its continued success.

Seven of the 18 auxiliary squadrons were transferred to regular fighter and bomber groups during 1937. 603 had been a candidate for transfer to army co-operation and that was being reconsidered.

The War Clouds Gather

After the deceptive lull of 1937, the coming year was to be a time of intense activity. Events in Europe had become increasingly grave. In October 1935, Italy invaded Abyssinia. The Germans moved into the Rhineland in 1936, the year which saw the start of the Spanish Civil War and in 1938 the invasion of Austria took place as well as the Czechoslovakian crisis. As a direct consequence of the worsening

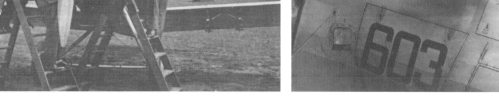

Turnhouse c. 1934-1938. Hawker Hart I with groundcrew.   603 Squadron gunner.

international situation between 1935 to 1938, the dark clouds of war began to form over Europe.

Financial provision for the RAF had at last begun to rise. The annual total of 'Air Estimates plus Defence Loans' rose from £17.7 million in 1934 to £27.5 million in 1935 and £50.1 million in 1936. 1937 saw the figure more than doubled to £137.6 million and the total for 1938 would be £200 million.

As of 1 January 1938, the 603 Nominal Roll was:

HAC The Earl of Stair.
S/L Lord G.N. Douglas-Hamilton.
S/L Chaplain, Reverend J. Rossie Brown.
F/Ls: F.H. Tyson (Adjutant), T.M. McNeil (Admin), I. Kirkpatrick (OC C Flight), E.H. Stevens (OC A Flight), J.L. Jack MBE, MC, (Armament), G.A. Reid (OC B Flight), H.F. Webb (Equipment Officer), T.C. Garden (Accountant Officer), I.G.L. Dick (Medical Officer).
F/Os: I.D. Shields, P. Gifford, J.G.E. Haig, G.L. Denholm, J.M. Shewell, F.W. Rushmer, G.A.G. Thomson, H.K. Macdonald, J.L.G. Cunningham, G.T. Wynne-Powell.
P/Os: J.A.B. Somerville, R. McG. Waterston.

Officer Commanding B Flight, F/L George Reid, was a popular and hard-working member of the pre-war Squadron. Before the outbreak of WWII he transferred to the Volunteer Reserve and became Assistant Chief Flying Instructor to Wing Commander I.E. Chalmers Watson at the Edinburgh RAFVR Centre. (See appendix for brief history.) Chalmers Watson had been appointed to the post by Scottish Aviation Ltd and was also a pre-war veteran of 603 Squadron.* George Reid did not return to 603 during the war but as a Beaufighter pilot flying operations in the same theatre as his former Squadron, he was later killed during an attack on the Greek island of Kos.

In February 1938, 603 were re-equipped with Hawker Hinds. This was a developed version of the Hart, but with a 640hp fully supercharged Rolls-Royce Kestrel V engine.

Perhaps due to unfamiliarity with the new type, a tragic and avoidable accident took place on 26 March. It was a standing order that no aircraft was put away without being refuelled. This was not done in the case of a B Flight Hind. Even more regrettable was that the F700 was completed by the fitter, indicating that all checks and servicing had been carried out. Flying Officer C.A.G. Thomson and AC2 R.H. Scarret, his air gunner, took off and during the flight the engine failed and the aircraft crashed killing both crew members. The accident was quickly reported to Turnhouse and Flight Lieutenant Ted Colbeck-Welch flew the CO over the crash-site. Along with F/L Tyson, Colbeck-Welch was immediately summoned to Group Headquarters in London for searching and crucial questioning. The fitter was subsequently court martialled.

In March 83 (B) Squadron moved from Turnhouse to its permanent base at RAF Scampton and the Station Headquarters closed on 15 April 1938. This re-organisation threw a considerable burden on 603's administration.

---

*During the war W/C Chalmers Watson AFC was employed initially as a Test Pilot on American aircraft when they arrived at Scottish aerodromes. He later became a squadron commander at an OTU and on a number of occasions was shot up by intruders. He was later reunited with George Denholm and Black Morton at Acklington with 1460 Turbinlite Flight. By D-Day he was with a Mosquito squadron flying ground attack missions. He became a Squadron Leader Night Operations, Station Commander of two RAF Stations, and No.142 Airfield. He was awarded the AFC.

On 1 April 1938, S/L Lord Geordie Douglas-Hamilton completed his term of office and relinquished command. He was promoted to wing commander and awarded a well-deserved AFC having steered the Squadron through four of its most difficult formative years. When he took over in 1934, the main responsibility had rested with regular NCOs. All flying training had been carried out by the adjutant and assistant adjutant. The percentage of trained men to establishment was under 60%. He left a fully self-sufficient unit, as highly trained as any in the Auxiliary Air Force. His efforts were recognised when, later that year, 603 won the Esher Trophy as the most efficient auxiliary squadron. On relinquishing command he was transferred to the Auxiliary Air Force (AAF) general list with the rank of Wing Commander. Ahead lay high office and great honours. A wartime

Esprit de corps. F/Sgt Jock Prentice (veteran) of 603, and other members of the Squadron (including Olly Mevlin, Ben Middlehurst, Jock Struthers, George Maclaren and Ian 'Micky' Campbell) admiring the Esher Trophy won by the Squadron for all-round efficiency among AAF Squadrons, 1938. The Squadron was to win the trophy once more in 1951.

Group Captain, the Right Honourable The Earl of Selkirk became successively Paymaster General, Chancellor of the Duchy of Lancaster, First Lord of the Admiralty, UK Commissioner for Singapore and Commissioner General for South East Asia.

The new commanding officer was Squadron Leader Ernest Hildebrand Stevens, OC A Flight. The command was a task he relished and a position of which he was immensely proud. He was a gregarious, amusing character known by his close friends as 'Steve' but more popularly as 'Count' due to his apparent aristocratic appearance and professional standing as a lawyer.

By now the Squadron had acquired one of the new Link trainers, an excellent machine for simulating blind flying on the ground and it was put to good use.

Distance between home and Turnhouse never affected the enthusiasm and attendance of 603 members. Patsy Gifford, OC B Flight, was a solicitor who later became a burgh procurator fiscal and town councillor. In 1931, whilst studying law in Edinburgh he joined 603 and became an enthusiastic 'weekend flyer', regularly attending two weekday evenings a week during the summer months. He owned a selection of fast cars and when travelling to and from Turnhouse used their capabilities to the full. His job as a practising solicitor in the family business (which still bears the Gifford name) was in stark contrast to his interests and he continued to spend his

Pat Gifford, c. 1937.

Patsy aka 'Nanny' with his Frazer Nash, 'ninety in third!'

Summer camp, July 1938, Ramsgate.

free time satisfying his great interest in aviation, later boasting that he could cover the 95 mile journey from his home in Castle Douglas, Kirkcudbridgeshire, to Turnhouse in 80 minutes in his Frazer-Nash sports car which he claimed could do 'ninety in third.' This comment was quickly adopted by the other pilots as a light-hearted war-cry. Legend has it that the local police were familiar to Gifford's transgressions of the speeding laws but despite lying in wait they never managed to catch him. In fact, in order to avoid the inevitable confrontations, Ted Colbeck-Welch occasionally flew to Castle Douglas to collect Patsy prior to a weekend's flying. Patsy was much respected by the other men. It was during his years at Sedburgh School that he developed his great aptitude for sports. His two sisters were much admired by his fellow officers and Gifford himself is remembered as having had a number of pretty girlfriends. George Denholm recalled his colleague:

> Gifford absolutely loved flying and he utterly relished the war when it came. He did not drink, because he did not like it, but would sometimes have a glass of sherry to show he was prepared to join in occasionally. I think his mother was American and was very charming, a quality which he inherited to a fair degree. In the phrase of the time he could shoot an imperial line – for example about being upside-down (airborne) 'With nothing on the clock .' Another side of his character was that he gave a lot of thought to the technicalities of air-fighting and I think he was the first man I ever heard decry the bullet pattern used for eight-gun fighters at the beginning of the war. He soon decided it was useless.

In June 1938, Pat Gifford was promoted to Flight Lieutenant with effect from 1st April. From 9-23 July the annual summer camp took place at Ramsgate, Kent, and included the prestigious pipe band. As a gesture of appreciation for them, the airmen organised a collection amongst themselves for a handsome mace for the drum major. This was designed, manufactured and presented in time for the Remembrance Service. It was re-presented to the re-formed 603 Squadron in 2000 and today is on display in the entrance hall of the Town Headquarters.

Ramsgate was the first occasion the unit had camped at a civil aerodrome and the absence of normal RAF facilities meant more work for the specialist sections but the station commander at Manston and Squadron Leader Eckersley-Maslin of the Thanet Flying Club provided invaluable assistance. Whilst there the unit was inspected by the AOC 6 (Aux) Group who subsequently carried out the annual inspection at Turnhouse on 16 October.

During summer camp, almost the entire complement of auxiliary airmen crossed the Channel to spend a day in Calais, each man immaculately turned out in matching blazer, straw boater and flannels. This was the sort of outing for which Sergeant Angus 'Angy' Gillies had joined 603 and he wrote a colourful account for the 1938 magazine, which reflects the ésprit de corps during a worsening international situation:

Our Day Out

Old Calais had never been so gaily decorated since that memorable day when the 'Little Corporal' had blown a kiss to a fast-receding St. Helena before landing once more on the shores of his beloved France.

Yes, something was surely in the wind; slowly the news had filtered out, starting with a whisper of incredulity and rising to a veritable crescendo of exultation. The Boys are coming – no, not the Yanks – the 603 Bomber Squadron. And so with an 'Oh, la, la,' young ladies made a bee-line for the beauty parlours, and the old gentlemen, who had brought their noses with them from the East, with a 'Vara Goot,' got busy inverting cards marked 6 and transforming threes into eights with the skill of a master-hand.

The cause of all this fuss – US – See us as we made for the boat, heads up, chests out, and swinging our arms. Why even 'Little Willie' of A Flight had a go at the Goose-step, we all felt so happy.

Alas, we had not reckoned on Old Father Neptune grinning in the background; poor Little Willie was the very first to make his acquaintance half an hour after we had sailed and, if we had started a competition for Mal-de-Mer, he would have been an easy first. There he sat with head between his knees, intoning the names of every Channel swimmer he had ever heard of and swearing that every one of them must have been plumb crazy.

Of course, you couldn't blame Willie for being prejudiced against the sheet of water we were hurtling over, for he was really a gentle little soul and had become the regimental pet, when we learned that his reason for joining up was because his Dad bred canaries and so he felt he had flying in his very bones.

But all things must come to an end, so in due course we found ourselves disembarked and making our way into town, one that was in some respects not unlike our own Newhaven.

Soon we came to a parting of the ways, breaking off into groups, each with its own idea of enjoyment; the intelligentsia, for instance, were going to sample the thrill and excitement of the local museum. For us it was the fair ground for an hour or two, and we brought Nobbie Blank along with us under protest; he thought he should really join the museum fans, but we reminded him of his promise to help us along with the language difficulty.

Nobbie had told us that this was easy – just buy a book of French phrases and start off like this: 'How are you?', 'I am well,' and 'Father he is well,' and 'Mother she is well.' He maintained that by the time you had bored through the medical history sheets of the fourth or fifth generation you would be able to talk French like an old soldier intoning Hindustani.

Nobbie made his purchase from an old second-hand shop and came out with the book under his arm as pleased as Punch. His second purchase caused this same pride to have a mighty fall; he had been looking for a nice stuffed parrot to send to a well-endowed maiden aunt, and for a likely bargain he chose a shop owned by one of the Eastern gentlemen already mentioned.

From here he emerged like a raging tornado, but minus the book; this, he explained bitterly, he had left as part payment for the stuffed remains of a bird that evidently died in great agony. The old gent had looked at his book and then informed him that what he really was carrying was a Yiddish Street Directory.

Nobbie was nothing if not volatile, and soon he was staring with open mouth at a gentleman who swallowed swords for a living. Yes, it sure was a great Fun Fair, and soon we were to have a demonstration of telepathy with a vengeance. One of the boys treated a couple of urchins to a turn on the roundabouts, and in a jiffy we were surrounded by the youth of all France, also it appeared to my startled imagination, part of Belgium as well.

This embarrassing situation brought our visit to an untimely end and left us with an hour or two before our return to the boat. What better than 'to trip the light fantastic,' any old where. Nobbie hailed our suggestion with joy, but little did he know what was in store for him. Time and again he had told us that he had missed 'greatness' by inches. Well, now he was going to get it, all at once, thrust upon him the minute we had taken our seats in the Dance Hall which he himself had chosen on account of its colour scheme. In explanation of what followed I must state that he had not looked on the wine when it was red; of course I admit he may have given it a glance in passing – if you know what I mean. He was at the 'At peace with the world' stage, and, when a lady asked for the pleasure of a few rounds of 'ze dance,' he simply could not offer the frozen mitt, although she was a decided outsize. Nobbie was no baby himself, and when you get around 19 stone, a few ounces either way makes little difference. Soon the dance floor felt that something had happened, and trembled with apprehension.

Compared with these two frail creatures doing their act, all-in wrestling was but a Kindergarten Minuet, and an elephant stampede but the toddling footsteps of a year-old child. When Madam started doing the real thing the audience definitely sat up and took notice. Of course the old Frenchies had seen dancing of all sorts in their time – can-cans, apache hops, and other simple little things – but never anything like this, for, when Nobbie noticed his partner getting fresh, he kept the Union Jack firmly fixed in his mind's eye and started some old Plantation prancings that would have turned a real negro green with envy.

Time had flown and we nearly missed the boat; as Nobbie would insist on halting every now and then to demonstrate a step or two he had forgotten to let loose when he was upholding the honour of the 'Old Country.'

The journey home: a riot of harmony; but, alas, when we left the boat – high heads, swelled chests, and swinging arms were all gone – we were much too tired. What a day! Lots of fun and no harm done, as the song says, and everybody happy, which is the only fit and proper finish to a day out.

Not to be outdone, Count Stevens booked the front two rows of the Prince of Wales Theatre in London and invited all his officers and their wives. He caused some hilarity by getting up from time to time to number off his party with his umbrella to ensure that all had arrived safely.

On 24 July the ORB records: 'Squadron ceased to function as a bomber squadron and became a fighter squadron, was transferred from 6 Group in Bomber Command to 12(F) Group in Fighter Command.' In early August, Lord Stair relinquished his appointment as Honorary Air Commodore of 603, a position he had held for eight years and in which had always shown great interest in Squadron activities.

September 1938 saw the crisis over Czechoslovakia reach its height. The Fleet and Auxiliary Air Force were mobilised and at Turnhouse trenches were dug, ugly red brick machine-gun emplacements sprang up at strategic points around the perimeter and gas masks were issued to personnel. Although 603 were placed on alert, it was not felt necessary for all personnel to remain on the station. Key personnel were, however, required to be either at the aerodrome or within easy reach.

On 27 October 1938, 603 became a fighter squadron in 12 (Fighter) Group and eventually came under the control of 13 Group. AC Quinnell's message in the 1938 magazine read:

The most important event during the year 1938 was the Air Council decision that Auxiliary Air Force squadrons should be regarded as first-line units. The Crisis in September, when the fighter squadrons were called up and moved to their war stations ready to take their place side by side with the regulars in the defence of this country, showed that this confidence in the efficiency of the Auxiliary Air Force was justified. The other auxiliary squadrons would have played their part as well.

As a result of the recognition of the auxiliary squadrons as first-line units, it was decided to bring into effect as soon

Empire Air Day, Oct 1938. RAF Turnhouse.

as possible the policy whereby all Auxiliary Air Force squadrons should be placed in regular groups and to change the role of some of them, so that their services could be used to the best advantage in the general scheme of defence.

The scheme involved the transfer from 6 Group of ten auxiliary squadrons, some to be converted to fighters and others to become general reconnaissance squadrons. The latter are for the protection of shipping, which is a new responsibility for the Auxiliary Air Force.

The transfer of these squadrons, which commenced in October, was completed by the end of November. Among the squadrons to leave the Group was 603 (City of Edinburgh) Squadron, which in October changed its role from a bomber to a fighter squadron and was transferred to 12 (Fighter) Group.

During the period 603 Squadron has been under my command, it was a matter of satisfaction to me to see the fine spirit that prevailed amongst the officers and airmen, regulars as well as auxiliaries, to make this Squadron a success. I have watched with interest the process of welding it into an efficient fighting unit. As a bombing unit it had reached a high standard of efficiency, and on its change of role to fighter, I have no doubt it will maintain the same high standard of efficiency which has always characterized its efforts. I regret the Squadron leaving my command, but I shall always look back with pleasure on my association with 603 Squadron and I shall follow its progress with the greatest of interest. The Squadron has my best wishes for its continued success.

On 7 November 1938, Flying Officer K.T. Thompson was posted from 77 Squadron for administrative duties and the Armistice Day parade service was held at Murrayfield Parish Church.

No.41 Squadron was welcomed to Turnhouse in November and Squadron Leader J.S.T. Adams and his men provided 603 with valuable insight into their new role. 603 were now re-organised to form two operational flights and one training flight. It was hoped that the latter would start ab initio training of airmen pilots in the near future.

On 12 December F/O Ted Colbeck-Welch was posted to 600 (City of London) (F) Squadron as adjutant. By March 1944 he was based at Headquarters 10 Group. He returned to 603 Squadron during the post-war years and ultimately achieved the rank of Air Vice-Marshal, CB, OBE, DFC.

In a New Year's message, Count Stevens wrote: 'We look forward to 1939 knowing, and determined to show, that we are worthy of the confidence placed in us as Scotland's first Fighter Squadron.' Sadly, early into the year there was to be another fatal accident.

603 cricket team. From left to right: J. A. G. L. Dick; G. T. Wynne-Powell; T. C. Garden; Rev J. Rossie Brown; P. Gifford; G. C. Hunter; R. Waterston; J. A. B. Somerville; G. Denholm; ?; J. S. Morton and D. K. A. MacKenzie.

1939

As of 23 January F/L H. Moreton Pinfold was posted to 603 from 502 (GR) Squadron as adjutant and to assist with the conversion from bomber to fighter squadron. Nicknamed 'Hook' by Pat Gifford (a weak pun of his name, Pin-fold) Moreton Pinfold was an experienced pilot and instructor and was to provide 603 with a valuable source of expertise during his time with the unit.

F/L Frank Tyson was promoted to Squadron Leader and posted to HQFC for intelligence duties. Pilot Officer I.E. Pease transferred from the RAFVR to 603 Squadron with effect from 13 January, but on 18 February the inexperienced Pease was killed during solo training when his Hawker Hind crashed at Kingsley Wood near RAF Kinloss.

On 30 February 603 Squadron was re-equipped with the Gloster Gladiator Mk I. The aircraft came from 54 (F) Squadron at RAF Hornchurch which was being re-equipped with the new Spitfire Mk I. The aircraft sent to 603 were part of the second production batch of 180 prepared to Air Ministry Specification F.14/35 (as amended in 1936) and built at Gloster Aircraft Co. Ltd., during 1937. Standard of preparation was similar to the first batch but with universal armament mounting under lower wing. The first 37 aircraft were equipped with Lewis guns outboard (these were later later changed to Vickers Mark III or V, and later to Brownings), the next ten had Vickers 'K' gas-operated guns, with 100 rounds per gun, the remainder had Colt/Browning 'Star' guns. They were powered by 840hp, Bristol Mercury IX engines. Hook Pinfold organised the conversion programme for the Squadron when the Gladiators replaced the Hinds. The latest programme for Gladiators to Spitfires was made more difficult by the extensive alterations being made to Turnhouse at that time. Great piles of soil and turf littered the area during landscaping operations to provide drainage for what was a frequently sodden airfield. The airfield surface was then levelled. Dispersal sites and air-raid shelters were built at intervals around the perimeter and the maintenance site was cleared and extended to accommodate new buildings. An extension to the officers mess was provided in the form of a wooden hut and some of the officers were seen, during available time whilst on duty, working on the roof, in uniform, including their service caps! The work on the aerodrome provided a number of unnerving hazards when the pilots brought their aircraft in to land.

On 27 March Pilot Officer L.L.W. 'Bambi' Bamber was posted in from Central Flying School as assistant adjutant.

15 April 1939 was a proud day for 603 when the coveted Lord Esher Trophy, awarded to the best

Gloster Gladiators being refuelled at Turnhouse, c. 1939.

Refuelling Gladiator Is, Turnhouse, c. 1939.

Turnhouse c.1938/39. Seated from left to right: ?, Somerville, Denholm, Stevens, K Macdonald and Peel.

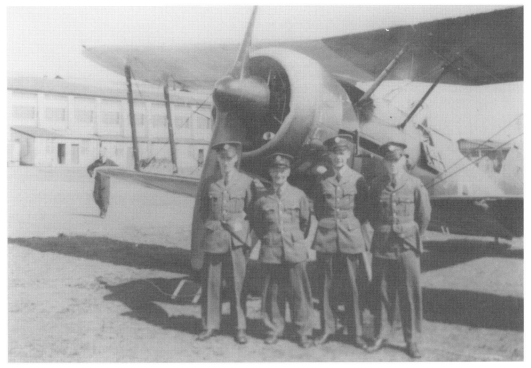

Top: A Squad Maintenance Flight, taken at their last peacetime summer camp in 1939.
Bottom: Black's groundcrew. Third from left Albert Day MBE.

OPPOSITE PAGE:

Top: May 1939, Empire Air Day at Turnhouse.
Middle left: Gifford, Kirkpatrick and Rossie Brown, Turnhouse 1938/39.
Middle right: Ivone Kirkpatrick, 'Kirk'.
Bottom: Hawkinge 1939, 603 Squadron summer camp. From left, Sheep, Black, Ken, Patsy, George, Hamish and Ian.

Top: Patsy at Hawkinge 1939. 'Dawn Patrol'.
Left: 'Cowboy' and Count Stevens.
Right: Hawkinge, summer camp, 1939. Black Morton with his aircraft.

auxiliary squadron, was presented to the unit by the Air Officer Commanding-in-Chief (AOC-in-C) Air Chief Marshal Sir Hugh Dowding GCVO, GCB, CMG. The Squadron gave an impressive flying display in their Gladiators.

On 20 May the Empire Air Day at Turnhouse attracted a vast crowd of 17,500. The Benevolent Fund benefited greatly from such an impressive turn out by the Scottish public. It was the last air day they were to enjoy.

On 23 April trainee architect, William Anderson Douglas (90896), joined. Born in Edinburgh in 1921, Bill Douglas underwent limited flying training with 603 in between work commitments before being mobilised on 24 August 1939.

On 17 June 603 took part in the combined parade of the army and air force units in Edinburgh and on 22 July the annual summer camp was held at RAF Hawkinge and was a memorable occasion. The ground crew (including the fully equipped pipe band) and stores travelled down by 'special train' but the departure of the pilots in their Gladiators was delayed due to poor weather conditions. When they eventually departed Turnhouse they carried out a scheduled stop en route at Digby where they were reunited with F/O Ken Macdonald who had just completed a photographic course at Reimanns in London. Ken, an excellent photographer, took many photographs during the stay at Hawkinge as did Black Morton.

Whilst at Reimanns Ken started a relationship with Mardi (Marguerite) which only ended with his death in the Battle of Britain. On 22 July he wrote to Mardi from RAF Digby, where he eagerly awaited the arrival of his 603 colleagues, and told her of his adventures since the couple were last together. Clearly, he is in high spirits and his letter provides a valuable insight and captures something of the atmosphere of the times in the build-up to war. At that time Ken's brother, Don, was studying at Peterhouse, Cambridge, where Ken had also been a student a few years earlier. En route to Digby Ken arranged to meet his brother with a view to cadging a lift for the remainder of the journey:

So I got to Cambridge and scanned the platform in vain 'till just as the train was starting off again when I saw him strolling along – so I nipped out of the train – then he said he couldn't motor me up there and there were no more trains or buses – so we just went and had gallons of beer and felt grand. After a bit he produced a couple of tickets for a dance so we rolled along. It was a dance given by the university to visiting foreigners – no British undergraduates allowed – so we were about the only people there who could 'Spika da English!.' Colossal fun – hundreds of Scandinavians and dark sinister looking Slavonic beauties. Don was in enormous form and a colossal time was had by all. Then we had to climb into Peterhouse and I slept on Don's sofa, more or less – then climbed out at some ungodly hour and tried to get organised without success, came back, had the hell of a breakfast in Peterhouse and then took Don's car and collected a garage chap to bring it back and set sail for here. But after a bit I got him to drive and just faded out until we arrived here at 11 a.m., only to find that the chaps were weather-bound and hadn't left Edinburgh. So it was now 4.30 and I am still here and look like remaining so indefinitely 'till they arrive. I don't think they have started off yet! I have absolutely nothing with me, not even an overcoat and may be here for weeks at this rate [Ken had sent some of his clothing and personal effects in advance of his arrival at Hawkinge, the rest was sent home to Edinburgh]. My aeroplane is here alright so I thought I would go for a fly around 'till the chaps came – but being Saturday afternoon I couldn't do so for some technical reason (giving the airmen too much trouble – or some nonsense). ...all that terrific frenzy to get here by 11 a.m. and now hours of nothing – that's life! Wish you were here…

Eventually, the rest of the men arrived and, reunited with Ken, flew south to Hawkinge. Whilst at camp Mardi and Ken arranged to meet in Deal. Mardi brought along a friend, Betty Toombs, who immediately found a friend in George Denholm and the relationship quickly blossomed.*

On 3 August, with 603 back at Turnhouse, P/O Bamber's short stay with the unit came to an end

---

*In 2001, Betty travelled from Fife to Hampshire to be with Mardi during the latter part of her struggle against cancer. She was at her bedside when her friend passed away.

603 Squadron, September 1939.

when he was posted to 10 Flying Training School at RAF Ternhill.

By 7 August Ken was back at 'Goodtrees', the family home in Murrayfield, Edinburgh, from where he wrote another bubbly letter to Mardi who was by then at her family home in Norfolk. Clearly, he had fallen for her:

> …here I am sitting in the garden at home in glorious sunshine with no shirt on. It is terrific being here and everything seems so incredibly clean and full of flowers after the attic in London and peaceful after the roaring pace of camp… The troops behaved amazingly well on the way home – reputed never to have behaved so well before. George and all the chaps arrived back yesterday. Ian [Ritchie] travelled by train with me on Saturday night as he had to be back by Sunday. Mardi, listen – you must come up here next week at latest. My mother is expecting you and Toombs [Betty Toombs, later Betty Denholm]. My mother loves having as many 'Young People' about the place as possible. George and Ian are just as insistent that you both come North.
>
> It was wizard that you were at Deal last week… I loved seeing you, despite the crowds! Now I want to lead you through the gates of the Highlands into our fairyland of hills and glens – here every burn breathes its story and romance and the music and poetry of life in this earth lie beneath every stone and in every tuft of heather… Come North…

Mardi did take up Ken's offer to visit Goodtrees and while there the couple visited the Isle of Skye. As Ken had anticipated, she was overwhelmed by the beauty of the Coullin mountain range.

At Turnhouse preparations were made to receive the new Supermarine Spitfire Mark Is with which the unit was to be re-equipped, replacing the Gladiators, and relevant stores and equipment were ordered.

On 23 August 1939, 603 Squadron was embodied into the Royal Air Force. All personnel were told to report to Town Headquarters (THQ) or Turnhouse as 'call out' notices came tumbling through post boxes.

Like so many others LAC Harry Ross received his 'Notice of Calling Out' through the post from the 603 adjutant, Moreton Pinfold. It was stamped '23rd August 1939' and requested his immediate presence at RAF Turnhouse. Hook also sent out urgent recall notices to men who had left the Squadron but were still on the Auxiliary Air Force Reserve of Officers (AAFRO). This included F/O Jack Haig.

In addition to the arrival of the reservists at Turnhouse, others also turned up whose arrival had not been expected. Accommodation was soon full to overflowing and other accommodation was hastily organised including straw palliasses in one of the hangars! Pinfold and his wife were unceremoniously evicted from their married quarter to make way for a number of female ATS drivers whose duties at Turnhouse were far from clear. The tension was eased somewhat by the impromptu sing-songs and entertainments during the evenings and airman D. Skinner recalls how the atmosphere in his hut was lightened by a dramatic rendition of Burn's epic poem 'Tam O'Shanter'.

John Rendall, an airman at the time, remembers being at the cinema in Edinburgh when a notice was projected on the screen calling 603 Squadron personnel to report to Turnhouse immediately. John recalls having to go home and get his kit, by which time he had missed the last bus to Turnhouse and walked until the local police gave him a lift.

By 1800 hours on 23 August nearly all serving personnel had reported at Turnhouse fully kitted and prepared for hostilities.

Ken Macdonald received his Form 1445D – Notice Of Calling Out – under the Reserve and

Town HQ, rifle range, after war broke out.

Auxiliary Air Forces Act, 1939 – on the 23rd and events gathered pace as the country headed towards war. On the 29th he received a letter from Mardi and immediately went about composing his response. His letter provides us with an important insight into the atmosphere of the period:

To-day we are having a holiday – we have been off-duty all day 'till tea-time and from 5.30 'till 11.30 we are to be allowed to leave the Station. So just before 'pushing off' I am writing this in case I don't get another chance for some time.

Don has left for the south. He left soon after you... short as our trip was, it was one I shall ever remember. That last lap to Mallaig with the glow of that heavenly day vanishing behind the Coullin like a silent lullabye in a million blues. Though we hardly stopped to look at it, it is something I shall never forget. And the awesome, towering, majesty of the Coullin overhanging Loch Cornisk, when voices echoed and humanity is spell-bound at its own utter insignificance. I can imagine God Almighty sitting in just such a place on the Day of Judgement.

I still don't believe there can be war. But, if there is, there should be no better preface to it than just that trip we had. For so far as I can see, the only way to look on such a war is in the way the Chinese do, that is, in its relation to thousands of years. How utterly negligible then is a petty squabble such as this, or our lives or our deaths, and particularly the self-inflated little twerp, Hitler!

What if we all go for glory – what the hell difference will it make... to the Coullin or the Thames or Wales or anything else that really matters. Nothing man-made is of the least importance – and nothing Made by God can be destroyed or even spoilt by us, even at our worst...

I have now returned after being into Edinburgh. It is 11.15. I went home for dinner, and then after dinner went to the Aperitif, met some chaps and had a drink or two, then a quick whip around all the joints, but everywhere practically empty. Lots of beer though and now feel in enormous form! Here comes George with a colossal cigar!! And here is Hamish [Somerville], as he says, screeching and waving a bottle, and also with a cigar. Now we are all here waiting for Nannie to come and tell us to get organised. Must stop... lots of love, and remember, nothing matters so much except the beautiful things

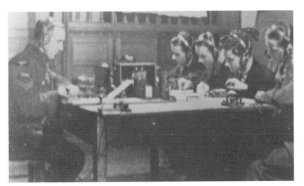

Town HQ, radio, telephony and morse training. Readying for action.

Pilot Officer Don Macdonald, taken early in 1940 at the family home in Murrayfield.

Ken Macdonald, at the family home Goodtrees.

and they will go on and on and always be there for us no matter what happens.

Ken's younger brother, Don, graduated from Peterhouse in August 1939 and, following a short holiday at the family home, was sent to SFTS at RAF Cranwell for flying training. He was commissioned in the RAFVR as a Pilot Officer on 8 November. He had been a member of the Cambridge University Air Squadron, based at Marshalls Flying Club, just outside Cambridge, where he had known Peter Pease and Colin Pinckney who have yet to enter the story and with whom he later served in 603 Squadron. The destiny of Ken and Don and the parts they played in the history of the Edinburgh Squadron is as fine an example of spirit, courage, and sacrifice as seen in any unit at war.

At the outbreak of war, 603 were the most efficient squadron in the Auxiliary Air Force, and Trenchard's vision of 20 years earlier had been fully realised. Many factors contributed to this success:

- a strong local identity and very real ésprit de corps had been created
- personnel were carefully selected
- training was very thorough
- there had been close and continuous liaison with the regular RAF
- co-operation and understanding had developed between men who had served together continuously for a number of years
- the Squadron had been well served by successive Commanding Officers, adjutants, regular and auxiliary NCOs

The Squadron's capabilities were soon to be put to the ultimate test. Within a year, five of its auxiliary pilots and four airmen had been killed and five pilots and five airmen wounded. Not long afterwards, the last of the pre-war pilots would leave the Squadron. The pride and ésprit de corps would however be safeguarded by the indomitable ground staff. Throughout the war and whatever their role, 603 would remain 'The Edinburgh Squadron'. As Scott Kennedy wrote in 1943:

The story of the Squadron's development over the 14 years to 1939 is the story in miniature of the development of that excellent institution, the Auxiliary Air Force. It has been said the RAF and the Royal Navy acquire ésprit de service rather than ésprit de corps. Not so the Auxiliary Air Force. Esprit de corps clearly distinguished all AAF units. The reason is not far to seek. Unlike the personnel of RAF squadrons and of ships of the Royal Navy, the personnel of auxiliary squadrons was not affected by changes and postings. Recruited locally, volunteer membership remained more or less static. Thus pride in squadron had opportunity to develop. All ranks grew to know each other thoroughly over a period of years. The distinctive 'A' badge, of which AAF members are justly proud, became the symbol of close comradeship denied to many a regular unit.

Such comments hold as true today as they did then.

CHAPTER 3

TO WAR WITH SPITFIRES!

The war-warning signal 'DIABOLO' was received at RAF Turnhouse on 24 August 1939 and by that evening the Gloster Gladiator Mk I fighters had been dispersed around the perimeter of the grass airfield. At 13.00 hours the following day the gun batteries situated at various locations either side of the Forth were ordered to fuse their shells and those at Pettycur, Kinghorn and Inchgarvie reported 'ready for action'.

On 1 September 1939, F/O Tommy Garden was posted to RAF Turnhouse. He had been with 603 (accounts branch) since 13 January 1935 (when his commission was gazetted). By March 1944 Garden was at Headquarters, Transport Command, Harrow.

On the eve of the declaration of war on Germany, Ken Macdonald wrote to Mardi again from his room in the officers mess. By that time Mardi had joined the WAAF and been posted south:

> High-Ho…,
>
> Yes, they do seem to have tried their worst on us, but I guess you can't enjoy belonging to the almighty British Empire and being allowed to do exactly what you want without having to fight for it every now and then. Anyway, as George [Denholm] said last night, '…there's nothing like a war for developing one's sense of humour!'
>
> Thanks a million for your letter…love hearing from you. I wish you could come up here – colossal fun.
>
> Today we have been working like blazes digging dug-outs and piling up sand-bags so that we are now all nearly dead. But we shall be tough guys when they declare peace. I'm feeling like a horse already.

RAF Turnhouse. Improvements and defences under construction. XT-H 'Hell' in background. September 1939.

A notice of calling out.

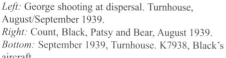

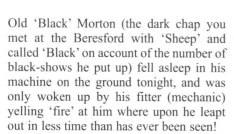

Left: George shooting at dispersal. Turnhouse, August/September 1939.
Right: Count, Black, Patsy and Bear, August 1939.
Bottom: September 1939, Turnhouse. K7938, Black's aircraft.

Old 'Black' Morton (the dark chap you met at the Beresford with 'Sheep' and called 'Black' on account of the number of black-shows he put up) fell asleep in his machine on the ground tonight, and was only woken up by his fitter (mechanic) yelling 'fire' at him where upon he leapt out in less time than has ever been seen! We went night flying the other night, simply marvellous, almost better than day – but then it was a wizard night, not so good on a punk one – but actually it was much easier than I had supposed, feel rather like a night-hawk. Must stop for tonight… before I fall asleep… The Londoners will make you laugh alright… they're marvellous people – peace will be pretty wizard to look forward to.

Lots of love.

Ken

At 11.15 hours on 3 September 1939, war was declared and 603 Squadron was placed 'on a war footing' for the first time in their history. The ORB provides a list of primary personnel in the unit at that time and almost all played a part in the coming conflict. Of the 24 officers, ten did not survive:

CO: Squadron Leader E.H. Stevens
Chaplain: Squadron Leader J. Rossie-Brown.
Armament Officer: Flight Lieutenant J.L. Jack MC.
Accountant Officer: Pilot Officer J. Smith.
Adjutant: Flight Lieutenant H. Moreton Pinfold.

A Flight: Flight Lieutenant Pat Gifford, Flight Lieutenant George L. Denholm, Flying Officer H. Ken Macdonald, Flying Officer J.A.B. Somerville, Pilot Officer Ian S. Ritchie, Pilot Officer Jim S. Morton and Pilot Officer George K. Gilroy.
B Flight: Flight Lieutenant Ian Kirkpatrick, Flying Officer Fred W. Rushmer, Flying Officer J. Laurie G. Cunningham, Flying Officer G.T. Wynne-Powell, Flying Officer Robin McG. Waterston, Pilot Officer Charles D. Peel and Pilot Officer Graham C. Hunter.
AAF Reserve of Officers: Flying Officer J.G.E. Haig.

Pupils: Pilot Officers D.K.A. MacKenzie, W.A. Douglas and C.E. Hamilton, Pupil Pilot R. Mackay. 803170 LAC Barnes J.H., 803576 LAC McLaren G., 803488 LAC Pritchard E.W., 803581 LAC Shepherd J.D.

No one knew how quickly hostilities would commence and the days leading up to the actual declaration of war had been chaotic. The pilots were at high readiness in the cockpits of their Gladiators at their dispersals around the airfield at Turnhouse, whilst the ground crews made shelters in the large drainpipes left over from airfield drainage modifications.

For the defence of Great Britain at the outbreak of World War II, 603 Squadron was a 'first line' unit equipped with 16 Gladiators '1st line echelon' and two more 'reserve echelon' and able to contribute 19 trained pilots, four experienced ground officers and 215 highly skilled airmen who worked well as a team and were able to carry out major repairs and maintenance. The pilots had sound flying experience on different types of aircraft in a variety of conditions, from the sub-zero temperatures of winter flying in the mountainous regions of Scotland – when the ground crews were able to keep the aircraft airworthy despite the numbing cold – to extensive flying over sea and summer flying over the south-east corner of England. Although inexperienced in times of war, the men of 603 formed a well trained, efficient and dedicated fighting unit, familiar with the command structure and administration of the Royal Air Force and immediately able to integrate into it.

The success of the Squadron was also linked to its close association with Edinburgh. It had been an inspired move by Trenchard when he decided to attach the auxiliary squadrons with a geographical location. The people of Edinburgh saw their Squadron very much as an elite unit.

With 603 Squadron operational, it would no longer be responsible for flying instruction and only trained pilots would be accepted. C Flight (the training section) was disbanded and its personnel integrated into A and B Flights. As a consequence Pilot Officer Bill Douglas was sent away to undergo the full flying training syllabus at a Flying Training School.

The process of establishing a full ground control organisation was underway and Hook Pinfold helped establish the operations room, Sector HQ, RAF Station Turnhouse, on the north side of Turnhouse Road. From here all operational flying would be controlled. Construction of the operations room block had recently been completed and the room itself was akin to a small theatre – approximately 60 feet across with two stories and situated within a heavily reinforced, air-conditioned, self contained block. The roof consisted of a deep stratum of rubble sandwiched between two layers of concrete. There was no natural light and the doors were bomb-proof.

Left: September 1939, A Flight line astern.
Right: September 1939. Yellow Section, echelon port.

Trenchard's visit in April 1926. From left to right: Philipson, Jack, Trenchard, unknown.

Approximately 40 people staffed the ops room including controllers, plotters, representatives of the Army and Royal Navy, Observer Corps and numerous runners. Annexed just off was the filter room. This consisted of a telephone exchange or series of switchboards where intelligence was initially received (mainly from the Observer Corps and RDF stations), collated, cross-checked and abridged by the staff before being passed to the adjoining room where it would be displayed on blackboards, maps or the plotting table – 'ops table' – situated in the centre of the room with its simple outline map (squared off using the British modified grid system) of the area of responsibility – 13 Group and its sector airfields. All enemy raids were plotted by the WAAFs who were given instructions via telephone headsets which plugged into jack sockets situated in the edge of the table. Coloured counters (either red, yellow or blue) represented enemy formations and these were moved into position by the plotters using magnetic rakes.* The sector airfields with their squadrons were listed on the 'tote' board on the back wall which indicated squadron states – 'available' through to 'returning home' – as indicated by lights providing the controller with an ongoing reference.

The Turnhouse controller at the outbreak of war was Squadron Leader Bob Johnstone and from his elevated position he had a clear view of the plotting table and tote board. He was passed weather details, including cloud cover. He also had a direct line to the Headquarters of 13 Group, Fighter Command in Newcastle. As sector controller, Johnstone could monitor the progress of an approaching enemy raid and contact the appropriate fighter station and order specific squadrons to intercept. Also present in the operations room at Turnhouse during October/November 1939 was Second Lieutenant Iain Horne of the Scots Guards who had many friends in 603, including Count Stevens.

By October 1939, Britain was divided into four Fighter Command groups: 13 Group was commanded by AOC Scotland and Northern Ireland Air Vice-Marshal Richard Saul; 12 Group, commanded by Air Vice-Marshal Trafford Leigh-Mallory, covered the Midlands and most of Wales; 11 Group was commanded by New Zealander Air Vice-Marshal Keith Park and covered the City of London and the area from the Isle of Wight across to the east coast; and finally 10 Group was

---

*The colour of the counters was changed every five minutes according to a colour-coded clock. This system enabled the controller to see the 'age' of a plot and assisted with its update or removal so that all information on the ops table could be guaranteed to be no older than 15 minutes.

commanded by another New Zealander, Air Vice-Marshal Sir Quintin Brand, who was responsible for the area of South Wales and the west of England. 11 Group was to bear the brunt of the majority of German air raids during the Battle of Britain and consequently the greatest amount of RAF fighter activity. Headquarters, Fighter Command during the battle was at RAF Bentley Priory, Stanmore, Middlesex. Air Chief Marshal Hugh Dowding was the Commander-in-Chief and his staff were able to compile a complete picture of approaching enemy raids once their approach had been detected by the Chain Home RDF stations at their various coastal locations. It was here in the filter room that information on incoming aircraft was relayed by landline from all the RDF stations around the coast. These plots were then laid out on their own ops table (covering all groups) and once the aircraft track was clearly established the information was then relayed to the group HQs and the individual sector stations (airfield). Additional information was provided by the Observer Corps which, by the outbreak of war, consisted of 30,000 observers and 1,000 observation posts, each equipped with a telephone, grid map, height estimator, and coloured map markers. The observers plotted enemy aircraft visually once they had passed over the coast (observers were ineffective at night and in cloud and rain). This information went to the Observer Corps centre before being passed straight to sector stations and group headquarters. The group commanders then had the responsibility of deciding which of their sectors to mobilize. The sector station commanders then had to decide which of their squadrons should fly on a particular sortie. Once airborne, aircraft were controlled by radio-telephony, direction finding (R/T-D/F). This process was designed to take just minutes to initiate. Whilst the whole system was dependent on early warning and continuous observation, the heart of the system was the RDF.

On many of the early days of war the 603 F540, Operations Record Book (ORB) states 'No movement of aircraft'. According to F/L George Denholm, until the Squadron was re-equipped with Spitfires the pilots invariably sat around waiting for something to happen. It could be seen as fitting that it was George who flew the first patrol flown by the Squadron after being placed on a war footing when, on 5 September 1939, he took off at 21.30 hours in a Gladiator for a 40-minute flight. No enemy aircraft were encountered. Individual aircraft numbers were not recorded in the Squadron diary.

The next flying action took place on 8 September, when at 20.00 hours B Flight, Blue Section was sent on patrol in pursuit of a 'supposed enemy'. The section landed again without incident.

On 11 September the Squadron carried out 'practice attacks and night flying,' as they did again on the 14th when that day saw the arrival of the first of the new RAF fighter which was to have such a profound effect on the conflict, the now legendary Vickers Supermarine Spitfire Mark Ia. 603 were one of only 11 squadrons to be equipped with the latest fighter and they were justifiably proud of that fact.

'Leaving their mark'. P/Os Reid and Waterston engrave their names on the roof of the extension to the officers mess. Turnhouse, 1939.

The next day seven more aircraft were delivered to Turnhouse and pilots of both flights began to accumulate what was to be many hours of 'handling flights' at RAF Grangemouth, situated further west along the Forth away from the then operational Turnhouse. On this day long-serving Squadron member F/O 'Jack' Haig, affectionately known to his colleagues as 'Old Gent' was posted to 12 Group Pool, Aston Down. Having effectively left the Squadron he had been working full-time as a salesman for a paper company in Derby. The group pool provided him with the opportunity to brush up on his flying skills.

On 16 September five more Spitfires arrived and the following day, with the help of a number of experienced pilots recently posted to the unit for the specific purpose of assisting with the conversion to type, the pilots of B Flight were released to begin training in earnest, initially with handling flights at Grangemouth.

First flight in a Spitfire

The Spitfire Mk I, powered by the Rolls-Royce Merlin III delivering 1,030hp* and fitted with a Rotol or de Havilland constant-speed airscrew, could achieve 362 mph (582 km/h) at 19,000 feet (5,795m) and was a delight to fly. It was positive in control, capable of incredibly tight turns and was a steady gun platform. To the pilots of 603 Squadron who came to love and cherish the Spitfire, it was a fighter pilot's dream. An opinion shared by many.

The 'A' type wing fitted to the 603 aircraft, had roots strong enough to take the undercarriage legs but they folded outwards which provided a less stable platform than the Hurricane. With forward vision impeded by the nose of the Spitfire the risk of taxiing accidents was high and the pilot had to zig-zag his aircraft into position. The wing also carried eight .303-in (7.7-mm) calibre Browning Mk II machine guns which fired a combination of ammunition including de Wilde tracer, used for sighting – the last 25 rounds were all tracer, providing the pilot with an indication of when his ammunition was about to run out. Each ammunition pannier carried 350 rounds, giving just over 14.5 seconds of firing time.** Pilots were taught to fire short accurate bursts. In an attempt to understand the fire power, a one-second burst fired at an enemy aircraft amounted to 160 rounds which weighed 2.8 lbs (1,134 gms). With a muzzle velocity of 2,400 ft/sec a burst of fire thrashing into the cockpit of an enemy aircraft from close range was devastating, as Brian Carbury, who specialised in getting in close, later proved. The weight of all 2,800 bullets was approximately 38 lbs (34,020 gms). Unlike the Hurricane, the thinness of the wing meant each gun was housed in three separate bays which took even an experienced and practised crew ten minutes to re-arm.

The gun-sight was the Barr and Stroud Type GM 2, reflector incorporated with adjustable ranging lines for wingspan and range. Each aircraft was equipped with the TR 9D high frequency radio transmitter/receiver but the performance was often a cause for complaint by the 603 pilots and it was upgraded to VHF (TR1133) which gave greater range and clarity. Squadrons could only communicate if they had the same equipment. Every squadron equipped with the Spitfire felt supremely fortunate.

Pilots were usually converted to Spitfires via Harvards or Masters, single-engine monoplanes with retractable undercarriage equipped for dual flying, but it was decided that the pilots of 603 would convert directly from Gladiators to Spitfires and they adapted very quickly but not without a great deal of hard work. The Spitfire's vastly superior performance to that of the Gladiator's 253 mph came, not just as a shock, but a great thrill to the pilots.

During conversion it was quite usual to see the 603 adjutant, Moreton Pinfold, standing on the wing-root pointing out the instruments, controls and levers to each pilot for the first time who, during the preceding days, had read and re-read the manual as well as having spent time sitting in the cockpit going over procedures in his mind, reviewing the characteristics and controls of the Spitfire and absorbing as much information as he could. When ready, Hook jumped from the wing and – with the propeller in fine pitch, the engine primed, switch on – the pilot signalled to the airman by the accumulator (external starter battery) and as the pilot touched the contact button the airscrew

---

*The later Mark II, with the slightly more powerful Merlin XII, produced 1,140 hp giving greater performance at altitude.

**According to the 603 pilots, and backed-up by their combat reports, each gun was equipped with 350 rounds as opposed to the commonly stated 300 rounds per gun. This point was also confirmed by the veteran ground crews.

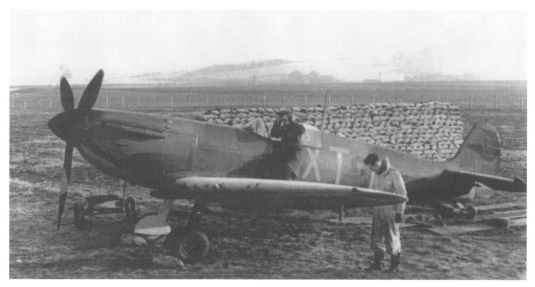

RAF Turnhouse, 1939. XT-H 'Hell'. P/O Colin Robertson and WEM (wireless, electronics, mechanic).

turned, falteringly at first, before clouds of dense blue/grey smoke was emitted from the streamline ejector 'Siamese' exhausts and the Merlin roared into life, whipping the smoke into a frenzy and dispersing it in seconds. The pilot taxied out onto the airfield and, having lined the aircraft up, opened the throttle; as he did so he was forced back into his seat by a surge of power way beyond anything experienced in the Gladiator. He corrected the slight swing as the aircraft bounced off the uneven surface of the airfield and rose smoothly into the air. The wheels were unlocked prior to retraction and then pumped up manually with the long-handled undercarriage lever. Immediately after take-off the inexperienced pilot could be spotted, his aircraft undulating, almost in time as he pumped the undercarriage lever.

The Spitfire was now in its element, a state of the art monoplane, enclosed cockpit, retractable undercarriage, flaps, supercharged engine and variable pitch airscrew and a major technological step forward and each 603 pilot saw his first flight as a never to be forgotten experience. They claimed that when they climbed into the cockpit and fastened the Sutton harness they felt they were strapping the aircraft to themselves, becoming a part of what was a tremendous fighting machine with great power and sensitivity of touch – the Spitfire 'practically flew itself'.

In the early days, the 603 pilots found heavy handling of the controls caused problems. In flight the field of view was excellent but there was a blind spot behind the tail. During the early flights, as the pilot grew in confidence, he cautiously began to put the agility and performance of the aircraft to the test including medium and steep turns and powered dives. At slower speeds he discovered just how well it performed.

In preparation for landing the pilot put the airscrew into fine pitch, slid open the hood, lowered the undercarriage and initiated a turn across the wind, selected flaps down and pointed the nose at the landing strip. Initially the 603 pilots found that they approached too fast compared with the Gladiator (even the aerodynamics of the Hawker Hurricane, the Spitfire's counterpart in the coming Battle of Britain, caused it to slow on landing). The Spitfire with her beautifully streamlined shape sliced through the air with minimum resistance and appeared to float before the wheels touched down. Although it was important to maintain speed prior to landing (about 140 mph), in order to avoid the stall and disastrous spin into the ground, the pilots were initially alarmed by this advance in aerodynamic technology, but once the early problems were overcome the Spitfire reigned supreme, a dream to fly and outstanding in combat. After touching down, the pilot brought the stick gently back as the aircraft lost speed, 'flaps up' was selected and the pilot zig-zagged back to dispersal, his body high on adrenaline, his life as an aviator never to be the same. At that time the final approach to the airfield was head-on, which sometimes resulted in tragic consequences.

Years later P/O (then Wing Commander) Ian Ritchie reflected on his time at Grangemouth: 'The grass was very long and the runways long enough for the greenest of the green to put his first Spitfire through his first tentative circuits and landings.'

On 19 September three more Spitfires arrived. The next day another single Spitfire brought the total to 17. On that day F/L Jack MC was promoted to Squadron Leader (Honorary) with effect from 27 August 1939. Meanwhile, B Flight continued to acquaint themselves with the new aircraft at Grangemouth where plenty of difficulties were encountered. Although by this time the twin-bladed airscrew had been replaced by a three-bladed, the early production Spitfires were to undergo a number of modifications during the months ahead. These included: replacing the twin pitch airscrew with a variable pitch and upgrading the radio antennae. The undercarriage hand pump was superseded by a hydraulically operated selection box although the hand pump was retained for a while, just in case. In anticipation of what lay ahead, a number of pilots got their fitters/riggers to purchase a suitable rear-view mirror from Edinburgh and attach it to the front canopy. The poor forward visibility posed a great threat during taxiing and the problem was never fully overcome. Despite much hard work and many hours flying it was a while before the pilots honed their flying skills with the Spitfire. In due course, they gained some combat experience when they came up against the slower bombers of the Luftwaffe which gave them time to adjust and open fire. Such occasions became more frequent but their baptism against fighters would be devastating, despite many of the unit having accrued many hours on type.

The newly arrived Spitfires had yet to be fitted with the eight Browning .303 machine guns and these were delivered separately, each gun packed in solid grease. Cartridges and links were delivered in other boxes and all ammunition had to be belted-up. Most of the .303 ball ammunition delivered to 603 at the outbreak of war was left over from WWI, but once this was exhausted new supplies arrived from the manufacturers ready belted. Until this occurred the long tedious task of belting-up manually was carried out by the ground crews. The armament section, under Squadron Leader Jack, was already at full stretch so the boxes of links and cartridges were loaded onto lorries and taken under armed guard to Town Headquarters where they were assembled into belts by a number of young lads under the supervision of the padre, James Rossie Brown.

Soon after the arrival of their new aircraft many of the senior pilots in the Squadron claimed one for themselves, knowing it would inevitably be flown by others, which they personalised by attaching names and logos. These eventually included: Walter Scott, Waverley, Portobello, Corstorphine, Nae Bother, Stickleback, Excaliber, Ard Choille, Walter McPhail, Port o' Leith, Aorangi, Bidar, Auld Reekie, Eboracum, Tigger, Blue Peter, Scottie, Sredni Vashtar, and The Bairn, usually flown by the least experienced pilot!

B Flight continued with its handling flights at Grangemouth until 25 September, when it was the turn of A Flight. On the 27th Red and Yellow Sections were recalled to Turnhouse to patrol Leith and Crail while Green Section B Flight was sent to patrol over Leith and Dunbar. No enemy was sighted although the section was fired upon by the destroyer, HMS *Hastings*, the crew believing the aircraft to be enemy. None of the 603 Spitfires were hit and they returned to Turnhouse. A Flight continued conversion training at Grangemouth through to the end of September but tragedy struck on 1 October 1939, at 17.45 hours when, according to the Squadron ORB: 'F/O J.A.B. Somerville was killed at Grangemouth Aerodrome, while taxiing in Spitfire L1047, when Spitfire L1059, flown by P/O Morton, collided with him on landing.' Black Morton had practically landed his Spitfire on that of Somerville, the airscrew of which slashed into the cockpit, grievously injuring Somerville. He died shortly after. Black's log book records: 'Practice Fighter Attacks 1 & 2. – Crashed.'

At that time the pilots had been approaching the airfield straight-on, rather than using a curved approach which enabled them to see what lay in their path. 'Hamish' Somerville was an experienced pilot, popular and enthusiastic and a lively character during time off. He was given a full military funeral with the padre fittingly conducting the service. Operational flying continued from Grangemouth and Turnhouse that day with three night sorties totalling 1 hour 40 minutes flying time. On 2 and 3 October, patrols continued, both day and night. On the 4th the Squadron flew day patrols only.

F/O J. A. B. 'Hamish' Somerville's funeral in 1939. The 603 padre leads the party.

On the 6th, S/L Jack was posted to Staff, 25 Armament Group. A significant influx of regular experience occurred on this day when Pilot Officer Brian J.G. Carbury and Pilot Officer Colin 'Robbie' Robertson were attached to 603 from 41 Squadron at Catterick, for flying duties. Carbury was posted to A Flight whilst Robertson was posted to B. Flying Officer John C. Boulter was also attached from RAF Station Usworth for flying duties and was posted to B Flight where he soon acquired the nickname 'Bolster'. He had been recalled from the Reserve of Air Force Officers (RAFO) at the outbreak of war. The contribution made by these three new arrivals in the conflict which lay ahead was considerable. Robertson was involved in the aerial fighting on 16 October, before being 'grounded' for a period following a riding accident. Boulter was to survive the Battle of Britain with a number of 'kills' to his credit and the reputation as a fine pilot and leader, while Brian Carbury would become the Squadron's highest scoring 'ace' during the Battle of Britain, managing to shoot down five enemy aircraft in one day in the process. The charismatic Robertson and Boulter were destined to die in tragic accidents before the end of WWII.

At 11.30 hours on 7 October P/O Graham C. Hunter crashed in Spitfire L1023 and was seriously injured. He had been approaching Turnhouse in hazy conditions when his aircraft stalled and crashed on the edge of the airfield. Hunter was admitted to the military hospital situated within the walls of Edinburgh Castle (today the hospital is home to The National War Museum of Scotland). He was discharged on 4 November and after a period of sick leave returned to 603. During the coming months he underwent remedial surgery and went before countless medical boards in an attempt to regain his A1 flying category.

Also on 7 October, Pilot Officers Bill Douglas and Douglas 'Ching' Mackenzie were posted to 7 FTS at Peterborough, in order that they complete their flying training away from what was now an operational RAF Station at war.

On 8 October the Squadron flew more daytime patrols. There were no operational flights for the next seven days. Flying Officer L.J. Fry was attached from RAF Station Church Fenton for 'flying duties'.

On 11 October eight of the Squadron's Gloster Gladiator Mk Is were handed over to 152 Squadron at RAF Acklington. On the 14th F/O Fry ceased attachment with 603 and returned to Church Fenton.

During the morning of 15 October, pilots of A Flight flew

Pat Gifford in October 1939, with Gladiators in background.

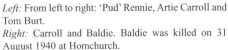

Left: From left to right: 'Pud' Rennie, Artie Carroll and Tom Burt.
Right: Carroll and Baldie. Baldie was killed on 31 August 1940 at Hornchurch.

their Spitfires down to 7 Armament Training School (ATS) at RAF Acklington, Northumberland, where they remained for the day. There, in perfect weather conditions, they underwent two short flights during which they carried out air firing practice over the ranges at Druridge Bay. They returned to Turnhouse during the late afternoon where, after dark, the Squadron practised night-time landings.

The 15th also saw the arrival of another experienced regular when 25-year-old Pilot Officer John R.C. Young was posted to B Flight from 41 Squadron at Catterick where he had been Central Flying School (CFS) representative, flying instructor and adjutant. Whilst at 41 Squadron he had

Artie Carroll, Turnhouse, 1939.

known Brian Carbury and Colin Robertson. John Young (later Wing Commander Young AFC, Official Historian for the Battle of Britain Fighter Association) was already a very experienced pilot with over 700 hours logged with Canadian Pacific Airways. When the airline closed down in 1936, he returned to England and was granted a commission in the RAFO. In July 1939, he passed the full instrument rating course at CFS, Upton, before moving to 41 Squadron. He was due to take on the duties of CFS representative, flying instructor and adjutant with 603 but the latter post was already in the process of being taken over by P/O Alen Wallace. Nevertheless, he assessed the flying ability of the pilots in the Squadron and made recommendations for furthering their training, which didn't go down well with the AAF hierarchy. He first flew with 603 on the 19th. Yet to be issued with an Irvin jacket, he was subsequently given the one which had previously belonged to 'Hamish' Somerville, complete with patch covering the large gash made by the airscrew from Black Morton's Spitfire. A colourful, eminently likeable character, John Young reflects on his time with 603 with affection:

> When I arrived the Squadron was more or less in mid-conversion, compared with 41 Squadron which was fully operational by day and night. The 603 pilots were, by comparison, infants and I wasn't much better. The day after I arrived at 603 Squadron they intercepted the German raiders which attacked the Naval shipping in the Forth. The pilots were naturally cock-a-hoop at their success.
>
> But they were good pilots by and large… Squadron Leader Stevens was a charming and extremely clever man utterly unsuited in some essential respects for the task set him. Late in

the war he became a highly respected Group Captain in operations at Fighter Command.

Moreton Pinfold was the peacetime adjutant and Squadron CFI. He was negotiating to become a Fighter Squadron CO during my early days. He was successful.

Mr Dalziel, Warrant Officer of 603, was the best and fairest warrant officer I had the privilege of knowing.

Alen Wallace, adjutant, grounded at the time but an early pilot with 603, was a great cohering force in the Squadron.

'Albert' Barton was the Intelligence Officer of whom I have the happiest memories (and his wife, Monique from Belgium). Albert provided a contrast in style and a gaiety seldom equalled.

The only memories I have of Patsy Gifford are of admiration for his qualities even after only a few days' acquaintance.

Ian 'Bear' Ritchie was great at 'Racing Demon'* and a good companion at dispersal. It was he who named me 'Dobbin'. He was of good solid value.

'Bubble' Waterston was the navigational instructor to the Squadron, in spite of the fact that Robertson was also a qualified navigation instructor and had been sent to 603 having been briefed to do just that.

Robertson was winner of the Sword of Honour at Cranwell and came with me from 41 and was an armament specialist and gunnery instructor. It was he who invented fabric covering over the gun ports (tested by me to improve aileron control, badly needed on early Spitfires). He was also inventor of the 'Lethal Tunnel' – gun harmonisation for the eight-gun Spitfire and Hurricane which directed the bullets into a 'tube' approximately 250 yards in front of the aircraft – as accepted by Fighter Command. The guns of the Luftwaffe fighters were aligned to fire straight ahead.

Robbie Robertson was seriously injured in a riding accident in May 1940, the residual effects of which may have been a contributing factor to his death in a flying accident in 1943 whilst a flight commander with 25 Squadron. Interestingly, John was appointed President of the Court of Enquiry. John continues with his memories of his time with 603 Squadron:

Black Morton believed that the key to success in combat was *élan* and that training in instrument flying was *infra* dig. Although we got on very well, George Denholm seemed to think we were always arguing. I think they were light-hearted endless arguments about how one should conduct oneself. He maintained that dash and spirit were all, whilst I maintained that without high technical skills those essential qualities would be wasted (and it was my job to see he acquired them). Black became a very successful fighter pilot and very successful in life after the war.

Haig was rather old for a fighter pilot. I liked him but didn't really get to know him.

My memories of 'Sheep' Gilroy are vivid, particularly for having acquitted himself so well in shooting down a Ju88 with only 83 hours total flying time in his log-book. We maintained our good friendship over the years after the war and shared a mutual interest in bee-keeping.

I got on very well with 'Razz' Berry – which I have always spelt 'Razz' and on which he never sought to correct me if it was wrong. All the other pilots spelt it that way too. Razz was a very competent pilot. Very keen, quietly confident and well-liked, we all enjoyed his boyish charm but of course he lacked experience.

I had a great relationship with Stapme Stapleton but he could be a bit slap-happy.

I knew Brian Carbury from our time together with 41 Squadron although, once again, he was another in the other flight to me. As an instructor I never had reason to be concerned with him because he was such a competent pilot. He left 41 Squadron to join 603 a few weeks ahead of me and we came together again while the Squadron was at Prestwick over the Christmas period of 1939/40.

---

*Racing Demon is a card game which John describes as a kind of competitive patience with each player having his own deck of cards.

George Denholm succeeded to flight commander and he was very keen on battle training and breaking away from interceptions, which suited me very much in that it was one of the great problems – getting away from the engagement. He was meticulous in this. For me, he epitomised all those qualities of calmness and resolution one would hope for in one's flight commander.

As I left the Squadron, Richard Hillary had just joined B Flight. He was at Oxford when war was declared. I regret I really did not know the men of B Flight as well as those of A Flight when we were either at Dyce or on alternate shifts at Montrose [usually night flying]. Although I knew them we did not have friendships. I later met Hillary when he was convalescing. He was an introspective man.

Flying with friends meant their loss was all the more poignant. The RAF policy seemed to be to post people to where they would have a good chance of being *simpatico*. When you think about it the City of Edinburgh Squadron was a bit if a mixture really. I found the politics bewildering. There was this distinct Scottishness, some of the officers wore tartan for dining-in nights in the Mess and on Burns Night when the piper came around the table making this excruciating noise, in such a tiny room.

While some of those who were attached to the Squadron found it difficult having no family or friends in the area, I did not feel the same way as my wife and son were living nearby. Robertson had also married, a girl from Stirling. I didn't necessarily agree with having your wife and children living nearby. Later, I would be flying missions and later that same night I was home in bed with the wife – it was too much of a contrast.

I thought all the men of 603 were very nice and I felt I got on very well with all of them. May I say that I am sure 603 under George Denholm was perhaps 'the greatest of them all' and of course laid the foundation for a lifetime of friendship.

CHAPTER 4

'FIRST BLOOD THE AUXILIARIES'
MONDAY 16 OCTOBER 1939

After dark on 15 October 1939 the first inbound Scandinavian convoy, NH0, made its way south, down the Scottish east coast. It was en route from Gibraltar to Methil on the north shore of the Forth. As well as a number of cruisers their escort included the Royal Navy destroyers HMS *Jackal, Janus, Jersey* and *Jervis*. The log book of HMS *Jervis* records that they were zig-zagging astern of the convoy when at 11.00 they were rejoined by HMS *Mohawk* which had been carrying out a sweep towards Norway along with a number of other naval vessels during the hours of darkness. *Mohawk* was a Tribal class destroyer which had been launched in June 1937 and completed 12 months later. At the outbreak of war she was part of the 4th Destroyer Flotilla, with the Mediterranean Fleet, where she had been since February 1938. Following allocation to the Rosyth command the ship was immediately ordered to return home. En route she was to provide part of the escort for a Scandinavian convoy due to leave Gibraltar. At 00.00 hours on 16 October the convoy was near the Bell Rock. Later that morning the cruisers along with *Jackal, Janus* and *Jersey* sped ahead of the convoy to their moorings east of the Forth bridge leaving *Mohawk* and *Jervis* to escort the convoy up-river towards Methil. By mid-afternoon on 16 October, the two destroyers were still making their way up the Forth towards Rosyth. Ahead of them were the cruisers HMS *Edinburgh* and *Southampton* of the 2nd Cruiser Squadron, commanded by Sir Edward Collins, which had only recently arrived at their moorings east of the Forth Bridge.

At 14.35 hours on Monday 16 October 1939, a Junkers Ju88 dive bomber screamed down from the skies above the naval shipping anchored offshore from South Queensferry, east of the Forth rail bridge on the Firth of Forth. As the Luftwaffe bomber pulled out of its dive, two bombs were released from the under-wing pylons and fell into the sea, exploding close to two Royal Navy cruisers. In accordance with the Luftwaffe plan, the British defences had apparently been caught by surprise. In reality the approaching bombers had been tracked and their arrival reported but the decision to respond had been late in coming.

Earlier that morning the first shots of the war had been fired over the British Isles. At 09.20 hours the Chain Home (CH) Radio Direction Finding (RDF) station at Drone Hill, Berwickshire, on the east coast of Scotland, detected enemy aircraft approaching from across the North Sea. They were two Heinkel He111s of *Kampfgeschwader* 26 (KG 26) *'Vestigium Leonis'* (Lion), based at a Luftwaffe airfield near the village of Westerland on the German peninsular of Sylt, situated just south of the German/Danish border, and briefed to carry out a pre-raid armed reconnaissance of the Forth area in order to confirm the whereabouts of HMS *Hood*. The Stabs Staffel of KG26 had been engaged in long-range armed reconnaissance of the North Sea and Scottish sea areas in what became known to the Luftwaffe air crews as the 'watery triangle'. With a number of German Rb30 cameras fitted in place of the port bomb racks the Heinkels could effectuate tactical reconnaissance photography and in some cases actually engage targets. These missions were a marathon affair and in most cases amounted to a round trip of 1,000 miles and called for a high level of flying skill, endurance, and alertness from the crews.[1]

It would have required a very high resolution photograph to allow the German photographic interpreter (PI) officers to have recognised the Spitfires of 603 Squadron on the ground at Turnhouse

Left: Ju88 of KG/30 and He III of KG/26, Westerland, Sylt.
Top right: Crew of the KG/30 Ju 88, 16 October 1939.
Right: Ju88 of KG/30.

prior to 16 October. Whilst German intelligence denied the existence of Spitfires in Scotland in the lead up to the raid, the Luftwaffe crews were aware that Spitfires were present.[2] This despite the assurances from the German hierarchy keen to boost morale by playing down the existence and numbers of the RAF's latest fighter in the area.[3]

At 09.45, the Observer Corps of 36 Group reported a visual sighting of an unidentified aircraft moving at high altitude south-west over Dunfermline heading towards the Royal Navy base at Rosyth and another aircraft was sighted and tracked by the Observer Corps posts of 31 Group, Galashiels. Both Observer Corps groups correctly identified these aircraft as He111s. One of the Heinkels subsequently flew eastwards at high altitude over the naval dockyard at Rosyth where it took photographs.

Just three minutes after the 36 Group sighting, the three Spitfires of Blue Section, 602 (City of Glasgow) Squadron, AuxAF, led by Renfrewshire farmer Flight Lieutenant George Pinkerton with Flying Officer Archie McKellar and Pilot Officer Paul Webb, took off from the airfield of RAF Drem with orders to patrol May Island in the Forth estuary at Angels Five (5,000 feet). The history

October 1939. An early start, George in the cockpit.

16 October 1939. L1049 at dawn. LACs Baldie and Carroll in the background.

of the great Glasgow squadron is inextricably linked with that of their sister auxiliary squadron in Edinburgh. But at no time were they more united as a fighting force than on this date, when, together, they left an indelible mark on history as well as the memories of the Scottish folk over whose territory they fought to defend.

At 09.35 hours, a few minutes before Pinkerton and his section took off from Drem, the RDF station at Drone Hill had suffered the first of two shut-downs due to a faulty NT57 valve, the result of which has been incorrectly considered by some to have had a crucial effect on the outcome of the day's aerial activity. Although the RAF sector controller's RDF capability was somewhat reduced, the RDF stations at Saxton Wold, Danby Beacon and Ottercops Moss, ably assisted by the men of the Observer Corps, were still available and provided an invaluable service.[4]

At 10.08, one of the reconnaissance Heinkels was identified by lookouts onboard HMS *Edinburgh* (it has been inaccurately recorded on numerous occasions over the years that the Heinkels were Ju88s which actually carried out the attack later that day). The visibility was fair and the German crew was able to establish the position of several Royal Navy vessels before heading on a reciprocal course for home. It was spotted over Drem at 10.11.

Flight Lieutenant Pinkerton and Blue Section of 602 Squadron had duly arrived over their designated patrol area over the Isle of May, a desolate, rocky, island situated in the mouth of the Forth estuary, 12 miles north of Dunbar and six miles south of Crail. The old chapel was abandoned a long time ago and the only occupants at that time were the members of the anti-aircraft battery.

Pinkerton patrolled the airspace for 20 minutes before receiving orders to head south towards the coast at Dunbar. The instructions gave the section leader an inkling that something was up. During the flight the staff at Turnhouse operations room continued to track what they believed to be an intruder and vectored the pilots to the area until they spotted a speck in the distance. As they closed it became obvious that it was an intruder and at 10.21 Pinkerton dispensed with the assistance from Turnhouse, ordered his section into line astern for a No.1 attack, and led an interception of the enemy aircraft. As they did so the Heinkel turned 45 degrees to port and dived for the available cloud cover. Pinkerton fired 720 of the available 2,800 rounds from his eight .303 Browning machine guns from extreme range, hoping to hit the fleeing foe before it made safety. Archie McKellar fired 1,000 rounds while Paul Webb, Blue 3, never found himself in a position from which to open fire. The 1,720 rounds fired by Pinkerton and McKellar were the first, unsuccessful, shots to be fired during air fighting over the British Isles during WWII at the start of a busy day for both the Glasgow and Edinburgh auxiliary squadrons. Interestingly, it was also the first combat action against the enemy in which the new Supermarine Spitfire Mark Ia was involved. The Heinkel was last seen heading eastwards 20 miles east of Dunbar and later landed back at Sylt. Blue Section, 602 Squadron, landed back at Drem at 10.44.

At 10.45 hours Green Section of 602 Squadron were also sent up from Drem to intercept unidentified aircraft. They were first vectored to Dunbar, then back to provide top cover over their own airfield when at 11.22 hours another sighting of a reconnaissance Heinkel He111 was reported. The CO of 602 Squadron and Glasgow city stockbroker, Squadron Leader Douglas Farquar, was informed by operations that he could investigate if he thought it necessary. The casual invitation needed little further prompting and minutes later he led Red Section away from Drem on a course to intercept, but unfortunately the enemy aircraft had already made good his getaway to the south-east. It had last been seen circling the 360-foot masts carrying the transmitter aerials at Drone Hill before heading out to sea.

Having provided top cover for Drem, Green Section 602 Squadron were then ordered on a heading which took them out to sea before returning to their airfield to refuel prior to being sent off again, this time north towards RAF Montrose. It was discovered that a number of plotting errors had led to the section being sent on reciprocal courses to the sightings, directly away from the unidentified aircraft!

As lunchtime approached the aerial activity lessened and, apart from standing patrols, the 602 Spitfires were recalled and refuelled. Both sections of A Flight had carried out search patrols, both reporting an above average amount of 'chit-chat' over the R/T. Several pilots had instinctively felt that the action had been a precursor to something more serious. In fact, indications of enemy activity continued throughout the remainder of the morning of 16 October through both intercepted radio traffic and occasional sightings of high-flying aircraft.

In the operations room at Turnhouse, S/L Bob Johnstone sat with his eyes glued on the 'ops table'. On his left sat Flight Lieutenant Tommy (Tiger) Waitt, the senior operations 'B' officer who had before him a telephone and switchboard through which he had direct contact with the squadron control officers at 602 and 603 Squadrons at Drem and Turnhouse respectively. As Tommy Waitt studied the operations room map he relayed his orders to the squadrons through Bob Johnstone but not before he had jotted his instructions down on paper which were then passed to the controller for initialling before being sent to the teleprinter for transmission and filing at 13 Group Fighter Command HQ in Newcastle. As air activity on the morning of the 16th began to develop it was by this means that the Air Officer Commanding (AOC Scotland and Northern Ireland) 13 Group, Air Vice-Marshal Richard Saul was kept informed. Through his direct telephone line to Bob Johnstone he himself would later become involved in the action.

Bob Johnstone had the responsibility of making the tactical decision of which squadron should be deployed, and how many aircraft should be sent up to intercept the enemy or patrol the airspace over potential targets, in order to maintain control over and maximise the use of his resources. His fighter resources were valuable and had to be used prudently, he also had information before him which would indicate if the aircraft were being refuelled and rearmed and therefore vulnerable to attack. Having directed Spitfires of 602 and 603 to intercept the incoming enemy aircraft Bob Johnstone provided vectoring until the pilots made a visual sighting of the German aircraft. They would then dispense with his services. Fighter control and radio communication provided Johnstone with the opportunity to introduce tactical updates if another enemy force appeared to be heading unopposed towards a specific target.

At 11.00 hours Green Section of A Flight 602 Squadron, consisting of the CO Squadron Leader Douglas Farquar, along with Flight Lieutenant Sandy Johnstone and Flying Officer Ian Ferguson, were ordered to patrol the airspace over May Island. From May Island the three Spitfires headed north towards Dundee and the Firth of Tay. With the insistence of the controllers that enemy aircraft were in the area the three pilots searched the heavens for bogeys, praying to be the first in action. During the patrol Farquar's radio went unserviceable and Sandy Johnstone took over leadership of the section. Following a report of unidentified aircraft in the vicinity of Drem, at 11.22 Green Section were ordered to 'investigate, if you think necessary', suggesting some doubt on the part of the Turnhouse controllers. In response, Green Section continued their search northwards in what was a strong south westerly wind and good visibility but saw nothing but sea, sky and cloud. Sandy Johnstone felt that there was something out there but it was like searching for a needle in the proverbial haystack. In all probability, he felt that it was likely that the enemy were coming, but towards Edinburgh and not targets in the south.

With the section getting low on fuel and frustrated at their lack of success, the pilots were ordered to return to Drem. By this time they had drifted about 40 miles east of Peterhead and having been airborne for more than an hour and a half their fuel levels were critically low. Sandy Johnstone recalled that '…Drem was beyond our prudent endurance so I brought the boys into Leuchars to refuel, in spite of Drem being visible in the distance.' At most they had 15 minutes flying time remaining and with little chance of making their own airfield, the Coastal Command airfield at Leuchars was a better option. On landing, the ground crews, used to working on Lockheed Hudsons, re-fuelled the Spitfires while Douglas Farquar telephoned Drem to report their whereabouts and to get permission to take lunch in the officers mess.

The morning's activities continued when at 11.39 hours George Pinkerton led McKellar and Webb of Blue Section on another patrol from Drem. On this occasion they were ordered to patrol the airspace over St Abbs Head (near to Drone Hill RDF Station), a rocky outcrop of coastline just north of Eyemouth. The patrol landed back at Drem at 12.43 hours, the pilots having sighted no enemy aircraft.

The operations room at Turnhouse received regular reports of sightings throughout the morning of the 16th and 602 was called upon to intercept in favour of 603 because they were based at the airfield from which the earliest interception could be mounted and as a result they had at least one section airborne for most of this time. The Turnhouse controllers became increasingly concerned as reports of sightings of enemy aircraft came in not just from the Observer Corps but also the anti-aircraft batteries whose aircraft recognition skills were not so reliable. Airborne traffic in the Forth area also included a number of Sea Skuas from HMS *Merlin* carrying out training flights out of Royal Navy Air Station (RNAS) Donibristle. These plots made matters worse as they were often mistaken for enemy aircraft. After a while the number of reports of unidentified aircraft increased beyond the capability of the limited fighter resources which couldn't possibly respond to them all.

By 16 October 1939, the RDF screen was not fully developed and was experiencing problems that day, although it still managed to report the raiders as they approached the coast. Over the years, attempts to apportion blame for the lateness of adequate warning and response have been directed at the Observer Corps, RDF stations and the operations room at Turnhouse. When one considers the rapid rise in the level of aerial activity on 16 October, apportioning blame is inappropriate and all parties did all they could. Assessment of what went on in order to improve operations would have served greater purpose than to blame men who were indeed working to the best of their ability. It should also be remembered that our various defence systems had yet to be tested in times of war and were still undergoing development (and construction in some cases).

The Chain Home RDF Station at Drone Hill was situated on high ground (225m/asl) off the A1107 Cockburnspath – Coldingham road and played a part in the defensive screen around the east coast of Britain in WWII and more specifically as far as this history is concerned, on 16 October 1939.

A name for this system of detection was not immediately indicative of its method of operation. In accordance with British concerns about security, and in order to deceive spies into believing the towers that were beginning to appear around the British coast were part of a system of radio direction finding, it was suggested that the use of the term 'RDF (R.D. and D/F)'. Thus when German reconnaissance aircraft provided photos of the sites they believed them to be part of a radio communication system by which ground control could guide interceptors towards incoming enemy aircraft (with the RAF fighters tied to their respective airfields), when in fact they were radar sites. In September 1943, in order to conform with United States terminology thereby preventing confusion between allies, it became known as 'Radar', an acronym for 'Radio Detection and Receiving' referred to by Watson Watt as a 'synthetic palindrome invented by our friends the Americans'.

The technology was first developed in 1935 and by 1937 manned by trained operatives. By way of the filter room, the information received at the RDF Station was quickly passed to the sector fighter stations, giving the controllers a fairly accurate picture of all aircraft in the air covered by the RDF network. There was a six-minute time lapse between RDF observation and the plot appearing on the map. Interceptor squadrons were allocated by the group controller and scrambled by the sector controller who directed them to meet the enemy.

The Chain Home – CH – Type 1 system consisted of four 360-foot high towers constructed of steel girders with transmitter aerials slung between them. In addition there were four 240 foot high

Left: Kommandeur of KG/30 Hauptmann Helmut Pohle who led a raid on 16 October 1939. He was shot down by Spitfires of 602 Squadron.
Middle: Helmut Pohle aged 92.
Right: Oberleutnant Hans Storp. Shot down by 603 Spitfires off Port Seton on 16 October 1939.

wooden towers on to which the receiving aerials were fastened. The site itself covered approximately 155,000 square metres, was conspicuous and attracted the attention of German tactical photo-reconnaissance aircraft. The range of the CH system was intended to be 100-200 miles and to a height of 15,000 feet but the average range of 80 miles was adequate for the threat from across the Channel. The system could not detect aircraft below 1,000 feet which would confirm the Germans' lack of intelligence on RDF prior to the Forth raid as the approaching Luftwaffe bombers flew at a height which was easily detectable. The power supply came from the National grid and diesel or petrol generators were to be established as a back-up for each system in the event that the local power supply was cut.

At the Luftwaffe airfield on Sylt, in addition to the Heinkels of KG26, was the first wing of Luftwaffe *Kampfgeschwader* 30 Verband (1/KG30). They were one of the first groups to be re-equipped with the new and aptly named *Wunderbomber*, the Junkers Ju88 A-1. Originally proposed as an unarmed *Schnellbomber* (high speed bomber) it relied on superior speed to avoid interception by enemy fighters.[5]

By the outbreak of war the Luftwaffe had only 12 Ju88s in front line service. Based at Jever they operated as 1/KG25 under their recently appointed Gruppenkommandeur Hauptmann Helmut Pohle who later led the raid on the shipping in the Forth on 16 October. On 7 September 1939, the two *Staffeln* of KG25 were re-designated, becoming 1/KG30 which began a period of intensive training and familiarisation with their new aircraft prior to frontline operations. On the morning of 26 September 1939, nine He111s of 4/KG26 and four Ju88s of 1/KG30's 'readiness flight', commanded by Leutnant Storp, carried out an unsuccessful attack on the Royal Navy aircraft carrier HMS *Ark Royal*. Storp would feature prominently in the events of 16 October.

With the failure of the raid against *Ark Royal* Pohle was summoned to attend a high level meeting in Berlin where Göring told the Gruppenkommandeur of 1/KG30:

Pohle, we have *got* to have success. There are only a few English ships making things difficult for us. The *Repulse*, the *Renown*, perhaps the old *Hood* as well. And, of course, the carriers... once these are out of the way, the navy's *Scharnhorst* and *Gneisenau* will dominate the seas out to the Atlantic Ocean.

With Pohle's assurance to Göring that his crews were ready and lacking only the opportunity, it was agreed that 1/KG30 should move to Westerland on the peninsular of Sylt. The unit had only to wait a week.

On 15 October a reconnaissance He111 of KG26 spotted a British battlecruiser, believed to be HMS *Hood** off the east coast of Scotland. Early the next morning she was again sighted about to enter the Firth of Forth. It should be noted at this stage that what was believed to be the *Hood* was actually HMS *Repulse*.

---

*HMS *Hood* was launched in 1918 and weighed 42,100 tons. It was later lost in battle with *Bismarck* with the loss of all but three crew.

Pohle was 32 and a veteran who had previously served as General Staff Officer at the Air Ministry in Berlin, had seen combat in the Spanish Civil War and had test-flown the Ju88 at Rechlin. His ability was highly rated and it was hoped his appointment would bring the Luftwaffe its first crucial success. According to Pohle:

> On 16 October, 1939, HMS *Hood* was on her way to Rosyth in the early hours of the morning, and being shadowed by German maritime reconnaissance. At 8 a.m. I got the order to attack the *Hood*, but only on sea. The order was quite definite. Do NOT attack when she is in dock.

The reconnaissance aircraft were Heinkel 111s of KG26, also based at Westerland which were spotted at 10.00 hours by the Observer Corps and shortly after by the lookouts onboard HMS *Edinburgh** anchored just east of the Forth rail bridge. At 11.30 hours, during their return flight over the North Sea, the Heinkels came within wireless range of Westerland and details of weather conditions over the target area were transmitted. But, significantly, the brush with Spitfires from 602 Squadron confirmed fighter presence in the Dunbar area. The information was passed to Pohle who had seen the Heinkels depart earlier that morning.

Pohle deduced that the Spitfires were from Drem which was deeply worrying as fighter escort of his bombers was not an option due to the long range of the mission. The sleek new RAF fighter was thought to be fast (actually, at least 60 mph faster than the Ju88) and the climbing rate of the Spitfire gave them little chance of escape before being intercepted and the prospect of being fired upon by single aircraft armed with eight .303 machine guns was formidable. Nevertheless, at 11.55 hours, before the two Heinkels of KG26 had returned, the sound of 24 Junkers Jumo 211 engines pierced the morning quiet at Westerland as Pohle led four groups of three Ju88 each with a four-man crew onboard, away from the airfield over 450 miles of sea on a daring daylight raid to Scotland.

Another senior 1/KG30 pilot under Pohle's command was the aforementioned Leutnant Hans Sigmund Storp whose first mission from Westerland had been the attack of the *Ark Royal*. Born in 1914, Storp was the son of a forester and became interested in flying from an early age. He gained a diploma for flying at the age of seventeen and had a career as an officer in his sights. In 1932 he joined the navy and as a cadet he sailed around the world onboard the cruiser *Koln*. Storp transferred to naval flying duties and was given the opportunity to fly practically every type of aircraft available at that time. As a marine pilot he served for nine months in the Legion Kondor in the Spanish Civil War and gleaned much experience. For his service in Spain he had been awarded the Iron Cross. On his return to Germany he was sent to the Luftwaffe testing and evaluation centres at Travemunde and Rechlin, where he test flew the first Ju88s.

Early on 16 October Storp assessed the sunlit morning as being 'The right sortie weather.' He then telephoned his girlfriend Elizabeth and arranged to meet her that weekend. It would be six years before they saw each other again. A few hours later he became the first pilot shot down by Spitfires over Britain – the victim of 603 Squadron. He later reflected:

> I shall never forget this raid as long as I live. Radio silence was ordered, to surprise the enemy, if possible. We crossed the North Sea at a speed of 400 kph, in fine flying weather. Four men flew in each Ju88 – the pilot, co-pilot, radio operator and gunner. All of us were tense in expectation. We knew it would be no Sunday afternoon stroll. The main question agitating all our minds, shall we get to our goal unnoticed. We held our English enemy in great respect, especially his Spitfires. For us it was still a gentlemen's war, and not yet the brutal affair it became later. Our machines flew steadily. We were busy keeping direction. Engines all going uniformly.

The part Pohle and Storp were to play as bomber pilots in WWII was destined to be short. They did not to return to Germany that day. Two other Ju88 pilots of KG30 who featured prominently in the raid on 16 October were Horst von Riesen and Sonny Hansen.

---

*HMS *Edinburgh* was launched in 1938. Weighing 10,000 tons she was eventually sunk by our own forces after being crippled by German torpedo attacks on a convoy returning from Archangel, N. Russia, on 2 May 1942.

Prior to the raid, as noted Pohle had attended a meeting in Berlin which was presided over by Göring himself who demanded success and promised '…Everyone who helps in getting rid of those ships will have a house of his own and all the medals that are going.' During the same meeting the German Chief of Intelligence, Major Beppo Schmid, informed Pohle: 'There's no fear of our bombers running into British fighters up there.' Whilst this comment was perhaps meant to boost confidence and ally fears, it was disingenuous. When asked about this some years later Pohle was positive that: 'The attack order of the German General Staff said there were no Spitfires in Scotland,' but on the morning of 16 October Spitfires had been encountered (by KG 26) near the target area.

Pohle led his 12 aircraft in scattered formation of four sections of three aircraft across the inhospitable North Sea, each aircraft carrying two 500kg bombs. The Ju88 A-1's maximum bomb load was actually more than double that which was carried on 16 October, but the long range of the mission kept the load of each aircraft to 1,000kg. With WWII in its second month this would be the first air-raid over mainland Britain by Germany's new air force. Although the spirit of Pohle's crews was good, they dreaded having to ditch in the inhospitable North Sea or face interception by Spitfires – even at that early stage the reputation of the now legendary fighter was all pervading.

Just before 13.10 hours, flying at an altitude of 23,000 feet, the leading group of Ju88s approached the half way point of the North Sea crossing. Peering through the breaks in the cumulus clouds the air crews could make out the wave crests which appeared to confirm the south-westerly wind direction as reported earlier by the reconnaissance He111s. Constant awareness of wind direction and speed was vital for accurate navigation.

At 12.25 hours, the Drone Hill RDF station went out of service to enable the engineers to fit the replacement amplifier valves. By this time the enemy bomber formation was well on its way across the North Sea, heading almost directly at the Drone Hill site. Although the RDF station was an important unit, its shut down was far from disastrous and the formation was reported to be approaching Britain by other stations well before it arrived.

At this time Green Section of 602 Squadron were re-fuelling at RAF Leuchars having spent the previous hour chasing an apparently non-existent 'bogey' as far north as Montrose.

Back in the Turnhouse operations room, F/L Tommy Waitt had been due to go off duty at 13.00 hours, but was asked to stay on at his post as things became more hectic. The pilots of 603, including Pat Gifford, Ken Macdonald and Robbie Robertson were intrigued by the morning's aerial activity. At Drem, 602 Flight Lieutenant George Pinkerton and Flying Officer Archie McKellar were served lunch as they discussed events. Their CO was still at RAF Leuchars where he along with Ian Ferguson and Sandy Johnstone had gone to the officers mess to grab some lunch. They, like the 603 pilots, were intuitively aware that something was about to happen. At 13.26 hours Red Section 602 Squadron once again took off from Drem with orders to patrol Crail at 'Angels Five' (5,000 feet).

Just before 14.00 hours, with the rest of the group having drifted apart and scattered over a widespread area, the co-pilot in Pohle's Ju88 spotted the British coastline approximately 20 miles ahead. They had marked Berwick-on-Tweed as the place on the map where they should make landfall (they were using a British Ordnance Survey map of southern Scotland purchased in London the year before). From Berwick (not to be confused with North Berwick) their route to Rosyth was marked out. Pohle recalled: 'I came straight as an arrow from Westerland to the south coast of the Firth of Forth, just over the anchor place of the cruisers.' Against his original plan, he led his section in to attack from the east, into the sun, and not out of it. Storp, leading the second section, carried out his attack as planned, from the west (a consequence of the suddenness of Pohle's attack was that most eyewitnesses recalled the bombers attacked from the west).

Due to the intense air activity that morning a certain amount of confusion reigned at the Turnhouse control room. The aircraft of KG30 flew into an area which had already experienced a number of sightings of unidentified aircraft, most false. Whilst there were several reports of enemy aircraft having been sighted in the airspace over Dunbar (one of which was from a searchlight crew who reported six Henschels at 13.25 which turned out to be the Sea Skuas from RNAS Donibristle), it is likely that some of these were accurate as, according to Pohle, he brought his section over mainland Scotland in the Dunbar area, north of his intended landmark of Berwick-on-Tweed. His course took his section more or less straight towards the Forth rail bridge, south of Drem near

Haddington and over the south shore of the Forth over Port Seton. With the other two Ju88s flying at a distance of a quarter of a mile each side of his own, he now had a visual of the instantly recognisable 340 foot high spans of the Forth rail bridge and continued on his heading straight for it. As he did so he began his descent from 23,000 feet to 12,000 feet, from which he planned to carry out his attack. Being in such close proximity to the fighter airfield of Drem the crew would have been on the look out for RAF fighters and tension at the prospect of interception would have been heightened. As they progressed their Junkers gradually became more recognisable to those on the ground.

Fourteen-year-old David Watson was on his way back from Dunbar to Edinburgh with his parents when, at the summit of Pencraik Brae – part of the A1 between East Linton and Haddington – he spotted aircraft which appeared to be flying west. He recalled: 'The sun roof of my father's Austin Ten was open and I recall standing up to get a better view. I could see the crosses on the aircraft.' It was after returning to Edinburgh that the teenager learned of the air-raid. It is most likely that the aircraft spotted by David Watson was the section led by Helmut Pohle. Eyewitnesses in Tranent saw the aircraft a few minutes later over Port Seton where Pohle crossed the south shore of the Firth of Forth. Now flying up the Forth, Pohle next passed Inchkeith Island situated below on his right in the middle of the river (whilst Inchkeith was manned by a detachment of the 7/9 Royal Scots Regiment it had no anti-aircraft armament at that time).

A few minutes after Pohle crossed the Scottish coastline Storp led his three Ju88s, his crewmen fully alert to the threat from fighters, across the coastline high over the intended landmark of Berwick-on-Tweed. Five minutes later, with his navigator continuing to confirm identification of navigational points en route, they passed to the north of Lauder and a further seven or eight minutes saw them pass over the area to the north of Gladhouse Reservoir. Far off to the right he spotted the Firth of Forth which he allowed his eyes to follow until he spotted the top of the spans of the Forth bridge. The weather conditions were still good with puffs of broken cloud at approximately 4,000 feet but clear visibility otherwise.

The reliability of the Observer Corps cannot be over-stated and their first confirmed sighting of enemy aircraft in the skies over East Lothian came at 14.20 hours. (The RDF could not detect aircraft once they had moved overhead and inland. The plotting of their route was down to visual sightings by the Observer Corps, but even then only during daylight hours.) Two minutes later F/L Cairns Smith in the Drem watch office was instructed by Turnhouse operations room to inform Blue Section of 602 Squadron to take off and patrol the airspace over Dalkeith at 20,000 feet. A matter of minutes later the three Spitfires took off from the steeply sloping airfield at Drem but as they began their climb towards Dalkeith, they were diverted on a reciprocal course with orders from the Turnhouse controller to 'Investigate two unidentified aircraft over Tranent, Angels Two'.

At 14.27 hours the anti-aircraft battery (RSG 1), situated in Dalmeny Park, to the west of Edinburgh, had been busy practising loading (blanks) when the battery commander reported (having accurately identified) three Junkers Ju88s flying up the Forth at an altitude of 10,000 feet. ARP Wardens in Queensferry watched the aircraft circling overhead. No warning or alarm had been received up to that moment. At 14.30 Blue Section 602 Squadron, reported that apart from having seen a section of Spitfires landing at Drem (Red Section returning from patrol over Crail) they had seen nothing. At that moment George Pinkerton's R/T immediately crackled into life again with the voice of the Controller informing his section: 'Enemy aircraft bombing Rosyth, patrol five miles north of present position.' At the same time the battery commander in Dalmeny Park reported seeing the aircraft over the Forth Bridge. Naturally keen to open fire, he was not given the order to do so for a further 11 minutes when reports were received that the Forth Bridge was being bombed. Three minutes after the first bombs had been dropped the battery crew were finally given permission to open fire and the only air raid sirens to sound were in military establishments. No sirens mounted in public areas were sounded during the German raid. The delay provides a further insight into the confusion and indecision which reigned at the time.

That morning Air Chief Marshal Sir Hugh Dowding and his staff at Fighter Command HQ, Bentley Priory, had watched the continuation tracks of the enemy force develop as information from the RDF chain came in. He knew that once the enemy force had flown over the coast and inland, tracking the enemy was more problematic. In referring to the lack of air raid warning, Hugh Barkla, who was also at HQ Fighter Command, stated:

What went wrong was due to an over-reaction to a series of false alarms. The allocation of 'hostile' identification to a track had been too lightly made, and the subsequent despatch of fighters to intercept had risked there being a shortage of fighters ready to deal with genuine raiders. The authority to name a track 'hostile' was then restricted to too small a number of Controllers. With improvements in communications and in procedure in Movement Liaison, the number of unidentified tracks decreased, and the accuracy of identification of hostiles improved. It would have been remarkable if such a novel and complex system had not suffered some such swings.

16 October 1939. A bomb explodes next to HMS *Southampton*, destroying the pinnace and admirals barge. No one was killed.

I have always believed that it was entirely due to the C-in-C over-ruling the statutory procedure and taking on himself alone the decision on whether the radar tracks were to be given the identification 'hostile'. The junior officers and the scientists in the Fighter Command Filter Room at the time were in no doubt but Sir Hugh Dowding incomprehensibly, held back. Fortunately, the consequences were not serious, though earlier warning to the fighters might have enabled them to shoot down more bombers. The official records may have drawn a discreet veil over the C-in-C's aberration... but the last thing that any of us would have wished was to record anything unfavourable to Lord Dowding. It was thanks to him that scientists were at HQFC in the first place, and it was he who widened our belief to cover all aspects of operational decision making.

Arriving over the Rosyth dockyard at 14.30 hours, Helmut Pohle attempted to locate HMS *Hood*. The large cruiser he found and which he mistook for the *Hood* was in fact HMS *Repulse*, sister ship to the *Hood* and almost exactly the same in appearance, hence repeated misidentifications by the reconnaissance aircraft and German intelligence. Even whilst flying overhead Pohle still saw before him HMS *Hood*. But *Hood/Repulse* was in the dockyard at Rosyth and therefore not a legitimate target. Being a disciplined Luftwaffe officer he was not tempted to break his orders but instead chose to attack one of two cruisers which lay ahead in the Forth anchored offshore from North Queensferry on the east side of the Forth rail bridge. These were HMS *Edinburgh* and HMS *Southampton** and legitimate targets. HMS *Mohawk*, *Jervis* and the aircraft carrier HMS *Furious* were also heading up the Forth and would soon become legitimate targets for 1/KG30.

It was 14.27 and as Pohle tipped his aircraft into an 80-degree dive he picked out the *Southampton* through the Lotfe bombsight. As Pohle attacked, Storp approached from the south-east. Pohle later recalled events:

I came straight as an arrow from Westerland to the south coast of the Firth of Forth, just over the anchor place of the cruisers. I could see the *Hood* already in the dock of Rosyth. A stationary target, perfect for dive-bombing but we were strictly forbidden to attack this sitting duck. However, in the Forth lay HMS *Southampton* and HMS *Edinburgh* at anchor. I attacked as the first of twelve Ju88s the *Southampton*. But during the dive suddenly there was an almighty crack as the top part of the canopy flew off, taking the rear gun with it. Although after the dive-attack I was now flying with my crew in a half-open plane, I nevertheless remained in the area to observe the results of the other aircraft.

---

*HMS *Southampton* was launched in 1936 and weighed 9,100 tons. It caught fire in action with Luftwaffe bombers on 10 January 1941 and was lost.

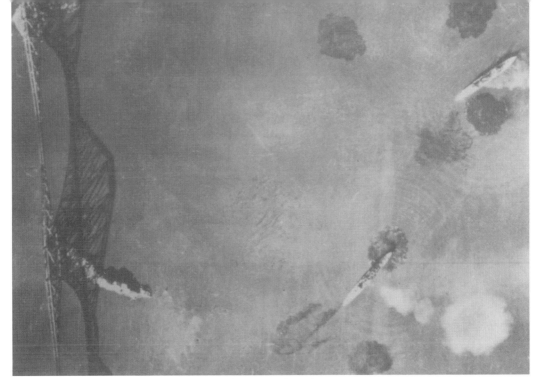

Top: Photograph taken by one of the attacking Ju88s of KG/30 on 16th October 1939, showing the Forth Bridge and evidence of bombing attack on *Southampton* (bottom) and *Edinburgh* (top).

Right: HMS *Edinburgh* under attack from Ju88 which has just pulled out of a dive. Note flak.

After the dive-attack from 12,000 feet to 1,800 feet, when I released the bombs, I continued down to 900 feet. I turned right and flew outside the famous bridge in reverse direction. This was to the north coast of the Firth of Forth, to see the other attacks. However, low over the sea and back would have been better!

The design fault which caused the cockpit canopy to blow off had occurred during testing at Rechlin. It also took with it the MG15 machine gun which was for the defence of the Junkers from above and behind.

The approach of the bombers had been watched by workmen busy building air-raid shelters beneath the arches of the bridge at North Queensferry. One, Adam McMahon, had noticed the bombers approaching along the north shore of the river and watched as one aircraft circled over Rosyth. This may have been the aircraft of Pohle himself as he tried to locate the *Hood*. The explosion of Pohle's two 500kg bombs occurred at 14.35 hours.

As the bombing started, Bill Maxwell, who was driving the Cowdenbeath ambulance onto the ferry at Hawes Pier, Queensferry, at the time, immediately set about the evacuation of his patients to the nearby shelter where they were given tea by the VAD (Voluntary Aid Detachment).

According to schoolgirl, Ella Boyle:

I was with my mother, father and younger brother visiting friends in Jamestown near Inverkeithing. I went out to play with my brother and the two children of the family we were visiting.

I can remember two planes flew over and some smaller planes that were much faster arrived and we heard the guns. This happened right above us. The two that were attacked flew over the Forth towards the bridge and we saw the bombs fall. It looked like they were trying for the bridge, at this time we did not realise that they were bombs and kept watching. None of the bombs hit the bridge but hit the water where spouts of water went into the air and I felt pain in my ears. A ship that was almost under the bridge was hit with a bomb and I saw men jumping from the ship into the water. At this time my father and mother came running up the hill, grabbed us and took us to the house. As this was happening I watched one of the bigger planes being shot at and pieces falling off. My mother and father took us into the house and I could only listen to the engines and shots being fired.

A few days after, I was at a funeral and saw two coffins. My mother told me it was two of the Germans from the planes we saw.

With his attack now complete, Pohle recovered altitude and maintained position, circling over Inverkeithing, from where he was able to observe attacks made by the second wave led by Storp at 14.38. In the absence of his canopy it was very draughty. He was also about to attract fire from the anti-aircraft gunners.

It was at 14.38 hours, just as the second Ju88 dived to attack, that the battery commander at the Dalmeny Park anti-aircraft unit was finally given the order to open fire. Almost simultaneously the batteries at Dalmeny, Donibristle, Mire End and Primrose Farm barked into life, the sky filling with the white puffs of bursting anti-aircraft shells. It is significant to mention the inherent dangers that this particular form of defence brought on the inhabitants below. Within seconds a lethal deluge of hot shrapnel rained down beneath the action with consequent casualties. In addition to the anti-aircraft guns of the city defences, the considerable fire power of HMS *Repulse* was also brought to bear.

P/O Ian Ritchie and a number of his 603 Squadron colleagues were enjoying an afternoon off in Edinburgh when the AA guns opened fire, alerting them to the fact an air raid was in progress. Eager to get back to Turnhouse and participate, the pilots dashed to their car in Frederick Street and drove at high speed back to the airfield. Unfortunately, they were too late to be of use.

As the raid began, activity in the Turnhouse operations room became frenetic. It was further hampered by the arrival of local top brass which didn't help matters as they crowded in to see what was going on. At Turnhouse the 603 padre was about to drive to Edinburgh in order to visit P/O Graham Hunter in the military hospital in the castle. His progress was brought to a rapid halt by the sound of the air-raid siren. Clambering out of his car he ran to one of the airfield's machine-gun posts and took charge of the Lewis gun, to the derision of the personnel. The aircrew and ground crew had an excellent view of the diving bombers and the puffs of anti-aircraft fire. They were only three miles from the southern end of the Forth bridge. One of the ground crew was Jim Marshall who sought cover in an air-raid shelter with a number of colleagues: 'I remember the day well as it was the only time I spent in an air raid shelter during the entire war!' At South Queensferry civilian passers-by were enjoying the mild autumnal weather when at 14.30 they witnessed aircraft diving down from the west towards the shipping anchored offshore. Moments later great spouts of water confirmed the ships were being bombed. In response the AA batteries then began to open fire. A single Naval Fairey Swordfish was suddenly caught in the same airspace as the dive bombers and the bursts of AA gun fire. The crew were from RNAS Donibristle, Fife, and had been practising torpedo bombing in the Forth estuary off Aberdour.

After passing to the north of Gladhouse Reservoir, Storp headed north-west passing to the south of the village of Roslin and over the Threipmuir Reservoir before continuing on the same heading towards the Forth, now only five minutes away. As he did so he dropped the nose of his Ju88 in order to bring the aircraft down to its attacking altitude of 12,000 feet. The Luftwaffe crews were aware that Turnhouse aerodrome, with its RAF fighters, lay below them to the east but unaware at that moment in time that the fighters of 603 Squadron were climbing to intercept. As recorded in the

603 Squadron ORB, Yellow Section took off from Turnhouse and, as the Spitfires climbed, Storp's section flew overhead and across their path en route to Rosyth. Unlike Pohle, Storp intended making a wide right-hand sweep to take his section over the dockyard. This plan of attack would allow them to make a more rapid exit from the area, out towards the North Sea. Storp estimated initiating his attack at 14.38:

> Suddenly we sighted the coast. We turned inland to approach the bridge from the west. Now it becomes a question of attack, each machine by itself. I have the sun at my back. Nothing is to be seen of any anti-aircraft defences. But where is the *Hood*? To our disgust she was in dry dock, and by Fuhrer's orders, there must be no bombs dropped on land. So the *Hood* is safe from us.
>
> But in front of the big bridge in the Firth of Forth, I espied a few boats. I tell the others over the radio: 'We attack!' Then I put the plane's nose down, and take a ship into my sights. So down to 2,500 feet goes the dive, and I slowly recognise that I have a cruiser in my sights. Later I heard that it was the *Southampton*. And still no anti-aircraft defence. At 2,400 feet I let my two bombs loose. Slowly I bring the machine out of the dive, but I still go down to about 800 feet. We see that our bombs have hit the cruiser.

Both Pohle and Storp later claimed their bombs had hit the *Southampton*. Storp was confident his bombs had been *aimed* at the *Southampton*. It is known that one of the 500kg bombs penetrated three decks of the battlecruiser, passing through the port hangar and the boy seaman's mess-deck before exiting near her bow near the waterline. At that point the bomb, with its 220kg of amatol, TNT or trialen, exploded, sinking the Admiral's barge and a pinnace which were moored alongside and peppering the ship with lethal shards of shrapnel. The trajectory of the bomb had actually been fortuitous. There were three casualties on board *Southampton* and seven on the cruiser *Edinburgh*. Although there were no deaths one naval rating was seriously wounded.

On 18 November an account of the raid by Mr A. Neilson was published in *The War Illustrated*. On that day he happened to be driving along the coast road alongside the Firth of Forth with his wife. As the bombing began they were adjacent to *Edinburgh* and *Southampton* giving them an uninterrupted view of events:

> Suddenly there was a loud cracking noise which seemed to be within the car, and which I immediately diagnosed as a broken ball-brace. Again! But this time the cracking noise was a few hundred yards away and easily recognisable as machine-gun fire. I stopped the car and jumped out just in time to see a great volume of water shoot up within a few yards of one of the cruisers. 'Air Raid!' I called. 'Come out, quick!'
>
> The attacker had gone, but presently the cruisers started loosing their shells to a height of about 6,000 feet. Up among the white puffs of smoke my wife spotted something. 'Look, there he is!' As she spoke the machine banked and came down in a fast dive from the west. Down, down he came, until directly over the Forth Bridge he released two large bombs whose course we were able to follow until they plunged into the river within a few yards of one of the cruisers.
>
> Several times this happened, and of the bombs which were dropped I should say more than one was as near as thirty yards from one or other of the cruisers. Certainly, a lucky day for them. Right behind us in a wood an anti-aircraft battery blazed away, and as we were not more than 400 yards [actually nearer 1,000] from the cruisers the noise was terrific, and all about us we could hear quite distinctly the orders given on the ship's loud-speakers.
>
> As we were on rising ground and looking down on the scene we had a perfect view of the whole affair. My wife was a bit afraid to start with, but I insisted that we were tremendously fortunate to get such a view and that we might never have such an opportunity again. I may say it was fairly obvious she was satisfied on this point – but not just in the way I intended her to be. I continued to reassure her, however, and pointed out that there was not a chance in a million of a bomb dropping near us as the marksmanship was far too good for that. The danger of shrapnel dropping on us was slight as we were too close to the guns. One large piece did, however, land within fifty yards of my car. What I did not tell her and what I dared

not think about was my secret fear of what would have happened to us if one of the bombs had made a lucky hit where the raider was aiming. It was a most thrilling experience which I should not have missed for a great deal.

Whilst eyewitness accounts from civilians are notoriously unreliable they are often the only testimony available. However, as there were a great many witnesses to the events of 16 October, the common denominators allow us to establish a reasonably accurate record of what happened. Nevertheless, a number of inaccuracies have been perpetuated over the years, the most common being that the German aircraft which carried out the bombing were He111s. Another was that the aircraft dropped a number of bombs before going round again for another run. The Junkers carried just two bombs and these were dropped during the culmination of just one dive attack. The fact that Pohle was circling over Inverkeithing, observing the success of the other aircraft in his unit, may have given eyewitnesses the impression that just three Ju88s carried out repeated attacks instead of what was actually several waves of aircraft.

The staff in the L.N.E.R. control office in Waverley Station were unaware of what was actually going on over the railway bridge until the controller responsible for the Edinburgh to Inverkeithing line received a telephone call from the signalman in the box at Forth Bridge North, situated on the northern approach viaduct to the bridge, who informed them that German bombers were all over the place. At that time no air raid sirens had sounded but initial doubts concerning the credibility of the signalman's claims were quickly dismissed when he opened the window of his signal-box and held out the telephone handset. The high pitched sound of aircraft engines intermingled with the crescendo of exploding bombs and anti-aircraft fire confirmed that the signalman had not been drinking! Alex Farish was one of the controllers on duty at Waverley that day. His son Brian recalled:

At this time a far more important decision had to be taken, and that concerned the safety of passengers on board the 2.30p.m., Edinburgh to Dunfermline train which had stopped at Dalmeny Station and was then ready to proceed over the Forth Bridge. After some hurried consultation it was agreed to let the train run – after all, the sirens had still not sounded and there was just the chance that this was only a major exercise! Lady luck rode that train that sunny October afternoon.

One passenger on the train was Mr Carter, an Edinburgh commercial traveller. His recollections of the event proved to be very accurate:

Anti-aircraft fire opened up, and the bombs were dropped, but nowhere near the ships, except one, which fell right at the side of one of them. There was a terrific spray and we thought at first it had been hit. We were then allowed to proceed, but more planes came over. We were on the bridge when the last bomb was dropped. The train went slowly, and the planes were swooping overhead. The bombing was concentrated on the larger ship. The attackers had a very hot reception.

The mother of 603 Squadron's Flight Lieutenant Laurie Cunningham was on the train and witnessed events. She later recalled being anxious that her only son was about to become involved in combat in the sky above her.

Many people later expressed concern that three waves of bombers were allowed to attack and, according to the Air Ministry, drop 40 bombs, unchallenged by RAF fighters.[6] At that stage the only opposition to the enemy bombers had come from the shore and ship-based AA guns. The first three waves carried out their attacks between 14.30 and 15.00 hours. The fourth wave was possibly an hour behind, having failed to navigate across the North Sea with the precision of the other three, and therefore making landfall further north along the Scottish coast. It was recorded that they approached the bridge at approximately 16.00 hours. It was following the third wave that RAF Spitfires appeared on the scene. Cecil Gibson maintains clear memories of that day: 'I got off a bus to see what turned out to be the air raid on the Forth Bridge and remember thinking that a Spitfire was rather close to a Blenheim. So much for aircraft recognition!' Cecil later served with 603 Squadron as a member of the ground crew during the 1950s and has retained many fond memories from the Vampire period just prior to disbandment.

As each of the German bombers completed their attack they fled eastwards along the Forth towards the North Sea. A few minutes after Storp's attack all hell broke loose when his wireless operator/rear gunner cried out the German equivalent of 'Spitfires are attacking!' 603 Squadron's Yellow Section had caught up with him.

It is recorded that the aircraft flown by Storp, Pohle and von Riesen attracted the attention of Spitfires whilst the others attempted to make their escape either straight along the Firth of Forth, by hugging the north bank of the river, or by flying low over the rooftops of Edinburgh. It is likely most all 12 aircraft were pursued and attacked by Spitfires at some stage. It is a quirk of fate that the first and second aircraft shot down during WWII should be flown by the two most senior and experienced pilots in KG30.

A common recollection was that the German aircraft were met by an impressive fusillade of gun fire, not just from the anti-aircraft guns onboard the Royal Navy cruisers, but also from the shore-based AA guns, once they had finally been given permission to open fire. Some of these AA batteries were manned by the local Territorial Army Regiment (the 94th [City of Edinburgh] Heavy Anti-Aircraft Regiment of the Royal Artillery). Their armament was not the most up-to-date and included a circa 1917 naval three-inch gun which had been designed to shoot down aircraft during WWI travelling at just 100mph. James Clark was an apprentice in the civilian building trade who happened to be working at the Royal Naval base at Port Edgar on the south side of the Forth, just east of South Queensferry. He recalled the arrival of the second and third waves of German aircraft from the west:

> Suddenly there was the sound of gunfire; this came from the anti-aircraft batteries. Then the sound of sirens [Royal Navy base at Port Edgar]. On looking up we saw two planes flying over the bridge with the puffs of bursting shells following them. I remember everybody on the site had gathered out in the open and were cheering the gunners as these shells burst closer and closer. None of us ever having been in an air raid before, we didn't appreciate the danger; we soon did, when a naval officer bore down on us, with a big lump of jagged metal in his hand and politely told us to get into the bloody shelter. Gerry didn't stop for very long. After we got the all-clear we went back to work. On finishing we had to walk past the base hospital, there we saw them removing the wounded who had been brought in from the ships that were in the Firth of Forth at the time of the raid.

At 14.30 hours, just as Helmut Pohle was approaching the Forth Bridge, Red Section, 603 Squadron, led by 29-year-old F/L Patsy Gifford, were ordered to scramble and vectored towards Drem. At 14.35, in response to a report by the Observer Corps of unidentified aircraft moving westwards over Dalkeith, S/L Bob Johnstone from his position in the control room at Turnhouse, ordered up Yellow Section. F/L George Denholm led Pilot Officers 'Sheep' Gilroy and 'Black' Morton away from Turnhouse on a westerly heading. Legend has it that while watching Yellow Section take off, Gifford had been impatient that his section had not been the first to be ordered into the air and, aware that an attack on his home soil was in progress, he had telephoned the station commander, W/C Don Fleming, and sector controller, Bob Johnstone, and badgered them into letting him get airborne. However, the Squadron ORB and Black Morton's log book confirm that Gifford's section took off five minutes prior to Denholm's section.

As soon as Yellow Section were airborne Black spotted what was probably the third wave of Ju88s away to the north over the Forth Bridge launching their attack on the shipping. Pohle could be seen circling in the background in Ju88A-1, 4D+AK 'Anton-Kurfurst', hoping to witness any success achieved by the other aircraft in his unit.

George Denholm later recalled that his section were hardly off the ground when they found themselves engaging the enemy bombers. To the south of the airfield at approximately 3,000 feet seemingly heading towards the airspace over the Threipmuir Reservoir, Black spotted three more aircraft. The leading aircraft was 1 Staffel's Ju88 A-1, 4D+DH 'Dora-Heinrich' commanded by Storp with his three other crew members, Feldwebel Hans Georg Hielscher, who was due to be married the following January, Feldwebel Hugo Rohnke and rear gunner Obergefreiter Kramer. Having successfully carried out their attack they were now flying a reciprocal course to that which they had flown to the bridge.

George, Black and Sheep attempted to intercept Storp's section of Ju88s and came within firing range over Colinton where Yellow Section split up to make individual attacks on their prey and pursued them to the east of the city, witnessed by a nearby searchlight crew. George and Black's initial attack was on the Ju88 flown by Storp. Black Morton's diary entry provides an insight into the ensuing combat:

> Very nice day, cloud 2-3/10, cumulus, 3,000'. Slight ground haze, no wind.
> About 2.25 'A' Flight ordered off. Red – P.G. [Pat Gifford], Ken [Macdonald], Robbie [Robertson] to patrol Drem. Yellow: George [Denholm], Sheep [Gilroy], Self took off 3-4 mins after Red. At about 2,000' to West of airport fired on by A.A. – 4 bursts in line 400' to right of us. Almost immediately saw 3 or 4 E.A. circling over Forth Bridge alt. 5,000', informed George, but had already spotted 3 E.A. to South of us, 3,000'. Pursued in line astern. E.A. making for bank of cloud over Currie. Did not identify all E.A., but one definitely Heinkel [all now known to be Ju88]. Followed Sheep through gaps in cloud, George in lead, firing at 1 E.A. At other side of cloud no sign of George, Sheep pursuing one turning to Port. I took starboard and followed it through two more clouds, shooting short bursts from low No.1 position. E.A. speed 190-200 mph. E.A. fired tracer, reddish brown puffs. Very strong impression of two or more guns firing. E.A. swung east in 3rd cloud. Over Dalkeith got in a burst of about 8-10 secs from high No.1. E.A. failed to make the next cloud and started to lose height, swinging to the North towards Wallyford. At end of this long burst I was shaken to see something black fall off E.A., shied violently at it.
> Was approaching to make a further attack when 3 Spitfires shot past me from above. They had obviously not seen me so I broke away and returned to re-arm. The last I saw of E.A. was about 500' over Port Seton being vigorously attacked by Red. E.A., eventually came down in sea off Port Seton, very badly shot up. 1 dead went down with aircraft, 3 prisoners.
> P.G. [Gifford] considers E.A. his trophy; but feel inclined to dispute it; as from my own observations and report of prisoners E.A. was partly disabled (port engine u/s) before Red section appeared. Whether this was due to my fire or to previous fire from George is unknown. I certainly hit him for one air gunner was killed. This must have been the lower, as Red report fire from top gunner up to last moment and I was certainly shot at from below at beginning of engagement.
> I was so excited that I failed to identify type of E.A. – prisoners report it as He111. Was surprised to find no trace of being scared, though crouched down a bit when tracer observed going by.

Storp later recalled the moment the Spitfires came within range and began their pursuit of his Ju88:

> Then I commit my biggest mistake. I climb. Suddenly, out of a serene sky, machine guns firing at us. My co-pilot calls out, 'Spitfires behind us!' But the first spatter of bullets had hit us. My left engine was out of action. I took violent evasive action. Ten to twelve Spitfires were after me. I resemble a hare shot and wounded, but still chased. My gunner had been killed in the first burst. I pressed my bird down. To get away was our only thought. But the Spitfires curved around us like devils. One burst after the other made a sieve of our Ju.
> The hell-like flight went right over the roofs of Edinburgh. Here we had respite for some seconds. The British did not shoot when over the city. My only thought was that the machine should not go down on land: it should not fall into enemy hands. I steered towards the sea. Where had the British hunters come from so quickly? Why had we not spotted them earlier? These were the thoughts that kept me busy while I was steering. My bird was finished. At about 700 feet the elevators went out of action. The machine capsized, nose forward, and fell into the sea like a stone. In the last second I was able to throw off the roof of the cockpit.
> I was thrown about 70 yards, still fastened to my seat. I came to under water, [and] swam to the surface.

It would seem that whilst George Denholm may have inflicted damage prior to the attack by Black in L1049, it was most likely Black's second burst (8-10 seconds from a high No.1 position) which knocked out the port engine of the Ju88 and killed Kramer, the wireless operator/rear gunner. This was later confirmed by Storp himself. In response to Gifford having reported return fire from the upper gun position late in the combat, Black diplomatically accepted that he must have silenced the *lower* gun position (ventral gondola) but, in order for Gifford to have experienced return fire, Morton *could* have killed the upper gunner and his MG15 was then taken over by the flight engineer/ventral gunner. All reports state that the Ju88 was pursued from above and behind by the RAF fighters. The upper gun position would therefore provide a clearer shot at the pursuing Spitfires.

It is interesting to note that Sheep and Black recorded in their log books flying times of only 10 and 15 minutes respectively for this patrol. Black also incorrectly identified the Ju88 as a He111. The latter comes as no surprise as the Ju88 was a recent addition to the German Air Force.

At 14.35 the peace and quiet of Roslin village was shattered by the sound of a single German bomber as it made its way east, followed almost immediately by gunfire. Later that day PC James Henderson submitted a report:

> About 2.35 p.m. on Monday, 16th October, 1939, an air plane flew in a westerly direction at a very high altitude over Roslin. About five minutes later I saw a plane, which I was of the opinion was the same one, flying in an easterly direction over the same course. A few seconds previous to seeing it the second time coming out of a large cloud, there was a burst of what sounded like machine gun fire coming from the direction of this cloud. A minute after it appeared from the cloud, four other planes appeared behind it also travelling eastwards. Those four planes flew in and out the cloud for a few minutes, and the sound of gunfire came from them. They then flew in a north easterly direction.
>
> Same afternoon I interviewed Joseph Thomson, Farmer, Langhimm Farm, Roslin, who informed me that after the planes left the cloud referred to two of them flew over his farmhouse, and a number of empty cartridge cases fell from them on to his farmhouse and steading. These cartridge cases, which are forwarded herewith, appear originally to have been live tracer cartridges.
>
> The direction taken by the planes would take them over the searchlight post at Gowkley Moss, Roslin, and into the vicinity of Glencorse Barracks.

It is likely PC Henderson actually saw *three* Spitfires pursuing a Ju88, a total of four aircraft. This was almost certainly Yellow Section. Having made contact over Colinton, the bomber was pursued over Roslin and Laighill Farm, situated just north of the village, where Joe Thompson was showered with spent cartridge cases from the Spitfires as they roared over his farmhouse in pursuit of their prey.

At Swanston Cottages, Herbert More, one of a number of eyewitnesses at Hillend, reported seeing two bombers coming under attack from Spitfires before seeking refuge in a bank of low cloud. According to a report given to the *Evening News*, one of the bombers was seen to flee on a north westerly heading in the direction of Auchendinny. It was this aircraft, flown by Storp, which Red Section, led by Patsy Gifford with Ken Macdonald and Robbie Robertson came across at 4,000 feet over Carberry Hill as they headed west back towards the city after a patrol which had taken them on a heading towards Haddington. Eyewitnesses described the Spitfires flying low overhead followed by a 'terrific roar'. In trying to establish the height of the aircraft at this time the reports given by the eyewitnesses on the ground conflict with those given by the pilots – the latter provided the more accurate record of the two.

Yet to encounter the enemy bombers, Gifford eagerly took up the chase. Perhaps a little too eagerly. As he made his first attack the bomber veered sharply to port to avoid the gunfire. They were dealing with an experienced pilot. It was now heading north towards the Forth. Patsy, Ken and Robbie each made an attack. Pieces of wreckage were observed falling from the aircraft and one engine was out of action – the result of the earlier attack by Black Morton of Yellow Section. Bearing in mind that attack had also killed the gunner, it would explain the lack of return fire at this stage of the pursuit. At Cockenzie School the children were startled by the low flying aircraft as they flew overhead, the crackle of gunfire sharp to their ears.

John Donaldson, who had earlier witnessed Pohle's section flying towards the Forth Bridge witnessed a number of Ju88s being pursued east over the Forth and the end of Storp's part in the war:

The bombers were being hotly pursued by Spitfires, low-flying and blasting away with machine guns. I had an excellent view of the one shot down into the sea off Port Seton. Another flew over our head making for the hills with spent bullets hitting the shed behind us.

John Dickson, of Links Road, Port Seton, was the skipper of the 35-foot yawl *Dayspring*, which was used for line fishing. At 04.00 hours on the morning of the 16th the *Dayspring* left port on the two and a half hour journey to May Island where John and his crew would shoot lines. In such a small vessel a trip so far offshore was an adventurous one and took courage and years of experience. Onboard with John were his sons William and John (junior) and brothers Andrew and Sandy Harkness. As John headed back to Port Seton he and the lads were initially quite unaware that an air raid was in progress when the Ju88 of Hans Storp came into view pursued by the Spitfires of Patsy, Robbie and Ken, with Red 1 in the process of delivering his final attack. The crew of the *Dayspring* looked on as the Luftwaffe bomber flew out over the river with smoke trailing from one engine. Approximately four miles offshore from Port Seton the elevators failed and the nose of Ju88 *Dora-Heinrich* reared up before it dived into the waters of the Forth in a great white splash. The time was 14.45 hours.

John Dickson estimated that the aircraft flew over the Forth at approximately 100 feet with undercarriage lowered and hit the water about a mile from his vessel. His son, John, called out: 'You'd better go and see if they're alive.' He later recalled his father '…was not keen as he thought they might have guns and could attempt to take the boat to Germany.' His brother, William, was harder and thought that as they might have bombed Edinburgh and killed innocent civilians they should just leave them. Nevertheless, John Dickson set course at full speed to render assistance. It took the *Dayspring* half an hour to cover the distance and the crew noticed that the Junkers remained afloat for about five minutes and, while the fishing boat was still a considerable distance away, it slipped beneath the surface. As they neared the site, any apprehension regarding the possibility of attack and hijacking of the boat by the German airmen had gone but as John (senior) could see no sign of survivors in the water he believed they must have gone down with the aircraft and that his efforts had been in vain. However, as he drew closer he spotted three survivors clinging to an air-filled float and a rope was thrown out to them. Whilst two of the Germans swam towards the *Dayspring*, the third was so reluctant to release his grip from the float, out of desperation he grasped the rope between his teeth and was hauled in. All three were relieved to be pulled shivering and exhausted from the icy waters of the Forth. The skipper saw that one of the Germans was wearing an Iron Cross (Storp) and had a cut on his face. As the three airmen sat on deck he noticed the others had similar injuries. John Dickson and the lads provided food, cigarettes and thick dry jumpers to put on over the Germans' wet flying clothing. In response they expressed their gratitude by vigorously shaking the hand of every crew member who were by now aware they were not in the least bit hostile or aggressive. They considered themselves lucky to be alive and informed them that the fourth member of their crew had gone down with the aeroplane.*

A small number of local people had already started to gather as the *Dayspring* pulled alongside in Port Seton harbour. All three survivors managed to walk unaided up the harbour steps, half an hour after they had been rescued. On arrival Storp told a German speaking local that: 'We had no chance to get away... our plane was just too slow'. Although none of the airmen was seriously injured, each had sustained cuts and bruises and was suffering from hypothermia, and Hielscher had received a blow to the ribs and was subsequently put on a stretcher. According to John Dickson (junior): 'All three men were very grateful for being rescued, and the leader, who spoke English fairly well, took a heavy gold signet ring with the German eagle on from his finger and gave it to my father.' The fisherman duly accepted the gift. John junior still wears the ring today.

The following day divers went down to try to find the wreckage of Storp's aircraft. They located it in about 100 feet of water, attached lifting gear and the aircraft was raised. Despite the salvage operation the body of the gunner was never found. Storp later confirmed that he had been killed

---

*Newsreel showing Storp's capture was later shown in a cinema in Stockholm in neutral Sweden. It was seen by a friend of Storp who sent a cable to his family in Germany informing them that he was alive, whilst they had assumed he had been killed.

during the first attack by (Black Morton's) Spitfire. The cold waters of the Forth became the grave for Obergefreiter Kramer.

All three were taken to Cockenzie Police Station, situated in Port Seton, where local GP Dr. Black administered first aid. PC Henry 'Harry' Stevenson was on duty at the time and some years later his daughter Barbara, then a schoolgirl, recalled:

> …my father was too busy trying to balance his Fine Book (local people who had been fined at the Burgh Court paid their fines at the Station) and did not take too much notice of the air activity overhead. By the time I arrived home from school, chaos reigned. I think the whole population of the Burgh had gathered at the Police Station as news had travelled fast that Germans had been brought in to the harbour on a fishing boat and were in the Police Station. There were no instructions in the Police Manual for dealing with this type of incident!
>
> Calls went out for dry clothing for the airmen, but one lady suggested a clothes rope might be more appropriate! The local publican sent a bottle of brandy round to the Police Station and I recall my father saying the airmen greatly appreciated that. Military Intelligence Officers arrived and the prisoners were taken by ambulance to Edinburgh Castle, taking with them our hot water bottles to help keep them warm. Alec Craig had provided

F/L Pat Gifford with his Spitfire nicknamed 'Stickleback' after claiming the first 'kill' of the war; the German bomber he shot down on its raid over the Forth was the first to be shot down on British soil.

some clothing for one of the airmen and when it was returned there was an Iron Cross in the jacket pocket. Although he was tempted to keep it, he thought it best to return it to the prisoner.

> On the evening of the 16th, Flight Lieutenant Gifford arrived at the Police Station to have a word about the day's events… while my mother made the visitor a cup of tea... I went out to try and find them – no personal radios in those days! We duly located them and they returned to the office and talked over the day's events. I thought Flight Lieutenant Gifford was terribly handsome and from then on my ambition was to join the WAAF!

It is interesting to compare the friendly and supportive assistance given by the residents of the Burgh of Cockenzie and Port Seton at a time when the attacks by the Luftwaffe on our cities had yet to begin, with the reaction of the British public to downed German aircrew as the war progressed. An excellent example of the change being the experience of 603's own Sheep Gilroy in August 1940.

The three Germans were taken under escort from Cockenzie Police Station to the military hospital at Edinburgh Castle*, which had been partially transformed earlier that year into a small hospital for military personnel for minor operations, accidental injury caused during training and convalescence and were beset by many questions both official and unofficial. However, they must have welcomed the relief of being able to climb between the dry sheets of their hospital beds, but even then they were not left alone. Despite a guard on the door a couple of press photographers managed to get into the room. Having taken their photographs they were about to leave when the garrison commander arrived on the scene and all hell broke loose. The photographers were escorted from the castle as the guards faced a severe reprimand. The photograph was indeed a coup, the first to be taken of Luftwaffe prisoners of war during WWII.

---

*Today the National War Museum of Scotland occupies what was the wartime military hospital in Edinburgh Castle, in particular the NWM archive occupies one of the wards.

Newsreel footage of Storp's crew arriving at Edinburgh Castle Hospital, 16 October 1939.

By that time, the Gruppenkommandeur of KG30 was also a prisoner, aboard HMS *Jervis* with two of his crew dead and a third fatally wounded. Storp later met his commanding officer again whilst in captivity in Canada. He commented:

> That the Spitfire pilots shot down only two machines was not the fault of the Spitfire pilots, but because of the late warning they received. Spitfire group pilots visited us the same day in hospital, bringing cigarettes and chocolate. We thought this very fair, and have not forgotten this to this day.

The senior army officer in charge at the castle at the time visited Storp on the ward. Two of the three aircrew were busy thumbing through the pocket size editions of the English dictionary thoughtfully given to them by their captors. Having introduced the prisoner to his companions as Hans Storp, he asked him if he was being well treated: 'Yes, thank you sir,' Storp replied in perfect, well enunciated, English.

Lurid details of supposed injuries to the Luftwaffe crew were published in the national and, in particular, local newspapers, but apart from 27-year-old Hielscher the only other injuries consisted of cuts and bruises. With so much ammunition having been expended in their direction, the three survivors had been very lucky.

While Storp had been attempting to evade the pursuing Spitfires his Gruppenkommandeur was also being intercepted. On reaching their appointed position over Tranent George Pinkerton, leading the three Spitfires of Blue Section, 602 Squadron, had been informed by control that: 'Enemy aircraft bombing Rosyth, patrol five miles north of present position'. He then spotted an aircraft approximately three miles ahead, flying east over a bank of cloud. Ordering his section into line astern he prepared to attack but his attention was drawn by Archie McKellar to three dark planes which were closer on the port side. He led Blue Section round to come down on their tail. These turned out to be naval Sea Skua training aircraft of HMS *Merlin* from RNAS Donibristle (155 Brigade AA battery later recorded that the Skuas had hampered their effectiveness at Donibristle). The aircraft were unfamiliar to the 602 pilots and George Pinkerton later recorded: 'These chaps never knew how close they came to being shot down.' Pinkerton then resumed his plan to intercept the enemy aircraft he had originally spotted, this aircraft was being flown by Pohle. Having left his orbiting position over Inverkeithing he was now heading home. By this time F/O Paul Webb had broken away from Pinkerton and McKellar and lost visual contact with them. The other two Spitfires of Blue Section climbed through the bank of cloud and continued their pursuit of their quarry from the position of superior altitude. George Pinkerton spotted the German through a gap in the clouds, switched his radio to transmit and called out: 'Villa, Blue Section,

Tally Ho, Buster', and with the aircraft of McKellar following close behind he dived from above, with superchargers at full boost, to get into a position behind the German bomber. During this initial dive the Spitfire of McKellar almost overhauled that of Pinkerton as he opened fire closing to 50 yards before breaking off his attack. As the Ju88 attempted to reach cloud cover McKellar opened fire, riddling the port wing before breaking off. The Ju88 dodged in and out of the broken cloud cover, with Pohle at the controls desperately trying to shake off his attackers, and each time he re-appeared either Pinkerton or McKellar were there to open fire. The vigilant Observer Corps subsequently logged the sound of aircraft firing at 14.43 hours, in the vicinity of Elie.

At 14.15 hours a third wave of Ju88 bombers was spotted crossing the coast near Dunbar, heading west before turning south in the direction of Haddington. At the same time the six Spitfires of B Flight, 603 Squadron roared over the grass airfield of RAF Turnhouse and took to the skies with instructions to patrol North Berwick at 3,000 feet. A short while later the instructions from the sector controller at Turnhouse were amended by his superiors at 13 Group, Fighter Command, who had overall responsibility for Scotland and Northern Ireland, and the controller at Turnhouse was told in no uncertain terms: B Flight too low at 3,000 feet, get them up to the correct height.'

There is evidence that there was some tension between the Turnhouse sector controller and 13 Group, Fighter Command, which is hardly surprising considering this was the first time that Fighter Command tactics were being tested and that inevitably flaws were appearing. At 14.51 hours Red Section, 602 Squadron were scrambled to patrol over their airfield at Drem. This was in order to extend a theoretical defensive line of fighters across East Lothian and the Forth.

At the controls of his Ju88, Helmut Pohle used all his experience in an attempt to shake off the Spitfires of Pinkerton and McKellar, or at least minimise the opportunity for them to open fire. Eventually, and in order to maintain a course home, he was forced to leave what little cloud cover there was and make a dash eastwards. He was now flying in clear skies over the sea with the two fighters to the rear and above. The Spitfire of Pinkerton appeared to be to his starboard side while that of McKellar was on his port. Which ever way Pohle turned he couldn't avoid flying into the firing line of one or other of the faster more manoeuvrable RAF fighters. With the leading Spitfire now only 50 yards behind, Pohle pulled back hard on his control column in order to shake off the fighters but in doing so he presented Pinkerton with a view of the upper surfaces and he immediately opened fire, sending a burst from his eight Brownings smashing into the German bomber, shattering the cockpit and claiming the life of Pohle's co-pilot and gunner and wounding the radio operator. A burst from McKellar's Spitfire damaged a wingtip of the Junkers. Bullets from Pinkerton and McKellar's aircraft hit the starboard engine while McKellar smashed the port engine with the last of his 'pellets'. With fuel streaming from his ruptured wing-mounted fuel tanks, Pohle dived towards a merchant ship and levelled out at 500 feet over the Forth. He later recalled:

> I was surprised by a Spitfire which I could not get away from. Also, we could not defend ourselves with the rear top gun as it had gone with the canopy. After another attack during which two of my crew were killed, one of the engines failed and began to smoke. Flying with one engine I managed another 20km, when – some distance off the Scottish coast – flying in an easterly direction, the next Spitfire attack destroyed the second engine too.
>
> Without both engines I must go down [to sea level]. I saw a trawler and aimed to [bale out] near to the ship with my parachute, but the fourth man of my crew, the gunner of the rear below gun, was badly wounded. [I hesitated] and was just able to clear the trawler before ditching the Junkers, although the sea was running at strength. The crew of the trawler – I hoped it would be Norwegian, then neutral country – rescued me as well as my fourth crew member. However, I collapsed on the deck with concussion and face injuries. My crew man died from his injuries the next day. A few days later I regained consciousness. A white bed and a nurse. I thought I was in Norway. However, I was in the Royal Navy Hospital at Port Edwards [Edgar], near Edinburgh. At the head of the bed stood... an RAF intelligence officer. About ten days later I was transferred to a military hospital in Edinburgh Castle. After that and shortly before Christmas I was taken to the Tower of London and finally off to No.1 PoW Camp, Grizedale Hall/Westmorland. Later I heard one of my two bombs – each 500kg, hit the *Southampton*.

Pohle had been attempting to reach the *Hornum*, a rescue trawler the German navy had positioned off the east coast of Scotland. He made one last attempt to gain altitude before dropping 'like a stone' into the icy waters of the North Sea. The members of Balcomie Golf Club on Fife Ness had an excellent view of the death of the bomber. The force of the impact with the sea smashed the perspex nose of the Junkers. With their ammunition exhausted Pinkerton and McKellar circled the aircraft before Pinkerton flew towards the merchant vessel and flashed an SOS with his downward inverted signal lamp and waggled his wings, before returning to the Junkers. By now petrol was seeping from the holed fuel tanks, creating coloured streaks on the surface of the sea. With the merchant ship having set course for the downed aircraft, Pinkerton and McKellar returned to Drem.

Pohle was transferred to the destroyer HMS *Jervis* (by which time his colleague was dead) where he was interrogated by the ship's Paymaster, Lieutenant Ralph Engledue, who spoke some German. As a consequence of his facial injuries Pohle lost consciousness again and the interview was terminated. The Observer Corps post 36/B2 recorded the crash as having occurred at 14.55 hours, three miles east of Crail. The second enemy aircraft to be shot down in WWII. 602 had lost out in the race to score the first kill to 603 by just ten minutes. George Pinkerton later filled in his combat report and recorded the time of the combat as being 'about 15.00 hours'. The log book of HMS *Jervis* records:

1450/16	German A/C sighted. Action Stations.
1453/16	German A/C shot down by own a/c. Proceeded full speed on co. 042 degrees to pick up survivors and wreckage.
1520/16	Stopped and lowered boat.
1625/16	Proceeded with one wounded and one dead German airmen co. 220 degrees, 30 kts.
1705/16	Stopped off Methil. Lowered whaler to pick up Lt. Robins.
1723/16	Hoisted whaler.
1725/16	Proceeded Rosyth.
1830/16	Secured alongside *War Nizam*.
1950/16	Lighter alongside. Dead German lowered into it.
2145/16	German prisoner taken aboard launch for despatch to Hospital, Port Edgar.
2145/16	Slipped from oiler.
2215/16	Secured alongside Jupiter at Y berth. Mohawk on inside.

The log of HMS *Jervis* states that 602 had shot down Pohle's Ju88 eight minutes after Storp's aircraft splashed into the waters of the Forth. This is the narrowest margin when examining the evidence of whether it had been 602 or 603 that had shot down the first enemy aircraft of WWII. George Pinkerton's Combat Report increased the margin to 15 minutes. The fact that Gifford had landed back at Turnhouse at 14.55 followed by Macdonald and Robertson at 15.00 also provides further confirmation which can be supported by those on the ground at Turnhouse. On landing Gifford completed his combat report stating the time of his attack as being 14.45. By December 1941, the matter was still in some dispute and Count Stevens, by then a wing commander, asked Air Intelligence for a ruling. On 28 December 1941, Air Intelligence replied:

...from this record you will see the first aircraft to be destroyed was by 603 Squadron at 14.45 hours on 16th October 1939 and the second by 602 Squadron at 15.00 hours on 16th October 1939. As these two were the first enemy aircraft destroyed by Fighter Command during the present war it clearly gives the honour of the first blood to 603 Squadron.

Despite this ruling the argument rumbled on. By the end of 1941 the matter had been referred to Fighter Command who gave the following response on 24 January 1942:

CLAIMS OF 602 AND 603 SQUADRONS REF DESTRUCTION OF FIRST ENEMY AIRCRAFT.

1. With reference to the above subject, it has now been established that the first enemy aircraft to be destroyed by Fighter Command was shot down by 603 Squadron at 14.45 hours on the 16th October 1939. 602 Squadron destroyed an enemy aircraft at 15.00 hours on the same day.

2. 603 Squadron therefore has the honour of destroying the first enemy aircraft during the war: Copies of the Combat Reports are enclosed.

The basis for the decision was the records compiled immediately after the event by pilots and trained ground observers. The subsequent analysis by Air Intelligence gave them no other option but to conclude that the first victory was Patsy Gifford's and the other 603 pilots involved. Sadly, by that time he was dead.

Meanwhile, at the Coastal Command base of RAF Leuchars, 30 miles to the north-east, the Spitfires of Green Section of 602 Squadron were being refuelled after their abortive patrol towards Peterhead. Unaware that there was an air raid over the Edinburgh area, Douglas Farquhar wandered over to the mess to find out what was going on. He came rushing back to his two colleagues and announced: 'For Christ's sake get a move on, those aren't Blenheims – they're ruddy Germans!' The three German aircraft the pilots of 602 Squadron had spotted were in fact the fourth and final wave of Ju88s which had drifted a considerable distance north and were now heading south-west towards the target.

Air Vice-Marshal Richard Saul at 13 Group Fighter Command HQ in Newcastle kept Fighter Command HQ at Bentley Priory updated and at 14.45 he informed Air Chief Marshal Hugh Dowding, C-in-C of Fighter Command that he '...had Tally Ho from four sections'.

602 Squadron continued to be as involved in the action as 603. Flight Lieutenant Dunlop Urie intercepted a Ju88 off Kirkcaldy around 15.00 hours which he pursued on a south-easterly heading over the river towards North Berwick to St Abbs head and finally off the coast of Eyemouth where he discontinued the chase and returned to airspace over East Lothian. According to Urie, during the pursuit:

> …Two Spitfires of 603 Squadron joined us and also had a go. When we reached St Abb's Head he was still flying on one engine and I decided there was no more we could do. He had been shot at by five fighters and I would be very surprised if he would cross the North Sea. Undoubtedly if we had closed to 200 yards he would have been destroyed. This is with hindsight. Our orders were very clear and given many times over.

Dunlop Urie highlights a problem experienced by many fighter pilots during the early aerial battles. Gun harmonisation at 400 yards was ineffective and Pat Gifford was one of many who sought to have the guns of 603 re-harmonised to 250 yards, a significantly more effective range. Had the guns been harmonised to 250 yards prior to 16 October, 602 and 603 Squadrons would have achieved greater success.

At Kincraig Point, near Earlsferry, signals officer Captain Lamb had been watching a convoy including escorts *Jervis*, *Mohawk* and *Furious*, moving up the Forth towards the boom defence. A few minutes later at 15.20 hours an enemy aircraft was spotted overhead. This was probably part of a section which had initially made landfall further north than the other aircraft, having been visible from RAF Leuchars. In order to reach the target the three bombers had flown south-west towards the Forth. En route they spotted the convoy and one of the pilots chose a military target to attack while the other two maintained course for the naval vessels east of the Forth bridge (it is possible that they also noticed that the '*Hood*' was already in dock thus it was decided that one aircraft should take the opportunity to attack an alternate military target at sea). The other two Ju88s were the last to be seen over the target area and one of them subsequently flew low over Turnhouse at 16.00 hours and was chased over the Scottish capital by Robbie Robertson and Black Morton. At 15.25 hours, 30 minutes after Pohle's initial attack, it proceeded to dive-bomb HMS *Mohawk* which was between Kincraig Point on the north shore of the Forth and Gullane on the south shore. The two 500kg bombs exploded within 50 feet of *Mohawk** peppering the vessel and crew members with lethal shards of shrapnel. The blasts and subsequent machine-gun fire resulted in 25 casualties with 13 ratings and two officers killed. John Keer was serving onboard at the time:

---

*HMS *Mohawk* was launched in 1937 and weighed 1,870 tons. It was later torpedoed in action with Italian destroyers in the central Mediterranean on 16 April 1941.

I ran to my action station which was 'A' Gun on the fo'csle, a 4.7 inch gun (Twin). I arrived there with Petty Officer Buffer. We saw something like a barrel land in the water right next to the ship. It exploded and both Petty Officer Buffer and I fell to the ground wounded by flying shrapnel. The next thing I knew I was being picked up off the deck with a bit of shrapnel sticking out of my head. One minute we were all laughing and joking; the next many were dead and injured.

On the bridge of HMS *Mohawk* was the ship's captain, Commander Richard Jolly, an oppressive disciplinarian who was very unpopular with his crew. During the attack by the Ju88, shrapnel penetrated the bridge hitting him in the stomach. The wound was very serious but he refused repeated requests to go below deck for treatment uttering the now immortal words: 'Leave me, go and look after the others.' 15 officers and other ranks were killed. The list of dead would rise by one more. The attack on the *Mohawk* caused by far the greatest loss of life during the raid on 16 October.

At approximately 15.30 hours Pilot Officer Hector MacLean of 602 Squadron intercepted a Ju88 at 5,000 feet over May Island. During MacLean's pursuit of the German bomber, his Spitfire nearly collided with one of 603's which had also latched onto the tail of the Junkers. The two fighters missed each other by inches.

Two Spitfires flown by 602's Douglas Farquhar and Ian Ferguson approached the Forth rail bridge, where Farquhar's attention was drawn by the anti-aircraft fire to an enemy aircraft approaching from the north-east and set off in pursuit. It had been tracked by the Observer Corps before approaching Rosyth and as the anti-aircraft shells burst in the airspace around his aircraft, the German pilot would have been unaware of the token gesture being made by the Earl of Elgin to bring him down with rifle fire from the garden of 'Broomhall', near Limekilns. The Ju88 was pursued towards Bo'ness where it dropped its bomb load near the burnt out wreck of the former naval depot ship HMS *Caledonia* (once the Cunard liner *Majestic* which had been taken to the Forth to be scrapped in 1937). The German pilot then tried to make good his getaway and turned east towards the sea. As he flew over Turnhouse Golf Course, his aircraft was met by another token effort to bring it down. The Reverend James Rossie Brown, the 603 padre, was manning a machine-gun post on the airfield at Turnhouse when the aircraft flew over. Later, in the mess, one of the pilots said to Rossie Brown: 'Padre, that was a very short burst you fired at that Hun.' It is said that in reply he uttered the now immortal line: 'Yes, it passed too quickly out of my diocese!' An official release later referred to 'The Fighting Padre of the RAF'.

Meanwhile, in the Edinburgh Castle military hospital 603's P/O Graham Hunter, who was still awaiting a visit from the padre, rushed to the windows along with his fellow patients in response to the sound of anti-aircraft gunfire in the distance but also the sound of small arms being fired by the Argylls from the castle itself at a passing Ju88. With the windows open, the temperature in the ward dropped and the army nurses herded the patients back to bed.

Meanwhile, onboard HMS *Mohawk*, Commander Richard Jolly brought his ship with its many casualties onboard, including himself, at full speed the 25 miles to Rosyth. A passage which lasted over one and a quarter hours, during which time his voice had become so weak that he could not make himself heard and his orders had to be repeated by the navigation officer, who was himself wounded. *Mohawk* tied up safely alongside Y berth, Richard Jolly rang off the main engines and immediately collapsed. Just under five hours later, he died. His had been an exceptional display of courage and devotion to duty. Royal Navy fatalities as a result of the air-raids over the Forth thereby increased to 16 killed and forty-four wounded, almost all onboard *Mohawk*.

Another Ju88 was intercepted by 603's P/O Robbie Robertson as it headed south from the bridge 'following the railway line north of the aerodrome at 150 feet' towards Edinburgh and home. Robbie had re-armed and re-fuelled at Turnhouse and had taken off at 15.40 hours for his second patrol of the day. 20 minutes later witnesses watched him chase the Ju88, with its sinister black crosses, north of the airfield at Turnhouse at an altitude of nearer 300 feet. The gunners manning the airfield gun emplacements resisted the temptation to open fire in case they hit the Spitfire by mistake. Nevertheless, they, along with the 603 padre, cheered on their man as he roared past. On seeing the two aircraft approaching, Black Morton rushed to his own Spitfire and, without obtaining permission, took off. The Squadron ORB confirms his take-off time as 16.00.

Whilst keeping Robbie in his sights as he pursued the German north-east towards Leith, Black

Above: Armourers of 603, 1939.
Right: 603 ground crew, October 1939.

attempted to gain ground by flying east, straight across the centre of Edinburgh. Thus began a most spectacular low-level chase across the rooftops of the Scottish capital, Robertson close on the tail of the German with Black to the south, racing towards Portobello and a successful interception. Eyewitnesses spoke of seeing the aircraft (Robertson and the Ju88) very close together, and hearing the rattle of machine-gun fire although Robbie claimed he withheld fire whilst over the city until they reached the suburbs. Robbie's chase continued over Raeburn Place and past the Royal Scots Club in Abercromby Place where a meeting was in progress. Legend has it that as the Ju88 roared past within sight of those at the table, the Chairman exclaimed: 'My God, that's a Jerry!' Apparently, after a moment's silence, the meeting continued as if nothing had happened.

Black finally caught up with his colleague and the German intruder south-west of Portobello and immediately opened fire. At 10 Hamilton Drive the masonry was pitted by several bullets and two of his spent .303 rounds drilled holes in the upstairs parlour window. The home belonged to Lord Provost, Sir Henry Steele. The bullets smashed the mirror of an antique display cabinet, damaging one small Japanese vase in a valuable collection of ivories and china. Sir Henry later recovered one of the bullets from the room and returned it to 603 Squadron at Turnhouse (a few years later the position of Lord Provost was occupied by Will Darling – corset maker to three queens – and HAC to 603 Squadron). Alexander McMillan, Sir Henry's chauffeur, recalled that at about four o'clock he heard the deep drone of aircraft engines and on hearing the crackle of machine-gun fire dashed inside to warn the household. From the back door he heard bursts of gunfire and saw one big machine with two of our own fighters close behind. McMillan got the impression that bullets were spraying down on the house. Chris Prentice was just three and a half years of age when he witnessed the Junkers fly over Duddingston View pursued by the 603 Spitfires as he played in the street.

That afternoon *The Adventures of Robin Hood* starring Errol Flynn and Olivia de Havilland was showing at the Portobello cinema. As 13-year-old James Dick emerged into the High Street and daylight at the end of the afternoon showing, he saw a German aircraft 'house high' being chased by two Spitfires. At 7 Coillesdene Crescent, Portobello resident Mr H. Robertson later recounted how he found a spent bullet on a bed in his house: 'It crashed through the window, pierced the bedclothes, struck a bedside table and finished up lying on a pillow.'

By assessing all eyewitness accounts of this pursuit and pin-pointing their locations it became apparent that the bomber could not have flown over *all* the sites. It should therefore be accepted that more than one Ju88 flew over the area and whereas many eyewitnesses referred to the aircraft as being 'overhead' the Junkers and Spitfires were actually at a greater altitude and distance away than was perceived by the civilians. Portobello resident Mr J. Hall-Livingstone who worked in the city recalled:

I caught the 6.14 p.m., train home to Portobello where I lived and all the talk in the carriage was of German raiders who had as was supposed then, tried to bomb the Forth rail bridge. On arrival at my home my mother told me that she watched a German plane from our house pursued by Spitfires fly low over Portobello. The local children had been collecting cartridge cases that had bounced from the roof-tops. Two of which adorned our mantlepiece for many years.

More serious was the story of painter Frank Flynn who was at work on the upstairs windows of 45 Abercorn Terrace, Portobello, when the bomber flew along the street, its twin Junkers Jumo radial engines creating a sudden and deafening roar. His mate Joe McLuskie was footing the ladder in the garden below at the time. According to Frank Flynn, as the bomber passed them it was lower than the top of the steeple of St Philip's Church, across the road from them. This is unlikely, although the perspective would have given him this impression when he had his fleeting glimpse of the German bomber as it sped by. Flynn later told reporters: 'Just then my pal said, "Something has hit me", and the next minute he crumpled to the ground. I went down the steps to him and saw that blood was pouring from his waistcoat.' Joe McLuskie was rushed to Leith Hospital in a Police Ambulance where he underwent emergency surgery to remove a bullet which had entered his side and was found lodged near his stomach. Houses in Morton Street and Joppa Road, Portobello, were also damaged and one woman found a bullet in her child's pram after the combat had passed over her garden. As he attempted to get a better view of the dogfight one workman fell from the scaffolding on which he was working, but was unhurt.

It is most likely that the majority of bullet 'strikes' were actually .303 calibre – from the guns of the Spitfires flown by 603's Black Morton and Robbie Robertson. This included the round that hit Joe McLuskie and those that did the damage at the Lord Provost's house. A number of the rounds recovered that day were .303 calibre. The empty cartridges raining down from the ejection chutes on the underside of the wings of the Spitfires added to the cacophony of sound and to some it gave the impression they were being shot at. Black reported that he had fired all his ammunition at the Ju88 in two long bursts over Portobello and had seen no return fire from the enemy aircraft. Robbie later reported that he too had held his fire as he flew low over Princes Street but had killed the German gunner soon after during an initial burst, which seemed to be confirmed by the lack of any further return fire. Black later recorded in his diary:

About 4.10 one EA observed approaching aerodrome from West at <500 feet, Spitfires in attendance. Took off independently – with cockpit door open – had to make steep turn at 0 feet at 100 mph to avoid Moth taking off at same time. Did not remember to put up u/c till over Corstorphine Hills. EA followed coast over Leith Docks. By taking short cut caught up at about Portobello power station. Opened fire from 500 feet quarter. Long range used in order to put him off as I thought he would bomb Portobello power station (groundless fear). Got off all rounds in two big bursts. After first two or three seconds was misled by incendiaries and used them instead of sight, most seemed to pass just in front of his nose; but second burst from astern seemed quite good. I saw no return fire. EA's speed 160-180. EA was at about 200-300 feet. After my second attack EA swung inland over Newhalls and then east again over Musselburgh. There was a Spitfire in attendance so I returned home. The other Spitfire turned out to be Robbie who had followed EA from up the Forth and reckoned he'd killed the gunner – hence no return fire. EA crossed coast at 140 mph and disappeared out to sea at 0 feet. Very disappointing result of engagement as he should have come down.

I found on return that I had no authorisation to go off; but it seemed to be OK. What a thrash. If all our battles are like this day's party it's going to be a lovely war. The Spitfire's a grand battle-wagon. It seems a wonderful thing that all these bullets didn't cause lots of civilian casualties in Portobello. I was very scared of this; but there appears to have been but one man and some furniture in the Lord Provost's house which looks as though it could do with it.

Notes: Apparently this chap got home about 9 at night having gone all the way on one engine. He crashed on landing as his undercarriage was shot up. He certainly deserves his

Iron Cross. Later reports are that there was another Hun who went away on one engine under similar circumstances after being shot at by 602. Only one of these two got home so we got a 'half' after all.*

Back at the Forth rail bridge a further interception of the intruders was made shortly before 16.00 hours when 603's F/O John 'Bolster' Boulter became detached from his section – F/O Fred Rushmer and F/O Geoff Wynne-Powell – and caught up with a Ju88 near Inverkeithing. Potato pickers at Spencerfield Farm watched as Bolster chased the Junkers through the deadly puffs of anti-aircraft fire from the battery at RNAS Donibristle and out to sea over Aberdour. Boulter broke off his attack and returned to base. He was unable to confirm if his attack had been successful as the German aircraft disappeared into the sea haze.

By 16.30 hours most of the Spitfires of 602 and 603 Squadrons had returned to their respective airfields to eagerly recount their exploits of that day.

Soon after, the respective squadron intelligence officers began to collate the day's combat claims. 11 pilots submitted combat reports (Form 'F'). Initial claims wrongly identify one He111 and one Do215 as being destroyed. The initial claim increased to three enemy bombers shot down with two others seen going out to sea with one engine out of action. One of these was flown by Leutnant Horst von Riesen. Later, Colonel von Riesen wrote:

…over Rosyth we found *Hood* safely in dock – where we were not allowed to harm her. Just to the east of the Forth Bridge there were some small warships, however, and I decided to attack one of these. I selected one and carried out a diving attack, but scored only a near miss.

During the dive a heavy flak shell must have exploded quite close to our machine. A loud bang momentarily drowned the sound of our engines, and then a strong wind howled through the cockpit. The right engine cowling had been blown off and the cabin canopy buckled inwards. Then, as I was climbing away, my radio operator suddenly shouted over the intercom that there were several fighters about two kilometres away, diving on us. I looked in the direction he was pointing and as soon as I saw them I knew that I would need all the speed I could possibly squeeze out of my Junkers if we were to escape. I pushed down the nose and, throttles wide open, dived for the sea. But it was no good. The Spitfires, as we soon recognised them to be, had had the advantage of speed and height from the start and they soon caught up with us. As I sped down the Firth of Forth just a few metres above the surface, I could see clearly the splashes from the shells from the shore batteries, as they too joined in the unequal battle.

Now I thought I was finished. Guns were firing at me from all sides, and the Spitfires behind seemed to be taking turns at attacking. But I think my speed gave them all a bit of a surprise – I was doing more than 400 kilometres per hour [250 mph], which must have been somewhat faster than any other bomber they had trained against at low level – and of course I jinked from side to side to make their aim as difficult as possible. At one stage in the pursuit I remember looking down and seeing what looked like rain drops hitting the water. It was all very strange. The I realised what it was; those splashes marked the impact of bullets being aimed at me from above!

I had only one ally: time. Every minute longer the Junkers kept going meant another seven kilometres further out to sea and further from the Spitfires' base; and I had far more fuel to play with than they did. Finally, however, the inevitable happened: after a chase of more than twenty minutes there was a sudden 'phooff' and my starboard motor suddenly disappeared from view in a cloud of steam. One of the enemy bullets had pierced the radiator, releasing the vital coolant and without it the motor was finished. There was no alternative but to shut it down before it burst into flames.

My speed sagged to 180 kph [112 mph] – almost on the stall when flying asymmetric – and we were only a few metres above the waves. Now the Junkers was a lame duck. But when I looked round, expecting to see the Spitfires curving in to finish us off, there was no sign of them. They had turned round and gone home.

---

*On 31 May 1940, P/O Robbie Robertson was awarded the DFC for the part he played on 16 October 1939 and for his expertise as a gunnery instructor.

Even so, we were in a difficult position. With that airspeed there lay ahead of us a flight of nearly four hours, if we were to get back to Westerland. During our training we had been told that a Ju88 would not maintain height on one engine – and we were only barely doing so. Should we ditch there and then? I thought no; it was getting dark, nobody would pick us up and we would certainly drown or die of exposure. An alternative was to turn round and go back to Scotland, and crash land there. One of my crew suggested this but one of the others – I didn't know who – shouted over the intercom 'No, no, never! If we go back there the Spitfires will certainly get us!' He was right. The thought of going back into that hornets' nest horrified us. So we decided to carry on as we were and see what happened. We preferred to risk death coming from drowning or the cold, rather than have to face those Spitfires again.

Gradually, as we burnt our fuel and the aircraft became lighter, I was able to coax the Junkers a little higher. The remaining motor, though pressed to the limit, continued running and finally we did get back to Westerland.

So it was that I survived my first encounter with Spitfires. I would meet them again during the Battle of Britain, over the Mediterranean and during the Battle of Sicily. It was not a pleasant experience.

Officially, although a number of Ju88s were badly damaged on 16 October, only two were confirmed destroyed. Years after the war it was learnt that a third Ju88 had failed to make it back to Sylt.* Having been raked with machine-gun fire and with unknown dead and/or injured onboard, Sonny Hansen's Junkers eventually crashed miles off-course in Holland killing all onboard. Hansen had been born at Newstead in the Scottish Borders!**

At 16.20 the Observer Corps A2 post at Athelstaneford, near Haddington, sent out an observer to investigate a report that an aircraft was believed to have landed nearby. At 16.40 the A2 post reported that the aircraft was again airborne and seen heading east in the company of a second aircraft. The perspective was deceptive; the aircraft had not landed but was 'contour chasing' – flying at extremely low level – in an attempt to avoid interception by Spitfires of 602 and 603. At 16.55 the same post reported seeing a twin-engine bomber, followed a few moments later by another, fly past at such low level that the aircraft were momentarily hidden behind woodland. Emerging from the other side they were last seen heading out to sea. This was the last confirmed sighting of the raiders on 16 October 1939.

The pilots of 602 and 603 were exhilarated by the day's action and hoped a further wave of bombers were on their way, but as the day drew to a close it became obvious the action was over.

Later that evening the adjutant, Moreton Pinfold, accompanied by P/O Benson (not to be confused with P/O Noel Benson, yet to enter the story) went to the Military Hospital to interrogate the three injured German airmen.

The AOC, AVM Richard Saul, flew in to congratulate all concerned. Messages were also received from the Chief of the Air Staff, Sir Cyril Newall and the AOC-in-C Coastal Command, Sir Frederick Bowhill. On the 17th ACM Sir Hugh Dowding, AOC-in-C Fighter Command, telegraphed 'Well done, first blood to the Auxiliaries'. One of the many congratulatory telegrams received by 603 Squadron reads: 'Nice work boys, Turrnhoose uber alles!' whilst another was addressed to 'Hun Crashers, Edinburgh.'

Despite the absence of any air-raid warnings in the city and with a great many civilians therefore still on the streets, it was fortunate that there were no fatalities caused by shrapnel from the anti-aircraft guns.

---

*In July 1953, 14 years after the raid on shipping in the Forth, 603 had their annual summer camp at Westerland airfield on Sylt where the countryside was reminiscent of Kent during the Battle of Britain – blue skies and fields of golden cereal crops. Sylt was something of a 'German riviera' for the whole of northern Europe, the playground of millionaires. The pilots recalled the famous nudist resort named 'Abyssinia Beach' which most, but not all, were too shy to visit and the price for flying low over the area was court martial!

**See Appendix for the story of Sonny Hansen and the third Ju 88 which was lost on 16 October.

Sheep in his aircraft. Note wing white with frost and early canopy without bullet-proof windscreen, October 1939.

Whilst civilian eyewitness accounts and reports by pilots suggest that a far greater number of German aircraft had been shot down by the two Scottish auxiliary squadrons, the Luftwaffe actually lost three aircraft with eight aircrew killed and four taken prisoner. After Helmut Pohle had recovered consciousness in Port Edgar Hospital in addition to the fractured skull and facial injuries he had incurred (see page 76), he was also suffering from having had three of his front teeth pushed in, as a result of the crash, which were subsequently straightened with a clamp, which was turned every second day. At the time he had little confidence in the treatment and thought: 'This is the famous Scottish thriftiness.' That evening he received a visit from one of his 602 assailants, George Pinkerton, along with Squadron Leader Douglas Farquar, Officer Commanding 602 Squadron. The comradeship of fellow airmen superceded the fact that already lives were being lost in the war.

At the end of October Pohle was taken by stretcher to the Military Hospital in Edinburgh Castle where he was put in a single room with a restricted view overlooking Princes Street, guarded round the clock by a sentry. There he received the best of medical care. One day John Kerr and Petty Officer Buffer who had been injured during the attack on the *Mohawk* found themselves in the same company as Pohle. Kerr remembers him being very nervous: 'All the time he acted as if someone was going to give him a pill, he even hesitated before drinking a cup of tea.' When, at the end of 1939, Pohle eventually arrived at Grizedale Hall in Westmorland, as the senior officer with the most 'time in' he came to know Oberleutnant Franz von Werra, the Luftwaffe fighter pilot who became famous as 'the one that got away', the only German PoW to make a successful home run during WWII after having been shot down over Kent by P/O Stapme Stapleton of 603 on 5 September 1940. Von Werra was planning an escape and required the Hauptmann's permission. Helmut Pohle was later sent to Canada. On returning home after the war Pohle discovered the Nazi propaganda machine had presented his mission on 16 October 1939 as a success and that he was a national hero. This was something he found hard to live with, particularly in light of the fact he had been shot down. To him the raid had failed and at a high price. For many years after returning to farming in his homeland his recollections of that day haunted him, in particular the memory of his navigator's brains spattered over the inside of the front windscreen after a burst of machine-gun fire had smashed through the perspex. After many years he found he was able to record his memories of 16 October 1939 and, with affection, his time in Edinburgh. Although he had not been shot down by 603 Squadron, whilst in hospital he received a visit from a 603 pilot:

One day – I remember gloomy – I had a visitor, Flt Lt Gifford at my sick bed. He was the pilot who had shot me down [602's George Pinkerton had shot him down]. I am sorry to say, there was not much conversation because of my tiredness. But the visitor gave just the right impression of a nice young officer of the Royal Air Force. I was violently shaken to hear of the death of Flt.Lt. Gifford during May 1940.

During the last week of November I was allowed to take a walk around the [battlements] of the Castle with the escort of my private and his rifle. One of them explained to me all the objects of interest of your marvellous town. For this walk I got a kind of jogging suit, a sky blue blouse, white trousers and a red band. I didn't know what to do with the band. Now I got the instructions: HM Queen Victoria had introduced this suit for sick soldiers and the red band must be for the British colours around the neck. As a through and through conservative much have I admired your great Queen Victoria... especially because Europe is obliged to her moreover for the washout W.C. [a reference to the flushing toilet and Pohle's belief that Queen Victoria or Prince Albert were behind the invention]. I put the red band around my neck with pleasure.

The 603 ORB for 16 October recorded:

Enemy Air Raid of 12 Aircraft attacked Naval vessels, dropping some 40 bombs near the Forth Bridge.

From 14.30 to 16.30 hours.

Aircraft Type & No.	Pilot	Time Up	Down
Spitfire			
L1070	F/Lt. P. Gifford	14.30	15.55
L1050	P/O C. Robertson	14.30	15.00
L1061	F/O H.K. Macdonald	14.30	15.00

Red Section shot down 1 enemy aircraft (thought to be a Heinkel 111) East of Dalkeith. Aircraft fell into the sea at Port Seton. Enemy aircraft believed to be one of three intercepted by Yellow Section. 3 prisoners were rescued from crew of 4.

Aircraft Type & No.	Pilot	Time Up	Down
Spitfire			
L1067	F/Lt G.L. Denholm	14.35	14.55
L1049	P/O J.S. Morton	14.35	14.55
L1048	P/O G.K. Gilroy	14.35	14.55

Yellow Section intercepted 3 enemy aircraft near Dalkeith and despite the fact that the enemy aircraft broke formation and took advantage of clouds, rounds were fired at each one of them. L1048 received 1 bullet through the top engine cover. Damage to enemy not known.

Aircraft Type & No.	Pilot	Time Up	Down
Spitfire			
L1050	P/O C. Robertson	15.40	16.30
L1049	P/O J.S. Morton	16.00	16.15

Intercepted one enemy aircraft thought to be a Heinkel 111 over Rosyth at very low height. Enemy pursued out to sea with starboard engine not running, and return fire from rear gunner suspended.

Aircraft Type & No.	Pilot	Time Up	Down
Spitfire			
L1021	F/O J.L.G. Cunningham	14.45	16.00
L1020	P/O B.J.G. Carbury	14.45	16.00
L1022	P/O C.D. Peel	14.30	15.20

Patrolled North Berwick and later Rosyth but did not sight enemy.

Aircraft Type & No.	Pilot	Time Up	Down
Spitfire			
L1024	F/O F.W. Rushmer	14.45	16.00
L1026	F/O G.T. Wynne-Powell	14.45	15.55
L1046	F/O J.C. Boulter	14.45	16.00

Section did not intercept but F/O Boulter became detached and delivered an attack on Heinkel 111 flying East from Aberdour. Result of attack not known. Thick ground haze which, accentuated by bright sun, made weather more use to the enemy than us.

Cumulus: 5/10 – 6/10 to 6,000 feet.

Summary:

Pilots	Officers	Airmen
Establishment	11	10
Available	17	

Aircraft:		
Establishment	21	
Serviceable	13	
Unserviceable	2	

Hours Flown:
Action against enemy air force : 14 hours 40 minutes (21 sorties)
Training : 3 hours 40 minutes
Total : 18 hours 20 minutes
Rounds Fired: 16,000
Enemy aircraft destroyed: 1

The pilots of both 602 and 603 Squadrons learned a great deal on 16 October 1939. It was felt that the enemy camouflage was more effective than that of the RAF. Some pilots thought that the anti-aircraft fire provided an indication as to the whereabouts of the enemy bombers, but that to continue to attack whilst they were still amongst the puffs of exploding anti-aircraft shells was obviously fraught with danger. The subsequent interrogation of Storp and his crew revealed that they had great respect for the Spitfire and were fearful of it in combat.

It was recorded in the 13 Group Operational Record Book that the Spitfire pilots were learning to compensate for the 'downward kick' of the aircraft when the guns were fired. Whilst a nucleus of experienced pilots in the Squadron had amassed a great many hours flying, since they had been re-equipped with the Spitfire, live firing opportunities had been scarce and marksmanship was therefore unquestionably poor, despite many of the pilots having been to 7 ATS at Acklington for live firing off Druridge Bay the day before!

The pilots were also at a disadvantage with outmoded tactics which had evolved during a previous era of aerial combat. With statistics to work with, the gunnery experts at Fighter Command made an important discovery. The arrangement of the guns mounted in the wings was such that their fire converged at a point 400 yards in front of the aircraft, but it was the inaccuracy of the guns themselves, caused by slight movement in the mountings (gun chatter), the recoil from which caused the nose of the aircraft to drop by five degrees, and the loss of velocity of the ammunition when firing from such a great distance, which conspired to cause the bullets to spread out over an area of approximately 18 feet by 36 feet by the time they reached this point. It was calculated that this gave a density of 7 or 8 bullets per square foot and this was reduced yet further when shooting with deflection. The calculated density was actually massively overstated. Nevertheless, such dispersed fire was insufficient to cause lethal damage to an enemy aircraft particularly if passing through it at high speed. The guns were therefore re-harmonised to a point 250 yards ahead (producing a 9 x13 foot spread). Thus the effects of inaccuracy at this shorter range were reduced and a much more concentrated area of fire was achieved. However, long before this advice was passed on to the squadrons and at a time when unauthorised re-harmonisation of the guns was a court martial offence, many experienced pilots had ordered their ground crews to re-harmonise the guns for 250 yards and in some cases even less in order to maximise effectiveness. The success of 603 during the Battle of Britain, still nine months away, signalled a vast improvement in aircraft handling and marksmanship which was thanks largely to the dedication of George Denholm who committed himself to ensuring his pilots continued to improve their flying skill, including formation attacks and dogfighting.

During the evening of 16 October a joint communiqué by the Admiralty, Air Ministry and Ministry for Home Security was released:

> This afternoon about 2.30 a series of bombing raids began. These were directed at the ships lying in the Forth and were conducted by about a dozen machines. No serious damage was done to any of His Majesty's ships.
>
> One bomb glanced off the cruiser *Southampton*, causing slight damage near her bow, and sank the Admiral's barge and pinnace which were moored empty alongside.
>
> There were three casualties on board the *Southampton* and seven aboard the cruiser Edinburgh. Another bomb fell near the destroyer *Mohawk*. This bomb burst on the water and the splinters caused 25 casualties to the men on the deck of the destroyer. Only superficial damage was caused to the vessel which, like the others, is ready for sea.

The press were subsequently issued with an official account of events for publication on Tuesday 17 October. Under the circumstances it was fairly accurate:

> Victory over the first German bombers to raid Great Britain since the war began has been largely shared in by men who, a few weeks ago, were Scottish stockbrokers, lawyers, and sheep farmers. At least two of the four enemy raiders accounted for during Monday's raid on the Forth were shot down by British fighter aircraft. They beat off the raiders in such a way that not more than half the German aircraft are believed to have returned home. About twelve or fourteen bombers took part in the raid. Apart from four which were brought down by British fighters, and anti-aircraft, and naval gunfire, several are thought to have been too crippled to complete the passage of the North Sea. No pilot claims to have brought down one of Monday's raiders single-handed. Their defeat was a team job. One running fight began over the Pentland Hills. British fighters chased a German bomber away from the Pentlands, and it crashed into the sea off Port Seton. Shots from several aircraft helped to cripple it, but the 'coup de grace' was delivered by an auxiliary pilot who, before the war, practised as a lawyer [Gifford]. He had taken a bet that he would be the first member of his squadron to bring down a German plane. Swooping low over Edinburgh, a Squadron Leader, who was a stockbroker in civil life [Farquar], chased another enemy raider out to sea. Two other members of his squadron, a sheep farmer [Pinkerton] and the manager of a firm of plasterers [McKellar], shot down a bomber off Crail.

Press coverage of the raids on 16 October revealed something of the excitement felt at the time and there was an initial feeling of euphoria that little damage had been inflicted. In contrast, German radio broadcast the following account:

> On Monday between 2.30 and 3.15p.m., German bombers made a successful attack on British warships in the Firth of Forth. Two British cruisers were hit, in spite of tremendous efforts on the part of the British Air Force to repulse the attackers. Two British chaser planes were shot down and two German planes are missing.

Late on the 16th the padre, Rossie Brown, eventually managed to pay Graham Hunter a visit in the military hospital in Edinburgh Castle. In a letter to S/L Jack written on 17 October he recounted events of the previous day:

> This letter did not get posted yesterday owing to the excitement. I was in the station car ready to visit Pilot Officer Hunter who was in hospital when the siren went. Rushing to my machine-gun post I had a fine view of the Boche Dorniers dive bombing towards the Forth. Also of shells bursting round them and our Spitfires attacking. It was a thrilling sight and when news came through that Patsy Gifford had got one down, we were all in great form. Later on a crippled Boche flew along the railway line north of the Aerodrome at about 150 feet with two of our boys chasing him. Unfortunately, they hadn't a bullet left, but the Boche came down all right in the Pentlands. When the show was over I visited Hunter and found

him in wonderful form and very sorry to have missed the doings. Returning to the Mess I found everyone very happy and Gifford, naturally, quite the hero of the hour. It was a great matter that, while not less than four and possibly six Boches were brought down, there was not one RAF casualty. I was particularly glad that Gifford should be the first Auxiliary Officer to have brought down a Boche. When I again visited Hunter just after the raid I found three German airmen also in hospital. They had taken part in the raid and had been picked up out of the sea by a fishing boat. I chatted for a little to two of them in German and found them very decent fellows, although I was a little taken aback when one of them gave me the Nazi salute.

I must try to get this letter posted today whatever happens. I am now Mess Secretary, no one else was available [F/L Jack was the previous Mess Secretary]. Heaven help the Mess. Why did you go to Oxford? I am afraid it will be a real mess if I have anything to do with it.

Ever yours

'Rossie'

Whilst his recollections of the combat are inaccurate, the rest provides a little of the atmosphere of the occasion.

Patsy Gifford was interviewed by A. Scott Kennedy of *The Scotsman*. To the pilots at Turnhouse, Kennedy was a loyal friend. The article was reproduced in a booklet published in 1943 in aid of the inauguration of the 603 Squadron Benevolent Fund. By that time Pat had been killed and because the country was at war when the article was published, his name is left out:

Shortly after the excitement had died, I found myself congratulating the leader of the section of 603 City of Edinburgh (Fighter) Squadron who was responsible for shooting down the first raider in the first air raid on this country. We had come upstairs to his bedroom in the Mess to escape from the banter in the ante-room. I was privileged to be the only journalist present, which was just as well, because it was a small bedroom with no chairs. Sporting gun-cases, a squash racquet or two, and some fencing foils filled the corners. We squatted on the bed and talked. Although in civil life a solicitor, and a particularly hearty solicitor at that, my young friend seemed to prefer that I should do most of the talking. And that was just what I didn't want to do. Then I remembered that 'line shooting' is not encouraged in the Air Force. I think it was my 'line' that Edinburgh, Scotland, the whole country, the whole world in fact, Goering and all would like to hear something about it, that got us started. Gradually I was able to piece the story together.

'Well,' he said, with that cheerful laugh, which alas, none of us will hear again. 'Well, I'm glad for two reasons – a) for the Squadron's sake, and b) I've won my bet.' Red Section, comprising three Spitfires, had taken off at 14.30 hours. At 14.55 hours Red Section leader landed at his base with the first Nazi 'in the bag.' Twenty-minutes from time of take-off to landing and the job was done.

They were on patrol over East Lothian at 3,000 feet. Visibility was not specially good. There was an autumn haze between them and the ground. 'Things were shimmering a bit.' Overhead were big patches of heavy cloud with clear sky lanes between. 'Look-out, there's a twin-engined job to starboard,' he heard his No.2 [Ken Macdonald] call on the radio telephone. Almost immediately an enemy bomber, a Heinkel, appeared out of the cloud. He was flying fast, and he was coming towards the Spitfires, head on! Evidently spotting them, the German swung off into a handy patch of cumulus, but not before his guns had attempted to rake the approaching fighters.

Red leader spoke a few words over the radio telephone and threw his machine into a stiff climbing turn. The others followed tightly. 'He dived away, and I stayed above him long enough to make certain that he was a Hun. There was no doubt about his markings. Then I went down in a stiff dive, came up under his tail. He filled the gun-sight, and I let drive before pulling out. My other boys followed. Before they'd finished, I had regained my height and position and went in again. Perhaps I was a bit too close, but there he was. I gave him a long burst. He was responding with all his armament; tracers were shooting past me, and I got a glimpse of a gunner behind twin guns. We went in again and gave him some more, and I saw he was hit forward. Bits of fabric were dropping off, and I thought I saw a red glow inside the fuselage. I broke away as the Heinkel's guns flashed again. At that moment one of my chaps came in at speed with his eight firing. We were now over the coast and as the German sought a lower course, we simply sprayed him with bullets. I could see our fire furrowing the water.' Then came the end. The Heinkel was badly crippled. The rear gunner was silent. 'As soon as the Spitfire in front of me had broken away after giving him another burst, I went close in and gave him all I had. He flopped into the sea, and as we circled overhead we saw that he was sinking. One man was swimming, and some boats were approaching. We returned to our station, and, after re-fuelling and re-arming, took off again.' So first blood was drawn in the first air raid of the war by the Edinburgh Squadron.

There is no mention in the report by Kennedy of the fact that when Pat arrived on the scene the Ju88 was already under attack from Black Morton's Spitfire and that he had flown between the German and Black's aircraft in order to attack. Black was further annoyed by Pat's actions after returning to Turnhouse to re-fuel and re-arm. By the time Red Section touched down, Yellow Section were already down with the Spitfire of George Denholm stuck in the soft mud at the far end of the landing strip. He had come in too fast and had overshot into the boggy area and available ground crew personnel were attempting to drag George's Spitfire free from the mud. Sheep Gilroy's Spitfire, L1048, had been hit by return fire from a Ju88. A round had passed through the top of the engine cowling and was being inspected by ground crew and pilots alike. Although minor, this was the first Spitfire to sustain battle damage. Black was a junior pilot and as a consequence, while waiting for his aircraft to be re-fuelled and re-armed, Pat Gifford's section landed and demanded he was given priority over Yellow. This was carried out particularly efficiently with the ground crews working flat out as the exhilarated pilots swapped details of their own experiences. The intelligence officer hastily noted down what details he could gather from them. Red Section took off again, leaving George, Black and Sheep annoyed and impatient to get airborne again.

As a legacy of London's vulnerability to aerial bombardment during WWI many pundits, including H.G. Wells, prophesied that British cities would be pulverised from the air by an intensive bombing campaign. And, following the raid of 16 October when the euphoria subsided, in its place began the recriminations.

The main bone of contention was the fact that whilst air raid warnings had been sounded in military establishments only after the raid had begun, no air raid warning had been sounded in the city itself. The Edinburgh *Evening News* published an article which alleged that whilst the capital had not warned its people of the impending air raid, the sirens in Perth and some districts of Fife had been sounded. This article fanned the flames of discontent. In actual fact the military bases had quite naturally gone on alert as soon as the air raid began and these sirens had prompted the civilians living nearby to make their way to the nearest shelter. The local siren at Port Edgar had sounded three minutes after the first bombs had fallen, but only after the siren at Rosyth had been clearly heard from across the river. This was followed by the sounding of the works hooter at the South Queensferry Distillery. At South Queensferry, where the sirens did provide warning of the air raid, many chose to remain outside in order to watch the action overhead. The citizens of Edinburgh only became aware that an air raid was in progress and not a practice exercise when the AA guns opened fire to the north followed by the spectacle of Spitfires pursuing bombers overhead. Except for those in military establishments, no sirens were sounded in Edinburgh that afternoon and it was that point which became the target for criticism. The concern expressed by the lack of adequate warning in some areas prompted the Lord Provost, Henry Steele, to state that he was 'very annoyed' and determined to get to the bottom of the matter. His reaction may have been attributable in part to the fact that his own house had been raked with gunfire. He was yet to discover that it was .303 calibre and not 7.92mm!

Following the raid a report was sent from the police station at South Queensferry to the Chief Constable at Linlithgow:

I beg to report that an Enemy Air Raid commenced about 2.30 p.m. on this date over the Firth of Forth in the vicinity of the Forth Bridge, where H.M.S. Edinburgh and H.M.S. Southampton were at anchor a short distance east of the Bridge and south of Inchgarvie Island. Four attacks were made on the warships by three enemy aeroplanes, ten or twelve bombs being dropped between the ships and the Forth bridge. Two small boats tied to H.M.S. Edinburgh were damaged and sunk and so far as is known there was one casualty on that ship, a naval rating being seriously wounded. No bombs dropped on land, at least within this county, but shrapnel fell at the Town Harbour, South Queensferry (in the sea), on Hawes Brae and at Newgardens House, Dalmeny. Shrapnel also fell at the house occupied by David Drummond, Water Superintendant, Queensferry Road, Kirkliston, and Peter McGowan, (24), farmer of Wheatlands Farm, Kirkliston was slightly wounded on the back by shrapnel while working in a field on that farm.

No Air Raid Warning Messages were received and the first intimation of the Air Raid was machine gun fire from an aeroplane followed by the explosion of a bomb being dropped in the vicinity of the Forth bridge. The siren at Port Edgar then sounded, followed by the local signal on the Distillery siren, and bomb explosions and the noise of anti-aircraft gun fire from the local units. What is believed to be the 'tail' of an enemy plane [actually the rear canopy of Pohle's aircraft] fell east of the Forth bridge into the water, floated north-westwards and was later picked up by a picket-boat from Rosyth along with other small pieces of wreckage.

The actual raid in the first place would last about 50 or 60 minutes, and about 3.50 p.m. the 'Raiders Passed' signal was sounded at Port Edgar, followed by the same signal on the local siren. About 4 p.m., however, the signals sounded the 'Air Raid Warnings' and a plane was sighted over Port Edgar but was driven off by Anti-Aircraft Gun fire from the surrounding batteries and the two warships.

It has now been ascertained that a 2Ib, anti-aircraft cartridge was picked up, unexploded, in the drive about 400 yards east of Leuchold House, Dalmeny, and two anti-aircraft shells were found, also unexploded, at Kirkliston, one on Almondhill Road and the other on the street at the crossroads in the village. These shells have been attended to by Inspr. Duncan, Linlithgow. Some slight damage was done in Kirkliston, one pane of glass in a window at 9 Queensferry Road, occupied by Mrs Jane Hood or Robertson being broken by part of a nose cap and several telephone wires are down in the district. All this slight damage is believed to have been caused by the shrapnel from anti-aircraft fire.

Fortunately at the time of the raid, few people were on the streets and the police succeeded in getting them under cover very quickly. There was little or no panic and the public in the district behaved very well.

The final 'Raiders Passed' signal was sounded about 4.35 p.m. on the Port Edgar siren, followed by the local signal here. There was no air raid message received by telephone at Port Edgar and they sounded all signals on hearing the Rosyth siren.

In the House of Commons the following day, Prime Minister Chamberlain answered the question as to why there had not been an air raid warning in the Scottish capital:

As the attack was local and appeared to be developing only on a small scale, and as our defences were fully ready, it was not considered appropriate in this particular instance to issue an air raid warning, which would have caused dislocation and inconvenience over a wide area. The responsibility for issuing air raid warnings must be left to the competent authorities, but the circumstances in which warnings had been issued would be carefully reviewed in the light of the experience gained.

The press were unhappy with the PM's explanation regarding the absence of warnings. *The Scotsman* wrote:

The truth is that the competent authority was extraordinarily fortunate over Monday's experience, and only the lucky fact that there was no loss of civilian life… What would have been done to the competent authority if, for example, a bomb had been dropped on a train passing over the Forth Bridge, as might have happened? If it is wise, the competent authority will not cease to bless its good fortune, and take the escape to heart.

On the subject of air raid sirens the paper wrote:

> An amazing feature of the attack was that many places, including Edinburgh, sounded no air
> raid sirens, and people stood in the streets gazing up at aerial dogfights, unaware that it was
> the real thing. Even officers of the defence forces were for a time under the impression that
> all the planes were British. One explanation of the absence of warning was that earlier there
> had been British bombing practice on the Forth.

Also unhappy with the PM's response, following a meeting with the Edinburgh ARP Committee,
Lord Provost Henry Steele waded in with his own comments: 'It was apparently the feeling of the
Committee, however, that the matter could safely be left where the responsibility lay – namely, the
Air Ministry and the Edinburgh Fighter Command' at Turnhouse. Fighter Command HQ itself was
responsible for issuing air raid warnings. Air Chief Marshal Dowding was aware that a number of
false alarms had caused confusion that day. Apparently, in view of this he had overruled the
established procedures in favour of holding back for further confirmation that it was a genuine
attack. This would explain why no one was actually instructed by the authorities to sound the sirens.

Every available aircraft in 602 and 603 Squadrons took to the air that afternoon in search of the
enemy raiders. No blame can be levelled at the pilots if they were ordered to investigate sightings
in one area when in fact the Germans were in another. Regardless of the fact that Drone Hill went
off the air, the raiders were continually tracked by other RDF stations along the east coast until they
passed overhead when Observer Corps correctly identified the aircraft and posts of 31 Group
Galashiels and 36 Group Dunfermline tracked them inland. Sir Hugh Dowding was so pleased with
the performance of the Observer Corps he sent a message of congratulations. Confusion lay with the
reporting of sightings by other 'observers'. These reports came from search-light and anti-aircraft
batteries and ultimately Spitfires were sent up to intercept what were probably friendly aircraft.
Importantly, mistakes made on 16 October 1939, were noted and by the time the Battle of Britain
occurred Dowding had an extremely effective and comprehensive early warning system at his
disposal. Each aspect of the system had a vital part to play in the air battle against the Luftwaffe and
Britain's ultimate victory.

Whilst no civilian lives were lost as a result of the bombing on 16 October, later air raids by the
Luftwaffe against Scottish targets claimed the lives of many civilians in Edinburgh and its suburbs.

Barrage balloons were important in reducing the effectiveness of air attacks on civilian and
military targets, particularly from dive-bombers, and there was a definite lack of them over the
military installations along the Forth. Their absence had been a significant lapse and, following the
raid, improvements to the balloon barrage around the shores of Britain were made, in particular a
complete barrage was taken down in Glasgow and was flying again 24 hours later over the Firth of
Forth.

The following year the work of the Auxiliary Air Force balloon squadrons was brought to the
public's attention when a film was released by the GPO Film Unit entitled 'Squadron 992' in which
the officers and airmen of the RAF played the starring roles. The film also included a detailed and
particularly evocative reconstruction of the German air raid of 16 October. Significantly the film
was directed by Brazilian Alberto Cavalcanti who later became friends with 603's Richard Hillary.
At one time Cavalcanti considered turning Hillary's best-seller *The Last Enemy* into a film.
Squadron 992 is a drama documentary which includes action footage of a Spitfire of 609 Squadron,
based at Drem at the time, chasing a German bomber (actually a Blenheim I) at low level over the
East Lothian countryside before finally being shot down and its crew rescued by the crew of a
fishing boat.

John Dickson at the tiller of the *Dayspring* and its neighbour boat took part in the reconstruction
of the rescue of Storp's crew. With accuracy in-mind, filming initially took place at the original sites
of Port Seton and offshore at the crash-site but this attracted a great many onlookers who gathered
along the coastline to catch a glimpse of the action. Unfortunately for them the Navy was unhappy
that such a large number of people were gathered in one area and ordered the film crew to move.
This they did, and filming actually took place on a Saturday afternoon in the Forth to the east of
Inchkeith. The water off Port Seton may have also been getting a little too rough for filming. In
order to include a convincing Aryan German in the part of Storp, Port Seton resident Jack Nicholson

Recovery of one of the Ju88s lost on 16 October 1939.

(a medical student who later qualified as a GP) was given the role simply because he had blue eyes and blond hair! Even at the new location progress still did not go unhindered as the army arrested the film crew and the Dicksons on suspicion of spying and locked them up until their position was clarified! John Dickson's son, John, still lives in the area and at the time of writing had the tiller from the *Dayspring* in his garden.

On 17 October, with a heightened state of tension, 603 flew daytime patrols. F/L Ivone Kirkpatrick was admitted to hospital for the removal of his tonsils. Sergeant Ronald 'Ras' Berry was posted to the unit for flying duties. Paperwork completed in July which confirmed his commission had been lost and he had to wait until December to be confirmed as a pilot officer RAFVR. That afternoon an excited crowd gathered along the harbour at Port Seton. A rumour existed that local fishing trawlers *East Lothian* and *Andrina Falconer* were heading back to port having salvaged one of the crashed German bombers. A large contingent had left with the boats, including RAF officials, the Receiver of Wrecks and cameramen. The trawlers returned with wreckage including a wheel and undercarriage leg of a Ju88 which were taken to Turnhouse in the back of a truck.

The first of the funerals for the dead took place on the morning of Friday 20 October, when six Royal Navy casualties were buried with full military honours at Douglas Bank Cemetery near Rosyth. The youngest was 18-year-old Ordinary Seaman Bernard Roebuck who had been serving onboard HMS *Mohawk*.

The bodies of Pohle's crew members, Kurt Seydel and August Schleicher, which had been recovered from the wreckage of the Junkers in the sea off Crail, were taken to St Philip's Church, Portobello on 19 October where they remained overnight under police guard, each coffin draped in the *Reichskriegflagge*. On the 20th the two coffins were removed from the church and placed on an RAF trailer for the short journey to Portobello Cemetery, escorted by 60 officers and airmen from 602 and 603 Squadrons. The funeral cortege moved sedately down Brunstane Road and Milton Road to the cemetery (a house in Brunstane Road still bears the 'spang' marks from .303 rounds fired from one of the Spitfires) and vintage film of this part of proceedings exists. Thousands lined the route. Sergeant 'Angy' Gillies was put in charge of the funeral party and prior to the occasion he had been carefully coached by a regular warrant officer in the direction and marching of the funeral party and of the ceremony itself. Dignitaries at the funeral service included the Lord Provost Steele, Regional Commissioner Tom Johnston, AOC 13 Group, Fighter Command, AVM Richard Saul, and officers and airmen from both Scottish auxiliary squadrons, although the majority of pilots and ground crews from both squadrons were at a state of readiness and did not attend. The service was conducted by S/L Rossie Brown and a firing party of ten fired a volley over the graves following which the 603 pipe band played *Over the Sea to Skye*. F/O Robin Waterston was on leave and numbered amongst the service representation at the funeral. On returning home he told his younger sister Jean that the Germans had been given a splendid send-off and hoped he would be given the same in the event of his own death. Sadly, when the end came for the extremely likeable young Scotsman, his send-off could not have been further removed from the event he had witnessed in Portobello.

In 1959 the bodies of Gefreiter Schleicher and Unteroffizier Seydel were moved to the German *Soldatenfriedhof* at Cannock Chase, Block 3, graves 477 and 478 respectively. Years later the 603 padre revealed that, unbeknown to anyone, he had felt compelled to write to the bereaved families of the German dead via the International Red Cross. In his letters he informed them that their sons had received a proper Christian burial and that he regretted the loss of life so soon after war had been declared.

19 October 1939. Funeral cortege of the bodies of Unteroffizier Kurt Seydel and Gefreiter A Schleicher. 603 pipe band and Squadron members formed the funeral and firing party.

CHAPTER 5

EARLY ENCOUNTERS/THE PHONEY WAR

Over the next few days 603 Squadron continued with day and night patrols. Pilot Officer Claud Eric Hamilton and Pupil Pilot Ronald MacKay along with LACs McLaren, Barnes, Pritchard, and Shepherd, were posted to 11 E&RFTS, Perth. Claud Hamilton was from Cairns, Midlothian and joined 234 Squadron at St Eval on 12 September 1940. The following month he sailed from Gibraltar on the aircraft carrier HMS *Argus* and was in the first flight of six Hurricanes which took off from the deck on 17 November to Ta Kali, Malta, where he joined 261 Squadron. On the night of 11/12 April 1941, Hamilton was to claim a Ju87 destroyed. On 12 May 1941, 261 Squadron was disbanded and Hamilton was attached to 185 Squadron. On the 14th he was shot down by Oberleutnant von Kageneck of III/JG 27 and fatally wounded. Claud Hamilton is buried in the Naval Cemetery, Capuccini, Malta. He was 20 years old.

Ron MacKay was born on 13 April 1910. After completing his flying training he was sent to 234 Squadron at Middle Wallop, three days before Hamilton, on 9 September 1940. While returning from a routine sortie on the 25th he baled out and was seriously injured. His Spitfire, X4182, crashed near St Mawgan. He was released from the RAF in January 1946 as a Flight Lieutenant.

Turnhouse, October 1939. Caister, Peel and Boulter play cards at dispersal.

According to the ORB, between the hours of 14.35 and 15.25 on 22 October 1939, F/L Patsy Gifford (L1070), P/O Robbie Robertson (L1050) and P/O Black Morton (L1049) were sent up:

Red Section ordered to intercept enemy aircraft reported to be attacking convoy off St Abbs. Section contacted 1 Heinkel 111 4 miles from the shore, pursued it out to sea and shot it down 7 miles out, after it had turned back towards the shore, presumably endeavouring to force-land as near the coast as possible. 3 of the crew of 4 were seen to escape in a collapsible boat and the section, after refuelling, returned to the scene and were successful in guiding HMS *Gurka* to pick up the prisoners. Spitfire L1049 landed at Turnhouse…. Spitfire L1050 received one bullet through a flap.

While training flights continued, 603 carried out a total of 11 sorties during the day totalling 10 hours 10 minutes. The pilots fired 5,000 rounds for one enemy aircraft destroyed. Black recorded:

22/10. Fine – cloud 8/10 3,000' – Hazy – light W wind.
Abt. 4.00 Red to take off. Failed to start engine immediately and lost P.G. [Pat Gifford] and Robbie [Robertson] in haze, followed them to Patrol 5m N of St Abbs. Failed to contact until after Tally-Ho from Robbie – the second (first abortive) – suddenly saw E.A. pursued by two Spitfires flying N abt. 3 miles to W, climbing to bank of cloud. Followed and kept below base

93

Top: 22 October 1939. The inspector general inspecting Tigger's wound.
Left: Cowling removed. Two bullet exit holes can be seen to right of underside.
Right: Two bullet holes can be clearly seen to left of Black's head.

of cloud 500' thick and turned to E as probable course of E.A. At end of cloud E.A. emerged abt. half mile from me with two Spitfires above and to port of him. One peeled off and attacked in gaps of clouds without breaking away between bursts. When he finished I went in, as other machines had disappeared. After a stern chase, delivered burst of 8-10 secs. from high No.1. E.A. was now in clear sky, above wispy cloud. On returning from breakaway found E.A. swinging round to port and losing height. No signs of return fire so went up to <300' and put in the rest of my ammunition. After first attack Patsy exhorted me 'For God's sake be careful with your pellets – I've none left.' E.A. then came down quite quickly on a glide – trying to regain coast. He made a nice landing in the sea, and the chaps clambered out into a rubber boat. I rather thought the Hun put down his wheels on the glide down; but have since been pooh-poohed. He certainly had them up when he landed.

After a jig round the convoy, we came home at great speed. 'I have shot down one 'Dornier' periodically on the RT. E.A. was He111 – probably old type as fuselage was rather Anson-like.

On landing found I had a bullet in the sump and only $1/2$ a gallon of oil out of $51/2$ left – workshops said 2 minutes more would have seen the works solid. It was very fortunate I didn't know about it at the time or I'd have been as windy as hell; but having got home I wasn't so scared. I shall be jolly careful not to jig about 10-15 miles out to sea after next time.

This affair of the engine just shows how vain it is to try and say who is responsible for the death of a bomber unless it comes down like a high pheasant. George may well have been responsible for our first one and Patsy and/or Robbie were very probably responsible for this one, though I certainly had all the fun of seeing this one down even if, as I rather think, it wasn't mine really.

This report was written in Black's personal diary and reveals something of a fighter pilot's thought process post-combat, as well the difficulty in confirming who actually shot down what enemy aircraft, a problem which persisted throughout the war.

The next day Ras Berry carried out his first flight with the Squadron from Turnhouse in Spitfire L1022. There was no operational flying and F/L George Denholm was attached to RAF Station, Northolt, Middlesex, for a ten-day Air Fighting Course.

On 24 October, P/O Brian Carbury received news that he had been posted to 603 Squadron – his attachment to the unit since 6 October, had become permanent.

On the 27th 603 handed over eight Gladiators to 141 Squadron, at Grangemouth.

Just as the events of 16 October had slipped into the realms of legend for both 602 and 603 Squadrons, so did Saturday 28 October 1939. Between 09.15-10.25 hours the following were in action: F/L Patsy Gifford (L1070), P/O Robbie Robertson (L1050), and P/O Sheep Gilroy (L1049). The ORB reads:

1 enemy aircraft by a patrol of 602 Squadron and RED SECTION on patrol 14,000 feet over the Forth, the aircraft was sighted owing to anti-aircraft bursts. RED SECTION attacked the enemy after a section of 602 Squadron had done so, and the enemy aircraft, which proved to be a Heinkel 111 (new type) was shot down near KIDLAW, 6 miles south of Haddington. 2 of the crew were dead from bullet wounds, the pilot was wounded, and the observer unhurt. The aircraft was riddled with bullet holes but was not extensively damaged on landing.

Action against enemy air force	: 11 hours 40 minutes (12 sorties)
Training	: 30 minutes
Total	: 12 hours 10 minutes

No. of rounds fired: 5,600.
Enemy aircraft destroyed: 1

The victim of this combat later became known as the 'Humbie Heinkel'* – the joint victim of 602 and 603 – a He111 of KG26, the unit which had carried out the long-range armed-reconnaissance missions over the Forth prior to the raid on 16 October.

---

*An MG15 machine gun (No.2640-38) from the Heinkel, with magazine, is currently on display in the National War Museum of Scotland in Edinburgh Castle.

Heinkel He 111 of Stab KG/26 aircraft No. 5449 coded 1H+JA. The first German aircraft shot down over British (Scottish) soil by fighters of 603 and 602 Squadrons.

Another shot of the Heinkel He 111.

Patsy off Dunbar in XT-A, October 1939.

Leutnant Rolf Niehoff and his crew were flying Heinkel He111, 5449, code 1H+JA, when they set out from Westerland over 'the watery triangle'. Initially they flew over the Firth of Forth (Luftwaffe target area 416) but were unable to take any photographs due to cloud cover before flying over the Firth of Clyde at an altitude of 6,000 metres.

At 10.45 the Heinkel had been spotted flying over Drem and Yellow Section, 602 Squadron, led by Flight Lieutenant Hodge, was ordered off to pursue the intruder. They failed to make contact but were diverted to investigate an unidentified aircraft near May Island. This was soon located and identified as an enemy machine and the three Spitfires slipped into line astern ready to attack. As they closed in, a burst was fired before it was realised that the bogey was in fact an Avro Anson. The section broke off their attack but the pilot of the Anson had been struck in the jaw by a bullet.

From the Clyde, Niehoff instructed his pilot to return to the Forth area at an altitude of 5,000 metres where Niehoff found the cloud had thinned noticeably. While the crew could see the Forth area, so could the anti-aircraft crews who greeted the bomber with an effective barrage but as the 3rd (Scottish) Anti-Aircraft Division report for the day states that 'No AA gun stations opened fire' it must therefore be assumed that the barrage came from the considerable number of naval vessels at anchor off Queensferry. These included the destroyer HMS *Mohawk*, keen to exact revenge for the damage and loss of lives on the 16th, and the cruisers HMS *Belfast* and *Edinburgh*, the latter having also been a target on the 16th, but both of which became famous in later years.

13 Group had already been alerted to the presence of the aircraft and Spitfires of the Edinburgh and Glasgow squadrons were on patrol when it returned to their airspace – Red Section of 602 led by F/O Archie McKellar were on patrol over Turnhouse whilst 603's Red Section led by Patsy Gifford were airborne over the Firth of Forth, with Gifford excited at the prospect of further success. Both units were drawn to the presence of Niehoff's Heinkel not by radio direction but by the puffs of anti-aircraft fire.

Whether by good marksmanship or good fortune, one of the first rounds exploded close to the fuselage of the He111 which effectively sealed the fate of the bomber and its crew. As the crew felt the impact of the explosion, Niehoff ordered his pilot Unteroffizier Kurt Lehmkuhl, to jettison the bomb load and dive towards the refuge of the thinning cloud cover below (the navigator is in charge of the Heinkel 111 rather than the pilot, whereas the pilot is in command of a Ju88). The cover was inadequate and at 10,000 feet the Spitfires of 602 were first to latch on to the tail of the Heinkel with 603 diving down from 14,000 feet to follow up with a second attack. 602 then carried out a second attack before each section alternated until the Heinkel was riddled from bow to stern and from one wingtip to the other. The Spitfires maintained their position behind carrying out line astern attacks until moments before the bomber crash landed. The port engine had been struck first, followed moments later by the starboard. The aluminium fuselage was raked with fire, the perspex and instruments were shattered and the control cables severed. Despite suffering agonising pain when a considerable burst of .303 rounds punched through the rear seat in which Kurt Lehmkuhl was strapped, the young Luftwaffe pilot miraculously managed to maintain control of the aircraft. Behind Lehmkuhl and Niehoff lay the bullet-riddled and bloody bodies of wireless operator/air gunner Gefreiter Bruno Reimann and flight engineer/air gunner Unteroffizier Gottlieb Kowalke who had not been so lucky. They had both been shot dead whilst changing the ammunition drums on their MG15 machine guns. It was too late to bale out as the Heinkel had lost too much height and, with the dead engines smoking, there was only one option. Despite his wounds and terrain which was not suitable for a forced landing Lehmkuhl skilfully slowed the aircraft to a stall, just prior to touching down with minimum forward speed. The Heinkel crashed onto a hillside between High Latch and Kidlaw, just to the east of the village of Humbie and slid along the ground, smashing through a drystone wall which tore off the starboard tailplane. The bomber continued to bump and skid along the ground for quite a distance, despite it being uphill, before coming to rest with its back broken and the familiar perspex canopy shattered and hanging off. Niehoff surrendered to the police who he recalled as being 'friendly' when they arrived on the scene and although he had managed to avoid the gun fire from the Spitfires, his back had been broken. Lehmkuhl was carefully taken down the hillside on a home-made stretcher (actually an old gate), and taken to hospital in Edinburgh. The bodies of his two crew members were also taken away on the gate before being removed to the hospital morgue.

One of the first on the scene was Second Lieutenant Iain Horne from Turnhouse ops room who had also been privy to the action of 16 October. As soon as he was aware the Heinkel was down, dressed in the uniform, including traditional kilt of the Scots Guards, he and two of the female plotters jumped in his car and drove at breakneck speed into the Lammermuirs. On arriving at the crash site Iain was disappointed '...there didn't seem to be any blood about, which was very disappointing as we were angry at what the Germans were trying to do.' If he had ventured into the fuselage where the bodies of Reimann and Kowalke were found Iain would have discovered plenty. The dead were buried on 31 October in adjacent graves in Portobello Cemetery.

Niehoff was later to recall that after supervising the removal of his fellow crew members he was taken to the local police station, from where an army captain took him to a large country estate, the HQ of an army unit, where he was given lunch as their guest. After he had dined he was taken to the guardroom at Edinburgh Castle, where he was interrogated by RAF officers for the rest of the afternoon. He recalled that they expressed a particular interest in his aircraft's self-sealing fuel tanks and the fuel injection system. During Niehoff's stay in the castle hospital Iain Horne and his two female companions paid him a visit. Iain recalls the German pilot being '...very arrogant, although perhaps we may have misinterpreted this attitude as at that time we had no idea he had broken his back in the crash-landing. He was also supremely confident he wouldn't be shot down but at the same time edgy, because I believe he thought, having been captured, he would be shot! He tried to impress a nurse in the hospital with his knowledge of English swear words!'*

Later Niehoff was taken to London by train where he spent a few days in the Tower of London. There it was discovered that the persistent ache in his back was due to a fracture of the spine received

---

*Although an army officer, Iain later became a pilot in the RAF. Following flying training at Grangemouth, where one of his instructors was Brian Carbury, Iain was posted to an Army Co-operation unit. He later joined the RAF and flew the early Mustang mostly during daylight operations and was flying night ground-attack missions with a Mosquito squadron in preparation for the D-Day landings.

in the violent impact of the crash-landing. Following four months of treatment in Woolwich Hospital he was eventually moved to 1 Prisoner of War Camp, Grizedale Hall, before being transferred to Canada in 1941. After the war, Niehoff returned to Germany where he had a successful career in the modern Luftwaffe, retiring with the rank of major.

The Heinkel was officially credited to both 602 and 603 Squadrons with no credit given to the anti-aircraft gunners. Niehoff later remembered there being only four machines attacking his aircraft when there were actually two

603 ground crew. Turnhouse 1939.

sections, a total of six aircraft. F/O Archie McKellar confirmed in his combat report the presence of three other Spitfires, in addition to his own section, which followed his section in to attack the Heinkel (these were flown by Gifford, Robertson and Gilroy). However, it would appear that the other two Spitfires in McKellar's section broke away or lost their leader during the attack, thus confirming Niehoff's sighting of the four Spitfires – McKellar, Gifford, Robertson and Gilroy. The damage to the Heinkel clearly indicated an improvement in the marksmanship of the pilots since 16 October.

The RAF expressed great interest in the wreck of the Heinkel. Sergeant 'Angy' Gillies was particularly impressed at the ease of access to the engine compartments for servicing. The engines were removed, packed up and sent to Rolls-Royce at Derby while the airframe was taken to the Royal Aircraft Establishment at Farnborough for detailed examination.

On 29 October, Sergeant James R. Caister was posted to the Squadron for flying duties. According to John Young, 603 was bolstered by:

> ...people like Caister. He was on his third tour as a fighter pilot, having completed his first tour as far back as 1935, need I say more?! He was a bit older than the rest and was an example of the backbone of the pre-war RAF. I remember very well him talking to George Denholm one day and saying: 'Well, I did this tour and then went back to my trade, and then

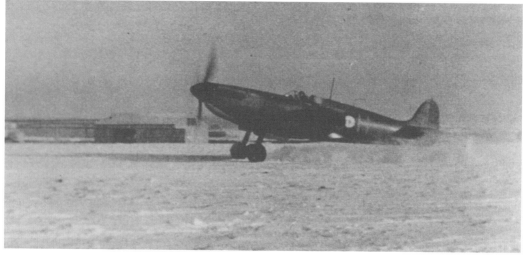

XT-H, November 1939.

I did another tour as a fighter pilot, and then went back to my trade.' He then came to us.

'Bill' Caister, as he was known by his colleagues, was 33 years of age and the Squadron's first regular sergeant pilot.

At the Squadron's conception, the class divide between officers and other ranks had been considerable. The peacetime lawyers, solicitors and managers, in addition to members of the aristocracy who made up the hierarchy of the unit, were wealthy and held positions of authority and status within the community. Fast cars and flying was something the wealthy could afford and there was a vast divide between those men and the other ranks until war brought about the need for pilots from

October/November 1939. A Flight, F/O Ken Macdonald, Turnhouse cricket pavilion, at readiness.

other walks of life. Nevertheless, the class divide continued and following the outbreak of war little had changed and Bill Caister and Ras Berry found life difficult until they too were commissioned and conditions eased a little, but they would always be from the 'wrong side of the tracks.'

On 1 November 1939, there was no flying and F/O Fred Rushmer left for a course at Bircham Newton on instruction of recognition markings on Coastal Command aircraft. The next day saw no operational flying, but practice flying continued and George Denholm returned from attachment to RAF Northolt where he had completed a Fighter Instruction Course.

By now, CFI instructor F/O John Young had completed his assessment of the 603 pilots. Despite their early success it was obvious the weakness lay in their lack of combat experience. Count Stevens was still in charge of the Squadron but no longer flying operationally when he decided that 603 should retain some of its Gladiators for night operations. John Young opposed this on the grounds that the extreme sensitivity of the Spitfire's controls as well as the lack of night flying experience of the pilots, rendered such a proposal unsafe. According to John his recommendations on training had never been well received by Count Stevens and this latest matter did nothing to improve relations between the two:

When I first arrived at 603 Squadron I found myself in rather a difficult situation. I'd been appointed Instructor and Adjutant and for reasons not apparent to me at the time, I found that 'Shag' Wallace had been appointed de-facto Adjutant (29.11.39) and that my position as instructor was challenged. I decided not to actively challenge this situation because my experience on Spitfires was limited but on the other hand, with a Central Flying School Instructors rating and an Airline Transport Pilots Licence, in many ways I was more experienced than the pilots there and I took the view that the briefing from CFS that my job with the auxiliary squadrons of 41 Squadron – 603 and 609 were attached to 41 Squadron – was to see, not that they performed well in battle, which was never in dispute, but that they got home safely, which was nothing like as certain and indeed there were a number of flying accidents.

I was faced with the fact that my predecessor was not supportive of me and was advising the Squadron that it should fly Spitfires by day and Gladiators by night. I had very limited experience as a night-fighter pilot, in fact I had very little experience as a fighter pilot, but I had more night-flying experience than most other pilots in the air force. I therefore came to the conclusion that of the aeroplanes postulated as a night fighter, the Gladiator was the least suitable. Flying the Gladiator at night was like trying to balance a pea on the end of a pin, and I decided against it. On the minus side of the 603 problem was that two pilots had recently been killed, one of which was killed in a collision at Grangemouth (Somerville). This occurred because the pilots were doing straight-in approaches and not curved approaches.

To improve my morale they gave me Somerville's Irvin jacket, complete with the hole punched through it by the propeller that killed him. In other words I was not welcome at 603.

F/O Ken Macdonald at readiness at the cricket pavilion.   Pat Gifford (far left), Turnhouse cricket pavilion.

I discovered later that all this was to do with 'Count' Stevens himself.

Having just come from 41 Squadron where I had an admirable squadron commander, Squadron Leader Adams, who led from the front, Stevens had no intention of either leading from the front or even flying a Spitfire at all.

I wrote a letter citing all the problems I was having to the Chief Flying Instructor at the Central Flying School. Unfortunately he was killed in a night flying accident whilst teaching an ATS girl to fly in a Harvard. It is my understanding that my letter reached Lord Dowding, because of the death of its intended recipient, and Lord Dowding came to Turnhouse during December 1939 and briefly interviewed me, talked to the people of 603 Squadron and other Scotsmen who were anxious to make their mark, as it were. The long and short of it was that while I was on leave over Christmas (the Squadron was at Prestwick at the time) a man called Collingwood turned up at the mess at Turnhouse with his wife with orders to take over command of 603 Squadron. He was told by Stevens to go away on the basis that as an auxiliary he could only be moved with his agreement, and of course he was a highly qualified Edinburgh lawyer.

In my opinion Stevens was not the right man to be a squadron commander of a fighter squadron. He was very well off, somewhat devious and knowledgeable in legal matters. I believe that in the more suitable environment of Fighter Command, where he worked in the operations department, he was highly successful. But it is my belief that it was his family wealth and seniority that produced him that position. Black Morton liked Stevens a lot but to me he wasn't the kind of man that I envisaged as suitable for running a fighter squadron – and remember that I had come from a military background and I'd known and seen at work the COs of 78 and 10 Squadrons in my bomber days and I'd seen 'Fanny' Adams, as he was called, as CO of 41 Squadron. I'd also seen the CO of RAF Catterick at work. They were all men who led from the front. Stevens walked around with his arm in a sling and I took the view that if his arm was in a sling at least he could have pushed the throttle forward and pulled it back again. I've heard since that he dislocated his shoulder if he operated the hood of his Spitfire. Well, why didn't he operate it with his right hand? He was simply the wrong man for the job. He shot himself which was an excessively sad and dramatic end.

The outcome of this was that Stevens was over-ruled and the Gladiators were not to be used. Spitfires were to be flown by day and night. Another interesting point which John had observed whilst working with the pilots was that since his accident Graham Hunter was experiencing problems with his eyesight. The MO rejected this but years later at a dinner Hunter admitted that John had been right.

On 3 November, Fred Rushmer returned from Bircham Newton and the duty pilots carried out fighting patrols from Turnhouse. There was no flying the following day and F/O Laurie Cunningham was attached to RAF Leuchars for 'experimental work'. John Young was attached to 609 Squadron at Drem and Graham Hunter was discharged from the Military Hospital at Edinburgh Castle and granted 28 days sick leave.

There was no flying on 5 November, some practice flights on the 6th and, again, no flying on the 7th. For the following three days the pilots carried out fighting patrols and practice flying. On 10 November Robbie Robertson's posting to 603 Squadron from 41 Squadron was confirmed with effect from 24 October 1939.

Practice flying went ahead on 11 November and on the 12th, Laurie Cunningham returned to the Squadron from RAF Leuchars and Pilot Officer C.O. Bean, RAFVR, was posted to the Squadron for adjutant's duties with effect from 29 October 1939.

The following day, F/L Ivone Kirkpatrick returned from sick leave, still unfit for flying duties.

On 14 and 15 November, the Squadron pilots carried out fighting patrols and practice flights. On the latter Patsy Gifford received news of his promotion to Squadron Leader and posting to 3 Squadron at RAF Kenley, flying Hurricanes, in preparation for his taking command.

On 16 November F/O Geoff Wynne-Powell left for Harwich where he was to undertake liaison duties with the convoys.

There was no flying on the 17th and on the 18th, S/L Patsy Gifford left to take his new post and F/L George Denholm took over as A Flight commander. After his departure, Ken Macdonald was quick to acquire Gifford's Spitfire, L1070, 'Stickleback'. Gifford's career after leaving 603 is worthy of mention at this point.

On the 28th Pat Gifford was awarded the DFC for his role in the action on 16 and 28 October, although he was of the opinion that his part in the destruction of a third enemy aircraft on 22 October should have also been mentioned (George Pinkerton of 602 Squadron had also been awarded the DFC for his success on 16 October).

On the morning of Friday 10 May 1940 the pilots of Gifford's 3 Squadron were scrambled to intercept an unidentified aircraft approaching the south coast. After a fruitless chase the Hurricanes landed back at Kenley to be greeted with the news of the German 'Blitzkrieg' assault on the Low Countries and their imminent departure to Merville, France, as part of the air echelon of the 63 Wing Air Component. After a brief and somewhat sketchy pep talk by Gifford the

Top: P/O D. K. A. 'Ching' Mackenzie, Sgt 'Ras' Berry and P/O G. Wynne-Powell.
Bottom: Patsy and George, November 1939. George took over A Flight from Patsy.

pilots hastily packed the minimum amount of kit aboard their aircraft and departed for France.

Patsy Gifford led his squadron on their first patrol over France on Sunday 12 May. At 11.20 the next day, flying Hurricane L1846, QO-B, he led six Hurricanes on patrol over the Wavre-Louvain area. At approximately 13.00 hours eight Henschel 123s of II(S)/LG2 were sighted flying at low altitude by Red Section and the Hurricanes engaged the enemy aircraft. In the ensuing combat two Hs123s were shot down, one He111 and one Do17.

At 15.45 hours on Tuesday 14 May, flying L1610, Gifford led 12 Hurricanes to the airfield at Berry-au-Bac, where they refuelled before taking off to patrol the airspace over the Sedan battlefield at 15,000 feet, as part of the cover for the 75 Wing attack force of 29 Fairey Battles of 88, 103 and 226 Squadrons. North-west of Sedan the Hurricanes of 3 Squadron encountered a large force of

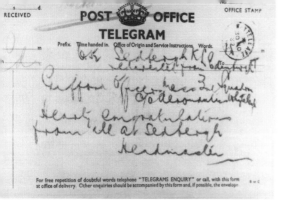

Left: Telegram of congratulations following award of DFC and promotion to S/L for Pat Gifford.
Right: 603 Squadron Spitfires led by F/L Pat Gifford in XT-A, L1070 'Stickleback' over Stirling, November 1939.

Ju87s in two waves escorted by Bf109s of I/JG54. In the ensuing combat, 3 Squadron claimed one Hs126, nine Ju87s, six Bf109s and one Bf110 destroyed, with two Ju87s probably destroyed. Fourteen Battles failed to return.

On Wednesday 15 May, Gifford led a dawn patrol in L1610, over the Sedan-Dinant area. As the result of what has been recorded as an 'accident' he forced-landed at Wevelgem and returned to his squadron unhurt. At 17.30 the next day Gifford took a patrol in P2825 over the Wavre-Louvain area when a German aircraft was sighted. Sgt Basil Friendship recorded:

> 'Patsie' [sic] Gifford sighted a Messerschmitt and chased it. Wilkie (Sgt. Wilkinson) and I followed as it dived down to low level over – as it turned out – the German front lines. Terrific light AA fire encountered. Wilkie broke to the right and I broke to the left, then circled a pom-pom type gun which was firing at me. I zig-zagged, climbed and dived until I was out of range. Squadron Leader Gifford did not return but I didn't see him hit the ground.

Sergeant 'Wilkie' Wilkinson also recorded:

> We gained some height to have a better look around when from out of nowhere came a Messerschmitt 110, which shot down Sqn Ldr Gifford. I managed to shoot down the 110. I moved into position to get a full deflection shot that sent the enemy plane into a long curving dive with one engine pouring smoke. I turned my Hurricane on its wing as I realised I had more 110s on my tail. As a Hurricane could out-turn a 110, I thought I had out-smarted the Huns. Glancing ahead, I saw a Messerschmitt 109 approaching head-on, with flashes indicating shell-fire emerging from his nose. There was no time for any sort of logical thought. I held my line, as did the other pilot, then opened fire at about 200 yards. The enemy aircraft screamed over my head and I never knew if I killed the pilot or not. When I returned to Merville, Walter Churchill had received confirmation from the front line that the CO had been shot down and that I had got the 110.

Wilkinson's action of not deviating from his head-on course with the 109 probably saved him from a more serious outcome. The Bf110, 2N+HH of 1/ZG1, crashed near Walem, one mile north of Mechelen. The pilot, Leutnant Heinrich Brucksch, and his gunner, Gefreiter Heinz-Werner Roth were killed. However, Hauptmann Adolph Galland of Stab/JG27, who was yet to achieve fame, reported having downed a Hurricane at 18.30 hours, one mile south of Lille. But since Sgt Wilkinson produced an eyewitness account of the Bf110 shooting down Patsy Gifford, it would seem that it was Wilkinson's Hurricane that Galland had attacked. Whilst it would appear that the 110 had claimed the life of Gifford it is not inconceivable that it had been Galland.

Patsy Gifford DFC (in forage cap, above cockpit) with 3 Squadron before they left for France.

With confirmation of the death of S/L Patsy Gifford DFC, F/L Walter Churchill took command of 3 Squadron. The sad news was passed on to Patsy's family and his many friends in civilian life and in 603.

Back with 603, during November Flight Lieutenant 'Hook' Pinfold was posted to Montrose as a flying instructor. He had hoped to be sent to an operational squadron with a command in mind but due to the urgent need for new pilots his request was not granted. He had been a very important asset to the unit during what was a critical stage of their development. He was very popular and was greatly missed. He went on to achieve the rank of Group Captain before retiring.

On 19 November, the 603 pilots continued with daytime fighting patrols and practice flights and Geoff Wynne-Powell returned from his liaison duties with the convoys. For the next week fighting patrols continued unabated. On the 25th, due to lack of accommodation P/O C.O. Bean moved out of the officers mess having been told to live locally and draw marriage allowance. At 16.30 on 27 November S/L Stevens attended a conference at Turnhouse which included the controllers and COs of all squadrons in the sector under the direction of W/C Don Fleming to discuss matters relating to operational duties in the sector.

On the 28th, as fighting patrols continued by day as well as practice flying, it was recorded in the ORB that F/L Pat Gifford had been awarded the DFC.

There was no flying on 29 November and George Denholm took five days leave during which time he married Betty Toombs at Linlithgow with members of A Flight present whilst B remained on standby at the airfield. The couple had met at the 603 summer camp at Hawkinge.

F/L Ivone Kirkpatrick left Turnhouse for an appointment with the CMB at RAF Halton and pre-war veteran of Turnhouse, P/O Alen 'Shag' Wallace, so nicknamed on account of his bushy moustache, reported for duty as adjutant, with effect from 29 November 1939.* The next day saw the duty pilots once again on patrol. Throughout November Ras Berry flew just two operational sorties, both in L1026.

On 1 December 1939, the airfield at Turnhouse was very soft and had large pools of water after the previous night's rain and gales for which warnings had been given. Although there was no operational flying, practice flying still took place.

By the next morning the ground was still soft but much of the surface water had drained away. Practice flying was the only aerial activity.

On 3 December, available pilots flew further fighting patrols by day and practice flights. All Squadron aircraft were moved into the hangar overnight after a gale warning. The next day the pilots gained further experience with patrols and practice flying. F/O Ken Macdonald collected a Spitfire from RAF Northolt and flew to RAF Catterick where he stayed overnight. The Squadron aircraft were again moved into the hangar for the night after another severe weather warning, this time for snow, which proved accurate as the morning of 5 December dawned revealing two inches of snow on the aerodrome. Ken Macdonald landed at Turnhouse after the short flight from Catterick.

The next day saw the Squadron pilots carry out more 'fighting patrols by day' and 'practice flying'. Ivone Kirkpatrick was granted a further 34 days sick leave. The Squadron ORB recorded: '358860 Sgt/Pilot Caister crashed Spitfire K9996 on Turnhouse aerodrome due to soft nature of ground.' On landing the wheels of the Spitfire had sunk into the muddy surface and the Spitfire nosed over onto its back. Bill Caister was unhurt and a photograph shows him examining his aircraft with airmen equipped with fire extinguishers looking on (see page 105).

A section was sent from Turnhouse to Montrose to protect the FTS flying training expansion. Encounters with the enemy were rare during February-March 1940. The occasional reconnaissance aircraft soon took flight on seeing the approaching Spitfires rising up to confront them.

On 7 December more practice flying took place. This day saw further patrols and between 12.10-12.50 hours F/O Laurie Cunningham (L1021), P/O Brian Carbury (L1020) and Sgt Ras Berry (L1025) sighted a formation of seven Heinkels heading for the airfield at Montrose and engaged them. This was the 603's first attack on an enemy formation. Previously they had only pursued

---

*Although an experienced pilot, Alen Wallace did not fly operationally during WWII and by March 1944 was based at Headquarters, Air Training Corps, Blythwood Square, Glasgow.

Top left: Bear helping to fill sandbags at dispersal. Turnhouse, 1939.
Top right: Ken attempting to evade a friendly attack, November 1939.
Middle: XT-H and XT-E over The Ochils, November 1939.
Bottom: Even the flight commanders can have fun! F/L George Denholm at dispersal with his car in the background.

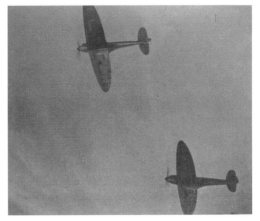

Top: B Flight dispersal. Robin Waterston eating with unknown who has his shotgun at the ready!

Middle left: 603 officers out on the town, Edinburgh 1939.

Middle right: Ken and Sheep over Dundee.

Left: December 1939. Caister's first somersault.

single enemy aircraft. Cunningham singled out one from a formation of three which dived to sea-level as it turned east, the gunner firing wildly at the Spitfire. During Cunningham's second attack no fire came from the rear gunner, who had probably been killed or injured and black smoke then streamed from one engine. Carbury meanwhile had got himself into a position whereby he made a frontal attack on another Heinkel and noted that white smoke began to pour from both engines. Such a method of attack required precise judgement as to when to break away and in what direction. Carbury was to use the method again during the Battle of Britain. Ras recalled that things seemed to be getting out of hand and that the only course of action was to 'plough the fields and scatter!' He dived on the starboard Heinkel and fired all his ammunition later claiming a damaged. The enemy aircraft turned and headed back over the North Sea with all available speed. The Spitfires were at the limit of their endurance and had to return to Montrose without confirming the fate of the enemy aircraft. I/KG26 lost two bombers but it is unclear if 603 or 72 Squadron did the damage. 603 were only credited with three damaged.

The Squadron ORB – 'Detail of Work Carried Out' included the following information:

Blue Section were ordered to Patrol Arbroath and when crossing Kirkcaldy en route signal received that seven enemy aircraft were observed south-east of Montrose. The section sighted enemy aircraft (Heinkel 111) in two Vic formations of four and three aircraft line astern about 600 hundred yards apart. F/O JLG Cunningham attacked No.3 of the second formation (3 enemy aircraft) in a No.1 attack. This formation dived to within 50 feet of the sea turning eastwards. Fire was returned from the rear gunner of the enemy aircraft. On delivering second attack no fire was returned from rear gunner of enemy aircraft and black smoke issued from port engine of enemy aircraft. P/O BJG Carbury carried out a frontal attack on port aircraft of the first enemy aircraft formation and on completing this white smoke was observed issuing from both engines. Sgt/Pilot Berry carried out a No.1 attack on starboard (No.4) enemy aircraft of the first formation. Of the interception there was no confirmed positive result. No camera or cine camera guns carried.

Although this attack was made against a lone raider, it was later written of the New Zealander:

By some extraordinary manoeuvre Carbury had put himself into a position to make a frontal attack on the leading formation. Such attacks were sometimes made in the Battle of Britain by very experienced pilots cool enough to fly on through the concentrated fire of the enemy formation's front gunners. It needed fine judgement to decide when to break away and in what direction. A very experienced Battle of Britain fighter pilot – Wing Commander 'Paddy' Barthrop later wrote 'Bloody Dangerous!!!' There are one or two lunatics who revelled in it.

This was the combat in which Ras achieved his first success. Years later he reflected on the action:

I was airborne for almost an hour and the weather was foul. It was very hectic perhaps the first real ops for many pilots airborne that day (R/T transmitters had been left on to complicate matters).

The following two days saw no flying of any sort but on 10 December patrols were carried out during the day with the whole Squadron at readiness by 06.30. Although there was no operational flying the next day, the pilots were busy with practice flying exercises. Geoff Wynne-Powell was admitted to the Military Hospital at Edinburgh Castle after a recent bout of illness where he was diagnosed as suffering from appendicitis.

On 12 December there were practice flights but no operational flying. F/O Fred Rushmer was granted six days leave and F/O Laurie Cunningham (GD) was appointed to take over command of B Flight in his absence. F/O John Young ceased to be attached to 609 Squadron at Drem and returned to 603. The ORB records the long overdue news for Ras Berry: 'Sgt/Pilot R Berry appointed to a commission GD Branch RAFVR w.e.f. 1.12.39, and with seniority from 29.4.39.' Ras's promotion had taken eight months from when he had first been notified! As a pilot he had already impressed those around him and his climb up the promotion ladder would end with the delightful Yorkshireman as an Air Commodore. Nevertheless, many of the ground crew personnel remember that both Ras and Bill Caister were treated badly by certain officers in the squadron in the period following their arrival.

The next day saw no operational flying but yet more practice flights. The regular flying meant the experienced pilots in the Squadron had accumulated between 160-200 hours on type by August 1940 but they had gained no relevant experience for when they would come up against the faster, agile German fighters. They had, after all, only encountered the slower, lumbering bombers. Although there was danger from return fire, to the 603 pilots the bombers seemed liked sitting ducks.

Prestwick and Montrose

There was no flying on 13 December and at 21.45 hours instructions were received for the Squadron to move to Prestwick, situated on the south-west coast of Scotland. The next day saw no operational flying but there was practice flying. All stores and equipment were packed up by the MT section and ready for transportation when the movement instructions were cancelled.

14 and 15 December saw no flying at Turnhouse but at 19.30 hours on the 15th the Squadron again received orders to prepare for an immediate move to Prestwick.

The next day saw a bustle of activity as the unit prepared to move. There was no operational flying but practice flying continued and the Squadron remained at readiness during the move. According to John Young: 'We moved to Prestwick over the Christmas period of 1939/40 in order to provide protection for the 1st Canadian Division when they sailed up the Clyde in such ships as the *Empress of Britain*.' The pilots were to provide top cover for the incoming troopships from Halifax, Nova Scotia, packed full of Canadian servicemen.

Personnel were transported by Ensign aircraft while the equipment and stores were moved by road. The ground staff at Prestwick were billeted in local civilian houses and transport had to be arranged to and from the airfield. The Squadron headquarters and officers mess were established in the 'Old Mill' house and during the evenings The Red Lion became the popular meeting place. The Old Mill was hardly home from home and the pilots recall it being cold and damp.

Prestwick, December 1939-January 1940. Sheep and Ken wrapped up against the cold. Note the mill on the left in which the officers mess was situated.

On the day the Squadron moved to Prestwick Pilot Officer B. Gerald Stapleton reported for duty from 32 Squadron at Biggin Hill, F/O Jack Haig reported back from 12 Group Pool, and P/O J.E.A. 'Albert' Barton (A&SD) was attached to 603 Squadron from Intelligence at RAF Turnhouse.

The Squadron carried out flying patrols by day on 17 December and F/O Fred 'Rusty' Rushmer returned from leave and took over command of B Flight from Cunningham. No flying took place on the 18th and Pilot Officer Noel J.V. Benson reported for duty from 145 Squadron (detach) at Montrose. Following his work on conversion to Spitfires Sergeant/Pilot W.W. Thompson also reported to 603 from 219 Squadron, based at Catterick with detachments at Scorton, Leeming and Redhill. John Young remembers the evening the officers were joined in the mess by a distinguished visitor:

> Lord David Douglas-Hamilton visited us at Prestwick and was in some way the centre of attention as we sat around our fireside. All the Douglas-Hamilton brothers were *so* different. I knew them all well and Lord David was the hardest. He later became Officer Commanding 603 Squadron in Malta.

With no operational flying, practice flying continued on 21 December and following his crash on 7 October, P/O Graham Hunter reported back with the Squadron but cleared for ground duties only. On 22 December practice flying was the only aerial activity by the 603 pilots. P/O Gerald Stapleton had only been with the unit for six days when he crashed at Prestwick in Spitfire K9997. He had

Snowballs in the Irvin leggings! Bubble and Charles, Prestwick. Winter fun at Turnhouse!

found the only soft piece of ground on the airfield when he managed to tip his Spitfire onto its nose whilst taxiing after landing. For this error he felt the wrath of the older and considerably more experienced (although only slightly more senior in rank) F/O John Young who remembered: 'The airfield surface at Prestwick was good, firm and dry. Gerald turned his aircraft over on a bad patch just in front of our dispersal. He knew about it but didn't understand the implications.' Whilst both pilots confirm the aforementioned cause of the accident, the mishap was officially recorded as a result of the undercarriage selector lever not being in the locked position.

Whilst taxiing T6 Harvard P5866 at Prestwick aerodrome on 23 December, F/O Bubble Waterston unwittingly operated the retractable undercarriage lever instead of the wing flap lever. As a result of the sudden drop onto the grass surface of the airfield the Harvard was damaged.

From 24-28 December there was no operational flying and the pilots continued to accrue experience during daily practice flying. There was no flying at all on the 29th and Pilot Officer G.I. Thompson reported to 603 from Porthcawl. The only aerial activity for the final two days of the month was yet more practice flying.

1940

From 1 to 3 January the pilots carried out practice flights but on the 4th and 5th they practiced their flying skills but in conjunction with co-operation flying with the searchlight and anti-aircraft units.

The 6th saw yet more practice with no operational flying and for the following two days bad weather curtailed any flying. More practice flying followed on 9 and 10 January and on the latter F/L George Denholm, F/O Jack Haig, F/O Ian Ritchie and P/O Robbie Robertson were attached to Montrose. There had been an increasing number of German air attacks on shipping, fishing fleets and ports and the four aircraft were sent to Montrose for convoy protection duties. At dispersal, they acquired three old wooden huts: one was the Flight Commander's office, one for the pilots and the third for the ground staff. By the summer the huts had been replaced by new larger ones.

At that time Montrose was a training station and home to No.8 Service Flying Training School (flying: Hart Trainer/Special, Audax, Hind, Gauntlet I, Fury, Tutor, Gordon, Shark II, Don, Master I & II, Hurricane I, Moth Major, the Battle V, Avro Anson I and Airspeed Oxford I & II aircraft). This somewhat complicated the life of the operational fighter pilots. There were usually three aircraft at readiness for immediate take-off. The remainder of the pilots were either 'available' (ready to take-off within half an hour) or 'released' (allowed to leave the aerodrome). With the Germans sending over single raiders from Sylt there was adequate strength at both Dyce and Montrose to deal with that threat. When a 'bandit' was detected by the elementary radar headquarters at Beach Ballroom at Aberdeen, operations would ring through and the corporal at the telephone in the pilots' room would call out 'Red Section Scramble'. A red Very light was fired to clear the air around the base of training aircraft, and within minutes Spitfires would be in the air and the leader would be given a course over the R/T to intercept the enemy.

Despite the red flare, taxiing on the airfield was risky for the Squadron pilots with training aircraft also on the move. Several serious accidents occurred.

A Spitfire from 603 being refuelled during a visit to RAF Lossiemouth during early 1940. Pilot is F/O Waterston.

On the 11th 'fighting patrols by day' took place. F/L Ivone Kirkpatrick was attached to RAF Turnhouse.

The 12th and 13th saw the Squadron carry out yet more patrols and practice flying. On the latter Sgt W. Thompson crashed while flying Spitfire XT-A, L1070, 'Stickleback' undershooting on landing at Prestwick in bad visibility, having been assisted during his approach with instructions via the R/T. The Spitfire was damaged but repairable and Thompson was lucky to escape unhurt.

On 14 January patrols and practice flying continued. The section at Montrose became a flight when F/Os Fred Rushmer and Laurie Cunningham, P/Os Ras Berry, Charles Peel, Noel Benson, Gerald Stapleton and Graham Thomson were also attached. Ras recalled that he flew more frequently from there and experienced combat for the first time. The responsibility of the flight was to be the same as when it was a section, '...to be available to intercept aerial attacks on shipping'. George Denholm, Jack Haig and Ian Ritchie ceased to be attached to Montrose and returned to Prestwick.

Ken Macdonald received a letter from Mardi who was serving at a radio listening post in Kent (she spoke fluent German) in which she records that she was having a 'cracking time.' On 14 January Ken wrote back:

I am in the very depths of depression – Stickleback was written-off yesterday. I lent it to our new start Student Pilot and he undershot coming in, and crashed it upside down in a field beside the aerodrome. Now it lies a twisted wreck – bloody awful.

The pilot was heaved out quite unhurt although he came down a pretty resounding crack. Now I have no aeroplane of my own, and no machine in the Squadron is either as fast or as new and well trimmed or reliable as old Stickleback. [Alec] Mackenzie is almost in tears.

George, Ian and Co., return today.

Love…

Ken

While flying continued on 15 January, John Boulter and Brian Carbury were also attached to Montrose to further strengthen the flight. The cycle of movement continued when Robbie Robertson returned from Montrose to Prestwick. The next day saw further practice flying.

With only practice flying on 17 January, the Squadron received instructions to remove the remaining part of 603 from Prestwick to Dyce. So off went George Denholm, Ken Macdonald, Jack Haig, Black Morton, Sheep Gilroy, Bill Caister and Sgt Thompson. On landing Thompson committed another *faux pas* when he put his Spitfire onto its nose. S/L Count Stevens and P/O Alen Wallace travelled by road, as did a bus containing other airmen.

From 18 January, the Squadron left Prestwick – the Station Flight moved to Dyce and B Flight to Montrose.

Dyce and Montrose

Their task was to provide air defence for the north-east coast of Scotland including convoy and coastal shipping protection in the North Sea. The operation was code-named 'Viken Zero' – Viken being the Squadron radio call sign.

Dyce lies about five miles to the north-west of 'the granite city' on the road to Inverurie and on the south side of a bend in the River Don. On the east side of the airfield is the small town which gave it its name. About three miles to the north-west, the land rises steeply to the Hill of Marcus which is about 700 feet in height.

The aerodrome was opened on 4 July 1934 as a grass strip by Eric Gandar Dower, a great pioneer of Scottish aviation. He ran Aberdeen Airways which became Allied Airways (Gandar Dower) Limited operating routes between Aberdeen, Wick, Thurso, Orkney and Shetland. Although the Auxiliary Air Force used Dyce before the outbreak of the war it was in 1940 that the military development of the airfield gathered momentum. Three surfaced runways were built and the RAF took over the western side of the airfield – where the civil airport buildings were subsequently located. They shared the field with the civil aircraft of Gandar Dower throughout the war, but it seems to have been an uneasy co-operation with the civil aviators feeling that they were always the poor relatives of their military counterparts.

The airfield elevation is 215 feet. The land rises far to the west and south to become the high mountains of the Grampians whilst to the north and east, it is relatively flat and low lying for the 20 miles or so to the fishing towns of Peterhead (also known for its Victorian prison) which faces east to the North Sea, and Fraserburgh on the north facing coast. The land is used for farming with sheep and cattle in evidence.

In good weather, the flat coastal plain with its patchwork of yellow and green fields can be beautiful. If the air is gin clear with a bright, clear blue sky, visibility can seem limitless, but often, the beauty is tempered by the chill wind which scurries the three hundred miles or so from Scandinavia across the North Sea. In bad weather, the wind drives the rain and snow unmercifully before it – lashing into unprotected faces, freezing hands and causing icing problems for aircraft in the air as well as creating the backbreaking effort of keeping runways and taxiways clear of snow.

During the first day the Squadron flew patrols in addition to practice flying. The remainder of the personnel and stores left Prestwick by road on its journey to Dyce. John Young reflects on conditions:

Five Spitfires of 603 on formation flying exercise, 1940.

I have many nice memories of 603 Squadron while at readiness in the old flying club at Dyce. Life was nothing if not up and down. Down on a dreary day, on readiness or available, when we slept to pass the time or played Racing Demon, a game which certainly gave a welcome lift to the day. On one occasion somebody delivered a lovely cheddar cheese which we had with biscuits one lunchtime – a kindly donation to the Squadron. Dyce was a reasonable surface and there was a particularly nice station commander who was very helpful. The work we did from Dyce was largely convoy protection and it was from there that we intercepted 'Weather Willie'. There were many happy days there and I was very happy with George Denholm's running of A Flight. He was quietly and firmly confident, and capable. When the A Flight group photo was taken during early 1940, I was still on leave at Prestwick after the move to Dyce.

Dyce, March/April 1940. From left, Sheep Gilroy, Ian Ritchie, Bill Douglas, Count Stevens (skipping) and George Denholm.

On the 19th, P/Os Robbie Robertson and Albert Barton left Prestwick and flew to Dyce.

On this day a He111 was intercepted and shot down into the sea. The reconnaissance He111 'Weather Willie' was of I(F)Obdl. and initially attacked by Sgt Bill Caister in K9998 on a lone convoy patrol between 12.05-13.15. At 12.35 Jack Haig (L1048), Ken Macdonald (K9995) and Sheep Gilroy (L1057) were scrambled and attacked the Heinkel 20 miles east of Aberdeen. The weather was extremely cold and the pilots found the inside of their perspex canopies iced up. To their advantage, the enemy aircraft was easy to spot and

Jack, Sheep and Ken, Dyce, January/February 1940.

launching their attack from the quarter the 603 pilots continued to fire until their guns stopped. They could not claim definite results but the Heinkel had been hit and was seen heading east, losing height. It eventually crashed into the sea and wreckage was later spotted in the water. On returning to Dyce 55 minutes later, the armourers confirmed that many of the Spitfires' machine guns had frozen up in the extreme low temperatures, causing them to fail. The ORB included details from Bill Caister's combat report:

> While on patrol for the protection of shipping from aerial attack off Aberdeen, overheard instruction by R/T to Red Section to patrol Aberdeen at 25,000 feet, therefore climbed and observed Heinkel 111. Carried out a No.2 attack opening fire at 400 yards and closing to 300 yards while Red Section were also attacking. No evasive action was taken by enemy aircraft and very little fire was observed from the rear gunners.

The ORB 'Details of Work Carried Out' also included a composite of the combat reports from the three pilots involved. The greatest contribution came from Red Section leader, Ken Macdonald, who always wrote lengthy summaries of his combat, much appreciated by those who later sought to produce detailed accounts of this period of action:

Sheep victorious, Dyce, March 1940.

Recognised an enemy aircraft Heinkel 111 and prepared to make No.1 attack, so section was ordered to stern attack at 13.05. No.1 Spitfire carried out No.1 attack from slightly below, fire being opened from 350 yards and closed to 250 yards. Intense cloud trail was created by Heinkel making observation very easy but obscuring it from astern.

Port Nos.3 and 4 guns did not operate on the Spitfire due to intense cold.

No.2 Spitfire delivered a No.1 attack opening fire at 500 yards and closing to 300 yards as another Spitfire was observed slightly to port of Heinkel.

No.2 Spitfire carried out a second No.1 attack opening fire at 300 yards closing to under 100 yards. On landing it was found that only one Spitfire gun had fired due to extreme cold. No evasive tactics were employed.

No.3 Spitfire gained height to port of Heinkel while other Spitfires attacked and then delivered an attack between Nos.1 and 2, opening fire at 300 yards closing 50 yards. When coming up behind the Heinkel the Spitfire was caught in the cloud formed by the enemy aircraft which froze to the windscreen. A second attack was delivered from the port side to avoid the cloud… A third attack was delivered from the starboard side and the top gunner could be seen returning fire.

The combat was broken off when ammunition was exhausted about 60 miles out at sea. The enemy aircraft was losing height.

Ras Berry was quick to find a solution to the problem of ice accretion on the inside of his canopy. He carried a small tin of glycol and a stick with a sponge on the end so he could de-ice his screen when necessary. Others thought of carrying a cloth soaked in glycol but when they reached down to pull the rag from its secure place they discovered it too had frozen solid!

The cold weather was an ever-present factor and the poor conditions prompted John Young to speak with his Flight Commander, George Denholm: 'I persuaded him that the Squadron should practice the so-called Z, Z, bad weather approach to the airfield. This method was practised with some success…'

By now Gerald Stapleton had acquired the nickname 'Stapme'. He also remembers the adverse weather conditions at Montrose: 'The weather could be so foul and when the wind blew in off the North Sea, over the dunes on the eastern seaward side, it was bitterly cold and flying conditions were impossible…'

From 20 to 30 January daytime patrols and practice flights continued. On the 22nd Ivone Kirkpatrick was posted to take command of No.2 Ferry Pilots Pool and Geoff Wynne-Powell reported to CMB Halton for a medical board. On the 24th pilots from B Flight undertook night-flying practice, albeit for a short duration and on the 30th P/O Graham Hunter was collected by F/L Ian Dick, the Medical Officer at Turnhouse, and attached to the station for medical observation, part of his on-going assessment following his accident the previous autumn. On the 31st an initial patrol was curtailed because of snow which continued to fall throughout the day.

During February 1940, the Squadron carried out fighting patrols by day and practice flying as and when the weather allowed. On the 2nd Fred Rushmer received news of his promotion to Flight Lieutenant.

On Friday 3 February the ORB recorded a party representing 603 attended the joint funeral of the German airmen shot down on 19 January.

F/O John 'Dobbin' Young and P/O Ian 'Woolly Bear' Ritchie in the crew room.

Behind the gun butts at Montrose. The ground crew's hut was soon replaced.

B Flight dispersal at Montrose, February 1940. On left is XT-M L1021 'Auld Reekie'.

Between 11.37 and 12.50 on the 9th Green Section, comprising F/O Laurie Cunningham (L1026), F/O Robin Waterston (L1046) and P/O Stapme Stapleton (L1022), were sent up to intercept a Heinkel 111. Visibility was very poor and they landed at Montrose with no confirmed results. The ORB reads:

> Green Section were ordered off to investigate aerial attack on shipping 10 miles east of Arbroath... Heinkel 111 was sighted by Green Leader who was too close to open fire. Green 2. [Waterston] delivered a No.1 attack and fired 800 rounds before Heinkel 111 climbed into the clouds and escaped.

Meanwhile, at Dyce, Bill Caister flying XT-T (K9998) nosed over on landing as a result of the sticky mud-covered surface of the aerodrome. The aircraft was left balanced on the tip of its starboard wing, propeller boss and two blades. Caister managed to slide open and lock back the canopy before dropping open the access hatch. He then climbed out and jumped to the ground. His ground crew secured a rope to the tail unit of the Spitfire and it was pulled back over onto its undercarriage. The only damage was to the propeller. The caption to the photograph (opposite) taken of the Spitfire balanced on its nose reads: 'Now I know why you have three-bladed airscrews!'

Patrols continued and on the 14th Wing Commander Menzie and Squadron Leader Wood from 13 Group visited Dyce aerodrome in connection with R/T reception and concern about the surface of the airfield. On this day S/L Stevens was attached to RAF Station, Turnhouse. The next day 603 saw completion of the telephone tie line – a direct private line put in by the GPO from B Flight dispersal, Montrose, to A Flight situated in the flying club at Dyce.

On 16 February as the Squadron carried out patrols by day F/O Charles Peel was admitted to the Officers Nursing Home in Edinburgh for an operation on his leg to remedy an unrelated problem with his knee. B Flight also carried out practice flying at night from Montrose.

On the 20th P/O Alen Wallace relinquished his commission in the RAFVR on appointment to a commission in the Auxiliary Air Force.

On the 22nd Red and Yellow Sections of A Flight were forced to land at Montrose due to the poor conditions at Dyce. On the 24th Count Stevens returned to 603 Squadron from Turnhouse and on the 27th Alen Wallace received news of his appointment to Flying Officer. For the remaining days of the month through patrols and practice flights the pilots continued accumulating flying hours and experience.

On 1 March, W/C Don M. Fleming travelled from operations at Turnhouse to visit Dyce. According to John Young, 7 March 1940:

> ...was a bright day and made up for the dull days. A bandit had been reported over Elgin way and was taking a short cut home via Aberdeen. Both sections – Red with George in the lead, Colin and A.N. Other and Yellow with Laurie Cunningham, Razz and I – had been brought to immediate readiness and were standing by our aircraft all togged-up chatting when 'Scramble Red Section' went up. George was away and as they climbed the bandit went right overhead steering SE, going out of sight in the clear blue sky. It was deep ocean blue. Soon we heard the bandit was down in the sea and George and A.N. Other returned. I will always remember because I was still standing, having been brought to readiness by my aircraft L1070 'Excaliber' when George ignored Barton, our 'Spy' [Intelligence Officer], came over and said, completely conversationally 'As you were saying Dobbin...' The rest is lost in my admiration for his complete *sang froid*. George Denholm and Robertson had shot down 'Weather Willie'. Weather Willie [although referred to by the 603 pilots as a singular was actually any one of the Heinkel He111s of KG26] flew over at high altitude on armed reconnaissance missions and transmitted and whose transmissions were being de-coded and so provided very useful information on German radio traffic. The Squadron shot down 'Weather Willie' on March 7 simply because he transgressed our unspoken rules by venturing too far and going over to look at the fleet. He came over Dyce in clear weather and was whopped! Robertson accurately pinpointed the position in the sea of the survivors of the He111 as 60 miles E magnetic from Carnoustie. Robertson's aircraft eventually needed refuelling and re-arming and I volunteered to take off and take over from him which, after a moment or two was agreed.

Top left: Caister's accident on 9 February 1940.
Top right: Robbie in XT-H. Note that he has installed his own mirror.
Middle right: Sheep has yet to follow suit.
Middle left: Dyce, March/April 1940. Bill Douglas, George Denholm, Sheep Gilroy and Ian Ritchie.
Bottom left: Dyce, A Flight, 1940, in the flying club. From left to right: Jack Haig, Ken Macdonald, George Denholm and Bill Caister.
Bottom right: RAF Montrose, home to 8 SFTS and B Flight 603 Squadron.

Following Robertson's directions, I did a rough calculation and set off at about 1,000 feet to locate them. Sure enough, at my ETA I saw a large oil slick but no Germans. With revs at 1850, max boost, I had hours of endurance yet. Heading due west, sure enough Colin was right. Carnoustie back again due East but this time much lower. Oil slick again and then into the sun – the dinghy, was it a dinghy? Lower yet. Yes, a mere dot but what to do? Even lower. They were waving. I was not as friendly and to indicate they were my prisoners I went lower beside them and gave a burst of eight guns dropping cartridge cases in a shower quite close. The waving ceased and I orbited the site as I climbed until radio contact was re-established and a fix confirmed, pinpointing their position for rescue. My radar position was ascertained from the new CH Station that had been completed not long before. By then high Cirrus had begun to fill the sky from the south and west and though the sea was mirror smooth the sunlight was filtered to a pale yellow. I dived down again to see if they were still there and then up again. An Anson (N6837) was sent from RAF Leuchars, piloted by Squadron Leader Scott (of 38 Coastal Patrol Squadron, I seem to remember) and took over from me. I climbed and re-fixed my position because tides are strong in that coastal sea, then went down and guided Scott to the dinghy by now sitting on a long oil streak spread by the tide. A launch from the local air firing range eventually reached the area and picked them up. I recall the sea being blue, mirror smooth, with a dot on it. How low do you have to be to see a dinghy in a *rough* sea! I was in the air 2 hours 15 minutes in L1070. Remember, a Spitfire on long range exercise only used 27 gallons an hour and we had 92 useable gallons. We later heard the crew had been picked up, interrogated and later shifted to Canada. Credit was rightly put on Robertson whose initiative in accurately pinpointing the site of the ditching was, of course, the prime factor in this rescue. The next day we were guests of S/Ldr Scott in Anson N6837 for a one hour patrol – to see how the other half or halves of the air force worked. I remember we actually had a sandwich meal and coffee on board, what luxury. Thirty years later I was at a conference to spruce up the TAF weather code and had lunch with the head of the German aviation weather service. I told him the story of 'Weather Willie' taking an unauthorised short cut. It turned out the observer was his brother. I have not yet taken up his offer of a tour round the Deutsche Welterdeinst. Alas, Colin is unable to share it with me.

The 'A.N. Other' to which John refers was Sheep Gilroy.

The Edinburgh RAF Volunteer Reserve unit was also busy at this time preparing its personnel for war.* While its headquarters was in the Scottish capital, flying training was carried out at Grangemouth. In a pamphlet, published by the RAF Benevolent Fund early in 1940, the RAFVR unit lists its instructors as, amongst others, F/Os Fred 'Rusty' Rushmer, Laurie Cunningham and Robin Waterston. Another name which appeared was that of F/L Chalmers Watson who had been with the Squadron during the early 30s flying the Wapiti and had left 603 to join the RAFVR as the unit's Chief Flying Instructor as appointed by Scottish Aviation Ltd, along with other 603 veterans F/Ls George Reid and David Young. The Chalmers Watson family features later in the story. By March 1944, W/C Chalmers Watson AFC, was stationed at RAF Ibsley, Hampshire.

On 8 March 1940 Squadron Leaders Ross and Tidd travelled to Dyce from Turnhouse to make an assessment of conditions, returning the following day. Charles Peel was discharged from the Officers Nursing Home and attached to RAF Turnhouse as non-effective sick, supernumerary. For the 603 Squadron personnel, life was becoming increasingly busier and even Ken Macdonald's letters to Mardi became less frequent, for a number of reasons. From Dyce on 8 March he wrote:

Darling,

I'm terribly sorry about not writing for such ages. In the last month I have only written one letter in all – that home, after weeks of trying to get down to writing. I don't know why it is – I used to enjoy writing letters, but nowadays I just can't get into the right frame of mind for it. Partly because nothing happened and partly because there is so little time, but

---

*See appendix for brief history of Edinburgh RAFVR Unit.

mostly because my brain and imagination is rotting so fast that I just cannot think past my immediate environment. Not since I finished your Chinese book have I read anything. I am thoroughly fed up with this war. We are on readiness – or have been 'till recently – from 7 a.m. 'till 7.30 p.m., which doesn't leave much time off. Steve* and George have both been away which left me as Commanding Officer. Yesterday we got a Hun at 27,000 feet. Sheep got it – Robbie, Caister (our Sgt/Pilot) and self were on to it. But of course although I was leading the section I was stooge as usual and the only one not to shoot. We had a 20 minute chase after him out to sea as we had to climb from ground-level. Sheep was patrolling on his own at the time and had a start on us. Halfway up to him in formation it seemed that Robbie and Caister were not flat out although I was, so I told them to go ahead in front if they could go faster, which they did (Firefly isn't a patch on Stickleback – which could leave anything). Sheep got there first and had a crack at him, we were 80 miles out [to sea] by then. Whereupon the Hun dropped his wheels and turned back towards Scotland. So I yelled to the chaps NOT to fire – thinking that maybe we could escort him right back to land and perhaps even get him to land on our aerodrome. Robbie left off his attack immediately having only fired one burst and we escorted him down (he had one engine done in) but he went into the sea about 60 miles from land. Caister had shot at him on the way down. One chap was picked up and has since said that he intended to try and make Leuchars aerodrome. What a scoop if we had forced it down whole on one of our aerodromes. It is my ambition to bring a Hun back alive + machine. But of course it might have been a dodge to get into low cloud and escape.

Funny thing too – coming back we all got separated and hit land in rather thick weather and followed coastline west thinking I was on north side of Moray Firth – and meaning to go on 'till I could identify Inverness and thence home – but damn me if I didn't meet the Forth Bridge! So altogether I do feel a 100% stooge, having led my section into battle from the rear and being the only one not to fire a shot. I quite seriously expect a rudey from God** when he sees the combat report. However, last night we had a piss'p – and tonight a hangover otherwise absolutely nothing has happened. George and Toombs are back tonight, but I haven't seen them. Soon I shall be getting another 12 days leave – within the month I guess. Can't quite decide what to do – if only spring were right here. I should like to go to Skye and see that old chap again if I had someone to go with.*** London is fun, but I feel I want something to stir up my imagination and senses a bit – London is so glittering and unreal that it truly deadens your senses or at most artificially stimulates them like (and with) alcohol. This war is so bloody silly I feel I would like to do something real.

I have to go down to Turnhouse soon to receive a razzberry from the Wing Commander on account of Stickleback because it seems it was all my fault for not warning Thompson that it had a poor 'pick-up' – although of course he had flown it before. As one says 'That's life!'

…sorry about all this tale of woe… I adore getting your letters and always do, even if I don't write back… That letter of yours is the only letter I have had in the last fortnight. I suppose it has been my turn to everyone.

All the boys are in good order. Sheep had German Measles (Hitler's secret weapon) but it only took him 3 days to shoot them all down – yesterday was his 4th day. You just can't keep a good Sheep down. Ian too is back from flu. Black is here and sends his love and promises to write you in a day or two.

We have never been in such a woman free existence ever since we came here. None of

---

*'Steve' was another, somewhat friendlier, nickname of S/L E.H. 'Count' Stevens, used by a number of his closest friends.

**This would most probably be the AOC 13 Group, AVM Richard Saul.

***It is most likely that Ken and Mardi stayed in the Sligachan Inn during their visit to Skye the previous year, in which case the 'old man' was in fact Norman Collie, the famous mountaineer and scientist. Richard Hillary stayed at the Sligachan Inn in March 1940 and also refers to Collie in his book *The Last Enemy*.

us knows any nor sees any. In fact we never get off the Station more than once a week. As we are on 'till 7.30 (getting later and later) it is about 9 o'clock by the time we are washed etc: then the pubs shut at 9.30 up here and Aberdeen is 25 minutes by car away. So you see we are a bit foxed for frollies. But it saves money – which is why one comes to Aberdeen I suppose. Must 'push-off'!   Lots and lots of love.

On the 11th, the Squadron were busy with operational and co-operational flying as well as practice flights. Count Stevens and Ken Macdonald visited RAF Turnhouse where Ken was to spend some time familiarising himself with the tasks of controller. On the 13th P/O Brian Carbury returned from attachment to RAF Turnhouse where he had undergone familiarisation of fighter control.

On the 16th AVM Richard Saul, AOC 13 Group, W/C Chamberlain and S/L Woods visited Dyce. Whilst at Dyce the AOC and Chamberlain spoke with Ken Macdonald who was still awaiting a 'razzberry' for the accident in which Sgt Thompson had pranged Stickleback. In a letter written to Mardi later that evening Ken informed her of the eventual outcome:

This is just nothing at all except a note to tell you that I'm becoming a little fed up with flying up and down the coast round here day after day. I informed the 'Gruppe' that I was about to do a 'Sector Reconnaissance' (whatever that is!) and went over the clouds to Skye. It was heaven winging along Loch Alsh [Kyle of Loch Alsh] and along to Kyleakin peaceful as ever although not in sun – clouds were down on the Coullin, but on turning Northward up the scattered coast there was sun shining ahead on the snow on those wild hills I had meant to show you. What a view and what a coast for yachting. I wished for time and petrol to go to Mallaig, I shall next time. Came back by Durnoch Firth and Tain. Feel glad now, it all only took an hour and a half and yet it was like a glimpse into another world and good to see it still exists unchanged. I could almost see us drinking beers outside that pub in Kyleakin. All the boys are out tonight at one party or another – but I've got to such a state of unreliableness I just can't stand messing around in the very depressing 'ultra-modern' cocktail bars in Aberdeen. Good beer in a country local – now *that* is *pints* different. Really am getting fed up with being sociable at all. If it wasn't for 'the boys' who are of course a never-ending source of amusement of whom I could never tire, I would go mad with Mess life. Like Garbo 'I want to be a lawn.'

'God' was here today – 'quite affable' (as you would say). I can't take him much though, I must say.

I also went home for a couple of quick nights last week – partly to see the Wing Commander to get a razzberry re. Stickleback. He was damned decent though and only read through a letter from 'God' saying I had incurred his displeasure or some rot and then he said 'Well, you won't be hearing anything more about that. I hear you got a Heinkel the other day etc etc etc. Come and have a drink.'

Firefly has turned out a dud – won't start and goes very slow, and not very well or nice to fly. So I got thoroughly fed up and, as luck would have it, we got another almost (in fact quite) split new and the very latest model Spitfire the other day – so, by a very shrewd piece of work, I bagged it and gave Firefly the breeze. This one now is without doubt the finest yet. It starts instantaneously and out flies and out climbs all the rest and flies straight and level as a planet at all speeds. It is a miracle – but as yet without a name.

Have just started 'Gone With the Wind' – marvellously written… My letters are incredibly 'ego' but excuse – difficult to picture anyone else's world these days. I consider we have put up a devilish black over Finland, and now blaming Sweden makes it all quite nauseatingly worse – we'll see. Lots of love from Black.

Ken

On 17 March, Group Captain Carnegie was another high-ranking officer to pay A Flight a visit. Pilot Officers Douglas Mackenzie and Bill Douglas were posted back from 7 FTS, Peterborough, where they had been sent to complete their flying training. Whilst Mackenzie was destined to lose his life in a tragic accident, Bill Douglas eventually became one of the longest and most dedicated servants of the Squadron.

Dyce, March 1940. Seated, from left to right: F/O J. G. E. Haig; F/L George Denholm; S/L E. H. Stevens; F/O H. K. Macdonald; F/O Alen Wallace. Standing, from left to right: Sgt J. R. Caister; F/O I. S. Ritchie; F/O J. S. Morton; P/O G. K. Gilroy; P/O A. Barton and W/O J. Dalziel.

Between 08.45 and 09.10 on the 17th Red Section (George Denholm [L1067], Robbie Robertson [L1050] and Jack Haig [L1048]) intercepted an enemy aircraft off Peterhead and Aberdeen. The ORB recorded:

> Red Section: Ordered at 08.42 to investigate unidentified aircraft off Aberdeen and Peterhead.
> Red 1. Intercepted enemy aircraft possibly a Ju88 off Aberdeen about 09.15 and fired a burst of 2 seconds before enemy aircraft was lost in clouds. No fire was returned from enemy aircraft. Red 2. Did not see enemy aircraft. Red 3. Intercepted enemy aircraft off Peterhead about 09.20 and after firing a burst of 4 seconds the enemy aircraft disappeared in clouds. From the description the enemy aircraft was a Dornier. No cine film was exposed.

On 19 March tragedy struck when P/O G.I. Thomson was killed in Spitfire L1026, which crashed on North Clochtow Farm, Slains, Aberdeenshire due to an error in judgement of position in poor visibility.

The next day John Boulter was hospitalised following an accident in Spitfire XT-D, L1022, when he collided with an Oxford while landing at Montrose aerodrome. Sadly, an accident in almost identical circumstances claimed his life.

On 21 March, P/Os Douglas Mackenzie and Bill Douglas were sent to B Flight. On the 25th Sheep Gilroy escaped injury when his Spitfire, K9926, collided with an Avro Anson during take-off from Dyce aerodrome. Both aircraft had been in the process of taking to the air. Night flying took place at Montrose and John Young recognised a particular shortfall associated with this:

> One of the problems I had with 603 was that they had no night-flying experience and it was my job to see that they underwent the necessary practice on Spitfires. This was carried out at Montrose.
> The question arose from us instructors as to how we were going to get Gilroy into line and motivate him to, amongst other things, accumulate the necessary five hours night-flying and to check that his instrument flying was alright. It was a great problem because the fact was he wasn't interested in doing anything else than being a day-time fighter pilot. Underneath his very nice, thoughtful exterior was a young man in a hurry. He was sometimes impatient with me as I tried to impart the importance of, amongst many things, *more* instrument flying and *more* formation attacks.

Montrose, 1940. XT-D collides with an Airspeed Oxford. Boulter and two of the Oxford crew were injured. B Flight dispersal is in the background with two 603 Spitfires and pilot's hut in front of gun butts.

Another picture of the wreckage after the collision of XT-D and an Airspeed Oxford.

On 1 April the weather was extremely bad and no flying took place from either airfield. F/O Alen Wallace and P/O Albert Barton visited Captain Fletcher of the coastguards to investigate reports of bandits received from the Bridge of Don the previous night. By now 603 Squadron had accumulated a great many flying hours during the standing patrols between Dundee and Aberdeen and the Spitfires began to run out of engine hours.

The 2nd, 3rd and 4th of April saw sufficient improvement in the weather for patrols and practice flights to resume. On the 4th Flying Officer Hector MacLean of 602 Squadron was sent over from Drem in LO-E, L1040, to reinforce the unit. It was the first time a member of his family had returned to the airfield by air since his uncle, then Lieutenant A.C.H. MacLean, had been seconded from the Royal Scots to the RFC and reported there for duty in 1913.

In actual fact B Flight did not require MacLean himself, only the aircraft but as he later recorded, his Spitfire, 'E-Edward', was the slowest aeroplane in 602! Years later Hector MacLean recalled his time at Montrose and the difficulties landing at the aerodrome:

...one did indeed require a steady hand to cope with the sudden loss of air speed when your aeroplane passed over the dunes as it approached from the sea. It was, I think, caused by the west wind rising over the dunes leaving a patch of calm air below just in the touchdown area inside the aerodrome. Although I approached with a good margin of flying speed the Spitfire dropped out of my hands onto the grass just beyond the dunes. Fortunately the undercarriage took it so I taxied in rather sheepishly to the 603 dispersal, which looked rather like a poor relation at the north end of the aerodrome. Either 603 did not notice or they were once more too polite to comment! It turned out they did not really want me; but they needed 'E' for Edward having run out of engine hours on their North Sea operation, named Viken Zero. The object was to catch the wily Heinkels and Ju88s who had been sneaking in under the radar cover to bomb and strafe merchant ships and fishing boats, and even light houses. This did not improve their reputation on the east coast of Scotland, but in spite of that I had to admit a grudging respect for the German air crews engaged on this work. They were hard to find but when we did they would be outnumbered, outpaced and out gunned. Without handy cloud cover they were doomed. In August the situation would be reversed. We would be up against German fighters, not just bombers, and we would be heavily outnumbered. The enemy must soon have got wind of 603 and Dyce and Montrose, because they became fewer and hard to catch.

Flight Lieutenant 'Rusty' Rushmer, a courteous and efficient auxiliary officer was in command of the detachment.

Despite not being required, Rusty Rushmer allowed Hector MacLean to take part in four patrols before returning to Drem on 10 April.

The Squadron fighting patrols continued on a daily basis in addition to practice flights. On 7 April, following a period of office duties after the operation on his leg, Charles Peel ceased to be attached sick at RAF Turnhouse and proceeded to B Flight. On the 9th, news came through that Germany had invaded Denmark and Norway. The next day Jack Haig crashed his Spitfire on landing at Dyce. He was unhurt in the incident.

On the 14th 603 was ordered to move from Dyce and Montrose to RAF Drem. The station commander at the time was Group Captain Charles Keary, who had been 603's first adjutant. 603 were replaced by 602 Squadron and the Viken Zero standing patrols continued unabated from Montrose. 602's Hector MacLean later recorded:

In the pilot's hut we were connected with Dyce by a special operational line which terminated on a small plate with a little black flap. This would fall down with a buzz if the control room required our services. In filthy weather we would sit in the hut at night at readiness watching the flap which used to quiver behind a catch before it fell. Frequently it only just quivered but did not fall. Sighs of relief, but we were sorely tempted to file a groove under that catch. Chewing gum would have been too obvious!

... Montrose housed a busy flying training school, operating Airspeed Oxfords and Miles Masters. On the station we were tolerated with mixed emotions. Our aeroplanes were envied, but our airmen did not quite match up to the servile demeanour expected in a flying training school. Inevitably their flying program would be interrupted by repeated operational scrambles with Very lights fired from the watch office to warn training aircraft out of the way while we took off. Unfortunately some pupils were too slow. One of the masters got in the way and clattered into my aircraft as we careered out from our dispersal. Fortunately there were no injuries – we faced a nerve-wracking enquiry as the result of which the fighters and myself, as section leader in particular, were found one third to blame; but I went unpunished and unrepentant. Indeed I was lucky to be alive because the Master was carrying a practice bomb which could easily have exploded and blown us all to Kingdom Come.'

... I have pleasant memories of Montrose. The mess was comfortable and the beer, which was brewed locally by a Newcastle company, was the best I've ever tasted. Our cars ran well on a little extra 100 octane petrol milked from the bowser, without which we could have been stranded car-less as the result of frequent moves which gobbled up petrol. The Montrose people were very hospitable.

The flying instructors, who included some RFC pilots in their forties, were men of steel charging off into the black with night-flying pupils. They did a real job for the RAF and must have trained hundreds of pilots.

Drem

By 15 April 603 Squadron had completed its move to Drem via Turnhouse where work continued on the airfield. According to John Young:

My earliest memories of RAF Turnhouse was that the airfield itself was terrible. The surface was really unsuitable for winter operations and indeed was being extensively re-surfaced and re-turfed when I arrived. The condition of the airfield at Grangemouth was a bit better than Turnhouse, but the grass was very long. In fact they had to give up Turnhouse quite soon after and the whole Squadron was shifted over to Drem while the work was being carried out [14.4.40]. We moved by means of BOAC Ensign aeroplanes. I didn't fly one of the Squadron Spitfires at the time and was therefore not selected to fly one of them to Drem.

The land on which RAF Drem was established was owned by Dr Chalmers Watson, a relative of 603 veteran and CFI for the Edinburgh RAFVR unit, Flight Lieutenant I.E. Chalmers Watson. Dr Chalmers Watson was responsible for producing the very first herd of tuberculin-tested milking cows in Britain. His wife was the former actress, Lily Brayton, who had played the leading role in Chu Chin Chow on the London stage during WWI. The couple lived in Greywalls, a large house next to Muirfield Golf Club in Gullane, where many of the 603 officers were entertained whilst at Drem. Today the house is a hotel.

Top and bottom: 603 Squadron ground crew, April 1940 at Drem.

Charles Keary had left 603 before the outbreak of war to take over as OC RAF Drem, then the home of 13 FTS. The new CO imposed the strict discipline and spit and polish routines associated with such pre-war establishments. He was enthusiastically supported by his staff but all his efforts came to an abrupt halt in October 1939 when 602 (City of Glasgow) Squadron moved in and the flying training school moved out. Whilst 602 took its flying very seriously (it was from Drem that they intercepted the Luftwaffe Ju 88s on 16 October 1939) it had its own interpretations of the Kings Regulations and Air Council instructions. Keary probably felt he was fighting a losing battle and for the former member of their unit things were not likely to change with the arrival of 603!

Drem was an aerodrome with a severe slope, which accounted for a large percentage of the accidents there. Many veterans recall that in the early days it was also an airfield where the long grass was an ever-present problem. There were some basic wooden huts, a wooden mess and a number of hangars. Once again the airmen were billeted off the base. There was no night landing guidance system as 'Batchy' Atcherley's famous Drem lighting had yet to be invented. The landing path was therefore marked with gooseneck flares and a Glim lamp at either end. The only other aid was a Chance light. During Hiram Smith's stay at Drem at the end of 1939 he had experimented with a slide projector to facilitate the correct angle of approach at night – red meant low, white correct and green too high. This ingenious experiment was subsequently forgotten.

Each flight had a system of rotation of its available pilots. Three groups of three pilots were placed on the staggered states of readiness and those left were in a position whereby they could apply for leave, carry out practice flights, or sit around. This system allowed all pilots to accumulate valuable flying hours, formation flying experience and hone their navigation and general flying skills on type. Naturally the experienced, senior pilots led each section and in many cases this was continued with the No.2 being the next most experienced pilot and the No.3 being the least. This intense period of flying activity had gone a long way towards honing their flying skills. But, as noted, what little combat flying those in the unit had experienced had been against Luftwaffe bombers, not fighters and it was tragic that once the Squadron moved south to 11 Group, despite the many hours that the pilots had spent working hard in the air, death came swiftly for the experienced and inexperienced alike.

On 15 April the ground crew personnel hastily went about their duties while the pilots carried out fighting patrols and practice flying. John Young reflects on an incident involving Ras:

> We thanked God for his preservation on one occasion when he was descending into Drem in bad weather. The controller was not very skilled and for some reason or another he was descending him from south to north, instead of east to west. Razz saw the heather of the Lammamuir Hills in front of him, and pulled back on the Spitfire control column so hard that he bent the wings. New wings were fitted and the aircraft flew all the better for them!

On the 17th, Pilot Officer Bill Douglas crash-landed on a ploughed field close to the aerodrome at Drem, whilst attempting to land in a rain storm. The undercarriage of the Spitfire, K9956, 'Eboracum' (York), dug into the soil and the aircraft nosed-over onto its back. Fortunately the pilot was unhurt and managed to struggle free from the inverted cockpit.

On 19 April the Squadron carried out 'fighting patrols, practice flying and night flying'. It is no wonder that photographs taken prior to the Squadron's move to RAF Hornchurch, show a number of the pilots looking very tired. Some of their personal letters confirm this. Once the fighting in the south began, it would be unrelenting and exhaustion soon resulted in loss of life.

On 20 April, the pilots flew fighting patrols and night flying exercises. S/L Rossie Brown returned from leave as did F/L Fred Rushmer. The following day saw practice flying during the hours of daylight and darkness.

On the 22nd, with practice flying the only aerial activity of the day, F/L George Denholm returned to RAF Turnhouse where he was attached for a period of duty in the operations room. F/O Geoff Wynne-Powell was posted back to 603 following a period with 13 Group. The next day flying was again intense with fighting patrols and practice day and night flying.

On 25 April, F/O Laurie Cunningham was granted 12 days leave and P/O Albert Barton was attached to 602 Squadron at Dyce, for intelligence duties. The duty pilots carried out practice flying only. The next day the pilots carried out patrols and practice day and night flying. The Spitfire was not best suited for the latter, as it was difficult to see clearly over the nose of the aircraft when approaching a flare path at night and the flames from the

17 April 1940, Drem. Bill Douglas' 'York' crashed on approach.

exhaust disrupted the pilot's night vision. A good example of this was when P/O Stapleton jumped by parachute after the undercarriage of his Spitfire L1025 had been damaged while attempting a night landing. Stapme was ordered to climb and bale out but landed heavily and damaged a knee. He kept the injury from the MO in case he was taken off flying. In 1998, after years of discomfort, the knee was replaced.

On the 28th, F/O Robin Waterston returned from leave to find 603 preparing for a move from Drem to Turnhouse. The next day saw no flying, P/O Barton rejoined and P/O Dudley Stewart-Clark was posted from Abbotsinch. There was no flying on the last day of April 1940.

On 1 May the duty pilots carried out practice flights and P/O Black Morton returned from leave. On the 3rd, F/O Wynne-Powell and Black Morton travelled to RAF Ternhill to ferry two Spitfires to Drem. The next day Count Stevens travelled to Turnhouse in advance of the move there.

Turnhouse and Dyce

On 5 May, the Squadron carried out the move from Drem to Turnhouse but to the dismay of Charles Keary, 602 Squadron moved back in! S/L Rossie Brown ceased attachment to Turnhouse and returned to 603. P/O Albert Barton ceased attachment to 603 and returned to Turnhouse. S/L Stevens was notified that he was to be posted away but, such was his opposition to a move away from 603, on reporting to Turnhouse he quickly let his feelings be known to his superiors.

On 7 May, P/O Bill Douglas was posted to 3 Bomber and Gunnery School, Aldergrove as a staff pilot. He moved to 3 BGS, Evanton on 3 July and 7 OTU, Hawarden on 5 September. On 16 September 1940 he joined 610 Squadron at Acklington.

On 10 May fighting patrols were carried out by the duty pilots. The ORB recorded: 'All leave stopped. J.C. Boulter and I.S. Ritchie recalled. Holland and Belgium invaded by Germany,' which gave added motivation to the pilots in their practices. On 11 May 1940, A Flight 602 Squadron moved to Dyce were they joined forces with pilots of 603 Squadron for the first time. Hector MacLean provides an insight into events of this period:

> During our short stay George Gilroy and I were ordered about 2.00 am to investigate a bogey at 25,000 feet. As I was climbing up through the night I decided on plenty of oxygen and gave myself an extra 5,000 foot dose. On the way up the R.T. was infested with music and German voices singing, but at 25,000 feet there was no enemy to be seen. Suddenly I began to feel happy and light-headed. More oxygen perhaps? Then I saw it; the oxygen tube was hanging down loose and disconnected to my mask. There was no time to connect it because I had been without oxygen and was in the process of passing out, so down I went to 15,000 feet in double quick time. Woken from my slumbers and in a hurry to get off the ground I had omitted the elementary precaution of connecting my oxygen tube, and then my attention had been distracted by that wretched German singing. It was a strange business. I have never met anyone else who encountered a similar experience. I was probably hamming into a German programme transmitting from an unusual range as far as Aberdeen.

On 13 May, F/O 'Wimpy' Wynne-Powell received news of his posting from 603 Squadron to Headquarters 13 Group and he left for Leuchars on the 16th. The New Zealander had been with the Squadron for some years and did not fly during the coming battle. He subsequently joined Bomber Command and by November 1943 was OC 623 Squadron, at Downham Market, flying Stirlings.

The next day news came that Holland had surrendered and the fighting in Belgium had intensified. 603 flew patrols, co-operation and practice flights. John Young's spell with them came to an end when he was posted to 249 Squadron at Church Fenton and served with them during the Battle of Britain after which he was given a roving commission to assist newly formed units. He was nicknamed 'Dobbin' by Ian Ritchie, a nickname relating to his well intentioned but laborious school-masterish manner towards the younger pilots in the Squadron whilst carrying out his instructions but doing nothing that would damage the precious Spitfires and/or themselves.

Left: B Flight at readiness. P/Os Noel Benson, Ras Berry and Stapme, and F/O Bubble Waterston working on his car.
Right: RAF Turnhouse, June 1940. P/Os Wimpy Wynne-Powell, Ras Berry and Noel Benson.

On 15 May Flying Officer R.S. Nicholson (Medical) was posted in.

Around this time a number of important modifications on the Spitfire Mk I were carried out by the 603 ground crew personnel. The de Havilland variable pitch (*fine* for take-off and *coarse* for the rest of the flight) three-bladed propeller was replaced on all aircraft in a matter of days by the new de Havilland (or Rotol) three-bladed constant speed (CS) propeller. This new airscrew would adjust automatically to suit any chosen throttle position, giving an overall improved engine performance. A further addition to the Spitfire at this time was the installation of a crow bar in the door flap of each aircraft. An upgrade of the original canopy of the Spitfire included a small pop-out panel designed to reduce the airflow over the hood, the resistance from which invariably meant the pilot had great difficulty opening the canopy in emergencies. The crow bar was for the purpose of levering the hood off its runners in the event of the pilot finding himself trapped even after punching out the panel. Some of the 603 pilots also chose to add their own rear view mirrors until they became one of the official modifications.

Another upgrade was the two-step rudder pedals which were fitted to all frontline Spitfires prior to the Battle of Britain. The upper step was about six inches higher than the lower. In normal flight the pilot sat upright with his feet on the lower pedals but prior to combat he placed them on the two upper pedals which had leather straps, providing a means of keeping the feet in position throughout the rigors of combat. By raising the legs and feet the body was given a more horizontal posture thus improving the pilot's 'blacking out threshold' by at least 1G. This allowed him to maintain tighter turns while retaining his senses.

In the spring of 1940, the RAF replaced the 87 octane fuel used in operational aircraft with 100 octane. In order to use the new fuel engines were modified and ultimately gave improved performance at heights below the full-throttle altitude of 16,500 feet for the Sptifire MkI. This higher octane fuel allowed an increase in supercharger boost from +6 lbs to +12 lbs without risk of detonation and damage to the engine. A pilot could select the boost for a maximum of only five minutes by advancing the throttle 'through the gate' to the fully forward position. This emergency power facility increased maximum speed by 25 mph at sea level and 34 mph at 10,000 feet. It also improved the fighter's climbing capability between sea level and full throttle altitude which was a vital factor during the Battle of Britain.

A further addition to the Spitfires of 603 was the IFF (Identification Friend or Foe) equipment which added approximately 40 lbs to the weight of the aircraft.*

On 16 May all pilots were recalled as a precaution in case of an attempt to invade Britain, although some leave was still granted.

On 17 May the Squadron duty pilots carried out day and night practice flying and Pilot Officers Bill Douglas and Douglas Mackenzie were confirmed in the rank. This was an intense period of patrols, day and night practice flying. Following the recent surgery to his leg, F/O Charles Peel travelled to RAF Halton on the 22nd for an appointment with the CMB hoping to be certified A1b – fit to fly.

---

*The wire aerials strung between the tips of the tailplane and the fuselage reduced the maximum speed by 2 mph but as the lack of such equipment was the chief cause of the infamous 'Battle of Barking Creek,' being able to identify the aircraft on radar from that of the enemy justified the minor reduction in performance.

There was no flying on 23 or 24 May, but on the latter the Squadron pilots attended a lecture given by Flight Lieutenant Blackadder who had recently returned from an intense period of aerial combat during the Battle of France. During the day, F/O Peel returned from RAF Halton having achieved an A1 fitness rating. The following day the 603 pilots were given another lecture this time by Wing Commander Harry Broadhurst who like Blackadder came to relate his experiences of the air fighting in France and the fighter tactics used. Things were hotting up.

On 27 May, F/O John Boulter's move to 603 became permanent when he was posted from RAF Usworth. On the 28th Belgium capitulated and the Squadron carried out patrols, co-operation day and night practice flying. The next day Bolster left Turnhouse to transport 'secret documents' to HQ Fighter Command and returned on 1 June. On 31 May, F/O Barton was posted from 603 to RAF Station, Dyce.*

A famous occasion in the history of 603 Squadron occurred on 2 June 1940, when AVM Richard E. Saul, AOC13(F) Group, presented them with the Squadron badge with the motto 'Gin Ye Daur' (If You Dare). Co-operation and day and night flying were the aerial activities of the day.

On 5 June, P/O Stapme Stapleton crashed Spitfire N3236 on Turnhouse airfield when both flaps and then brakes failed. He had circled the aerodrome three times, each time failing to get down. He was successful on the fourth try. According to Bert Pringle his rigger/fitter:

> He abandoned three previous attempts to land before he finally managed to get down on the fourth. When we examined his aircraft it turned out that the compressed air bottles were faulty. Stapme was lucky, the only injury he received as a result of the crash-landing was a small cut to his forehead.

For some time Count Stevens' shoulder problem had persisted. When pulling the canopy of the Spitfire closed, his right shoulder was inclined to dislocate. This happened repeatedly and eventually led to surgery to rectify the problem. As a result he never flew operationally throughout WWII. Because it was possible for a pilot to close the canopy of a Spitfire with one hand, it has been suggested that, as war became inevitable, Stevens used the problem to avoid combat. What is known is that Stevens was enormously proud of the Edinburgh fighter squadron and saw the arrival of regular officers who were posted to the Squadron at the end of 1939, an intrusion. This despite the fact that they were actually more experienced and were there to offer their particular instructional skills to the unit.**

Following the declaration of war the Air Ministry had sought to 'regularise' the position and on 4 June 1940, sent a regular officer, Squadron Leader W.A. 'Jack' Satchell, to Turnhouse from 5 OTU Aston Down to take over command of 603. He had just completed a Spitfire conversion course after his escape from France and the advancing Germans. Satchell was an excellent fighter pilot and his war record makes interesting reading. Jack and his wife drove up from Lincolnshire, arriving at Turnhouse during the afternoon. The Squadron had not yet realised the full ramifications of embodiment and Stevens was of the belief that they were still living in the elitist pre-war atmosphere. His reception of Jack and his wife was unacceptably cold and, expressing quite unbelievable discourtesy, Stevens did not even invite them into the mess for tea

May/June 1940. 7 ATS Acklington. Jack Haig, Sheep, George Denholm and Ian Ritchie relax during gunnery practice.

---

*By March 1944 S/L Albert Barton was stationed at RAF North Weald.
**It should also be noted that it was an unwritten rule that the CO of an auxiliary squadron should not be sent to fight.

South Queensferry, June 1940. Ching and Sheep.   Ken juggling at South Queensferry.

following their long journey. He merely told them that 603 Squadron could only be commanded by an auxiliary officer and bade them goodbye. Satchell consulted Group HQ who, on this occasion and for reasons unknown, concurred and sent Jack to 141 Squadron at Grangemouth as supernumerary Squadron Leader. He was eventually given command of 302 Squadron, the first Polish fighter squadron to be formed in England, which he commanded during the Battle of Britain. Incidentally, when Jack Satchell was later posted overseas Mrs Satchell stayed at Bo'ness but had no means of transport. Betty Denholm, who lived nearby, was very kind to her and helped her out during this period. Later, Jack Satchell saved the life of Lord David Douglas-Hamilton, who was 603's CO at the time whilst in Malta.

S/L Stevens was appointed as one of three controllers at Turnhouse as well as being nominally CO of 603. On 5 June he was posted 'supernumerary non-effective sick' with his on-going medical problem and F/L George Denholm was appointed acting squadron leader and took command. Count Stevens remained in touch with the Squadron up until his untimely death in 1949.

This period of intensive flying continued and on 8 June, Pilot Officer Don Macdonald was posted to 603 from SFTS, RAF Cranwell. The next day Pilot Officer Douglas Mackenzie inadvertently raised the undercarriage after landing in Spitfire N3026. The aircraft was damaged.

On the 12th, Fred Rushmer, Ken Macdonald and Laurie Cunningham were promoted to Flight Lieutenant but their delight was tempered by the death of a good friend, P/O Douglas Mackenzie, who was killed when his Spitfire crashed near Balerno, Midlothian. Douglas, known as 'Ching' by his friends, had been a trainee chartered accountant when he joined 603 in 1938. His Spitfire, L1050, took off from Turnhouse at 01.10 hours and crashed at Bol of Bere Farm in the Pentland Hills after he was apparently dazzled and disorientated by a searchlight battery. The wreckage of his aircraft was buried on impact with the marshy ground where it remained for many years before re-emerging over a period by the will of nature and stripped for souvenirs by the farmer, Mr Prentice, when he came across it. Once the mud had been removed, the guns were found to be in pristine condition. Ching Mackenzie was a tall, good-looking Scot whose premature death was deeply felt by his colleagues.

On 13 June, co-operation and day and night flying practice took place. Sheep Gilroy crash-landed on Turnhouse aerodrome with the undercarriage of Spitfire L1048, still retracted. Some modification had been made to his aircraft and he was preoccupied with this as he approached the airfield, touched down smoothly but was surprised to hear the tail wheel running along the ground but no landing wheels. At that moment he realised he had forgotten to lower his undercarriage.

On 14 June 1940, the Germans entered Paris. For the next nine days the pilots of 603 Squadron flew no patrols, only day and night practice flying and co-operation flying with searchlight and anti-aircraft batteries.

Above: Scamel (who doesn't feature in the story), Ching and Sheep bathing. Inset: Ching snatches Sheep's towel.

Below: Bubble Waterston wrestling with a colleague as his girlfriend (Patricia Allt, at her home in Edinburgh) looks on.

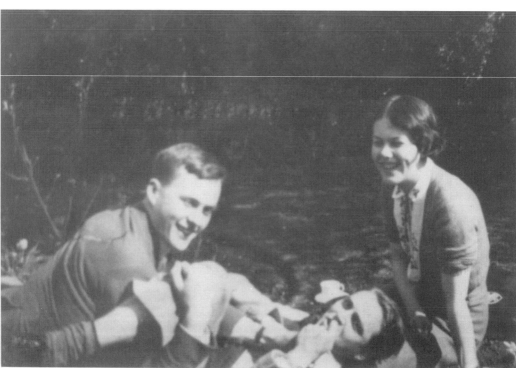

Left: 'Tigger' at Turnhouse, June 1940.
Right: RAF Montrose. F/L Pat Gifford (pilot) and F/O Ken Macdonald as passenger. Miles Master is behind the gun butts.

On 16 June, Pilot Officer Graham Hunter travelled to RAF Halton to go before yet another medical board. The round-trip of three days to travel to the Queen Mary RAF Hospital at RAF Halton, Buckinghamshire, appear before the CMB, and the return trip to Scotland had by now become a monthly occurrence.

Brian Carbury's Spitfire MK I 'Aorangi' XT-L. He soon had the XT-W code.

Although 603's time at Turnhouse was busy, the personnel also made the most of their time off. Since the outbreak of war, leave was freely granted to the pilots and on an almost weekly basis right up until they moved south they were away visiting friends and relatives. During the evenings the nearest watering hole for the officers was the Maybury Roadhouse, a white art deco building on the east end of Turnhouse Road, which still exists today. Many of the pilots frequently travelled into the capital where they visited clubs and pubs. On occasions these outings became lengthy drinking sessions. Although they visited the Balmoral which later extended an open invitation to the officers of 603, one of the favourite hostelries was the D'Guise night club, part of the Caledonian hotel. There were the inevitable high jinks and Charles Peel was one of the liveliest characters in the Squadron. On one occasion a drinking game involved the laying of a bottle of whisky on a table with the top jutting out over an edge. Many recall Peel lying under the table, in-line with the bottle top, and on the given order the top was removed and the young flying officer drank as fast as he could. In those days they also drove back to the base having had a skin-full. There were frequent mishaps!

Dyce and Montrose

On 21 June B Flight moved to RAF Montrose and Graham Hunter travelled to the Military Hospital at St Hughes College, Oxford. The doctors at his last medical board had recommended further surgery to try to correct his injuries. In his absence, he was posted from 603 Squadron to RAF Turnhouse as non-effective sick.

Squadron Leader Stevens had also been before the CMB at RAF Halton and returned to Turnhouse on this day.

On 24 June the duty pilots flew night-fighting patrols, co-operative and practice flights. P/O Don Macdonald was sent from Turnhouse to join B Flight. The next day France stopped fighting against Germany and Italy at 00.35 hours.

On 26 June, Turnhouse was bombed in what was the first ever air raid against this RAF station and the first on Scotland in the war. It was a night raid and Flight Lieutenant Ken Macdonald was ordered up to intercept any intruders. Ken later recalled the events of that night for a radio broadcast:

Post-Script to the News
By
Flight Lieutenant H.K. Macdonald
June 27th 1940

Tuesday's was the first night raid over our part of the coast. When the enemy were detected I was ordered to go up and *look* for them – that was between midnight and one a.m. I flew around, peering into the gloom – and for some time all I could see was an occasional searchlight beam snooping around the sky. I'd almost begun to think the Hun had managed to get away, when I suddenly spotted, a long way off, flashes on the ground and in the air. 'Ah, anti-aircraft fire.' I thought, 'that means an enemy.' So I went over to have a look, and when nearly there, I saw a Heinkel sliding across the sky really beautifully floodlit by our searchlights. Anti-aircraft fire was going off absolutely all round it. It really was a magnificent sight. After all, I had – well, what you might call – a ringside seat.

I could just imagine the feelings of the chaps at the other end of these searchlight beams – *and* the feelings of the ack-ack gunners too – turning their handles and twiddling their knobs, 'in action' at last on their first night raid – the first time searchlights up this way have had a chance to catch the enemy. You see, we can always have fun flying, whether the enemy calls round or not. But the searchlight and anti-aircraft boys have to sit there in the open, wet or fine, and just wait… However, now they really were at it.

There was a terrific firework display in progress, and the Heinkel looked to me rather like a puzzled old woman suddenly caught in a spotlight. I'd come up more or less from behind and there he was, just ambling along, not quite knowing what to do. As a matter of fact I imagine the pilot was pretty well dazzled with all the lights on him. I got into position right behind and just below, got my sights on him, and pressed the gun-button. A shower of sparks flew out of the enemy, and clouds of smoke, and he wallowed a bit. Then he went down in a slow spiral dive into the darkness. That was the last I saw of him – though I did catch the glare of his incendiary bombs on the ground. He must have jettisoned these as he dropped.

Incidentally, while I am talking about this raid, there is one rather important point. When you hear the sound of aeroplanes at night don't immediately jump to the conclusion that they must be German. Remember many of them are our own fighters on patrol or chasing after the enemy.

One thing about this night fighting is that you feel much more the lone wolf than you do by day. We operate more on our own, but of course with our allies. The guns and searchlights. I expect you've wondered as you've watched the searchlights at work how much good they'd be. As a matter of fact we've wondered too what chance they had of lighting up a raider without lighting up *us* as well. Well now we've had our answer. Co-operation between ground and air defences really was one hundred percent.

This version of events was re-written by Ken for the broadcast. The original was more in fighter-pilot parlance. Ken's sister, Ewen, recalled hearing this broadcast during the evacuation of her family from Kent to a village near Chester.

When the alarm was first raised, Flying Officer Jack Haig was airborne in Spitfire N3190. Running low on fuel, he requested permission to land but, with the possibility the intruders were still in the area, control replied: 'Negative we can't switch flare-path lights on or bombs will find target.' Jack stooged around for a while staring anxiously at his instrument panel before deciding to climb over open countryside and turn his aircraft towards The Lang Whang (the A70 Edinburgh to Moffat road). As he did so, to his horror '…the motor went phut'. It was too dark to force land: 'Fortunately, as I was heading out towards the hills I received orders to bale out.' This he did successfully but sprained an ankle on landing. Jack's aircraft subsequently crashed near Harperrigg Reservoir. It was some time before the sirens signalled the 'All Clear' and a rumour had begun to circulate that a German parachutist had been seen to come down in the Pentlands Hills area. Meanwhile Jack hobbled to the first cottage where the occupants were non too friendly, believing him to be the enemy. Having quickly convinced the farmer he was a Scot, he was given a lift back to Turnhouse in a lorry. As they approached the airfield the lorry and its passengers crashed into a bomb crater!

Since the retreat from France and the evacuation of Dunkirk, 603 was keen to get involved.

Despite the attack on their airfield, with the ensuing offensive action against the Luftwaffe bombers, the duty pilots still managed to carry out a hectic schedule of day and night fighting patrols, co-operation and practice flying, as was the case on 28 June, the day Pilot Officer A.G.C. Colquhoun joined B Flight and 25-year-old F/O Robbie Robertson was seriously injured in an accident while out horse-riding locally to the aerodrome. Having been knocked unconscious in a fall from his horse, he was taken to the Military Hospital at Edinburgh Castle where doctors diagnosed a fractured skull. Local newspapers later included details of the riding accident when announcing news of his marriage: 'For two weeks he lay unconscious, during which time his fiancée, now his wife, kept vigil at his bedside.' It has been said that this injury may have contributed to the cause of the accident on 12 December 1943, in which he was killed.

Robertson was born in Falkirk in 1915, where his father, George Robertson, ran the family plumbing business at Howgate, Falkirk. Colin was one of three children, an older brother George, a younger sister, Maisie, and a younger brother, Richard, whom Colin was particularly close to. He had joined the RAF as a 'Halton Brat' but won a scholarship to RAF Cranwell where he excelled as a student pilot and fencer, winning a number of medals for the latter. He passed out from Cranwell as recipient of the Sword of Honour. He was described by his 603 colleagues as a fun-loving, likeable Scot who immediately settled in and was popular with both pilots and ground crew. LAC John Rendall recalled the time he was instructed to install one of the newly arrived bullet-proof windscreens on Robertson's Spitfire XT-H 'Hell':

Top: RAF Montrose, 1940. XT-H 'Hell' of Colin Robertson. Miles Master is in background with Macdonald and Gifford.
Bottom: Flaps down on approach to RAF Montrose.

The task involved about eighty bolts and our knuckles were skinned by the time we finished the job. It took a while because you had to avoid over-tightening the bolts in case the [perspex] forward canopy cracked. When the task was complete we stood back to admire our work. At that moment Robertson came in to the hangar and stepped up on to the wing to have a closer look. Impressed by the new thick piece of laminated glass which offered him extra protection he mumbled a few words along the lines of 'We'll see how tough it is,' picked up one of the spare bolts and flung it at the glass from point blank range. To our amazement the windscreen crazed and we stared at each other in disbelief. The job had to be started all over again with a new piece of glass. Afraid that he had prompted an adverse reaction from us, the much amused Robertson leapt from the wing and retreated from the hangar to leave us to it.

He was a very nice chap who willingly chatted with the ground crew chaps unlike some of the others during the earlier days of the war and pre-war.

B Flight, Montrose, July 1940. Back: Corps Harry Barnes and Cantley; F/Sgt Mackie; Sgts Angy Gillies and Sanderson; Corp Murray. Front: P/O Ras Berry; F/L Fred Rushmer and P/O Noel Benson.

On 29 June Graham Hunter was discharged from hospital in Oxford. Sadly, Graham failed in his bid to rejoin his colleagues as a fighter pilot and went on to play a valuable part working with RDF and radar. By 1944 he was at RAF Ventor, Isle of Wight and at the time of writing he and Geoff Wynne-Powell are the two remaining survivors of the pre-war Squadron.*

Meantime, the 603 pilots continued with day and night patrols and practice flying. On the 30th A Flight moved from Turnhouse to Dyce and Ras, flying Spitfire N3105, recorded: 'I fired at a German a/c – no result.'

July 1940

603 Squadron were in action from 1st and 2nd and throughout July carrying out patrols in defence of the Scottish east coast, whilst practice continued. On the 3rd Pilot Officers Philip Cardell and Bill Read and Sergeant Pilots Jack Stokoe and Alfred Sarre were posted from 263. Cardell was sent from Turnhouse to B Flight while Read, Stokoe and Sarre were sent to A Flight.

On 3 July a Ju88A-2 (4D+1IS) of 8/KG30 was shot down by the Green Section Spitfires of Flying Officer Carbury, and Pilot Officers Berry and Stapleton, offshore from Montrose. At 14.05 Ras Berry had been the first to spot the German raider flying at 9,000 feet and heading south. Having established the aircraft as a Ju88 the pilots closed for attack but as they did so the German pilot began evasive manoeuvres and flew into a large bank of cloud. The Spitfires followed and Brian Carbury instructed Ras and Stapme to remain above the cloud whilst he stayed below in the event the Ju88 re-emerged. The Ju88 reappeared above the cloud and Ras carried out a head-on attack firing a two-second burst. Carbury and Stapme followed him in firing short bursts. Stapme recalled there being no return fire from the German gunners. The German pilot jettisoned the bomb load and dived for the cloud but the three Spitfire pilots pressed home their attacks. Carbury carried out a No.1 attack closing from 250 to 50 feet, Ras delivered a further head-on attack and two No.1 attacks before running out of ammunition. Stapme fired approximately 215 rounds during a No.1 attack, opening fire from 300 and closing to 150 feet. The enemy aircraft was visibly damaged and lost height before finally crashing into the sea. Brian Carbury dived down in search of survivors and spotted an oil patch and three crew in lifejackets. A rubber dinghy was seen nearby. Carbury managed to attract the attention of a number of trawlers in the vicinity, one of which later picked up one survivor. Of the crew of four, Feldwebel O. Heidinger, Unteroffiziers F. Rabe and P. Wieczoreck were killed and Unteroffizier R. Hehringlehner was rescued

---

*Post-war Graham Hunter lived in St Andrews with his wife but latterly moved south to be near his daughter at Malmesbury, Wiltshire. Despite the injuries received in 1939, which negated any wartime flying career, today he is an enthusiastic golfer.

from the icy waters of the North Sea and taken prisoner. The pilots had been scrambled at 13.46 and landed back at Montrose 50 minutes after the combat without further action.

Ras later recorded his assessment of the patrol and his 'share' (recorded in his log book as 'destroyed' whilst flying XT-N, L1046):

> I claim this destroyed myself, although two others fired at it fifteen minutes before without result.... The thing was that fifteen minutes later I found him again in the cloud and I went straight in and gave him a hell of a long burst, head on, and he went straight down into the sea. I did not see him go down because of the cloud, but it was confirmed and the crew may have been saved.

Red Section at Dyce shot down two German aircraft during two separate interceptions, which were later confirmed destroyed. The ORB recorded:

Red Section:

Time Up: 15.43 hours. Time Down: 16.40 hours.
1. S/L GL Denholm
2. P/O D Stewart-Clark
3. Sgt Arber.

'Section attacked He111, 25 miles NE of Peterhead. E/A came down in sea. All Red Section received hits in their machines.'

The three Spitfires attacked the 'He111' at 16.00 hours which turned out to be a Ju88 of 8/KG30 which crashed as stated above at 16.15 hours. The crew were reported missing.

Red Section:

Time Up: 18.58 hours. Time Down: 19.23 hours.

1. F/O IS Ritchie
2. P/O Gilroy
3. Sgt Caister

'Red Section attacked Ju88 off Stonehaven. E/A seen by Coastguards to crash into the sea.'

Montrose July/August 1940. B Flight dispersal. On ground are XT-M and XT-R flown by Hillary and Waterston. Airborne is XT-R flown by Boulter.

AC1 George Knox with 'Auld Reekie'. He painted many of the names on the 603 Spits at the start of war.

The Spitfires of Ritchie, Gilroy and Caister shot down yet another Ju88 of 8/KG30. The four crew members were not found. Red Section landed safely back at Dyce.

On Thursday 4 July, the Squadron was involved in more daytime patrols and more practice, to maximise the pilots' experience before the fighting began in earnest. S/L Stevens returned from Prestwick and on the 5th he proceeded to Perth, Leuchars and Arbroath and on the 6th to Montrose and Dyce to assess the bases. 603 also saw the arrival of a new Intelligence Officer, Pilot Officer W.L. Blackbourn, who had been posted from 602 and remained the 'Spy' for a considerable period. P/O Colquhoun was posted to RAF Drem.

On 6 July three new pilots arrived who had been posted to 603 on completion of their conversion training on Spitfires at 5 OTU, RAF Aston Down. Pilot Officer Richard Hillary* and Flying Officers Colin Pinckney and Peter Pease arrived at RAF Turnhouse from where they were allocated to one of the detached flights – Hillary and Pease were sent to B Flight and on entering RAF Montrose, they reported to the station CO, Air Vice-Marshal H.V. Champion de Crespigny** while Colin Pinckney was sent to A Flight. Hillary was known to his friends simply as 'Richard' or 'Dick', but soon after their arrival Colin Pinckney and Peter Pease gained the nicknames of 'Pinker' and 'Popper' respectively. Richard Hillary later wrote fondly of his experiences with 603 Squadron in his best-seller *The Last Enemy*, published on 19 June 1942. His friendship with Pease and Pinckney meant a great deal to him and he referred to it as 'The Triangle of Friendship'. None of the trio survived the war.

By that time F/L Fred 'Rusty' Rushmer was the established B Flight Commander. The 30-year-old was very popular and a good pilot. One of his closest friends was 23-year-old F/O Robin Waterston. Robin used to take Rusty back to the house quite regularly for tea, sometimes with Laurie Cunningham. Rusty and Robin were to die within a week of each other.

Junior members were required to undertake a period of induction before being made operational, which included some menial tasks. One such duty was when A and B Flights were on standby for night-flying operations as it was often the task of newcomers to light and extinguish the flare path to enable the two members of the section on night-flying operations to take off and land. The two fighters took off at ten-minute intervals, so the junior pilot had to jog up and down the flare path, lighting or extinguishing the goose necks as he went numerous times! George Denholm was also keen for them to undergo a week of practice interceptions and attacks on Blenheims capably flown by 248 Squadron (based at Dyce and then Sumburgh) with a detachment at Montrose before becoming operational.

As the new arrivals were settling in, Red Section from Dyce shot down a 'Do.215', 100 miles east-north-east of Aberdeen. The Squadron ORB recorded the following details:

---

* For the complete story of Hillary's life see: *Richard Hillary*, by David Ross. Grub Street 2000.

**AVM Champion de Crespigny's office has survived and today forms part of the main building of the Montrose Aerodrome Museum Society.

F/L Fred Rushmer, P/O Brian Carbury and P/O Noel Benson, B Flight, Montrose, 1940.

6.7.40

Red Section:

Time Up: 12.29 hours. Time Down: 13.37 hours.

1. P/O Gilroy

2. P/O Stewart-Clark

3. Sgt Caister

'Red Section attacked Do.215, 100 miles ENE of Aberdeen. EA crashed in flames into the sea.'

Red Section had actually shot down a Messerschmitt Bf110 of *AufklarungsGruppe* of the *Oberbefehlshaber der Luftwaffe*, at approximately 13.15 hours. The crew were not found.

At that time some of the more experienced pilots in 603 were taken off operational flying and underwent a two-week term of duty as trainee controllers in the operations room at Turnhouse. This was intended to provide a greater level of knowledge of the system of fighter control.

As the intensity of the air battle in the south increased, the details which filtered back to 603 made the pilots and ground crews impatient to play a more significant part. In addition to being an operational unit whose daily routine had involved being up at first light, and stood down late into the evening with the occasional excitement of an interception, the CO had ensured an intensive programme of flying exercises was carried out simultaneously for those not at readiness. As a consequence of the long hours and hard work the pilots were already very tired but had yet to experience intensive fighter versus fighter combat.

CHAPTER 6

THE BATTLE OF BRITAIN

I remember my youth and the feeling that will never come back any more – the feeling that I could last forever, outlast the sea, the earth, and all men; the deceitful feeling that lures us on to joys, to perils, to love, to vain effort – to death; the triumphant conviction of strength, the heat of life in the handful of dust, the glow in the hearth that with every year grows dim, grows cold, grows small and expires – and expires, too soon, too soon – before life itself.

Rudyard Kipling

Whilst 10 July was later officially recognised as the start of the Battle of Britain, to squadrons based in the south of England plus those who had been involved in the defence of the country for some time it was just another hectic day in the remorseless increase of air activity by the Luftwaffe over Britain. Ironically, some had already lost their lives or received wounds that prevented further input in the conflict prior to this date. They were not to receive the 'Battle of Britain Clasp' in official recognition of this. Even if their sacrifice had occurred only a matter of hours before or after the specified dates they did not receive this award to go with their 1939-45 Star.

603 in formation. Loch Long, June 1940. XT-A is nearest to camera.

The pilots of 603 Squadron saw no flying on 10 July but by now the frequency with which German reconnaissance aircraft and bombers appeared in the airspace over the east coast of Scotland had also increased. They were also aware of what was going on in the south and were keen to do their bit.

**The Men of 603 (City of Edinburgh) Fighter Squadron
in the
Battle of Britain**

The pilots who served in 603 Squadron in the lead up to and during the Battle of Britain were a diverse group of individuals united by a common interest in flying which had consumed their weekends, some weekday evenings and, ultimately, taken them to the fight against the Germans. The latter they did with great enthusiasm, determination and courage. They had chosen to be fighter pilots as opposed to serving in any other service. To them it was glamorous and disassociated from warfare as they knew it. They were committed to opposing the despotism which had advanced as

136

far as the other side of the Channel and threatened the freedom of Great Britain. Some expressed the opinion to friends and family that such was the intensity of the fighting there was every chance they wouldn't be coming back.

A total of 47 pilots flew with 603 during the Battle of Britain of which 13 were killed between 10 July and 31 October 1940. In all, 23 of the 47 pilots who had flown with 603 during the battle had been killed by the end of hostilities.

A pen-portrait of each pilot is presented here in alphabetical order, with the exception of the then Commanding Officer, who heads the portfolio.

George Lovell Denholm, RAF No.90190, was born on 20 December 1908, to William Andrew and Minnie Scott Denholm (née Lovell) at the family home 'Tidings Hill', Cadzow Crescent, on the shores of the River Forth at Bo'ness, West Lothian where, legend states 'the lassies used to climb the hill to see if the whalers were coming home.' Tidings Hill had been built by George's parents who had moved in on 10 December 1908. George was born shortly after. The big new house was equipped with a number of luxuries of the period, including central heating.

George had two younger brothers, Jimmy who died aged ten, and Michael who sadly also died around 1950. His father ran a well-established coal exporters and pit-prop/timber importers based at Bo'ness on the Forth, which was, from medieval times until the late 19th century, the third largest port in Scotland. William Denholm died when George was only fifteen.

George was educated at Cargilfield Prep School and Fettes School. Before attending university his mother and uncle advised him to gain some experience of life and arranged for him to 'learn a thing or two' at a tough Glasgow office in order for him to appreciate university and his good fortune. He hated Glasgow and was very unhappy. In an attempt to help her son find a more enjoyable environment in which to learn Minnie Denholm and the uncle sent the young George to St Johns College, Cambridge, where he was extremely happy. He studied Economics and Law but according to Betty '…didn't excel. He was an adequate student, nothing more.' At Cambridge he learnt about guns and artillery in the University Cadet Corps and also how to ride (contrary to myth he was never a member of the Territorial Army). He worked with horses and gun carriages 'thoroughly enjoying the experience.'

On graduating work in the family business soon became boring (although post-war he did find happiness in the business) and George sought excitement in the air, taking private flying lessons during his spare time with the Civil Aviation's, Edinburgh Flying Club Ltd at Macmerry and East Fortune, both in East Lothian. His closest friend, George Gilroy, also learned to fly at Macmerry and the two were later to serve together in 603 Squadron AuxAF. In June 1933, George Denholm joined the Squadron after Count Stevens (later OC 603 Squadron) and Douglas Shields, suggested that he might apply (it is possible Stevens and Shields were instructing at Macmerry where they became friends with George). Competition was intense but he was accepted and his commission as Pilot Officer (AuxAF) was gazetted on 27 June of the same year. Promoted to Flying Officer (AuxAF) on 27 December 1934, he qualified as a flying instructor in July 1937, and was promoted to Flight Lieutenant on 8 January 1939. Pre-war, George shared a room in the officers mess with Ken Macdonald on the Saturday night of flying weekends.

George's leisure pursuits were not solely connected to flying. He was a competent skier, enjoyed sailing, riding and tennis but admitted to being a poor golfer. To the dismay of his opponents he played with only a four iron and a putter in his bag!

George married Betty Toombs on 29 November 1939 in Linlithgow. Betty recalls with amusement: 'the 603 pipe band massed outside the church vied with the organ inside to create a horrible noise!' The couple lived at Tidings Hill, Bo'ness where Betty remained throughout the Battle of Britain. She ventured south on just one occasion: 'I didn't like what I saw of the war. Some of the sights were so unexpected. I was terrified when the bombing occurred.'

With the embodiment of 603 Squadron on 23 August 1939, George was called to full-time service. He reflected on that initial period:

Betty Denholm.

We did no training as far as I remember in the first days of the war but waited continually for things to happen. We had however followed the prescribed Fighter Command training, but in practice it was not carried out according to the 'book'. The airfield at Turnhouse was grass and as it happens I myself got bogged in the middle of the Forth raid.

By that time he was an experienced flight commander who had been considering retiring from the Squadron at the relatively advanced age of 31. It was the fact that he was considerably older than most of the younger pilots and had a much respected air of authority, discipline and organisation about him that led to his being given the nickname 'Uncle' George. As their leader during the Battle of Britain, his paternalist instincts were evident in his concern for the welfare of his longstanding friends in the Squadron, as well as the young, inexperienced newcomers. His nickname, whilst initially relevant to his age, also became appropriate for this reason. He was less well known by the nickname 'Demon', which was occasionally used following the battle and attributed in response to the reputation he had gained during that hectic period.

George was a respected and popular member of 603 who took his job very seriously. In the months leading up to the Battle of Britain he ensured his pilots constantly practised flying skills and in particular fighting tactics – formation attacks and dog-fighting – hoping it would put his men in good stead for the battle that lay ahead. At the time of the battle he was 32 years of age, was very experienced, and had accumulated a great many flying hours.

Ivor Kenneth Arber, RAF No.156944, joined the RAFVR as an airman u/t pilot (742741) in December 1938. Called up on 1 September 1939 he did his advanced flying training at 8 SFTS Montrose which he completed in May 1940. He joined A Flight 603 Squadron at Dyce shortly after as a sergeant pilot. Arber was commissioned as a Pilot Officer on 22 August 1943, promoted to Flying Officer on 29 February 1944 and Flight Lieutenant on 30 August 1945. He was awarded the AFC on 1 January 1945. He left the RAF after the war and was commissioned in the RAFVR as a Flying Officer on 31 October 1947, and promoted to Flight Lieutenant (RAFVR) on 31 December 1948. He died on 1 September 1952.

George John Bailey RAF No.106355, joined the RAFVR as an airman u/t pilot (741820) on 26 July 1938, and did his elementary flying training at 9 E&RFTS Ansty and 13 E&RFTS White Waltham. He was called up at the beginning of October 1939 and posted to 5 FTS, Sealand. With training complete he went to 234 Squadron on 4 May 1940. Bailey shared in the destruction of a Ju88 on 8 July and another on the 27th. He was posted to 603 Squadron at Hornchurch on 10 September.

Noel John Victor Benson RAF No.33485, was born on 11 December 1918. The Benson family lived in Cedar Croft Cottage in the beautiful North Yorkshire village of Great Ouseburn, in what was very much a farming community. Noel was the eldest of three children. He had a brother, Brian J.N. Benson (born 10 May 1920) and a sister Margaret. His father, Dr Joseph Benson was a respected physician and surgeon but worked from home as the local pharmacist. His wife, Olive 'Daisy' Benson, ran the household. She was 29 when Noel was born.

The three children also did their share of the chores, mainly looking after the animals, including a number of horses. From an early age Noel suffered from asthma and he left his brother and sister to look after the horses, the likely cause of his condition, whilst he developed his great talent for woodwork. In addition to the stables, Cedar Croft had an enormous garden with an additional twelve acres of land. In the garden there was a shed in which there were tools and machinery for Noel to exploit his interest in woodwork. His standard of workmanship was high and he quickly moved on to more challenging projects. The children all had bicycles and with the river Ouse only a short ride away they used to spend summer days bathing. Noel decided to make a small sail boat. He made a marvellous job of it and they had many hours of fun sailing down the river. Noel named it 'Imada'.

Noel was a fearless child and had been keen on planes from an early age and with the local aerial activity from RAF Linton-on-Ouse he quickly developed a fascination for flying. But, like so many

Noel, Margaret and Brian Benson.

Noel with friends shortly before the war.

others who were destined to join the RAF, it was a flight arranged by his father which saw Noel smitten by the bug. During a trip from Montrose to York the air was a little turbulent which upset Daisy and Margaret Benson who were not at all keen on flying, but the boys enjoyed themselves, after which Noel lived for flying and nothing else.

The Benson children initially attended school in Harrogate before the boys were both sent away to the exclusive Sedbergh School, North Yorkshire. Noel did not excel at any sport in particular, unlike his contemporaries in 603 Squadron, although he enjoyed most sports. He was, however, an outstanding academic.

On leaving Sedburgh, Noel chose a career in the RAF but before embarking on his chosen path he enjoyed a period of rest during which he bought his first car. A short while later Brian also bought a car and the two young men developed a fascination for engines. They carried out their own servicing and maintenance work and dismantled the engines simply for the fun of it. His sister Margaret remembers:

> It was problematic with petrol rationing but they drove everywhere. I remember the two boys going into York one day to look around the showrooms looking to buy (or part exchange) a new car.

Although Noel had few friends in the village he did have one in particular who was the son of a wealthy farming landowner. When his friend announced he was to be married, his mother arranged an elaborate wedding. Margaret was aware that: '...the boy was not only wealthy but also in a reserved occupation and didn't have to fight.' Naturally, Noel was invited to the wedding and it was a great occasion. Shortly after, in April 1938, he entered RAF College, Cranwell, as a Flight Cadet. With a love of flying and all things connected to the subject he found both practical and academic course work easy 'One day he flew over the garden (in an aircraft with an open cockpit) and came very low, so we waved to each other. Mother was there too,' Margaret recalled. He graduated as a Pilot Officer on 23 October 1939 and the whole family travelled to Cranwell for his passing out parade. His sister again: 'Noel was so proud. After the war we went to see the chair which had his name on. It was rather moving.'

His first posting was to the 11 Group 'Pool' at St Athan where he spent only one week before being posted to 145 Squadron at Croydon, equipped with Blenheim 1Fs, which had been reformed on 10 October. On 18 December 1939,

Broody Benson at Montrose. June/July 1940.

Noel was posted to B Flight 603 Squadron at Montrose. (It is interesting to note that 145 Squadron moved to Drem with detachments also at Dyce and Montrose on 14 August 1940. These circumstances may have led to Noel opting for a move to the Edinburgh fighter Squadron.) Both pilots and ground crew remember Noel being very professional and always appearing smart and 'clean cut'.

It was at Montrose that he met Richard Hillary who described him: 'Broody Benson, nineteen years old [actually twenty-one], a fine pilot and possessed of only one idea, to shoot down Huns, more Huns, and then still more Huns'. He was affectionately nicknamed 'Broody' by the rest of the Squadron because his colleagues were quick to latch on to his habit of sitting in the dispersal hut for periods of quiet contemplation, ignoring all that went on around him. In truth there was more to this as described later in a letter from George Denholm to Broody's father, 'he was always so despondent if, for any reason, he was not allowed to fly' and '... had a habit of pondering over the many problems confronting him'. Margaret remembers their time together after he travelled north:

> After joining 603 he only had short spells of leave and it passed very quickly. He just came and went. He was a quiet chap anyway and didn't mention anything while home on leave, he was not allowed to anyway. Only problems with the car were discussed!

Ronald Berry RAF No.78538, was born in Hull on 3 May 1917 to Mr and Mrs W. Berry of 28 Kelvin Street. He became known as 'Ras' Berry after somebody wrote those letters before his surname on his flying log book and it stuck for the rest of his RAF career. (The spelling is most commonly 'Ras', although some 603 pilots maintain it is 'Razz'. Berry himself accepted either spelling.)

He was educated locally at Riley High School and at eleven years of age went to Hull Technical College. On leaving college he took the position of clerk in the St Andrews Engineering Company at Hull Docks. After 18 months he went to work at the city treasurers office at the Guildhall as a clerk on salaries and income tax. After seeing an advert in a newspaper during the early part of 1937 he and a friend in the same office joined the RAFVR in April 1937: 'It was not easy to get into the RAFVR and I got myself really fit by running around my local park.' Later, after achieving success, at no time was praise for Ras's achievements more cordial than from his former colleagues at the city treasurer's department. Having joined them as a 17-year old, the city treasurer kept a photograph of Ras alongside a model of a Spitfire bearing the Hull coat of arms.

Ras undertook flying training on the Blackburn B2 at the weekends at E&RFTS, Brough: 'Having gone solo I realised that flying was going to be something that I was really going to enjoy.' All his annual leave from the time that he joined until war broke out was spent flying. In August 1937 alone he flew 35 times and was taught aerobatics! By July 1938 the full-time contingent of RAF officers at Brough had been joined by Brian Carbury who was later to fly with Ras in 603 Squadron.

Called up as a sergeant pilot in February 1939, Ras was initially sent to 66 Squadron at Duxford flying Spitfires:

> Winter time in a Spitfire, in strange country, I certainly had my hackles raised a few times. Taking off for the first time, they briefed me and said, 'Don't break it', and off I went and ran out of airfield before you could say 'Jack Robinson', and pumping the wheels up was a new experience. I had never flown a monoplane before, and it was exhilarating to say the least, but it was hairy. There I was in winter time, the visibility wasn't all that good, no complaints but it certainly brought me down to earth about what flying a fighter would really be like. It was the acceleration that impressed me most, I did a few quick turns, I was too frightened to do anything aerobatically, I really took to it. I never had any criticism of this aircraft.

After three weeks he returned to Brough and Hawker Hinds but the experience had put him in good stead for his next posting. In July 1939 Ras was granted a five-year commission but the paperwork was lost and he was to wait until December before his commission came through. In October 1939, after a short spell at gunnery school, he was then posted to 603 Squadron at Turnhouse. He arrived on 17 October 1939, and was attached to B Flight and first flew on 23 October (A/c No.L1026). In

November 1939, he flew two sorties in Spitfire L1022. Ras's early experiences off the Scottish east coast prompted him to persuade one of his ground crewmen to buy a rear view mirror from Halfords which was subsequently bolted to the canopy of his Spitfire to enable him to see behind. Ras was commissioned on 1 December 1939: 'Based on my flying not my IQ!' Richard Hillary later recorded his initial impressions of the powerful Yorkshireman in *The Last Enemy*:

F/O Ras Berry DFC by Cuthbert Orde.

> Pilot Officer Berry, commonly known as Raspberry, came from Hull. He was short and stocky, with a ruddy complexion and a mouth that was always grinning or coming out with some broad Yorkshire witticism impossible to answer. Above the mouth, surprisingly, sprouted a heavy black moustache, which induced me to call him the organ-grinder. His reply to this was always unprintable but very much to the point. Even on the blackest days he radiated an infectious good-humour. His aggressive spirit chafed at the Squadron's present inactivity and he was always the first to hear any rumour of our moving south.

His last operational sortie before moving south to Hornchurch was on 22 August in a/c R6626 of which he recalled: '...served me well during the Battle of Britain.'

John Clifford Boulter RAF No.37757, was born in Barnes, London. In March 1933, Boulter was placed on the Reserve of Air Force Officers (RAFO), later the Royal Air Force Reserve of Officers (RAFRO). In April 1936 he became active again when he was granted a short service commission in the RAF. On 18 April he went to 7 FTS Peterborough and was subsequently posted to 1 Squadron at Tangmere on 25 October. He moved to 72 Squadron at Church Fenton at its reformation on 23 March 1937, and was later at RAF Usworth from where he was sent to Scotland on 6 October 1939, to provide some regular RAF experience for 603 Squadron at Turnhouse,. He joined B Flight where he quickly acquired the nickname 'Bolster' and became a popular member of 603. Believing him to have served in the army at some stage, his colleagues gave him the additional nickname of 'Brown job'. Boulter's bizarre activities became legendary. Richard Hillary later wrote: 'Then there was Boulter, with jutting ears framing the face of an intelligent ferret, always sleepy and in bed snoring when off duty.' He was also one of the pilots who visited Invermark Lodge and Tarfside.* Stapme Stapleton recorded: 'He used to stand drinking, leaning on the bar all evening, talking and quietly watching the antics of the more active. By the end of the evening, at kicking-out time, he would simply release his grip on the bar and fall flat on his face!' When 603 flew south in August 1940, he was one of the most respected pilots in the unit.

Boulter by Orde drawn at Drem shortly before he was killed.

---

*While off duty at Montrose, some of the pilots were invited to stay at Invermark Lodge. While there they befriended a number of children in the village of Tarfside.

Alfred Denmark Burt RAF No.49994, was born on 27 July 1916 and educated at Brockenhurst County School. He joined the RAF on 7 September 1932, as an aircraft apprentice (566159) at RAF Halton, Buckinghamshire. There he trained as a fitter II (airframes and aero engines). He passed out on 26 July 1935 and was posted to 4 Squadron as a Leading Aircraftman (LAC). Burt applied for pilot training and on 18 January 1938 he began a course at E&FTS Filton. On 27 March he moved on to 10 FTS at Ternhill. On 30 October he was posted to No.1 Electrical and Wireless School, Cranwell as a staff pilot. With the outbreak of war, Burt moved to 46 Squadron at RAF Digby and just two weeks later he was sent to 611 Squadron at RAF Digby. On 21 August 1940, he claimed a share of a Do17 shot down off the Lincolnshire coast. On 4 October Burt was posted to 603 at Hornchurch.

James Russell Caister RAF No.44827, from Rye, East Sussex, was born on 19 October 1906 and joined the RAF as an aircrafthand (358860) on January 1924 aged 18. He later applied for pilot training and subsequently saw service in Palestine between the wars as a sergeant pilot. Known as 'Bill' to his fellow NCOs, Caister joined A Flight of 603 on 29 October 1939. Bill was powerfully built and very tough. A keen athlete and capable boxer, he often sparred with some of the NCOs and airmen in their billet, including AC.1s Arthur 'Artie' Carroll and Alec Mackenzie with whom he became good friends. Born and brought up in Leith, Alec was himself a very capable boxer who took the sport very seriously, was regularly seen running in the streets of Leith and went on to achieve some success. Today, Alec Mackenzie and Artie recall with amusement the excellent nights out they used to have when off duty when together with Bill Caister they visited the Tartan Club in Aberdeen.

Brian John George Carbury RAF No.40288 was born in Wellington, New Zealand, on 27 February 1918. His father was a veterinary surgeon. The family later moved to Auckland where Brian was educated at New Lynn and Kings College (1932-34). He had a reputation as a fine athlete, playing rugby, cricket, and tennis, was a gymnast, fencer, an excellent swimmer – becoming a member of the water polo team – and was also a member of the local cycling club. He could play the guitar and, significantly, was an excellent marksman with the rifle. It has been said that Brian gave his outdoor activities priority over his academic studies.

On leaving college he worked as a shoe salesman for the Farmers Trading Co., Auckland, but soon became tired with the job and in June 1937 at the age of 19 he travelled to England. He apparently failed in his attempt to join the Royal Navy, for which he was deemed to be over-age, but successfully applied for a short service commission in the RAF and began his flying training on 27 September 1937, at 10 E&RFTS, the Bristol Flying Training School, Yatesbury.

In June 1938, he was posted to 41 Squadron at Catterick, which was at that time flying Hawker Fury Mk II biplanes. Here he met John Young, who was an instructor and adjutant of 41 Squadron, and Colin 'Robbie' Robertson with whom he would later serve in 603 Squadron. A sergeant pilot at Catterick later wrote:

> ... Brian came to 41 Squadron in 1938, and was in A Flight with me. He was with us until posted to 603 Squadron just before the war started. Not like other officers, he used to chat freely with the sergeant pilots and airmen; there were a few others from overseas, who also disregarded the 'class barrier' – a couple of Canadians and another New Zealander.

Sometime around the end of July he joined the full-time RAF contingent at RAF Brough, Yorkshire, as an instructor, where the unit was known as 'Harston's Air Circus'. Ras Berry was also there at this time and Brian would later become the highest scoring pilot of 603 Squadron with Ras achieving second place on the list.

A rare photograph (opposite) taken on 27 July 1938, shows Brian astride the nose of Hawker Hart K3879, which Australian Dereck French crashed on landing. French later distinguished himself as a bomber pilot, receiving the DFC and Bar before returning home after the war where he resides today. The crash, he recalled, was: '...due to my poor show-off flying'. In October 1938, Brian returned to 41 Squadron at Catterick.

41 Squadron converted to Spitfire Mk Is in January 1939, and on 6 October Brian was attached to A Flight, at Turnhouse to assist with 603's own conversion to type. His temporary position became permanent on 24 October 1939, following the outbreak of war.

In line with the trend at the time Brian had his ground crew paint the name of 'Aorangi' on the port cowling of his Spitfire in white enamel paint. Aorangi is a Maori word which has been used to name the highest mountain in New Zealand, and is also the name of the largest of the Poor Knights Islands, situated off the northern coast of New Zealand. Generally, the word could most appropriately be taken to represent: 'lofty, high in the sky – above the others'. Richard Hillary was immensely impressed by Brian Carbury's skill as a fighter pilot and later included a thumbnail sketch of him in *The Last Enemy*:

> Then there was Brian Carbury, a New Zealander who was six-foot-four, with crinkly hair and a roving eye. He greeted us warmly and suggested an immediate adjournment to the mess for drinks. There was little distinctive about him on the ground, but he was to prove the Squadron's greatest asset in the air.

Promoted to Flying Officer on 27 April 1940 (w.e.f 7 March), when the Squadron moved south on 27 August he was to achieve considerable success, becoming one of the top-scoring pilots during the Battle of Britain.

Brian Carbury and Arthur Slocombe.

Philip Melville Cardell RAF No.80815 was born in Great Paxton, Huntingdonshire in 1917 to Harold and Elsie Cardell. He had a younger brother, Teddy, with sister Margaret the youngest of the children. Philip was educated locally at a private school at Little Paxton. The family owned a large farm and were quite wealthy. Harold Cardell was known by the locals as the 'Squire'; a large imposing man with great authority. After leaving school Philip saw his future running the family farming business. During his late teens he owned a MG convertible sports car. Family friend, Mrs Richards, remembers Philip:

> He used to dash around the village in his fast car. He was quite reckless. When he had gone to war we used to say that his recklessness and willingness to throw himself into the task in-hand would bring him success or get him killed. When we heard that he had been killed we were greatly saddened but not that surprised. He was a nice boy. Not particularly bright and did not go to university. He was dashing, good-looking, stylish and determined to be successful at all he did.

Joan Palmer had known Philip from childhood as 'the boy next door …about five feet eight inches tall, sturdily built and very good-looking.' They would become engaged and fond memories of Philip have stayed with Joan for over 60 years. During his late teens Philip became interested in learning how to fly, a natural and fashionable progression in those days for a young lad with money and a fast car. He learnt at Marshall's Flying School, Cambridge during 1936/37, a private flying club which was home to the Cambridge UAS. His younger brother, Teddy, also joined him there. The cost of a flying lesson at that time was one pound ten shillings an hour in a Tiger Moth, and two pounds in a Puss Moth.

During an air display at Marshall's in 1938, Philip's enthusiasm was elevated onto a different plain when three Spitfire Mark Is from 19 Squadron, Duxford, put on a flying display led by Squadron Leader H.I. Cozens. The Squadron had only been equipped with this new aircraft one month earlier and the tannoy system informed the crowd that this was the fastest aeroplane in the

The Cardell family, Great Paxton, Cambs. From left to right: Teddy, Margaret, Philip, Harold and unknown.

world. It is a coincidence that one of the Spitfires that Philip saw fly that day was K9795 which saw service with 603 Squadron from 29 September 1940, during the Battle of Britain. Compared with the aircraft types he had been familiar with, the Spitfire must have been an awesome sight. Philip was smitten and he knew what he wanted to fly next.

By February 1939, 50 Group had commandeered 22 E&RFTS, Cambridge, and soon started the direct entry RAF officers course where eight civilian instructors taught thirty-two pupils. Weekend flying by the 'VR' was done on Tiger Moths, Hinds, Harts, and Audaxes, the supercharged version of the Hart and Fairey Battles. 22 E&RFTS was without doubt the best operated and most productive of all these schools.

Philip joined the RAFVR in May 1939 as an airman u/t pilot (748036) and along with his brother was one of the first VRs to be called-up when war was declared. Having qualified as a pilot in late 1937, Philip had considerable experience by this time. The decision to commit himself to full time service was his. As a farmer he had been in a reserved occupation. His brother had also been commissioned in the RAFVR and like his older brother, became operational.

Sent to 15 FTS at Lossiemouth in January 1940, Philip began flying on No. 6 Course Initial Training School (ITS) on 2 January. He flew solo sometime during the first week. On 18 March 1940, he completed the ITS syllabus and began work on the advanced training (ATS) program. This he completed on 8 June. He was commissioned as a Pilot Officer on 10 June 1940. From 10-23 June he converted to Spitfires at 5 OTU at Aston Down, where he amassed just over 20 hours flying time. Bill Read, Jack Stokoe and Alfred Sarre, also from No.6 Course at Lossiemouth, were also there. Fifty-six years later Jack Stokoe remembers Philip as being: '..an extremely nice person.'

On 23 June, Philip, along with Read, Sarre and Stokoe was posted to 263 Squadron at Drem, in the beautiful East Lothian countryside. Following the sinking of HMS *Glorious* on 8 June during the return voyage from Norway, with the tragic loss of some of the pilots and ground crew, 263 had been re-established at Drem on 10 June, flying Hurricane Is. Philip began conversion to Hurricanes on 26 June. The squadron moved to Grangemouth on 1 July and, being due to convert to the new twin-engine fighter, the Westland Whirlwind, Philip and his newly arrived associates were offered the choice of staying with 263 and converting, or remaining on single-engine fighters, in which case they would be posted. Hence on 3 July, Philip and his colleagues were posted to 603 Squadron and travelled the short distance across country to Turnhouse where they were then sent to the two detached flights protecting the north-east Scottish coast and off-shore shipping. Philip went to B Flight at Montrose while Jack Stokoe, Alfred Sarre and Bill Read went to A Flight at Dyce. Within three days Philip would be joined by Richard Hillary who later recorded his first impression of Philip as appearing: 'Bewildered, excited and a little lost.' Philip was quickly nicknamed 'Pip' by his fellow pilots.

John Laurence Gilchrist Cunningham RAF No.90194. Laurie Cunningham was born in Burntisland, Fife in 1917 and educated at Edinburgh Academy. On completion of his education he very reluctantly joined the family grain merchant business. He joined the AuxAF in early 1935 at the age of 18 and his commission as acting Pilot Officer AuxAF was gazetted on 6 May of that year. He appears as a fresh-faced young man on the front row of the 1936 Squadron photograph. He was promoted to Flying Officer in January 1937 with effect from 6 November the previous year. By 12 March 1940 he was a Flight Lieutenant and one of the more experienced members of 603. He was

Blue Section leader with B Flight when Richard Hillary arrived and he later recollected his memories of Cunningham in his book: 'Larry [sic] Cunningham had also been with the Squadron for some time. He was a Scotsman, tall and thin, without Rusty's (Rushmer) charm, but with plenty of experience.' In order to look older than their years, a number of the Flight were at that time trying to grow a moustache. Laurie was the least successful and quickly abandoned the idea.

He was one of the pilots of B Flight who visited Invermark Lodge and played with the children there; but he is remembered as being of a rather more serious nature than the others, and was less inclined to 'let himself go'. Maybe something to do with the fact that he had developed a close relationship with 16-year-old Rhoda Davie! On moving south with his Squadron, his time became all too brief.

Andrew Smitton Darling RAF No.740544, one of the less well-known members of 603 was from Auchterarder, Perthshire and joined the RAFVR around August 1937 as an airman u/t pilot. He was called up on 1 September 1939, and was with 611 Squadron at RAF Digby at the beginning of the Battle of Britain. On 21 August 1940, Darling shared in the destruction of a Do17 off the Lincolnshire coast. On 27 September 1940, he was posted to 603 Squadron at Hornchurch.

Robert Basil Dewey RAF No.42815, was from Portsmouth. He joined the RAF on a short service commission in August 1939 and was an acting Pilot Officer as of 23 October 1939 and confirmed at that rank on 18 May 1940. Dewey completed his flying training and as a Pilot Officer was then sent to 5 OTU Aston Down on 18 May 1940, for conversion training on Spitfires. He joined 611 Squadron at Digby from Aston Down on 9 June. Dewey was posted to 603 Squadron on 27 September.

Peter Grenfell Dexter RAF No.41680, was born in Durban, Natal, South Africa on 5 June 1918. He joined the RAF on a four-year short service commission as an acting Pilot Officer on probation in the general duties branch on 4 March 1939 (with effect from 29 December 1938). He was graded as a pilot officer on 30 September 1939 (on probation). With initial training complete Dexter was posted to 16 Squadron at Old Sarum, Wiltshire, on 3 January 1940, where he flew Lysanders IIs with army co-operation. In April his squadron was sent to Bertangles, France, to join 50 Wing. According to the squadron ORB, Dexter's first operational flight with the unit was on 9 May 1940, with A.C. Webb as his gunner, when he took part in an air observation patrol flying Lysander II L4795. On 21 May, in fine weather, the squadron sent four tactical reconnaissance sorties and one photographic from Lympne, Kent. Whilst flying Lysander II (L4795) on one of these, of the Arras/Cambrai/Amiens area, he was attacked by nine Bf109s. In the ensuing mêlée Dexter exhibited great airmanship and courage in that he managed to shoot down one of the fighters with his forward-firing .303 machine gun before manoeuvring his aircraft to enable his gunner, Aircraftman Webb, to shoot down a second. Despite severe damage to the 'Lizzie' Dexter managed to fly his aircraft back to base. For this remarkable achievement, against the latest and vastly superior German fighter he was awarded the DFC (gazetted 22 July 1940).

His army co-operation unit was withdrawn to Redhill on 28 June 1940. In early August Dexter was posted to 7 OTU, Hawarden, and after converting to Spitfires he joined 54 Squadron at Catterick on 3 September and flew operationally with the squadron on five occasions. Thirteen days later on 16 September and with very few flying hours on Spitfires he joined 603 at Hornchurch.

George Kemp Gilroy RAF No.90481. George was born on 1 June 1914. He was an only child who later gained a reputation as an excellent shot, a fine shepherd and sheep/cattle breeder. His family home was 'Kingledores' situated on a large estate at Tweedsmuir and they were close friends with the McKerrows of 'Polmood' house, just a mile away, the only other home in the immediate vicinity. As a teenager Mary McKerrow came to know George through her father:

George used to come over for shooting or drinks with my parents. I was about 14 at the time George was a few years older than me (19+). Although he was an excellent shot he really didn't come across as someone who would eventually go to war, become a fighter pilot and kill. It really was a surprise, even to this day, that he did so and was successful.

Left: Sheep. Later in the war with his own aircraft.
Right: George Gilroy (second right), during a hunt on the land around his family home at Tweedsmuir.

Young George became a sheep farmer and was involved in all the traditional pastimes associated with the lifestyle into which he had been born. Many early photos show George dressed in tweeds on shooting expeditions. Later his profession led him to being nicknamed 'Sheep' by his fellow pilots. Some of his colleagues, including their wives, also referred to him somewhat more affectionately as 'Mouton', the French for sheep. He joined the AuxAF in 1938 following flying lessons at Macmerry where George Denholm had also learnt to fly. His commission as an acting Pilot Officer was gazetted on 10 November of that year. He was promoted to Pilot Officer and called to full-time service on 23 August 1939. Sheep was one of the first Spitfire pilots to see action on 16 October 1939. When the Squadron moved south to Hornchurch he was in the thick of the fighting.

Claude Walter Goldsmith RAF No.72152. One of three South Africans in the Squadron during the Battle of Britain, Stapleton and Dexter being the others. Born in 1917, Goldsmith was from Dersley, Transvaal and was educated in England at Cheltenham College and Imperial College, London, where he studied mining. He was a member of the London University Air Squadron in 1936 and was commissioned in the RAFVR in March 1938. Called to full time service on 10 October 1939, he was promoted to Flying Officer on 9 December. He had been posted to A Flight at Dyce in July 1940, after having initially served in a Lysander unit with the army co-op. Keen to fly the Spitfire he applied for a transfer and was sent to 603 Squadron. He travelled south to Hornchurch with 603 on 27 August.

John Galloway Edward Haig RAF No.90189. Known as 'Jack' by his colleagues, Haig was from near St.Andrews, Fife, and before the war had worked as a paper-salesman with the Guardbridge Paper Company, Derby. He joined 603 Squadron, AuxAF, early in 1932 and was commissioned as a Pilot Officer (AuxAF) on 11 June of that year. For four weeks out of five he attended lectures and dutifully went about his flying training. He was promoted to Flying Officer (AuxAF) on 11 December 1933. In June 1938 he went onto the Reserve of Officers (AuxAFRO), as he explained: 'I stopped about nine months before the war. The gilt had worn off flying a bit by then.' Nevertheless, when war came he rushed north to rejoin his unit. Recalled for full-time service on 24 August 1939, he was promoted to Flying Officer. Twenty years later he believed the effort was worthwhile: 'After all, we'd been trained for this for six years. We were just as good as the regular RAF. It was a job to do and we did it.'

On 15 September Haig was sent to 12 Group Pool, Aston Down and following a flying refresher course and conversion to Spitfires he was posted back to the Edinburgh Squadron on 8 December. By now Haig was one of the oldest and most experienced members and was with A Flight at Dyce before travelling south to Hornchurch.

Peter McDonnell Hartas RAF No.41407. Joined the RAF on a short service commission in October 1938. He was with 4 Ferry Pilot Pool sometime in 1940 before being posted to 7 OTU at Hawarden on 3 September 1940, where he converted to Spitfires. On 16 September he was posted to 616 Squadron at Kirton-in-Lindsey and moved to 603 at Hornchurch on the 24th.

Richard Hope Hillary RAF No.74677. Richard Hillary was born in Sydney, Australia, on 20 April 1919, sharing the same birthday as Adolf Hitler. His father worked for the Australian government and moved to England when Richard was three. When Richard's father was posted to Khartoum to work for the Sudanese government he sent his son to Hawnes School in Bedfordshire followed by Shrewsbury School and Trinity College, Oxford where he studied history. Whilst at Shrewsbury he gained a reputation as an oarsman which reached a pinnacle at Oxford when he stroked the Trinity VIII to the Head of the River in 1938 and helped retain the title the following year. Richard was tall, athletic, and his good looks ensured he had little trouble attracting the ladies. He joined the Oxford University Air Squadron (OUAS) but initially made little progress as he attempted to row his way into the Oxford VIII. He gradually lost interest in the strict training routine along with the realisation that he was unlikely to succeed against the bigger, fitter and more skillful oarsmen in the university and so he directed his attention towards writing and the OUAS. By the time war was declared he had gained his air proficiency certificate and been accepted by the RAFVR. His first ITW was in Oxford but he completed the majority of his training at 3 ITW at Hastings along with a number of his university/OUAS colleagues. From Hastings he was sent to 14 FTS at RAF Kinloss and on completion of the course was posted to No.1 School of Army Co-operation, at Old Sarum flying Lysanders. The Battle of France left Fighter Command with a shortfall of trained fighter pilots and Richard along with several of his colleagues was sent to 5 OTU Aston Down to convert to Spitfires. From there he went to 603 Squadron on 6 July where he flew with B Flight during the early days of the Battle of Britain. On moving south to Hornchurch Richard quickly established himself as a competent combat pilot.

Peter Howes RAF No.74332. From Wadebridge, Cornwall, Howes was born in 1919, and educated at Oundle School and St John's College, Oxford, where he read natural science. He joined the Oxford University Air Squadron on 24 January 1939, and was on the same induction as Richard Hillary, with whom he became friends. Peter Howes features in his bestseller *The Last Enemy*, and they were together throughout their pilot training.

On 15 June 1939, Howes joined the RAFVR as AC2 (aircraftman 2nd class) u/t pilot, service No.754281. Called up on 3 September 1939, he was sent to No.1 ITW at Hastings on 3 October before going to 14 FTS at RAF Kinloss on 20 November. Flying training was completed by 14 May 1940, and the next day he attended No.1 School of Army Co-operation at Old Sarum. On 23 June 1940, Howes was sent to 5 OTU at Aston Down to convert to Spitfires. From here, on 8 July, he joined 54 Squadron at Rochford which subsequently moved to Hornchurch, where he was reunited once again with Richard Hillary. On 11 September he moved to 603 Squadron.

Keith Ashley Lawrence RAF No.42133, was born in Waitara, near New Plymouth, New Zealand on 25 November 1919. He attended Southland Boys High School, Invercargill from 1933 until 1936 when he went to work as a bank clerk in the National Bank of New Zealand in Invercargill. He remembers there being plenty of Scotsmen living in the area. In February 1938, he enrolled on the Civil Reserve of Pilots and in June successfully applied for a short service commission in the RNZAF. On 1 February 1939, Keith left for the UK in the RMS *Tainui*. On 13 March he went to 10 E&RFTS, Yatesbury and on 28 May he moved to 5 FTS at Sealand. From OTU he joined the newly reformed 234 Squadron at Leconfield on 6 November which were equipped with Blenheims. By March 1940 the unit had converted to Spitfires and Keith saw considerable action during the period July-August 1940. He shared in the destruction of a Ju88 on 8 July, the Squadron's first victory. On 12 July he damaged a Ju88 and on 24 August he damaged a Bf110. On 7 September he claimed a Bf109 destroyed and a Do17 damaged. Keith remembers:

> We were with 10 Group at Middle Wallop and, as I remember it, were generally ordered to 'patrol Brooklands at Angels 20,' where we came under the control of 11 Group. In 234 Squadron during this period we lost sixteen Spitfires in six weeks.

On 9 September, having requested a move to a frontline fighter squadron after 234 was withdrawn, Keith was posted to 603 at Hornchurch.

Harold Kennedy Macdonald RAF
No.90193 and **Donald Kennedy
Macdonald** RAF No.74679.

Harold Kennedy Macdonald was
born in Murrayfield, Edinburgh, on
24 February 1912. His father was
known by his middle name, Harold,
therefore, in order to avoid confusion
in the family household Harold junior
was known as 'Ken'.

Harold Macdonald was a solicitor
and prominent figure in the local legal
business with the company Morton,
Smart, Macdonald and Prosser. The
business still exists today on York
Place, Edinburgh. The profession
eventually brought him wealth and a
comfortable lifestyle in an opulent
part of the Scottish capital, affording
such luxuries as nannies for his
children and a chauffeur-driven
Rolls-Royce. The family enjoyed
many holidays on the continent where

Don and Ken on Ken's new motorbike. At Goodtrees aged 14 and 16.

Ken and Don were given plenty of freedom to express their sense of adventure.

As a child Ken, who was the apple of his mother's eye, was frequently quite ill and the very best
of medical care was bestowed upon him by his parents at the slightest sign of an ailment, various
doctors and surgeons being brought to their home to help with his difficulties, the most significant
being breathing problems which continued for a number of years and at one stage the experts feared
a lung tumour.

He seemed to grow naturally out of what was a sickly period of his life and was enjoying good
health by the time he was in his twenties.

During WWI Harold Macdonald served away from home and on his return in 1918 the
Macdonalds moved into a luxurious new home called 'Goodtrees' in Murrayfield.

Ken was educated at St Monica's School in Edinburgh where it was noted that he was slack with
his work which eventually led to extra coaching during the summer holidays of 1920. Following the
Christmas holiday of 1920 Ken was sent to Cargilfield, a well known prep school, and during the

summer holiday of 1923 he suffered the first of many serious asthma
attacks. Doctors were called out again and he subsequently underwent
further surgery.

In 1925 he was sent to the prestigious Loretto, a tough school where
the main sport was rugby. At the age of 16 Ken found an effective and
absorbing distraction from his health problems, his father provided funds
for him to buy a brand new motorbike and a black MG convertible. His
mother confirmed the upturn in his health and happiness in her diary:
'…he could think of nothing else, is always covered in oil and giving me
endless alarms being late and going in for trials etc.' Ken gained a
reputation in his neighbourhood for fast driving and during his days with
603 he gave lifts to members of the ground crew who waited at the
junction of Murrayfield Road and Corstorphine Road as he motored by
on his way to Turnhouse. They found the trip hair-raising! Ken's sister
was greatly influenced by her brother's interest in cars and mechanics
and remained an enthusiast for the rest of her life.

Ken grew up tall and lean, his voice noticeably deep and he had
inherited his father's looks whereas Don was shorter, broader and had

Ken at Goodtrees.

inherited his mother's looks. The beautiful spacious gardens at Goodtrees had a tennis court at the far end to the house. As children Ewen, the older sister, and her brothers played there and as teenagers entertained their friends during the summer months on their own private court. Even though the tennis court was in the garden he still dressed appropriately in whites and blazer. Ewen, described him as '…sleepy and laid-back, like his mother. He attracted the girls in large numbers but he was not that interested at the time.' Nevertheless, they fell for him. In comparison, Ewen described her younger brother, Don, as '…outgoing, jolly, and a bit of a practical joker… he was always pulling pranks of one sort or another. He was great fun.'

Mardi and Ken.

Aged eighteen in September 1931, Ken left Loretto for Peterhouse College, Cambridge, were he became an oarsman of repute.* He continued to suffer asthma-related respiratory problems and was prone to relapse when conditions were cold and damp but generally his health had improved markedly. Nevertheless, it is surprising that he was later able to achieve A1 category, flying fitness.

On 29 June 1934, Ken graduated from Cambridge. Despite expressing a preference for following a career as a professional photographer, the influence of his father prevailed and Ken agreed to follow him into the legal profession becoming a 'writer to the signet' (solicitor) with the Edinburgh based firm of solicitors of which his father was a partner.

Somewhat bored with work, Ken became a 'weekend flyer' when he joined 603 Squadron AuxAF in early 1935. His commission as an acting Pilot Officer (AuxAF) was gazetted on 4 March. He was yet another individual from the period who had found the excitement of fast cars and motor bikes irresistible, and when the opportunity came to take that excitement to a new high by learning to fly, being able to afford to he eagerly took up the challenge.

During the summer holiday of 1935 the family travelled to Scandinavia where they had a wonderful time. A day's sailing prompted the now immortal phrase from the boy's mother:

There was an old home-made boat by the loch-side [fjord] which Don took out to the middle of the loch but I was thankful when I saw them again on dry land. I'm not built to be the mother of heroes – they tell me – and I fear they are right.

May Macdonald's words were to prove prophetic and have been regarded as such by family members during the years since 1940. On their return Don fulfilled a dream when he too was bought a motorbike.

Ken and Don's sister married Kent farmer Robert Mount and the couple lived in 'Denstead' farmhouse. In the period before the war Ken was always eager to drive all the way down from Edinburgh to Kent in his sports car in order to visit his sister. Ewen recorded that her brother would brag that he 'could cut ten miles off the journey by cutting every corner!' In 1935, when 603 flew south to camp at Hawkinge, he brought the Squadron over Denstead. When war came Robert Mount stayed behind to run his farm and carry out his duties on a local AA battery while his family were evacuated to Great Bellow near Chester. While based at Hornchurch, Ken occasionally flew over Denstead in his Spitfire and provided an aerial assessment of the condition of the farm. Ken was promoted to Flying Officer (AuxAF) in January 1937 w.e.f. 4 September 1936.

In 1938, Ken was particularly depressed following the end of a relationship, so he decided to pursue his love of photography which stemmed from his time as 603's officer-in-charge, photographic section, in 1936. He took his camera everywhere and took many pictures. He travelled to London to further his photographic skill at Reimanns where he lived in a rented attic flat in Victoria. Ken met Marguerite (known as Mardi) at Reimanns and the couple went out together for more than three years. She retains many fond memories of him:

---

*By January 1932 he was Captain of Boats at Peterhouse, competed at Putney for a place in the college First VIII but having failed to win a place, he eagerly supported his university Blue Boat in the Oxford v Cambridge Boat Race.

He was sort of part poet, part philosopher, part artist. He totally changed my life. I only knew him for about three years but I looked at life totally differently. But I've always felt that he couldn't cope with what was coming. He had too much imagination and he felt terribly frustrated. It was a tragedy waiting to happen.

Mardi eventually married Black Morton.

On 16 July 1939, Ken left Reimanns and travelled to Hawkinge for the summer camp where he was reunited with his girlfriend Mardi who had joined the WAAF and was based at the station.* Following 603's return to Turnhouse, Ken returned to the family home in Edinburgh and, to his parents' delight, went back to working at his father's business. His return to the legal business didn't last for long. Ken was called to full-time service on 24 August 1939, and he was involved in several of the early engagements of the war over the Scottish east coast. At the start of the Battle of Britain, Ken was with B Flight.

Born in Murrayfield on 20 August 1918, Don was Ken's younger brother by five years and was educated locally at Bilton Grange before being sent to Marlborough School, Wiltshire, from 1932 to 1936. His sister wrote: 'He was a bright boy and did very well.' He also learnt to play the bagpipes. From Marlborough he, like his brother, went up to Peterhouse, Cambridge, where he read medieval and modern history. As an undergraduate he joined the Cambridge University Air Squadron and learnt to fly at Marshall's Flying School. Once qualified he was able to further his flying skill by joining the RAFVR, also based at Marshall's. During the two years Don was a member of the CUAS, he knew Peter Pease and Colin Pinckney. After graduating from Peterhouse he went to RAF Cranwell for flying training. Unlike his brother, Don was a member of the RAFVR. He was called to full-time service in November 1939, having been commissioned as a Pilot Officer on 8 November and posted to 603 Squadron. He was with A Flight in early July 1940. On arrival his knowledge of navigation was judged to be 'technically lame' and he was immediately sent on a course at an aerodrome in South Wales, at the end of which he took a week's leave before rejoining 603. He had minimal experience by the time they travelled south to Hornchurch.

Don at Goodtrees.

Brian Radley Macnamara RAF No.25123, was born on 2 June 1915. He was seconded to the RAF from the Royal Tank Corps on 8 November 1938, with the rank of Flying Officer. After completing his flying training he was posted to No.1 School of Army Co-operation at Old Sarum in September 1939. In October he joined 614 Squadron at Odiham, flying Lysanders. In August 1940, he volunteered for Fighter Command and on the 22nd was sent to 7 OTU Hawarden. After converting to Spitfires, MacNamara was posted to 603 Squadron at Hornchurch, arriving on 1 September during an immensely busy period.

---

*Mardi had initially been sent to join the staff of the top secret code-breaking unit at Bletchley Park. But when her superiors discovered she could speak fluent German she was sent to Hawkinge where her job was to listen in to the radio transmissions of the Luftwaffe aircrews. During the Battle of Britain she moved to Kingsdown right on the coast just south of Deal.

James Frederick John MacPhail RAF No.42014, joined the RAF on a short service commission in February 1939 with the rank of acting Pilot Officer confirmed on 29 April 1939. He was known as John by many of his RAF colleagues. On completion of training he was posted to 26 Squadron flying Lysanders. He was promoted to Pilot Officer on 6 November 1939. He also served with 41 Squadron at West Malling prior to volunteering for Fighter Command in August 1940. On 21 August he was sent to 5 OTU, Aston Down for conversion training to Spitfires. On 31 August he was posted to 603 at Hornchurch. MacPhail reported for duty with Brian Macnamara and 'Robin' Rafter on 1 September [the records incorrectly state he joined earlier]. MacPhail had a lively, boisterous personality and always took an active part in the infamous mess games. A number of photographs show him attempting to carry out the 'de-bagging' of a fellow officer whilst at West Malling. He met his match when he came up against Stapme Stapleton on one particular occasion while at Hornchurch.

Ludwik Martel RAF No.76812, was born in Poland on 5 March 1919. During the latter stages of the German occupation of his country Martel managed to escape, arriving in England in early 1940. In May he was commissioned in the RAF and on 6 August he was transferred to the Polish Air Force (PAF). During mid-September Martel was posted to 54 Squadron at Catterick but was moved to 603 Squadron at Hornchurch on the 28th. He remembers his time with the unit with great affection: 'My posting to 603 was one of the most happy and enjoyable periods of the last war. The Squadron was under the command of S/L George Denholm and thanks to him it was a very happy and efficient unit. I will never forget those days.'

Henry Key Fielding Matthews RAF No.40551, joined the RAF on a short service commission in November 1937. On 5 March 1938, he was posted to 9 FTS at Hullavington and subsequently joined 64 Squadron at Church Fenton on 17 September. In June 1940, Matthews was with 54 Squadron at Hornchurch when, on 9 July, he shared in the destruction of a He59. He destroyed a Bf109 on 12 and 25 August before being moved to 603 on 30 September, as part of the on-going effort to redistribute pilot manning levels – compensate for losses – within the Hornchurch-based units.

David Alexander Maxwell RAF No.84962, joined the RAFVR around July 1939 as an airman u/t pilot (754510). He was called up on 1 September and completed his training at 22 E&FTS at Marshall's, Cambridge, and 5 FTS, Sealand. Pilot Officer Maxwell arrived at 7 OTU, Hawarden, on 17 September 1940 where he converted to Spitfires. On 30 September he was posted to 611 Squadron at RAF Ternhill and moved to 603 at Hornchurch on 24 October.

James Storrs Morton RAFVR No.72026, RAF No.90727. Morton was born in Wellington House, Bridlington, Yorkshire on 24 April 1916, to Harold and Donna Morton who had been married nine months earlier on 23 July 1915, when the family home was in Blackheath. Doctor Harold Morton was a six-foot-five-inch former England rugby international with the nickname 'Tiny'. Jim was the eldest of four children. The others were Anthony S.M. Morton (born 1923) who became an Admiral in the Royal Navy, John R.C.M. Morton (1927) who died in Australia some years ago and Hannah, the youngest. At the age of nine Jim was sent to St Anselm's Preparatory School, Bakewell, Derbyshire, where he boarded. Whilst there his parents moved to a larger house in Flamborough Road, just 300 yards from the beach. He moved to the reputable Loretto School, Musselburgh, where he gained a reputation as a fine rugby player and the nickname 'Black' because of the colour of his hair. There were two Mortons in the school at the time, one with blonde hair and Jim with his black hair. Later, colleagues incorrectly believed his nickname was a play on the coal mining connotation or even that he had 'put up a black' (the RAF expression for gaining a black mark from those in authority) since joining the RAF.

In 1934/35, while Black was away at school, tragedy struck the Morton family when the mother was drowned whilst swimming offshore from their local beach at Bridlington. Harold Morton hired

Above: Jim 'Black' Morton. Sailing was his great passion.
Above right: Black in relaxed mode.
Right: Black and Mardi in later years at Woodcote Manor, the family home.

a nanny to help bring up his children and eventually remarried. The couple produced a son, Jay, a step-brother to Black ten years his junior. From Loretto, Black went to Pembroke College, Cambridge where he read chemistry, physics and physiology.

In February 1936, he joined the CUAS and attended the summer camps of 1936 and '37 at RAF Abingdon. By the time he left Cambridge he had gained his A licence/air proficiency certificate. Black also became a very fine yachtsman.

In November 1937, he graduated from Cambridge with a degree in engineering and began working for the Fife Coal Company at Cowdenbeath Colliery where, as a trainee manager, the colliery owner offered him prospects of senior management. However, he was required to spend time at the seams and quickly became disillusioned. His search for more excitement during his spare time led to him joining the RAFVR in July 1938, undertaking 'casual training' at RAF Turnhouse. In May 1939, he joined 603 and his rank of acting Pilot Officer (RAFVR) was gazetted on 23 May 1939. He was subsequently granted a commission in the RAF. He was called to full-time service on 24 August 1939, and his rank of Pilot Officer was confirmed on that date. His first combat experience came on 16 October 1939 for which he received a Mention in Despatches on 29 February 1940. He continued to be involved in some of the early action along the east Scottish coast. On moving to Hornchurch on 27 August he was again involved in the thick of it.

Peter Olver RAF No.84963, was born on 4 April 1917, at Leamington Spa. He was educated at Eniscote Lawn Preparatory School and Bromsgrove. He later studied mechanical and electrical engineering. After working in a business in which his father was general manager and director, Olver moved to the Derbyshire and Nottinghamshire Electric Power Company, as a power development officer. Around March 1938, he joined the RAFVR at Derby, but had done little flying prior to being called to full-time service on 1 September 1939. There was quite some time lapse before he was sent to 3 ITW, Hastings. During early April 1940, he went to 22 E&RFTS, Cambridge, and was posted to 5 FTS, Sealand on 25 June. On 17 September, with his training completed he was sent to 7 OTU, Hawarden where he amassed only ten hours while converting to Spitfires. On 29 September, Olver was posted to 611 Squadron at Digby and on 24 October 'I caused myself to be posted to 11 Group, where the action was and so joined 603 at Hornchurch.'

Arthur Peter Pease RAF No.72447, was born in London on 15 February, 1918. The eldest son of Sir Richard and Lady Pease of Prior's House, Richmond, Yorkshire, Peter was educated at Eton from 1931-36 in the house group of C.J. Rowlatt. At Eton he had been a talented schoolboy; initially he was renowned for his beautiful treble voice and he recorded: 'O for the wings of a dove'. Later, he edited the school magazine. His academic and social achievements at Eton were outstanding.

In 1936, he was sent up to Trinity College, Cambridge, where he read history. He and his close friend Colin Pinckney, whom he had met at Eton, joined the University Air Squadron and undertook flying training at Marshall's Flying School. By September 1938, he had applied for and been granted a commission in the RAFVR.

Peter had been in his final year at Cambridge when he was called up during early October 1939. He was sent to No.1 ITW at Jesus College, Cambridge, after which he continued flying training at 22 E&RFTS, Cambridge. On completion he was initially sent to No.1 School of Army Co-operation at Old Sarum, where he met Richard Hillary and their brief friendship began. Sometime during this period Peter attended a night skating party where he met Denise Maxwell-Woosnam who had joined the ATS and was stationed at a training unit in Cheshire at the time. Daughter of Max Woosnam who, in the 1920s was captain of Manchester City (the only amateur in the side), played tennis at Wimbledon, led the Davis Cup team and scored a century at Lords for England. Denise recalls her first meeting with Peter: '…a bit of glamour in a not very glamorous situation. This tall figure unwrapped itself from the car and it was Peter and that was that.' The couple were quickly engaged. According to Denise: 'Everything happened quickly in war, you saw everything as through a telescope at the wrong end.' Denise was eventually posted to an ack-ack battery in Vange, Essex. On 23 June 1940, Peter was sent to 5 OTU, Aston Down, where he converted to Spitfires. On 6 July he joined B Flight, 603 and achieved his first success on the 30th. Richard Hillary later wrote of Peter:

> Peter was, I think, the best-looking man I have ever seen. He stood six foot three and was of a deceptive slightness, for he weighed close on thirteen stones. He had an outward reserve which protected him from any surface friendships, but for those who troubled to get to know him it was apparent that this reserve masked a deep shyness and a profound integrity of character. Softly-spoken, and with an innate habit of understatement, I never knew him to lose his temper. He never spoke of himself, and it was only through Colin [Pinckney] that I learned how well he had done at Eton before his two reflective years at Cambridge, where he had watched events in Europe and made up his mind what part he must play when the exponents of everything he most abhorred began to sweep all before them.

Charles David Peel RAF No.90199. Born in London on 3 May 1919, Charles Peel was the younger son of Lieutenant Colonel W.E. Peel DSO. The family home was in Haddington, East Lothian. On leaving the army his father became a race horse owner/trainer. Charles was educated at Cheltenham College from September 1932 until July 1937. He began his ab-initio flying training with 603 in December 1937 and was commissioned as a Pilot Officer (AuxAF) on 25 February 1938. He worked locally at the time of joining the Squadron as an apprentice chartered accountant. As was the case with a number of the other pilots, young Charles also owned a fast sports car. He also possessed a small accordion which he could play. One of the ground crew was also a competent accordionist and Charles lent his instrument to him in order for him to entertain his colleagues. He also acquired a bulldog puppy which he named Shadrak and which eventually had to be left at home due to the problems it caused at the aerodrome.

Called to full-time service on 25 August 1939, Charles was promoted to Flying Officer the same day. He was destined to be the Squadron's first wartime casualty.

David John Colin Pinckney RAF No.72520, was born at the family home of Hidden Cottage in Hungerford on 6 December 1918. He had an older brother Brian, born on 7 April 1915, and three sisters. His father J.R. Hugh Pinckney was a senior member of the India tea industry who had been educated at Trinity College, Cambridge. Unable to serve during WWI due to poor eyesight, Hugh Pinckney was in the War Trade Intelligence Department, for which he was awarded the CBE. He was to bear the loss of his two sons in World War II with great fortitude.

Colin's early life was very similar to that of Richard Hillary and Peter Pease – boarding school from an early age followed by university, a period of travel and death in action with the RAF. Of Colin, Richard wrote:

> He had a bony, pleasantly ugly face and openly admitted that he derived most of his pleasure from a good grouse-shoot and a well-proportioned salmon. He was somewhat more forthcoming than Peter but of fundamentally the same instincts. They had been together since the beginning of the war and were now inseparable.

Colin was six foot three inches tall, had brown hair and was slender in build. In contrast his brother was shorter and more rugged, broad, athletic and very powerful. While Brian was easygoing and amiable Colin had a more delicate sensibility. He attended school in St Neots in 1927, and followed the same route as his father and older brother when he was sent to Eton, where he gained a reputation for being idle for which he was frequently punished. However, his reputation was tempered by personal charm, as borne out by his housemaster:

> Colin, perhaps, has mixed feelings on leaving Eton. Mine are not, for I am very sorry that he is going. I know that he has been in a quiet way a good influence in the House.... I admire immensely his attitude of independence towards public opinion – he never bothered to ingratiate himself with his fellows... If he is somewhat idle, he is one of the best advertisements for idleness I have ever come across, and if he has acquired only a small part of his charm from Eton, his time here has certainly not been wasted.

Brian and Colin Pinckney. Both loved shooting and fishing.

His idleness did not prevent him from getting seven credits in his school certificate in 1935, or when three years later he sat for his Tripos in Anthropology at Cambridge from coming within a few marks of first class honours.

Colin was admitted to Trinity College, Cambridge, in 1936, nearly two years after his brother, and graduated in 1939. Brian Pinckney had entered Trinity College in 1934 but did not graduate and left to join the family business after one year.

Colin's interests at Cambridge would perhaps appear culturally apart from the norm in the modern age, in that one so enthusiastic and efficient at fishing and hunting wild-fowl could also be an avid bird watcher and lover of nature. Colin also decided to join the University Air Squadron and underwent flying training at Marshall's Flying School where he flew the Tiger Moth followed by the Miles Master.

An example of his independence was when he went on an extensive tour of Canada during the summer of 1938, experiencing many adventures on the way.

In December 1938, with his flying training with the UAS complete and having qualified as a pilot, Colin successfully applied for a commission in the RAFVR in order to continue to develop his flying skills.

The following summer Colin again visited the Western Hemisphere but on this occasion he headed farther south to Jamaica and Spanish Honduras. As the situation in Europe deteriorated and became ever more warlike Colin was prompted into making an early return to England. He caught a coach north to New York where he found that war had been declared and all shipping to Europe at a standstill: 'I had hoped to return to work, not to war.' When, after a week's delay he embarked for England, it was indeed a return to war. His notification of call-up for service with the RAF was waiting for him at Hungerford. On reporting for duty in early October 1939, his first posting was to No.1 ITW at Jesus College, Cambridge, from where he received further flying training at 22 E&RFTS at Marshall's before being posted to No.1 School of Army Co-operation at Old Sarum during late May 1940. Interestingly, the Pinckney family descend from a knight of one of William the Conquerer's lords who, having loyally served their Norman King during the invasion, subsequently settled in Old Sarum. On 23 June Colin was posted to 5 OTU, Aston Down and after converting to Spitfires was sent to 603, joining A Flight on 6 July.

Harry Arthur Robin Prowse RAF No.42358, joined the RAF on a short service commission in May 1939 and on the 30th of that month he began his ab-initio training at 8 E&RFTS, Woodley. On 11 August he was sent to 13 FTS, Drem, and completed his training at 15 FTS, Lossiemouth. On 6 January 1940, Harry was posted to No.9 Bombing and Gunnery School (BGS), Penrhos, as a staff pilot and on 16 May he was sent to No.4 Ferry Pilot Pool. In June, just prior to the fall of France, he was shot down by anti-aircraft fire near Lille. He managed to force-land his Hurricane in a field and return to England by ship from Cherbourg. On 3 September 1940, Prowse was sent to 7 OTU, Hawarden, and on the 16th, after converting to Spitfires, he joined 266 Squadron at Wittering. On 20 October, he was posted to 603 at Hornchurch at a time when '...most of the Battle of Britain excitement was over.'

William Pearce Haughton Rafter RAF No.42572. 'Robin' Rafter was born on 17 July 1921, the son of Sir Charles and Lady Rafter of Harborne, Birmingham. Sir Charles had served in the Birmingham police force for 37 years, rising to the rank of Chief Constable. In 1932, Robin was sent to Shrewsbury School where he gained a reputation as an outstanding sportsman. He was the novice boxing champion for 1933. Richard Hillary was there at that time. In 1935 Robin's father died and the following year he was sent to Cheltenham College to finish his education.

On leaving Cheltenham, Robin joined the RAF receiving a short service commission on 26 June 1939. Having volunteered and been accepted for aircrew training he was sent to 6 Civilian Flying School (CFS), at Sywell in Northamptonshire. On 2 September 1939, having obtained his civilian flying licence, he then went to 12 FTS at Grantham in Lincolnshire, but was sent to 10 FTS at Ternhill just three days later to complete his flying training. Here he gained his 'wings' brevet. He was promoted to Pilot Officer on 1 February 1940 and was posted to No.2 School of Army Co-operation at Andover to undergo training on twin-engine aircraft. On 17 March 1940, on completion of his course, he was then sent to No.1 School of Army Co-operation at Old Sarum. From here he went to Andover on 26 April where he remained on supply flying duties until 7 May when he was posted to 225 Squadron at Odiham, Hampshire. On 10 June, 225 moved to Old Sarum and Robin was engaged on coastal reconnaissance flying in Lysanders even after the Squadron was again moved to Tilshead. On 22 August 1940 he was sent to 7 OTU at Hawarden where, after converting to Spitfires, Robin was posted to 603 at Hornchurch. His arrival coincided with that of Brian Macnamara and Jim MacPhail on 31 August. He was with a frontline squadron with just 15 hours training on Spitfires.

William Albert Alexander Read RAF No.80822. Bill Read was born on 11 August 1918 in Palmers Green, London and went to school in Mill Hill. On leaving school he became a junior publisher's assistant and worked on Richmal Crompton's *Just William* proofs which appealed to his sense of humour.

He joined the RAFVR in July 1938 as an airman u/t pilot (741635) and began his flying training at 21 E&RFTS, Stapleford Tawney. By the time he was called up to full-time service at the outbreak of war, he had logged 46 hours and 40 mins flying time.

Bill went to ITW at Selwyn College, Cambridge in November 1939, and was posted to 15 FTS Lossiemouth on 1 January 1940, along with Pip Cardell, Alfred Sarre and Jack Stokoe, in whose company he remained throughout the time of his training and ultimately his service with 603 during the Battle of Britain.

As part of No.6 Course he began flying with the initial training school on 2 January. On completion of this on 18 March, he moved on to the Advanced Training School (ATS). He passed out from 15 FTS on 8 June 1940. On the 10th Bill's promotion to Pilot Officer was promulgated and he was posted to 5 OTU at Aston Down, where he began conversion training to Spitfires the following day. On 21 June he completed his course and on the 23rd was posted to 263 Squadron at Drem, where he began converting to Hurricanes. On 1 July the squadron moved to Grangemouth. At that time 263 were converting to twin-engined Westland Whirlwinds and Bill was given the choice of staying and converting to this type or remaining on single-engine aircraft. He chose the latter and on 3 July was posted to A Flight 603 Squadron, where he soon acquired the nickname 'Tannoy' because '....he kept chattering on the radio.' After being blooded in combat on 24 July he flew with 603 throughout the Battle of Britain.

Ian Small Ritchie RAF No.90198, was another squadron member who was a writer to the signet (solicitor) in civilian life.

Born in 1910, he gained a degree in Law at Edinburgh University and LL.B., and went to work in the city for Dove, Lockhart, Mackay and Young W.S. When his local squash club played RAF Turnhouse he met George Denholm for the first time. George suggested that Ian might like to join 603 Squadron and learn to fly. This he duly did and he began his ab-initio flying training in December 1937. Ian Ritchie and George Denholm remained great friends until Ian died.

Ian Ritchie's rank of Pilot Officer (AuxAF) was confirmed on 15 February 1938. He was given the nickname of 'Woolly Bear' (shortened to 'Bear') by his colleagues on account of the contrast between his impressive powerful build, and his kind, quiet and gentle demeanour.

On 23 August 1939, he left behind the antiquated wood and leather decor as well as the peace and calm of his solicitor's office in York Place when he was called to full-time service. He was also promoted to Flying Officer. Like George Denholm, Bear was 30 at the time of the Battle of Britain. The two friends were well aware of the large age difference between themselves and the youngsters coming into the Squadron just prior to the battle, particularly in the case of Bear with his prematurely greying hair. Nevertheless they were very supportive and provided a necessary and much respected level of experience and maturity for the newcomers.

On 3 July 1940, Bear saw action when he shared in the destruction of a Ju88, recalling that his section carried out a piece of precise blind formation flying through a wall of cloud in which they made two precise course changes before emerging into brilliant sunlight at 14,000 feet to execute the unsuspecting Junkers! Prior to flying south with 603 he recalled flying five patrols in a 26-hour period.

Frederick William Rushmer RAF No.90192. Fred 'Rusty' Rushmer, so nicknamed by his fellow pilots because of his dark red hair, was born at Sisland, Norfolk on 12 April 1910. He was the youngest of 11 children and tragically the first to die. The Rushmer family were farming landowners and quite well-off. Their family home was Manor Farm, Thurlton. As a young man he, like so many of his 603 colleagues, had owned a fast sports car. In Fred's case an MG. He had been an engineering draughtsman in civilian life and, while he was at his first place of employment in Norwich, had won the opportunity to experience flying in a competition entered by all the lads in his office. This first flight was at Horsham St Faith (now Norwich Airport). Having moved to Edinburgh to take up a job at Bruce Peebles Engineers in the city he joined 603 Squadron. His rank of Pilot Officer (AuxAF) was confirmed on 19 October 1934. He was promoted to Flying Officer (AuxAF) on 19 April 1936. On 23 August 1939 he was called to full-time service and promoted to Flying Officer. He was one of the most experienced pilots in the Squadron at this time and was appointed leader of Red Section. Promoted to Flight Lieutenant on 12 March 1940 he was made commander of B Flight when it was sent to Montrose. A common memory of Rusty was that he was far too nice to be a fighter pilot. In *The Last Enemy* Richard Hillary described their first meeting:

Rusty Rushmer (aged 22) and his father.   Rusty, aged 21.

As we came in, half a dozen heads were turned towards the door and Rushmer, the Flight Commander, came forward to greet us. Like the others, he wore a Mae West and no tunic. Known by everybody as Rusty on account of his dull-red hair, he had a shy manner and a friendly smile. Peter [Pease], I could see, sensed a kindred spirit at once. Rusty never ordered things to be done; he merely suggested that it might be a good idea if they were done, and they always were. He had a bland manner and an ability tacitly to ignore anything which he did not wish to hear, which protected him alike from outside interference from his superiors and from too frequent suggestions from his junior officers on how to run the Flight. Rusty had been with the Squadron since before the war: he was a Flight Lieutenant, and in action always led the Red Section. As 603 was an Auxiliary Squadron, all the older members were people with civilian occupations who before the war had flown for pleasure.

On 30 July 1940 Rusty had shared in the destruction of a He111 south-east of Montrose. During what was his first experience of combat his own aircraft had been hit by return fire.

Alfred Richard Sarre RAF No.197053. 'Joey' Sarre, as he was known by his fellow 603 pilots, joined the RAFVR during March 1939 as an airman u/t pilot (745543). He was called up on 1 September 1939, and following ITW he was sent to 15 FTS at RAF Lossiemouth where he began flying training with No.6 Course, Initial Training School (ITS) on 2 January 1940. He was on the same course as Pip Cardell, Jack Stokoe, and Bill Read. With the ITS training completed on 18 March, he moved onto the Advanced Training School (ATS) which he successfully completed on 8 June. On the 10th he went to 5 OTU, Aston Down, and conversion training to Spitfires began the following day. With a total of just over 20 hours flying time he completed his training on 21 June and was posted to 263 Squadron at Drem on the 23rd, where he began converting to Hurricanes on the 26th. The Squadron moved to Grangemouth on 1 July.

263 Squadron were about to convert to the twin-engine Westland Whirlwind and, like his associates, when offered Joey made the choice of remaining on single-engine fighters. He was posted to 603 on 3 July, arriving at A Flight, Dyce where he made his first flight with the Squadron on the 6th. He became very good friends with Jack Stokoe.

Francis David Stephen Scott-Malden RAF No.74690. Born on 26 December 1919, at Portslade, Sussex, David Scott-Malden was educated at Winchester College, where he met Black Morton, and won a scholarship to Kings College, Cambridge where he gained first class honours in his Classic preliminaries, and won the Sir William Browne Medal for Greek verse in 1939. He also shot at Bisley.

'Scottie' joined the University Air Squadron at Cambridge in November 1938 and on completion of his initial training in June 1939, he joined the

RAFVR (NCO No.754343). He was commissioned on 3 October and called to full-time service in October 1939. On 1 January 1940, he was posted to FTS Cranwell and in late May, after completing his flying training, he was posted to No.1 School of Army Co-operation, Old Sarum. He was at Old Sarum while Richard Hillary, Peter Pease and Colin Pinckney were there, but left on 10 June when he was sent to 5 OTU, Aston Down, where he converted to Spitfires. He was on the same course as Bill Read, Pip Cardell, Alfred Sarre and Jack Stokoe. On 3 October when Scottie was posted to 603, he was reunited with Colin Pinckney. By then Richard Hillary was in hospital and Peter Pease had been killed.

Scottie's part in the unit's wartime history was to be significant, both as a fighter pilot and leader.

John Flewelling Soden RAF No.42903, joined the RAF on a short service commission during August 1939. He was sent to 9 FTS and with training complete he went to 5 OTU, Aston Down on 10 June to convert to Spitfires. He was on the same course as Scott-Malden, Sarre, Stokoe, Cardell and Read but remained for three days further training. On 26 June he was posted to 266 Squadron at Wittering. On 15 August Soden shared in the destruction of a He115 floatplane. The next day his Spitfire, K9864, was severely damaged in combat with Bf109s over Canterbury. With slight wounds to his legs he made a forced landing near Oare, Faversham. On 14 September Soden joined 603 at Hornchurch.

Basil Gerald Stapleton RAF No.41879, was born in Durban, South Africa on 12 May 1920. His father, John Rouse Stapleton OBE, had been born in Thurlby, near Stamford, England and had a distinguished career in marine radio service and broadcasting.

In 1935, Gerald and his older brother Deryck (later Air Vice-Marshal Deryck C Stapleton CB, CBE, DFC, AFC, RAF [Retired] were sent to King Edward VI School, Totnes, Devon.

On 23 January 1939 Gerald applied for a short service commission in the RAF. Gerald was sent to 13 E&RFTS, Civil Flying School at White Waltham for his ab-initio flying training, which was privately run by de Havilland. It was here that he learnt to fly Tiger Moths, to this day one of his favourite aircraft.

On 15 April he was sent to 13 FTS at Drem for flying training and on 21 October 1939, with training complete, he was initially sent to a detached unit of 219 Squadron at Redhill, flying Blenheim Is, but the next day he was sent to 11 Group Pool (attached) at St Athan for operational training where he remained until 20 November 1939. Having converted to Hurricanes, from St Athan he was posted to 32 Squadron for a brief period before going to 603 on 16 December 1939 when, he recalled, '...it was decided to send a number of experienced, full-time pilots to the auxiliary squadrons to complete their establishment of pilots.' On arrival he had to convert to type having previously flown Hurricanes. The Spitfire became his favourite.

His rank of Pilot Officer was confirmed in appointment on 23 January 1940. By that time Gerald was married to Joan but did not qualify for 'married man's allowance' or a married quarter. The couple therefore found it hard to make ends meet.

On 26 April 1940 at Drem, Gerald was forced to bale out of his Spitfire at night.

Following B Flight's move to Montrose he acquired the nickname 'Stapme' from an expression used by Captain A.R.P. Reilly-Ffowll in the *Daily Mirror* cartoon strip 'Just Jake'. Reilly-Ffowll was always chasing attractive women

Stapme Stapleton and his brother Deryck.

and one of his expressions when he saw a woman was 'Stap-me, what a filly!' Gerald used to cut the cartoon from his paper and stick it on the notice board in the dispersal hut. This irritated his flight commander, Fred Rushmer, who preferred that the board be kept for official notices only!

Stapme became great friends with Bubble Waterston, one of the experienced members of the Squadron, and together they were responsible for creating what was to become a legend: the story of 'the children at Tarfside.' He saw combat in defence of the Scottish east coast and southern England through the summer of 1940.

Dudley Stewart-Clark RAF No.78535, was one of a number of local men in the Squadron, from West Lothian. He was born at Dundas Castle, a member of the wealthy Coates family, the manufacturers of fine threads, and enjoyed a comfortable lifestyle. He was educated at Eton and joined the RAFVR around May 1939, as an airman u/t pilot (748218) – possibly having undertaken initial flying training as a member of a UAS. He was called up on 1 September 1939, and at Abbotsinch until 29 April 1940, when he was posted to A Flight, 603 Squadron, at Dyce. His rank of Pilot Officer was promulgated on 17 April 1940, and he was involved in the early action off the north-east coast of Scotland before moving south.

Dudley Stewart-Clark's grave in Pihen-les-Guines, France.

Jack Stokoe RAF No.60512, was born the son of coal miner on 1 February 1920 in West Cornforth, County Durham, otherwise known as 'Doggie'. He received a good education and so employment in the mines was not an option. He started work at 18 as a council technical assistant. Promotion within the council was slowed by the influx of miners who received preferential treatment so, keen to further his career within the technical clerical system, he travelled south and took up a position in the chief inspector's department of Buckinghamshire County Council in Aylesbury, taking lodgings nearby.

Living away from home, weekends and evenings were tedious so, in search of an inexpensive and exciting hobby, he joined the RAFVR in June 1939, as an airman u/t pilot (748661) where he did his weekend flying at 26 E&RFTS, Kidlington, Oxford. Between 17 June and 5 September he amassed a total of 53 hours 45 minutes of flying time.

With war looming Jack was emphatic, he wanted to be a fighter pilot *not* a bomber pilot. He was called to full-time service at the outbreak of war and given the honorary rank of sergeant. On 5 September he was sent to No.1 ITW, based at Magdalene College, Cambridge, where he underwent four months of 'lectures and still more lectures' but no flying. He recalls about half the intake were randomly selected for fighter pilot duties, the remainder going on to fly bombers after ITW.

On 1 January 1940, he was posted to 15 Flying Training School (FTS) at Lossiemouth where, as part of No.6 Course he began flying training with Sergeant Joey Sarre and Bill Read and Philip Cardell with whom he would later serve. He took his first solo flight on 9 January and recorded in his log book: 'That feels better!' He completed the first half of the course at ITS (Initial Training School) on 18 March and on 8 June completed the second half of the course with the ATS (Advanced Training School) at 15 FTS. While at 'air firing school' he achieved 45 hits out of 100, when a normal score was 5-15. Under the heading: 'proficiency of pilot on type' his instructor recorded: 'average'. On the same day he learned that he was being sent to 5 OTU at Aston Down.

Jack Stokoe at Lossiemouth with a Harvard.

Still in the company of fellow 603 pilots to-be Jack was at Aston Down from 10-23 June, where he converted to Spitfires. He amassed a total of 20 hours 25 minutes on Harvards and Spitfires and completed the course on the 21st. His log book was signed by Flight Lieutenant 'Prosser' Hanks, veteran of 1 Squadron which had been in the thick of the air fighting in France during May of that year. On 23 June 1940, Stokoe was posted to 263 Squadron at Drem.

On 26 June, along with his three associates from the course at Aston Down, he began converting to Hurricanes. The Squadron moved to Grangemouth on the 28th where Jack continued his training on Hurricanes. On 3 July he had his last flight

Jack Stokoe with his sweetheart.

with 263 Squadron. The unit was about to convert to twin-engine Whirlwinds and Jack, like Cardell, Read and Sarre, was given the choice of converting, or remaining on single-engine fighters. He chose the latter and on 3 July was posted to 603 Squadron's A Flight. He took his first flight in a Spitfire with them on 6 July and during the weeks until the move south he amassed more than 80 hours flying time. Of his colleagues he wrote:

I did not know all the people in the Squadron. Some were on leave, some in the other flight and, inevitably, there was the officer/NCO divide. There was a big divide in 603 in this respect as it was an auxiliary squadron and the RAFVR NCO was a world apart. I recall the red-lined tunics of the officers and that the NCOs and officers only mixed at dispersal/readiness. At other times they were in their own messes and quarters.

Jack being rescued from the sea after having been shot down whilst with 54 Squadron at Hornchurch, 1941.

John Mawer Strawson RAF No. 741453 (Sergeant), 120105 (Squadron Leader), DFC, was born to a yeoman Lincolnshire family on 13 July 1916, at Stragglethorpe House, near Cotgrave, Nottingham. The eldest son of William Henry and Lois Elizabeth Strawson of Marnham, Nottinghamshire, his parents were farmers and, in addition to John, had five other children – two younger brothers and three younger sisters. Initially educated at High Pavement School, and Radcliff-on Trent, Nottingham, he was later sent to a preparatory school in Ruthin, North Wales. At the age of 16, with his schooling complete, he went into business as an egg merchant at the Old Vicarage at Low Marnham in Nottinghamshire, where his family had recently moved. At first he was reliant upon a motorbike to get about but as he became more successful he purchased a lorry on the side of which the Strawson name was proudly displayed. With the business running smoothly he went in search of interests away from work and decided to take advantage of his growing fascination for flying (he was also aware that war was looming). On 18 April 1938 he joined the RAFVR as an AC2, being promoted to sergeant the following day. He underwent flying training at 27 Elementary and Reserve Flying Training School, Tollerton, Nottingham, where he flew Hawker Hinds and Harts, and Miles Magisters. He first went solo on 11 June 1938 aged 21.

Strawson was recalled from the reserve on 3 September 1939, reporting to Nottingham TC mobilisation station and on 29 December, following a lengthy wait, was sent to 3 ITW, at Tollerton. He then went to HQRC Pool on 7 March 1940 before moving to 14 FTS at Cranfield, Bedfordshire, on 11 May where he underwent training, having already worked his way through the syllabus at Tollerton before the war. The advanced part of the course was on North American T6 Harvards. On 31 August he was sent to 7 OTU, at Hawarden, where he converted to Spitfires. On 16 September he was made operational and sent to 616 (South Yorkshire) Squadron at Kirton-in-Lindsey. During the early stages of the Battle of Britain 616 had suffered heavy losses whilst operating from Kenley and had to be withdrawn first to Coltishall in Norfolk and then to Kirton. Redesignated a 'C' class squadron the surviving pilots were given the task of carrying out familiarisation training of the replacement pilots in readiness for combat. One of the new influx was Sergeant John Strawson.

On 3 October 1940, Strawson was posted south to Hornchurch, initially to 41 Squadron but on arrival was immediately assigned to 603 to fill the space recently left by the death of a pilot.

Patrick Hugh Richard Runciman Terry RAF No.1190615. Sergeant Pilot Patrick Terry joined the RAF on a short service commission in January 1936 (officer's No.37725) with the rank of acting Pilot Officer confirmed on 30 March. On 25 October 1936, on completion of his flying training, he was posted to 19 Squadron at Duxford. His rank of Pilot Officer was promulgated on 3 February 1937. On 16 September 1937, Terry was posted to SHQ staff at RAF Halton. His promotion to Flying Officer was confirmed on 3 November 1938 and on 2 February 1939, he was sent to 111 Squadron at Northolt. On 12 September 1939, he resigned his commission.

Terry's second spell in the RAF began in 1940 when he rejoined as a pilot. Having completed further training he was posted to 72 Squadron at Biggin Hill on 3 October, as a sergeant pilot. He was posted to 603 later that month.

Robin McGregor Waterston RAF No.90197, was born at 58 Netherby Road, Trinity, Edinburgh, on 10 January 1917. Soon after his birth the family moved to 8 Wardie Road, Leith. Robin was the second youngest (and youngest son) of eight children born to James Sime and Mabel Waterston. James Waterston was educated at the Edinburgh Institution from 1885 to 1890 and became director of George Waterston & Sons Ltd, the famous Edinburgh firm of stationers and printers. During his working life James Waterston also developed many other business interests. All the sons of James and Mabel Waterston attended Melville College (formerly the Edinburgh Institution). John Leslie Waterston attended from 1909 to 1917 and on leaving travelled to Australia. He returned to Edinburgh in 1931 and joined the Royal Scots. Phillip Blair Waterston attended from 1916 to 1926. He travelled to New Zealand and in 1932 he died as the result of injuries received in an accident.

Robin was educated at Melville College from 1922-35. He was made a prefect in 1934 and selected for the 1st XV for the season 1934-35. As a young man he was fascinated by things mechanical and it was with great reluctance that he took a job in insurance with the Alliance

Bubble Waterston. Always a keen mechanic, even as an officer!

Assurance Company which his father had arranged for him. He loathed being stuck in an office and accident assessment on behalf of the company gave him an excuse to get out into and around Edinburgh. It also gave rise to a lucrative pastime when he renovated motorbikes which had been damaged or written-off and charged a fee accordingly. He had a fascination for flying from an early age and was a keen modelmaker. At the Pathhead flower show in 1938 he exhibited a collection of 30 model aircraft he had built from scratch or cast in metal. His younger sister Jean helped with the display. She is still involved with the show today. After a restless year in the insurance business Robin finally succeeded in getting his own way. On 6 September 1938, at his first matriculation, he gained his Scottish Universities Entrance Board Learning Certificate, with a 'higher' for English and maths and a 'lower' for science and French, and began studying for a science (engineering) degree at the University of Edinburgh.

He joined 603 (City of Edinburgh) Bomber Squadron, AuxAF, and his commission as a Pilot Officer (AuxAF) was gazetted on 3 February 1937. Once in the Squadron, he was keen to put on an overall, roll up his sleeves and work on the aircraft engines, such was his mechanical prowess. The sight of an officer with his sleeves rolled up working on the engine of one of the Harts was certainly unusual.

He was awarded his 'wings' in July 1937 and promoted to Flying Officer (AuxAF) on 3 March 1938.

Soon after joining 603 Squadron, this good-looking young man was nicknamed 'Bubble' by his fellow pilots and even 'Delectable Bubble' by P/O Colin 'Robbie' Robertson. The nickname is thought to have been given on account of his bubbly, effervescent personality and the *Water*-ston connotation (some incorrectly assumed his nickname was 'Bubbles', a corruption of the original pronunciation), however, George Knox, who was a member of Robin's ground crew believes the name was attributed in response to his likeness to a ruddy-cheeked young lad in a billboard poster advertising Pears soap. The painting, produced by Sir John Millais in 1886, is entitled 'Bubbles' and is of a youngster blowing bubbles from a clay pipe. It was acquired by Pears for £2,200 and used for promotion once the soap tablet had been added to the painting.

It was during 1938 that he met Patricia Greenhouse-Allt whose father was the director of music at St Giles Church, Edinburgh. It is possible Robin knew Dr. Allt from his days at Melville College where he taught music. Robin and Pat who, at fourteen, was five years his junior, were still going out together when he was killed. They shared many wonderful times particularly at the Allt's family home, a flat on the corner of Melville Street and Stafford Street. In 1938 he shared a month long summer vacation with them at their holiday home in St Andrews. At that time he owned a Norton motorbike but eventually graduated to an MG convertible sports car. In 1938, Robin took Pat to the summer ball at Turnhouse where she recalled how splendid he and the other officers looked in their dress uniform.

Robin was still studying for his engineering degree when he was called to full-time service on 24 August 1939 and given the rank of Flying Officer. He was with B Flight in July 1940 when Richard Hillary arrived and he later included a thumb-nail sketch of Robin in his book:

'Bubble' Waterson was twenty-four, but he looked eighteen, with his short cropped hair and open face. He, too, had been with the Squadron for some time before the war. He had great curiosity about anything mechanical, and was always tinkering with the engine of his car or motorbike.

During the time at Montrose several pilots decided to name their aircraft with Richard Hillary's 'Sredni Vashtar', XT-M, L1021 (formerly 'Auld Reekie') probably being the most famous. George Knox was one of Bubble's loyal ground crew right up until the time he flew south to Hornchurch. He remembers being asked to paint the words 'Ard Choille!' (the war-cry of the McGregor clan, pronounced 'Ard

Coil') on the starboard cowling of Bubble's Spitfire. He used white enamel paint and Bubble was so impressed he asked George to paint the McGregor coat-of-arms on the port cowling. Unfortunately, there was not the variety of colours available but the next time he was on leave in Edinburgh George bought a number of tins of modelling enamel paint from Woolworths and completed the task by adding the coat-of-arms under the white lettering of Ard Choille, much to Bubble's delight.

No matter what he was involved in, he forever exhibited a joyful, youthful exuberance and an unconscious charm. His unquestioning acceptance of everyone in the Squadron for what they were made him without doubt the most popular member with officers and ground crew alike.

Shortly before moving south to Hornchurch with 603 and knowing he would soon be in the thick of battle, as a gesture of his gratitude for all the good times he had shared with the Allt family he presented them with a gift of a cast-metal Spitfire plated in gold and mounted on a bakelite plinth.

Archie Little Winskill RAF No.84702, was born in Penrith, Cumberland, on 24 January 1917. He joined the RAFVR in April 1937, as an airman u/t pilot (740365). According to (Sir) Archie:

I have been a lucky survivor in aviation from 1937 to 1982. Before the war, twice I successfully landed a Hawker Hart in a field – once because of engine failure, and secondly through bad weather between Stirling and Glasgow. Weather forecasting was unheard of in those days!!

At the outbreak of war he was called to full-time service. From September 1939 until June 1940, Winskill was a staff pilot at BGS Catfoss. He was commissioned in August 1940, and converted to Spitfires at 7 OTU, Hawarden before being posted to 72 Squadron on 4 October. On the 17th he moved to 603 and first flew with the Squadron on the 20th.

The ground crew
Amongst the many 603 ground crew personnel present at Hornchurch were: John Barrington Smythe Mackenzie – known as 'Tails' because of his ability on the dance floor of the pre-war Edinburgh halls – who served with 603 throughout WWII and, until his death in 2002, was Chairman of the 603 Association; Bob Wilson, who also served with the Squadron during the whole of the Second World War; Bill Smith and Reg Cockell, Jim Skinner, James 'Chic' Cessford, George Knox, Bubble Waterston's fitter; Alec Mackenzie, Ken Macdonald's fitter; Harry Ross who, according to Richard Hillary, was killed at Hornchurch during the lunchtime raid of 31 August 1940; Freddy Marsland and 'Tug' Wilson, Richard Hillary's rigger and fitter; Bert Pringle, Stapme Stapleton's fitter; Jackie Crooks, Artie Carrol, James 'Spanky' McFarlane; Tommy Devlin; George Mullay, the oldest ground crewman in the Squadron; Angy Gillies; AC1s Forrest, Adams, Ritchie, Worthington, Dickinson and Reynolds; and LACs Dickson and Baldie.

Ground crew, Montrose, July 1940.

Whilst Ken Macdonald had initially been against war and believed the nation was being let down by its politicians, by now he was all for fighting for what he saw was a just cause, particularly as many of his friends were engaged in the conflict with one force or another. During June, Ken took a few days leave and travelled south to visit some of his old haunts. In a letter written to Mardi on 11 July he provides a further insight into the period. His opening comments are in response to the recent promotions amongst the pilots of 603 Squadron, including his own to Flight Lieutenant:

> Colossal show – at this rate we should have the old Force cleared out of braid, tape and whatnot in no time at all.
>
> Thanks for your letter... I have been wanting to write to you for ages, but you've just no idea how impossible it is... I don't suppose I ever told you... I had 4 days around the 22nd June. I went south and stayed at '76' [his old accommodation in Victoria]. I went to Reimanns which was emptier than ever and closing down that day... Otherwise it rained the whole weekend and it was all a bit melancholy.
>
> I have been a terrific stooge lately. One of my lugs packed up about a couple of weeks back [as a child Ken had been plagued with sinus problems and had undergone surgery on a number of occasions] and the other was pretty phoney too, so that I couldn't hear the local bombs dropping at all and just paid no attention. So it does put me off flying – as it was high altitudes that caused it (sudden ups and downs coupled with hay-fever and blocked up schnozzle etc.) – anyway there I was on the ground with the boys bringing down rights and lefts all around me like driven grouse while I heard not a sausage – and I was always looking in the wrong direction.
>
> Now I have been bumped down here [Turnhouse] to be controller for a fortnight. Damned stupid! I can hear fine now and can flap like anything with the rest of them once again! So if there is the hell of a shambles in this sector anytime inside the next fortnight you will know what it's all about.
>
> Meanwhile it's damned nice living at home and doing not very long, and set, hours a day and being able to read and write in peace – quite like peace time again – almost call my soul my own. I go about now with an enormous Ghat ('equalizer') these days [RAF issue pistol] – great fun. I'm sure I shall loose it off at someone bending over one day!
>
> Lots of Love
> Ken

On the 11th Ken proceeded to RAF Turnhouse for a spell on controller duties, P/O Colquhoun was posted to RAF Drem, and the Squadron continued with patrols and practice flying, particularly for the new arrivals. On Friday 12 July, A.M. Bulletin No.1107 announced: 'His Majesty The King has been graciously pleased to approve of No.110 (City of Toronto) Squadron, Royal Canadian Air Force, being allied to No.603 (City of Edinburgh) Squadron, Auxiliary Air Force.'*

On this day Yellow Section, 603 Squadron (Sheep Gilroy and Sgts Bill Caister and Ivor Arber) took off at 12.43 from Dyce and shot down He111 H-3, 1H+FT, of 9/KG26 over Aberdeen. Unfortunately, the German bomber crashed on to the town's recently opened ice rink, the resulting fire destroying the aircraft and the new building. The crew of four – Leutnant Huck and Unteroffiziers Plischke, Skokan and Kerkhoff – were killed. Wreckage from the Heinkel was taken away and dumped at the 'race course' situated on the outskirts of Aberdeen. The city race course had actually closed many years prior to WWII and the site became the city rubbish dump but retained its original name. Kids who salvaged pieces of the wreckage inadvertently created a myth which has perpetuated over the years by stating that the Heinkel had crashed on the race course.

On Saturday 13 July P/O Don Macdonald, younger brother of Ken, made a forced landing at Montrose when the connecting rod went through the crankcase, causing the Merlin engine of Spitfire L1024 to seize. Since his arrival at B Flight, Don had undergone a number of sector

---

*This was the third alliance of a unit of a Dominion Air Force to a unit of the Royal Air Force. The first, announced on 15 August, 1938, was that of 21 (City of Melbourne) Squadron, Royal Australian Air Force, and 600 (City of London) (Fighter) Squadron, Auxiliary Air Force; the second announced on 19 January, 1939, was that of 22 (City of Sydney) Squadron, Royal Australian Air Force, and 602 (City of Glasgow) (Army Co-operation) Squadron, Auxiliary Air Force.

reconnaissance flights to acquaint himself with the local terrain. He struggled with the task which was not altogether surprising as throughout his entire flying training he had only flown over the flat Cambridgeshire and Lincolnshire countryside. This difficulty had not gone unnoticed and Fred Rushmer and Laurie Cunningham assessed Don's reconnaissance and navigational skills as being 'technically laim' and later that same day he departed for South Wales, where he underwent further training with 417 (General Reconnaissance) Flight at St Athan.* On this day the Squadron were also involved in operational night flying in addition to the now familiar daytime routine of patrols and practice flying. The next day saw more practice flying and daytime patrols.

The morning of 15 July dawned cloudy and overcast. F/L Laurie Cunningham was replaced by F/L Ken Macdonald after his term on controller duties at RAF Turnhouse and returned to B Flight at Montrose. At 11.55 two Spitfires of Yellow Section, Black Morton and Dudley Stewart-Clark, were scrambled and at 12.15 spotted He111 H-3, 1H-EK, of 2/KG26 as it emerged from the thick cloud 15 miles east of Peterhead. It was to prove a most unfortunate move by the pilot with such generous cover available. The Spitfires carried out a hurried three-quarter attack before the German pilot, Oberleutnant Ottmar Hollmann, managed to disappear into the cloud once again. The Spitfires returned to Dyce. The short attack however had been extremely accurate. Later that day, four of the crew, Hollmann, Obegefreiter Probst, Unteroffizier Walz and Obegefreiter Prefzger, were picked up from their dinghy in the North Sea. The fifth member of the crew, F. Reinhardt, had been killed. The crew members were able to confirm that having climbed from their ditched aircraft into the dinghy they had counted over 200 bullet holes. (It is intriguing that the state of mind of the crew was such that they were able to count the holes in their aircraft having just been in combat, shot down, ditched in the sea and taken to their life raft.) The surviving crew members were taken to Fraserburgh as PoWs.

As well as his log book, Black Morton kept a diary of his combat experiences. Of this patrol he wrote:

Cloud 10/10, 1500-2000' over land. 7/10-10/10, 500-200' over sea, wind light west.

1150. Yellow [Section] (self and Dudley Stewart-Clarke [sic]) to seek bandit, Banff, below cloud. On way diverted to Peterhead. Emerged at Cruden Bay 600' to meet sea mist (down to 200') climbed over this and turned N to P'head. When off there D [Dudley Stewart-Clark] reported unidentified to starboard flying S to SE and went to investigate: turned round and pursued A/C. D went in before I could identify but return fire was enough for me. Later saw it was He111 with large cross outlined in white on side. Hun was by now in cloud but usually dimly visible. D finished his attacks. I then did two diving attacks from the quarter (starboard) without visible effect, though return fire (from twin guns) ceased. EA now going NE towards denser clouds. Speed was low, definitely less than 100 and I overshot badly while manoeuvring for position. Cloud got thicker and in addition my windscreen was badly oiled up (J) and the reflector-sight partially pegged out, making shooting in cloud hopeless.

Four Huns paddled ashore in their rubber boat and report they were shot down by us. The twin fire noticed was due to fire through side windows. Dudley knocked out one rear gunner – who was replaced – and one engine (hence oil on his A/C). I probably got the other engine, though Dudley may quite well have got both. The Huns didn't seem quite sure when the second engine got hit. I lost him in the cloud, he was forced landing towards the coast.

D reports his AC covered with Hun oil. When last seen (20 miles out) Hun was apparently OK though going slowly. We had no hits. A very unsatisfactory and untidy battle. The nearness of the sea below the cloud was rather a drawback. However, we're both pretty confident we hit him.

The next day flying activity intensified with day and night-time patrols, co-operation and practice flying.

---

*417 (General Reconnaissance) Flight was established at St Athan on 15 July 1940.

CHAPTER 7

THE SQUADRON'S FIRST
BATTLE OF BRITAIN CASUALTY

On Wednesday 17 July, with the poor flying weather continuing, 603 were busy with daytime patrols, co-operational and practice flying and again saw action. A raid had taken place on the Imperial Chemical Industries factory at Ardeer, Ayrshire by He111 H-3s of Major Victor von Lossberg's III/KG26, flying from Stavanger, Norway, and the aircraft were heading home in a straggled formation as Spitfires of 603 caught up with one of them. Red Section, of Ritchie, Morton and Stewart-Clark, shot down He111 H-3, 1H+KT, of 9/KG26, 25 miles north-east of Fraserburgh at 16.12 hours. Two crew members, Oberleutnant Lorenz and Unteroffizier Beer, were seen by the Spitfire pilots to climb into a rubber boat. They later became PoWs but Unteroffizier Liedtke and Gefreiter Heimbach were killed. It was reported that Red 2, Black Morton's Spitfire was hit in the starboard mainplane by an armour piercing (AP) bullet.

At this time more and more Luftwaffe units were being established in Northern France and the German army's plans to invade Britain, Operation *Sealowe* (Sealion), had been finalised. The troops from twelve 'crack' divisions had been chosen with air cover provided by Luftflotte 2 and 3.

Following this patrol Black recorded in his diary:

Fine, hazy, some cloud above 20,000' and out to sea at 7,000'. Wind very light, southerly.

About 3.30, Yellow [Section] (Ian, self and Dudley) patrol Frazer burgh [sic] 20,000'. When in position, ordered to steer SW 12,000' and then Aberdeen 25,000' almost immediately told Hun bombing Peterhead 20,000. Then Frazerburgh 20,000'. Sighted He111 flying E, 18,000' 6-8 miles N. Frazerburgh 6 miles off. Hun saw us when we were about 1-2 miles away and opened up (black smoke) and started gentle dive. Ian went in to identify positively, I pulled out to starboard quarter (into sun). Ian then attacked and I got into position on starboard quarter when Dudley shot over my head and attacked. I let Ian and he finish and then went in. Hun was doing massive turns and diving, but nothing very steep. I opened with about 30 degrees deflection with no visible effect; but soon got into excellent position dead astern at 250 degrees. The return fire, which had been fair, stopped and almost immediately the starboard engine and most of the rest of the Hun were obscured by a large cloud of black smoke and a shower of bits fell out of the starboard engine. I thought it was going to blow up so broke away. The black smoke died away and was replaced by a long trail of white smoke and steam. Hun was now at about 9,000' making for a bank of cloud at 7,000'. Ian then made another attack and I followed him. There was return fire again, but it seemed poor (all below). Hun then turned round west and headed for the land, losing height. He force landed quite well but not as well as the St. Abbs chap. One chap seemed OK and got out on to the wing. He appeared to be helping a second. I could see a man still sitting in the top rear-gunners place. The machine was settling down and I couldn't read the letters. I climbed up and set off for home keeping careful course and time.

I reported Huns as 25-80 degrees from Frazerburgh. They were picked up later in the evening. Two of them – we'd got the rear gunner and his replacement. They were frightfully grateful at the trouble we took to pick them up and also for not being shot at as they descended. There was no need to tell them we'd no more cartridges.

I had one bullet in starboard main plane, but we've patched it up with fabric for the present.

F/O Charles Peel, flying with A Flight in Spitfire K9916, did not return from a patrol on this day. While on detached duty with 603 from 41 Squadron as an instructor F/O John Young met solid resistance when he had recommended Peel be given further training:

F/O Charles Peel, who was lost on 17 July 1940, 603's first casualty in the Battle of Britain.

> Colonel Peel and his wife had a house near Drem [Haddington] and I had recommended that as Peel was so inexperienced he should be sent to an Operational Training Unit for further training. The Peels put on a party at which they tried to get me to rescind my decision, but the long and short of it was that, in my judgement, Peel's flying, in particular his instrument flying, was inadequate and this was born out when he died while flying from Montrose. I believe he dived out of control into the sea. I felt very sad for his mother who was a wonderful person.

Charles Peel was a Flying Officer at that time and, aware of his own failings, it is tragic that in this case he was not as willing as Don Macdonald to accept the situation and take good advice. It is also sad that John Young was seen as a pedant by a number of the senior officers in the Squadron and not simply as someone doing his job.

The exact circumstances relating to Peel's disappearance will never be known although, as the weather was not good for flying, he may have lost his way, suffered some kind of mechanical failure and/or run out of fuel before he could reach land. It may be that his aircraft was hit by return fire from an enemy aircraft. What is easiest to assume is that when he went down it was in an area where his recovery was least likely, and the North Sea became his grave.

Thursday 18 July 1940 was a very busy day for 603. Generaloberst Hans-Jurgen Stumpff's Luftflotte 5, based in Scandinavia, had started to increase the regularity of operations directed at the north of Britain. At 10.00 hours three Heinkel 111s of KG26 attacked Montrose unopposed. At 10.08 Green 1, Ras Berry was ordered to patrol Montrose at cloud base and managed to intercept one of the bombers at which he fired two short bursts '...which very probably crashed'. He landed again at 11.20. At 14.17 hours the three Spitfires of Yellow Section flown by Flying Officer Ritchie, and Pilot Officers Morton and Read were sent up to intercept a convoy-spotting Dornier Do 215 10 miles east of Aberdeen. They all fired at the enemy aircraft but did no apparent damage. They landed back at Dyce at 15.53. Yellow 2, flown by Black Morton, had a very fortunate escape when his Spitfire, L1049, Tigger, was hit eight times by accurate return fire during the exchange with the German gunners. He later recorded in his diary:

> Cloud 10/10, 1000-3000' inland and to coast. Cloudless but slightly hazy out to sea. Wind light W.
>
> About 2.30, Yellow [Section] (Ian, self, Read) patrol Colliston 3000'. Then steer SE and orbit A/C sighted by Read flying NW 2000' 3m W of us. I pulled out to starboard to identify and Ian went in behind. A/C Do215. Ian did astern attack and E/A then turned round to SE. As he turned I saw Read about 600' behind apparently going in to attack. I told him to wait; but got no answer and as Hun was in nice position for beam attack, delivered one, developing from full beam to astern chase as Hun did steep evasive turns and dived to 500'.
>
> Return fire was good and I felt two hits in starboard wing. Then an explosive or incendiary went off with a hell of a flash right in front of my face. It tore a hole in the top cowling and the camshaft cover. I gave him one more burst and broke away in a flat shielding turn, which appeared to fox the gunner. Hun then jettisoned his bombs (about 10). Ian did another attack and I then finished my rounds in a quarter attack and returned home at speed, as I didn't know what damage was done.
>
> On landing I found I had eight bullet holes. One in port tail plane, cutting trimmer chains – never realised how much one uses the trimmer till it wouldn't work. One in port mainplane, one in starboard mainplane. This stopped two guns (192) after 50 rounds by cutting their

belts. One glanced off starboard oleo leg, taking most of the fairing, one glanced off the radiator fairing. Two in airscrew. One of these was the one which went into the top cowling. If it hadn't hit the airscrew it looked as though it would have hit plumb in the middle of the windscreen. The last one hit the port side engine bearers and broke up, one bit cut a deep groove in the crankcase, another went through the main oil pipe (fortunately only a small bit) another bit cut a groove in the main petrol feed. There can't have been much more than a good thickness of bumf left.

Ian had no hits and Read lost us after his first abortive attack – he was actually breaking away when I thought he was approaching.

Notes: This may have been one of the new heavily armoured Huns as:

i.   His performance was rather like 'trailing his coat' for us.
ii. Ian and I both fired all our pellets with no apparent effect and both thought we were shooting well.
iii. There is a report of six Spitfires of a reputable squadron attacking a Do215 without effect.
iv. The tail swastika was on a red ground – possibly a special distinction. Certainly both the evasive action and the return fire were well above average.

By that time a number of the A Flight pilots had named their aircraft after characters in the children's story 'Winnie-the-Pooh' by A.A. Milne.*

At 16.25 hours two Spitfires from Red Section, Red 1, Sheep Gilroy and Red 3, Sgt Bill Caister, were again sent up to intercept a He111 from KG26 over Aberdeen. Sheep fired all his ammunition but was then hit by return fire, damaging the glycol cooling system of his Spitfire, R6755, forcing him to land near Old Meldrum at 16.40 hours. Red 3, Bill Caister, did not sight the enemy and returned to base at 17.03. Red 2 had trouble taking off and did not take part in the engagement.

At Montrose a Miles Master trainer, piloted by a student of 8 FTS, taxied into a parked 603 Spitfire, N7881, causing some damage.

Finally, late into the evening, between the times of 22.25 and 22.45 hours, 603 achieved success. During a raid on a convoy off Aberdeen by Ju88s of Major Fritz Doensch's I Gruppe, KG30, Bill Caister attacked a Ju88 and fired four bursts at a range of 100 yards closing to 50 yards, damaging the enemy aircraft. Caister reported that having fired at the Ju88 it then dived steeply into low cloud and was not seen again. He was confident that it would crash into the sea, but owing to cloud and darkness was unable to follow it. The enemy aircraft later crashed in Aalborg, Denmark with a wounded crew member on board.

On Friday 19 July flying continued by day and night. Bill Caister was again in action when he intercepted an enemy aircraft in Spitfire K9995. His own aircraft was hit by return fire but he returned to Dyce safely. Meanwhile, Don Macdonald was finding South Wales less agreeable than Cambridge, Cranwell and Montrose and was keen to rejoin his squadron. On 19 July he wrote:

We don't actually get much time off on this navigation course, but from what I've seen, the country is flat and uninteresting…. the towns and villages ugly and dirty, and the Welsh village people nothing like as friendly as in the North. Furthermore the Huns bomb us every night here – the bombs make a lot of noise but do very little damage which is most reassuring! Jolly nice… Ken getting leave. I've been thinking of him and his guns which I

---

*The original illustrations for the books (before Disney produced their own simplified version of the cartoon characters in 1936) were by E.H. Shephard. Black Morton named L1049 'Tigger' and, whilst it is not known for sure, it is likely Ian Ritchie named his Spitfire after the 'Bear' himself. The artwork was ably undertaken by those of the ground crew most gifted with a paintbrush. B Flight had AC1 George Knox, as noted earlier.

Born in London in 1879, Ernest H. Shephard won a scholarship to the Royal Academy of Arts and later worked for *Punch* magazine as a cartoonist and illustrator. Shephard's drawings appeared in many books for adults and children but he is best known for his illustrations of Winnie-The-Pooh and his friends in the Hundred Acre Wood. E.H. Shephard died in 1976.

should think were practically red-hot almost the whole of last week! I'll be back at Montrose this time next week...

On Saturday 20 July 1940 Pilot Officer R.G. Manlove, a ferry pilot, was delivering a new Spitfire to B Flight at Turnhouse when he crashed on landing. The aircraft, R6752, was repaired on-site and later flew operationally with 603.

At 11.35 hours Blue Section took off from Montrose led by F/L Laurie Cunningham with F/O Bubble Waterston and P/O Stapme Stapleton and shot down Dornier Do17P, A6+HH, 30 miles east of Aberdeen. The aircraft crashed into the sea in flames at 12.05, the crew, Leutnant Heur and two NCOs were reported missing with one NCO known to have been killed. Stapme's memories of this incident are still vivid:

Montrose was a very exciting time for us because we had German aircraft to intercept. The 20th of July was the first time I fired my guns in anger. We had a lot of German aircraft over on reconnaissance missions and that was when I shared a Dornier Do17 with Bubble. There were three of us; Cunningham was leading with Bubble as his No.2 and me as his No.3. Cunningham approached the bomber, but for some reason he didn't fire at it. Later, after we had landed, he told us that he had gone up to the aircraft to identify it, which was bloody nonsense! So Bubble went in and opened fire and I followed behind and did the same. For some reason Bubble refrained from carrying out another attack but when I closed in I could see the dorsal gun pointing straight up, instead of at me, which indicated that the rear gunner had been hit! I then flew in close formation alongside the aircraft and was able to make a note of its squadron letters and numbers before it landed in the sea. I got on the radio to tell them where it was so they could get a fix on me and get the Air Sea Rescue crew out to pick up the surviving crew members. When I returned to base they told me that they hadn't sent anybody out to rescue the crew because the weather was too rough, but it certainly was not. I had to land at Dyce after that patrol because, much to my amazement, my oil pressure gauge showed naught, but the temperature wasn't going up! So I realised that I couldn't have lost my oil because my temperature gauge was OK. I remember once when 'Uncle' George was A Flight Commander at Dyce, he landed and he had what I remember as being a glycol leak, and the engine was still going, it hadn't seized. The manufacturer's engine identification brass plates fixed to the side of the engine, saying 'Rolls-Royce' etc, had melted and were buckled, but the engine was still running! That gives you some idea of the quality of the Rolls-Royce engine.

Why he got his nickname – P/O Noel 'Broody' Benson. F/L Fred Rushmer is on his right.

On 21 July P/O Noel Benson returned from leave having spent the time with his parents at the family home at Great Ouseburn in Yorkshire. On the 22nd S/L Stevens was discharged from RAF Hospital, Cosford, following surgery on his troublesome shoulder, and granted 22 days sick leave.

The Squadron was in action again between 14.47 and 16.00 hours on Tuesday 23 July. B Flight, Blue Section with Flight Commander, Rusty Rushmer, Ras Berry (R6626) and Broody Benson (N3229) took off at 14.47 and shot down a Dornier Do17P 75 miles east of Aberdeen at 15.30 hours. The enemy aircraft crashed into the sea and all four crew members were killed. The Spitfires of Blue 1, Rushmer and Blue 3, Benson received hits from accurate return fire, but despite the damage they managed to nurse their aircraft back over the 70 miles of the North Sea, landing at Montrose at 16.00 hours. Whether as a result of the damage received or not, the starboard undercarriage leg failed on N3229 during landing causing damage to the wing tip.

That same day the CO, S/L George Denholm, landed at Montrose with the undercarriage of Spitfire N3026 still retracted. The aircraft was damaged in the ensuing crash but repairable and the CO was unhurt.

Left: N3229, XT-N, 23 July 1940. Flown by Noel Benson, this aircraft had been hit by return fire from a Dornier Do17 prior to crash-landing.
Right: Another shot of Noel Benson's aircraft after crash-landing.

Don Macdonald was granted six days leave. Having only recently completed his flying training and an additional course deemed necessary due to his lack of navigational skill, he sadly lacked flying hours on type. Perhaps a period of intense flying practice would have been more appropriate than a motoring trip to the west coast of Scotland.

At 07.00 on Wednesday 24 July the Spitfires of Red Section, Sheep Gilroy, Jack Haig and Bill Read, damaged a Heinkel He111 H-3 of III/KG 26 over the North Sea between Aberdeen and Peterhead. The port engine and rear gunner were put out of action but as the enemy aircraft lost height it disappeared into low cloud and was not seen again. The Heinkel made it back to base on one engine with three wounded NCOs on board and crashed on landing. Damage was assessed as being 25%. The next day patrols and practice flights continued.

For 26 July the ORB recorded: '...fighting patrols by day. Co-operation, operational and practice flying. P/O George Gilroy landed at Dyce and put Spitfire N3288 on nose in mud. P/O D. Stewart-Clark returned from leave.' By the end of July Sheep had been involved in the shooting down of seven enemy bombers whilst flying with A Flight from Dyce and had accumulated valuable experience for the battle ahead.

On the 28th, F/L Ken Macdonald returned from six days leave which he spent at the family home in Murrayfield. A friend remembers seeing him at the local swimming baths and recalled how desperately tired he looked. The fact that he was still keen to attend the local balls at this time was an indication of how much he loved dancing. Once the fighting began from Hornchurch, Ken rarely left his room when off duty and when he did it certainly wasn't to go dancing. The responsibility of being deputy CO and the effect the fighting was having on him was most probably the reason for this change. Photographs of Bubble Waterston taken during July/August also show him looking tired and dark around the eyes (see page 176).

At 11.47 on Monday 29 July, Red Section – Bill Read, and Sgts Bill Caister and Jack Stokoe – took off from Dyce and intercepted two intruders. The ORB states: 'Red Section sighted 2 He111, 12 miles west of Aberdeen. There was thick cloud. Red 1 fired at e/a whch jettisoned its bombs into the sea. E/a was lost in cloud and no damage was seen. Red 2&3 did not get close enough to fire.'

It wasn't long after arriving at Montrose that Richard Hillary and Peter Pease were made operational. In *The Last Enemy* Richard wrote that the B Flight Commander, Rusty Rushmer, made him operational after he was almost shot down by Brian Carbury during a practice flight, stating that: 'I think it will be safer for everyone'.

On 30 July the weather was again overcast and at 11.45 Green Section – Rushmer, Berry and Pease – took off from Montrose and intercepted a Heinkel 111, 40 miles east of the base. The bomber was shot down into the sea. There were no survivors and one body was seen floating on the water. The Spitfires landed again at 12.35.

This attack on Heinkel He111 H-4 of 8/KG26 was Peter Pease's first operational combat experience and he was credited with a 'share' or a third of the kill. Ras, flying Spitfire R6835, was also credited with a share. His aircraft was hit by return fire along with that of Flight Commander Rushmer. Both were repairable. KG26 had mounted a small number of raids against

Above: Colin Pinckney, Richard Hillary and Peter Pease. Peter Howes in inset.
Right: B Flight, Montrose, August 1940. F/Ls Laurie Cunningham (left), and Rusty Rushmer (centre), with P/Os Stapme Stapleton (standing) and Richard Hillary.

P/O 'Broody' Benson (right), B Flight Montrose, August 1940.

Scottish cities from their base in Norway. Whilst the slow Heinkels and the faster more agile Ju88s were relatively easy targets there was still significant risk from return fire. These early skirmishes provided little in the way of preparation for fighter versus fighter combat.

On 31 July, following an invitation from the Earl of Dalhousie to the pilots of 603 to stay at his hunting lodge at Invermark, Glen Esk, F/O Brian Carbury was granted six days leave and, along with a number of colleagues from the Squadron, was one of the first to take advantage of the offer. Of those that stayed at Invermark Lodge, Carbury became one of the more successful hunters. A talent which seemed typical of the accomplished fighter-pilot 'ace' was that they were also good shots with the full-bore rifle or, more particularly, the shot gun where an understanding of good deflection shooting was a necessity. The scenery in Glen Esk is stunning and in stark contrast to the airfield at Montrose with its frequently inhospitable weather conditions, the most memorable being the icy wind that blew off the North Sea. In the quiet of Glen Esk the pilots could relax in the hunting lodge with the option of stalking the hinds (the male stags that needed to be culled seasonally), shooting grouse (which took place during two or three days in August), and fishing in Loch Lee, which was situated just 200 yards from the lodge which overlooked the water from a prominent position. On returning to Montrose Brian Carbury wrote of his experiences in a letter home dated 8 August 1940:

We have a lodge near here… way up in the hills and we usually go up there for one or two days and have lots of good fishing and shooting grouse, hare, rabbits and now stag. Last week I got me a young stag, 24 rabbits and four trout. It is marvellous getting up there away from it all and not having to worry about dress or anything.

The Children of Tarfside

Montrose and Dyce only required one section at 'readiness' at any time, therefore, with the remainder of the Squadron's compliment of pilots either 'available' or 'released', time away from the base was always possible. Unless you lived close by there was not a great deal to do during the daylight hours and after dark the mess was home to those who had come from far away. While at Montrose Stapme Stapleton's girlfriend visited and they married at a church in the nearby town. Richard Hillary and Peter Pease occasionally drove to Dyce to see Colin Pinckney; from there they drove into Aberdeen for a night out. Therefore, the offer from Lord Simon Ramsey, the 16th Earl of Dalhousie, to use his hunting lodge at Invermark was greatly appreciated. Boulter, Berry, Cunningham, Hillary, Carbury, Waterston and Stapleton were just a few who made the 20-mile trip inland from Montrose. However, despite the stunning surroundings Bubble and Stapme soon became bored with fishing and shooting and on a bright sunny day towards the end of July whilst staying at the lodge, they were driving from Invermark towards Tarfside on their way back to the aerodrome in Bubble's MG convertible, when they chanced upon a scene which captured their imaginations. The local families and holiday-makers were enjoying a picnic on the grass next to Migvie Farm while watching, as well as participating in, the Loch Lee games, a mini highland games. It was an event which had been going for many years. Back in 1940 most of the cottages in Glen Esk were holiday homes as they are today. Many of the inhabitants in the glen during those momentous summer months were in fact made up of locals, estate workers, shepherds, ghillies, game keepers, evacuees and holiday-makers. The Tarfside kids consisted of the children of a number of the holiday-makers staying in holiday cottages, the children of the local inhabitants and evacuees from nearby Brechin who were lodging with the locals; some also stayed in the lodge. The two pilots were made welcome and participated in the games with Stapme leading the way. They stole the hearts of the children and were asked to come and play with them the next time they were on leave. They found the invitation irresistible and the parents were grateful for the additional distraction. Back at Montrose the pilots occasionally flew along the glen during practice flights, providing an impromptu flying display before the eyes of the enthralled children. Although it was only for a period of a few weeks, while they were on holiday in the glen, to visit the children at Tarfside became a popular getaway for the pilots. With the Loch Lee games over for another year, the pilots took the children on a picnic to Glen Mark, swimming in Loch Lee where they also played on a German dinghy captured from a Heinkel which had been shot down by the Squadron. On another occasion, following a day of games they finished off by telling stories to the youngsters in the hayloft at a farm called Migvie between Tarfside and Invermark. During their second visit Bubble and Stapme took Richard Hillary who was in their section of B Flight. When his book was published in 1942, the world found out about Tarfside and thus the legend of the 'Children of Tarfside' was born. Hillary wrote:

> Bubble and Stapme would both come up to Invermark but neither of them shot. How they employed their few hours of freedom will, I think, come as a surprise to a number of people, for they must have seemed from the outside as typical a pair of easy-going pilots as one could expect to meet anywhere. Stapme with his talk of beer, blokes and carburettors, and Bubble with his absorption in things mechanical, might have been expected to spend their leaves, respectively, in a too-fast car with a too-loud blonde, and in getting together with the chaps in the local pub. In point of fact they played hide-and-seek with children.
>
> Tarfside was a tiny hamlet a few miles down the road from Invermark, and to it this summer had come a dozen or so Scots children, evacuated from the more vulnerable towns in the district. They went to school in Brechin, a few miles from Montrose, but for the holidays they came to the mountains, under the care of Mrs Davie, the admirable and unexacting mother of two of them. Their ages ranged from six to sixteen.
>
> How Stapme and Bubble had first come upon them I never discovered, but from the moment that I saw those children I, too, was under their spell. That they really came from Brechin, that thin blooded Wigan of the north, I was not prepared to admit; kilted and tanned by the sun, they were so essentially right against that background of heather, burns and pine. They were in no way precocious, but rather completely natural and

unselfconscious. In the general confusion of introductions, one little fellow, the smallest, was left out. He approached me slowly with a grave face.

'I'm Rat Face,' he said.*

'How are you, Rat Face?' I asked.

'Quite well, thank you. You can pick me up if you like'.

I gave him a pick-a-back, and all day we played rounders, hide-and-seek, or picnicked, and as evening drew on we climbed up into the old hayloft and told stories. Stapme, Bubble and I striving to outdo one another.

I lost my heart completely to Betty Davie, aged ten. She confided to me that I was her favourite and I was ridiculously gratified. She was determined to be a school teacher, but with those eyes and the promise of those lips I did not doubt that her resolution would weaken.

It was with regret that we drove back to the aerodrome, and with the latent fear that we should not get back to Tarfside. We drove always straight to the dispersal point, each time expecting the greeting 'Tomorrow we move south'. Out before the huts crouched our Spitfires, seemingly eager to be gone, the boldly painted names on their noses standing out in the gathering dusk.

Richard told the story of Sredni Vashta the ferret, and the Wizard of Oz. His death was later announced in the local paper under the heading: 'Last of the Long-Haired Boys'. Some of the children kept the cutting believing that all the RAF pilots who had visited the glen had been killed. Invermark Lodge, the glen and its quite breathtaking setting has not changed since the summer of 1940.**

When B Flight received orders to return to Turnhouse it was with immediate effect and no time to say goodbye to their young friends in Glen Esk.

August 1940

By 1 August the RAF Fighter Command Order of Battle showed that 603 had 11 aircraft ready for combat with four more unserviceable and 20 pilots on state. No commanding officer is noted at this stage as George Denholm had still to be confirmed in the position.

Poor flying conditions reduced the number of operations on both sides of the Channel and, similarly, also caused a great number of flying accidents with the experienced as well as trainee pilots. On Friday 2 August Sgt Ivor Arber crashed his Spitfire, R6717, at Inkhorn, Aberdeenshire. Despite the aircraft being a write-off, Arber was unhurt.

On Saturday 17 August 603 Squadron received orders to prepare for a move south to Hornchurch in Essex. A and B Flights were recalled to Turnhouse on 23 August in readiness. The following day, after 15 years in the RAF, Bill Caister was commissioned.

---

*Today, Graham McCrow lives in Carnoustie. He has retained many memories of the summer at Tarfside when, as the youngest, he had been considered something of a burden by one or two of the older children and nicknamed 'Rat Face'.

**In 1998 Stapme returned to the glen prompting a local resurgence of interest.

CHAPTER 8

OUT OF THE FRYING PAN...
SOUTH TO 11 GROUP

The news that 603 would be moving south was exciting for all, but in particular Broody Benson, as Richard Hillary recalled:

> Broody was hopping up and down like a madman. 'Now we'll show the bastards! Jesus, will we show 'em!' Stapme was capering about shaking everyone by the hand, and Raspberry's moustache looked like it would fall off with the excitement. 'Eh, now they'll cop it and no mistake', he chortled. 'I've had just about enough of bulling about up here!' Even Boulter was out of bed, his ears twitching uncontrollably. Our relief squadron was already coming in, plane after plane engining down over the boundary. Rusty quickly allocated us to sections, and 'B' Flight roared twelve strong across the aerodrome, dipped once over the mess and headed south.

The Squadron were to wait anxiously for another four days before the move south was finally confirmed. On 26 August the CO of Turnhouse, Lord Geordie Douglas-Hamilton, offered them a couple of days grouse shooting on his estate. The original party had consisted of Peter Pease and Colin Pinckney with A Flight pilots Sheep Gilroy and Black Morton. Peter had to drop out as he was on duty and Richard Hillary volunteered to take his place. The weather was awful and Richard, cold, wet, and making little attempt to hide his misery, found some consolation in the hospitality on offer. Sheep and Black had to return for duty that night but Richard and Colin stayed for a hot bath, dinner and the promise of more shooting the next day, if it wasn't raining. At 02.00 hours Richard and Colin were awakened by one of the ghillies who had received an urgent telegram from Turnhouse:

SQUADRON MOVING SOUTH STOP CAR WILL FETCH YOU AT EIGHT OCLOCK STOP – DENHOLM.

By ten the next morning they were back at Turnhouse. On the 27th Bill Caister was granted seven days leave to get married and, with his recent promotion, enjoy a double celebration.

During that period the pilots had been eager to become involved in the battle being fought in the south of England but were concerned that they had yet to come up against the Messerschmitt Bf109E-3 & 4 (Emil).* The plodding Heinkel III and the slightly more formidable Junkers Ju88 armed only with MG15 machine guns had provided easy victories. Once news of their move to 11 Group came through naturally there was a great deal of conjecture as to how they might fare in fighter versus fighter combat. The Bf109 (Me109, as the pilots themselves referred to it) was still relatively unknown to the 603 pilots who gleaned information on the 109's performance limitations from RAF air intelligence briefs, supplemented by discussions with battle-weary pilots from other squadrons who had been posted to the relative tranquillity of 13 Group for a rest. They discovered the 109 was a *very* good fighter. Its advantages lay in its high speed, good performance above 25,000 feet (7,625m), acceleration in a dive and the negative-g capability of the fuel injection system employed by its Daimler-Benz DB 601A engine. The aircraft was armed with two 7.9mm MG 17 machine guns (1,000 rounds) mounted on the engine and a Rheinmetall MG FF 20mm Oerlikon cannon mounted in each

---

*Interestingly, a little known fact is that the Bf109F (Friedrich) was operational in small numbers during the Battle of Britain and Werner Mölders was one pilot who flew the variant.

wing. At that stage of the war the use of cannon in fighters was still very much in the development stage, an example of which was the early attempts to arm the 109 with an engine-mounted 20mm MG FF which fired through the propeller boss. This was initially beset with problems not least of which was the effect of vibration on the engine and overheating of the breach. As a consequence, and contrary to myth, this armament was used only by a few senior pilots during the main part of the Battle of Britain. Nevertheless, the thin-cased 20mm Mine rounds fired at RAF aircraft from the two existing cannon (supplemented by incendiary and armour-piercing rounds) resulted in atrocious damage to both aircraft and pilot when they exploded on impact.* Whilst the entry and subsequent explosion within the aircraft's skin caused

Turnhouse, August 1940. 'Auld Reekie', Cunningham's aircraft, with his own rear-view mirror fitted. Note the patched gun port. A member of the ground crew is warming up the engine.

enough damage, the shell splinters also took a terrible toll on aircraft and the frail human body of the pilot. The early production Spitfires carried no armour protection for the pilot and as a consequence of the initial experiences of RAF fighter pilots, including the Advanced Striking Force (ASF) in France, armour protection in Spitfires and Hurricanes was ordered. In response the 603 ground crew personnel hastily carried out the modifications on their Spitfires before the Squadron headed south: a 3mm light alloy cover was fitted over the upper fuel tank to deflect rounds striking from a shallow angle, a $1^3/4''$ (41mm) thick chunk of laminated glass was bolted to the front windshield to provide protection from rounds fired from head-on, and 73lbs of armour plating was fitted to the cockpit behind the pilot's seat (including a $1/4''$ thick piece of stainless steel behind the pilot's head). Many pilots had been killed as the result of being shot in the back and head from behind and this point had gone unheeded by Fighter Command until that time.** However, there were limits to the amount of weight that could be added to the aircraft without incurring unacceptable penalties. Officialdom stated that by installing the steel plate, the speed of the aircraft would be reduced by three miles an hour. Possibly, the surviving Hurricane pilots from the Expeditionary Force returning from France may have told them that the loss of three mph was of no great interest to a dead pilot. Hector MacLean would lose the lower part of his right leg when a cannon shell exploded in his cockpit during the Battle of Britain, cutting short his input in this period of the conflict. The cannon round had entered his Spitfire from behind and even if the armour plate had extended far enough down to protect the pilot's legs the armour was not thick enough to stop a cannon shell. Interestingly, in order to save weight the armour behind the pilot's seat was tapered, being thinnest at the top and getting thicker towards the base of the seat. By this time rear-view mirrors had also been fitted.

However, the 109 did have its failings: a relatively poor combat radius of action and, as a result of its considerably higher wing loading, inferior turning performance compared with the Hurricane and Spitfire. The range could have been increased by using the 66 Imp gallon (300 litre) *Zusatztank* (drop-tank) but the issue of these came too late for use in the battle. On 25 July 1940 an 11 Group

---

*The MG FF 20mm Oerlikon cannon carried 60 rounds of ammunition per gun, firing 8-9 rounds per second with a total firing time available of approximately seven seconds. Whilst just one shell could prove lethal the low muzzle velocity limited the penetration power and the low rate of fire proved more suitable to the marksmen than the less experienced fighter pilots. Improvements were made with the later MG FF-M which was fitted to the E-4 variant of the 109. The only difference between the E-3 and 4.

**Whilst the Bf109 was fitted with back and head armour for the pilot, reports on a number of wrecked 109s reveal the existence of an additional armour plate in the fuselage which the Luftwaffe had begun fitting in the field from July 1940. During the Battle of France, Luftwaffe pilots realised just how vulnerable they were: under their seat was the L-shaped, self-sealing fuel tank in which 88 gallons (400 litres) of 87 octane fuel was carried!

Bulletin to pilots read:

> A recent experiment with a captured Me109 shows that this type is exceptionally well armoured against fire from directly astern. Even point five A.P. failed to penetrate... Head-on and deflection shooting should be increasingly employed as opportunity offers. There is no evidence yet that armour protection has been provided for the engine.

In the years since the Battle of Britain, family members of 603 pilots recall the apprehension and trepidation expressed by their sons or brothers as the air activity increased around the shores of Britain, but overall they remember the determination and enthusiasm expressed by them that the Germans had to be stopped and that they were only too willing to fight and, if needs be, die. Both Rushmer and Waterston believed they would not be coming back, but unlike contemporary warfare, their cause was clear and unequivocal.

Bubble looking tired, August 1940.

Information had been filtering back that the squadrons of British and allied fighters were fighting a desperate battle against a far greater number of Luftwaffe bombers with fighter escort but were holding their own (analysis of German records after the war showed that the Luftwaffe had the following aircraft available for the air attack on Britain: 1,200 Heinkel and Dornier bombers; 280 Junkers Ju87 dive bombers; 769 Messerschmitt Bf109s; 220 Bf110s and 140 reconnaissance aircraft). Whilst the number of available RAF fighters was actually comparable with that of the Luftwaffe the overall number of Luftwaffe fighters *and* bombers was superior, with guns being fired at the RAF pilots from both enemy fighters and bombers alike. Thanks to Lord Beaverbrook a revolution in aircraft production had taken place. Three days after becoming Prime Minister, Winston Churchill appointed Beaverbrook Minister of Aircraft Production and he did not care who he antagonised when he cut through red tape. Churchill wrote of him:

> This was his hour. His personal force and genius combined with so much persuasion and contrivance, swept aside many obstacles. New or repaired aeroplanes streamed to the delighted Squadrons in numbers they had never known before.

Air Chief Marshal Sir Hugh Dowding, AOC-in-C, Fighter Command, commented:

> We had not the supply of machines necessary to withstand the drain of continuous battle. Lord Beaverbrook gave us those machines and I do not believe that I exaggerate when I say that no other man in England could have done so.

Each night during the height of the Battle of Britain Beaverbrook would call Air Vice-Marshal Keith Park to ask how many aircraft he needed. Beaverbrook then proceeded to make every effort to get them supplied. Replacing pilots was a different matter.

Post war, the RAF analysts, with the help of captured German records, divided the Battle of Britain into five key phases, commencing on 10 July 1940 and ending on 31 October, a total of 114 days. This was the first battle in history which changed the course of an entire war without any participation by land or naval forces.* The preliminary phase began on 10 July with attacks on Channel convoys and the south coast ports. Dowding noted in a report to the Secretary of State for Air that this was the day on which

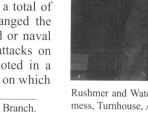

Rushmer and Waterston, officers mess, Turnhouse, August 1940.

---

*Air Narrative Vol.II, The Battle of Britain July-Oct 1940, Air Historical Branch.

Watch office crew, Turnhouse, 1940.

the Germans employed: 'the first really big formations – seventy aircraft – intended primarily to bring air fighter defences to battle on a large scale.' The second phase of the battle began on 8 August when daylight offensive operations intensified. On the 12th the Luftwaffe began heavy attacks against airfields and on the 19th Air Vice-Marshal Keith Park, AOC of 11 Group, which was responsible for the defence of the whole of south-east England, and into which 603 Squadron would be moving, sent a directive to his group and sector controllers:

> The German Air Force has begun a new phase in air attacks, which have been switched from coastal shipping and ports to inland objectives. The bombing attacks have for several days been concentrated against aerodromes, and especially fighter aerodromes, on the coast and inland. The following instructions are issued to meet the changed conditions:
>
> (a) Dispatch fighters to engage large enemy formations over land or within gliding distance of the coast. During the next two or three weeks we cannot afford to lose pilots through forced landings in the sea.
> (b) Avoid sending fighters out over the sea to chase reconnaissance aircraft or small formations of enemy fighters.
> (c) Dispatch a pair of fighters to intercept single reconnaissance aircraft that come inland. If clouds are favourable, put a patrol of one or two fighters over an aerodrome which enemy aircraft are approaching in clouds.
> (d) Against mass attacks coming inland, dispatch a minimum number of Squadrons to engage enemy fighters. Our main objective is to engage enemy bombers, particularly those approaching under the lowest cloud layer.

In another directive, Keith Park summarised the tasks of his fighters in order of priority in the event of invasion:

> 1.) To avoid being attacked on the ground and when taking off.
> 2.) To destroy bombers and fighters attacking fighter aerodromes.
> 3.) To continue operating from inland aerodromes – Sectors and Satellites – whilst these are being attacked.
> 4.) To destroy enemy aircraft in the following order of importance:
>   i.) Transport aircraft.
>   ii.) Dive bombers.
>   iii.) Reconnaissance aircraft and high bombers.
>   iv.) Fighters which will be attacking our bombers and army co-operation aircraft.

Left: The wives at Tidings Hill, summer 1941, the home of George and Betty Denholm.
Right: 603 husbands and partners taken during the same get-together.

From 16 August, Luftwaffe bombers attacked the London area. During a five-day period between 19 and 23 August there appeared a comparative lull in the air battle, before heavy attacks against fighter airfields in the south-east began on the 24th, when central London was also bombed. In retaliation the RAF attacked 'military objectives' on the outskirts of Berlin. By this time the Germans believed that Fighter Command was on the verge of collapse and saw the latest phase as an attempt to finish them off. Night attacks also intensified. It was during this phase that 603 Squadron joined the fray.

The news that reached the pilots of 603 only served to agitate and make them all the more enthusiastic to be a part of the great air battle and, by achieving success, acquit themselves well in combat. Many of the pilots had already gained some combat experience, albeit against bombers, but those that had not felt they still had something to prove and were keen to do their bit. For some, that first baptism of fire would be so terribly short. With many patrols flown in recent months they had enjoyed plenty of time to scan the airspace around with the only adversary coming in the form of slower bombers. A first encounter from an unseen foe which was a fast fighter with a tactical height advantage would be very different…. A few seconds of devastating, withering cannon and machine-gun fire, the massive flow of adrenaline, the heart pounding, seemingly out of control; deafening, shuddering bangs as the Spitfire is hit, the instruments disappear in front of the pilot in a welter of exploding glass, the body jerks spasmodically in reaction to the impact of bullets, cannon shells, and shrapnel; feelings of being hit with great force in the parts of the body not protected by the armour plate but no pain, the Spitfire slowing perceptibly, the cockpit starting to fill with smoke and petrol fumes with the terrifying threat of fire. Sheer panic has already overwhelmed the inexperienced pilot, the feeling of claustrophobia is heightened in the cramped cockpit, visibility feels limited, more so by goggles and oxygen mask, the flow from which does not seem to keep up with demand; the body wet from perspiration under flying clothing and beads of sweat running down the face. The smell of rubber and chamois, occasionally vomit, in the mask. A quick look to see where the enemy is, seeing nothing but the blinding sunlight above and behind, an attempt to take evasive action or to get out of the stricken aircraft, but too late, the delay, although just a few seconds, has been too long and without evasive action the crippled aircraft is still prey. Perhaps a cry for help from the physical and mental pain of their plight... a Mother's face... then nothing….

When the Squadron travelled south the personnel left behind their families and loved ones, including Betty Denholm, Patricia Greenhouse-Allt, Bubble Waterston's teenage girlfriend who was destined never to see him again; Ras Berry's fiancée Nancy Watson; Bill Caister's fiancée; Jack Haig's fiancée, Diana Holt; Eltider Wallace; Joan Stapleton; Jack Stokoe's wife; Evelyn, Sheep Gilroy's girlfriend; and Ian Ritchie's wife. Already in the south were Mary, Fred Rushmer's girlfriend and, in service, Mardi, Ken Macdonald's girlfriend and Denise Maxwell-Woosnam, Peter Pease's fiancée.

Tuesday 27 August 1940
At 11.00 hours the pilots took off from Turnhouse and flew down to Hornchurch in Essex, and into the heat of the battle. The movement of the Squadron was the responsibility of Air Chief Marshal Sir Hugh Dowding AOC-in-C Fighter Command and Air Vice-Marshal Keith Park, commanding 11 Group. Dowding's chain of command reached from his headquarters in Bentley Priory at Stanmore, Middlesex, to Group HQ (including 11 Group at Uxbridge) and from there to the sectors such as

Sector D at Hornchurch which covered the area roughly between Southend and Folkestone. The 603 ORB for this day reads: 'All flying personnel and 38 other ranks proceed to Hornchurch.'

Fighter Command and the Air Ministry did not hesitate in sending 603 to the harder-fought front line of southern England. They were to relieve the battle-weary 65 Squadron which had only five aircraft and 12 pilots left. They were sent to Turnhouse via Church Fenton to rebuild and shortly before the 603 Squadron Spitfires left, 65 Squadron landed. According to the log books of Jack Stokoe and Black Morton, with George Denholm leading, the pilots flew for 55 minutes before landing at Linton-on-Ouse. They then flew to Church Fenton – 15 minutes

Bill, Ken, Sheep, Black, Patsy, George and Ian.

away – before flying for a further 50 minutes to Hornchurch. The weather that day consisted of low cloud and drizzle. Noel Benson, Colin Pinckney, Richard Hillary and Pip Cardell waited for four unserviceable Spitfires to be repaired and finally left Turnhouse at 16.00 hours by which time the dull, overcast sky gave way to clear skies and sunshine. They eventually arrived at Hornchurch at 19.00 hours. Broody led with Colin navigating in the 'pocket'. Richard and Pip, the least experienced, flew either side stopping en route at Church Fenton to refuel. The Squadron had already lost its first pilot in the Battle of Britain. Of the 24 who travelled south, either by air or road, nine more would lose their lives along with four members of the ground crew.

As the Spitfires took off that morning a Bristol Bombay also departed Turnhouse. Onboard were 22 members of the ground crew including five riggers and five fitters under the command of Sergeants Gillies and Mackenzie. They had the minimum of equipment with them and had to borrow a great deal on arrival at Hornchurch.

Peter Pease did not fly down with the Squadron but chose to take his car. His fiancée had decided to take a week's leave and travel to Edinburgh and stay with an uncle in order to be near Peter at Turnhouse. As Denise disembarked at Waverley Station she was greeted by Peter with his luggage packed and loaded aboard his car. The couple drove south together, stopping overnight at Prior's House, the Pease family home. After the war Denise reflected on the atmosphere in the car:

> It was a pretty grim journey when one looks back on it, as he must have known the state of the casualty lists, and I had seen daily the little Spitfires whirling like wounded butterflies to the ground. But neither of us said anything – there was really nothing to say. When we arrived at Hornchurch he had to go straight and fight – and I saw him about every other day in between battles for an hour or two.

Having travelled all the way to Edinburgh to be near Peter, she was now back at work, only 17 miles from Hornchurch.

As the eager and confident pilots arrived in the airspace over Hornchurch, they swung their Spitfires over Upminster before racing in low over the turf of Hornchurch airfield and breaking gracefully downwind for the circuit and landing. On arrival the pilots were met out on the tarmac by the Station Commander, Group Captain Cecil A. 'Boy' Bouchier DFC who, at the welcome address, told the pilots that at 12.00 the following day they would be put on readiness. From now on, things were going to be very different to what they had been used to with an atmosphere much changed to the relaxed surroundings of Dyce and Montrose. Everyone around them seemed tired and the mess bar lacked the familiar jocular banter. S/L George Denholm, now finally confirmed as OC 603 Squadron, spent the rest of the day in consultation with the commanding officers of the other squadrons. Later, as an Air Commodore Bouchier recorded his memories of that first meeting with the pilots of 603 in the *Wings for Victory* 603 Squadron Benevolent Fund magazine published in 1943:

I'm so glad I have been asked to write a few words about the City of Edinburgh Squadron, because, although my words may not do justice to the occasion, your squadron did all their instinctive air fighting from my Station, and I am, therefore, in some respects, perhaps the person best qualified to give you 'something of a picture' of how they fought in the most momentous battle that this country of ours has ever been called upon to fight – the Battle of Britain.

It was my great good fortune throughout 1940 to command a large Fighter Station adjacent to the East End of London, and whose task it was to protect London, the Thames estuary, and Kent. It was there, at Hornchurch, that 603 Squadron came to me on the morning of the 27th August 1940. I shall never forget their coming! Could this really be a Squadron, I thought, as I went out to meet them on the tarmac on their arrival. The CO, on getting out of his Spitfire, had his little 'side-hat' perched on the back of his head; he meandered towards me with bent shoulders, hands in his pockets, followed by, what seemed to me then to be, the motleyest collection of unmilitary young men I had seen for a very long time. I was not impressed. Good heavens! (I suddenly remembered) it's an Auxiliary Squadron. Ah! I thought, that explains it, but what have I done to deserve it?

How wrong I was! And yet, somehow, I feel that 603 will forgive me for those first impressions. You see, the RAF Station at Hornchurch was always my spiritual home, and I was very proud of it. I had grown up there in peacetime with No.54, 65 and 74 Fighter Squadrons – those early 'Regular' Squadrons which were the first to bear the brunt against the German Luftwaffe, and who fought so valiantly during Dunkirk and afterwards. They were truly magnificent. One by one, battered and weary they departed from my Station in a blaze of glory to quieter parts of the country to recuperate and fill up their ranks again, and thus it was that there came to Hornchurch other 'Regular' Fighter Squadrons, eager and fresh for the fray, to take their place.

Into this line of succession of 'Regular' Squadrons there suddenly dropped No.603, the Auxiliary Squadron from Edinburgh. How could they possibly cope with what they would be up against? How could they, an Auxiliary Squadron, be expected to acquit themselves in the same manner as my long line of 'Regular' Squadrons had acquitted themselves? Shades of Malan and Tuck and Bader, and hosts of others! – the very salt of the earth; the cream of our Fighter Squadrons! How could 603 live in such company, I wondered. Those were my thoughts as I went out to greet them on their arrival.

How I was made to eat my unspoken words – literally made to eat them, for did I not attend the Squadron dinner the CO of 603 gave in London to celebrate the shooting down of their 100th Hun from Hornchurch? What a dinner that was! Even as we ate and drank, we could hear the bombs bursting and the guns booming over London – for London was 'getting it' again – but what did we care? – 603 had got a hundred Huns.

As I write, memories come crowding in upon me, and from their store I give you this of 603. They were, I think, the greatest Squadron of them all.

Within an hour of their arrival at Hornchurch they were in the air again to give battle to the Hun over Kent and the English Channel, charging through the perpetual smoke and haze of the Hornchurch area and the hazards of the London balloon defences. From that moment until the Battle of Britain had been won, 603 stayed with me at Hornchurch. No Squadron was ever regarded more highly. No Squadron ever went to war with such quiet grace, with so little fuss, or with more determination. During the whole time they were with me (and they did not leave until the Battle of Britain was over and won) I never heard them complain once, yet they were ever appreciative of all the little ways in which we strove to help them.

No.603 Squadron was not a Squadron of giants; they were not even a Squadron of personalities. I'm sure they will not mind me saying that. 603 was composed of a collection of quiet and serious young men: men from the city desks of Edinburgh and the fields of the Lothians, led by one whose quiet personality wrapped his Squadron round as with a cloak, and made of them by his concern for them and by his leadership and example, a great and valiant Squadron.

I, and all those who served with me at Hornchurch, will remember 603 with pride and affection for as long as we live. I follow still their fortunes in the Middle East, where they are still carrying on the good fight, and I am sure will continue to do so until the last battle of all has been won.

If room can be found for this poor tribute of mine to a very great Squadron, I shall be very happy in the thought that it may bring back some pleasant memories of those heroic days to so many of the original members of the Squadron who were my friends, and who are still serving their country in various parts of the world.

The 603 pilots were shown the intelligence room, area maps, codes etc., and were instructed to report back at 11.00 hours the next morning to complete the briefing. Ras Berry exhibits his sense of humour when recalling his arrival at Hornchurch:

I was walking around the hangars that night and remember meeting a chap who was to become the top-scoring pilot from New Zealand. His Spitfire had been hit, and what he had to say about being hit is unprintable, so I won't repeat it.....'Fucking hells snakes he hit me!' He was later in my Wing in North Africa.

The New Zealand pilot was Flying Officer Colin F. Gray of 54 Squadron (later Group Captain Colin Gray DFC**, DSO).

Like so many pilots in 603 Ras also developed an affinity with the calm, relaxed voice of the controller at Hornchurch issuing urgent instruction to the pilots, via the tannoy system, with no hint of concern in his voice. It had a lasting effect on those that were fraught with tension at that time. The voice was that of Ronald Adam. His real name was Ronald G.H. Adams and he had been a fighter pilot in World War I. On 7 April 1918 he was shot down by 'the Red Baron', Manfred von Richthofen, wounded and taken prisoner. On 2 December 1914 when he was only 17 years old he had been commissioned temporary Second Lieutenant into the 15th (Reserve) Battalion of the Middlesex

Ken at readiness.

Regiment. He later transferred to the Royal Flying Corps where he qualified as an observer before moving on to pilot training. He served with 18, 44 and 73 Squadrons. 73 Squadron was based in France at the time. After being shot down by the Red Baron he spent the next eight months in various hospitals before being repatriated on 17 December 1918. After the war Adams qualified as a chartered accountant but found his life lacked excitement and moved into theatre management. He took on the Embassy Theatre in London and moved into the acting profession itself. It was at this time that he changed his name slightly, dropping the 's' at the end of his surname. His film career began in 1936 and his tall figure and distinguished demeanour guaranteed him many 'character' roles in an outstanding film career which included: 'Q' Planes, The Lion Has Wings, Song of Freedom, Escape to Danger, Angels One-Five, The Lavender Hill Mob, Captain Horatio Hornblower R.N., The Million Pound Note, The Man Who Never Was, Reach for the Sky, amongst others. During WWII he rejoined the RAF and was, amongst a number of appointments, the fighter controller at RAF Hornchurch during the Battle of Britain. By the end of the war he had attained the rank of Wing Commander. He died on 28 March 1979 aged 83. Ronnie Adam is fondly remembered by those who flew from Hornchurch during the battle.*

A number of wives now also travelled south to be near their husbands. Joan Stapleton moved into a house in Romford, from where Stapme travelled to Hornchurch early each day. During early September Ras travelled to Scotland to marry Nancy. On returning south the Stapletons invited the couple to share their rented accommodation with them thus halving the burden of the bills. At that time both wives were pregnant.

---

*See appendix for 'Readiness at Dawn', a short story by Ronnie Adam.

603's arrival at Hornchurch. From left to right: Sgt 'Angy' Gillies; Bob Wilson on pipes; 3rd from left Tommy Devlin; second from right George Mullay.

Within a few days of arriving Sgt Angy Gillies led his ground crewmen out to dispersal with Bob Wilson dressed in the traditional regalia of the Squadron piper, and George the mascot with his handler. In truth, it was a publicity stunt arranged by the media. Bob couldn't play the pipes and to the veteran ground crew members George the goat was not popular: 'Its coat was tatty and it stank but, nevertheless, it served its purpose in the publicity photographs.'

The line-up had changed somewhat during the previous 12 months, since its embodiment into the RAF. As well as the inevitable postings to and from the Squadron, Hamish Somerville had been killed at Grangemouth, Ching Mackenzie had been killed when he crashed during a night flight, Charles Peel had failed to return from a patrol which had involved combat over the North Sea, and injuries suffered by Graham Thompson in a flying accident at Turnhouse put paid to any further wartime flying.

Most of the Squadron had amassed a great many hours flying the Spitfire. Some including George Denholm, Sheep Gilroy, Stapme Stapleton, Bubble Waterston, Laurie Cunningham, Black Morton, Patsy Gifford, Dudley Stewart-Clark, Ras Berry, Ian Ritchie, Ivor Arber, Bill Caister, Ken Macdonald, Robbie Robertson and Peter Pease had already seen some action. By the time 603 returned north to be rested two months later, they had inflicted heavy losses on the Luftwaffe, but in doing so had suffered a terrible mauling of both experienced and inexperienced pilots alike.

Of the 3,000 pilots that are listed as having flown in the Battle of Britain, approximately 1,000 actually fired their guns at the enemy during combat. With hindsight it was realised that the newly-arrived pilots needed about five patrols, involving combat, in order to gain the experience to have any idea what was going on around them, ie: developing situation awareness of the proximity of enemy aircraft; taking *effective* evasive action to avoid being shot down; handling the aircraft with reasonable aptitude under stressful circumstances; remaining reasonably calm

P/O Bubble Waterston's XT-K 'Ard Choille'.

enough to act effectively; and ultimately to mount an attack of their own and survive that particular patrol. An understanding of this would help the historian to comprehend why experienced and inexperienced pilots were so often shot out of the sky within this initial five-patrol period.

The Squadron performed brilliantly throughout the battle. Brian Carbury was to achieve the highest number of enemy aircraft destroyed by any member of the unit and was one of the top five highest scoring allied pilots in the RAF for the same period. He was also one of very few who received both DFC and Bar during the battle and his confirmed claims for five enemy fighters destroyed during one day was remarkable.

In Scotland they had been used to having just one section of three Spitfires at readiness. On arrival at Hornchurch they found three squadrons at readiness! The RAF airfields were being bombed, although on the day of their arrival, after early reconnaissance activity over much of the south-east by enemy aircraft, no attacks materialised out of the gloom of a dull, overcast and drizzly morning. The Luftwaffe were reassessing their strategy.

Hornchurch was a hive of activity with various squadrons and supporting crews dashing about in lorries or on foot attempting to keep up with their work loads, aircraft taking off and landing with great frequency. What greeted the eyes of the pilots and ground crews of 603 on arrival must have been quite daunting. They were now right in the front line.

Ras Berry remembers the new lifestyle to which he had to adjust:

Half a dozen pilots would sleep at dispersal in readiness for surprise dawn attacks. This entailed being up at 04.30 hours, with the Spitfires warmed-up by 05.00 hours. The first sortie was usually about breakfast time, the last being at about 20.00 hours. We had egg, bacon and beans for breakfast which was sent over from the Mess. Other times we ate whenever we could. Some didn't even live to enjoy breakfast.

This photograph includes Bill Read, Pip Cardell, Joey Sarre and Jack Stokoe who all joined 603 before the Battle of Britain and fought during it.

CHAPTER 9

'GIN YE DAUR'

Wednesday 28 August 1940

The distinctive sharp crackle of gunfire could be heard by civilians and servicemen alike who, from their position on the ground, were witness to events as they developed high in the sky over the Kent coast. Vapour trails graphically told the tale as enemy and RAF fighter pilots fought for advantage over each other, before opening fire – other less experienced pilots simply flew their aircraft as best they could, praying that they were not being hunted by a superior combat pilot.

From out of the sky two trails seemed to curve away from the mêlée and streak vertically downwards towards the Channel. From altitude both were not trailing water vapour but glycol and smoke, both were diving at terminal velocity and rotating slowly with no visible deviation from the plunge to the sea below. To the onlookers it appeared as if the two pilots were making no attempt to escape or they were either dead or wounded, unable to react as they hung in their harnesses until the Spitfires impacted with the surface of the English Channel in a great splash of foaming white water, their aircraft exploding into pieces.

No aircraft parts or bodies were ever found and the pilots posted as 'missing'. Apart from the moment they were attacked, caught fire, and broke formation, there were no official eyewitnesses to the end of the two courageous individuals. Their families were never to receive their bodies for burial and after an initial period of hope that they may have landed in France, they gradually accepted the fact they would never be coming back. For some this process took years, for others the experience was too traumatic. Both mothers were destined not to survive the ordeal.

****

Officially the Battle of Britain was 48 days old by the time 603 arrived at Hornchurch, by which time they had been officially credited with 18 enemy aircraft destroyed during the fighting off the north-east coast of Scotland. The official start date of the battle had little bearing on what had been happening. The air battles over England did not just start on 10 July; many fine men had been killed or maimed as a result of combat in the skies over southern England since France had fallen. Although, by then the fighting was in earnest, British airfields were being bombed relentlessly in an attempt to eliminate the RAF in preparation for an invasion. The demand on the RAF fighter pilots and the entire ground crew was enormous. There had to be aircraft and pilots available to deploy against the relentless waves of attack from the Luftwaffe aircraft as the Germans sought to achieve air superiority.

Since 24 August large numbers of RAF fighters had been ordered into the air against massed formations of Luftwaffe aircraft as they approached the coastal areas of Kent, Sussex and Hampshire. Initially the first fighters to become airborne were usually successful in intercepting the Germans over the coast but the German tactics of splitting their formations once they were over land confused the Observer Corps. It therefore proved impossible to guide subsequent fighters on to the enemy formations with any accuracy. The result was that more than two-thirds of the fighter force failed to make contact with the enemy. To take effect as from 27 August, but used for the first time on the 28th, Keith Park, ommander of 11 Group, covering the vital south-eastern defence airfields and approaches to London, instructed his fighter leaders to pass a coherent sighting report back to their controller before going into attack. They were to use the traditional call of 'Tally-Ho' and give the position, course, strength, and height of the enemy aircraft. This system was eventually used to great effect but an 11 Group bulletin for the attention of pilots only confirmed initial problems:

Reporting of 'Tally Ho' by Formation Leaders

From combat also Unit Intelligence reports, it is observed that occasions continue to arise when only half the Squadrons despatched to engage heavy attacks make contact with the enemy. This is due primarily to difficulty experienced by ground observers in reporting the progress of raids flying at high altitude in a clear sky, or above cloud layers when the reporting is done by sound only. To enable Sector and Group Controllers to direct all fighter Squadrons to the enemy formation leaders send a brief enemy sighting report in the following form, whenever humanly possible: 'Tally Ho! 50 bombers, 30 fighters, Angels 20, proceeding North MAIDSTONE.'

During the early days of the war the 603 pilots occasionally used the 'war-cry' 'Rooki, Rooki!' when diving to attack the enemy, but there is nothing of the Doric about it. During his service in Palestine, Bill Caister had picked up the expression – which describes how a troublesome young boy would be seized by the scruff of the neck with one hand while the other hand takes hold of the seat of his pants in order to throw him from the room. The idea caught on after he mentioned it to his fellow pilots.

The attacks on the RAF airfields continued, but the might of the Luftwaffe, with its familiar three-phase pattern, was now no longer directed at 10 and 11 Groups but almost entirely at the airfields of 11 Group. Park was reliant, now more than ever, on other group commanders for reinforcements to maximise the effort in order for his group to survive. The Luftwaffe were also carrying out extensive night bombing against British targets.

The morning of the 28th dawned fine but chilly with 5/10 cloud over the Channel. Apart from the odd confrontation with reconnaissance Dorniers early that morning the first raid of the day was reported to be building up over the Pas de Calais just after 08.00 hours. The Hurricane pilots of 79 Squadron who were moving forward to Hawkinge at the time, sighted the Heinkels and provided the controller with the required information before going into the attack. A total of 44 aircraft attempted to engage the bombers. Once again the airfields were the target and as they crossed the Kent coast over Deal they split into two groups, the Dorniers of I/KG3 attacked Eastchurch while the Heinkels from KG53 attacked Rochford (later Southend Airport) just after 09.00. The heavy German fighter cover of Bf109s overwhelmed the RAF fighters and 79 Squadron were lucky not to lose any aircraft as they attempted to halt the Heinkel attack. 615 lost one Hurricane with the pilot injured as they attempted to attack the Dorniers with 501 Squadron, but 264 were bounced by Bf109s, and of the 12 that took off, eight returned and of those only three were serviceable. Two pilots and two gunners were killed. Refuelled and rearmed, the crews of the remaining three were eager to get back at the Germans during the next raid. Although the bombers managed to get through to Rochford, damage was light due to the flak around the airfield, but one hundred bombs fell on Eastchurch. Despite extensive damage to the grass airfield and the destruction of several light bombers it was not put out of action.

Following their failure earlier that morning the Dorniers of II and III /KG3 attacked Rochford aerodrome at 12.35 hours, heading up the Thames estuary at 18,000 feet. RAF fighters of 1 and 54 Squadrons were scrambled to intercept the raid and achieved limited success with 54 shooting down a 109.

While the ground crews were busy refuelling and rearming the aircraft, the south Kent RDF stations reported that a number of high flying enemy formations were approaching the south and south-east. Several flights were protecting the sector airfields and six groups of fighters were vectored on to the incoming raids. These enemy aircraft turned out to be not bombers but five Gruppen of Bf110 and Bf109 fighters, and as wave after wave of enemy fighters approached the coast and 11 Group Sector, a fighter versus fighter confrontation occurred. This was just what the German commanders had intended and just what Park had been trying to avoid. It was the bombers that had to be stopped, which meant not allowing his fighters to be kept occupied by the Luftwaffe fighters.

It was during the afternoon raid by the Luftwaffe that 603 Squadron was involved for the first time since moving south from Turnhouse. That morning Richard Hillary had bumped into his college and flying training colleague, Peter Howes, who was with 54 Squadron at Hornchurch whose Spitfires were dispersed close to those of 603:

> On the morning after our arrival I walked over with Peter Howes and Broody. Howes was at Hornchurch with another squadron and worried because he had as yet shot nothing down. Every evening when we came into the mess he would ask us how many we had got and then go over miserably to his room. His squadron had had a number of losses and was due for relief. If ever a man needed it, it was Peter Howes. Broody, on the other hand, was in a high state of excitement, his sharp eager face grinning from ear to ear.

It is worth considering the physical and psychological state of Howes compared to Benson, the man who had been involved in combat recently and the new arrival, eager for his first experience. Benson would not have long to wait.

The first defensive patrol took off from Hornchurch at 12.27 to intercept the second major Luftwaffe raid of the day. It consisted of possibly twelve of the most experienced members of the Squadron: S/L Denholm (XT-D, L1067 'Blue Peter'), F/L Ken Macdonald (XT-E, R6752), F/L Rushmer (XT-N, P5489), F/L Cunningham (XT-U, R6351 'Auld Reekie'), F/O Ritchie (XT-X, R6989), F/O Boulter (XT-S, N3267), F/O Waterston (XT-K, L1046 'Ard Choille'), F/O Haig (XT-A, L1070 'Excaliber'), F/O Carbury (XT-W, R6835 'Aorangi'), P/O Gilroy (XT-H, N3288 'Hell'), P/O Berry (XT-V, R6721), and P/O Morton (XT-G, R6735 'Tigger').

Ordered to patrol the Chatham area, when they were 20 miles west of Canterbury they saw approximately 12 Bf109s in vics of three at an altitude of 22,000 feet. The 603 Spitfires were at the same height. They were ordered into sections, echelon starboard. As they approached the enemy aircraft the German fighters scattered. Dogfights ensued but only Red 1, George Denholm, was able to engage an enemy aircraft before the rest escaped into the cloud.

The types of patrol were referred to by several names, sorties, defensive patrols and fighting patrols. George Denholm, flying Spitfire L1067, Code XT-D, claimed one Bf109 probable on landing and his interpretation of events was as follows:

Ras climbing into his Spitfire at Hornchurch during the Battle of Britain with 'Spy' Blackbourn in attendance.

> When 20 miles west of Canterbury we saw 12 Me109* in vic's of three at 22,000'. I was at the same height and got onto the tail of a Me109, followed it through a cloud, and fired at a range of 80 yards with a two second burst, firing 240 rounds. The enemy aircraft went into a vertical dive with a long trail of white vapour, which I thought was glycol fumes. After that I did not see the enemy aircraft again. It was noticed that the Me109's had yellow noses, but no yellow wing-tips. The experience of the Battle made me a little doubtful if the organisation of a squadron into 2 Flights, each of 2 Sections of 3 aircraft, was ideal. It was, of course, undesirable to make any sweeping change during the Battle, and I relinquished my Command shortly after its termination; but the weakness lay in the Section of 3 when it became necessary to break up a formation in a 'Dog Fight.' The organisation should allow for a break up into pairs, in which one pilot looks after the tail of his companion. A Squadron might be divided into 3 Flights of 4 (which would limit the employment of half-Squadrons), or it might consist of 2 Flights of 8, each comprising 2 Sections of 4...

---

*Originally designed by Bayerische Flugzeugwerke (Bf), of Augsburg, the Bf109 and Bf110 were test flown on 28 May 1935 and 12 May 1936 respectively. Despite the reformation of the BF company in 1938 as Messerschmitt AG, the designations of the existing products never changed. Despite evidence from nameplates of captured and shot down aircraft, and from the interrogation of captured German pilots these aircraft were consistently inaccurately referred to as the 'Me 109' and the 'Me 110'.

RAF combat reports frequently referred to the formations of enemy 109s as being in vics of three – sometimes in sections of five – when the enemy fighters actually flew in pairs and fours – *Rotte* and *Schwarm*. The RAF pilots simply took it for granted that the Luftwaffe flew the same formations as they did, in sections of three.

All 12 aircraft returned to Hornchurch landing at 13.30 hours. Noel Benson and Richard Hillary were on the ground eager to hear from the returning pilots. Richard later wrote:

> They started coming in about half an hour after we landed, smoke stains along the leading edges of the wings showing that all the guns had been fired. They had acquitted themselves well although caught at a disadvantage of height. 'You don't have to look for them,' said Brian (Carbury). 'You have to look for a way out.

Although he recalled this incident as having occurred on the day the Squadron arrived at Hornchurch it was the day after. At 15.55 603 was again sent up on a defensive patrol. On this sortie the pilots were: S/L Denholm (XT-D, L1067), F/L Ken Macdonald (XT-E, R6752), F/L Cunningham (XT-U, R6751), F/O Boulter (XT-S, N3267), F/O Ritchie (XT-X, R6989), F/O Carbury (XT-W, R6835), P/O Gilroy (XT-H, N3288), P/O Morton (XT-G, R6735), P/O Berry (XT-N, P9459), P/O Read (XT-Z, R6808), P/O Don Macdonald (XT-K, L1046), and F/O Pease (XT-V, R6721).

For Berry, Read, Pease and Don Macdonald this was their initial patrol and, therefore, first opportunity of combat since moving south. When they were between Canterbury and Dover they saw eight Bf109s with yellow noses in 'lose vic formation', about 15,000 feet above them,

Ras Berry, in pre-Hornchurch days.

with another 30 Bf109s above the loose vic formation. 603 were in sections line astern. As 603 attacked the loose vic formation the other 109s dived to attack. Black Morton claimed a 109 destroyed:

> As No.2 of Yellow Section flying sections astern in a southerly direction over Canterbury at 24,000' I observed about eight Me109's 2,000' above and on the port beam 800 yards away. The enemy aircraft crossed over us into the vein. I pulled up onto one Me109's tail but stalled. On recovery I observed another to the NE of me. I approached this and attacked an Me109 pursuing a Spitfire. He emitted a long trail of white smoke and dived for cloud. I followed and found him SE over the Channel. At 6,000' he flattened out a little and I got within range at 300 yards and fired 2 bursts, one of six and one of four seconds, closing to 150 yards. During the second burst flames came from behind the cockpit. I left him at 4,000', burning fiercely and still diving steeply east, as I was approaching the French coast. I returned at sea-level.

Sheep Gilroy destroyed a Bf109E-4 (0941). Badly wounded, the pilot, Leutnant Landry, managed to bale out of the burning Messerschmitt and on landing was taken prisoner, although he clearly posed no threat. He died of his injuries on 23 September. His aircraft crashed at Church Farm, Church Whitfield at 16.25 hours. Sheep recorded:

> While in a position north-west of Dover at 20,000' I observed one Me109 going to attack a Spitfire. I got into position behind it and fired a burst of about six seconds from a range of 150 yards closing to 40 yards. The Me109 put its nose down and I gave a two second burst while allowing for deflection. The enemy aircraft went on fire and the pilot opened his hood, which flew off, and came down by parachute.

He fired a total of 1,200 rounds of ammunition. The incident was witnessed by Winston Churchill during a tour of inspection of Dover Castle. A short while later he also visited the crash site. Flying his first sortie with B Flight since arriving at Hornchurch, Ras Berry claimed a 109 probable:

> When approximately over Dover the squadron split up on sighting several Me109's. Looking above three Me109's crossed my bow in line astern. Shortly after, on my beam a Me109 was firing and I immediately whipped up my aircraft and round and found myself on his tail, and at close range pumped lead into it until it opened into a heavy cloud of smoke. On returning again, another Me109 was attacking from quarter astern. I steep turned to the right and got on his tail and he dived. I followed him and attacked, some bits fell from the enemy aircraft. As my ammunition was expended I broke off combat and returned to base.

Ras opened fire at 100 yards, firing the entire 2,800 rounds in three bursts, each of five seconds duration. He recalled:

> We were off on patrol at 30,000' in the Dover area, and it was our first encounter. Unfortunately for me the chap on either side of me got shot down in flames, and that was typical. We were in these vic-three formations and out they came, down out of the sun and that was when we started to learn our fighter combat, from then on. These two just got shot down as quick as that and I turned round and got into a dogfight, I thought I got one Me109, I definitely got another but credited with only a probable.

It was Ras's first encounter of the day but the Squadron's second. It had been section leader F/L Laurie Cunningham in XT-U, Auld Reekie, and P/O Don Macdonald in XT-K, Ard Choille who he witnessed losing their lives. Their flaming aircraft plunged into the sea with the pilots, dead or alive, still in their cockpits. Ard Choille was the usual aircraft of Bubble Waterston, who was rested from this patrol.

F/O Brian Carbury, flying with B Flight claimed a Bf109 damaged with bits of the wings seen dropping off and white smoke coming from the front of the engine after a beam attack over Hawkinge at an altitude of 30,000 feet:

> Approximately over Dover I sighted the enemy aircraft (six Me109's). As they attacked leading sections, we kept in vic, but broke as Me109 came down, I followed two through the cloud, with three following. I fired a short two second burst at one Me109 from 300 yards closing to 200 yards, smoke emitted from front of cockpit and carried on at about 45 degree's dive for France, so I left him. I sighted another Me109, gave a full deflection burst but lost him in the cloud. I also lost the rest of the Squadron, so returned to base.

Ten Spitfires landed back at Hornchurch at 17.20 hours following which Laurie Cunningham and Don Macdonald were posted 'missing' later 'killed in action'. The Squadron had been caught at a height disadvantage at 16.45 hours over the Channel off Dover when both men were shot down during a single diving attack by 109s of II/JG3. Laurie was 23 years old and an only child who cared greatly for his young cousin, Jean, who has retained proud childhood memories of him:

> I was only 11 when he died. Laurie was a much-loved only child and his death aged only 23... devastated his parents. He was my favourite cousin and I have never forgotten him. He always had time to talk or have a game with me as a small girl, so he must have been a kind young man. One tends to remember people at the age they died and it is hard to imagine him as he would be now, had he lived.

P/O Don Macdonald, with camera, at the family home in Edinburgh, 1940.

His mother never recovered from the trauma of losing her only son and she took her own life on the eighteenth anniversary of his death.

Don Macdonald also failed to survive what was his first combat sortie from Hornchurch. He was killed eight days after his 22nd birthday. Like Laurie, Don's body was never found. Both are remembered on the Runnymede Memorial (George Denholm represented Don's father, Harold, who was very frail by then, at the unveiling of the new Runnymede Memorial by HM the Queen on 17 October 1953).

Don had not been due to go up on the patrol but he had begged Uncle George to let him do so. George tried hard to stop him as he realised he was 'pretty raw', however, he was eventually persuaded against his better judgement by Don's determination and enthusiasm. At the time of his death he only had approximately 25 hours on Spitfires. In contrast, Laurie Cunningham had over 200. The Squadron had been bounced by 109s and neither stood much chance. A change in tactics reduced the risk and George Denholm and Ken quickly learnt to lead the Squadron on a reciprocal heading to that given by the controller and when sufficient height had been gained they would turn and fly towards the enemy having negated or at least reduced any height advantage. But in the case of Laurie flying experience had made no difference. Don's rigger was AC1 John Mackenzie. Sixty years later, aged 85, he reflected with emotion on the loss of his pilot:

> We worked 24 hours a day on the Spitfires to keep them airborne. We were always on standby and I was very aware that the pilot's safety – his life – was in my hands. I was responsible for the whole of the airframe; the fuselage, wings and undercarriage. Every day I took off all the curlings – the metal coverings around the plane – inspected everything and put it all back again, sometimes in a howling wind or torrential rain. I also checked the oxygen bottles were full because the pilot depended on it to breathe at high altitudes, and made sure that the windscreen was clean and highly polished, which was important because spots of dirt could affect the pilot's vision. There was a small rear-view mirror in which the pilot could check for enemy planes coming up from behind, and this had to be spotless as well. Sheep Gilroy was famous for his sharp eyesight. He could spot a bandit before anyone else and no one dared let a speck of dust settle on his windscreen! Our base at Hornchurch took a terrible hammering during the battle. Wave after wave of German bombers and fighters swept over us. Seeing those bombs coming down at you was frightening. I remember one lad who was running, screaming with terror. I caught him; 'Just remember,' I said '..if your number's on one of those bombs, you'll get it, no matter how fast you run.' But the most horrible thing was when a young pilot joined the squadron, we got his plane perfect for take-off and gave him the thumbs up, only for him to be killed on his first flight in combat. I got through by saying my prayers every night. I always believed I would survive. If you lose faith you are in trouble.*

Ken had been flying the same patrol as his younger brother, whom he doted over. He later informed his sister, Ewen, of events just prior to Don's death:

> I looked down the line of planes and saw Don looking at the controls slightly wondering what was what – then off we went. Don was a sitting target and hadn't a hope. It was rather like a Formula 1 car at Brands Hatch which you'd never seen before. We'd hoped he'd landed in France where his knowledge of French and German would help get him back. We hoped he was well, would be OK and get back, several pilots did, but it was not to be and we should not hope...

Almost exactly one month later they were to be reunited.

Flying Officer Ian Ritchie had also been hit during the attack by II/JG3. He returned to base severely wounded in the back and hand. An armour-piercing round had gone through the rear of the fuselage, passed along the inside of the aircraft, before penetrating the lower and thickest part of the

---

*John Mackenzie had been an auxiliary with 603 since 1937, in civilian life he was a chiropodist until he was called up in August 1939 when 'the squadron became our lives.' Post war he ran a chain of shoe shops in Edinburgh. He married Margaret in 1947 and they had three children. As a widower he was a proud and dedicated Chairman of the 603 Association. He died in October 2002 aged 87.

armour behind the pilot's seat. Unfortunately, the core of the projectile managed to penetrate the metal and entered the muscle in Bear's lower back one inch to the right of his spine. The bullet struck the sciatic nerve and his body went rigid as it was wracked with excruciating agony. Automatically, he put his aircraft into a dive to evade further attack levelling out at 18,000 feet. Bear had always dreaded baling out but having assessed the condition of his Spitfire he was relieved to discover that although it was badly damaged it was still airworthy. Through a sea of pain and with his uniform and flying clothing saturated in blood he managed to locate the Thames and set a course back to Hornchurch where, fighting off unconsciousness, he carried out an excellent landing. After taxiing to dispersal he was grateful for the oblivion, passing out in the cockpit of his aircraft as it came to rest. His ground crew, assisted by medical staff, carefully removed him from the cockpit and he was taken by ambulance to Oldchurch Hospital, Romford, where he remained for ten weeks. His Spitfire was assessed as having Category 2 damage and repaired. The story goes that he was later visited in hospital by Earnest Shephard who had heard that some of the 603 Squadron pilots had named their aircraft after the characters he had drawn for A.A. Milne's book as related earlier. He was also aware that the ground crews had attempted to produce likenesses of the characters on the cowling of the Spitfires. He was so taken by the idea he went away and had a set of stencils depicting each of the Pooh characters made and sent to the Squadron in order for them to produce the best possible likenesses.* Bear's Battle of Britain was over and there followed a lengthy recovery from his wound. He suffered acute sciatica for the rest of his life. While in hospital he received news of his promotion to Flight Lieutenant.

In response to the RAF losses caused by being 'bounced' ACM Dowding later wrote:

> Some of our worst losses occurred through defective leadership on the part of a unit commander, who might lead his pilots into a trap or be caught while climbing by an enemy formation approaching 'out of the sun.' During periods of intense activity promotions to the command of Fighter squadrons should be made on the recommendation of Group Commanders from amongst Flight Commanders experienced in the methods of the moment. If and when it is necessary to post a Squadron Leader (however gallant and experienced) from outside the Command, he should humbly start as an ordinary member of the formation until he has gained experience. Only exceptionally should officers over 26 years of age be posted to command Fighter Squadrons.

Although officialdom decreed his age an apparent disadvantage, George Denholm was held in the highest regard by the pilots in his charge. His paternal instincts towards the younger pilots were evident but he cared greatly for all the men in his Squadron. Their subsequent loss was deeply felt by him.

The last patrol of the day occurred at 18.36 hours and consisted of: S/L Denholm (XT-H, N3288), F/L Ken Macdonald (XT-E, R6752), F/L Rushmer (XT-N, P9459), F/O Haig (XT-A, L1070), F/O Waterston (XT-S, N3267), F/O Pinckney (XT-B, N3056), P/O Hillary (XT-W, R6835), P/O Benson (XT-P, N3105), P/O Stapleton (XT-R, L1024), P/O Berry (XT-L, L1020), and Sgt Sarre (XT-G, R6753).

The nucleus of Denholm, Rushmer, Ken Macdonald, Haig, Waterston, Stapleton and Berry were scrambled with Richard Hillary, Colin Pinckney, Noel Benson and Sergeant Joey Sarre about to gain their first experience of intensive air to air combat. Although the pilots were prepared to fly any of the Squadron aircraft, some had a Spitfire they had named and flew regularly. Bubble Waterston was forced to take up XT-S, N3267, on account of his own having been lost during the previous patrol. With the arrival of X4273 on the 30th, Bubble had his ground crew paint his XT-K on the fuselage and he once again had his own aircraft. It was lost the very next day.

---

*During the 1990s the stencils appeared in an auction catalogue and were spotted by Mardi Morton. Hoping to acquire her late husband's 'Tigger' she informed her children of her intentions. They secretly agreed that should bidding go higher than their mother could afford, they would continue the bidding on her behalf. Unfortunately, they were eventually sold to an American for an astonishing £8,000 with Mardi and her children having fallen by the way. However, they were allowed to look through the waxed-card stencils only to discover Tigger was missing from the set!

Left: F/O Robin Waterston and F/O John Boulter.
Right: F/L George Denholm, taken in the early months of war.

The 11 Spitfires took off from Hornchurch and when ten miles west of Manston they saw ten Bf109s at 20,000 feet. The Squadron flew over the top of the enemy formation and dived in echelon starboard, attacking them out of the sun. The pilots later recalled the 109s had yellow noses and were in vic formation. At 19.36 hours George Denholm, leading A Flight, destroyed a 109 which crashed in a field near Dover:

> In combat against 10 Me109's when 10 miles W. of Manston at 20,000 feet, I singled out a Me109 and made two stern attacks at it, and after the second attack, it appeared to be in difficulties. I was then able to make two quarter attacks and the pilot, who had been heading for France, turned back towards the coast and glided down to land. I saw him hit high-tension wires and crash into a field W. of Dover. I fired 1,700 rounds.

Sid Eade and his 14-year-old son from Truckshall Cottage, just below Beachborough, witnessed the dogfight. They watched as the aeroplanes roared over Newington and out to sea where Denholm gave the 109 another burst. Executing a perfect 'u-turn', the German increased power to clear the terraced slopes of Hythe, narrowly missed Saltwood Castle, and then flew through high-tension cables which created a terrific flash before belly-landing near the railway tunnel on Copt Hill Farm at 19.15. The pilot, Feldwebel Otto Schottle of I/JG54, with bullet-grazed face and head wound, leapt from the burning machine, Bf109E-1 (6204), and walked calmly towards the Eade's cottage, neatly hurdling a fence en route. Bubble Waterston claimed a 109 probable while flying with B Flight:

> I saw ten Me109's 5,000' below me and attacked one out of the sun. I fired two short bursts at about 150 yards, both astern attacks and saw the Me109 dive vertically, emitting a stream of white glycol smoke. I was unable to follow it as I was attacked by another Me109.

Ten of the 11 Spitfires returned to Hornchurch by 20.12 hours. Pilot Officer Noel 'Broody' Benson was reported missing, later confirmed killed. One of the first to die during the first day of operations from their new front-line airfield, Broody was bounced by Bf109s of I/JG26. During the few seconds of combat he experienced over Kent he was unable to fulfil his earnest intention... 'To shoot down Huns, more Huns, and still more Huns' as recalled by Richard Hillary. Locals at Leigh Green witnessed the final act of the pilot of a Spitfire as he struggled to steer his burning aircraft away from their hamlet before it crashed in flames in a field on Great Hay Farm, Leigh Green, Tenterden at 20.30 hours. (Years later the remains of his aircraft were recovered.) His body was thrown clear on impact and found close by. In respect of this action, those who had seen him die asked the owners of Leigh Green Post Office to display a photograph of Broody in their shop,

Top: Noel Benson's crash site at Great Hay, Green Leigh, Tenterden. Taken some time later.

Middle left: Noel's grave in St Mary's Churchyard, Great Ouseburn, following the burial.

Middle right: Noel's grave today.

Bottom: Some years after the tragedy, Joseph and Daisy Benson at the family home.

which they did for many years. He was 21 years old. At the end of one of Noel's last visits home, his sister Margaret recalls seeing Brian walk round to his brother's car and tell him that 'he wished he could break his legs so he couldn't go. They both went off in their cars and that was that.' The family requested a civilian funeral with no service personnel present although Broody's 603 colleagues were just too busy to attend. It was a fitting occasion and the grave was left adorned with an impressive display of brightly coloured wreaths and flowers. On his gravestone were inscribed the words: 'Battle of Britain, One of the Few, How bright these glorious spirits shine'. Margaret reflects on a strange but comforting experience after the loss of her older brother:

> After Noel's death I was shopping with my mother in Harrogate. There were three airmen over the road from us on the opposite pavement talking together. Without saying a word Mum and I acknowledged our disbelief on realising that the middle man was Noel. We walked on, still not saying a word, but knowing it was him.

Confirmation of Broody's death did not reach the Squadron until the following day after the crash recovery team had been to the site. The irrepressibly exuberant Broody Benson was dead. Perhaps the flames reached the cockpit before he could get down, and thus he crashed. It is of course possible he had been wounded and was unable to function properly. Perhaps he was hoping for further good fortune following his lucky escape of a few weeks previously when he had brought his damaged aircraft back over 75 miles of inhospitable North Sea. We will never know all the details. Broody, Don and Laurie had needed to be alert, fast thinking, fast reacting, tactically aware and skilful combat pilots at one with the aircraft and familiar with the 109 in combat. Above all they had needed luck. Unfortunately they were quite naturally lacking some of these critical attributes.*

The losses this day were a terrible blow to the men of the Squadron. It had been a devastating baptism in the air battle over southern England with 603 having lost three outstanding pilots by the end of their first full day at Hornchurch. But it was just the beginning.

The following day Black Morton found time to record the events of the 28th in his diary. In a short period of time, Black experienced trepidation as he flew into combat, exhilaration in the fight as well as fear of being a victim, the tragedy of seeing good friends die, and courage and perseverance, to name just a few of the emotions. It is no wonder that such men found life difficult post war after experiences such as these. His account, which we are fortunate to have, is a valuable piece of reflection on what these men endured. On 28 August Black was one of the lucky ones. However, his luck was destined to run out:

> Cloudless over land. Thin cloud 22,000' over Channel. Wind light W. Visibility excellent (1555-1720).
>   Squadron ordered off just before four. Patrolling at 29,000' just inland from Deal flying about SE. I was Yellow 2 to Ken [Macdonald] with George [Denholm] leading. About 8 aircraft suddenly appeared from E about 1,000' or less above and flying into the sun. I didn't

---

*Noel's younger brother, Brian, had intended following his father and train as a GP. However, following the death of Noel he decided he should also do his bit and joined the Royal Corps of Signals (RCS). The Benson family suffered further tragedy when Brian was killed in Germany on 15 April 1945, aged 24. He was by then a Captain RCS. According to Margaret: 'The death of Brian finished my parents off entirely. I did my bit for the war effort by working for the RAF at Harrogate doing mainly administrative and secretarial duties but after the boys were killed I worked at home as it was such a busy house with the surgery and all the animals to look after.' Although they both lived long lives, Joseph and Daisy Benson never recovered from the grief of losing their sons. Dr Benson died on 10 September 1957, just short of his 82nd birthday and is fondly remembered in the village. His wife died on 23 March 1961 aged 72. Noel and his parents are buried in a beautiful spot overlooking the Ouse Valley in what is the new extension to the churchyard at St Mary's, Great Ouseburn. Although Brian's name appears on the headstone of his parents' grave his body was never brought home and remains in Germany. His parents never managed to visit the grave. Following the death of her parents, Margaret was keen to remain at Cedar Croft Cottage but the task of looking after the house and gardens became too great. She later married and moved out to live with her husband in Winchcombe, Gloucestershire. He has since passed away and she travels to the family grave at Great Ouseburn once a year and any other time she happens to be in the area. Noel's godfather/cousin, Viner-Brady, was the instigator behind the Battle of Britain Memorial Window in Westminster Abbey.

see them until they were almost over us and even then didn't tumble until I was annoyed to see crosses on their undersides. I didn't think anyone else saw them either for there was no cry of 'Fritz' till about the time I saw them. Forgetting I was about 30,000' I pulled the nose up hard to have a crack at one as he went over and of course promptly spun which was almost certainly an excellent thing, as one of the following ones would have had an easy shot at me.

As I recovered at about 26,000' I saw a dogfight developing to the NE of me and two aircraft to seaward spinning down into the cloud at about 22,000'. I couldn't see whether they were E/A or not, but it appears likely that they were Laurie [Cunningham] and Don [Macdonald] – both missing. George, I think, was shouting 'keep together' at this time, so I made to join two or three Spitfires wurzling near me at my own height, rather below the general dog-fight. There were now a Hell of a lot of 109s about – probably having come down from above when the fun started – and the dog-fight was a rather amazing sight. Fortunately there weren't any in our direction. I made to join up with the Spitfires between me and the main fight; but on the way I saw a 109 chasing a Spitfire just below me. I gave chase and soon got a shot from about 300' with slight deflection from starboard. I saw bits of incendiary or De Wilde and the E/A turned violently to starboard and made for cloud at 22,000' leaving a wispy white trail. I was now pretty close to him, but not in a position to shoot. I lost him in the cloud but met the swirl he made going through. When I got through he was well ahead, diving steeply SE for France. I gave chase and was about 400-500' behind when at 6,000' or so he flattened out. I then gained rapidly and got to about 200' and was just going to fire when he saw me and dived steeply, showing his underside. I took a straight deflection shot. Two good bursts with strikes visible both times. In the second, flames appeared on the under surface – quite small at first, but growing quickly. At 4,000' he was still going down steeply – more so than before and burning very fiercely – great long red ones with a big black trail.

We were now about 3/4 way over the Channel, so I turned for home and dived to sea level. On the way down I noticed I was being followed so pressed the tit and kept very close to the water. The chap was 6-800' behind and I was slowly gaining. I kept on at sea level to the bottom of the cliffs near Hawkinge and came up and did a tight circuit of the old airship hangar, but the chap had gone.

I felt rather relieved in the Channel as I thought most of my rounds were gone. Actually I had about 100 left per gun. 'Tigger' with the tit pressed and the dive from 4,000' was doing a steady 320 with a great long trail of smoke. I wonder if the Hun claimed anything.

While I was near the coast George called and said reform W of Hawkinge at 4,000' so I joined him but no-one else turned up for a bit and as I thought I was about out of bullets, I came home.

When I got back most people had already landed, including 'Bear' [Ritchie] who had mistaken 3 109s coming to beat him up for Spitfires coming to form up. He had a cannon hit near the fuselage and by the tail, which blew a big hole in one side and made the other side look like a cheese grater. Also several bullet hits. One came up the fuselage, punched a neat hole in the THICK armour and lodged in his back – not deep though. Two hits on the back of the thin plate from incendiaries which just dented it. One ploughed through the top of the hood and lodged in the top of the armoured windscreen. Several odd bullets in the tail and wing roots – Very lucky Bear. Laurie and Don are missing and Broody Benson is reported down in flames on last night's show. All rather much – four pilots gone and only four confirmed fit – George, Sheep and Razz [plus Morton himself]. Winston is reported to have watched Sheep's from Dover. It burnt too.

This was the first time we met 109s. We saw some in the morning but some way off and only George had a shot – inconclusive. The remarkable thing was the speed at which they appeared from a clear sky and how near they were before we saw them. I may have been lucky and picked a dud, but he didn't seem very good at getting away other than going flat out for France. This is a very different business from up North. I've had an empty feeling in my middle all the time – rather like, only much worse than, before a big football match. I expect it will wear off though.

Ken seems to be taking Don's going very well, though I don't expect there's much hope.

Thursday 29 August 1940

The recent increase in night-flying activity by enemy bombers continued with all three Luftflotten involved with 121 towns attacked in addition to the cities of Birmingham, Manchester, Nottingham, Bristol, Leeds, Newcastle and Liverpool which experienced the heaviest bombing raid yet. The morning of the 29th dawned with no activity on the radar screens and allowed time for a re-shuffle by Dowding of a number of tired and weary squadrons. This included 264 Defiant Squadron at Hornchurch, which was sent to Kirton-in-Lindsey and replaced by 222 Squadron flying Spitfires which joined 603 at dispersal on the east side of the aerodrome.

The weather was cloudier than the previous day and there were a number of showers with bright intervals. The morning remained very quiet and the pilots discussed tactics in an attempt to avoid a repeat of the previous day's losses. Unfortunately, little expert guidance was available. The weather brightened after lunch and the first build-up of enemy activity – a raid on the Kent/East Sussex area – occurred at 15.00 hours, at which time a small number of Dorniers and Heinkels were sighted below and ahead of an enormous screen of more than 500 Bf109s and 150 Bf110s. A number of squadrons were sent up to intercept but it had been a trap to lure the RAF fighters and to get as many more airborne and into the fray as possible, thus keeping them occupied and away from the large formations of bombers that were to follow.

F/O Peter Pease.

It became clear to the German commanders that the RAF were unwilling to suffer the inevitable high number of losses likely when large numbers of allied and German fighters met in combat. That evening the Germans reverted to a number of free chases by 109s over the English coast in a further attempt to lure the RAF fighters into action.

603 Squadron took off at 15.15: S/L Denholm (XT-D, L1067), F/L Rushmer (XT-N, P9459), F/O Boulter (XT-S, N3267), F/O Carbury (XT-W, R6835), F/O Pease (XT-V, R6721), P/O Stapleton (XT-R, L1024), P/O Hillary (XT-M, L1021), P/O Read (XT-Z, R6808) and Sgt Sarre (XT-A, L1070).

The 'L' series Mark I Spitfires were by that time quite tired and easily out-performed by the newer aircraft. Joey Sarre was given L1070 Excaliber (formerly Stickleback) for this patrol. One of the stars of 16 October the previous year it had been one of the Squadron's first arrivals and had seen a great many flying hours since, having also been badly damaged in a crash-landing while 603 were at Prestwick. The composite patrol report for the day read:

> At 15.15 hours nine aircraft of 603 Squadron took off to patrol Rochford at about 24,000'. When in position they were ordered to Deal. While over the cloud slightly inland from Deal, they saw eight Me109's coming down on them, also a further six Me109's inline astern. These six did not make any attempt to attack. A dogfight ensued, and it was found that the 109's operated in pairs, and when one attacked it dived, No.2 diving as well.

Confusion continued amongst the 603 pilots regarding the formations used by the Luftwaffe fighters, as an 11 Group bulletin to pilots records:

> 603 Squadron report being attacked on 29/8/40 by 8 Me.109's flying in a formation of one aircraft leading a second in line astern then behind the second E/A came two sections of three E/A in line abreast one section behind the other.

What they actually saw were the pilots flying in pairs and fours, as described earlier on page 187. During this patrol Richard Hillary claimed a 109 probable while flying Spitfire L1021. It was his first claim. His recollections of his first kill in *The Last Enemy* compensates for the lack of a combat report and tells us something of that experience:

As they came down on us we went into line astern and turned head on to them. Brian Carbury, who was leading the section, dropped the nose of his machine, and I could almost feel the leading Nazi pilot push forward on his stick to bring his guns to bear. At the same moment Brian hauled hard back on his own control stick and led us over them in a steep climbing turn to the left. In two vital seconds they lost their advantage. I saw Brian let go a burst of fire at the leading plane, saw the pilot put his machine into a half roll, and knew that he was mine. Automatically, I kicked the rudder to the left to get him at right angles, turned the gun-button to 'Fire,' and let go in a four second burst with full deflection. He came right through my sights and I saw the tracer from all eight guns thud home. For a second he seemed to hang motionless; then a jet of red flame shot upwards and he spun out of sight. For the next few minutes I was too busy looking after myself to think of anything, but when, after a short while, they turned and made off over the Channel, and we were ordered to our base, my mind began to work again.

It had happened.

My first emotion was one of satisfaction, satisfaction at a job adequately done, at the final logical conclusion of months of specialised training. And then I had a feeling of the essential rightness of it all. He was dead and I was alive; it could so easily have been the other way around. I realised in that moment just how lucky a fighter pilot is. He has none of the personalised emotions of the soldier, handed a rifle and bayonet and told to charge. He does not even have to share the dangerous emotions of the bomber pilot who night after night must experience that childhood longing for smashing things. The fighter pilot's emotions are those of the duellist – cool, precise, impersonal. He is privileged to kill well.

While flying with B Flight F/O Boulter destroyed a 109 while in his regular Spitfire, N3267. He delivered his attack at 16.10 hours over Deal at an altitude of 23,000 feet, at 16.00 hours:

Whilst on patrol with 603 Sqn I noticed a formation of Me109 aircraft above and to the front. I informed the leader of 603 Sqn of their presence and turned to intercept them. As I did so I received a bullet in the cockpit, distracting my attention from my target.

When trying to rejoin my squadron, I saw five Me109's and engaged one of them. It broke away, and I was able to carry out a quarter attack, causing a trail of grey-white smoke or vapour to pour out of the undersurfaces.

Boulter had opened fire at 200 yards, closing to 50 yards, firing 800 rounds in a seven second burst. He failed to mention in his report that he had been wounded by the bullet which entered his cockpit. The damage to his Spitfire was quickly repaired. The aircraft that Boulter shot down was a Bf109E-1 of III/JG3 flown by Unteroffizier Pfeifer. The pilot was reported as missing. At 16.00 hours while flying with B Flight, Stapme Stapleton claimed a 109 destroyed:

When on patrol with 603 Squadron we sighted enemy fighters just south of Deal. P/O Read and myself broke away from the squadron to engage two Me109's who were circling above us. P/O Read engaged the first and myself the second. After firing short deflection bursts the Me109 which I attacked went straight down out of my sight with smoke issuing from the engine. I then broke away and climbed into the sun.

Stapme opened fire from a range of 150 yards with 2x2 second bursts with no more than 30 degrees of deflection, firing a total of 480 rounds. He was credited with a probable.

An important point that is worth considering is that one of the major differences between the Spitfire and the 109 was the fuel injection that the German fighter possessed. If attacked from behind the German pilot could push the 'stick' forward and, with the throttles wide open, dive straight down, under power. The Merlin engine of the Spitfire had a gravity-fed carburettor and such a manoeuvre would lead to a momentary loss of power due to sudden fuel starvation, leaving the pilot unable effectively to pursue his prey and vulnerable to attack himself. The Spitfire pilot would therefore need to roll away and dive at the same time, ensuring the 'carb' received the necessary downward pressure from gravity to provide a continuous flow of fuel. When the Messerschmitt 109 carried out this manoeuvre there was a visible puff of smoke from the exhaust ports, giving an inexperienced pilot, in pursuit of the German, the impression that he had hit him, when he may not have. Bill Read reported:

Whilst patrolling as Red 3 at 23,000' and still climbing, enemy aircraft were sighted crossing above us. I overshot Red 1 (Stapleton), and made a steep right hand turn, finding a Me109 turning above and in front of me. I pulled up nose and fired a short burst from the port quarter. The e/a turned on its back and fell into a spin. I was quickly engaged by other Me109's and thus lost sight of it. But another pilot saw it spinning down (P/O Hillary). In the course of the ensuing dogfight I fired at three more 109's (head-on and two beam attacks), but could not observe effect of fire as I spun myself .

F/L Rusty Rushmer, B Flight Commander.

Rusty Rushmer force-landed at Bossingham following the same combat, thought to be with aircraft of I/JG26. At 16.10 Rusty was slightly wounded and his aircraft, although damaged, was repairable. The records show that a Spitfire of 603 Squadron was claimed as having been shot down by Oberfeldwebel Wilhelm Muller of 2/JG26 over Dover. The claim was unconfirmed. At that time Muller had ten confirmed enemy aircraft destroyed to his credit.

A second raid developed between 18.04-19.00 hours in the Dover/Dungeness area and four squadrons were sent up, including 603 whose Spitfires were airborne between 18.10 and 19.30 and flown by: S/L Denholm (XT-D, L1067), F/L Ken Macdonald (XT-E, R6752), F/O Pinckney (XT-G, R6753), F/O Carbury (XT-W, R6835), F/O Pease (XT-V, R6721), P/O Gilroy (XT-H, N3288), P/O Read (XT-Z, R6808), P/O Stapleton (XT-R, L1040), P/O Hillary (XT-M, L1021) and Sgt Stokoe (XT-A, L1070). The ORB reads:

Ten aircraft of 603 Squadron left Rochford at 18.10 hours. When at 27,000' over Manston, they saw about 24 Me109's in line astern, weaving over their heads. The 109's made no attempt to attack, so 603 climbed and attacked. A dogfight ensued.

During this patrol Colin Pinckney was shot down and managed to bale out of his Spitfire but not before being burned about the face and more seriously his hands. Richard Hillary was also shot-up during the same combat and received minor burns before force-landing near Lympne. Both men were shot down by Ben Joppien of I/JG51.While leading Green Section of B Flight Brian Carbury destroyed a Bf109, over Manston at an altitude of 27,000 feet:

I was leading Green Section when enemy aircraft were sighted. We went into line astern, Green 2 and 3 attacked individual enemy aircraft. I climbed and saw two Me109's climbing below, so I carried out a frontal attack with slight deflection. A long burst and the enemy aircraft smoked and then blew up. I returned to base having lost the rest of the formation.

Colin Pinckney's report was written by the Intelligence Officer on his behalf:

F/O Pinckney claims a Me109 destroyed over Manston at an altitude of 27,000' while flying with 'A' Flight. He himself had to bale out as four Me109's of I/JG51 shot at him and damaged his machine. He is still in hospital and his report will follow. The Me109 was confirmed by the Observer Corps.

Colin's Spitfire R6753 Tigger crashed at St. Mary's Road, Dymchurch at 18.42 hours. (The wreckage was recovered in 1976 by enthusiasts of the Brenzett Aeronautical Museum. The F700 – the form completed by the ground crew which confirms all servicing and checks had been carried out – was found in the remains of the cockpit!) The aircraft was usually flown by Black Morton who expressed consternation at the loss of his regular Spitfire: 'Tigger – R6753 – shot down in flames near Dungeness. Colin Pinckney bailed out slightly burned after bagging one 109 confirmed. Rusty bailed out, Hillary crash landed and I think Stapme.' Stapme did not use his 'brolly' during the Battle of Britain. The Intelligence Officer (IO) was also responsible for logging a provisional report of Richard Hillary's claim prior to a full report by himself on his return to the Squadron:

P/O Hillary claims a Me109 destroyed, over Manston at 18.50 hours at an altitude of 27,000', this was confirmed by the Observer Corps. P/O Hillary forced-landed in the sea and is still in hospital.

This was Richard's first confirmed destruction of an enemy fighter but he was then shot down himself while acting as a 'weaver' to the Hurricanes of 85 Squadron; a situation that caused a certain amount of controversy. The report states that he was slightly burnt and his name was included on CC list 295 'slightly injured'. Having been hit Richard initially tried to make Hornchurch but he soon realised that his aircraft would not make the distance and forced-landed at 19.00 hours in the same field that Colin landed in by parachute. He was not able to complete a combat report before he was shot down on 3 September.

Richard's aircraft was not written-off. Spitfire I, L1021, 235, Sredni Vashtar first flew on 16 June 1939, went to 20 MU to have guns fitted on the 26th and then to 603 Squadron at Turnhouse on 15 September. Following Richard's forced landing it was repaired and used by 57 OTU until it was struck off charge (SOC) on 6 March 1945.

On 2 September the Air Ministry sent Michael Hillary a letter informing him that Richard had received 'slight injuries' while in combat. Colin provided his own interpretation of the events of that day in a letter home which stated:

F/L Laurie Cunningham with Spitfire XT-M Auld Reekie. Later this aircraft passed to P/O Richard Hillary who renamed it Sredni Vashtar.

> I was shot down during a patrol over Kent... After shooting down a German aircraft my own aircraft was hit and caught fire. I was forced to jump out of my aircraft at about 1,000 feet... Having landed all the local Home Guard were on the spot ready to arrest me, the lone parachutist, in case I was a German spy... Soon after I applied to join the Caterpillar Club for airmen who had to land by parachute... I also wrote to the Irvin parachute manufacturers to compliment them on the quality of their goods.

The burns to Colin's face and in particular his hands were severe enough to cause a great deal of pain and disability for the next few weeks. After treatment in hospital he was discharged and granted sick leave. After Richard had been shot down, Pinkers, who was himself still on sick leave at the time, visited him in hospital and provided an up-to-date bulletin of the Squadron's successes and tragedies.

After seeing him off in an ambulance, which he thought was rushing to his aid and not that of his colleague, Richard was invited to a brigade cocktail party which was taking place in nearby Lympne Castle where he dined and was given plenty to drink by his hosts until he was in no condition to return to Hornchurch that night. This may have been an excuse to make the most of the hospitality but shock must have also played a part and contributed towards his mental state. A short period before this relaxed, welcoming and convivial gathering, he was fighting for his life, and winning his own individual battle, with the German fighter falling to his guns.

Sergeant Jack Stokoe also claimed a Bf109 probable while flying Spitfire L1070 Excaliber:

> We were patrolling Manston at 27,000' in sections astern, when above us we observed about 24 Me109's flying in line astern.
>
> We climbed to attack and I chased one down about 5,000' without getting close enough to fire. I climbed back and closed on the tail of a Me109 which was following another Spitfire. I fired about five long bursts, closing from 800 to 100 yards, white smoke came from the 109,

and it spun gently down. I did not observe what happened then, as I was out of ammunition and had to shake a Me109 from my tail.

Stapme also claimed a 109 probable while flying Spitfire L1040 code XT-R, with B Flight, at 18.50 hours over Manston at an altitude of 29,000 feet:

When enemy fighters attacked our squadron I was separated from the rest. I climbed into the sun to 30,000', I sighted one Me109 just going into a loop, catching him with a full deflection shot of 5 seconds, he continued upwards and did a bunt, going downwards beyond the vertical.

Stapme opened fire at a range of 200 yards closing to 50 yards; in his short burst he used 550 rounds. He flew guard regularly and reflected on the anxieties the responsibility brought with it:

Was that just a spot in your vision or was it an enemy fighter? As you glanced around the sky spots in your vision could invariably move more slowly than the speed of your eye movement giving the impression that it could be an enemy fighter. Coupled with marks on your canopy you had to be extremely alert.

I found the enemy aircraft easy to spot against the blue sky. It was our anti-aircraft fire that quite often indicated to us the whereabouts of the incoming enemy aircraft.

Fortunately, he and Sheep were particularly good at spotting the German fighters. Stapme also reflected on the improvements the new Mark IIs brought to the squadrons, although they had yet to arrive:

The Mark II Spits' with the more powerful Merlin XII engines incorporating the Coffman cartridge starter and a pressurised glycol/water cooling system, had an increased 18lbs of boost which we used in the climb. Unfortunately this initially 'knackered' the gudgeon pin on the pistons until an improvement was made.

Those pilots who were able to make it back to their home base landed at 19.30 hours at the end of what had been a very climactic day after a surprisingly quiet morning.

Fine weather had spread over England during the day and continued into the night making conditions ideal for a continuation of the night bombing campaign. Two hundred bombers hit Liverpool and Birkenhead for the second night in succession; the cloudless sky allowing easy location of the target. The site was actually visible as a number of incendiary fires were still smouldering from the previous night's raid. Having flown in combat during the day, Ken Macdonald wrote home during the evenings, if he wasn't too exhausted. From his position at the 'front line' he tried to keep his parents informed of events. The day after Don went missing Ken sat in his room in the officers mess and wrote to his father. His letter provides us with an example of the spirit of the time. If he was fearful of his own destiny it is not evident and although his writing displays great emotion, it appears to indicate that he was maintaining a hard exterior and was simply getting on with the job of fighting the enemy, despite having lost his brother with the very real prospect of meeting the same fate. He knew it was essential he kept his mind focussed on doing his job. His colleagues depended on him and he couldn't afford to allow his true emotions to come to the surface. While most of the pilots took every opportunity to have a drink in the mess or get off base and travel to a nearby pub or even into the capital, it was typical of Ken that although he did join in, he preferred to retire early to his room for letter writing or reading, but these luxuries became nearly impossible as the battle wore on and sleep was the only choice. His optimism and spirit in the following letter in which he attempts to qualify the death of his younger brother and thereby temper his parents' grief is very moving and to be greatly admired. He himself had been prepared to climb into his aircraft just over two and a half hours after Don was reported missing and continue to go about his work with determination and courage:

My dearest Daddy,

You will I think have received an official signal informing you of Don. I am afraid it would be quite untrue to say that there is any likelihood of his turning up now. No one knows exactly what happened, but it is almost certain that he was attacked from above and behind by a diving Messerschmitt. We were patrolling high over Dover in a Squadron. The weather up there at 25,000 feet was sunny and clear. Suddenly just out of the blue came about 20 Messerschmitts. They managed I think to get Don and Laurie and then beat it for home. We got some of them. Don being in 'B' Flight was not in the same section of our Squadron Formation as myself – so I didn't see him much in the air.

We did four patrols yesterday. Don was not in the first two, but went in the third to relieve another pilot. It was from this one, his very first, that he did not get back. It was due to no fault of his and no lack of skill. It was mere chance that they should have singled out any particular one of us.

It was grand seeing him again when he arrived from Wales. I saw him on Tuesday [27 August] morning when he got to Turnhouse. And then he flew down that day and we laughed a lot together at dinner on Tuesday evening here.

It will be a tremendous blow to Mother and you and all of us. He was a grand chap. No-one so much fun to go around with. However it is all the luck of the game and we must take it as philosophically as we can. He could not have gone in a better way – nor is there any way he would have preferred. He enjoyed himself with us up to the hilt – and any loss there is, is ours and not his – and we can stand it as well as other people in a time like this. All my love to Mummy and you.

Ken.

Friday 30 August 1940

Bombing of a large number of British targets continued after dark. The battle was now entering a critical phase with the number and intensity of operations continuing to increase towards what would turn out to be an unimagined climax over the days ahead. The next 48 hours involved the fiercest fighting in the whole of the battle. The weather could not be relied upon to offer any respite as an extensive anti-cyclone was stationary over practically the whole of north-west Europe, and it would remain fine for some days yet. The day had dawned fine with a thin layer of cloud lying at 7,000 feet over south-east England, which caused some difficulty for the Observer Corps. Dowding and Park must have been in some way aware that such a climax was near. Over the next week and a half the resources of Fighter Command would be severely taxed.

Soon after dawn on the morning of the 30th a number of attacks were made by the Luftwaffe, mainly against convoys heading north from the Thames estuary, in an attempt to discover what fighter forces would react and from where.

The next raid, the main attack, dwarfed the first in that it consisted of three waves crossing the Kent coast on three sides at half-hourly intervals from 10.30 onwards. The first wave consisted of about 60 Bf109s (three Gruppen) which crossed at different points. Park believed there to be large numbers of bombers to follow, and did not react, his intention being to save his fighters at Hornchurch, Rochford, North Weald, Croydon, Northolt, Biggin Hill and Kenley.

At 11.00 hours his judgement was proven to be sound when the Observer Corps reported that raids totalling 40 Heinkels, 30 Dorniers, 60 Bf109s and 30 Bf110s were heading towards the Kent coast.

By 11.45 hours the situation had become so confused that it was impossible for the Observer Corps to identify which raids had been intercepted, 48 of them reporting dogfights overhead! All of 11 Group's fighters were airborne with ten squadrons in action and Park had to call upon 12 Group for reinforcements in the form of two squadrons from Duxford to cover the airfields at Kenley and Biggin Hill.

222 Squadron, situated at Hornchurch with 603, were hit hard as ten 109s bounced B Flight. They, like 603, had only recently arrived at Hornchurch from the north and had not been briefed, as they had worked their way up to operational status, on the updated tactics now being applied by those squadrons that had been in the thick of things. They were still flying in a close formation with a weaver. By the end of the day they had eight Spitfires shot down, with one pilot killed, two wounded and five aircraft lost.

At that stage the Luftwaffe commander Albert Kesselring changed his tactics quite significantly. Instead of waiting two or three hours before mounting his next assault, he followed the first at lunchtime with more bombers supported by Bf109 and 110s giving the RAF the absolute minimum time to recover from their previous sorties. Massive demands were made on the exhausted ground crews who exhibited total dedication towards the task of getting their fighters airborne once again, in the hands of equally exhausted pilots who had every faith that the men who had been working on his aircraft had done the best possible job in preparing it for further combat. As the ground crew watched the fighters in their squadrons take off they perhaps had a few moments to reflect on what had been and what lay ahead.

At 13.30 the enemy aircraft once again started to cross the Kent coast at 20-minute intervals. Apart from invaluable help from the Observer Corps, Fighter Command were blind. There was no assistance from the radar stations at Beachy Head, Dover, Pevensey, Fairlight, Foreness, Rye or Whitstable as the electricity grid had been hit during the morning raids.

With the RAF stretched almost to its limit the third and largest raid crossed the coast shortly after 16.00 hours. For the next two hours the RAF fighters fought against no less than 19 Gruppen of enemy aircraft as they crossed the English coast over the Thames estuary and Kent.

This third great aerial assault of the day consisting of 60 Heinkels with an escort of Bf110s aimed at Luton, Oxford, Slough, North Weald, Kenley, Biggin Hill and the Handley Page factory at Radlett.

The fighting that day had been the heaviest so far with Dowding's pilots flying 1,054 sorties. The fighting on 15 August had been spread over four Group areas but with nowhere near the intensity of this hot, sunny Friday in August. Twenty-two squadrons were in action, some as many as four times, almost all at least twice.

603 Squadron's involvement consisted of two sorties and began with the very first raid. At 10.35 hours just six Spitfires took off from Hornchurch to intercept the first wave of what was reported to be 80 Bf110s: S/L Denholm (XT-D, L1067), F/O Boulter (XT-S, N3267), F/O Pease (XT-V, R6751), P/O Morton (XT-E, R6752), P/O Berry (XT-W, R6735), and Sgt Sarre (XT-F, R6754).

Over Dover the 110s split and formed defensive circles of approximately 20 aircraft spiralling upwards. Black Morton claimed a Bf109 probable and a 110 damaged:

> As rearguard aircraft of the Squadron (six a/c), I was above and behind the formation at 32,000 feet over Deal when many bombers with Me110 formations above were seen at 20,000 feet. Squadron went into line astern, and dived. I encountered one ring of Me110's. One was in a convenient position and I fired from port quarter above for about two and a half seconds from 400 to 100 yards, when I had to break away to avoid collision as I was going very fast. A long plume of white smoke came from e/a's port engine and on tailing from my break away, I saw that it had dropped out from the formation and was losing height to the N/E. I then found another ring of Me110's and selected one, attacking from above on the port quarter, from 400 to 100 yards, finishing astern. Two bursts of 3 to 4 seconds each.

> E/A broke formation with white smoke coming from both engines. Spiralled down through cloud at 4-5,000 feet. On emerging from lower side of cloud layer 6/10, I saw e/a about 5 miles S.S.W. Lympne still spiralling at 3,000 feet with 2 Hurricanes pursuing it. I therefore left it to them and returned to base.
>
> No return fire from first 110, he probably did not see me. Some accurate fire, probably cannon, from slow rate of fire, from second 110.

Black delivered his attack at 11.25 hours west of Dover at an altitude of 17,000 feet. He fired a total of 1,185 rounds in bursts of one-and-a-half to eight seconds in length. That evening he wrote of this patrol in his diary, while events were still fresh in his mind:

> Haze high up and cloud 6/10 at 4,000-5,000'. Wind light 1035-1135.

Black Morton, early 1940.

Squadron ordered off but could raise 6 aircraft*. I did rearguard. We now knew the importance of height and got to 31,000' – I at 32,000' – between Canterbury and Dover. Saw about 80 110s and bombers in four tiers below us around 20,000'. Squadron went line astern and dived out of the sun on the topmost ring of 110s. I was a long way behind and didn't see the others after we started to dive.

I came down at full bore, for fear of 109's possibly following, and diving steeply got up a very high speed. One of the top ring of 110's was conveniently placed as I came down and I had a good shot with slight deflection from port and well above. I don't think he saw me as there was no return fire. I only got a burst of about 3 seconds before I had to break visibility to avoid hitting him. His port engine started smoking white and as I recovered I saw him leave the formation and lose height to the NE – towards Manston. He was going away and as I was now conveniently placed for a dive on another ring of 110's below, I left him.

This time I wasn't going nearly so fast and had time for two bursts from port coming astern (ring was going clockwise) of 3-4 seconds each at one. There was some return fire which I thought to be cannon as the puffs seemed to be coming slowly. There was also quite a lot of stuff going past in front and below me from the next chap in the circle. It looked rather like tennis balls going past. Both his engines started to smoke with large white streamers. I saw him leave the ring and lose height quickly in a left hand spiral down towards Lympne. I followed discreetly as there were now many 109's about and I couldn't see any of our chaps. He went into cloud at 5,000' and on coming out below I saw him at about 3,000' a mile or so away still spiralling and smoking. He had two Hurricanes beating him up so I left them to it as there was a lot of stuff about. However, I saw nothing else bar another Hurricane which I stalked – quite successfully too if it had been a 109 – and came home soon after. I was allowed a 'probable' for the second and a 'damaged' for the first. I expect the Hurricanes claimed the second as theirs. Anyhow, Intelligence would never find anything out, much too busy! I was the only chap to make any claims, which surprised me. I thought the others would have had a better chance than I had. Apparently, they all saw 109's and proceeded with more caution. George got going wrong way round to a circle of 110's and got hit in the engine, having to bale out of 'Blue Peter'. However, he's OK.

These rings of 110's looked incredibly like a school of dogfish I saw from Nuada, off Lismore – grey and sinister.

I must have been going very fast in the first attack – somewhere near 450 by the time it took to close the range. Yet the shooting was quite good – 1,185 rounds fired.

*This in spite of having brought 18 with us on Tuesday and another two having come down since.

Joey Sarre returned to Hornchurch with damage to the tail of his Spitfire received over Deal at 11.10 hours in combat with Bf110s of II/ZG26 which were supporting the bombers making their way to Hatfield to bomb the Handley Page Halifax works. As Black recorded, George Denholm was forced to bale out at 11.15 hours over Deal after his aircraft was damaged by enemy fire, also from 110s of II/ZG26. His aircraft Blue Peter crashed on Hope Farm, Snargate. On 22 September 1973 the Brenzett Aeronautical Museum recovered many parts from the crashed Spitfire including the instrument panel, most major controls and components together with many manufacturers plates. They also recovered part of the fuel tank cowling still showing traces of the red and gold lettering of the wording Blue Peter. George Denholm was invited down to see the display.

During the morning Richard Hillary had made his way back to Hornchurch arriving shortly after lunch. The Squadron landed at 11.37.

Scrambled again at 15.55 hours, the following Spitfires took off to intercept the last and heaviest raid of the day by the Luftwaffe: F/L Ken Macdonald (XT-E, R6752), F/O Boulter (XT-R, R6709), F/O Haig (XT-E, R6753), F/O Carbury (XT-W, R6835), F/O Waterston (XT-O, X4163), P/O Berry (XT-G, R6773), P/O Read (XT-B, N3056), P/O Morton (XT-S, N3267), F/O Pease (XT-V, R6751), P/O Gilroy (XT-H, N3288), Sgt Stokoe (XT-K, R6898) and Sgt Sarre (XT-X, R7021).

Bubble Waterston destroyed a 109 that was providing fighter cover for I/LG2 over Canterbury at 16.40 hours, but his own aircraft was hit during the combat returning to base with a punctured oil tank. The aircraft was repairable:

> When at 25,000 feet over Deal, I saw three Me109's in a vic at the same height as myself. I attacked the nearest one to me on the starboard quarter, firing a short burst. The Me109 dived steeply, then caught fire and crashed in flames in the Medway.

Waterston was flying with B Flight when he delivered his attack at 16.30 hours, north of Canterbury. Brian Carbury, now DFC, celebrated his achievement with the destruction of another Me109 at 16.45 over London. The Messerschmitt Bf109E-1 was of 3/JG27 and flown by Feldwebel Ernst Arnold who force-landed his damaged aircraft at Westwood Court, near Faversham, and was captured:

> I sighted three Me109's north of me, so I attacked the rear aircraft. The leading two aircraft turned for my tail. I got a good burst in and the propeller of the rear enemy aircraft stopped, started and finally stopped, with white vapour coming out behind. The enemy aircraft went into a glide for the east coast. I veered off as other enemy aircraft were closing in on me.

Brian Carbury was leading a section in B Flight when he delivered his attack at 16.30 hours, north of Canterbury at an altitude of 25,000 feet. He opened fire with a two second burst at 250 yards closing to 50, showing yet again that his success was due to his ability to get in close whilst firing, and continue past to re-establish a height advantage before commencing another attack. The same German aircraft was previously reported to have been shot down by Tom Gleave of 253 Squadron at 11.55 hours. Carbury's ability to hit the enemy fighter hard from close-in and to pull away from the initial attack and not be tempted to remain to 'mix it' in what was a vulnerable position, gives us some idea of why he was so successful.

Joey Sarre claimed a Bf109 probable and shortly afterwards was hit himself and forced to bale out at approximately 16.55 hours. The tail of his Spitfire was shot off in combat possibly by the same 109s that were protecting I/LG2. His aircraft was written-off in the crash at Addington Park, near West Malling. His combat details read:

> When on patrol with 603 Squadron at 25,000 feet, we sighted enemy formation at 20,000 feet, with enemy fighters above them. I became detached from the squadron and was attacked by a formation of four Me109's from the starboard quarter. I turned into them and opened fire. I was unable to see the result of my fire as my machine fell into a violent spin. On landing by parachute I was met by F/O Delg of West Malling, who had witnessed the combat through field glasses, and said he had seen one Me109 fall away and enter a steep dive, but had not watched the enemy plane crash.

Joey Sarre was with A Flight when they encountered 12 109s over Deal. He received an injury to his hand.

The Squadron had been at Hornchuch for only three days, however the intensity of the battle must have made it seem that they had been there for a much longer period. Already they would have been feeling the physical and mental strain. The physical strain coming from the hours without sleep, and the stresses on the human body strapped into the seat of a fast agile fighter being thrown about the sky. The mental strain coming from being in perpetual anticipation of what fate had in store. Would they be hit during the next patrol, would they be shot, burnt or simply blown out of the sky? This constant strain would have certainly taken its toll; remember the mental condition of Peter Howes when Richard and Broody met him at Hornchurch. He had been there longer than they, yet just a few days later they now had a better idea of what he had been experiencing. Some individuals would find the tension unbearable, rushing outside from the dispersal hut to vomit. Many looked drawn and tired, dark around the eye. The loss of their companions was not something they could afford to get emotional about. They had a job to do and such thoughts would detract from their ability to do it properly. One hour after landing it was the job of the CO George Denholm to make a check on who was missing. Sometimes there would be a telephone call from a pilot to say he was safe but inevitably there was the call from a rescue team with the number of an aircraft, and another name was wiped from the board. Richard Hillary wrote: 'At that time the losing of pilots was somehow extremely impersonal; nobody, I think, felt any great emotion – there simply wasn't time for it.' The apposite story of 43 Squadron's John Simpson is told in *Combat Report* by New Zealander, Squadron Leader Hector Bolitho, in which the author quotes from one of John's letters to him:

> I have never found a sign of morbidity over death among pilots. When war was declared, few of them expected to live very long. I have gone through the possessions of many dead pilots. In almost every case, I found a letter, 'To be opened in the event of my death'. I am sure that they never admitted this foreboding among themselves. But it was there. Death had already become their companion when they were training and afterwards, flying with their squadrons. The experience of death was not new to them when the war began. It was merely intensified and made more horrible. This risk was the price they paid for being allowed to live with the clouds, the wind and the stars. They came to know the heavens better than they knew the earth. Pilots and gunners and navigators shared this privilege although they seldom spoke of it among themselves. I think that the double risk of death, which was always with them, made them all the more grateful for life. Each time they landed they gave thanks. Perhaps it was in the form of drink. They drank to celebrate, never to stimulate false ecstasy or to drown depression. They drank to celebrate. It was, and is, one of the most enchanting aspects of their talent for pleasure.
>
> Life and death are not so very far apart for them. How many times have I seen a little group of bare-headed young pilots, so young that life was still a fresh gift in their hands, carrying a coffin into a church, or watching it being lowered into a dark hollow in the earth!
>
> But there is no remorse, even when some form of fear remains. They do not necessarily conquer fear. They adapt themselves to it and beat it into a positive part of their character. For their fear and their sensibility are one. The habits of the pilots show a frank, open-hearted acceptance of certain facts: that the price of double happiness must be paid for with the coin of double risk. So every living moment must be exhausted in joy. They resent idleness because it means waste of time from which pleasure might be wrung. This was true before the war, when the risks were those of peace-time flying. It is still true, with the added risks of war. It was true ten even twenty years ago when the Air Force was numbered in thousands. The gaiety of pilots has always been that of men who were prepared to die at any moment, in return for the privilege of enjoying the beauty and danger of flight. They knew the terms of their bargain when they learned to fly and they were prepared to keep the bargain when the time came.

Off duty many found an outlet in the form of heavy drinking sessions in the mess or a night out in London. In the mess they would usually keep to their own company because they were off when others were on. Having piled into the cars brought south by some of the pilots, the nights out in London could be quite wild; some stayed overnight but always ready to fly as and when required to do so, albeit sometimes a little worse for wear. Once in the air again and faced with the inevitable confrontation of a life and death situation, a few deep breaths of oxygen would soon have the head reasonably clear again and the senses alert!

On one occasion several 603 Squadron pilots managed to sneak past a reluctant doorman into a fairly exclusive club in the West End. It was after hours and they were looking to continue what had already been a lengthy drinking session. In the early hours the management tried to turf them out, as it was closing time, but the pilots refused to leave. The manager then threatened to call the provost but George Denholm informed the manager that the provost marshal was a squadron leader and so was he and anyway the provost was currently on leave. The party continued into the daylight of a new day with the manager tied up and locked in his own office!

CHAPTER 10

SUCCESS… BUT AT A PRICE

Saturday 31 August 1940

It has gone on record that this day was 603's best day as, of the 63 enemy aircraft destroyed, they accounted for 14 – the highest individual bag. Fighter Command sent up 978 fighter sorties, losing 39 aircraft in action. RAF airfields were bombed by the Luftwaffe, most of the important sector airfields being bombed twice.

There were several large scale attacks over the group area throughout the day, the first (08.05-09.43) developed over the Debden and North Weald areas of Kent. The second attack (10.00-11.15) was concentrated on the Thames estuary and two squadrons were sent up and intercepted the force.

From 12.00-13.45 hours an attack developed in the Kent, Thames estuary and Kenley areas and ten squadrons carried out an interception.

Between 17.30 and 19.30 hours a widespread attack developed over Kent, Thames estuary, Essex and London when 13 squadrons attacked the enemy.

Hornchurch was bombed at lunchtime at which time three more pilots had reported for flying duty with 603 Squadron. Pilot Officers Brian R. Macnamara and W.P.H. Rafter who had responded to the call from Fighter Command for more fighter pilots by volunteering to move from 614 and 225 Squadrons respectively, both army co-operation units based at Odiham, where they had flown Lysanders. They were sent to 7 OTU at Hawarden where they converted to Spitfires. Flying Officer Jim MacPhail, an ex-army co-operation and 41 Squadron pilot had converted to Spitfires at 5 OTU, Aston Down.

The first patrol of the day by 603 Squadron took off at 08.55 hours. The 12 Spitfires were flown by: F/L Ken Macdonald (XT-E, R6752), F/O Boulter (XT-S, N3207), F/O Haig (XT-P, X4274), F/O Waterston (XT-K, X4273), F/O Carbury (XT-W, R6835), P/O Hillary (XT-M, X4277), P/O Morton

Two remarkable photographs showing the bombing of Hornchurch airfield on 31 August 1940 by the Luftwaffe.

(XT-J, L1057), P/O Read (XT-F, R6754), P/O Gilroy (XT-H, N3288), Sgt Stokoe (XT-X, X4250), P/O Berry (XT-Y, R6626), and P/O Stapleton (XT-L, L1020).

The 603 fighters took off to join forces with the many other fighter units in an attempt to intercept the German fighters, thus leaving the bombers at the mercy of the Hurricanes. That was the general plan but in the mêlée that followed the initial first attack the fighters attacked the nearest available enemy aircraft. This was Richard Hillary's first flight in Spitfire X4277, the aircraft in which he was shot down on 3 September. During this sortie Carbury and Gilroy each destroyed a Bf109 while another 109 claimed destroyed appears in the Squadron diary but was unallotted. On his way to achieving 'ace in a day' (not strictly accurate as he already had two enemy aircraft destroyed to his credit) Brian Carbury claimed a Bf109E shot down over Canterbury:

> We were climbing over Canterbury at 28,000 feet when enemy aircraft were sighted. I warned VIKEN leader, and then led on diving on the near Me109 which turned over and spun in. The pilot jumped out by parachute.

Brian Carbury and Spitfire Mk I, R6835, forged probably the most successful fighter/pilot combination during the Battle of Britain. 'Viken' leader was Ken Macdonald. The enemy aircraft numbered 20 109s and Carbury launched his attack not long after 09.00 hours. He opened fire at 200 yards closing to 50 yards during which time he fired one three-second burst. It is possible that with this claim he shared in the shooting down of the ace Oberleutnant Eckhart Priebe (holder of the Iron Cross – First Class) of I/JG77 with F/L Denys Gillam of 616 Squadron. Priebe had continued to lead his Staffel into combat despite the fact that earlier, having selected a target, he found his own guns had jammed, possibly due to too much oil. His ploy worked for a while but the British fighters quickly became aware of his plight and the unarmed fighter soon received the attention of a number of Spitfires and Hurricanes. The complicated maze of pipes and rubber hoses that circulated the vital coolant in his aircraft was pierced and very soon the engine began to protest. During one of the final bursts of gunfire that caught his plane, bullets penetrated the slender fuselage behind the cockpit, one bullet entering the cabin and ricocheting back, striking him in the forehead.

At 12,000 feet above the beautiful Kent village of Elham, Priebe baled out and opened his parachute. The cut on his face was bleeding profusely and he had to wipe it away in order to read his watch which said 10.23 hours (09.23 hours BST). An RAF fighter flew around him, discharging bursts of ammunition as if in celebration of the victory. Sheep Gilroy claimed a 109 destroyed:

> P/O Gilroy attacked a stray Me109 in mid-Channel south of Dungeness. He saw it crash in flames in the sea. Later in the day P/O Gilroy baled out and is still in hospital. Report follows.

This report was written by the Intelligence Officer and a full report was never written. Gilroy was with A Flight when he attacked the 109 at an altitude of 25,000 feet. The 603 pilots landed again at 09.35 hours. Listed as the first patrol of the day, Jack Stokoe recorded in his log book: 'Interception – 2 Me 110's damaged. – Windscreen shot away. 50+ 109's. Rather too hot! Hand slightly damaged by windscreen splinters.' Bearing in mind it was an extremely hectic day, Jack's four entries are listed in reverse order. The second patrol (10.25 to 11.30 hours) is recorded in the log books of Jack Stokoe and Black Morton but is missing from the Squadron ORB. For this patrol Jack recorded: 'Interception 30+, 109's – No luck!'

Kesselring tried to tempt up RAF fighters by sending over a number of *Freie Jagd* or free-hunts (attempts to lure up the RAF fighters), but Park did not rise to the bait and kept his precious fighters/pilots on the ground until he was sure that the raid was for real. However, it did serve as an indicator to the controllers that an enemy bombing raid was likely to follow.

The next raid materialised in the form of two waves of Dorniers and Heinkels escorted by Bf109s and Bf110s, sent by Kesselring to attack Croydon and Biggin Hill. The Dorniers, flying at 2,000 feet, had almost made it to their target at Croydon unopposed, before the Hurricanes of 85 Squadron took off to intercept them at 12.55, just as the first bombs started to fall on the east side of the aerodrome. Led by Squadron Leader Peter Townsend, the Hurricanes caught up with the Dorniers over Tunbridge Wells, but as they climbed hard to attack the 110s the 109s fell on them from out of the sun. In the ensuing combat it was claimed that the Hurricane pilots had destroyed two 109s and one 110 for the loss of two Hurricanes with both pilots being injured. One of these pilots was Townsend, who later had a piece of cannon shell removed from his foot and had a big toe amputated. The Dorniers had succeeded in bombing Croydon and one hangar was destroyed in the raid.

Biggin Hill was hit hard by the two Staffeln of Heinkel He111s that bombed the aerodrome from 12,000 feet hitting two of the remaining three hangars, messes, living quarters, and more importantly, the operations room. All the repair work that had been carried out after the last raid was undone. Water and electricity mains and telephone lines, were once again cut. Hurricanes of 253 Squadron intercepted the Heinkels as they made good their escape and managed to shoot down one of their number. For the third time, at 12.35, 12 Spitfires of 603 were scrambled from Hornchurch to intercept: F/L Ken Macdonald (XT-E, R6752), F/O Boulter (XT-S, N3267), F/O Waterston (XT-K, X4273), F/O Carbury (XT-W, R6835), P/O Gilroy (XT-N, X4271), P/O Morton (XT-B, N3056), P/O Stapleton (XT-R, X4264), P/O Read (XT-F, R6754), F/O Haig (XT-P, X4274), P/O Hillary (XT-M, X4277), Sgt Stokoe (XT-X, X4250), and P/O Berry (XT-Y, R6626).

The intelligence patrol report reads:

> 12 aircraft of 603 Sqn left Hornchurch to patrol Biggin Hill at 28,000'. P/O Gilroy saw enemy aircraft above him, so the squadron climbed, but lost sight of them. They were then ordered to patrol base, where they saw about 14 Dornier Do17's at about 17,000', protected by Me109's and He113's. The squadron went into line-astern and dived to attack. A dogfight ensued. The He113's had white spinners and grey and white speckled camouflage on top of the wings.

The He113s that the Intelligence Officer refers to were Messerschmitt Bf109Es which were amongst the confirmed losses that day. The He113 appeared in all British recognition manuals of the early war period and RAF pilots frequently reported combats with them during the Battle of Britain. The existence of the He113 was actually an elaborate hoax by the Germans. Before the war the Luftwaffe had rejected the Heinkel He100 in favour of developed versions of the Bf109. In the spring of 1940, nine He100s were prepared for a remarkable hoax which was intended to convince the Allied intelligence services that a new high-performance fighter had entered service. The aircraft were photographed in lines bearing fictitious unit markings and victory bars. The propaganda ruse certainly fooled some RAF pilots during the Battle of Britain.

There were no casualties within 603 Squadron and Ras Berry claimed two 109s destroyed, with Brian Carbury claiming two He113s [Bf109s] destroyed. Richard Hillary claimed a 109 destroyed, Ken Macdonald a He113 [Bf109] destroyed and Black Morton a Dornier Do17 destroyed. Whilst Hillary had now claimed two destroyed and one probable, Brian Carbury had already eight enemy aircraft destroyed to his credit. Black's combat report was detailed:

> As leader of rearguard action I was above squadron at 32,000 feet when many bombers with escort were seen approaching Hornchurch at about 15,000 feet. Squadron dived to attack. I got in a short burst from starboard quarter on a Do.17 of formation. No results observed. On recovering from break-away I observed a Do.17 slightly apart from the main formation. I made to attack it and it lost height quickly. At 8,000 feet I observed a Hurricane also pursuing this a/c. I allowed him to make his attack and followed from the sun. I fired bursts totalling 10 seconds from quarter and astern. E/A was now flying at 500 feet at about 240 m.p.h. After my first burst cabin roof of e/a blew off. I made a second attack and finished my ammunition. E/A was now going slowly very close to the water. It forced landed on the sea near the French coast. I did not wait to see any survivors. No return fire in first attack, slight and inaccurate in second.

Black Morton was flying with A Flight during this combat and delivered his attack at 13.15 hours at an altitude of 15,000 feet. Years later Ras Berry recalled the morning and third patrol on this hectic day:

> The batman's knock on the door before dawn signalled the beginning of another day. The date was 31 August 1940 and we were required to report almost immediately for dawn-to-breakfast standby... This day began like most others – a quick cup of tea in the mess, a few quips from the chaps, then out to the three ton truck, which took the pilots to Squadron dispersal point, a hut on the far side of the airfield.

Wearing my Mae West, and after briefing by the C.O., I went to meet my ground-crew, two devoted airmen who treated and cared for my Spitfire like the thoroughbred she was. After that, back to the dispersal to report aircraft O.K. The Squadron came to readiness. It was still dark.

It was too early to play the usual Mah Jong or shove ha'penny. The pilots sat, or lay, around, waiting to scramble or to be relieved by another Squadron for breakfast.

As the sun mounted, it revealed a familiar pattern of weather, blue sky with high thin white wisps of cloud, a clear indication of a fine day ahead.

Then came the order: 'Squadron Scramble, patrol Thames Estuary, 30,000 feet, many bandits.'

In seconds we were airborne and climbing eastwards, stringing out to take positions which would leave us enough room to manoeuvre and to keep a good lookout. We were soon on patrol at 30,000 feet across the estuary. The French coast looked near.

...The Squadron was in the thick of a mass of wheeling, milling, Messerschmitt 109's which were protecting their big brothers, the Heinkel and Dornier bombers. The Squadron split up and in seconds I was in a dog-fight with an Me109.

The turn got tighter. The question was, which of us would straighten up – would the 109 roll over and disappear, or stay long enough for me to get a bead on him?

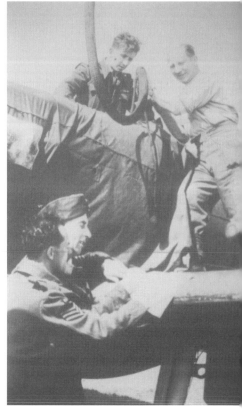

AC1 George Mullay refuelling. George was the oldest member of the 603 ground crews.

He left it too late, I got in a long burst, then another and he burst into flames.

Another quick turn to check that no one was on my tail. I could see several dog-fights going on around me, and hear quick, high-pitched calls: 'Look out behind you, so-and-so!'

Another 109 crossed below and in front. I waited a second or so and then rolled over and followed him. He never saw me, I gave him a long burst as I closed rapidly on his tail. There was a long trail of smoke and flame and he went straight into the ground. The next thing I knew was that the attack was withdrawing, badly mauled.

I returned to Hornchurch, my aircraft unscathed, to give my combat reports to the 'Spy' (Squadron Intelligence Officer).

Following the combat Ras reported:

Patrolling with squadron at 28,000' over Biggin Hill, I saw a protective fighter formation above bomber squadron. They formed a circle and soon split into combat. I stuck on the tail of a Me109 and closed in and fired two bursts of four seconds and the enemy aircraft broke up. I then caught up with another 109 and closed in and fired at close range. Pieces fell off the 109 and it sank out of control and broke up.

Ras was flying as Blue 2 of B Flight. The number of German fighters and bombers was estimated as 50. The attack was delivered at 13.15 hours over Biggin Hill, at an altitude of 28,000'. He opened fire at 100 yards closing to 20 yards, firing bursts of four seconds in length using a total of 2,800 rounds during the combat. Brian Carbury's report reads:

Enemy aircraft Me109 sighted and the squadron gave chase. I left and went for another formation which turned out to be friendly fighters. Heard over R/T that e/a were bombing home base, set course and saw e/a proceeding east. I was at 25,000', so we came down to attack bombers, but saw fighters He113 and Me109 above. I attacked the He113, he went straight down missing the rear of the formation and crashed straight into the ground. I carried out a beam attack on another He113 off to starboard. After one long burst he went on his back, pilot jumped out by parachute, and e/a crashed and burst into flames in a vacant bit west of Southend.

Carbury was leading a B Flight section against approximately 50 Dornier Do17s, 'He113s' and Bf109s in an attack delivered at 13.40 hours, west of Southend, at an altitude of 28,000 feet. He opened fire at 150 yards and closed to 50, firing bursts of two seconds. One of the Messerschmitts, a 109E-1, was 4806 flown by Oberleutnant Hafer. He managed to bale out but was found dead in Ingrebourne Creek on 2 September, his parachute unopened. His aircraft crashed in flames at Bridge Road, Rainham.

Richard Hillary's claim of a 109 destroyed was written-up by the Intelligence Officer based on available evidence from fellow Squadron members and the confirmation of his kill by the Observer Corps: 'P/O Hillary claims a Me109 destroyed, shot down over the Channel. He is at present in hospital report to follow.' Richard was with B Flight and was involved in the attack on approximately 50 109s over Dungeness, carried out at an altitude of 18,000 feet. He was later able to confirm that he opened fire with 3-5 second bursts at 200 yards and closed to a mere five yards! With George Denholm still recovering from having to bale out of his Spitfire during the previous morning's combat, Ken Macdonald claimed a 'He113' destroyed while leading 603. His report reads:

> After patrolling for some time with the squadron at 30,000' we were told to patrol base. On approaching base from the south I saw considerable a/c and anti-aircraft activity over base at about 20,000'. I put squadron into line astern and gave the order to attack. I selected an He113 which was coming straight in my direction but below me. I got a momentary burst in from almost vertically above but was unable to allow enough deflection. I then pulled out and did a steep climbing turn and came down again above him and behind him to the south. He broke away from the rest of the battle and turned south east at about 20,000'. I followed and after a bit gradually overhauled him. As I approached very close behind him he suddenly made a very steep turn to the right. I gave him a full deflection burst of about 2-3 seconds and he immediately emitted a long trail of white 'smoke' and went into a steep spiral dive. I watched him to see him crash, but at about 4,000' he pulled gradually out and proceeded SE flying low. I flew down from 20,000' and again overtook him flying at about 1,000' and about 350 mph. As I approached again he went into a gradual left hand turn and I gave him another burst of about 2 seconds from immediately behind having to pull up very suddenly to avoid him. He then flew down onto a field and rolled over and over. He came down approximately south or south east of Maidstone.
>
> The aircraft was of very good lines and appeared not unlike a Spitfire in shape, but in colour (seen as I always did with the sun behind me), it was easily different from the Spitfire owing to its different green and grey camouflage and its cross on the fuselage just behind the cockpit. It had a general appearance of neatness and compactness.

Ken was leading the Squadron as the leader of the Station Flight (A). His attack was delivered at 13.15 hours at an altitude of 20,000 feet. The enemy aircraft he claimed destroyed was a Messerschmitt Bf109E-1, (3652) of 1JG/77 flown by Feldwebel Walter Evers. It crashed on Court Farm, Hunton, Kent at 13.25 hours. Evers was severely wounded and succumbed to his injuries the next day. He was buried in Maidstone Cemetery. 603 Squadron landed at 13.56 hours. Jack Stokoe recorded in his log book: 'Interception – 15 109's. Balloon Barrage.'

At approximately 13.15, 40 minutes after 603 took off on patrol, Hornchurch was bombed. In contrast with the attacks of the previous day the raiders of Biggin Hill had flown in over the coast to the west of Folkestone as part of a two-wave formation. The second wave split from the first near Maidstone and headed for Hornchurch aerodrome where, due to the heat haze east of London inhibiting the Observer Corps from passing accurate plots on this particular raid, the Gruppe of Dorner Do17s had almost reached the airfield when the Spitfires of 54 Squadron, led by Al Deere, were just taking off. Deere's experience has gone down in history and he was clearly blessed with good fortune when he escaped with only minor injuries. The Cf. Form 540, 54 Squadron, 31 August 1940 reads:

> 13.15 hours. A large formation of enemy bombers – a most impressive sight in vic formation at 15,000 feet – reached the aerodrome and dropped their bombs (probably sixty in all) in a line from our original dispersal pens to the petrol dump and beyond into Elm Park. Perimeter track, dispersal pens and barrack block windows suffered, but no other damage to buildings was caused, and the aerodrome, in spite of its ploughed condition, remained serviceable. The squadron was ordered off just as the first bombs were beginning to fall and eight of our machines safely cleared the ground; the remaining section, however, just became airborne as the bombs exploded. All three machines were wholly wrecked in the air, and the survival of the pilots is a complete miracle. Sgt Davis taking off towards the hangars was thrown back across the River Ingrebourne two fields away, scrambling out of his machine unharmed. Flt Lt Deere had one wing and his prop torn off; climbing to a hundred feet, he turned over, coming down, slid along the aerodrome for a hundred yards upside down. He was rescued from this unenviable position by P/O Edsall, the third member of the section, who had suffered a similar fate except that he landed the right way up. Dashing across the aerodrome with bombs still dropping, he extricated Deere from his machine. All three pilots were ready again for battle by the next morning.

The Hornchurch Station operations record book states:

> Mass raids continued to be made against our aerodromes, again starting early in the morning. The first two attacks were delivered at 08.30 and 10.30 respectively and were directed at Biggin Hill, Eastchurch and Debden. The third attack was delivered at Hornchurch, and although our squadrons engaged, they were unable to break the enemy bomber formation, and about thirty Dorniers dropped some one hundred bombs across the airfield. Damage, however, was slight, although a bomb fell on the new Airmen's Mess which was almost completed. The vital damage. however, was to a power cable, which was cut. The emergency power equipment was brought into operation until repair was effected. Three men were killed and eleven wounded. 54 Squadron attempted to take off during the attack and ran through the bombs. Three aircraft were destroyed, one being blown from the middle of the landing field to outside the boundary, but all three pilots miraculously escaped with only slight injuries.

According to surviving ground crew of 603 and a number of pilots, including Jack Stokoe and Stapme Stapleton, the 603 Spitfires landed at Rochford at 13.56 hours, having been diverted as a result of the bombing of Hornchurch. Although it has been written that 603 returned to Hornchurch at 13.56 and subsequently took off again ten minutes prior to the second bombing raid of the day, ground crewmen of 603 recalled waiting at dispersal with their equipment at the ready for the Spitfires to return, but this did not occur until after the final patrol of the day. In *The Last Enemy* Richard Hillary refers to the lunchtime attack on the airfield which he says occurred as he was walking to dispersal:

> ...I heard a shout, and our ground crew drew up in a lorry beside me. Sergeant Ross leaned out:
> 'Want a lift, sir? We're going round.'
> 'No, thanks, sergeant. I'm going to cut across.'
> This was forbidden for obvious reasons, but I felt like that.
> 'O.K., sir. See you round there.'
> The lorry trundled off down the road in a cloud of dust. I walked on across the landing ground. At that moment I heard the emotionless voice of the controller.
> 'Large enemy bombing formation approaching Hornchurch. All personnel not engaged in active duty take cover immediately.'
> I looked up. They were still not visible. At the dispersal point I saw Bubble and Pip Cardell make a dash for the shelter... Our lorry was still trundling along the road [the perimeter 'Peri' track], maybe half-way round, and seemed suddenly an awfully long way from the dispersal point.

I looked up again, and this time I saw them – about a dozen slugs, shining in the bright sun and coming straight on. At the rising scream of the first bomb I instinctively shrugged up my shoulders and ducked my head… and then my feet were nearly knocked from under me, my mouth was full of dirt, and Bubble, gesticulating like a madman from the shelter entrance, was yelling, 'Run, you bloody fool, run!' I ran. Suddenly awakened to the lunacy of my behaviour, I covered the distance to the shelter as if impelled by a rocket, shot through the entrance while once again the ground rose up and hit me, and my head smashed hard against one of the pillars. I subsided on a heap of rubble and massaged it.

'Who's here?' I asked, peering through the gloom.

'Cardell and I and three of our ground crew,' said Bubble, 'and, by the Grace of God, you!'

I could see by his mouth that he was still talking, but a sudden concentration of the scream and crump of falling bombs made it impossible to hear him.

The air was thick with dust and the shelter shook and heaved at each explosion, yet somehow held firm. For about three minutes the bedlam continued, and then suddenly ceased. In the utter silence which followed nobody moved. None of us wished to be the first to look on the devastation which we felt must be outside. Then Bubble spoke. 'Praise God!' he said, 'I'm not a civilian. Of all the bloody frightening things I've ever done, sitting in that shelter was the worst. For me the air from now on!'

It broke the tension and we scrambled out of the entrance. The runways were certainly in something of a mess. Gaping holes and great gobbets of earth were everywhere. Right in front of us a bomb had landed by my Spitfire, covering it with a shower of grit and rubble.

I turned to the aircraftmen standing beside me. 'Will you get hold of Sergeant Ross and tell him to have a crew give her an inspection.'

He jerked his head towards one corner of the aerodrome:' I think Sergeant Ross won't be doing any more inspections.'

I followed his glance and saw the lorry, the roof about twenty yards away, lying grotesquely on its side. I climbed into the cockpit, and, feeling faintly sick, tested out the switches. Bubble poked his head over the side.

'Lets go over to the mess and see what's up: all our machines will be landing down at the reserve landing field, anyway.'

Richard had not gone up the previous day and, having flown all four patrols on 31 August in Spitfire X4277, was not at the aerodrome during the raids but in combat. Bubble also flew all combat patrols being tragically killed during the last. Nevertheless, the airfield was bombed, a number of 603 ground crew personnel were killed and wounded and Pip Cardell was on the ground at the time and had still to fly his first patrol from Hornchurch. The morning on which Richard was rested was actually 1 September (Hornchurch was not bombed on the 1st) when the whole Squadron was stood-down during the morning before they were once again in combat in the afternoon. Sergeant James Harry Ross does exist, survived the war and is a member of the 603 Squadron Association in Edinburgh. No sergeant was killed during the bombing of 31 August.

According to the log books of Jack Stokoe and Black Morton, the Squadron flew *four* patrols on 31 August, not three, as written in the ORB. This point is further confirmed in the private letters of Ken Macdonald. The 'missing' patrol in the ORB being the second of the day. The log books record the following times of the patrols for 31 August: 1.)08.30-09.35…..3 Bf109s destroyed. 2.)10.25-11.30. 3.)12.35-13.40…..6 Bf109s and 1 Do17 destroyed. 4.)17.55-19.00…..4 Bf109s, 1 Bf109 probable.

Hornchurch and Biggin Hill were bombed again shortly after 18.00 hours. This was the fourth attack on the RAF airfields that day. Erprobungsgruppe 210 accompanied three Staffeln of Ju88s and Bf110s dropping about 30 bombs on each target. Two parked Spitfires were destroyed at Hornchurch and another member of the 603 ground crew was killed bringing the total to four for the day with 11 wounded.

LAC 803238, Johnny Reilly, was on the aerodrome at the time. A veteran WEM* of 603 having originally joined in 1931, he remembered seeing his friend and fellow WEM, Jack Wright, emerge

---

*WEM – Wireless, Electrical, Maintenance technician.

from the smoke and dust following the bombing covered from head to toe in blood. Fortunately he was unhurt. A bomb blast had killed the chap next to him, spraying him with blood.

Although a force of 30 bombers had approached the airfield most had already dropped their bombs and apart from damage to dispersal pens, the perimeter track and airfield surface it remained serviceable. Nos 54 and 222 Squadrons were also airborne at the time attempting to fight off the raid on Biggin, with 603 having got airborne prior to the raid, having refuelled and rearmed at Rochford. The RAF Hornchurch ORB states:

> The fourth attack of the day was also directed at Hornchurch, and once again, despite strong fighter opposition and AA fire, the bombers penetrated our defences. This time, however, their aim was most inaccurate, and the line of bombs fell from them towards the edge of the aerodrome. Two Spitfires parked near the edge of the aerodrome were written off, and one airman was killed. Otherwise, apart from the damage to dispersal pens, the perimeter track, and the aerodrome surface, the raid was abortive, and the aerodrome remained serviceable. Our squadrons, which had a very heavy day, accounted for no less than 19 of the enemy and a further 7 probably destroyed. 603 Squadron alone were responsible for the destruction of 14 enemy aircraft. Although we lost a total of 9 aircraft, either in combat or on the ground, only 1 pilot was lost.

An aerial photograph taken of Hornchurch in 1941 (opposite) clearly shows where the bombs struck the airfield during the raids of the previous summer. By comparing the photograph with Joe Crawshaw's (222 Squadron ground crew) photographs (see page 230) taken of the dispersed Spitfires in 1940, it is possible to pin-point the position of Richard Hillary's Spitfire, XT-M, X4277, on the aerial photograph. Stapme Stapleton later heard about the attack on the airfield from colleagues:

> In twenty-four hours the airfield was serviceable again. They hit the airfield and not the hangars. It was a grass aerodrome with no actual runways. If they had hit the hangars some damage would have been inflicted. Daddy Bouchier was the CO and he got everybody onto the airfield filling in the bomb craters. He helped position the little yellow marker boxes on the airfield after the raid on the 31st in order to indicate to the returning pilots a safe strip to land on. The pilots returning from combat remember seeing this little figure scurrying about, hastily positioning these markers to help guide them in. There was one strip left untouched by bombs at the southern edge of the aerodrome, which we could still land on when we returned at the end of the day.
>
> Looking from south to north, 603 Squadron was situated half way along on the east side of the aerodrome with the hangars on the left-hand side and the administration block and that sort of thing, with the mess further over on the same side. We were very much a squadron, even in the mess, because you were off while the other squadrons were on and you never saw them. We had a wonderful controller, I don't remember his name, he used to say, '603 Squadron please get into the air as soon as possible, please get going chaps,' he spoke in such a mellifluous way. There was no urgency in his voice, no panic, nothing. It was a great influence.

As Ras Berry recalled earlier, the voice was that of Ronald Adams the actor and WWI fighter pilot, and it also had a calming effect on him. On 8 December 1940, the Edinburgh newspaper *Sunday Post* ran a feature on the pilots of 603 during that year with a headline referring to the success achieved on 31 August: 'Edinburgh Boys Bump Off 13 Jerries in One Day.' It included photographs of pilots Ras Berry, Stapme Stapleton, Brian Macnamara, Ludwik Martel, John Boulter and David Scott-Malden. (The article did not actually appear until the edition of 8 December 1940, thus explaining the inclusion of Martel and Scott-Malden who had yet to join the Squadron.) The actual score was 14 with the loss of only one pilot and two Spitfires.

The last patrol that 603 mounted took off at 17.51 hours and was led once again by F/L Ken Macdonald. (Whilst the Squadron AIR 20/2079 states that they took off at 17.51 the log books of Jack Stokoe and Black Morton state the time as being 17.55.) The patrol comprised: F/L Ken Macdonald (XT-E, R6752), P/O Berry (XT-Y, R6626), F/O Haig (XT-P, X4274), F/O Boulter (XT-S, N3267), F/O Waterston (XT-K, X4273), F/O Carbury (XT-W, R6835), P/O Gilroy (XT-N,

Top: Photograph of RAF Hornchurch showing filled-in crater marks from bomb damage inflicted during the Battle of Britain.
Bottom: F/L Fred Rushmer, B Flight Commander in XT-R.

X4271), P/O Morton (XT-B, N3056), P/O Read (XT-F, R6754), Sgt Stokoe (XT-X, X4250), P/O Stapleton (XT-L, L1020), F/L Rushmer (XT-R, X4264), and P/O Hillary (XT-M, X4277).

As a collective, this group of pilots had by this time amassed a total of over 2,500 hours on Spitfires with 603 Squadron. Over Woolwich they met formidable opposition in the shape of the Bf109s of I/JG3, with Carbury claiming another two enemy aircraft destroyed over Southend, but they also suffered the tragic loss of the most popular member of the Squadron, Bubble Waterston. His Spitfire had only been issued to 603 the previous day as a replacement. Due to the frantic nature of the aerial combat his loss was not witnessed by any of his colleagues but many eyewitnesses on the ground saw the Spitfire descend from the sky above. The most likely cause was that at 18.30 hours he had been shot down by 109s of I/JG3 during combat over London and was either dead or unconscious when his aircraft plunged into Repository Road, Woolwich. If he was still alive on impact, F/O Robin McGregor Waterston died instantly in the resulting crash. He was 23 years old. Back in Scotland his youngest sister heard the tragic news when her two young nieces ran up the path outside the family home shouting: 'Uncle Robin's dead!, Uncle Robin's dead!', too young to appreciate the heartbreak of the news that had been passed to them.

Contrary to popular belief, his aircraft did not break-up in mid-air as the result of damage received – it has been previously stated that a wing was seen fluttering down from the Spitfire. However, a Bf109 E-4 (1503) of I/JG3 flown by Leutnant Walter Binder was shot down over the same area, and during the early part of its subsequent plunge to the earth it lost a wing. The flaming aircraft spiralled to the ground, with the wing 'fluttered' down nearby. Binder was found dead in the wreckage. It was this aircraft that had been reported as having been seen breaking-up in mid-air and subsequently the details of the two crashes became confused.

Bubble's final direction before impact had been from the north-east and, in order to miss the barracks, he came down at an angle of about 45 degrees, which would have taken his aircraft over the rooftops on the north side of Wellington Street and caught the trees on the south side next to the barracks before crashing into the middle of Repository Road. Bombardier John Cross of the Royal Artillery (RA) was at that time based at the Royal Artillery Depot, Woolwich, with countless others, waiting to go overseas:

Bombardier John Cross whilst at Woolwich (with corporal stripes).

On the 31st, because of the aerial activity, we were confined to the ground floor of the barrack block when there was the sound of an explosion close to the west of the block. Shortly after, a sergeant announced that there had been a plane crash by the roadside and that a guard was required. I was told to take five gunners with rifles and to block the road at the south end of the incident, the intention being to protect the public from the dangers of live ammunition and to prevent looting. Similarly, another NCO took the north end.

On arrival at the site we were met with a tragic mess. The impact of the crashing Spitfire had resulted in the pilot being thrown through a corrugated parade shed at the side of the road. The impact was so great that his body was fragmented. His head was found on top of the shed.

My guard was kept busy holding back the gawping civilians who were arriving in numbers. Civilian undertakers arrived with a coffin, which was no more than a wooden box with a tarpaulin cover. Assisted by several gunners, we began the gruesome task of gathering the human remains. The job was carried out very thoroughly and it took us about an hour. During the operation we commented on how the pilot had just missed the north-westerly corner of the barrack block, on the corner of Repository Road and Wellington Street, and so avoided the loss of many lives. The fact that the shed remained un-repaired for many years served as a reminder of the sacrifice made by the brave young pilot.

Certain members of the public did attempt to encroach on the crash site and John Cross and his men were forced to use their rifles against the crowds of civilians. John was later reprimanded for pointing his rifle when a civilian took a dislike to the way the bombardier carried out his duty. They were not entirely successful in protecting the site from ghoulish souvenir hunters, however. A young lad called John Hodnett was shown a piece of RAF tunic by another youngster who told him he had found it at the crash site. Several others also managed to acquire small fragments of the aircraft as souvenirs. This was John Cross' first encounter with death, and many years later the effect that this experience had had upon him was still clearly evident.

The Spitfire disintegrated on impact. The Merlin engine was half buried in the road and the wreckage that remained attached was spontaneously engulfed in flames as the fuel tanks ruptured and sprayed a welter of flaming aviation fuel over the immediate area. Such was the devastation that little was left to identify the aircraft as having been a Spitfire. The instantly recognisable elliptical wings were smashed and subsequently burnt in the ensuing flames which ultimately produced the 'white ash' of incinerated aluminium.

The *Kentish Messenger* printed an article on 6 September which captured the atmosphere of the period and in particular the events that occurred over Woolwich on 31 August. Interestingly, the reporter includes a rather different version of the last seconds of Bubble's flight:

You would think it was just a summer shower coming on when the sirens sounded on Saturday morning, so unconcernedly did the womenfolk, caught at their delayed weekend shopping, take shelter. At one minute the business streets were thronged with a typical Saturday morning crowd; the next minute they were deserted as on a Sunday morning. This was the sixth air raid warning in twenty-four hours.... With unrehearsed precision the men and girls from the workshops and offices filed into the shelters.... Not all of them. There were little groups of women standing in the doorways of the closed shops, and as they had plate glass all around them they stood in the greatest peril. Fighters attacked the raiders and far away a blazing 'plane drifted slowly down and fell out of sight. Nearer came the bombers. Then the local guns went into action, and their peremptory banging produced puffs of exploding shells and the bombers veered away. Once more the fighters swooped into action. In the suburban gardens families stood by their Anderson Shelters spellbound at the remote battle overhead. They saw the formation of bombers break up before the attackers of the fighters. But as one lot sheered off another formation appeared. The sky twinkled with aircraft. Wings flashed in the sunlight, and it was plain that something was going on in the far-away depths of the sky. Then they saw an aeroplane that was not flying. It was tumbling over and over. It was a Messerschmitt fighter coming down, rolling down, turning on the axis of its body, for it had lost a wing. At the same time two pin-point flashes appeared from the tail of another aeroplane overhead, and it went into a dive. For a moment it pulled straight, then turned on its nose and came down vertically, obviously out of control and done for, but 'zooming' terrifically. Still a long way off, it fluttered a moment then dropped like a stone. Out of the remote and unreal it broke swiftly into the near and real, no longer there but here. Out of the sky it rushed roaring towards the earth, suddenly, terribly, exploded in the air and disintegrated in a thousand fragments. How unforgettable was the crash that followed, and the black column of smoke from an Airman's pyre. The Messerschmitt was still fantastically rolling its way down, but was now in flames, and soon it too became monstrously near to some watchers, who dived for their shelters, and trembled there while the thing hit the earth with an ear-splitting noise, and buried itself in somebody's back garden. Then from out of the upper reaches of the sky there drifted down a fluttering wing, presumably of the crashed Messerschmitt.... There was a rush to the places where the remains of the crashed 'planes were to be seen. All that was left of the machine that dived and exploded was a heap of white ash in a road and fragments of machinery scattered around. There was ample evidence of the efficiency of arrangements in the prompt way the police, wardens, fire service, ambulance, and soldiers were on the spot. But there was nothing much to do once the fire had burnt out, only to pick up the bits of engine and keep the crowd back. …the *Pathe Gazette* cameraman drove up in his car and the crowd stood and stared….

What the reporter actually witnessed when he saw the officials at the crash-site picking up the 'bits of engine' was in fact the recovery of all that was left of Bubble. The reporter expresses a degree of animosity at being held back by the 'efficient arrangements of the officials that attended to the crash scene.' This adds credence to the effort required by John Cross and his gunners in order to restrain the inquisitive and, to some degree, morbid onlookers who wished to get past his roadblock for a closer look. The reporter's interpretation of events leading to Bubble's Spitfire crash conflicts with that of Mr Pendercast who described the Spitfire diving straight into the ground from a steep angle, with no doubt in his mind that the pilot had not attempted to get his aircraft safely down:

As a fourteen year old at that time, I was continually ticked-off by my parents for often leaving the shelter and covered way during air raids to see what was happening. It was during one such time that I witnessed the final throes of the plane in what was virtually a vertical dive. My opinion was, and has remained so, that the brave pilot was in all probability either badly injured or even worse, or alternatively the plane's controls had been damaged during the combat to render it unresponsive, because the nature of the plane's dive was vertical with no apparent effort to ease or pull out of the dive. The point at which this observation was carried out was somewhat less than a quarter of a mile, as the crow flies. I still recall telling my family that it was a British plane and their reaction that I must be wrong as it must have been an enemy plane. I can quite definitely say that any suggestion that the plane 'broke up in mid-air' was quite incorrect as the view I had indicated that the plane was completely intact. I do realise that this version tends to fly in the face of the suggestion that this brave pilot deliberately steered the plane away from a built-up area, but in my view it in no way detracts from saying that Robin McGregor Waterston was a hero, for he was one of the 'glorious few'… one who I will never forget.

The Press later mentioned there had been a mid-air collision between two aircraft before they plunged to the ground and the aircraft which landed on the road (Waterston) disintegrated on impact with the tarmac. It mentioned that the body of the pilot was removed from the wreckage once the fire had been extinguished but did not name him. The scars in the road and surrounding buildings remained visible for some time. Typically, there are inconsistencies within these reports. Out of the great many servicemen and civilians interviewed who witnessed events, not one recalls seeing a mid-air collision between the two fighters, in actual fact they had come from two different directions and crashed in very close proximity to each other. It was also incorrectly stated that the fire in Repository Road was caused by the burning wing section of the Messerschmitt when it was Bubble's Spitfire.

Jack Stokoe was credited with shooting down Binder's Bf109 and his combat report and log book confirms the details: 'Interception – 1 Me109 Confirmed – 1 Me109 Damaged. Broke away from formation and attacked 2 Me109's climbing into sun over London.' Stokoe also claimed another probable during this patrol. One civilian eyewitness claims they saw the German fighter (Stokoe's 'confirmed' kill) initially dive out of control and lose a wing after it collided with the cable from a barrage balloon, before spiralling to the ground. Both of the attacks for which Stokoe made claims were reported as having been initiated in the airspace north of Southend. Bubble's Spitfire came from the north-east after a dogfight over Canning Town, Binder's 109 came from an east to west direction; they crashed in the same zone but came from different directions.

While it cannot be confirmed as to who exactly was responsible for shooting down Waterston, two Luftwaffe pilots claimed to have destroyed Spitfires during roughly the same time period and it is possible that one or other could have shot down the young Scotsman. Major Adolph Galland, CO of JG26 shot down a Spitfire over Gravesend while Unteroffizer Hugo Dahmer of 6/JG26 made an unconfirmed claim for a Spitfire destroyed, also over Gravesend. Galland had 26 kills to his credit at this time while Dahmer had seven.

As we can see, the many local eye-witness accounts provide two distinct versions of events that describe Bubble's final seconds. One version describes the Spitfire descending at a fairly shallow angle and seemingly under control suggesting that perhaps the pilot had been trying to find a safe place to crash-land without causing loss of civilian life. A romantic suggestion perhaps and a not uncommon one during the battle but a valid point considering the local terrain. Based on this information it is possible that Bubble was alive until or just before impact as he skimmed the rooftops looking for a place to put his aircraft down. He may have succumbed to wounds at the last minute, having made a controlled descent. This version ends with the aircraft diving in at a steeper angle once over the rooftops of Wellington Street, 100 yards from the crash-site and clipping the trees before crashing. The other version of events presented in the eyewitness accounts describes the Spitfire diving out of control, recovering briefly while still at altitude, before continuing its dive at terminal velocity and crashing onto Repository Road. We shall never know what really happened.

As the youngest son, and second youngest of eight children, Bubble's death was naturally a devastating blow to his family, his girlfriend Patricia Greenhouse-Allt and her family who had grown so fond of him. A notice announcing Bubble's death appeared in *The Scotsman* on 5 September 1940: '...Funeral on Saturday 7th September. Service at Crematorium, Warriston at noon. (No flowers, no mourning).'

Bubble's remains were removed from the crash-site, returned to his home and cremated at the Edinburgh (Warriston) Cemetery. There was a short memorial service in his memory attended by his family and friends. The 23rd Psalm was read out and the congregation sang the hymn 'For All the Saints'. His name appears on Panel 4 of the memorial.*

Pat Allt, who later married Geoffrey Hirst who had served with the 25th Indian Division during WWII, remembers Robin with great affection:

> Robin was a quiet, gentle, friendly person. There was also a bit of hero-worship on my part really. We used to go dancing at the Plaza in Falcon Avenue with my sister Vera and her friend Andrew Morrison who may have introduced Robin to me. His parents couldn't have taken me very seriously, I was only fourteen when we met. Robin was such a nice lad who could also be very quiet and liked to sit and read a lot. He was never forceful. He was very popular with my parents. I was still at school when I heard the news of his death. His funeral was the first I had ever been to and such a terribly sad occasion.

As a consequence, on leaving school instead of going to university Pat and a colleague were determined to do their bit and joined the WAAF in 1942.**

During the same combat over Southend at 18.30 hours on the 31st, Brian Carbury's Spitfire was hit by a 20mm cannon shell fired from a Bf109 of I/JG3, which knocked out the compressed air system and caused severe damage when an oxygen cylinder exploded. Carbury was slightly wounded in the foot but managed to return to base safely and was on patrol again after missing just one flight. His combat report reads:

> Enemy aircraft sighted over London and we attacked. Three of us attacked nine Me109's, the first went down straight and burst into flames; attacked four e/a which were in pairs, slipped up a beam attack, hit the glycol tank of one and rolled over and went straight down hitting a wood. A Me109 got on my tail, received one cannon shell and the air system punctured, so came home.

His aircraft, R6835, was eventually repaired and returned to operational use ten months later. In the three days from the 29 to 31 August he had claimed seven 109s destroyed – five of these in three

---

*See Appendix 23 for more information and comment.

**Patricia Allt joined the WAAF in 1942. She did her preliminary training at RAF Innsworth, Gloucestershire before moving to Cranwell for a six-week Radio/Telephony Course. From Cranwell she was posted to Drem, part of 13 Group. In May 1943 she attended 7 Radio School, Kensington and underwent a signals course for her commission. In January 1944, she attended OCTU, Windermere. As Section Officer Patricia Greenhouse-Allt, she then moved to 26 Group, Langley where she was at the cessation of hostilities and then 44 Group OAC, Gloucester and CAC and JATC Uxbridge.

sorties on the 31st – one at 09.00, two at 13.40 and two more between 17.50 and 19.00 hours. Some of the other pilots and ground crew in 603 were aware that Brian was a very talented fighter pilot and some pilots tried to follow his example by emulating his tactics. He initiated his attack at 18.25 hours north of Southend at an altitude of 25,000 feet. For each attack he opened fire from 150 yards closing to 50 yards, again firing one three second burst on each occasion. Very efficient.

At 18.20 Sheep Gilroy had a lucky escape. A few moments after shooting down a 109 of I/JG3 his Spitfire was hit and set alight over the Thames by 109s from the same unit. The initial diving attack by I/JG3 claimed the life of Bubble. Ten minutes later they also damaged the Spitfire of Brian Carbury. Slightly burnt and wounded, Sheep managed to escape from his stricken aircraft when he baled out over Ilford. It had been a warm day and he was flying without his tunic and with his sleeves rolled – nothing which identified him, particularly as an RAF pilot. As he drifted nearer the ground he expected a friendly welcome but noticed that below he had caused quite a stir with people running about excitedly. He also caught a glimpse of what looked like a gun. As he dropped lower he realised it *was* a gun and pointed at him! He waved in a friendly

Sheep Gilroy.

manner at his London welcoming committee but it became quite clear they had made their mind up he was a German. On landing, he was immediately surrounded. Faced with great hostility Sheep did not escape a battering before a bus conductress recognised his RAF blue shirt and rushed to his rescue. He was taken to King George Hospital, Ilford, where he was treated for minor injuries and, more severely, burns.

When the Mayor of Dagenham heard of the incident he was so appalled that he visited Sheep in hospital and, by way of an apology, raised a subscription with the support of several members of the public who had been responsible for his beating, and a £10 cheque was presented him for the Squadron. Subsequently, every time he shot down an enemy aircraft after that, he would buy a round of drinks, announcing to his fellow pilots that they were: 'On the Mayor of Dagenham!'

His Spitfire, X4271, crashed into 14 Hereford Road, Wanstead, but the engine, which had broken free from its mountings, fell onto the garden of number 12, the only casualty being a dog. The road was cordoned off for two weeks while the wreckage was cleared.

The remainder of the Squadron landed again at 19.00 hours with Ras claiming a third Messerschmitt 109 destroyed, which was later confirmed as being a Bf109E-4 (4+, Werknr. 1082) of I/JG3 flown by Oberleutnant Helmut Rau, which he had damaged in combat over the Thames estuary at 18.45 hours. Ras's report reads:

> As I had no oxygen, I had to leave the squadron at 22,000 feet and waited below in the sun for straggling enemy aircraft. After patrolling for 30 minutes, I saw a Me109 proceeding very fast. To overhaul him I had to press the emergency boost – indicated speed – 345. I caught the enemy aircraft off Shoeburyness. I opened fire at close range and fired all my ammunition until the enemy aircraft streamed with smoke and pancaked on the mud at Shoeburyness.

The Form F states that Ras Berry was with B Flight and attacked this 109 at 18.45 hours as it was returning to France, opening fire at 150 yards, closing to just ten, firing three bursts of five seconds totalling 2,800 rounds. Years later Ras recounted this combat:

> I reached the Hornchurch area at about 10,000 feet having run out of oxygen. I could see a large beehive of fighters around a straggling clutter of enemy bombers, and some flashes on the ground where bombs were falling. Then in my rear view mirror, I saw the flash of an

Me109 streaking across Hornchurch, heading east. I did a half roll, called on my Spitfire for all she could give, and chased after him.* I was mad after seeing those bombs fall.

Soon we were both at tree top height over the fields and villages of Southern Essex. I crept nearer and nearer until over the houses of Southend I was in range. I held my fire until I crossed the coast at Shoeburyness and was almost on the 109 when a film of oil on my windscreen hampered my vision, so I kept giving short sharp bursts and looking up to see the effect. Bits were falling off the 109 and without any warning it made a long turn and finally crash landed on the mud flats of Shoeburyness.

I circled for a moment and saw the enemy pilot standing beside his wrecked aircraft shaking his fist at me – a satisfactory ending to an eventful day.

Rau had forced-landed on the beach at Shoeburyness opposite the officers mess in the 'old ranges'. His aircraft was a write-off and was initially taken to the 'new ranges' at Shoebury before eventually being taken away and scrapped. The story has it that as Rau climbed out of his fighter the army commandant rushed down the beach with pistol in hand, accompanied by a number of gunners, to head off any attempt by the pilot to set fire to his aircraft. Rau was apprehended and taken to the guardroom where he spent the night. A good many myths have developed relating to the capture of Luftwaffe pilots during the Battle of Britain and over the years many have been accepted as historical fact. The story of Helmut Rau and Ras is no exception. Rau was described as a 'tall arrogant Prussian' when in fact he was quite amiable, short and stocky. It has been said that a dinner suit was found in a small case secreted in the cockpit of Rau's 109, perhaps for a dinner date in France later that evening, which is highly unlikely. The myth has also been perpetuated that Ras paid Rau a visit in the guardroom where the guard commander left the two alone. A short while later he heard raised voices and entered the cell to find the two struggling together, Rau accusing Ras of assaulting him. Ras never later referred to such an incident during lengthy interviews when details of his experiences were very forthcoming. Rau was taken to London the next day for interrogation.

As previously mentioned, Jack Stokoe had his claim for a 109 destroyed over south London at 18.20 hours confirmed as being a Bf109E-4 of I/JG3 flown by Leutnant Walter Binder. His combat report and his memories of that action leave little doubt as to the severity of the damage inflicted on the enemy fighter:

We were ordered to patrol base at 12,000 feet. As I was rather late, the formation took off without me. I took off alone, climbed into the sun, and rejoined the formation which was circling at about 28,000 feet. I observed two Me109's above, and climbed after them in full fire pitch.

The Me's kept close together in a steep spiral climb towards the sun. I pumped several bursts at the outside one from about 200 yards with little effect. I closed to about 50 yards and fired two more long bursts. Black smoke poured from his engine which appeared to catch fire, and eight or nine huge pieces of his fuselage were shot away. He spun steeply away and crashed inside the balloon barrage. I continued climbing after the other Me109, and fired two long bursts from about 150 yards. White smoke came from his aircraft, and he spiralled gently downwards. I broke away as I was out of ammunition, and failed to see what happened to him.

The Bf109s had been at 30,000 feet when Stokoe had attacked the first at 18.25 hours. Stapme claimed a 109 probable:

When patrolling in line astern with the rest of the squadron I sighted bomber formation below us on the port. With two other aircraft I climbed into the sun for a favourable position, to make an attack on the bombers out of the sun, when five Me109's engaged us.

These Me109's came out of the bomber formations climbing into the sun. Flying Officer Carbury engaged three Me109's and I engaged the other two. These two were flying in tight line astern. After giving the rear one a deflection burst of three seconds he pulled vertically upwards with white streams pouring from his engine.

---

*Ras used his boost over-ride which enabled him to use +12lb. boost and 3,000 rpm. The Mark II Spitfire was to provide 18lb. boost. A significant improvement.

Stapme attacked the Bf109s at 18.25 hours at an altitude of 25,000 feet north of Southend. This 'probable' was in fact the aircraft which crashed and burned near Whalebone Lane Gunsite, Chadwell Heath at 18.50 hours. The pilot of Messerschmitt Bf109E-4 (5339) of 3/JG3 was Oberleutnant Johann Loidolt who managed to bale out of the stricken fighter. It is possible that he was also attacked by Sergeant F.W. 'Taffy' Higginson of 56 Squadron as well as Stapleton and Carbury.

That same afternoon a series of low level raids aimed at the CH (Chain Home: long range early warning radar), stations in Kent and Sussex, and the CHL (Chain Home Low: shorter range for plotting low level flying aircraft), installation at Foreness, were carried out in an attempt to render the RAF blind once again. However, the damage was light and the units were operating again by the end of the day. That night the bomber offensive continued with Liverpool being hit for the fourth consecutive night. The continued inability of the night fighters to have any effect on the German bombers may have prompted the decision to withdraw the Defiant from daylight operations and train the two squadrons in night fighting. While the daylight losses of Defiants were unacceptably high, this decision was later proved to be valid as the Defiant became an effective night-fighting aircraft.

During the previous two days the Luftwaffe had carried out an enormous assault on the fighter airfields of the RAF that guarded London, having carried out 2,800 sorties. The intensity of the attacks on the airfields would never be equalled during the rest of the battle and the number of RAF fighters sent to intercept would never again be as great as during those two hot summer days in late August. The RAF flew 2,020 sorties with 65 fighters downed, 39 on the 31st. These were dark days indeed. The average of 115 pilots killed or wounded a week was double the output of the training schools and the actual situation was worse than it looked. Experienced pilots killed or wounded had to be replaced with inexperience. Peter Townsend of 85 Squadron recalls:

> Our strength was even sapped from within. On the morning of 1st September, Sergeant Geoff Goodman of 85, with only four guns working, shot down a Me109; the air lines to the other four guns had been blocked with matchsticks, sabotaged by some German sympathizer at the depot.

To the pilots and ground crews alike, 31 August must have seemed like an eternity. The Squadron had been in combat four times, in addition, their airfield was bombed on two occasions. During the lunchtime raid three 603 ground crewmen were killed, (the incident which inspired Hillary's fiction) LAC W.J. Baldie, LAC J.E. Dickson* and AC1 J. Worthington – all Edinburgh lads – when a bomb fell right in front of their lorry as it dashed around the perimeter track, blowing it onto its side. In addition, Sergeants Angy Gillies and Mackenzie and AC1 Forrest, AC1 Adams, and AC1 Ritchie were wounded. The survivors remember seeing the driver of the lorry blown out of the cab, his body landing a considerable distance away. Angy Gillies had also been in the lorry and was lucky to survive. The airfield was still serviceable and the pilots and ground crews were working as one in their attempt to repel the Luftwaffe. A fourth fatality, AC1 Dickinson, occurred during the last raid of the day. Most of the 603 ground crewmen witnessed the bombing but the experience was particularly upsetting for Artie Carroll. LAC Baldie and AC1 J. Worthington had been close friends of his since before the war who had shone during the annual Squadron sports days. Artie Carroll

Top: Hornchurch, September 1940.
Bottom: LAC Ernie Dickson, KIA Hornchurch 31 August 1940

---

*LAC John Ernest 'Ernie' Dickson was born in Edinburgh and educated at George Heriot's School in Lauriston Place. He joined 603 in 1932 with Angy Gillies and qualified as an FAE the same year but soon established himself as an expert with armaments.

Article from the *Sunday Post* (Edinburgh) 8 December 1940. The Squadron was actually credited with 14 kills. From left to right: P/O Ras Berry; P/O Stapleton; P/O Brian Macnamara; F/L John Boulter; P/O David Scott-Malden and P/O Ludwik Martel. The article features the action of 31 August, before Macnamara, Scott-Malden and Martel had joined the Squadron.

found his memories saddening despite the years that had passed: 'In just one day I had lost my two closest friends. Both were in the lorry which was hit by the blast from a bomb during the lunchtime raid. Baldie was a lovely chap, both were great athletes.'

A list of casualties inflicted on the Germans by 603 Squadron for the period 28-31 August whilst under the operational control of AOC 11 Group was included in Intelligence Bulletin 75. It credited the pilots with: 23 confirmed destroyed and 11 unconfirmed destroyed. A total for the period of 34.

Sunday 1 September 1940
From this day the Squadron ORB ceased to include the Squadron code and code of each Spitfire, although the aircraft numbers still appear next to the name of each pilot who flew the aircraft on patrol.

On this day Pilot Officer Dudley Stewart-Clark and Sergeant Bill Caister returned to the Squadron, Stewart-Clark from leave, Caister prematurely from his honeymoon. On the day the Squadron had departed for the south he had been married to a local girl and the couple left for a honeymoon in Pitlochry. Word soon reached him that 603 was in the thick of the fighting in the south-east, where he was born, and as an experienced RAF pilot he felt it was something he had trained long and hard for and should be part of. He managed to contact Dudley Stewart-Clark who agreed to pick up Caister in his Bentley before motoring to the nearest station where they '...shoved the thing on a rail "flat" at the end of the train and made off for London.' En route the truck with the Bentley became detached from the rest of the train and when they arrived in London they had to hire a car to get to Hornchurch. On reaching the aerodrome they found their colleagues were in the process of taking off to intercept enemy raiders. Dudley was not officially due to return from leave until the following day but Caister dashed around looking for his regular aircraft, which had gone: 'Luckily, I saw another in a corner of the field, ticking over, so I grabbed it and was soon in the thick of it. I found out afterwards it belonged to another squadron!'

In addition to the early tactical change of flying on a reciprocal course to that given by the controller in an attempt to avoid being bounced while climbing to intercept, the pilots also agreed to attack in pairs with one protecting the tail of his partner, who was the main attacking aircraft.

Some pilots wore their goggles with darkened lenses attached. Others didn't fly with their goggles in position at all. Richard Hillary wrote:

With spots on the windscreen, spots before the eyes, and a couple of spots that might be Messerschmitts, blind spots on my goggles seemed too much of a good thing; I always slipped them up on to my forehead before going into action. For this and for not wearing gloves I paid a stiff price.

Visibility was so important that during the fast turn around of the fighters by the ground crews when the aircraft were refuelled and re-armed, the oxygen cylinder was replaced and any problems with the aircraft were checked, the canopy and windscreen were wiped and buffed to remove the slightest blemish that could be mistaken for an enemy fighter at that vital moment. Equally dangerous was the fact that an enemy fighter may well be disregarded as being a spot of dirt. The closing speed of two fighters diving head-on to one another came as a shock to even the experienced pilot. Therefore, a moment's deliberation could be fatal. It was also important that the cloth used to polish the canopy was not in any way abrasive. The sun shining on a scratched perspex surface would be refracted and the glare intensified and magnified.

At 09.00 hours on 1 September the RAF Fighter Command Order of Battle stated that 603 had 13 aircraft that were combat ready with three more unserviceable. It also recorded that the Squadron had 18 pilots on state. With George Denholm still recovering from his experience on the 30th Ken Macdonald covered his flying duties.

On the 1st Dowding carried out the re-deployment of a number of squadrons, reflecting the need to bring fresh squadrons into the heat of the battle while re-appointing certain others that had suffered debilitating losses to aircraft and men, giving them the opportunity to re-group. At the same time it was realised that a nucleus of experience had to be maintained. Many of the pilots of the 'experienced' squadrons were both physically and mentally exhausted, vulnerable therefore in their current state. At the same time, to introduce inexperience was presenting the enemy with potential 'cannon-fodder'.

603 Squadron had only been at Hornchurch for five days. In that time Benson, Waterston, Cunningham and Don Macdonald had been killed. George Denholm, Sheep Gilroy, Colin Pinckney, Brian Carbury, Pip Cardell, Joey Sarre, Ian Ritchie, Rusty Rushmer and Richard Hillary had all been fortunate to have escaped from a variety of situations by baling out or forced-landing their aircraft, some receiving minor burns and wounds. They were already veterans, having to fly their Spitfires skilfully enough to shoot down enemy aircraft and avoid being shot down themselves. All this would have taken its toll and they would be starting to feel drained. The prospect of facing death each time they took off would have made each living second all the more valuable.

On the 1st there were four big attacks during the day. At 10.20 the Kent RDF stations reported enemy raids forming-up over France, and by 10.55 these aircraft were advancing over Dover over a front five miles wide which split into two groups of about 30 bombers each with the same number of fighters. They were heading for the airfields once again, with Detling, Eastchurch and Biggin Hill the targets along with the London Docks. Eleven squadrons were sent up to intercept. The groups divided again 15 minutes later, just as the fighters of 11 Group attacked, but they were unable to break through the heavy layer of protection offered by the Bf109s and 110s. Once again Biggin was hit, with a number of aircraft of 610 Squadron in the process of moving north to re-group being destroyed or damaged. 85 Squadron was to see action on two occasions on this day, firstly at 11.05 and then 13.50 hours, but time was running out. The Squadron had been badly depleted and the pilots and ground crews were near total exhaustion, and today would again bring heavy losses. It was only a matter of time before 85, which had been involved from the beginning, was annihilated. In fact by the end of the next seven-day period the equivalent of six squadrons would have been destroyed.

The next raid began at 13.00 with 170 enemy aircraft reported to be crossing the Kent coast 40 minutes later, and 12 squadrons were despatched to intercept. A third attack was carried out against Hawkinge and Lympne between 15.32 and 16.05 hours. 603 were rested during the morning but were airborne between 15.45 and 17.20 hours when the last phase of attacks was launched between 16.30 and 17.00 hours with Detling and Dover the targets. Kesselring sent over seven different formations consisting mainly of fighters. Park was not tempted into sending up his valuable pilots and so the Germans set about strafing the defences. Biggin Hill was bombed yet again, for the third time this day, when a small group of Dorniers swept in under the cover of the fighters and cratered the airfield but more importantly they managed to score a direct hit on the operations room when a 250kg bomb brought down the reinforced concrete ceiling. Despite this, two of the WAAF telephone operators remained at their posts throughout and were subsequently awarded Military

Medals for their courage and devotion to duty. Another amazing effort came from the Post Office engineers. Having just finished re-establishing the main London-Westerham cables, the Biggin Hill sector operations room communication lines were knocked out again and they spent the night patching lines through to a temporary operations room which had been set up in a village shop. As a result of their dedication the sector had full switchboard facility once again. At 15.45 hours 603 Spitfires were sent up for the first time on a routine operational patrol. Led by Uncle George in XT-D, X4260, the patrol also comprised: F/L Ken Macdonald (XT-E, R6752), F/O Boulter (XT-M, X4277), F/L Rushmer (XT-Y, R6626), P/O Morton (XT-B, N3056), P/O Hillary (XT-V, R6721), P/O Cardell (XT-L, L1020), Sgt Stokoe (XT-N, X4271), and P/O Read (XT-J, L1057).The intelligence report reads:

> Nine aircraft of 603 Squadron to go to Manston. When over Canterbury, Sgt Stokoe was at 3,000' and attacked a single Me109. P/O Cardell forced-landed owing to oil trouble. The rest of 603 saw nothing.

Sergeant Jack Stokoe's report while flying with A Flight, claiming one Bf109 destroyed in combat over Thanet reads:

> At about 16.30 we were patrolling Manston at 12,000' when control informed us Canterbury was being bombed. About five miles south of the town when at about 3,000' a Me109, silver with black crosses, dived past my nose flattened out about 50 feet up and headed south. I executed a steep turn, pushed in boost overide, and sat on his tail. At about 50 yards, I gave him one small burst with little effect, closed to 30 yards, and gave a slightly longer burst. Black smoke poured from him as I overshot him. The a/c crashed in a field, turned over two or three times and burst into flames in a clump of trees. 70 bullets were fired from each gun.

This Messerschmitt was probably a Bf109-E4 (4020) of III/JG53 flown by Oberleutnant Bauer who was killed in the crash, which occurred south of Chilham. Pip Cardell forced-landed at 16.45 hours due to a problem with oil temperature. This patrol had been his first since moving south from Montrose and had been a real baptism when you consider the intensity of the action in which they had become embroiled. The Squadron landed again at 17.25 hours following which Ken Macdonald was granted 24 hours leave. Ken chose to catch up on rest rather than leave the station.

The pilots spent many hours in or sitting outside the dispersal hut in pretty uncomfortable conditions. Dudley Stewart-Clark asked George Denholm if he had any objections to his improving matters. With his full support Stewart-Clark made a couple of phone calls to Harrods and the next day a van arrived with a delivery of easy chairs, rugs and curtains!

Monday 2 September 1940

Night bombing continued with the cities of Liverpool, Cardiff, Swansea and Bristol among the many targets attacked. By the evening of 1 September the night-fighter squadrons of 25 and 600 were moved nearer London. Martlesham Heath to North Weald and Manston to Hornchurch respectively, in preparation for what was thought by Dowding and Park at Fighter Command to be the imminent night attacks on the capital.

The morning of the 2nd dawned fine and warm. At 07.15 hours just inland from Calais at 12,000 feet gathered one Gruppe of KG3's Dorniers and stacked up to 20,000 feet its escort of one Geschwader of Bf109s for the first of Kesselring's four-phase attacks that were to occur this day. As they approached Deal 11 RAF fighters were scrambled to intercept, unfortunately only five were able to make contact due to the controllers maintaining standing patrols over the sector airfields. In the Maidstone area the bombers split-up and attacked Biggin Hill, Rochford, Eastchurch and North Weald. Gravesend received a few bombs on the outer edge of the airfield. 253 Squadron had initially failed to penetrate the fighter screen prior to the split, but nine Spitfires did manage to engage the Dorniers and Bf110s over Maidstone at 13,000 feet. 603 were scrambled to protect Hornchurch but when it was realised that the airfield was not under immediate threat of attack they were ordered forward and caught the German 109s as they withdrew over Kent.

Intelligence Patrol Report – 603 Squadron
07.28-0830 hours. 2.9.40

The squadron was ordered to patrol Hawkinge. When at 22,000', they saw three Me109's flying in line astern, which they attacked. Later the guard section attacked a further two Me109's. One pilot lost the squadron and saw tight vic's of about 50 Do17's and Me110's consisting of small vic's. He attacked the outside Me110. The Me110's had no yellow noses, but whitish grey wing-tips.

The patrol that took off from Hornchurch consisted of 12 Spitfires flown by: S/L Denholm (X4260), F/O Haig (R6752), F/O Boulter (R6626), F/O Carbury (X4263), P/O Caister (X4185), F/O Pease (P6721), P/O Morton (N3056), P/O Read (L1057), P/O Stapleton (X4274), P/O Berry (X4264), P/O Hillary (X4277), and Sgt Stokoe (X4250).

This patrol provided Bill Caister with his first experience of combat since the Squadron had moved down to Hornchurch, and no comparison could be made with his minimal experience gained north of the border a few weeks previously. This would be a shocking introduction to a much greater level of action, despite his vast experience.

Richard Hillary claimed a 109 destroyed in the combat but was shot down before he was able to find the time to write his combat report. The 603 Squadron Intelligence Officer, 'Spy' Blackbourn, prepared an interim statement for the records:

> P/O Hillary claims a Me109 destroyed, which he shot down into the sea. In a later engagement he baled out and is still in hospital. Report follows.

Hillary was flying with B Flight. His attack was delivered at 08.15 hours at an altitude of 26,000 feet, north of Hawkinge. It is possible that this was the flight during which he chased a 109 back to a point over the French coast:

> On another occasion I was stupid enough actually to fly over France: the sky appeared to be perfectly clear but for one returning Messerschmitt, flying very high. I had been trying to catch him for about ten minutes and was determined that he should not get away. Eventually I caught him inland from Calais and was just about to open fire when I saw a squadron of twelve Messerschmitts coming in on my right. I was extremely frightened, but turned in towards them and opened fire at the leader. I could see his tracer going past underneath me, and then I saw his hood fly off, and the next moment they were past. I didn't wait to see any more, but made off for home, pursued for half the distance by eleven very determined Germans. I landed a good hour after everyone else to find Uncle George just finishing his check-up.

Hillary was shot down the following morning and never flew again with 603; his combat reports were therefore never brought up to date. Sergeant Jack Stokoe claimed a Bf110 damaged:

> We were patrolling the Channel at 26,000' when enemy planes were sighted and I became separated from my squadron. Not contacting any enemy aircraft, I heard control say, gate to homebase 15,000'. I climbed to 17,000' and observed a mass of enemy bombers flying south towards me at 15,000'. They were flying in irregular vic's, but packed very close. There must have been at least 50 Me110's and Dorniers. I executed a steep turn and dived on a Me110 on the right of the formation, putting in two short bursts at about 100 yards range. I did not observe what happened then as my windscreen was hit and perspex was scattered into the cockpit. I slid away under the formation and glanced at my instruments to see if the engine was alright. It seemed normal, so I climbed and attacked another Me110 on the left of the formation, closing from 200 to 75 yards and firing several long bursts until my ammunition ran out. White smoke appeared from the port engine of the Me110 and it was losing height towards the coast. I spiralled down to 1,000' and headed for home base.

Jack was flying with A Flight, delivering his attacks at 08.15 north of Hawkinge, opening fire at 100 yards for two bursts of three seconds, firing 360 rounds. His hood was shattered during combat and the likely opponents were the Bf109s of I/JG2. He received a slight wound to the hand from a shard of perspex, his aircraft, XT-X being repairable. Jack Haig considered one 109 'definitely claimed':

> When on patrol at about 26,000' over Hawkinge, I saw two Me109's. I saw another Spitfire diving at the same e/a as me. The e/a dived vertically and then pulled up steeply. As it pulled

out I noticed a white stream coming from the port wing. I had not fired up to this point, but as the e/a was still proceeding on a westerly course, I opened fire and saw it burst into flames. Later I ascertained that it was Pilot Officer Berry who had fired at this Me109 before me.

Jack was with A Flight and delivered his attack at 08.15 hours. He opened fire from a range of 250 yards and closed to 100 yards firing a five second burst of 720 rounds. Ras Berry claimed a 109 destroyed:

> When on patrol at 26,000' over Hawkinge, I sighted two Me109's, which half rolled and dived earthwards. I followed one and as it pulled out of the dive I opened fire at 100 yards and fired an eight second burst to close range (50 yards). Smoke poured heavily from the Me109. I broke away and blacked-out. Later I saw a Me109 in flames. After landing I ascertained F/O Haig had also fired at Me109.

It was a rarity for Ras to experience a black-out, his stocky physique gave him a far greater tolerance to the effects of g-Force than the taller, thinner pilot. Ras was with B Flight and fired 1,400 rounds during this combat patrol. The claim by Berry and Haig was confirmed as being a Bf109E of I/JG51 shot down over Kent at 07.50 hours. The pilot Leutnant Gunther Ruttkowski was killed and the aircraft was a complete loss when it crashed at Nethersole Park, Womenswold, east of Barham. This aircraft was also claimed to have been shot down by Pilot Officer Gribble of 54 Squadron at 08.00 hours.

Three other Bf109s were shot down by the Spitfires of 603 but it has not been possible to confirm exactly who shot them down. A Bf109E of 8/JG51 went down over the Channel with the pilot, Leutnant Braun, rescued unhurt by a Seenotdienst. Another Bf109E of I/JG51 was shot down over the Kent coast at 08.00 hours and the pilot, Feldwebel Heinz Bar was rescued by Seenotflugkommando.* The final aircraft was another Bf109E of I/JG51, shot down over Kent at 08.00 hours. The pilot, Leutnant Helmut Thorl baled out and was captured unhurt. The aircraft crashed in flames at Leeds Castle, near Maidstone. It was also thought to have been shot down by Squadron Leader James Leathart of 54 Squadron. It is possible that one of the two German fighters shot down over the Channel was Carbury's claim, while Hillary or Stewart-Clark could have been responsible for the I/JG51 Bf109 that crashed at Leeds Castle. But with the Spitfires of 54 Squadron involved in the same combat it will never be confirmed as to who shot who down. The 603 Spitfires landed back at Hornchurch at 08.30 hours.

Around midday a larger formation of 50 Do17s with an escort of 250 fighters was plotted heading for Dover and this time the controllers sent their squadrons to intercept the enemy from the outset, with success not shown necessarily by the numbers of enemy aircraft shot down but by the fact that the raiding formation was broken early on. Four sections were also vectored from neighbouring sectors and a total exceeding 70 Hurricanes and Spitfires rushed to intercept the German armada fighters over Kent. Once again this attack by the enemy bombers and the following one were aimed at the airfields, drawing up all available RAF fighters into the air. The Luftwaffe force split into two and one unit attacked Debden aerodrome causing serious damage:

Intelligence Report – 603 Squadron
12.08-13.35 hours.

> Nine aircraft took off to patrol Chatham at 22,000'. When five miles east of Sheppey, they saw large sections of Me109's, about 10 vic's with eight or nine in a vic, above them. The squadron went into line-astern and climbed to attack. A dogfight ensued. Below the Me109's there were about 50 Do17's in vic's of five, with Me109's a little above them weaving. The Do17's were doing about 220 mph.

The nine Spitfires were led by Uncle George: S/L Denholm (X4260), F/L Rushmer (X4263), F/O Boulter (X4185), F/O Haig (R6752), P/O Berry (X4264), P/O Hillary (X4277), P/O Stapleton (X4274), P/O Morton (N3056), and P/O Read (L1057).

Fred Rushmer claimed a Do 17 destroyed:

> When on patrol with the squadron at 25,000', a number of Me109's were sighted. In the general melee at this height I became separated from the rest of the squadron and continued to patrol on the fringe of the clouds. AA fire aimed at a formation of 40-50 bombers with

---

*Oberstleutnant Heinz Bar, Knights Cross with Oak Leaves and Swords, was credited with 220 victories over the Western Front, North Africa and Russia. He was killed in a flying accident in 1957.

Me109's as escort flying at 15,000' towards the Isle of Sheppey attracted my attention.

I manoeuvred for a position ahead of the formation and selecting a target dived down and attacked a Do17 from a quarter ahead. I followed through the dive in the breakaway astern of the bombers and, on climbing up immediately, I saw a Do17 on fire diving into the Thames estuary. A further attack carried out in a similar manner on a second bomber had no apparent effect.

Rusty had been leading a section in B Flight. His attack was delivered at 12.45 hours, 5 miles east of the Isle of Sheppey at 15,000 feet. He opened fire at 300 yards closing to 50 yards while firing a three second burst totalling 750 rounds. George Denholm claimed to have damaged a Bf109:

When on patrol with 603 Squadron at 22,000' we saw about ten vic's of Me109's, eight or nine in a vic. I put the squadron into line-astern and climbed to attack. In the dogfight which ensued, I fired a short burst at a Me109 from about 150 yards. The Me109 dived and thick black smoke came from the engine in intermittent puffs. I left the enemy aircraft 30 or 40 feet above the water about ten miles from the French coast.

We then passed a Fw seaplane which was apparently scouting for pilots in the sea. The Me109 then pulled up stiffly and headed back over the seaplane. In the meantime I had broken off and made an attack on the seaplane but found that I had no more ammunition, so we returned home.

George also made his attack at 12.45 hours, 5 miles east of the Isle of Sheppey at 15,000 feet. He noted on his combat report that he saw approximately 80 109s. Black Morton claimed a 109 destroyed:

At 20,000' below cloud the Squadron encountered about 12 Me109's about 1,000' above. They circled to attack us from astern and we turned also. I met one Me109 head-on and gave a short burst with no effect. After a while the general melee became split up. I found one Me109 unattended climbing above me and gave chase. Opened fire from 300 yards on port quarter slightly below at 23,000'. Enemy aircraft saw me then and did a steep left hand turn into a dive. I got in a good long burst and observed much white smoke from below the e/a. The e/a then went into a vertical dive and I did not see it again.

Pilot Officer Berry who was in my vicinity reports having seen the a/c dive vertically into the ground. E/A was grey with very light wing tips.

Black was with A Flight and delivered his attack at 12.45 hours, 5 miles east of Sheppey at 21,000 feet. Richard Hillary claimed a 109 destroyed during this patrol and on this occasion managed to complete his combat report after he had landed:

When five miles off Sheppey, I saw a formation of Me109's. I chased one over to France and fired at it. I saw the enemy aircraft perspex hood break up, but as it was a head-on attack I was unable to see anything more of it. I then saw a squadron of Me109's at the same height as myself, 23,000', it was turning in formation. I attacked the outside Me109 with three short bursts and saw it spin down emitting black and white smoke. After a few seconds it caught fire.

Richard was flying with B Flight and delivered his attack at 13.05 hours. The Squadron returned to base and landed at 13.35 hours. A short while later Haig carried out a forced landing on the airfield with undercarriage retracted due to damage received in combat with Do17s, possibly of I/LG2, and 109s over the Thames estuary. Haig was unhurt and his aircraft, XT-E, repaired.

The last attack of the day approached the coast near Dover at 17.00 hours and consisted of 250 enemy aircraft. Kesselring still had this formidable force available despite the magnitude of the last raid. As the enemy aircraft approached a massive dogfight developed near Ashford between about 70 Hurricanes and 15 Spitfires in action with about 160 Bf109s. It only ended when the enemy broke off soon after the Dover barrage commenced firing. Several similar situations like this developed during this raid, high flying Bf109s diving out of the sun to attack the RAF fighters. The escorting fighters were flying much higher above the bombers than had been the case during earlier raids. This initially led to the belief that these groups of fighters were in fact a return to the free-hunt tactic, and for some days some controllers held back fighters mistaken in the belief that it was a lure when they were actually the escort. This ploy, although inadvertent, did produce some positive results.

The raids were successful in bombing the airfields once again at Biggin Hill, Kenley, and Hornchurch; with Brooklands, where the Hawker and Vickers factory were situated, being bombed for the first time. Despite 100 bombs being dropped on Detling by a Gruppe of Do17s not much damage was done, but the smaller raid on Eastchurch resulted in mass devastation because the bomb dump, containing 350 bombs, was hit and exploded. Every building for 400 yards was demolished as well as the severing of the drainage mains and power cables along with the telephone lines.

Dowding's suspicions were confirmed with the Brooklands raid, in that the Germans would go for the aircraft factories as the RAF combat losses mounted. Park agreed and a standing patrol was maintained. Unfortunately it had been drawn away over into the Kent airspace on this afternoon, so the raid got through. The final patrol of the day for 603 occurred in the late afternoon:

> Intelligence Patrol Report
> 16.04-18.20 hours. 2.9.40.
>
> Eleven aircraft climbed over base at 23,000' and saw a large solid triangle of about fifty bombers and at least fifty fighters, loose and in vic, stepped up to 20,000'. The squadron dived to attack and a dogfight ensued.

Nos 616, 249, 1, 54, 257, 303, 72, 46, 501, 253, 222 and 603 were all sent up. The eleven 603 Spitfires were flown by: S/L Denholm (X4260), F/L Rushmer (X4261), P/O Morton (X4259), F/O Carbury (X4263), P/O Berry (R6626), F/O Pease (P6721), Sgt Stokoe (X4271), P/O Caister (X4250), P/O Cardell (X4274), P/O Stewart-Clark (L1057), and P/O Hillary (X4277).

This was to be Dudley Stewart-Clark's first combat patrol since his return from leave and the Squadron's move south. Richard Hillary was flying the Spitfire in which he flew the majority of his patrols from Hornchurch; what he referred to in *The Last Enemy* as 'his' particular aircraft. During this patrol he claimed a 109 probable:

> I lost sight of the squadron and saw four Me109's in line astern above me. I climbed up and attacked the rear Me109, getting to about 50' of him before opening fire. The Me109 went straight down with thick smoke pouring out and I did not see it again.

His attack was delivered at 17.10 hours in the airspace over Hornchurch at an altitude of 20,000 feet. He was with B Flight at the beginning of the engagement. Pilot Officer Dudley Stewart-Clark claimed a Bf110 probable:

> I saw eight Me110's in loose echelon below me. I dived and made a head-on attack at the back Me109, which went into a spin with black smoke pouring out. I did not see the enemy aircraft again.

Stewart-Clark was with A Flight and delivered his attack at 17.10 hours at an altitude of 17,000 feet. It was quite common for the pilots to agree on a time of engagement after the event, and all record the same time in their reports. Brian Carbury claimed a 109 destroyed:

> I broke away down when the enemy aircraft jumped on us out of the sun, then climbed again and waited about for other friendly aircraft to join up with. Sighted three aircraft, so chased after them diving, as I was above them, and found them to be 3 Me109's in line astern going east. Carried out a rear beam attack on last enemy aircraft with no visible effect. I climbed up again and did a slight head-on deflection shot and his cockpit hood disappeared and the enemy aircraft went straight into the sea about ten miles off the coast, between Margate and Ramsgate.

Carbury was leading a section in B Flight and delivered his attack at 18.00 hours, off Margate, at an altitude of 15,000 feet. He opened fire at a range of 200 yards and closed to 50 yards, firing a single burst of two seconds.

At 17.25 hours Jack Stokoe's Spitfire was hit over Maidstone during combat with enemy Bf110 fighters, possibly of II/ZG76. He had been wounded and the fuel tanks in front of him had been punctured and he recalled seeing burning petrol seeping back into the cockpit. As the flames licked around him Jack told how he glanced down at his hands and watched transfixed as the skin peeled from the backs in white translucent layers. Opening the canopy only caused his situation to deteriorate as the airflow fed the flames which burnt more fiercely. After what were actually only seconds, Jack managed to bale out and he landed near a number of tall fir trees just south of the village of Warren Street. Admitted to the Leeds Castle Hospital he later went to St. Mary's Hospital, Sidcup. His Spitfire dived from altitude but was seen to level out within a few hundred feet of the ground and eventually crashed in flames north-west of Warren Street. Jack's log book reads: 'Rushed immediately to hospital and treated for severe burns of hands and face... Six weeks in three hospitals. What a life!!' It was sometime before the Squadron was notified of his whereabouts and until then he was posted missing. Jack's parents had died before the war and apart from a younger brother his father's sister was his nearest relative. She was sent a telegram stating her nephew was missing in action. Richard Hillary achieved success near French air space:

> I remember once going practically to France before shooting down a 109. There were two of them, flying at sea-level and headed for the French coast. Raspberry was flying beside me and caught one half-way across. I got right up close behind the second one and gave it a series of short bursts. It darted about in front, like a startled rabbit, and finally plunged into the sea about three miles off the French coast.

The remaining Spitfires of 603 landed back at Hornchurch at 18.20 hours. On this day Ken Macdonald's 24-hour leave pass expired and he rejoined the Squadron.

Keith Lawrence, who was to join 603 on 9 September, to help replenish the heavy losses at the beginning of the month.

Tuesday 3 September 1940

The cities of Birmingham, Liverpool, Cardiff, Castle Bromwich and Liverpool received the attentions of about 50 bombers during the night causing little damage and a few casualties. Bomber Command was also in action with long-distance raids on Milan and Turin. Dowding had assessed the strength of Fighter Command during the previous evening and decided against his own wishes to introduce a new system whereby certain experienced pilots were removed from their squadrons in the north to make good the losses of the squadrons in the south. This scheme was brought into full operation by 8 September but much against the advice of the squadron commanders who were struggling to build up morale and team efficiency in their units.

Park was forced once again to re-arrange his battle order. 85 Squadron was finally ordered from the front-line base of Croydon to rest and rebuild the squadron which by this time consisted of eight aircraft and 11 exhausted pilots, not forgetting the supporting ground crews. They made their way to Castle Camps near Cambridge. 111 Squadron were moved from Debden, which was hardly away from the intense fighting, to Croydon in place of 85. Since 8 August 41 Squadron had been reforming at Catterick; it was now on its way back to Hornchurch. Its place at Catterick was taken by 504 Squadron. 66 Squadron moved its 13 Spitfires from Coltishall to Kenley, relieving 616 Squadron, one of whose Flight Lieutenants remained behind to assume command of 66.

The first and main attack of the day, as it turned out, was building up at 08.30 hours behind the Pas de Calais and easily detectable by the long-range radar. The enemy force was delayed during its build-up, waiting for its escort of Bf110s. As it finally approached Kent, Fighter Command sent up 14 squadrons, three of which were in position over the Dover area in good time to attack the force. However, it was realised in time that the enemy force actually consisted entirely of fighters and the RAF fighters were ordered to retreat northwards to avoid combat. While this was going on 54 Dorniers, escorted by about 80 Bf110s, were flying up the Thames estuary at 20,000 feet. It was not clear whether the raid was heading for yet another assault on the North Kent airfields or whether it would turn north. The possibility also existed that the enemy formation may carry on its current heading, towards London. Park's controllers ordered all available fighters into the area and called for reinforcements from 12 Group. By 09.40 hours 16 squadrons, totalling 122 fighters, had been ordered into the air to patrol specific positions in the airspace over Essex and Kent, from the east of London to the south-east coast.

The enemy turned northwards just west of Southend at 09.45 hours, crossing the coast on the north shore of the Thames, and headed straight for the RAF Station and sector airfield at North Weald. As the fighters took off from their airfields in the area the Dorniers had time to swing around and carry out a text book attack in open formation from the north-east at an altitude of 15,000 feet. All of the hangars were hit, fire gutting two of them. Messes and administrative buildings were damaged, and the vital operations block was hit, but not destroyed. In all 200 bombs were dropped on the airfield, many of which were delayed action. The runways were heavily cratered but the airfield remained open. There were four deaths. The problem had been that the controllers had delayed too long before scrambling their fighters and it was only as the enemy bombers headed for home with their escort that the RAF fighters reached the altitude necessary to attack.

Although the cannon-armed Spitfires of 19 Squadron from Duxford initially found themselves in a position to attack, six of their number suffered stoppages as they engaged the Bf110 protection in an attempt to protect the bombers. The infuriated Spitfire pilots broke off their attack and returned to base leaving the Hurricanes of 1, 17, 46, 249, 257 and 310 Squadrons to attack in a multitude of waves in the company of eight Spitfires from 603. The Bf110 crews fought valiantly against the onslaught from the fighters and although they lost a high number of aircraft, with the Czech pilots of 310 Squadron having a particularly successful morning, the Luftwaffe Bf109 and 110 crews still managed to inflict a high number of losses on the RAF fighters as they tried to penetrate their defences and get to the bombers. The dogfights over the Colchester area produced a sky streaked with grey smoke trails from the damaged aircraft, some diving to the ground with the pilot having escaped his stricken aircraft and taken to his 'brolly', the white silk (Luftwaffe air crews were identifiable by their sky-blue parachutes) visible as he hung high up in the sky suspended under his canopy. Others were not so fortunate in that they were still in the cockpit as the aircraft plunged to the ground, dead or frantically trying to get out.

603 Squadron Spitfires were attacked by the 109s of II/JG26 that had arrived over the Essex coast and Thames estuary to cover the bombers' retreat, in an operation intended to make maximum use of the 109's limited range and endurance.

<u>Intelligence Patrol Report – 603 Squadron.</u>

<u>09.15-10.30 hours, 3.9.40.</u>

Eight aircraft took off from Hornchurch. At 22,000' over Manston they saw about six Do17's in vic at the same height and about 12 Me109's; above this formation was a further formation of 12 Me109's. The Squadron attacked the fighters, which they considered to be inferior to any they had encountered before. The Me109's had no yellow noses. P/O Stapleton took off with 54 Squadron and when south of Harwich, dived on to a Do17 and shot it down.

RAF Hornchurch, 1 September 1940. 222 Squadron Spitfires and Hillary's Spitfire XT-M being re-armed.

Sixty years later Stapme has absolutely no doubt he took off with his own Squadron. The 54 Squadron ORB states that 12 Spitfires took off on their first patrol at 10.15, one hour after 603. According to the ORB, the following pilots took off on this patrol in two vics and a singleton: S/L Denholm (X4260), F/L Macdonald (X4259), P/O Caister (L1057), F/O Pease (X4263), P/O Stewart-Clark (X4185), P/O Hillary (X4277), P/O Stapleton (R6626), and P/O Cardell (X4274).

George Denholm led 603 at the head of A Flight.* Pilot Officer Caister claimed a 109 destroyed:

When on patrol with 603 Sqn, 12 or more Me109's dived on the Squadron from above, a few miles east of Manston. Six Me109's broke away east from below and did not enter engagement. I attacked from astern, one Me109 and after a few seconds bursts it climbed steeply; closing up with a long burst I saw the e/a out of control. I had fired a few seconds burst at close range and broke off, and almost stalled. Turning away from the e/a I had attacked, I fired a few seconds burst at another Me109 almost dead ahead. This machine did not break off but passed me within a few yards distance. There appeared to be six streams of fire coming from the e/a. I did not observe any damage. I saw at least two and perhaps a third explosion on the water, either bombs or aircraft crashing. Turning round I looked for somebody of my Squadron. I noticed an aircraft in my mirror, but I was too far away for it to start firing. Spiralling down in a steep dive I lost it, and being short of petrol I refuelled at Manston, taking off immediately and returned to base.

Caister had been with A Flight when he delivered his attack at 09.45 hours over the Channel at 20,000 feet. He opened fire at 250 yards and closed to 50 yards, firing a burst of ten seconds. Peter Pease claimed a 109 destroyed during this patrol:

I saw one Me109 over the sea about 5,000' below me. I could see no other aircraft above or below me, so I dived to make a beam attack. When I was still out of range, the enemy aircraft did a half-roll and dived vertically. It never pulled out, and crashed into the sea.

Pease was with B Flight when he shot down the Messerschmitt 20 miles north-east of Margate at an altitude of 12,000 feet. His claim was confirmed as being a Messerschmitt Bf109E-4 of II Stab/JG26. The pilot Leutnant Eckardt Roch, the Gruppen adjutant, was missing at the time of the report and was later confirmed as having been killed in action. He had four kills to his credit. Stapme claimed a Dornier Do17 destroyed:

---

*Ken Macdonald was Denholm's deputy when the CO remained on the ground. 'Old Gent' (Jack Haig) and John Boulter also led the Squadron later in the Battle of Britain.

...I sighted a formation of 15 Do17's, accompanied by 20 Me110's. The enemy aircraft were flying in line astern and weaving about in 'S' turns. As we had some 8,000' on this formation, the squadron went into line astern and attacked the Do17's. I fired at a Do17 in my first attack, with no visible effect. I climbed up again into the sun and attacked a Do17 which had one engine stopped. I attacked on the starboard side, stopping the other engine with a deflection burst of four seconds.

Stapme delivered his attack 15 miles south-west of Harwich at 09.45 hours at an altitude of 20,000 feet. That evening, 54 Squadron, which had been one of the other squadrons operating from RAF Hornchurch with 603, flew to RAF Catterick. The Squadron ORB recorded:

The eventful and crowded life of the Squadron at Hornchurch came to an end on September 3rd, 1940, when the flying personnel went in a body to RAF Camp, Catterick. It was generally thought that the object of this move was to enable our pilots to get a well-earned and long anticipated rest after the daily pressure of combat at Hornchurch; but in point of fact the Squadron became operational soon after its arrival, and a little later heard that the flying members were to be dispersed to different units in the south leaving only a few to form the nucleus of an OTU. This was a shock to everyone – for all felt keenly the breaking up of a fine team of fighter-pilots who had been long enough together to have built up an espirit-de-corps and a strong tradition.

By 10 September 1940, only seven of the pilots that had flown to Catterick were still with the unit. Of the 54 Squadron pilots to depart, Pilot Officers Peter Howes and Ludwik Martel were posted to 603 and made a prompt return to Hornchurch. Of their new arrivals, Flying Officer Claude Goldsmith and Pilot Officer Peter Dexter were also destined to move to 603 Squadron at Hornchurch.

The 603 ORB shows that the Squadron suffered the loss of two aircraft with both pilots, Richard Hillary and Dudley Stewart-Clark, badly injured. During this combat, while flying Spitfire X4277 Richard was shot down by Hauptmann Erich Bode (pronounced Boder) of II/JG26 Schlageter at 10.04 off Margate. He had been very fortunate indeed in that, although grievously burnt, his unconscious body had fallen free from the cockpit. He had been unable to escape prior to this occurrence. Just four minutes later Hauptmann Bode struck again at 10.08 when he also managed to shoot down Stewart-Clark in Spitfire X4185, although the RAF pilot maintained control of the aircraft before finally deciding to abandon when he baled out over Creeksea Church, Burnham. He had received a bullet wound to the lower leg and was admitted to Chelmsford Hospital on landing. Although Bode was an extremely experienced pilot these were the first and second enemy aircraft he had destroyed in combat. Also on 3 September 1940 Feldwebel Hoffmann of 4/JG26 claimed to have shot down a 603 Spitfire at 10.20 am over Hockley. It was unconfirmed.

It is interesting to compare the official Air Ministry instructions to fighter pilots for carrying out the most efficient way of exiting a single-seat fighter after it had been hit. No doubt the provision of such a thorough procedure, knowing that in reality blind panic and terror would seriously detract from the pilot's ability to initiate these guidelines in full, was realised. Nevertheless, if mentally rehearsed in their entirety they could in part still lead to the pilot escaping from the disabled aircraft in the most adverse conditions:

The sequence of operations is most important, even if you are in a hurry. First, lift your seat to the full 'up' position, slide back your hood and lock it fully open. Undo your harness, take hold of the parachute rip-cord, and then either stand up on the seat and put the stick forward, or roll onto your back.... If you are on fire don't open the hood until the last moment, as it will draw flames into the cockpit. If your clothes are soaked in petrol, switch off the engine switches and leave the throttle open, otherwise as you get out the sparks from the exhaust may act like the flint in your cigarette lighter. Keep hold of the rip-cord as you leave the aircraft, but if you are very high there is no need to pull it for the time being. Pilots who have pulled the rip-cord immediately after getting out in a high speed dive have been badly injured. You will fall more slowly out of your aeroplane than in it, so do a delayed drop whenever you can. The '109' will also find you harder to hit with the umbrella shut than open. You only fall 1,000 feet in five seconds, so there is really plenty of time.

When you consider that these pilots had not been trained in parachute jumping and the first time they were to experience this was during combat, it is obvious that the fear of the free-fall was far less than that which they endured when plunging to earth in an uncontrollable aircraft and/or when confronted with the possibility of being burnt to death.

Richard Hillary had been hit at approximately 25,000 feet, whilst pursuing an already damaged enemy fighter, when he should have broken off his engagement in order to avoid the inevitable attack on his own aircraft. According to Richard, when he had initially tried to open the canopy it would not move back sufficiently on its runners to enable him to escape the cramped confines of his cockpit which had become a terrible blazing inferno. A blow-torch of searing heat blasted back against his body from the leg well, burning his trouser legs off in seconds and scorching his legs, his flying boots offering the only protection. Richard unfastened his straps in order to get a better purchase on the canopy handles. He was not wearing gloves. He had spurned the idea of wearing his goggles, apart from during take-off and landing, because he found them restricting. A practice shared by several other colleagues in the Squadron. Having pulled back the canopy far enough in order to bale out he lost consciousness and fell back into his seat.

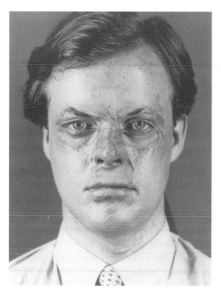

Richard's burning aircraft had been falling from the sky throughout his attempts to escape, and finally the Spitfire fell into an interminable screaming dive for several thousand feet more before, at a height of approximately 10,000 feet, it rolled over into an inverted position and Richard fell free, but before doing so his head had smashed against the inside of the canopy frame.

His brief period of combat with 603 Squadron in the Battle of Britain had come to an end, although he faced another battle in the months ahead. His parents were informed that he was posted 'missing' by the station adjutant at Hornchurch and three hours after his initial call he telephoned again with news that Richard had been picked up by the Margate reserve lifeboat, *J.B. Proudfoot**, but that he had been very badly burnt. On the return journey the lifeboat crew's abiding memory of him was of his pain-wracked words as he lay on the deck: 'How much further? How much further?' On landing Richard was rushed to Margate General Hospital.[7]

Above: Richard Hillary's face after his reconstructive surgery.

Below: His deformed hands.

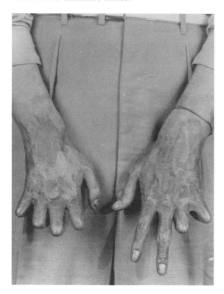

When his condition had stabilised Richard was transferred to The Masonic at Hammersmith. He eventually moved to the Queen Victoria Memorial Hospital, East Grinstead, where he came under the care of the brilliant New Zealand-born plastic surgeon Archie McIndoe (later Sir Archibald McIndoe). Following a lengthy and painful period of reconstructive surgery to his face and hands Richard travelled to America where he was encouraged to write about his experiences. He returned to England in November 1942 and his story was published in America

*Interestingly, for a period between March and June 1952, the *JB Proudfoot* was the No.1 lifeboat at Holy Island, Northumberland, where the only time it was called into action was on 25 June 1952, when its crew rescued two people from an aeroplane that had ditched in the North Sea.

as *Falling Through Space* and in England as *The Last Enemy*. He underwent staff training and for a while accepted that his injuries would keep him from returning to flying. However, a window of opportunity opened when Air Marshal Sholto Douglas told him that if he could get himself passed A1b medically fit, he would allow him to return to operational flying. On the morning of 8 January 1943, he and his radio/observer, Sergeant K. Wilfrid Fison, died when their aircraft crashed whilst undergoing night-fighter training with 54 OTU, at RAF Charterhall in the Scottish Borders. Richard Hillary was 23.*

Meanwhile the 603 Squadron pilots had re-grouped and were licking their wounds, the experienced pilots trying to give the new arrivals every chance they could to survive their first few encounters. They had only been in the front line for a week themselves during which time 14 of their Spitfires had been destroyed.

Assessing the Performance
In just one week of combat, 24 pilots of 603 Squadron flew a total of 164 patrols. Ras, Bolster and Black Morton achieved the highest number in this period, with Denholm, Ken Macdonald and Richard Hillary attaining the next greatest number. Nevertheless, the price of success had been high. During that time 603 had lost four pilots, and four ground crew killed with two more pilots seriously injured. Seven pilots had baled out and five more crash-landed their aircraft. It is also interesting to note how the pilots were rotated in order to give brief rests from combat patrols. Although some flew very little during this time, their period of frantic air fighting was to come.

As a Flight Lieutenant in the Battle of Britain, Freddie Rosier (later Air Chief Marshal Sir Frederick Rosier) assessed the requirements he believed were necessary to achieve success as a fighter pilot:

> The really good fighter pilot had a gift. He could scan the skies, take it all in, know how long he had to do something and then do it. Very few people had that gift. I think I was an exceptional pilot in peacetime, but I didn't have that gift. Eyesight was terribly important. You could pick out things long before anyone else. But when you were in the middle of combat, it was the facility to look around and instantly put it all into your mental computer to produce the right answers. Most people who looked around could only take in a certain amount.

Ras, Sheep and Brian Carbury were probably the natural combat pilots in 603 Squadron whilst the others who had been achieving success were rapidly learning the complexities of dog-fighting. While aim and range had to be correct in order to hit the target, camera guns showed that pilots frequently fired when well out of effective range. By analysing the films the pilots were encouraged to get in closer, a tactic which Brian Carbury practised to great effect, as mentioned earlier.

Many of the Luftwaffe fighter pilots had refined their tactics during and after the Spanish Civil War. In comparison, the RAF had had little opportunity to hone their tactics and skill in combat. An excellent example of an out-of-date tactic used by the RAF was the 'vic' formation flown by Fighter Command during the early days of the battle. This formation proved totally unsuitable but, interestingly, although the German pilots referred to the RAF's use of the vic as *Idiotenreihe* the Luftwaffe Jagdgeschwader had used the same method in Spain until they discovered by chance a more effective formation which they quickly adopted. Three groups of four aircraft would fly with some 800 yards between each formation. Each group was an open 'V' with a leader, two aircraft on one side and one on the other. This was the so-called 'finger four' because it resembled the fingers of a hand. The advantage was that all pilots in the formation could continually scan the skies. In combat the 'V' could instantly break into pairs – the basic formation for effective air fighting. Whilst a pilot is firing at an enemy aircraft, his eyes must be fixed on his target and during this time he is dependent on his wing man for protection. The RAF later operated the same system.

---

*In November 2001 a memorial was unveiled by HRH the Duke of Kent in memory of Hillary, Fison and all who died at Charterhall during WWII. Thanks to his best-selling book the name of Richard Hillary and that of his contemporaries and colleagues in 603 Squadron will live on. See *Richard Hillary* by David Ross (Grub Street 2000).

Early in 1941 Wilfred Duncan Smith (later Group Captain W.G.G. Duncan Smith, DSO*, DFC**) who joined 603 Squadron that year, noted:

> New formations and tactics were devised. A pair of aircraft as a fighting formation had come to stay. It was much more flexible than the old formations of three aircraft... we could manoeuvre more comfortably and fly at a much higher cruising speed.

Battle of Britain fighter pilot Wing Commander 'Dizzy' Allen later assessed the tactics of the RAF and believed that the most important factor in fighter combat was to see the enemy before they saw you and that a pilot with long-sightedness had a distinct advantage. In the traditional formation each pilot was required to keep an eye on the aircraft nearest to him with only the leader scanning the sky. The formation behind was therefore vulnerable to attack. Some units adopted the tactic of 'weavers' whose job it was to watch out for enemy fighters who might be getting in position to attack. But they themselves were vulnerable as they had no tail guard. Following the early losses 603 adopted the tactic of having a single section 'guard' watching over the formation from behind and at greater altitude. With a number of pilots possessing excellent eyesight, it proved reasonably successful.

The performance of the Spitfire was similar to the Messerschmitt Bf109 with each having superiorities over the other – the Spitfire had a tighter turning circle which was vital in air combat, the 109 had better performance over 25,000 feet and its fuel injection system provided a significant advantage. The critical limits of the Spitfire Mk I were therefore constantly kept in mind. Pilot fitness was also an important factor as dog fights were of short duration, extremely energetic encounters leaving pilots drenched in sweat. To survive being bounced by enemy fighters a pilot had to break sharply and dive away to avoid being hit. This exerted great forces on the body and brought about greying out and, more seriously, blacking out.* The resistance of each individual to blacking out varied. Under the effects of about 3 or 4 'g' the heart couldn't pump oxygen-enriched blood to the brain and this initially affected the eyesight. First he experienced a grey mist over the vision and, as the 'g's increased, the pilot eventually blacked out as he tried to shake the enemy fighter from his tail. The experience was described as like being: '...with your eyes open in a dark cellar with no lights on.' As the aircraft levelled out the 'g'-Force eased and the pilot was able to see again. Constant vigilance was vital and many lives were lost due to lapses in concentration. With pilots flying three or four patrols in a single day, fatigue set in and mistakes became inevitable and frequently fatal. During their early experiences adrenaline provided the pilots with a naturally occurring stimulant which kept them focussed, but as each day of intense fighting went by, so the flow of adrenaline lessened and the effect of fatigue became dominant from which inexperienced and experienced pilots alike became victims as a consequence.

Another important factor was the service provided by the dedicated ground crew personnel. On landing the engine and airframe of each aircraft were quickly checked for any combat damage and, if any was found, an estimation was given of how long it would take to repair. (If it was too great a task the aircraft was pushed into one of the large hangars to await collection for repair or written-off. A new Spitfire was made ready.) The fitter usually filled the fuel tank, often using a drum on wheels with a semi-rotary pump as bowsers were in short supply. The armourer removed the empty magazines, cleaned the guns before fitting new ammunition drums, cocked the guns and replaced the access panels securely. Patches were painted over the gun ports to prevent freezing, keep the guns free of foreign bodies which might jeopardise their operation, and signal to the armourer on landing that the guns had in fact been fired. The oil and glycol were topped up, where required, and the oxygen supply replenished. The fuel caps were checked and the gauges read, the radiator intake cleaned whilst the rigger tested the controls for movement. The WEM tried the radio, checked the gun-sight was working and that the spare bulbs (for the gun-sight) were in position. The compressed air system was checked for the flaps and the hydraulics for the undercarriage. Finally, the canopy runners were checked for smooth movement and, as noted earlier, both windscreen and canopy were cleaned and polished with a scrupulously clean soft cloth. The 'Form 700' was signed to certify all tasks had been carried out and that the aircraft was ready. All these tasks were done as quickly as

---

*The opposite to grey and black out is red out, when blood is forced to the brain rather than from it.

possible in the event that 603 were scrambled again but also ready to take off as quickly as possible and with an aircraft ready for combat in the event the airfield was attacked. Any mistake or misjudgement on their part, no matter how small, may affect the performance of any one of the aircraft's systems, thus providing the enemy with an advantage in combat. The 603 ground crewmen worked diligently and sometimes in the most appalling and basic conditions to serve their pilots to the best of their ability. They seldom had the time to carry out the regulation 20-hour inspection. Although there were a number of regulars amongst the mainly auxiliary ground crews before and during the Battle of Britain, an advantage 603 had over other squadrons was that there was little movement of staff to and from other units; 603's ground crews had worked together as a coherent team for a long time before the war, in some cases many years. They were a confident and experienced team. To many of the surviving ground crewmen the class divide between officers and NCOs was very evident and despite there being many fine men who were officer pilots, 603 was no exception. As mentioned earlier, among the pilots Ras Berry had a 'particularly hard time' when he first joined 603 as did Bill Caister but both were tough individuals and were commissioned soon after joining. Nevertheless, some saw their treatment as unforgivable. However, the majority of the officers had great respect for the NCOs and airmen. An excellent example being the relationship between Count Stevens and Angy Gillies; Ken Macdonald who had occasionally given Jim Skinner and other airmen lifts to Turnhouse in the years before the war, and Brian Carbury who talked to any man in the same polite way.

In appreciation of the work of the parachute packers at Hornchurch during the Battle of Britain, the surviving pilots of 603 presented each of them with a gold cigarette case.

By the end of the day Claude Goldsmith was sent to 54 Squadron, also at Hornchurch, and Boulter and Haig had been promoted to Flight Lieutenant and Black to Flying Officer.

Wednesday 4 September 1940
Between 09.00-10.15 hours an attack developed over Kent and the Thames estuary. Fifteen squadrons were sent up to intercept. Between 13.00-14.15 a further attack developed over the south coast to Shoreham, inland to Woking and over Kent to Gravesend and the estuary. Fourteen squadrons were sent up to intercept.

At 12.45 12 aircraft took off from Hornchurch with orders to patrol Gravesend. From there they were directed to Manston where Ken Macdonald and Joey Sarre became separated. At 30,000 feet they spotted six Bf109s, 4,000 feet below them and dived to attack. Macdonald fired bursts at one from astern after which it rolled over onto its back and dived vertically. Sergeant Joey Sarre also fired on a 109 without result. His engine began to misfire and he later forced-landed his Spitfire X4263 at Elstead near Ashford as a result of engine failure. Sarre was unhurt and the aircraft was repaired On the same day Pilot Officer Caister shot down a Messerschmitt Bf109E-1 of 3/JG27 off Dunkirk at 10.40 hours. The pilot was Feldwebel Wilhelm Harting who was wounded and later rescued from the sea. A similar sojourn near the French coast would bring the war to a premature end for Caister a few days later.

Thursday 5 September 1940
On this day there were two major attacks. The first between 09.40 and 10.40 hours crossed the coast between Dover and Dungeness proceeding to mid-Kent and the Croydon, Kenley and Biggin Hill area. Part of the formation broke away and headed north-east penetrating as far as Brentwood. Of the ten squadrons sent up to intercept five made contact, including 603.

Between 14.15 and 16.30 hours a second attack took place. One raid headed along the Thames estuary whilst the other went towards Biggin Hill. A third raid flew almost directly to Detling. To counter this atttack 13 squadrons, including 603, were sent up to engage the enemy. Of these 603 were one of nine which were successful, assisted by three others who had not been detailed to the raids. The outcome of the ensuing combat was the loss of eight Hurricanes and 14 Spitfires written-off.

603 Squadron had taken off from their forward base at Rochford at 09.30. Climbing to 29,000 feet they spotted 15-20 Dorniers approximately 9,000 feet below them with three more lower still, just south of Hornchurch. As the Squadron dived to attack they were engaged by the fighter escort of II/JG26's Bf109s. Black claimed a 109 damaged. Stapme was engaged by two fighters and managed to hit one, and later reported seeing glycol leaking from the radiator. As he attempted to

finish off the 109 he was fired on by another. F/L Fred Rushmer failed to return following combat with II/JG26, over Biggin Hill at 10.00 in Spitfire X4261. Rusty was posted as missing and his name later inscribed on Panel 4 of the Runnymede Memorial. Squadron records state that his loss occurred between 09.34 and 10.34 hours. In time, and by process of elimination, it became obvious he had been buried on 11 September, identity unknown, in All Saints Churchyard, Staplehurst, Kent. With little left to provide any clue as to who the pilot had been, bearing in mind that the country was at war, minimum effort had been spent confirming the identity and thereby offer the family some peace of mind knowing there was a recognised grave. It is no mere coincidence that the inscription 'Spitfire 5.9.1940' etched on a wooden beam in a nearby barn at Buckmans Green Farm, was carried out by farm workers who witnessed the crash and were moved to commemorate or record the tragedy.

At 10.00 hours on 5 September, during his first flight with 603, Pilot Officer 'Robin' Rafter was shot down by Bf109s of II/JG26 over Marden. Fred Rushmer had been leading his section and both were hit during a single diving pass. Robin was struck in the right leg by a piece of shrapnel from a 20mm cannon shell but more serious was the injury to his head. As the result of damage to the tail unit of X4264, his aircraft, suddenly plunged downwards, the centrifugal force catapulting him through the canopy. He managed to open his parachute, however, and landed safely at Marden. His Spitfire crashed nearby. He was admitted to West Kent Hospital in Maidstone but the Squadron were not notified of his whereabouts and he was posted as 'missing'. He was later transferred to the RAF officers convalescent hospital at Torquay and reported back to RAF Hornchurch on 7 November categorised 'non-effective sick'. He finally returned to 603 Squadron at Hornchurch on 26 November 1940.

Success for the Squadron came during the same combat in which Robin had been shot down, Stapme bringing down the Messerschmitt Bf109E-4 (1480) piloted by Oberleutnant Franz von Werra of Stab II/JG3 who became famous as 'the one that got away' in the book of the same name.* His aircraft forced-landed at Love's Farm, Winchet Hill, Marden at 10.10 hours and he was captured unhurt.

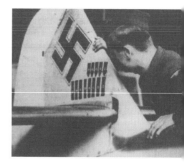

Above: Shot down by Stapme on Thursday 5 September 1940, Messerschmitt Bf109E-4 <+- (1480) of Stab II/JG3, flown by Oberleutnant Franz von Werra at Love's Farm, near Marden. Note army guard with RAF airman busy removing live ammunition.
Top right: Another photo of the aircraft taken sometime later with an RAF Sergeant examining the tail.
Bottom right: Hauptmann Franz von Werra, Gruppen Kommandeur, II JG/53.

The One That Got Away by Kendall Burt and James Leasor published by Collins with Michael Joseph in 1956. A film of the book was later made and starred Hardy Kruger as von Werra.

Von Werra's unit was initially attacked from above by 41 Squadron between Ashford and Maidstone whilst on a diversionary fighter sweep over Kent. Stapme caught up with his 109 at low level and fired several bursts, eventually forcing it down. The 603 ORB reports this combat as being between 09.34 and 10.34 hours and that Stapme:

> ...dived to attack bombers but was engaged by 109's. Attacked one and saw glycol but was then attacked himself and dived to evade. Attacked a lone 109 which forced-landed, pilot got out and tried to fire his aircraft by setting light to his jacket but was stopped by the LDV.'

Interestingly it also mentions that as he attacked the 109: '...the pilot broke away, waggling his wings.' In his combat report Stapme recorded:

> I was diving to attack them (the bombers) when I was engaged by two Me109's [the 'Rotte', the typical Luftwaffe tactical formation consisting of leader and wingman]. When I fired at the first one I noticed glycol coming from his radiator. I did a No.2 attack and as I fired I was hit by bullets from another Me109. I broke off downwards and continued my dive. At 6,000 feet I saw a single-engined machine diving vertically with no tail unit. I looked up and saw a parachutist coming down circled by an Me 109. I attacked him (the Me109) from the low quarter, he dived vertically towards the ground and flattened out at ground level. I then did a series of beam attacks from both sides, and the enemy aircraft turned into my attacks. He finally forced landed. He tried to set his radio on fire by taking off his jacket and setting fire to it and putting it into the cockpit. He was prevented by the LDV.

The parachutist being circled by the 109 was Robin Rafter of 603 Squadron. Rumours of the Germans murdering pilots as they hung defenceless in their parachute harnesses existed at this time. Stapme remembered the pursuit of the 109:

> I noticed that its airspeed had dropped dramatically and I pressed home an attack, followed by another before allowing the pilot to carry out a forced landing. I remember seeing my tracer strike the 109 and was concerned that I was firing at low level, with a village in my apparent line of fire.
> Contrary to the myth that has developed over the years, I have no doubt that the pilot was making no attempt to open fire on Rafter as he hung seriously injured in his parachute harness. He was merely concentrating on self preservation and happened to be circling in the vicinity of Rafter. The 109 was clearly disabled with the pilot looking to evade further attack and get his aircraft down. Why risk murdering the parachutist knowing that his aircraft was damaged and a forced landing, on enemy territory, was imminent?

It would appear that von Werra had had every opportunity to open fire on Rafter, who had also suggested that the German pilot had been in a position to shoot at him, but had not done so prior to being 'driven off' by Stapme. On landing Stapme had believed the pilot had been waving his jacket up in salute of his victorious attacker and so he waggled his wings. In truth the wave was a deception by von Werra who had actually been in the process of setting light to his jacket. The arrival of the LDV put paid to his plan when they dragged the burning jacket from the cockpit. Stapme learnt these facts before writing his combat report. At the time Stapme had no idea who he had shot down: 'It was sometime between the end of the war and when I moved to South Africa that I was told the name of the pilot I had shot down on 5 September, and of his reputation as the one that got away.' The aircraft Stapme saw 'diving vertically with no tail unit' was that of Robin Rafter, who had stated in his letter home that '...my tail must have been damaged'. The tragic story of Robin Rafter came full circle on 29 November 1940.

The rest of the 603 pilots landed at Hornchurch at 10.34. Ian Ritchie was discharged from Oldchurch Hospital, Romford and returned. The Luftwaffe night bombing raids continued apace.

Friday 6 September 1940
There were three major engagements. The first attack occurred between 08.45 and 09.45 hours over the Thames estuary where ten squadrons engaged the enemy. A second attack developed between 12.30 and 13.40 when the enemy force targeted the Chatham area. Seven squadrons engaged the

Top: 6 September 1940. P/O Bill Caister's Spitfire. He landed near Guines, France, and his aircraft XT-D soon attracted the attention of the local Luftwaffe personnel. *Middle:* Another shot of Bill Caister's Spitfire. By now the Luftwaffe ground crews have removed it to a dispersed site at their airfield. Note the 24" high lettering as opposed to the usual 30". *Bottom:* Bill Caister's aircraft was repainted and test flown at Rechlin. An intact Mk I Spitfire example.

enemy. A third attack occurred between 17.20 and 18.45 over the Thames estuary when three squadrons intercepted and attacked the enemy. Thirty-seven enemy aircraft were destroyed, 19 probables and 11 damaged.

Between 13.00 and 14.15 hours on this day 603 carried out an interception. During what was a sporadic engagement over the Channel off Manston, Caister's Spitfire, X4260, XT-D, was damaged in combat with Hauptmann von Bonin of I/JG54 over the Channel off Manston. Due to damage received or perhaps disorientation, he landed on the wrong side of the water. With his hydraulics system u/s Bill Caister was unable to lower the undercarriage of his Spitfire but still managed to carry out a perfect landing in a field near Guines in northern France. The aircraft quickly became the centre of attention of the Luftwaffe pilots and ground crews from the nearby airfield. It was lifted by crane and the undercarriage lowered before it was towed away and hidden in woodland close to their own dispersed fighters at Guines. As the propeller had been damaged during the landing, the ground crew replaced it and gave the Spitfire a coat of light blue paint before it was taken away for testing and evaluation at Erprobungsstelle 2 at Rechlin, Mechlenberg. The recently commissioned pilot officer with over 15 years service in the RAF had a brief meeting with von Bonin in the mess at Guines, after which he was taken away to spend the rest of the war in captivity but he was no model prisoner. Of his 4½ years as a prisoner five months were spent in the *Straflager* (punishment block). For the greater and latter period he was imprisoned in Stalag Luft III, Sagan, (PoW No.242), which became notorious for The Great Escape. Having been married for just over a week Caister was not to see his wife again until May 1945, when he was released as part of Operation Exodus (the repatriation of PoWs), which began on 7 May. He had been awarded the DFM on 13 September 1940. He left the RAF as a Flight Lieutenant on 8 June 1946. At 34 years of age, he had been the Squadron's first regular non-commissioned and the oldest 603 pilot to see action during the Battle of Britain.*

On 6 September, Ras Berry was granted 48 hours leave in order to get married. As he was packing, John Boulter tried hard to persuade him to accompany him to a 'naughty show' in London that evening, but Ras declined insisting that he had a train to catch from King's Cross and a wedding he really needed to attend! By 9 September he was flying again. Life moved quickly during this period. His bride, Nancy, travelled back south with Ras and the couple moved in with Stapme and Joan Stapleton in Romford. The Squadron now received news that Jack Stokoe was alive and in Leeds Castle Hospital. His family were notified accordingly.

Saturday 7 September 1940
The battle now entered its fourth phase when the Luftwaffe sent over the single biggest daylight raid of the war so far in an attempt to destroy the London dockland area. The raid developed around 16.15 hours with an enemy force which consisted of 300 bombers and 600 plus single-seat and twin-engine fighters as escort. They came mostly from the direction of Calais, crossing the coast between Dungeness and North Foreland before thrusting north towards the Thames estuary and London in several waves. It was an attempt by the Luftwaffe to attack the administrative and commercial heart of the country while drawing the RAF's depleted Fighter Command into a massive aerial battle. By 16.30 hours 19 squadrons had been despatched to confront the attacking force of the Germans as it approached the Thames estuary. The massive aerial combat which took place was to deplete Fighter Command still further (fortunately in aircraft, not lives), but it was to deliver a severe jolt to the German confidence and their feeling of invincibility. Eight Spitfires and 16 Hurricanes were written-off, while 42 enemy aircraft were reported destroyed with 23 probably destroyed and 25 damaged.

---

*After the war Bill Caister '...tried an MT course but soon got tired of that and tried my hand at market gardening. I would have tried my hand at anything but this seemed as good as anything. I couldn't grow a thing at first, but gardening friends of mine helped out and there you are' and waved his hand at an expansive vegetable plot on his centre in Colinton, Edinburgh. 'I make a fair living at it but I'm not sure I shall keep it up.' He received regular visits from former Squadron colleagues. Feeling restless, he later spent four months travelling around the USA in his Dormobile with his wife and son, James, also known as Bill (today a serving officer [Engineering] in the RAF), where he visited a woman who had 'adopted' him during his time in captivity and regularly sent him parcels and letters – which she continued to send him 20 years after the war! Bill emigrated to Canada but returned to live in the Scottish capital and died in 1994 aged 88.

Intelligence Patrol Report – 603 Squadron.
16.44-18.45 hours. 7.9.40.

12 aircraft of 603 squadron left Hornchurch to patrol base, when at 15,000 feet they saw a wave of fighters and bombers at 18,000 feet approaching base. Sqn.Ldr. Denholm turned into them and fired at long-range. The squadron then climbed and attacked. In all there were about four waves of enemy aircraft; the first was very well protected by fighters, the third appeared to have no escort of fighters, and the fourth was in very ragged formation. The Me109's and the He113's had yellow noses. About six He113's were seen in line astern. P/O MacNamara [sic] said he saw something about the size of a parachute bag coming from the port side of a He111 which was about to crash.

George Denholm ordered his pilots into echelon starboard and they dived to attack. The formation then broke up and each pilot fought individual dog fights. Later, tactic changes would ensure they fought in pairs, a leader with a wingman.

Brian Macnamara, who had joined the Squadron during the bombing of Hornchurch on 31 August, claimed one He111 destroyed. He had seen it diving south pursued by RAF fighters, but as he was in a good position to intercept, he did so, firing from astern. The bomber was seen to dive into the ground inland and blow up on impact. No combat report exists.

Brian Carbury claimed a Bf109 and one He113 [Bf109] destroyed. Both were seen to crash in flames. He also claimed a He113 probable which was last seen diving and streaming glycol:

> I was leading No.2 section and enemy aircraft were sighted above us in waves of bombers with fighter escort around, above and below. The sections were ordered echelon starboard. I attacked a Me109 which burst into flames. I dived, then climbed into the sun, sighted a string of He113's below me, so I attacked the last of the enemy aircraft twice, and glycol streamed out of him and he proceeded down in a dive. I climbed again to 30,000 feet and dived through another enemy aircraft formation, spraying the whole way down, but did not see any damage at the time. I climbed again and sighted two strings of He113's, attacked the last enemy aircraft and he burst into flames and went earthwards. I landed at Northolt, because I was out of ammunition, petrol and oxygen.

Brian Carbury was with B Flight. He estimated that there were four waves of 80 enemy aircraft which consisted of Bf109s, Bf110s, He113s and Do215s. It should be mentioned again that the existence of the He113 was an elaborate hoax by the Luftwaffe and all 'He113' claims were in fact Messerschmitt Bf109s. He delivered his attack between 17.00 and 17.30 hours over south London at 18,000-30,000 feet. He opened fire at 200 yards firing two-second bursts, closing to 50 yards, firing a total of 2,760 rounds. Still using the most reliable tactics his score continued to mount.

Black Morton dived headlong through the enemy formations at high speed, firing at anything that came into his sights. He claimed a He111 probable with white smoke streaming from both engines and then attacked several 109s which had latched onto a Spitfire. He later claimed one probable with glycol streaming from both radiators, and a second 109 damaged, glycol emitting from one radiator.

George Denholm forced-landed at base in Spitfire X4250, XT-X with a cannon shell in the mainplane after combat with the Bf109s of I/JG2 at 17.08. He was unhurt and the aircraft was repaired.

Following combat over south London at 17.20 hours with the same Bf109s of I/JG2, Peter Pease discovered his undercarriage would not lower and was forced to belly-land back at base. Peter was unhurt and the aircraft, L1057, was repairable.

Sergeant Joey Sarre was trying to recover lost confidence since being shot down on the 30th but once again fell to the guns of an enemy fighter. He baled out of Spitfire P9467 over the Thames. He was wounded and on landing was taken to hospital. Due to a mix up, news of his survival did not reach 603 Squadron and he was posted 'missing' and his family were informed accordingly.

At 17.25 hours Stapme was shot down during the same patrol and carried out a forced landing in Spitfire XT-L, N3196, at Sutton Valence. His aircraft was repaired and he was unhurt. George Denholm, Peter Pease and Stapme were probably victims of either Oberleutnant Heinz Ebeling or

Spitfire Mark Ia, XT-L, N3196. Photo taken surreptitiously following Stapme's force-landing at Forsham Farm, near Spark's Hall, Sutton Valence, Kent on 7 September 1940.

Hauptmann Joachim Müncheberg, Ebeling being the CO of the 9th Staffel and Müncheberg the CO of the 7th Staffel of JG26. Between them they had amassed 35 'kills'. Sarre was probably shot down by another outstanding 'ace' of JG26, Hauptmann Gerhard Schoepfel, CO of III Geschwader with 17 kills. The men of 603 had been up against outstanding combat pilots.

Stapme's aircraft had been badly damaged by cannon and machine-gun fire and with the loss of the hydraulics he looked for the first convenient place to crash-land. Soon after being hit he discovered that his aircraft had no aileron and flap control and he flew on until loss of forward speed and altitude enabled him to carry out a wheels-up landing. Visibility from his cockpit was practically zero as the radiator had been damaged and glycol was spraying onto the windscreen and through his open canopy into the cockpit:

> I didn't see or hear anything apart from the loud and shocking takatakatak! as the bullets and cannon shells hit my aircraft. My forward speed slowed noticeably as my Spitfire was hit and I rolled it onto its back and dived away from the danger. But the damage had been done; my aileron cables had been severed by the cannon shells and I could only fly straight and level. In that split second after realising I had been hit I must have blacked-out from shock. When I came to my senses I found my hands undoing my straps! I regained my composure, re-fastened them and headed inland. I glided, using intermittent bursts of the engine, about twenty miles. I opened the canopy and the glycol vapour streamed in. I had the radiator flaps fully open.

Having successfully belly-landed his aircraft in a cornfield adjacent to a hop garden at Forsham Farm, Forsham Lane, Sutton Valence, without any injury to himself, he climbed out, examined his aircraft and closed the hood. One cannon shell had exploded between the two central machine guns on the starboard wing, completely flattening the two guns. The .303 ammunition belts hung from holes in the aircraft's damaged wing surfaces. He glanced up to see an RAF pilot descending by parachute into an orchard close-by. He met up with him and found out that he was from a Hurricane squadron. The pilot was Sergeant Alan Deller of 43 Squadron. Having destroyed a 109 he himself was shot down following a combat over Ashford. He baled out and his aircraft, V7309, crashed and burnt out at Babylon Farm, Sutton Valence.

At the time of Stapme's arrival in the field, a couple were having a picnic in another field at Forsham Farm. Having witnessed Stapme's landing the couple offered both he and Deller a cup of tea before driving them to the King's Head in Sutton Valence in their Austin Ruby. After a number of drinks at the pub Stapme telephoned his brother Deryck at the Air Ministry who managed to arrange transport to return his younger brother to Hornchurch in the form of a chauffeur-driven camouflaged Humber Super Snipe station wagon. The audacity of a 20-year-old pilot officer! Black Morton's personal diary reads:

7.9.40. Slight haze. Wind light (1645-1840).

Squadron ordered off to intercept raid approaching Hornchurch – 12 A/C – I was rearguard. At 15,000' saw large Balbo* approaching from SE with much AA all round it. Balbo at 10,000'. Climbed hard to south and got to same level and to W. of Balbo. V. [very] powerful escort of 109 and 110. Squadron attempted a beam attack on the bombers; but we were in a poor position, being slightly below if anything, and had to wrangle to protect ourselves from the escort. I tried a dart at some 110s but had to take some v. [very] strong evasive action before I could get in range. Squadron became completely split up without anyone getting a shot.

I climbed hard towards Southend and was at 29,000' over there with one or two other A/C in the vicinity when we were told to reform over base at 20,000'. It was very annoying having to lose all that height and, as it proved, a gross error on ops' part for they again put us too low to do anything but get beaten up.

Five of us managed to join up over base at about 21,000'. Ken leading, Pease, Stapme and I think Brown ['Brown Job' – Boulter] and Tannoy [Read] though I'm not sure of them. Stapme was doing guard above. The rest of us were in vic climbing hard to get above a Balbo coming in from the same direction as the first one at about 21,000'. I suddenly saw a 109 sitting about 30 degrees behind Pease shooting like anything. He just seemed to appear suddenly as though he'd joined the formation. I was too surprised to do anything for a moment, meanwhile he half-rolled and pushed off. Pease was streaming glycol and went down in a gentle turn. He forced landed on the aerodrome OK. Stapme didn't see the Hun till too late. We split up after this and I found myself about 1500' below the Balbo, going the opposite way. There were a lot of 109s going along with it and I hoped they wouldn't pay any attention to me. They didn't, except the last chap who dived head on at me, shooting hard, though I didn't see any stuff nearby, I expect it was all behind. He evidently found he wouldn't get enough deflection on, for he rolled over on his back and had a shot from there – a most amazing performance – eventually he passed over my head without getting a shot.

I then saw another large Balbo to the south and went to do an attack on it. It was a most annoying sight to see these great formations coming in. Each with its cloud of flies buzzing around it and its escort of white and black AA bursts. In the middle of this great formation of bombers – 30 or so in tight vics astern – keeping on absolutely steady through all the AA and everything. There must have been at least six of them all coming in more or less at once from SE to S and converging on us down over Woolwich-Blackheath way. It was the most impressive sight I can remember.

One of the Balbos, Dorniers, I think, with only a small escort was in a fairly convenient position for me to do a diving beam attack from 2-3,000' above and to the west.

Just as I was beginning my attack I saw a Spitfire below and ahead being chased by a 109 so I dropped down on the 109 who didn't see me and got a very good shot from astern from 300 degrees to point blank. He pulled up as soon as I started firing and I don't think he had much of a shot at the Spitfire.

I could see strikes on his fuselage and port wing and much coolant came from both radiators, covering my windscreen so that I could hardly see to shoot. I was going much faster than he was and passed a few feet underneath him from where I could see big tears in the underside of his fuselage and wing roots. I pulled out to starboard as he went into a gentle dive turn to port in towards the middle of London. He was losing height fast and didn't

---

*Balbo was RAF jargon for a mass formation of enemy bombers, so-called after Marshal Balbo the Italian Minister for Air during the 1930s. In July 1933 he commanded a formation of 24 Savoia-Marchetti flying boats in a transatlantic flight. As Governor of Libya he was shot down and killed by his own anti-aircraft fire near Tobruk on 28 June 1940. The Luftwaffe equivalent of Balbo was 'Valhalla'.

appear to be flying very fast, so I expect his motor was done. I couldn't watch him long as I was almost immediately attacked by another 109. I did a very tight turn to port and found myself after one circuit above and to port of the Hun who had more or less carried straight down. I was wondering whether to go down after him when he pulled up and quickly got in range, doing a quarter attack from port developing into below and astern. I saw some strikes of incendiary or De Wilde on his engine and a big stream of coolant from his port radiator. I then had to break to avoid other 109s of which there seemed to be a lot about even though there were no bombers close by.

I then climbed up to the west trying to formate on another Spitfire for part of the way; but he wasn't having any. About 24,000' I was beaten up by a solitary 109, but I saw him and he missed and didn't come again. I eventually got to 26,000' when I saw another large Balbo coming from the South over Chislehurst way. While I was looking at them and deciding to have a crack I saw a most amazing sight – bombs bursting.

I suddenly saw a patch of brown smoke jump up south of the river in that loop west of Woolwich. It started about half a mile south of the river and moved north quite evenly. On the way they must have got a gas holder, for there was an enormous flame which lasted for about 10 seconds without any smoke to speak of. I watched it grow and die and by that time the whole of the loop of the river seemed to be one great brown cloud. The funny thing was I didn't see the raid that did it. I suppose I was some miles away really, though I seemed close.

By the time I'd finished looking at all this, the Balbo I was going to attack was geting close. It was made up of about 30 He111s in vics of 3 astern with an escort of 109s. It was about 5,000' below me and coming N or NW. I started a diving head-on attack from about 20 degrees on its port bow – more or less straight out of the sun and came in range about 30 degrees on port bow and 40 degrees above. I took the leader of the first vic and saw incendiary strikes on the nose and white smoke beginning to pour from both engines before I went past, going down past his tail at a very steep angle between the first and second vics. I saw the dark green tail of the starboard machine flash past and thought how big it was. I carried on down in the dive for a bit, coming up at 16,000' more or less underneath and to the east of the Balbo. Nothing had followed me down so I had time for a good look round.

The Balbo was still steaming on in good formation, except for a straggler or two in the rear, which was disappointing I'd hope to have shaken them. However, the leader had gone and the Balbo was led by the two remaining aircraft of the first vic. I had a good look for the leader but couldn't see him for certain, though there was a big machine flying south a couple of thousand feet below the Balbo and to the west of it which might have been him; but I was hopelessly placed for investigating so left him and turned west to find a quiet patch of sky to climb up in.

I was beginning to feel a bit weary by now and knew I could have very few cartridges left. However, control was constantly calling to tell us to stay up and harass the Hun even when our bullets had gone, so I thought I'd better climb up again. I couldn't see any more Balbos after the one I'd attacked, but there were a lot of 109s about in ones and twos and I was attacked twice on the way up to 30,000'. Fortunately I saw them both and got off; I took a quick squirt at one, but my guns stopped almost as soon as I pushed the tit. I was well over the west of London by this time climbing generally towards the sun and began to pick up the BBC on the RT. A chap was giving a religious talk, more or less of 'Prepare to meet thy God' lines which was a bit shaking.

I eventually got to 30,000' and cruised about without seeing anything until we were told we could land which I did forthwith as I was getting extremely short of essence.

When I landed, there was Pease and his A/C still strong. George with a hole in his port wing you could stand up and turn round in – I think I saw him in the first battle as I noticed an aircraft with a big white patch on one wing. He said it handled OK though rather left wing down. Stapme force landed. Sarre missing (he turned up later).

The award of the DFC to F/O Brian Carbury was announced this day.

Sunday 8 September 1940

There was only one attack by the Luftwaffe which spread over Kent and into the Thames estuary between 11.10 and 13.00 hours. There appeared to be two phases, the first crossing the coast north-east of Dover, circling over Dover and Dungeness before returning to France. The second phase passed the returning first phase, bombed Dover, partly turned out to sea where a section broke away and flew towards the Thames estuary, back through Kent and over the coast near Dungeness. An estimated 100 aircraft took part in the attack. Ten squadrons were ordered to intercept, including 603, but only four engaged the enemy with 603 not one of them. On this day Göring broadcast from northern France:

> Now is the historic hour when for the first time the Luftwaffe has struck at the heart of the enemy. After all of the provocative British attacks on Berlin the Führer decided to order reprisal blows against London. I personally assumed command of these victorious German airmen, who, for the first time have attacked London in broad daylight, accompanied by brave fighter comrades. They will continue to carry their orders to full execution.

This was another critical turning point in the battle, although, only the most senior commanders appreciated it at the time. In some cases the British air defences were being pushed to the limit. The summer of 1940 was not the long hot summer with day after day of clear blue skies that legend will have us believe. Had there been fine weather throughout the period of the battle, the outcome may have been different. As it was, there were days when it was overcast and wet, during which time British aircraft manufacture continued with minimum loss of aircraft and pilots due to enemy action. Aircraft production was therefore able to keep pace with the losses, thanks to the efforts of Lord Beaverbrook and the many people who worked in the industry. However, replacing pilots was another matter and, bearing in mind the length of time it took to train a pilot, there was a desperate shortage of experienced pilots and many young men joined the fray long before they were ready. Churchill later commented:

> This period (24 August – 6 September) seriously drained the strength of Fighter Command as a whole. The Command lost in this fortnight 103 pilots killed and 128 seriously wounded, while 466 Spitfires and Hurricanes had been destroyed or seriously damaged. Out of a total pilot strength of about 1,000, nearly a quarter had been lost. Their planes could only be filled by 260 new, ardent, but inexperienced pilots drawn from training units, in many cases before their full courses were complete.

The decision by the Luftwaffe High Command to switch the main thrust of its attacks from the RAF airfields to London ultimately gave 11 Group the much needed opportunity to consolidate but the seriousness of the situation was emphasised when on 8 September a No.1 Invasion Alert was brought into force. By this time exhaustion had long set-in with the 603 pilots. The long hours, the massive stresses and strains of flying battle, facing death each day as well as meting it out, the anticipation of combat as well as the combat itself, had taken its toll. Black Morton recorded in his diary:

> There are now too many battles and I am too tired to write accounts of them all. This one, however, is worth trying to write about. I was more impressed by it than I thought possible. The streams of Hun formations seemed endless and what with that and the attack on the Heinkels and seeing the bombing of the docks and the gas works go up and the BBC and controllers' exaltations I don't suppose I shall forget it.

Monday 9 September 1940

Overnight 120 British targets were bombed. Following a patrol Black claimed a He111 damaged. A new addition to 603 Squadron was the experienced New Zealander, Pilot Officer Keith Lawrence, who joined the Squadron from 234 Squadron at Leconfield where he had claimed their first victory on 8 July. Keith didn't fly an operational patrol with 603 until the 15th but made quite an immediate impact during what later became known as Battle of Britain Day. He plays down his contribution to the Squadron's success:

> My service with 603 at Hornchurch during the second fortnight in September 1940 can but qualify me as a part-time member of the Squadron with hardly even time to get to know the

regular members – Group Captain Bouchier, a cracking good station commander, our CO S/L Denholm, F/O Morton, P/O Dexter (South African) and of course fellow gate-crasher Sgt. Bill Bailey who was posted with me to 603 from 234 when the squadron returned to St Eval from Middle Wallop.

The efforts of the 603 pilots continued to receive recognition. Sheep Gilroy was awarded the DFC and P/O Bill Caister the DFM. Unfortunately, by that time he had been a PoW for a week.

There was only one engagement during the 9th. Around 16.30 hours a large-scale attack developed over south-east England involving an estimated 200 aircraft. After crossing the coast between Dungeness and North Foreland the raid headed north-west towards London. Twelve out of the 18 squadrons scrambled managed to intercept the enemy formations, including 603. The raid eventually petered out around 18.30.

603 were airborne between 16.55 and 18.30 and, out of a total of 32 destroyed, eight probably destroyed and ten damaged, against the loss of 12 Hurricanes and four Spitfires, they claimed three He111s destroyed, three more damaged, two Bf109s destroyed and a Do17 probable without loss to themselves. During the operation some interesting enemy radio traffic was intercepted:

I).   The control station of one group told bombers in the estuary 'If fighter defence too strong break off task at once' (17.14 hours).

II). A second control of another batch of bombers signalled 'If own fighter protection too weak, to break off task' (17.11 hours).

III). A third aircraft on ground station signalled '30 English fighters in estuary' (17.05 hours).

IV). A fourth control signalled to aircraft 'If fighter protection useless, return.'

Tuesday 10 September 1940
Enemy activity showed a marked decrease on previous days and was limited to small raids of single aircraft, most appearing to be reconnaissance patrols armed with bombs. Throughout the day, operating in sections of two or three, RAF fighter pilots were detailed to intercept with only 72 and 92 Squadrons managing to do so, claiming two destroyed and one probable. According to the 603 ORB P/O Peter Howes was posted to the Squadron from 234 Squadron when in fact he came from 54. Sergeant Pilot George 'Bill' Bailey also arrived at Hornchurch having been posted to 603 from 234 with Keith Lawrence. That night the bombing of British targets continued practically unopposed.

Wednesday 11 September 1940
Apart from a number of armed reconnaissance raids the day was quiet until 15.15 hours when a large-scale raid targeted the London riverside area (including Woolwich), Portsmouth and Southampton. Consisting of approximately 270 enemy aircraft the enemy tactics were to send a small force in advance to attack Dover and Deal and lure up the RAF fighters in the process, while a larger force proceeded to London. While this raid was in progress an attack on Portsmouth was carried out by 50-60 enemy aircraft. The raids continued until 16.45 with 21 squadrons ordered to intercept, all but two managing to do so. Later, between 18.00 and 18.45, a second attack was mounted on Dover and the shipping offshore (by 14 Ju87s) which 92 Squadron intercepted. An outstanding feature of the engagements on this day is that many more enemy bombers than fighters were destroyed, the ratio being 2:1.

603 Squadron were in action between 15.16-16.40 hours. The ORB reads:

12 aircraft left Rochford at 15.16 hours. At 28,000 feet over Rochford they joined up with 41 Squadron. When just south of London they saw a large formation of Me110's and He111's in vic's of five, vic's line astern at 20,000 feet going north. There were also some Bf109's above. No.41 Squadron dived to attack the bombers, followed by 603 in line astern. A dogfight ensued and the enemy formation turned south, dropping their bombs in open country over Kent. It was noticed that the Me110's had very pale yellow noses. There seemed to be fewer Me109's than usual, and they made no attempt to assist the bombers when attacked. The Me109's had yellow noses.

603 claimed one Do17 destroyed, one He111 probable and three more damaged, one Bf110 probable and another damaged. It was the familiar nucleus of 603 that was still knocking down the German fighters, and managing to stay alive. Those few had been joined by the latest influx of fresh blood who, in turn, were now being given the chance to prove themselves in battle.

P/O Jim 'John' MacPhail, (another one of the three new arrivals at Hornchurch during 31 August) claimed a He111 destroyed during this combat with what he perceived to be Bf109s, Ju88s and He111s:

P/O MacPhail.

> When on patrol with 603 Squadron and 41 Squadron I saw a large enemy bomber formation south of London moving in a north-westerly direction.
>
> The formation was protected by yellow-nosed Me109's. I dived on a He111 from its port beam. The enemy immediately took evasive action, turning sharply to its port and I was forced to break away to its rear. I saw my burst enter its fuselage.
>
> I climbed up and saw the enemy going southwards losing height. A Hurricane and Spitfire then dived and did stern attacks, one each, and the enemy turned to the right and I dived and did a head-on attack of two to three seconds, from a range of 150 yards to 50 yards, and saw tracer enter the centre of the fuselage. Two of the crew baled out, the wheels came down and the aircraft exploded on landing in the vicinity of Edenbridge. The crew landed in two fields slightly to the south-west of the aircraft. I received an A.P. bullet in the gun channel heater of my inner starboard gun.

MacPhail had been with A Flight and delivered his attack at 16.00 hours over the southern outskirts of London at an altitude of 22,000 feet. He fired bursts of three to four seconds. Brian Carbury was again successful when he claimed one He111 probable, which had last been seen with its wheels down and the starboard engine dead:

> I was flying Red 2, and our squadron joined up with 41 Squadron at 25,000 feet over Rochford. The two squadrons were vectored south-west and at 22,000 feet we sighted large formation of e/a below us. We went into line astern, 41 Squadron leading and peeled off.
>
> I attacked a stray He111K, stopped the starboard engine with one burst. The undercarriage fell out with the second, and the rear gunner baled out. Another burst made the port engine pour out white smoke. A short beam attack and a piece of the e/a fell away from the nose. I left as six Me110's formed a defensive circle around the e/a and went south.
>
> Out of oxygen, so landed at Hornchurch to refill and found only three guns in the starboard wing had fired, the rest had froze up. Returned to Rochford.

Brian Carbury had been with B Flight when he delivered his attack at 16.00 hours, south-east of London at 20,000 feet. He opened fire at 250 yards and closed to 50 yards during which time he fired a burst of three seconds which amounted to 210 rounds. The enemy aircraft consisted of: a Balbo of He111K and Ju88, escorted by Bf109, Bf110 and the fictitious 'He113'. Stapme Stapleton claimed one 110 probable, with both engines having been damaged:

> When patrolling with the squadron I saw a large Balbo of enemy aircraft approaching from the east. At that moment my oxygen gave out and I dived to 18,000 feet. Then I sighted a Me110 at 20,000 feet heading south-west.
>
> I did two beam attacks and damaged both engines. By this time I was over the coast at 15,000 feet. Glycol was streaming from both engines of the e/a but he was not losing much speed.
>
> After that engagement I came down to 4,000 feet over Dungeness. I sighted a Me109 at 2,000 feet heading for France. When he saw me he dived to 100 feet approximately and continued on a steady course. I caught up after five minutes of flying and gave it two long bursts from dead astern at 250 yards. Glycol issued from his radiator. By this time I could see the coast of France quite plainly, so I turned back.

Stapme delivered his attack at 16.25 hours initially south of London at an altitude of 20,000 feet. The enemy Balbo consisted of 100 Bf109s, 110s and He111s. He reflected on the dangers of getting in close:

> Closing to a range of 50 yards was not a problem if the enemy aircraft was a fighter, but closing to within 50 yards of a bomber was daunting. The enemy aircraft seemed massive, and if you opened fire and hit the bomber there was the risk of damage to your own aircraft from the large amount of debris that flew back at you.

Ras Berry also claimed a Bf110 damaged:

> Patrol over London at 28,000 feet, S/Ldr ordered line astern on sighting large Balbo of enemy aircraft – He111's, Ju88's, Me110's and Me109's. We peeled off and I dived onto a 110 which was in line astern with others. I fired two bursts into the fuselage of 110 and at close range saw bullets entering the fuselage. I broke off engagement, as my speed was then too great to hold position to fire.

Ras delivered his attack at 16.00 hours over south London from a range of 150 yards closing to 50 yards during which time he fired an eight second burst, expending 1,600 rounds of ammunition. Bill Read claimed a Bf110 damaged:

> I was patrolling in Guard section when enemy bomber formation was sighted. I did not dive to attack with the squadron, as I was well above them and seven Me109's arrived below me as I was about to dive. They climbed in line astern and I climbed as well, and they made off SW. I fired a short burst at the last one and then dived on the bombers. I executed a head-on attack from above on an escorting Me110. Just before I broke away, smoke was emitted from its starboard engine. I was travelling at high speed in the dive and did not observe further effect. I experienced no return fire from this aircraft, but I was right in the sun and probably my approach was not seen.

Bill Read's attack was delivered at 16.10 hours over south-west London. He opened fire, firing short bursts, from 400 yards closing to 100 yards expending 1,750 rounds. John Boulter claimed a He111 damaged 15 miles off Dungeness during the same patrol:

> At 15.16 hours 603 Sqn was ordered on patrol. After the initial engagement, I became detached from my squadron, and patrolled at approximately 20,000 feet between London and Dungeness.
> I saw a He111 proceeding south below me and dived towards it. As I approached, it was attacked by other friendly fighters; I joined in, and when I broke away after firing a burst of approximately two seconds, the e/a appeared to be losing height and brown smoke was coming from both engines.

Boulter delivered his attack at 16.10 hours at an altitude of 15,000 feet, 15 miles north-west of Dungeness. Pip Cardell claimed a He111 damaged during this patrol. He had now been flying on a regular basis since his first combat patrol in the south on 1 September:

> I saw a He111 going east, on which I made one stern attack, opening fire at 300 yards and closing to 40 yards. Then I did four quarter-attacks, when white smoke came from one of the engines. Having fired all my rounds, I broke off the attack.

Pip delivered his attack at 16.10 hours half a mile north of Margate at an altitude of 5,000 feet. The final claim on this day by a 603 pilot was for a He111, damaged by F/O Brian Macnamara:

> On sighting a large Balbo approaching London, the squadron formed line astern, peeling off and attacking the bombers. I found a lone Heinkel and attacked it from above and behind, slightly on the port quarter. After a prolonged burst I saw black smoke from the starboard engine. I broke away and again attacked from below and abeam, giving it a burst of three to four seconds. I was then forced to break away, as a number of other Heinkel's and some Me109's were firing at me.

Brian's attack was delivered at 16.00 hours at 15,000 feet south of London. He opened fire from 350 yards initially and closed to 100 yards firing a burst of six seconds, which expended approximately 1,500 rounds.

Having been discharged from hospital, Joey Sarre returned to Hornchurch where the welcome was not what he expected. Believing him to be dead, his colleagues thought they had been confronted by a ghost. He then returned to his billet to find his personal possessions had been packed up by the effects officer in preparation for sending home to his family. He then discovered his family had also been informed he was 'missing' in action. Until he made contact they believed him to be dead. The strain of battle on young Joey Sarre had been great and this latest experience pushed him almost to the limit. He knew only too well he had had more than his share of luck and his experiences had taken a severe toll. In an eight-day period, four of the Spitfires he had been flying were lost – Sarre having crash-landed twice, baled out twice. Four times he was convinced he was going to die, four times he had cheated death. He had reached breaking point.

Incredibly, at this late stage of the Battle of Britain, F/O Alen Wallace and the remainder of the 603 ground personnel, with all the maintenance equipment which had been left behind when the Squadron flew south on 27 August, finally left Turnhouse for the overnight journey to Hornchurch onboard a 'special train'.

Thursday 12 September 1940
The following message was sent to the sectors by the AOC, 11 Group in connection with the attack on the London area the previous day:

> The Group Commander sends congratulations to all Squadrons on their magnificent fighting this afternoon resulting in the breaking up of the heavy attack on London and aircraft factories in the suburbs. Of 21 squadrons despatched 19 squadrons intercepted and engaged the enemy inflicting heavy losses, thanks to the excellent team work between squadrons working in pairs and to the efficient work of Sector operations staff most of whom are working under very difficult conditions.

The day's activities consisted of single aircraft carrying out armed reconnaissance missions over south-east England. Interceptions resulted in the shooting down of one aircraft with two others damaged.

On the 12th Ken Macdonald wrote what turned out to be his last letter to Mardi from his room in the mess at Hornchurch. It provides an insight into his mental state at that time. Many of the 603 pilots are remembered as men who seemed so out of place fighting a war. Ken is a classic example of this:

> Darling…,
> Thank you from the bottom of my heart for your letters and the books. The latter only arrived five minutes ago – I read the 'first one' – it is wonderful. The only trouble about reading anything of this sort these days is that it all makes me want to live and revel right in… this beautiful natural world to such an overwhelming extent that it makes the uncertainty of this side-tracked hemmed-in existence scarcely bearable. Reading poetry reminds you of what else there is in life and makes you see the war in its proper perspective – but right now looking out of the windows at green fields, hills and trees which are unreachable and seeing heavenly paths winding into distant forbidden lands seems to make this prison almost more than I can reasonably stand.
> It is easier to limit one's mind to the Daily Mirror, punk gramophone records, what's for lunch and whether one's aeroplane is flying straight… although this may be easier, it is obviously futile and if one does so, we might as well be dead. So we have to go on and 'live' life to the hilt in books, music and poetry even if what that all means is a bit off the map at present… So thanks for all these things. I read them and they do me good – when I can take them.
> …A good joke happened here half an hour ago: The civilian sirens went round here. The Station loud-speakers announced (as they often do) 'There is absolutely no need for Station personnel to take cover.' Within ten seconds there was a deafening 'Wheeeeeee-ooo-wump! Wump! Wump! And everyone in the mess crawled under the tables and chairs while three

bombs dropped alongside the aerodrome. Immediately afterwards the loud-speakers announced 'Sorry about that everyone, sorry!'

Friday 13 September 1940
Heavy night bombing continued and one He111 was destroyed during the early hours by 25 Squadron. The raids on the 13th numbered 75, mostly by single aircraft whose pilots made good use of the cloud cover to evade attack as they flew over the coast between Winchelsea and Dungeness. Thirty interceptions were ordered with contact made by four fighter squadrons resulting in one He111 destroyed and one He111 and two Ju88s damaged. George Denholm received notification that Robin Rafter, reported 'missing' on 5 September, had been seriously wounded but was safe in West Kent Hospital, Maidstone.

Saturday 14 September 1940
During the morning and early afternoon many raids by single aircraft were carried out with four being intercepted. At 15.20 the first big attack of the day developed when approximately 200 bombers and fighters crossed the south-east coast between 15,000 and 20,000 feet, and headed north-west towards the outskirts of west London. Seventeen squadrons were ordered to intercept, only five managed to do so.

At 15.28 hours, 12 Spitfires of 603 Squadron took off and joined 222 Squadron over Rochford. At 24,000 feet, just south of Hornchurch, they spotted a large number of Bf109s above them in line astern at 28,000 feet. The 109s did not attack and, unclear as to what tactics to adopt, the pilots of 603 and 222 formed defensive circles. Occasionally, individual aircraft from 603 peeled off to attack stray 109s. Carbury, Boulter and Macnamara each claimed a 109 destroyed. Bolster shot down Bf109E-1, 3854, of I/JG77, flown by Feldwebel Ettler on a freelance fighter sortie over Kent which the Londoner witnessed belly-land in a field at Long Barn Farm, Boxley Hill, near Detling at 16.30 hours. Ettler was captured unhurt.

A second attack of approximately 200 aircraft developed between 17.55 and 19.00 and at 17.55 crossed the coast between Dover and Dungeness. One raid of 60 aircraft penetrated the IAZ, two others flew to Maidstone and Gravesend, while approximately 90 enemy aircraft remained in the area over east Kent. 603 Squadron was one of 19 squadrons sent up to intercept of which eight were successful. 603 was not one of them. An 11 Group Intelligence Bulletin for pilots reads:

603 Squadron on patrol 14/9/40 in company with 222 squadron sighted a formation of yellow nosed Me.109's in line abreast above them. The E/A went into line astern but did not attack. Later about 12 Me.109's in vics with white noses and white wing tips passed underneath them. About 5 He.113's were seen in the line astern and one pilot thinks there was an irregular white mark on the wing-tip of one of them.

Boulter once again claimed a 109 destroyed ten miles south-west of Maidstone.

By the end of the day the fighter pilots of 11 Group were credited with 14 enemy aircraft destroyed with two probables and ten damaged for the loss of one pilot confirmed killed with two others missing.

Pilot Officer John Soden was posted to 603 from 266 Squadron at RAF Wittering. That evening, in the comfort of his room, Ken Macdonald wrote to his sister:

I am afraid I cannot really encourage any hope for Don – no one actually saw him for certain go down, but we were attacked by surprise on our first engagement down here, and at least one Spitfire was seen to go down. I don't feel so terribly glum about it though – I feel mortified that he had so little chance – a lot was against him that day and in several ways he was terribly unlucky – but he enjoyed himself thoroughly right up to the last minute – it was marvellous being with him and now we are left without the warmest laughter we ever basked in – but that is our loss and not his.

How are you and Iona? And Wendy? [Ken's young nieces]. Write and tell me all about them. They are the ones that count these days.

In this letter Ken also writes about his brother-in-law, Bobbie, and Denstead, Ewen and Bobbie's farm in Kent, run by his parents while he was in service:

…I have several times gone and beaten him up on the way from a battle – but have never managed to spot him. Also I usually go and have a look at Denstead – just to keep an eye on it for you – it needs some weeding I think – just as peaceful as ever though. Were you at home on the 31st August? I bagged a Heinkel 113 (their 'Spitfire') [actually a Bf109] which crashed not very far west of Denstead – it dawned on me after that you might have been at home at the time.

We are having a fairly hectic time it can be fairly truthfully said – absolutely no time for anything.

We are standing-by from dawn till dusk at an instant's call every day. At nights we get bombed on and off regularly but so far pretty inaccurately, and they put out all the lights on the Station whenever there is something around – it is impossible to read or write or even shave or bath or anything. Today has, thank heaven, been wet and murky – so, except for a sudden patrol at 6.45 a.m. for an hour and a half – it has been fairly quiet (and this was to have been Der Tag!!).* We have been here three weeks now and I haven't set foot outside the Station. All the same it is all damned good fun and I thoroughly enjoy myself and feel pretty good – the only thing that gets me is this absolutely ceaselessly being chivvied-about and never being able to have one minute's relaxation to read a book in. About three days ago they moved our headquarters etc here [Hornchurch] from Turnhouse with which we now no longer have any connections whatever. We have 'moved in' here lock stock and barrel – presumably for the duration – or our duration! We have quite a few new pilots – in fact George (who has now twice had to descend gracefully on his 'brolly' – yesterday from Hastings being his last time), Morton, Jack Haig and I are the only ones operating at present whom you know of. Ian Ritchie, Sheep and Dudley Stewart-Clark are OK but in hospital.

On the whole though we have been doing not too badly and getting quite a good bag. The shooting this season is, as you will have gathered, excellent. They come over in 'Balbo's' of 50-70 bombers at once with clouds of fighters buzzing round them like flies – a sight well worth seeing and most impressive. But they don't like Spitfires and you can see their flesh creeping when they fight us. Also when we first got here we always seemed to be the only British Squadron in England and never saw anything but Huns by the hundred. But recently the sky is full of other Spitfires and Hurricanes – and this morning above the clouds we ran into 5 Squadrons of Spitfires – but no Hun – most comforting though and we all felt extraordinarily brave! The most amazing Squadrons are the Poles – and then come the Czechs. The Poles now fly Hurricanes and absolutely annihilate the Hun – it is all they live for and whereas we look on the whole business much as a day's shooting – to them it is their religion. They are charming chaps – tough as hell and think nothing of chasing the Hun from here to Paris and shooting them down there. They really are incredible – so are the Czechs. A Czech Squadron Leader's aeroplane was shot down in flames and he baled out from 300 feet above ground. He was aged 42. He came straight here and was quite annoyed when we wouldn't supply him with another aeroplane as he wanted to go and shoot some more down. He eventually phoned his own Squadron and demanded them to bring him one at once. Which they did and off he went again after the last staggering Hun, disappearing homeward!

I have led the Squadron several times when George has been brollying and so on – and, although I had a little to do with it, I was leading all through what was the record day to-date when we bagged 16 and lost none. I find the war at fairly close quarters encouraging. We have to fear Hitler, absolutely.

Ewen – write again sometime – letters are my only link with the outside world – I live for the postman – lots of love to you, Iona and Wendy, and Robbie (tell him to look out for me).

Ken is a little franker about his true feelings in his letters to Mardi (he tends to paint a softer picture in his letters home, perhaps in the hope he would lessen their concern). Nevertheless, this letter to his sister shows his indomitable spirit and provides a wonderful insight into the mind of a Battle of Britain pilot at the height of the conflict. Although he is tired, during the following 13 days, an immense amount of time in the scheme of things, his level of fatigue increased to mental and physical exhaustion. Nevertheless, his spirit remained right to the end.

*As this letter remained in his room throughout the following day, he added the bracketed comment before posting it.

Chapter 11

BATTLE OF BRITAIN DAY
SUNDAY 15 SEPTEMBER 1940

The air defence of this country can be finally assured only by victory over the enemy, and conversely it can only finally fail in our defeat.

Dowding

There were three major attacks during the day and 603 Squadron were involved in two. The first attack developed between 11.00 and 12.30 when two enemy formations headed towards London and the second between 14.00 and 15.30 hours. The third attack took place against Southampton between 17.45 and 18.30 hours and was a much smaller raid. Throughout the day 21 squadrons were involved in interceptions.

The 15th started misty but soon cleared leaving a little light cumulus at 2-3,000 feet. The bright sunshine provided ideal conditions for the German bombers.

At 10.50 the coastal RDF stations began to detect vast numbers of German aircraft forming up above their airfields on the other side of the Channel. RAF squadrons had been strategically deployed in advance of the attack. Churchill visited 11 Group's operations room and witnessed the build-up. The lights on the board indicated that 16 fighter squadrons had been ordered to intercept the enemy force of approximately 120 enemy aircraft which had crossed the English coast at 11.35 between Dungeness and North Foreland where the attack had split into two parts (15,000 and 26,000 feet) one headed straight for the Thames dock area, the other for west London. Churchill later wrote:

> These air battles on which so much depended, lasted little more than an hour from the first encounter. The enemy had ample strength to send out new waves of attack, and our Squadrons, having gone all out to gain the upper air, would have to refuel after seventy or eighty minutes, or land to re-arm after a five minute engagement. If at this moment of re-fuelling or re-arming, the enemy were able to arrive with fresh, unchallenged Squadrons, some of our fighters could be destroyed on the ground... Presumably, the red bulbs showed that the majority of our Squadrons were engaged...
>
> I became conscious of the anxiety of the Commander, who now stood still behind his subordinate's chair. Hitherto, I had watched in silence. I now asked, 'What other reserves have we?' 'There are none,' said Air Vice-Marshal Park.

Fifteen were successful in intercepting the enemy raiders. Scrambled at 11.20, 603 engaged the enemy between Dungeness and Dover. Uncle George fired a short burst at a 109, which emitted glycol and dived into a small cloud. He followed, firing another short burst and the Bf109E of 3/JG53 landed in the sea at 12.05. The pilot, Oberfeldwebel Alfred Muller, was wounded and taken prisoner. P/O Jim McPhail attacked a 109 which went down into a wood south of Detling. Ras Berry also claimed success when he shot down a 109 which crashed into the sea. Tannoy Read attacked a formation of what he described as Dornier 215s, which were actually Do17s, an almost identical aircraft. The engine of the trailing bomber began to smoke and dropped out of formation. Owing to the speed of his approach, Read overshot the target and did not see it again. The German bomber formation was harried all the way to London and dropped bombs at random on the capital, two of which fell in the grounds of Buckingham Palace damaging the Queen's private apartments.

Fortunately, the Royal Family was not in residence. As the bombers turned and retreated they were still chased and attacked by RAF fighters. The 603 pilots landed at 12.30 when the ground crews, not knowing how soon the next sortie would occur, swarmed all over the Spitfires, hastily going about their respective tasks with a level of dedication which was admired by the pilots as much then as it is today.

A second large attack developed between 14.00 and 15.30 hours and involved 230-250 aircraft. Crossing the coast between Hastings and Dover the enemy formation headed for London. A small part of the formation penetrated IAZ. Twenty RAF squadrons were ordered to intercept and all were successful with help from 602 Squadron and one aircraft of the Station Defence Flight, RAF Northolt. At 14.09, 603 were ordered into the air for the second time. The intelligence report reads:

> 13 aircraft took off to join 41 Squadron, which they did not meet. When at 21,000 feet ten miles south east of Chatham they saw about 200 Me109's and 110's making smoke trails at 18,000 feet, and under them about 15-20 He111's in vic's of five [at 20,000 feet], also another formation to the south. One pilot saw two formations of Do17's, 20 in each, unescorted, flying towards Biggin Hill, the leader of the second formation was white on the undersurfaces. An He111 was seen to land at Dishforth with three red bars on the upper surfaces of its wings.

Jim MacPhail and Sgt Bill Bailey each claimed 109s destroyed. Bailey's crashed south of Maidstone:

> When on patrol with 603 squadron SE of Maidstone, I saw a large formation of enemy aircraft. The squadron attacked and after I lost the squadron. I then engaged a Me109 south of Sheerness, which was flying south at 8,000 feet at about 180 m.p.h. I gave him a burst of about two seconds from dead astern and he immediately left a large column of smoke and fell through the clouds and I saw him crash south of Sittingbourne.

Bailey was flying with A Flight and delivered his attack at 15.00 hours. He opened fire from a range of 200 yards closing to 150 yards during which time he fired 480 rounds in a two second burst. The aircraft he had shot down was a Bf109E of I/JG53; the pilot Unteroffizer Schersand was killed. Bailey survived the war. P/O Keith Lawrence now claimed his first successes with 603, six days after his arrival at Hornchurch. An impressive start it was too: one Bf109 destroyed and two more damaged:

> As Yellow 2 on patrol with 603 Squadron, I went in to attack with the squadron a formation of approximately 30 Do17's and He111's 3,000 feet below. Due to the awkward approach and excessive speed on reaching the bombers, I pulled up to engage the Me109's coming down, one of which I chased and opened fire at 75 yards, and after about six seconds, and having closed to about 30 yards, it went up steeply and then fell away in a spin and was still spinning on entering the cloud. The 109 lost control at about 18,000 feet. I used the remainder of my ammunition on two Me109's which dived into the clouds. Range in both cases approximately 30 yards.

Keith's ability to get in close before opening fire was sure to bring some success. He was flying with A Flight when he delivered his attack at 14.50 hours, at a height of 20,000 feet, south-east of Maidstone. He expended 2,800 rounds of ammunition. His aircraft was also hit, although he was unaware of this until he returned to Hornchurch. As he climbed out of the cockpit at dispersal his rigger carried out a quick inspection of his charge before announcing in his broad Scottish accent: 'Look at this!' and pointed excitedly at a number of bullet holes in both wings.

Stapme Stapleton claimed one Do17 destroyed in the same combat. The aircraft was a Do17Z (3405) of 9/KG2 which crashed into the sea five miles north-east of Herne Bay at 15.15 hours. It had been on a sortie to bomb St Katherine Docks in London when it had been intercepted by Stapme and Pilot Officer B. Pattullo of 46 Squadron. During the attack its starboard engine had been severely damaged and the crew ditched the bomb load before crashing into the sea. Stapme reported:

P/O Keith Lawrence.

When patrolling with my squadron, I sighted 25 He111's and 50 Me109's. While diving to attack, I found myself going too fast to pull out on the enemy, so I continued my dive. About ten minutes later, I sighted two Me109's in light vic. I fired two deflection bursts at one and glycol streams came from his radiator. They dived into the cloud.

Later I saw one Do17 over the Thames estuary heading for the clouds. I did several beam attacks and he dived to 100 feet. He flew very low indeed and pancaked on the sea five miles NW of Ramsgate. I experienced no return fire.

Stapme recorded the time of his attack as being 14.50 hours, ten miles south of Chatham at an altitude of 20,000 feet and he fired 2,800 rounds. On his return to base he noticed a Do17 that had 'pancaked' on the sea in the Thames estuary and the crew were in the process of clambering out. Stapme saw a British convoy entering the estuary about five miles away and attempted to gain their attention as to the plight of the German airmen. As he got closer, the convoy opened fire on him, and he responded by promptly returning to base!

Ras Berry claimed a Bf109 probable, last seen in an uncontrollable dive with black smoke, and a Do17 destroyed, although he admits that the Dornier was also being attacked by others prior to him apparently finishing the German off:

The squadron was patrolling over Rochford at 22,000 feet. I sighted large numbers of fighters, Me109's, above and several vic's of three of He111's below. The squadron went into line astern and peeled off onto the bombers. As I dived I saw a Me109 attacking a Spitfire. I immediately split round and came on the 109's tail and at point blank range fired a long burst. The 109 with heavy smoke pouring out, went into a vertical dive into heavy cloud. Whilst patrolling around land over Southend, I sighted a Do17 homeward bound. A Hurricane and Spitfire approached me. We all attacked in turn. I gave a long burst on starboard engine with success, as I had to break away with oil all over my windscreen from the enemy aircraft. The enemy aircraft then glided down and pancaked in a field on the Isle of Sheppey. The crew of three climbed out and the aircraft began to burn slightly.

The crew of Do17Z-3, 2881 (Unteroffizier Wien, Feldwebel von Goertz, Gefreiter Schild and Gefreiter Weymar) were all captured. Ras delivered his attack at 15.00 hours ten miles south of Chatham, at a height of 18,000 feet. According to his combat report he fired an eight second burst from 100 yards and two bursts of two and four seconds respectively on the Dornier, closing to 50 yards, expending all his 2,800 rounds.

It is possible that Brian Carbury shot down the Bf109E-4 of Stab I/JG77 flown by Oberleutnant Herbert Kunze. The 109 crashed into a dyke near Stuttfall castle, Lympne, at 15.30. The pilot was killed and buried in the cemetery at RAF Hawkinge. Brian Macnamara claimed a Do17 damaged, having observed hits to the rudder and starboard engine:

After becoming separated from the squadron, I hung about the estuary for stragglers. I soon saw AA fire from the Isle of Sheppey and saw a Dornier just emerging from cloud. I carried out a stern chase and saw my incendiaries hitting his starboard engine and very soon black smoke came from it and the aircraft, which was steering east, started turning towards the Essex coast. I had to break away, as I had run out of ammunition and was troubled by heavy AA fire. I did not see what happened to the Dornier. Throughout this attack I was troubled by heavy AA fire, which did not cease despite the fact that I had commenced an attack on the enemy, and shells were continually bursting very close to my aircraft.

Macnamara delivered this attack at 14.45 hours over the estuary just east of Southend at a height of 10,000 feet. He opened fire at a range of 200 yards and closed to 150 yards in which time he had fired two bursts of eight and four seconds respectively expending 2,000 rounds. Uncle George had survived having been shot down on a number of occasions. He had also claimed his share of German aircraft. During this combat he claimed two Do17s damaged:

I attacked an He111 with a two second burst, diving from astern, then I fired a short burst at a Me109 but observed no results. Some time later I saw an unescorted formation of Do17's over the coast and made a diving frontal 1/4 attack on the port flank of the formation from out of the sun. I fired a short burst and dived through the formation and turned to make an astern attack. I saw the two Do17's at which I had fired lagging behind the formation, emitting black smoke. I was then fired at and flames started to come through my instrument panel which was broken, so I baled out.

George delivered his attack at 15.00 hours south-east of Maidstone at a height of 18,000 feet. His own aircraft R7019 was destroyed when it crashed on Warren Farm, Fairlight, near Hastings. He landed by parachute near Guestling Lodge. At 14.55 hours, while Uncle George was about to deliver his initial attack on the German Messerschmitt, Peter Pease was diving to attack enemy Heinkel 111 bombers of KG26 that had just dropped their bombs on targets in the West Ham area of London and were on their way back across the Kent countryside. The bombers had had a relatively easy run so far with the loss of just one aircraft that had been forced to break formation due to engine trouble and had been finished off by the RAF fighters. Their escorting fighters had driven off any other attempt to break through to the bombers. Such was Peter's determination to press his attack home that he neglected the defence of his own aircraft and was shot down by 109s south-east of Maidstone shortly after 15.00 hours. No RAF pilot saw his demise, however, it was witnessed by the Heinkel bomber crews and one in particular, Leutnant Roderich Cescotti, who later gave his memories of the attack on his own aircraft by one lone Spitfire:

> A few Tommies succeeded in penetrating our fighter escort, I saw a Spitfire dive steeply through our escort, level out and close rapidly on our formation. It opened fire, from ahead and to the right, and its tracers streaked towards us. At that moment a Me109, which we had not seen before, appeared behind the Spitfire and we saw its rounds striking the Spitfire's tail. But the Tommy continued his attack, coming straight for us, and his rounds slashed into our aircraft. We could not return the fire for fear of hitting the Messerschmitt. I put my left arm across my face to protect it from the plexiglass splinters flying around the cockpit, holding the controls with my right hand. With only the thin plexiglass between us, we were eye to eye with the enemy's eight machine guns. At the last moment the Spitfire pulled up and passed very close over the top of us. Then it rolled onto its back, as though out of control, and went down steeply, trailing black smoke. Waggling its wings, the Messerschmitt swept past us and curved in for another attack. The action lasted only a few seconds, but it demonstrated the determination and bravery with which the Tommies were fighting over their own country.
>
> Fortunately nobody was hurt, and although both engines had taken hits they continued to run smoothly. Ice-cold air blasted through the holes in the plexiglass. So the navigator, with more bravery than circumspection, opened his parachute pack and cut off pieces of silk which he used to block the holes. It was his first operational sortie and I suppose he thought he ought to do something heroic.

Despite over 30 hits on his aircraft, Cescotti's Heinkel was not seriously damaged and the pilot was able to maintain formation and get home. The flaming Spitfire with Peter still onboard dived into the ground at Kingswood near Chartway Street, south-east of Maidstone in Kent at 15.07 hours. The descent of the Spitfire was witnessed prior to the crash and the fighter was described as being very much alight with a large flaming hole at one wing root. Peter's body was removed from the wreckage and carried to a nearby shed until the undertakers arrived. The flaming pyre had caused some concern as the nearby field contained a cereal crop and could have easily ignited.*

---

*In August 1990, 50 years after Peter had been killed, local aviation artist Geoff Nutkins and his father, Frank, of the Shoreham Preservation Society carried out a dig of the site. The depth of the dig was to 12 feet and much of Peter's Spitfire was discovered and is now on display at a number of venues including the Nutkins' Shoreham Aviation Museum. The engine however, was not found and is thought to be still at the site. Amongst the many items discovered were cartridges which had exploded in the fire and pieces of parachute. In July 1991 a plaque and kneeler were placed in Broomfield Church and Sir Richard Pease [Peter's younger brother] and Denise Patterson [née Maxwell-Woosnam, Peter's fiancée in 1940] came to the dedication. It was Denise's first visit to the crash site and was a moving occasion. Peter's presence was felt by some of those at the church service, including Denise. The shed where Peter's body was taken after the crash has only recently been knocked down.

Peter was initially reported missing, then reported killed on 17 September. Official confirmation of his death came on 13 November. His body was eventually returned to his home in Yorkshire for burial in the family plot at St Michael and All Angels at Middleton Tyas. He was 22 and had been engaged to Denise Maxwell-Woosnam, to whom Richard Hillary dedicated his book, *The Last Enemy*, in which Peter, Denise and Colin Pinckney feature prominently. It was Denise who thought of the title believing 'It was Peter speaking to us.'

Peter had been a member of the Tory squirearchy, the family seat being Richmond, Yorkshire, and had been in his third year at Trinity College, Cambridge, when war broke out. His beliefs in his country, his society and his place within it were firm and secure and he was prepared to risk his life for them. Beneath his surface shyness he was well aware of the privileged life into which he had been born. It was accepted that he had the mental ability, the self-discipline and the inclination to follow a career of his choice in the diplomatic service. He is remembered as being modest, shy and utterly conventional. The Pease family had lost their dearly loved eldest son-and-heir and Richard Hillary and Colin Pinckney had lost a dear friend.

The afternoon he died, Denise had been with a group of her girls at prayer in a church in Vange. On hearing the sound of Merlin engines in the sky outside she glanced at one of the windows and saw a number of Spitfires pass by. She caught a fleeting glimpse of the code on the fuselage of one of the fighters. It was XT-B, carrying Peter on his last patrol although she wasn't to hear the terrible news for some days: 'I was on duty at Vange but so many planes came down all the time that nobody had any track: it was nearly a fortnight before I got a telegram from his parents, asking me to come to his funeral. That was the first I'd heard. One's world had ended.'*

By the end of 15 September 603 had accounted for four Bf109s destroyed, two more probably destroyed and one damaged, two Dornier Do17s destroyed and two more damaged. They had lost one pilot killed and two aircraft destroyed. Pip Cardell was granted four days leave and left the Station. He travelled home along the Great North Road to visit his family at Great Paxton. John Boulter's experience, leadership and skill was rewarded with promotion to flight lieutenant and command of A Flight.

Today, 15 September is celebrated as 'Battle of Britain Day' not because it was the day on which RAF fighters shot down the greatest number of German aircraft, for it was not, but because the loss of 56 aircraft was decisive in persuading Hitler to postpone plans for an invasion. Having been confronted by over 250 fighter aircraft flown with determination and courage, the morale of the Luftwaffe aircrews was suffering and they had seen no indication that the RAF had been on its last legs, despite what their own hierarchy had publicised. Overall, German losses for the day were substantial, although not nearly as high as claimed by RAF pilots at the time. But, significantly, the Luftwaffe crews and their commanders, also prone to extreme over-claiming, realised that Fighter Command was still a powerful force to contend with and was still capable of decimating daylight attacks by German bomber formations.

Hermann Göring, the sycophantic Reichskommissionar of aviation, forestry *and* hunting, as well as being the head of the Luftwaffe, treated the latter like his own personal air force with deputies Ernet Udet who, in 1935, had taken Stapme for his first flight, and Erhard Milch as his personal servants. When the fighting in the Battle of Britain was at its peak, his simple arithmetic led him to believe the RAF had almost totally run out of fighters, overlooking the fact that British production of fighter aircraft turned out twice as many new aircraft as the German factories – a vital factor in the defeat of the Luftwaffe in the Battle of Britain. Hitler was inclined to express disappointment with anything less than total success and so Göring made matters worse for himself in the process, by exaggerating the achievements of his air force in order to appease his Führer.

---

*Following Peter's death Richard Hillary and Denise found comfort in each other's company. Richard fell in love with Denise and wanted romance. His mother, who she knew as 'Marmee', treated her like a daughter. However, it was not to be. Emotionally she 'went into deep freeze' for several years before meeting the man she married. According to Denise: 'Richard was a born writer. Every paragraph, even in his letters, leapt into vivid life. And for my grandchildren it was required reading at school. It has a spiritual dimension. It stirs people.'

CHAPTER 12

THE MANY AND THE FEW

Monday 16 September 1940

Overnight there were three successful interceptions of enemy bombers resulting in two being destroyed and two more probably destroyed.

Just after 07.00 hours an attacking force of 200-250 enemy aircraft crossed the coast between Dungeness and North Foreland and continued towards London and the Thames docks. Twelve squadrons, including 603, were ordered to intercept but due to the amount of cloud only 17 and 222 managed to do so. From 10.45 onwards all raids consisted of single aircraft only and crossed the coast at various points between Dover and Shoreham-by-Sea dropping bombs indiscriminately. Raids had failed to reach the IAZ until 13.00 when they managed to penetrate and bomb south-east London. From 15.00 enemy activity dwindled due mainly to the poor weather conditions. From 16.30 activity was mainly single aircraft raids against targets in the Kent area. No contact was made by fighters sent up to intercept.

By now the Squadron had been at Hornchurch for three weeks and George Denholm was feeling the effects of fatigue: 'I have lost count of the number of times we have gone up to engage the enemy. It has certainly been the most crowded three weeks of our lives.' P/O Peter Dexter, who had already flown in action with the Squadron, was officially posted to 603 from 54 Squadron. Dexter, an experienced pilot, had already been awarded the DFC for his service during the battle of France. He provided experience in the face of recent losses and was in action the next day.

Tuesday 17 September 1940

Although the British were not aware of it at the time, Hitler had realised that obtaining air supremacy over England would be very difficult if not impossible. On this day he postponed Operation Sealion and reports reaching the War Cabinet indicated that invasion seemed less imminent and the invasion alert was relaxed to second level.

During the morning enemy activity had been minimal over the 11 Group area. Single aircraft were plotted over Kent and the Channel and several patrols of one, two or three aircraft were despatched to intercept. Only one was successfully carried out. At 14.30 a number of raids appeared off Cap Gris Nez and circled for half an hour before approaching the Kent coast. Of a force of 260 enemy aircraft 180 crossed the coastline and headed for London while the remainder stayed over the Channel. Nineteen squadrons were ordered to intercept of which four were successful, including 603 Squadron.

At 15.15 hours 12 Spitfires of 603 Squadron took off from Rochford and joined up with 41 Squadron. The ORB provides details of the pilots and aircraft flown: F/L Macdonald (X4259), F/O Haig (P9553), F/O Boulter (N3267), P/O Lawrence (X4394), P/O Read (P9440), P/O Morton (R6836), P/O Stapleton (X4348), P/O Soden (P9499), P/O Berry (X4347), P/O Howes (X4323), P/O Dexter (X4274), and Sgt Bailey (K9803).

At 25,000 feet over Chatham they saw a large number of 109s. Stapme attacked one which began leaking glycol and broke formation waggling its wings. As more 109s came in to attack, Stapme broke off his attack. Ras quickly appreciated the value of pairs as a fighting unit. Having sighted 109s he singled out one for attack and called on John Boulter to cover him. He opened fire and the aircraft began to smoke and dived down to sea level. Boulter then joined in the attack himself and although the 109 landed in the sea off Ramsgate, Ras and Bolster were only credited with half a probable each. P/O Soden claimed a third 109 probably destroyed. The pilots landed at 16.10. Ras flew four sorties that day.

The Squadron now received confirmation that the body of the pilot found in the wreckage of the Spitfire at Kingswood was Peter Pease. Sheep Gilroy was discharged from King George Hospital, Ilford.

Wednesday 18 September 1940
Night bomber operations by the Luftwaffe against British targets began almost as soon as dusk had fallen and as the night phase ended the early morning reconnaissance began prior to what amounted to four major attacks, all of which centred on Kent and the Thames estuary. At 09.00 hours a force of 100 enemy aircraft crossed the Kent coast between Dover and North Foreland before splitting up and heading towards London. 603 Squadron were one of 13 sent up to intercept. Only five managed to do so and as a result of the ensuing engagements one aircraft was claimed destroyed, six probables and five damaged for the loss of one pilot, who happened to be from 603.

The Squadron were ordered up at 09.08 hours. The pilots were: S/L Denholm (X4415), F/L Macdonald (X4259), F/O Haig (P9553), P/O Morton (X4347), P/O Read (P9440), P/O Lawrence (X4394), P/O Stapleton (X4348), P/O Howes (X4323), P/O Soden (P9499), and Sgt Bailey (K9803). The ORB reads:

> Ten aircraft left Rochford and joined up with 41 Squadron. When over Maidstone at 25,000 feet, 41 Squadron dived to attack something which 603 did not see. 603 then saw Me109's above them and also two vic's of five Me109's 2,000 feet below them. A dogfight ensued when the squadron dived to attack the lower formation. One pilot when attacking a Me109 at 28,000 feet, saw six Me109's on his tail. He dived and only three of them followed him to 10,000 feet and then went back to France.

George Denholm claimed a damaged 109:

> I saw two vic's of five Me109's pass at 20,000 feet underneath us and ordered the squadron to attack. We dived down. The Me109 which I picked out did one or two circles and then dived for home. I fired 1,600 rounds at it at ranges of about 150 yards and lost it in a layer of cloud, when he was emitting black smoke and not flying very fast.

George's attack was delivered at 09.45 hours at 23,000 feet over Maidstone. Shortly after Uncle George had seen the damaged 109 make good his escape, Peter Howes was shot down by 109s of Stab JG/26 and/or III/JG53. His Spitfire crashed at Kennington, near Ashford, at 09.50 with the 21-year-old still in the cockpit. 11 Group intelligence report No.58 provides further details of Peter's death:

> 603 squadron, on patrol with 41 squadron, at 25,000 feet over Maidstone were attacked from above and out of the sun by 30-40 Me.109's in no set formation. One pilot was dived upon by 6 Me.109's, three of which stayed above while the other three followed him down to 10,000 feet.

Peter Howes and Richard Hillary had been good friends, having been at Trinity together, and both having joined the OUAS and gone through each stage of their training at the same time. After converting to Spitfires at 5 OTU, Aston Down, Peter was posted to 54 Squadron, at Rochford, on 8 July. Like Richard, Peter could speak German, and during his time with 54 Squadron at Hornchurch he was called upon to translate for a captured German pilot. Al Deere wrote in his book *Nine Lives*:

> There was a surprise in store for us that evening when we returned to the mess, in the person of a Luftwaffe bomber pilot, who had crash-landed and was under escort in the writing-room. He had made a forced landing not far from the airfield and, together with a crew of three NCO's, had been brought to Hornchurch for safe custody. Full of curiosity to get a look at this specimen of Hitler's Aryan elite and, if nothing else, to poke faces at him, we hurried into the writing-room to be met by a rather small, dark and jack-booted officer who gave us a most haughty look as if to say, 'You can stare, but my turn will come.' Through the medium of P/O Peter Howe (sic), a squadron pilot who spoke German, we learned that the officer was in no way alarmed at his predicament and, indeed had assured Howe that Hitler would be in

London within two weeks. He didn't expect to remain a prisoner for long and for this reason thought it necessary to carry only toilet requisites in the event of being shot down!.....The cockiness of this German pilot certainly had the opposite effect from that which he had hoped to convey. To those of us who were feeling low and near breaking point it was like a shot of adrenaline, and with a rejuvenated spirit we faced the next day.

By the time Richard Hillary arrived at Hornchurch with 603, Peter had already been with 54 at the aerodrome for some time. He was physically and mentally exhausted. With so little experience and with the action being so frantic he struggled to survive against the odds. He was also very unhappy with his lack of success. Perhaps it was this disappointment or his response to an official circular that on 11 September he was sent from 54 to 234 Squadron at Middle Wallop, before being sent to 603 at Hornchurch. One week later he was dead. Despite being initially unhappy at having his plans for the future interrupted by the war, he had committed himself passionately to fighting the Germans. His remains were taken to the Woking (St.John's) Crematorium in Surrey.

During the same combat patrol in which Peter Howes was killed, Sgt Bill Bailey landed back at base with the fuselage of his Spitfire K9803 badly damaged by a 20mm cannon shell incurred during combat over Maidstone at 10.00 hours. The pilots drifted back to the aerodrome between 10.20 and 10.31.

The next attack occurred between 12.15 and 13.30 hours when a number of raids totalling approximately 250 aircraft crossed the Kent coast and headed towards London. Bombs were reported to have been dropped on Worthing, Gillingham and Hoo although this attack was believed to be 'tip and run'. There were also a few isolated raids in the Harwich area. At 12.25 hours 603 were ordered into the air. Eleven Spitfires took off from Rochford and consisted of S/L Denholm (X4415), F/L Macdonald (X4259), F/O Haig (P9553), F/O Boulter (R3267), P/O Berry (X4274), P/O Morton (X4347), P/O Read (P9440), P/O Stapleton (X4348), P/O Soden (P9499), P/O Dexter (R6836), and P/O Lawrence (X4394).

Whilst south-east of Kenley and still attempting to reach 25,000 feet they saw six 109s heading north-west. The 603 pilots continued to climb in order to achieve the advantage before attacking out of the sun. The Luftwaffe pilots then went into a gentle dive before forming a defensive circle but then dispersed almost immediately 'showing little fight or ability.' Ken Macdonald attacked one of the fighters which, in an attempt to shake him off, dived vertically down. Ken followed closely firing several short bursts. The 109 caught fire at 3,000 feet and crashed. The 109s were seen to take no evasive action which the 603 pilots found curious. Tannoy Read became separated and attacked the leader of four 109s flying in line astern. He opened fire aiming ahead of the formation which, as anticipated, flew through his burst. He then latched on to the last aircraft but having run out of ammunition broke away. Black attacked a 109 which slowed visibly with coolant streaming from its radiator. He was credited with a 'damaged'. The pilots made their way back to Rochford, landing around 13.40. Seven of the 17 squadrons sent up successfully intercepted the enemy formations.

Once again, Ras flew four patrols on this day. He flew two patrols a day for the remainder of September. His level of durability, alertness and concentration, as well as skill, was incredible and would explain how it was that neither he nor any of the aircraft he flew were ever hit. Pip Cardell returned from leave. Colin Pinckney visited Richard Hillary in hospital that evening and took him news of Squadron successes and losses.

Thursday 19 September 1940
Enemy attacks during the day consisted of isolated raids widely dispersed across Kent and Sussex. Some penetrated the IAZ and dropped bombs on the dock area of east London. One raid in particular crossed the coast at Hastings, flew to West Malling where it orbited the airfield then made for Hornchurch, passed into the IAZ and bombed the Surrey Docks where, it was reported, the streets in the vicinity were machine gunned. The raid re-crossed the coast between Dover and Dungeness. In addition there were a large number of enemy patrols consisting of single aircraft over the Channel between Beachy Head and North Foreland. Three raids were intercepted, the result of which was that two enemy aircraft were destroyed and one probably destroyed. 603's F/O Brian Macnamara was granted four days leave and left the station.

Friday 20 September 1940
Intensive night-time bombing raids by the Germans continued. Apart from a few reconnaissance raids, activity during the day was limited to one attack over north-west Kent and the Thames estuary between 10.50 and 12.00 hours and consisted of about 100 enemy aircraft, the great majority of which were fighters. The force crossed the coast between Dungeness and East Bay then divided, one part turned north-west towards the estuary reaching the Isle of Sheppey before turning back. The second part headed west and reached the Biggin Hill/Kenley area before turning back. No reports of bombs being dropped were received. During this attack ten squadrons engaged the enemy although weather conditions were not ideal for fighter action. Five failed to make contact, including 603.

Saturday 21 September 1940
There was only slight activity during the day, there being a number of armed reconnaissance raids which carried out some bombing up to 17.30 hours. One such raider flew over the Thames estuary before dropping bombs on the Mile End Road and Cambridge Road at 07.48. One raid was intercepted by three sections of RAF fighters and despite damage managed to escape over the coast at Littlehampton. Between 17.50 and 18.45 about 150 enemy aircraft took part in a raid over Biggin Hill, Kenley and London, the latter force splitting into several smaller raids one of which flew right over London, then east to Hornchurch. The vast majority of the enemy aircraft failed to reach London and returned back over the coast between Dover and Dungeness. Whilst there were a few reports of bombs being dropped no significant damage was reported to military or industrial targets. While 20 squadrons were detailed to intercept only one was successful and a bomber was damaged. The pilots of 603 remained on the ground and were able to take advantage of the lull.

Sunday 22 September 1940
Enemy activity this day consisted of raids by single aircraft. Morning activity was minimal but in the afternoon a number of raids crossed the coast between Beachy Head and Dungeness, the majority heading straight for London. Whilst a number of patrols were sent up to intercept, the only success was claimed by 607 Squadron when they attacked a He111. Brian Macnamara returned to the Squadron after his short break and confirmation was received that Bill Caister was a PoW. Whilst his wife and family were relieved to learn he was no longer 'missing', it would be a long time before they saw him again.

Monday 23 September 1940
Enemy activity was characterised by two attacks. The first at 09.00-10.15 consisted of approximately 100 aircraft, which crossed the coast at Dover and headed in a north-westerly direction towards the estuary. None reached the IAZ, and the raiders eventually turned and headed back to France on a reciprocal course. There were no reports of any bombs being dropped. Fifteen squadrons were already airborne, including 603, patrolling specified areas and seven additional squadrons were sent up to intercept. Of the total number in the air only nine made contact. Initial reports state that nine Bf109s were shot down with five probables and five damaged. At 09.25 hours 603 Squadron took off on defensive patrol with Ken Macdonald leading in X4259: F/L Boulter (X4248), F/O Carbury (X4164), P/O Morton (X4347), P/O MacPhail (N4394), P/O Berry (R6626), P/O Stapleton (N3244), P/O Dexter (N3100), P/O Lawrence (X4274), P/O Read (R6836), P/O Cardell (R9553), and Sgt Bailey (X4250) were also up. The 11 Group intelligence bulletin for the 23rd includes the following notes:

> 603 squadron at 32,000 feet, between Canterbury and Dover sighted some scattered pairs of Me.109's at 27,000 feet and attacked. They report that the E/A were camouflaged to resemble Spitfires, on the upper surface with red and blue roundels on the wing tips, the under surface silver grey with black crosses on the wings, and the lower half of the nose coloured yellow. Mistaking the E/A for Spitfires half of the section attempted to formate on some of them.

In a dog fight over Dover Jim MacPhail's Spitfire was hit and he baled out slightly injured. MacPhail blamed his being shot down on a stiff neck acquired during a boisterous mess game during which he foolishly thought he could get the better of Stapme. The South African had been observing MacPhail's antics and realised sooner or later he would take on more than he could handle! When

MacPhail dived at him he just bounced off the strong South African and ricked his neck in the process. On returning to Hornchurch MacPhail confronted Stapme in an attempt to apportion blame for the fact that his stiff neck rendered him unable to watch his tail! MacPhail's enthusiasm for wrestling and de-bagging was somewhat dampened after that. For reasons unknown, he did very little flying with 603 and his time with the unit was brief.*

Brian Carbury and John Boulter each destroyed 109s (Boulter's, 15 miles north of Dover) and Ken Macdonald claimed a probable. They landed again at 10.40. A second raid by the Luftwaffe occurred between 17.15 and 18.00 when about 50 aircraft crossed the coast and headed for north Kent and the Thames estuary. This force soon turned back and is believed to have consisted solely of fighters. 603 was one of 12 squadrons ordered to intercept but no contact was made.

Tuesday 24 September 1940
There were four major attacks during the day, two in the morning over Kent and the estuary, and two late on in the day on Southampton. In addition there were also a number of raids operating singly or in small numbers which continued throughout the day dropping bombs at random on targets in Kent and Surrey. 603 Squadron were not involved in the action. Brian Carbury's award of the DFC was promulgated. The citation reads:

> During operations on the north east coast Flying Officer Carbury led his section in an attack on two enemy aircraft. Both were destroyed. From 28th August 1940, to 2nd September 1940, he has, with his Squadron, been almost continuously engaged against large enemy raids over Kent, and has destroyed eight enemy aircraft. Five of these were shot down during three successive engagements in one day.

Sheep Gilroy returned to Hornchurch following his time in hospital. Having sufficiently recovered from injuries received on 31 August and a period of sick leave, he arrived at the aerodrome and was officially posted to the RAF station from 603 Squadron as non-effective sick until such times as he was A1 fit to fly. Pilot Officer Peter M. Hartas was posted to 603 from 616 Squadron. In an attempt to reduce the grief of losing their youngest son, and in a respite from the battle, Ken Macdonald wrote this revealing letter to his parents who had just returned from a short holiday:

> My Darling Mummy and Daddy,
>   I just received your letter – thank you very much. I expect you are quite glad to be home again, but I hope you both feel the better for your holiday. Thank you also for the clean clothes which were a God-send. We never seem to get much time to change clothes anyway – and go about in rather a state of sartorial disrepair.
>   This last week has been so far as we are concerned, rather quieter – due partly to the weather and also I think because the Hun no longer likes to bring his bombers over by day but waits for night time.
>   The weather, as you can imagine, is the ruling factor in this game. What we don't like is cloudless skies, as then the Hun is able to come over in masses together at all heights and it is an awful strain for us trying to keep the whole sky Hunless. Our first fortnight here we never saw a cloud – it was terrible. Since then we have had what you would call 'good weather', but we have had some cloud which divides the sky, so that we can either search below and pay little attention above, or search above. But his fighters dislike coming below

---

*On 11 September he claimed a He111 destroyed and a Bf109 on the 15th. He was promoted to Flying Officer on 6 November 1940. On 20 February 1941, MacPhail was ferrying Spitfire P8016 from 6 Maintenance Unit (MU) to 74 Squadron at Hawkinge, when he lost control of the aircraft and was forced to bale out. The Spitfire subsequently crashed at Oak's Park near Wallington, Surrey. Further misfortune followed on 4 March 1941. Whilst carrying out an air test in a Spitfire, MacPhail crashed at Belmont, Surrey. Initial hospitalisation led to a period at the Queen Victoria Cottage Hospital, East Grinstead, where he underwent plastic surgery. He became a member of the Guinea Pig Club and, along with the likes of Richard Hillary, Tom Gleave, Geoffrey Page, Eric Lock and 'Ben' Bennions, was on the first committee of that unique organisation. He was promoted to Flight Lieutenant on 6 November 1941 and was with 174 Squadron during the Dieppe air battle in August 1942. He was released from the RAF as a Flight Lieutenant in 1945, and died in 1963.

clouds and his bombers cannot bomb accurately from above them, and so they cannot co-operate and protect each other. Also of course they cannot bring over enormous formations in punk weather, and so we get the old 'hide and seek' tactics against single aircraft that we used to enjoy at Dyce. And so you see the whole game is infinitely variable (like 'Lawyering') and never dull or monotonous. What we would thoroughly enjoy now and then, and will soon be getting I expect, is thick fog which makes flying utterly impossible at all – then we have a rest!

We have been having on average one or two battles a day this week. Our job here is not so much to go for the bombers, but to shoot down their fighters which come over to escort them – [although] Spitfires are a bit better than anything they have, it is a more or less even fight, one single-seat fighter against another. There are, or used to be, always many more of them than of us but this doesn't actually count for so much. All our battles take place over either Kent, the Channel or the Thames estuary and now and then over London itself – though we usually get at them before they get that length. It is a magnificent sight to see all these fighters either in squadrons or all individually wheeling and diving after one another, glinting in the sun and making long 'smoke' trails, pure white, miles above the coast at 30,000 feet. There is no doubt that it is the highest form of warfare – there is nothing whatever sordid about it. It is gloriously exhilarating and calls for all one's dexterity and skilful tactics. Successful pilots I am certain are not those who just go hell-for-leather after the first Hun they see. There is a tremendous art in picking your man and equally as much in outwitting or out-manoeuvring the others. A few of the Huns are reasonably expert but the majority are unimaginative, and nine out of ten do exactly the same thing every time they are attacked. But of course they all need watching, and some of their reconnaissance and bomber pilots put up jolly good shows, such as one yesterday flying all over London below the clouds in broad daylight with everyone firing at him from the ground and fighters after him chasing him into the clouds – then out he would come again and again, eventually to get home safely.

So far since coming down here I have shot down three Huns by myself for certain. The first was a Heinkel 113 [Bf109] – their latest fighter and rather like a Spitfire (very nice looking). It crashed not far west of Denstead. It turned out to be, I think, the first 113 to be got down in England and the Intelligence were quite excited, only I think it was too bashed up to be much good to them. The next was a Messerschmitt 109 single-seater fighter crashed in flames south of Maidstone, and yesterday I got another '109' half-way across the Channel. Unfortunately, he only counts as a 'probable' as I couldn't wait to see him go into the sea as his chums were taking rather an interest in me, but when I left off there was petrol and smoke pouring from him and he was going vertically downward in an unhealthy manner.

I have of course fired at dozens of others, but could never sit about to watch what effect I had made owing to having to make myself scarce from the other ninety and nine which always seem to fill the sky. However, if we count these three and the four Huns out of the Heinkel 111 I got down at night up at Turnhouse that makes seven Huns I have personally accounted for and four machines which would cost the Führer something more than one Spitfire cost our Government. There are several Huns I have shared in up North and may have damaged down here – so that whatever should happen I shall feel that I have given the Hun a run for his money. If I can double this I shall have given him a run for Don's too. Please don't think that I am getting murderously blood-thirsty. Not at all. It is just a case of 'keeping the score' in the game.

We have been here four weeks today. So far I have declined to take any leave because if I do, it means that George who has all the office work as well, must also fly every time as only he and I have as yet led the Squadron. Also I reckoned that I could last this place out and get leave when we were moved elsewhere. Now the quotation for our stay here is three months, i.e. two more. If this is to be so, I think I shall probably give up the martyr attitude and take leave. The trouble is of course that George refuses to have any. Anyhow I feel fine just now and don't need any at present, although it would be nice to get off the Station for an afternoon or an evening. The days getting shorter is another God-send to us. Also with all this Invasion nonsense on the tapes, it would be a pity to miss it if it ever comes off. We are all secretly rather pleased at being here I think. At the risk of being incredibly bumptious – it would seem not unreasonably fantastic to presume that someone (whoever is responsible for our being there) considers we are not <u>too</u> bad, if they put us here at a time when – as the 'Daily Rags' put it – the future of civilisation, the world etc. etc. depends on the RAF. We definitely feel we are here with something to do. For instance, this is quite absurd but it captures the (or at least <u>my</u>) imagination. This afternoon one lone Hun bomber (probably only a reconnaissance aeroplane) was reported approaching London from the S.E. One aircraft was told to go and chase it. As I happened then to be sitting in my aeroplane I went up. I climbed right up miles above London where the sirens had all gone (damned silly), and there I was, the sole protector of the Heart of the Empire! Of course I never saw the Hun who probably never saw me, but anyway went home doing no damage. But with a streak of imagination he <u>might</u> have tried to drop a bomb on Westminster or the Houses of Parliament and messed up my view from Lambeth Bridge – or he <u>might</u> have dropped one on Madame Tamara [based in Sloane Square, the lady responsible for making the hand-knitted dresses worn by Ken's mother]… and I might have stopped him! What I mean is – it makes it worthwhile going up, quite apart from the fun of the thing…

Lots of love to you both

'Ken'

This letter was to be his last.

Wednesday 25 and Thursday 26 September 1940
Once again 603 were not involved in the action on the 25th which was confined mainly to combating a series of raids by single enemy aircraft (although there was one large scale which approached Portland from the south-east). Five of these raiders were intercepted, in only one instance was there no effective result.

Following a quiet morning when only four raids crossed the coast, activity in the early afternoon of the 26th consisted of isolated raids by single aircraft most of which crossed the coast between Dungeness and Beachy Head on reconnaissance missions. Very few bombs were reported dropped. Between 16.00 and 17.15 a raid of approximately 70 aircraft approached from the Cherbourg area and converged on Southampton which nine squadrons were sent up to intercept. Several raiders also appeared over the Kent coast, possibly as a diversion.

As September drew to a close 'practice flying' began to appear again in addition to patrols as part of the day-to-day activities recorded in the ORB. The need for the pilots to gain experience was obviously so great that they were risked being airborne in a hostile area. Night time bombing of British cities and towns in the south-east was particularly widespread.

Friday 27 September 1940
The first raid of the day did not involve 603 and occurred between 08.30 and 09.30 hours when a large number of individual incursions (mostly small) amounting to around 100 aircraft targeted London. RAF fighter squadrons formed a defensive circle around the capital preventing all but three raids from penetrating the IAZ. Two other enemy formations approached west London from the south-west.

The second attack began at 11.00 hours when two raids of more than 80 enemy aircraft crossed the Channel from Cherbourg. As they were heading towards Southampton fighters were sent up to protect the city, but the force turned away, crossed the coast at Swanage and headed for Bristol. Also at 11.00 five large-scale raids plotted as nearly 500 aircraft crossed the coast in the Dover area and aimed for London. Sixteen squadrons of 11 Group were sent up to intercept of which seven were successful, including 603: S/L Denholm (X4164), F/L Macdonald (X4489), P/O Morton (L4490), F/O Haig (X4275), P/O Dexter (N3100), F/O Pinckney (R6836), P/O Read (P9440), P/O Berry (R6826), P/O Cardell (N3244), and F/O Macnamara (X4348). The ORB reads:

At 11.46 hours, ten aircraft took off from Rochford to patrol Hornchurch at 18,000 feet.

P/O Pip Cardell RAFVR, Hornchurch September 1940. Photo shows Pip looking very tired, taken at dispersal during late afternoon just a few days before his death. XT-V, P9553 first saw service with 603 on 8 September. On 2 October it was shot down over Croydon with Dexter at the controls.

When at 18,000 feet over Maidstone, four Me109's went across the bows of the squadron. The squadron chased them and they turned east. When in mid-Channel, two of the Bf109's turned and came back towards England.

P/O Dexter DFC and P/O Cardell were together when P/O Cardell was fired at by two Me109's. P/O Cardell baled out from 500 feet, 400 yards out in the sea off Folkestone. His parachute failed to open, but he came up immediately and was seen floating head well above the water. The machine crashed near him. P/O Dexter circled for ten minutes calling up rival (other squadrons) and 603 Squadron, but got no reply. There were several people on the beach and he tried to attract their notice. As they showed complete apathy and no boats put out, he crashed his machine on the beach, and after much waste of time, he got a boat from a fisherman, but by then P/O Cardell was drowned. A naval launch arrived on the scene an hour later.

Annoyance is clearly evident in intelligence officer 'Spy' Blackbourn's reporting of the events surrounding the slow response to a pilot in distress, enhanced no doubt by Dexter's own interpretation of events. His anger can quite rightly be appreciated. Peter Dexter claimed one Bf109 destroyed during this patrol and his combat report reads:

Returning home with the squadron, I saw one Me109 making for France. After chasing it for some time, I engaged from the rear and fired until a white stream came from the starboard wing root. The machine rose to 500 feet and the pilot baled out.

At this time, P/O Cardell was engaging another 109, which he destroyed. I saw the aircraft hit the water. Five more Me109's came down at us out of the sun. After a short engagement, I saw P/O Cardell make for home. I followed him and observed him to be having difficulty with his aircraft. He baled out at 500 feet, a quarter of a mile off Folkestone beach, but his parachute failed to open.

I circled for ten minutes and as no attempt was made by the people on the beach to rescue P/O Cardell, I force landed on the beach, commandeered a rowing boat and picked up P/O Cardell. He had, however, by that time been drowned.

Peter Dexter made his initial attack which resulted in the destruction of a 109 at 12.00 hours at a height of 500 feet. He opened fire at 200 yards, closing to 50 yards in which time he fired several bursts and expended 1,500 rounds of ammunition. Blackbourn filed a combat report confirming the destruction of one 109 on behalf of Pip Cardell, as witnessed by Peter Dexter.

It was thought that Pip may have been wounded when he and Dexter were bounced by the five 109s, as he was busy finishing-off his 109. His Spitfire, N3244, was also damaged. He initially attempted to re-gain English soil but he was clearly having trouble flying his crippled Spitfire. As his failing aircraft neared stalling speed with the risk of it simply spinning out of control, he was forced to abandon it at 12.45 hours, close by the pier. Dexter, knowing that he could do nothing to help, watched in horror as Pip jumped and plummeted into the sea; his parachute left the pack but seemingly failed to deploy by the time he hit the water. Dexter repeatedly flew over Folkestone harbour and any potential rescue boats that were slow to put out. Furious at the attitude of the onlookers, in a better position than he to take action to help the stricken pilot, he made his decision. He lowered his flaps and crash-landed his Spitfire X4250 on Folkestone beach, crashing through barbed wire defences and stopping just yards short of an area where mines had apparently been placed. He climbed out of his cockpit and, still encumbered in his flying gear, ran to a group of six men who were attempting to launch two boats, but they lacked his sense of urgency. Hastily ditching his flying gear he helped to launch the first and jumped aboard the second.

When they reached Pip he was floating in his Mae West but all life was gone from him. It was a calm, windless day and the surface of the sea was smooth. The reason for his parachute not opening completely during his short descent was because the altitude was insufficient for an adequate deployment. The airflow drags the released 'chute from the bag and fills the silk canopy, but with insufficient airflow 500 feet had been too low for him to stand any chance over land. Over the sea, he apparently survived the fall but died soon after from several possible causes; drowning (as the IO notes in his report), wounds received in combat or, as is very likely, injuries received from the fall. Hitting the sea from that height would have been akin to hitting a brick wall. Either way his death certificate recorded: 'Multiple injuries received due to war service.'

In a photograph, taken in front of Spitfire XT-V P9553, just before he was killed, the strain is very evident. Having moved south to Hornchurch on 27 August, Pip had to bide his time until he flew his first patrol on 1 September. His first experience of combat with Luftwaffe fighters resulted in damage to his own aircraft and he forced-landed back at base. On 11 September he damaged a He111 over the Kent countryside, south of London. By the time of his death he had seen one month's action during the heat of the battle. He had been a very good pilot, had gained a great deal of experience, but was both mentally and physically exhausted.*

The combat report for the morning patrol of 27 September 1940:

> George Denholm claimed a Me109 probable out of a formation of four at 12.15 over Maidstone at a height of 18,000 feet. 'I saw four Me109's fly across the bows of the squadron about 400 yards away, so I ordered A Flight to attack. The 109's started to dive for France, except for one which became separated from the rest and of which I lost sight. I selected the nearest of the others and did a series of attacks on it from underneath at a range of about 400 yards, this being the nearest I could get to him. Eventually about half-way across the Channel, the other two which were above, turned back north again, and the one I was attacking, slowed up considerably, so that I was able to get quite close, but by this time my ammunition was exhausted.
>
> From the position in which I finished up, I could not see much, as he was right in the sun, but from reports from other members of the flight, it appears that the 109 was emitting a thick stream of glycol.
>
> I thought I was above at that point, so I dived into the haze which was over the sea and made for home.'

---

*See appendix 23 for more information and comment.

Brian Macnamara continued his run of success in the Squadron with a claim of a 109 damaged. His experience had been rewarded with responsibility:

I was Guard section leader when the squadron was proceeding north near Dungeness. I saw a 109 flying very low going south. I peeled off and chased it, firing continuously. I could see my incendiaries bursting on the machine and black smoke began to come from the engine and the enemy began to slow down and turn as if about to land on the water. However two Me109's suddenly appeared 200 yards ahead of me out of the haze and shooting at me. I was forced to turn and run. The enemy chased me till I had crossed the English coast. I flew about 20 feet off the water, taking violent evasive action and the enemy's bursts missed mostly through insufficient deflection. In fine pitch, with full throttle and the red lever pressed, I appeared to be drawing away from the 109's, as their fire slackened for the last mile or two and when I turned, they were further behind me than at the start of the action.

Macnamara's attack was delivered at 12.00 hours between Dungeness and the French coast. The height of the enemy fighter above the surface of the sea was just 50 feet when he attacked it, opening fire from 300 yards, firing one burst of three and one of 12 seconds as he closed to within 150 yards, expending all his ammunition.

The second attack occurred between 14.35 and 16.15 hours when three or four raids totalling about 100 aircraft crossed the coast in the Dover/Folkestone area and flew north-west across mid-Kent towards the Thames estuary.

603 were one of 13 squadrons sent up to intercept, of which ten were successful. The Squadron were airborne for their second patrol between 15.11 and 16.25 with Uncle George leading in X4164, F/L Macdonald (X4489), F/O Pinckney (R6836), F/O Macnamara (X4348), P/O Stapleton (P9553), P/O Morton (X4490), P/O Berry (R6626), and P/O Read (P9440).

Ken Macdonald and Ras Berry each destroyed a Bf109 with Ras and George credited with a third and one probable. At 15.50 hours Colin Pinckney claimed a 109 probable:

When on patrol with 603 Squadron, I saw 30 Me109's flying beneath us at 25,000 feet and after being ordered into line astern, attacked a single machine at the back of the formation. After my first burst from astern, enemy aircraft took evasive action by turning in towards me, with glycol streaming from its engine. I followed him down through cloud to 2,000 feet, attacking it from the quarter astern. Last seen, the enemy was a few feet above the ground near Herne Bay, with engine ticking over.

Flying with A Flight Colin attacked the 109 over Canterbury, opening fire at a range of 200 yards, closing to 75 yards in which time he fired several bursts, expending 2,000 rounds of ammunition. Back at the aerodrome Pilot Officer Robert B. Dewey arrived from 611 Squadron.

During combat on 27 September the pilots of 11 Group were initially credited with 88 enemy aircraft destroyed, 27 shared destroyed; 27 probable, 1 shared probable; 39 damaged, 2 shared damaged but 15 pilots were lost killed or missing. The efforts made by Fighter Command didn't go unnoticed by Churchill:

Message of Congratulations from the Prime Minister

Following message which has been suitably acknowledged has been received from the Prime Minister through Air Ministry, begins: Pray congratulate the Fighter Command on the results of yesterday 27th September. The scale and intensity of the fighting and the heavy losses of the enemy, especially in relation to our own, make September 27 rank with September 15 and August 15, as the third great and victorious day of the Fighter Command during the course of the battle of Britain. Ends. Please transmit to all other ranks.

Saturday 28 September 1940

The Spitfire trailed smoke as it circled high above the army barracks, the pilot desperately looking for a place to land. Losing height rapidly he unfastened his harness, disconnected the radio lead and oxygen supply and rose to bale out, opening the access hatch on the port side of his aircraft as he did so. Realising the likelihood that his aircraft would crash on a built-up area he dropped back down in his seat and continued to search for an open area. By now flames had spread back from his engine to the starboard wing of his Spitfire and were beginning to lick around the cockpit.

Below, a number of army personnel were the only witnesses to the brave act which was unfolding above them. It would remain etched on their memories for the rest of their lives.

The Spitfire approached the barracks and, with the trajectory reasonably assured, the pilot leapt from his stricken fighter. Almost immediately the aircraft flipped over and dived into the tarmac of the parade ground below, spontaneously bursting into flames.

As the pilot had intended, no lives had been lost, but as his parachute streamed from its pack, but before the canopy could fill with air, his body smashed into the ground a short distance from where his Spitfire had crashed. He had taken a terrible gamble and lost, sacrificing his life to avoid death or injury to others.

Soldiers on the parade ground had dispersed moments before the Spitfire crashed, taking cover in one of the barrack-block basements. The only injury was minor: in his haste to take cover one of the soldiers had fallen down the stairs, cutting open an eyebrow.

Three major attacks took place against London and Portsmouth. The first, between 09.50 and 10.45, consisted of raids totalling 60 enemy bombers and fighters crossing the coast between Dover and Dungeness at heights of 13,000-20,000 feet and heading towards London. Nineteen 11 Group squadrons were despatched, including 603 which took off at 09.40 and included the following pilots: F/L Macdonald (L1076), F/O Pinckney (R6836), F/L Boulter (X4429), P/O Morton (L4409), P/O Read (P9440), P/O Stapleton (X4348), P/O Soden (R6626) and Sgt Bailey (X4275).

Ken Macdonald was an experienced pilot and deputy to CO George Denholm and the manner in which he lost his life, as an example of premeditated courage, has seldom been equalled.

At 10.20, whilst the Squadron were still attempting to achieve a height advantage over the enemy, they were bounced from out of the sun and superior altitude by Bf109s of II/JG26 over Gillingham. Black claimed a probable 109. With Ken leading the Squadron in L1076, his aircraft was targeted by Oberleutnant Walter Schneider, CO of the 6th Staffel, and attacked during a single fast, diving, pass. His Spitfire was severely damaged and eventually crashed on the site of Brompton Barracks, home of the Royal Engineers. The soft-spoken, much-liked member of the Squadron, highly respected for his leadership, was killed while attempting to get his aircraft down safely. The number of pilots with the experience to lead the newcomers was dwindling, but even experience was no guarantee of survival.

With his aircraft badly damaged, Ken had dived away from the threat of further attack and headed for Hornchurch. The condition of his machine rapidly deteriorated and eventually caught fire forcing him to get his Spitfire down as soon as possible. He aborted an initial attempt to bale out preferring to steer his aircraft away from what appeared to be a densely populated area below. Like so many of the veterans of 603 Squadron he was used to flying over the open countryside of Scotland. The situation soon deteriorated to the point whereby flames were starting to engulf him and, with conditions becoming unbearable, Ken knew he was about to lose control. His last few minutes of life were witnessed by a number of military personnel on the ground, thus preserving the legend of Ken's sacrifice. Although he had claimed three enemy aircraft destroyed, in truth his score was nearer seven. Aware of this, he didn't place any great importance on his own achievements only that of the Squadron as a unit, and only ever mentioned it once in a letter home.

Albert B. Johnson was a 19-year-old Royal Engineer on sentry duty at the barracks and witnessed the whole episode. He later reflected on memories which still generate great emotion:

As a nineteen year old (and only just at that) I had been in the Territorials. Too young to go to France, I had no yardstick to measure bravery when I watched F/L Macdonald die, the first time in my life I witnessed death taking place although we were living in the Battle of Britain and could hear and watch it above us. The bombs were missing us at the time.

In later years I wondered if his extreme heroism had been recognised and so I wrote to Chatham and RAF Hendon. I was sent an article/extract from 'The Sapper' magazine in which an ex-major stated that the pilot of a Spitfire engaged in a dog-fight over the Barracks had landed safely a mile away whilst his plane landed on the Square at Brompton, making the writer of the article dive for cover in the basement.

For some time I then realised that my unique position high on the arch manning a Bren gun alone probably meant that I was the only person who, by the nature of my duty and the 'All Clear' having gone, had witnessed the entire occurrence, except of course the actual dog-fight. This must have been either very high up or some way away because I had neither seen nor heard any action that morning in a clear sky. The first drone of his plane over the estuary was no more than we were used to, flying at a fairly low height in no apparent trouble as if on his way back to the 'drome. A feint trail of smoke started as he circled over the Medway estuary, Rochester and Gillingham before losing sight of him behind the School of Military Engineering when he lost height. Perhaps he realised that his plane wouldn't reach the 'drome. I hadn't taken my eyes off him. I then turned away from watching him, as he had disappeared, when I heard a roar and turning quickly I saw him emerge low behind the SME with increasing smoke from his starboard wing. By the time he was just above me, slightly to my right, the starboard wing side [root] was covered by thick black billowing smoke and flame. The pilot clambered out, hung on the fuselage, looked down at me (there was nothing obviously wrong with him when he looked down at the Square and the Arch, having hurriedly climbed from the cockpit), put the plane into a nose dive, and leapt clear. Both he and the Spitfire plummeted onto the tarmac, his parachute barely emergent. There was a series of explosions as the ammunition went off and when this ceased someone ran and knelt down beside him... He had been shot down by Messerschmitts, 'Bounced' and slightly damaged as to render it impossible to continue... but he could have baled out earlier and saved his own life I'm sure. I learned from his sister that his younger brother went out on patrol and never came back a month earlier.

Ken climbed out of the cockpit of his Spitfire onto the port wing and jumped from approximately 400 feet. His parachute had barely left its pack when his body hit the ground. He had been too low and had died instantly in the fall. His Spitfire crashed onto the parade ground and exploded in a sheet of flame, uprooting one of a row of trees, and narrowly missing the barrack block by a matter of feet. Perhaps, as Broody Benson had done on the 28th and Richard Hillary on the 29th, Ken had been trying to coax his damaged aircraft back to Hornchurch but when fire broke out he realised he was committed to getting his aircraft down as soon as possible, as he was by that time too low to bale out. As the flames reached the cockpit and threatened death by fire he chose to jump and take

the risk his brolly may not open in time. Eyewitnesses on the ground were also convinced Ken had been trying to direct his aircraft away from the more densely populated areas that lay below him.

This brave act was also witnessed by Corporal F.E. Hesslewood, Royal Engineers, whose report was almost identical to Johnson's. Although it was officially recorded that Ken Macdonald's body landed on the parade ground of St Mary's Barracks, a quarter of a mile further on from the crash-site, Albert Johnson had an uninterrupted view of the square at Brompton Barracks where both pilot and aircraft came down.

Unusually, the crash made little impression on the surface of the parade ground, the engine had not

Wreckage of Ken's Spitfire.

Wreckage of Ken's Spitfire is removed by transporter.

been buried with the wreckage confined to a small area; perhaps confirming that it had dived in vertically from low altitude. Fanned by the light breeze, the flames of the ensuing fire scorched the leaves off the nearby trees. The Merlin engine, a piece of the fuselage and tail section and the undercarriage were evidence to onlookers that the remains had once been a Spitfire. A Queen Mary transporter took the wreckage away the following morning, after a number of photographs had been taken, leaving a scorched area with the uprooted tree as a sad reminder of the sacrifice made by this brave pilot. Today the trees around the parade ground are all new. The trees that were there during the war were all blown down during the hurricane of 1987. New saplings have since been planted and have practically reached the same size as their predecessors. It is interesting that the one replacing that which was uprooted by Macdonald's Spitfire is noticeably undersized compared with the rest.

The body of Ken Macdonald was removed and taken home to Edinburgh where he was cremated at Warriston Crematorium. He was 28 years old and had now been reunited with his younger brother Don. He claimed five enemy aircraft destroyed, three shared destroyed and two probables. In the memories of those with whom he served he left a reputation as a fine pilot, leader and a greatly respected man.*

At 12.25 formations of enemy aircraft began to appear over France and patrols were sent up as a precaution. Although this activity diminished by 13.30 formations crossed the coast near Dover and made for the capital followed by two more raids which flew inland over Deal. At 13.10, 603 was one of 12 squadrons ordered into the air to drive back the incursion and some of their 'old hands' reaped further success:

---

*For the Macdonald family, the time following 28 September was wretched. In a period of 31 days during the Battle of Britain they had lost both sons. Their mother, May, was naturally grief-stricken and husband, Harold, found her inconsolable. They received a standard format letter from the King and Ken's personal effects, including his dog-tags. The letter was preserved by May and Harold Macdonald alongside a photo of Ken. The couple received much warmth and support from friends and relatives but no amount of time would heal the loss of both sons. On receiving news of Ken's death Mardi was naturally devastated. Back at work she quickly discovered that she could no longer listen to the Luftwaffe radio transmissions without becoming distraught. The cries of 'Sieg Heil!' which some pilots cried when destroying an RAF fighter was just too much to bear as, to her, she was hearing Ken being shot down again and again. Her superiors were sympathetic and she was quickly transferred to another listening station, well away from 11 Group near Scarborough, where she had an opportunity to come to terms with her grief. Whilst Mardi persevered with her work, back in Edinburgh things had deteriorated even further in the Macdonald household. May had not recovered from losing both sons and as a consequence her own health took a downward turn and she refused all medical aid. She died on 18 December 1940, of what was described as a 'broken-heart', having suffered such a terrible shock. The shock was indeed real and harrowing, but in actual fact she allowed a stomach ulcer to become life threatening as a result of her loss of will to live. As a widower, Harold Macdonald eventually moved to somewhere more manageable and Goodtrees became an old folks home. In the years after the war, the family tragedy of the period was tempered in part by his surviving daughter and his grandchildren but the ghosts were all around him while he remained at Goodtrees. Ewen remained devoted to the 'City Squadron', as she called it, for the rest of her life. In 1989 she received a copy of Albert Johnson's account of Ken's death to add to her collection and sent it to George Denholm, who wrote back: 'Let me tell you that about the most heart-rending memory I have of 1940 is the shattering blow to your parents in the loss of Ken and Don. Much above other tragedies, that was the most tragic…'

BUCKINGHAM PALACE

The Queen and I offer you our heartfelt sympathy in your great sorrow.

We pray that your country's gratitude for a life so nobly given in its service may bring you some measure of consolation.

George R.I.

Left: Ken Macdonald's dog-tags.
Bottom: Ken's record of his mention in despatches.

By the KING'S Order the name of
Flight Lieutenant H.K.Macdonald,
Auxiliary Air Force
was published in the London Gazette on
24 September, 1941.
as mentioned in a Despatch for distinguished service.
I am charged to record
His Majesty's high appreciation.

Archibald Sinclair

Secretary of State for Air

Eight aircraft of 603 Squadron took off from Hornchurch and joined 222 Squadron on the Maidstone patrol line at 15,000 feet, 603 Squadron leading. They then saw smoke trails going east and climbed to investigate to 30,000 feet, but the smoke trails by that time had disappeared. Still on the Maidstone patrol line, 222 Squadron had to go down to 17,000 feet owing to the lack of oxygen and 603 saw about 16 Me109's in a straggling formation going west at 23,000 feet.

603 went into line astern and dived, chasing the Me109's westwards. The Me109's did not appear to see the squadron till they were fired upon, but Guard 1 of 603 was attacked by a vic of three Me109's, which peeled off and started to dive on him. Cloud cover 10/10ths at 1,000 feet.

Sheep Gilroy DFC destroyed a Bf109 which was seen to go down in flames:

Attack was delivered from astern after following enemy aircraft through a tight half-roll. Smoke followed by flames, issued from the enemy aircraft and it dived vertically with cowling and hood coming off. The pilot was not seen to jump, but he may have delayed opening parachute until reaching cloud.

Sheep was flying as Red 3 in A Flight when he delivered this attack at 14.32 hours, south-east of London at a height of 23,000 feet. He opened fire from a range of 200 yards, closing to 75 yards during which time he fired a seven second burst, expending 1,060 rounds. Despite deteriorating eyesight 'Old Gent', F/L Jack Haig, one of the longest standing members of the Squadron, claimed one Bf109 damaged:

When leading 603 Squadron and followed by 222 Squadron, we sighted about fifteen Bf109's below at about 25,000 feet. We dived down from 31,000 feet and came up astern of them. I fired a good burst at one and it dropped out of the formation with white smoke coming from it. I broke away and did not see it again, as one Me109 came diving down on me, and so I was fully occupied.

Haig led the squadron as A Flight commander and delivered his attack at 14.30 hours, in an area north of Maidstone at 25,000 feet. He opened fire from a range of 250 yards, closed to 50 yards and fired an eight second burst which expended 1,108 rounds. Tannoy Read damaged a 109:

I was patrolling as Red 2 with 603 Squadron at 31,000 feet when approximately 16 Bf109's were sighted below and to starboard, heading west.

The squadron was ordered into line astern and came round into a gentle dive, attacking the enemy aircraft from dead astern. The Me109 which I engaged did an abrupt stall turn, nearly colliding with another. It then dived and I followed, giving it further bursts. White smoke streamed from its port exhausts and I left it going straight down. I was forced to leave it, being attacked from behind by another Me109.

Read was with A Flight and had attacked the 109 at 14.35 hours, over Sevenoaks at 26,000 feet. He opened fire at a range of 300 yards and closed to 150 yards, firing three bursts of four seconds expending 1,950 rounds. Only six of his eight guns had functioned.

In response to a request for experienced volunteers to return to the harder hit squadrons in the south, P/O Claude Goldsmith returned to 603 and his dwindling group of friends. Pilot Officer Ludwik Martel was also posted from the same unit. Ludwik was the youngest Pole to fight in the Battle of Britain. That evening Colin Pinckney visited Richard Hillary in hospital and passed on the sad news of the loss of Pip, whose death had been confirmed earlier that day, and Ken Macdonald.

Sunday 29 September 1940

At 16.10 hours a formation of 70 enemy bombers and fighter escort crossed the coast between Dungeness and Hastings at heights plotted as 15,000-20,000 feet, and headed for Weybridge. At 16.05, as 11 pilots of 603 took off, further raids followed. Of the 18 squadrons sent to intercept, 603 were one of only two that were successful: S/L Denholm (X4490), F/L Boulter (X4489), F/O Haig (X4259), P/O Stapleton (R6738), P/O Berry (X4274), P/O Soden (P9499), P/O Hartas (R6626), P/O Lawrence (R6752), P/O Dewey (P9440), Sgt Bailey (N3099), and Sgt Darling (X4347).

Having climbed to 30,000 feet through dense (10/10) cloud cover over Beachy Head they spotted four aircraft in line astern below. Uncle George ordered Ras to go down and investigate and he subsequently attacked a 109 inflicting severe damage. He then had to take violent evasive action to shake off another 109 that had latched onto his tail. Ras then pulled hard on the control column and, with his natural resistance to g-Force, counter-attacked. He saw pieces fly off the 109 before it rolled over and, with smoke pouring from it, dived down into the cloud. No other 603 aircraft made contact. Clearly, the Squadron had not adopted Ras's recent practice of attacking in pairs. If he had had a wingman he may not have needed to take evasive action when the 109 attacked him. In sending Ras George Denholm had probably sent the best man for the job.

The recent influx of replacement pilots included Pilot Officer Henry K. Matthews who joined 603 from 54 Squadron.

Monday 30 September 1940
According to the 603 ORB, S/L Count Stevens finally left 603 on 30 September when he was posted to command RAF Station Ford.*

The day's activities saw five major attacks, one of which passed into 10 Group. Previously, raids tended to have more than one target but in each attack on the 30th the enemy concentrated on one objective. The first developed between 09.05 and 09.40 hours when an estimated 50 enemy aircraft (Ju88s and Bf109s were reported) crossed the coast in the Dungeness area and proceeded towards Mayfield. Two raids headed towards Slough but deviated west and north-east. During this attack a further 28 enemy aircraft were seen over the Channel but did not cross the coast. 603 were one of 13 squadrons ordered to intercept but were not successful. Perhaps the aircraft seen over the Channel were part of a second attack which occurred between 10.10 and 10.45 and again involving about 50 aircraft which crossed the coast between Dungeness and Hastings before heading for Biggin Hill. Seven squadrons were sent up but no interceptions were made.

Between 11.00 and 11.50 two raids approached Swanage and Portland with seven squadrons sent to intercept. No engagements took place, there were no reports of bombs being dropped and the raid passed into 10 Group.

The next attack took place between 13.07 and 14.00 hours with RDF stations having earlier detected the build-up of a large-scale attack over France. Three raids were plotted over Dungeness, two being small, probably all fighters, followed by the main raid of about 100 enemy aircraft, according to the Observer Corps, made up predominantly of bombers. The raids progressed towards Biggin Hill and on to London. The major raid wheeled over to the Northolt/Uxbridge area and, plotted at 20,000 feet this 'appeared to be a most determined attack'. Fifteen squadrons were sent up, the majority to fly the patrol lines. Eight engaged the enemy, including 603 which had been scrambled at 13.06 with George Denholm once again leading his pilots away from the aerodrome. The ORB reads:

L4490 S/Ldr Denholm	P/O BERRY 2 ME.109 Destroyed. F/O BOULTER
X4489 F/Lt Boulter	1 ME.109 Destroyed. P/O SODEN 1 ME.109
X4259 F/O Haig	Destroyed. P/O STAPLETON 1 ME.109 Destroyed.
X4347 P/O Morton	P/O MORTON 1 ME.109 Destroyed and 1 ME.109
X4274 P/O Berry	Probable. F/O HAIG 1 ME.109 Probable. P/O
P9499 P/O Soden	DEWEY 1 ME.109 Probable. SGT. DARLING 1
N3099 P/O Goldsmith	ME.109 Probable and 1 ME.109 Damaged.
P9553 P/O Stapleton	
P9440 P/O Dewey	
R6736 Sgt Darling	
R6752 Sgt Bailey	

*The previous attempt to post him away from the Squadron whilst still at Turnhouse was thwarted by Stevens himself when he refused to be posted against his will, a privilege given to members of the Auxiliary Air Force. He was either unaware or, as is more likely the case, chose to ignore the fact that 603 had been embodied into the RAF on 23 August 1939, and therefore governed by the rules of the RAF, not the AAF. However, Count Stevens was a strong-willed and particularly intelligent man who somehow managed to counter any attempts by the authorities from imposing such a move.

11 Group intelligence bulletin No.70 for 30 September records:

> 603 Squadron at 30,000 feet saw about 40 bombers in very tight vic's of 5 between 15,000-20,000 feet, protected by about 60 Me.109's at heights up to 25,000 feet in various formations and numbers. No single Me.109's were seen. The Squadron went into line astern and dived to attack the fighters as a result of which 6 were destroyed, 4 probably destroyed and 1 damaged.

It is possible that the aircraft claimed by Dewey is that which crashed and burned out at Kentwyns, Nutfield. Since moving south, Ras's score had increased by seven destroyed and two more shared victories, as his main objective when attacking the enemy was to get as close as possible before opening fire. Black Morton found time to write in his diary and poignantly refers to his close friend Ken Macdonald:

> Cloud 10/10 7,000' – 6,000'. Rising to SE Kent (13.00-14.25).

Squadron took off 11 A/C and climbed through 10/10 [cloud cover] from 6,000'-7,000' to 30,000' south of the river. I was leading Yellow [section] behind George. At 30,000' somewhere between Biggin and Maidstone saw about 40 bombers in tight vics at about 15,000' with many 109's up to our height flying towards London – we were flying SE. About 20-30 109's appeared 1,000' below us and to NE flying NW. Squadron went into line astern and attacked in LH wurzel. The Huns turned in towards us, but we came round on them. I got behind one in a LH turn and was just getting into range when the deflector sight bulb holder came off due to the 'G' in the turn. I stuffed it back, but it came off again when I tried to get on his tail. I put it back properly but the Hun took his chance and got away. There seemed to be a lot of them wurzling rather aimlessly and I soon got on to another's tail. I gave him a second burst from starboard quarter which took effect as he wobbled a bit then turned slowly over on his side and went down. There was a lot of Hun about so I couldn't see what happened to him, though I'm pretty sure he was hit hard.

I then saw another one in quite a good position and got back behind him. He must have been a closet [novice] for he was flying straight and level back to Hun-land. I gave him two very nice bursts from dead astern and slightly below. After the second he turned very slowly over on to his back and his nose dropped and he went down on his back, his dive steepened until he was going quite vertically and doing very slow aileron turns. He disappeared into cloud still going vertically. I think I must have got him right away for he never made any attempt at evasive action while I was shooting at him and he looked very dead the way he went down exactly like the one that went in near Sittingbourne. I was now a lot lower down than at the start – about 20,000' I should think, and there was no-one about so I made for a dog-fight to the east and found a 109 quite conveniently placed. I gave him two short bursts with a good deal of deflection from 30-40 degrees on port quarter and close range. The second being from 50 degrees or less. They seemed to take effect, for on the second burst there was an explosion in the cockpit, the hood flew off and the whole machine seemed to burst into flames. The first explosion had little or no smoke, but there was a good deal immediately after. I only saw him for a second or two after he blew up as I passed over him as he fell away and had to watch out for other chaps. Actually, if I'd been quick and not watching him I could have had a shot at another which crossed my path at about 40 degrees from port to starboard, but by the time I'd decided to have a shot he was in [a] bad position and [I] didn't get another shot before I was all alone again.

After a little while I saw two aircraft chasing each other well below me. I thought they were a Spitfire chasing a 109 but as I couldn't be sure I went down to see. It turned out OK so I watched. The Spitfire did only a short attack and then broke away north and started climbing up. I waited for him to come back, but he pushed off, so I went in to attack. The 109 had been hit as there was some thin vapour coming from his fuselage, probably petrol. He was diving fairly straight and very fast for the cloud. I got behind him and gave him a good burst after which there was a very big stream of coolant from both radiators. We were now quite near the cloud but the 109 levelled off and seemed reluctant to go into cloud at all. He dodged about a bit on top of the cloud and I got in one or two more bursts. The vapour streams had died down a lot now into a thin trail of steam or suchlike. The cloud was now beginning to have one or two holes in it and we went into one of these. We were just getting to the end of it when the 109 suddenly started to slow-up. I overshot badly and he got into cloud where I lost him. However, I thought he would probably come out again, if he was still able to, so made for the top and came out after about 3/4 of a minute to find the Hun steering a parallel course close to the cloud top and 500' away slightly behind. I started to turn in to attack again when two Spitfires suddenly dived down and the leading one gave the Hun a burst from dead astern. He immediately burst into flames and went down. I went down through the cloud and circled the fire with the other two to see who they were. They turned out to be Berry and Stapleton, Berry having shot him. After this I cruised about a bit getting down towards Folkestone but saw nothing but a Hurricane which I stalked but recognised in good time.

I came back shortly after this and waggled my wings at an AA battery near the oil works opposite Chatham to show we'd had a good afternoon. When I got back I found I'd only 8 or 10 rounds left per gun, so it's probably a good thing Berry came along, though I don't think the Hun would even have made it home by the way he was going and the glycol he'd lost.

It was one of the best shows the Squadron has had. I feel it makes up a little for losing Ken – quite a suitable revenge.

We got six confirmed – Razz 2 (one with some help from me), Bolster 1, Soden 1, Stapme 1, and self 1. Four probable – Old Gent [Jack Haig], Dewey, Darling, and self. Two damaged – Darling and self. All without a single bullet among us.

The Squadron returned to the airfield in dribs and drabs around 14.25. The fourth attack took place between 15.45-16.50 and seemed to be mainly directed against the Weybridge/Slough/Reading area. The attacking force consisted of about 180 aircraft stepped up between 15,000-25,000 feet and crossed the coastline on an eight-mile front between Dungeness and Hastings and headed for London. They then skirted south of the IAZ (where a few aircraft broke away from the main formation and penetrated into south-west London) and proceeded via Brooklands to the Reading/Maidenhead area, where they were given a hot reception by eight of 11 squadrons sent up to intercept. 603 were one of the eight, having taken off at 16.00 hours, and included: S/L Denholm (X4490), F/L Boulter (X4489), F/O Haig (X4259), P/O Martel (X4274), P/O Dexter (P9553), P/O Stapleton (X4348), P/O Hartas (R9499), P/O Goldsmith (N3099), P/O Matthews (X4347), P/O Dewey (P9440), Sgt Darling (P9440), and Sgt Bailey (R6752).

The enemy formation was scattered and made their escape over a wide area from Dover to the Isle of Wight. Peter Dexter, who had earlier received news of his promotion to Flying Officer, probably destroyed a Bf109 near Farnborough and damaged another. No further action was recorded and the pilots landed again at 17.50.

That day the Squadron received a signal from 11 Group HQ (A236, dated 30 September 1940): 'Group Commander sends warm congratulations to 603 Squadron on their successful fighting without casualties to themselves, showing exceptional leadership and straight shooting.'

The message was copied into the Squadron ORB from that period, which is today kept at the Public Records Office at Kew. The word 'without' has been heavily underlined by a latter-day 'reader' and following the exclamation mark added at the end of the sentence, the same hand had scrawled: 9 killed, 9 wounded, 1 missing, 1 PoW – In 30 days! It is inconceivable that Keith Park had not been anything but familiar with the statistics and aware that 603 had suffered greatly in the battle. With that in mind, it is most likely that Park's intended message was misunderstood during dictation or transcription.

The 30 September saw the final long-range daylight attack by German bombers on London. According to initial reckoning, since their arrival at Hornchurch, 603 had destroyed a further 60 enemy aircraft, to add to the 18½ destroyed over Scotland. 11 Group intelligence bulletin No.80 provides more specific details of 603's success throughout September: 37 enemy aircraft destroyed and 25 probable (a total of 55½ destroyed).

Tuesday 1 October 1940

The fifth and final phase of the Battle of Britain began on this day. Whilst heavy night-time attacks continued, attacks by fighters and fighter-bombers began. Although the threat of invasion began to slowly fade, 11 Group fighter squadrons continued to repel the Luftwaffe throughout October and were engaged in a number of fierce dog fights. By late autumn, Hitler concluded that the invasion of Britain was no longer practical and turned his attention towards the east and the invasion of Russia, which he carried out on 22 June the following year.

The day featured five main attacks, all during the afternoon. Four developed over Kent and targeted London, the other towards Southampton. Few interceptions were made and 603 were not involved.

Wednesday 2 October 1940

On this day the Squadron claimed five Bf109s destroyed, two probable and one damaged. The first phase of an attack by enemy aircraft occurred between 08.50 and 09.30 and was reported as a fighter sweep towards London. The second phase developed between 09.30-10.30, appeared over the Channel and swept in over Dungeness towards London. Reports suggested that the estimated 80 aircraft were all fighters. Sixteen squadrons were sent up to intercept, six of which were already airborne following the previous attack. The following 603 pilots took off at 09.29: S/L Denholm (X4409), F/L Boulter (X4489), F/O Haig (X4259), F/O Carbury (X4164), P/O Stapleton (X4348), P/O Dexter (P9553), P/O Martel (X4272), P/O Hartas (P9499), P/O Goldsmith (P9440), P/O Matthews (X4347), Sgt Darling (R6736) and Sgt Bailey (R6752). 11 Group intelligence bulletin No.72 reads:

> 12 aircraft of 603 Squadron when over Biggin Hill at 30,000 feet saw 15 Me.109 going N.W. at 23,000 feet. The Squadron formed into line astern and dived on to the E/A from out of the sun. F/O Carbury destroyed one Me.109 which he saw crash S.E. of Canterbury. F/O Haig destroyed a second which another pilot saw crash in Biggin Hill area. Sgt Bailey attacked a Me.109 which poured out glycol smoke and spun down. He watched it down to a few feet from the ground when its camouflage merged into the ground 5 miles S.W. of West Malling. P/O Hartas destroyed a Me.109, seeing it pour out glycol and smoke and spin vertically down. He followed it through cloud and saw a column of smoke where it had crashed five miles from Biggin Hill. F/O Boulter probably destroyed one Me.109, seeing one wheel down and white glycol smoke. The E/A turned on to its back and slipped in. P/O Martel damaged one (glycol smoke). Sgt Bailey reports fire from a rear gun on a Me.109 and believes it was cannon fire. One Me.109 was seen firing at another Me.109, result not observed.

At 10.20 P/O Peter Dexter was shot down over Croydon by 109s of III/JG53. Seriously wounded in the leg by a bullet or splinter(s) from a cannon shell, the same leg subsequently became trapped as he attempted to extricate himself from his aircraft. The Spitfire fell 15,000 feet before he finally managed to wrench his foot from the snagged flying boot, dislocating his knee in the process, and fall free. He was only just high enough for his parachute to deploy successfully. Spitfire P9553 crashed and burned out. It had been used as a back-drop for a photograph taken of Pip Cardell, just before he was killed. Up until that time its pilots also included Peter Pease. Dexter was admitted to Croydon Hospital. His leg injury was so severe it required reconstructive surgery. He remained in hospital for the next six

Left: F/O Peter Dexter. Photo taken whilst with 611 Squadron.
Right: His notice of death, sent to the family, see page 347.

months before moving to the officers convalescent facilities at Torquay. A few seconds prior to his aircraft being hit he managed to shoot down a 109, later confirmed as destroyed.*

Phase three of the Luftwaffe attacks of 2 October took place between 11.55-1300 hours and consisted of about 50 aircraft opposed by eight RAF fighter squadrons. The fourth phase occurred between 13.00-14.15 hours and involved 25 aircraft. Several targets in London were bombed. Ten squadrons were sent up. The final phase developed between 14.15-18.00 hours and included two attacks within this period. The first (14.15-15.15) crossed the coast over Dover/Dungeness with most heading for London. One raid branched off and headed for the Isle of Sheppey. Eight squadrons were despatched. The second attack (16.20-16.55) consisted mostly of fighters which crossed the coast over Dymchurch/Folkestone and flew towards the capital. Six squadrons were ordered to intercept. 603 were not involved.

Thursday 3 October 1940
Despite poor weather (10/10 cloud down to 300 feet with visibility down to as little as 500 yards) enemy activity continued although it was limited to flights by single/pairs of armed reconnaissance aircraft. No engagements were reported.

On this day Richard Hillary's promotion to Flying Officer appeared in the *London Gazette* and Sergeant Pilot John Strawson arrived from 616 Squadron. At this time 11 Group and 603 Squadron was coming through a particularly chaotic period but Strawson recalled with admiration the atmosphere of order imposed by Uncle George. By now the Luftwaffe tactics had changed since the combat-heavy days during the peak of the Battle of Britain. During October the enemy raids consisted mainly of bomb-carrying 109s known as Jagdbombers or Jabos. Although the damage caused by such raids was relatively insignificant in comparison with the attacks of the larger bomber formations, the swiftness with which

From left to right: unknown; Andy Darling and John Strawson.

they were executed saw the Germans on their way home having dropped their lethal load before the RAF fighters could intercept. In order to combat this method of attack Fighter Command implemented 'standing patrols' (also known as 'cab-rank patrols') over south-east England which consisted of fighters sent up in relays to patrol set lines (eg, 'the Maidstone Line') at 15,000 feet. When an incoming raid was detected the aircraft were vectored in the direction of and to the altitude of the enemy aircraft.

It had been five long days since the death of Ken Macdonald and during the evening Black Morton retired to his room in the officers mess and wrote to Ken's girlfriend:

My dear Mardi,
    I'm awfully sorry I've not been able to see you and talk about things during the last day or two, but I've just had my days off and it was only when I got back that I got your note and found you'd been about.
    We are still not quite sure exactly what happened; but this is the gist of what is rather a wonderful story.
    He was leading the Squadron when we were ordered towards the Hun before we'd got high enough. We were set on by about 30 – we were only 7 – and got split up. Ken's machine got badly hit; but he must have thought he could get it down all right. Then when he got down fairly low he evidently realised he couldn't get it down safely and started to get out. He got

*See Appendix 23 for Life after 603.

half out and then saw it was going to crash into a big barracks; so he got back into the cockpit again, steered it clear of the barracks and then jumped just before it crashed. The machine burnt, but he was quite clear of it. I think he was hit by the tail-plane as he jumped, so he could never know what happened. This story is still not for publication as I think the authorities want to get all the details before they give it to the world.

For sheer calculated bravery I think it's one of the most wonderful things I have ever heard. It's easy enough to do brave things in the heat of battle; but a thing like that when there is time to consider and decide coolly and when it would be so easy to do the other thing – and there would have been absolutely no blame in doing otherwise – is almost beyond comprehension. It is almost one of the things of which dreams are made; an ideal far beyond the search of ordinary men. And yet I'm not really surprised at it. It is just what I, knowing him well, would have expected; for his dreams and ideals were not just the idle ones of the ordinary man but things that were absolutely real to him.

After the incredulity at his going and then the burning anger at it, the knowledge of the manner of it is rather like the sun and wind on the hill after the muck and dirt of the town. There is something serene and sublime about a life that is completed like that, and not just ended as is the fate of most of us, that lifts one out of the sordid darkness of this world of fighting and makes me realise that life is not the dirty evil thing it so often appears.

I fear that nothing in the manner of his going will alter the blackness and emptiness of things and the sort of gnawing feeling of being lost. I feel somehow there is some purpose behind it all. I have had a singularly happy and untroubled life; but even so, I have since come to the conclusion that everything that happens to us is part of the scheme of things and is in the nature of a trial put there to improve us and to make us more fit for some purpose which God has in store for us later – rather in the manner of the old concept of the purifying fire.

Will you let me know when next you are to be in town; for I would like to see you. I think I should get a day off sometime next week. If you will let me know in good time when and where. I will do my best to fix it with George. I am sending two books which… I thought you might like to have back. I hear you are leaving Kingsdown. I think it's a good move.

God Bless
Black

Black and Mardi were destined not to see each other as planned. He too was shot down before the meeting could take place.

Friday 4 October 1940

The activity by enemy aircraft was restricted to raids carried out in nearly all cases by single aircraft. The morning raids made landfall between Beachy Head and Dover and returned along the same route. The raids concentrated on London and the south-eastern area of the group in most cases. During the afternoon the raids made landfall along the broad stretch of coastline between Shoreham-by-Sea and Hastings and reached a peak around 15.00 hours when about 15 raids were in 11 Group airspace and penetrated as far as the IAZ. Thirty-eight patrols were sent up to intercept. 603 were not involved.

The 11 Group intelligence bulletin for this day (No.74) announced the award of the DFC to S/L George Denholm. From his room in the sergeants mess, new addition, Sgt John Strawson, wrote home of his early observations since arriving at Hornchurch:

Dearest People,
Here I am sitting in my pyjamas at the table (we have an armchair and a stool, locker, cupboard, shelf and a lampshade too) in the room which I am sharing with Garvey.* It is 9.30pm and I am expecting lights to go out any minute – air raids – hence the pyjamas. I am

*Sgt pilot Leonard Arthur Garvey was from Birmingham and remembered as a fine athlete. He joined the RAFVR in June 1937 and was serving with 41 Squadron during his time at Hornchurch with Strawson. On 30 October, whilst Strawson was recovering from his injuries, Garvey was shot and killed in combat with 109s over Ashford. His Spitfire (P7375) crashed on Church Farm, Stanford. He was 26 and his remains were buried in Wilton Cemetery, Birmingham.

not cold because I have a leather jacket which I got today. It is the same sort as the one I showed you but not as new. It is all blackish (oil) and battle scared although I have looked in vain for bloodstains and bullet holes. I like it better than a new one as it will not look so 'sprog'.

I owe some of you an apology, you were right, I ought to have caught the earlier train. Not for the sake of being here, they didn't expect us or anything, but for comfort.

To tell you things as they happened. I got into London at 11 o'clock and after that can't remember the details but rode about in the tube trains and walked half way across the town from station to station eventually arriving with heavy kit and greatcoat and in a lather of sweat just in time to jump aboard an electric train which landed me about a mile from here. Then more walking and searching for the 'drome and I staggered in to the guardroom at 1am.

They fixed me up with a bed and thinking to have a wash tried to commit suicide by crashing my forehead against some rugged looking ironwork in the dark. After mopping up the blood and expressing my opinions about Hornchurch generally I had a fair night's rest. Rolling out about 9 o'clock I found the mess and breakfast. I spent the day introducing myself around and getting a room. Garvey arrived mid-morning and we share one.

That was yesterday. I have been messing about all today (Sat) getting a parachute and Mae West etc.

I like the Squadron Leader and Adjutant but have not met the other officers yet, incidentally, they are nearly all officers, only about two more Sgt pilots. There are three Squadrons here and ours is '603' whose home is in Edinburgh or somewhere up there. Lots of them are Scots. They have been down here a month and have the best record of the lot.

I think I shall like being here only I have been doing nothing important today as they have not had time to take notice of me, having been fighting nearly all day.

However, I am to go at dawn tomorrow morning so expect to do something. I am really quite lucky in getting down here where there is some real action and a chance to find out if you are any good or not.

Nearly all the work is done at the most amazing heights which is why Londoners seldom see the fights. Even on a brilliant day it would be hard to discern anything at the heights used and almost impossible to hear the planes unless they are 'all out'.

I was stopped there by all the lights going out and so had supper by lantern and am now finishing by torch-light in our room. There is an air raid on and a good one too, but that is the regular thing. The East End and out here are called 'Hells Corner' and rightly so. One can tell there's a war on here all right.

The noise of the AA guns is just like sharp cracks of thunder and is fairly continuous at night. If you go out you can see your way about by the big flashes from them, just like lightning. They do not keep me awake at all but I have not got properly used to them yet. Just now coming across from the mess I heard the whine of bombs (not screamers) away to the west. It is not a pleasant feeling and makes you want to run, which of course is silly.

Of course there is no danger of being bombed here at night, we are too far out and for daylight raids there are very good trenches indeed and of course the boys see that Jerry doesn't dare too much in daylight. Incidentally, they did quite well today. It always happens that the Spitfires meet enemy fighters and not bombers, the ME109 appears to be our favourite meal. The Hurricanes lower down deal with the bombers.

By the way, we do not go off in small numbers but the whole Squadron (12) at a time and often several of them. One pleasing thing about this sector is that it is almost impossible to get lost because of the river.

I understand that London had a pasting but did not see any damage coming through at night, but I did see some sights which I shan't forget, the tube stations.

Every underground station, and I passed through dozens, was absolutely packed with people, all sleeping on the floor on rags and blankets. They were everywhere, thousands upon thousands of them. You had to pick your way along little paths between them on the platforms, the ticket halls, passages. Staircases and even an escalator which was stopped. There were all kinds of people, odd ones and families and almost all classes. All about half undressed and so thick on the floor that not one more could have laid down.

They were quiet and mostly sound asleep at that time of night and lots of special police etc walking about seeing they didn't overcrowd too near the edge of the platform as the trains were running. I've never seen such a motley crowd anywhere, dirty urchins, prosperous business men (to look at), working youths, whole families and quite a lot of smartly dressed business girls. The air was pretty thick I can tell you. I suppose as the posters told me, 'they're all the same to Hitler'. Funnily enough no-one asked me for my ticket, not even at King's Cross. I suppose I could have ridden about free for ever.

All those people in the stations were not there for a raid but sleep there every night on principle.

Hornchurch is a properly built station (RAF) and the mess is quite nice though not up to Kirton Lindsey standard. I find that Kirton is voted the best station ever by anyone that has been there, including me.

We have had some excitement since I wrote that last bit. The place has been showered with incendiary bombs so we've had a busy ten minutes putting them out with sand. It's quite easy really and great fun dashing about with sandbags and shouting. There were lots of them and lit the whole place up like day. A garage and car were burnt out (object lesson)...

Lots of love to all

John

Saturday 5 October 1940

During the day the enemy carried out four attacks over Kent towards London, one over Poole, and another over Portsmouth.

A tip and run raid occurred between 10.00-1030 when about 24 enemy aircraft flew over Dover and on to Maidstone. A number of aircraft flew over the Thames to the Southend area. Six sorties were sent up to intercept.

The second attack occurred between 11.00 and 12.00 when two formations of about 25 aircraft flying at 20,000 feet crossed the coast at Dungeness and flew to the Biggin Hill area. A second formation of 100 aircraft crossed the coast, the majority believed to be fighters with two formations of bombers. Eleven squadrons were sent up to intercept.

603 Squadron took off at 11.10 with orders to climb to 25,000 feet to investigate activity in the Maidstone area: S/L Denholm (X4490), F/L Boulter (X4489), F/O Haig (X4259), F/O Carbury (X4169), P/O Berry (R6626), P/O Morton (K9807), P/O Read (P9440), F/O Macnamara (X4272), P/O Soden (N3100), P/O Martel (X4348), Sgt Bailey (N3099) and Sgt Darling (R6752).

Having spotted a number of He111s and Bf110s about 10,000 feet below they went into line astern to attack. Before they could reach the bombers they were intercepted by the escort which came out of the clouds above them. This situation once again highlighted the failings of the RAF tactics at this time. 603 formed a defensive circle and a series of dogfights ensued. Black, now one of the most experienced and successful pilots in the Squadron, was shot down by 109s of II/JG53 over Dover at 11.55 hours. He managed to bale out of his Spitfire but had been burnt about his forehead, neck and hands. His Spitfire crashed near Chilham. He played no further part in the battle and later recorded in his diary:

5.10.40. Written later. Cloud 2/10 about 3,000'.

Squadron took off about 11.20. I was rearguard. At about 30,000' near Ashford, Squadron went into line astern to dive on 110s and I think bombers, at about 20,000'. On the way down I saw a single 109 on our starboard beam diving towards our leading machines. I broke out and dived on him trying to come up under his tail. I went right past him and was unable to pull up on him and lost him. There were then 110s circling above me but I was too far below to get a shot so cleared off and climbed up. At 21,000' saw three 109s just above me (500') and about 1/2 mile E going E. They were climbing too. I set off after them and got to about 600 when they split. Two doing a gentle left turn and the third going straight on. I chased the two and was just getting into position about 400 slightly below and to their port quarter when I saw a single one coming at me from slightly above on my port. He was some way off –

RAF Hornchurch October 1940. A 603 Spitfire is in the middle of the airfield having run out of fuel on landing. The pilot stands near the tail.

400-500 – and I hesitated whether to make a quick shot or turn. I then started to turn hard left. As I went into the turn there was a very loud clang on my port side forward and, almost immediately, a lot of flame came up from my feet. I let go of everything and tried to open the hood using both hands. I got it back; but it slipped forward again and I was just thinking 'I can't do it again' when I opened my eyes for a fraction to have a look at things, I noticed there was no perspex left in it; whether it had gone from the heat or the shell I don't know. I then did a bunt to get out; but hadn't undone the straps. I got hold of the clip and pulled it out. It was a terrific effort and seemed to take ages.

The aircraft then did another bunt – whether I pushed the stick forward again or whether the machine just did it I don't remember – and out I went without touching anything. As I went out I waited for the bang as I hit the tail but it didn't come and suddenly there I was sailing through the air. At first I felt all legs and arms whirling around; but very soon became quite comfortable. The wind didn't seem very strong; but I began to feel very bad and thought I'd better pull the cord before I passed out. I did this with no difficulty and the brolly opened almost before I had time to wonder whether it would open. There was a biggish jerk and there I was suspended. The straps cut in a bit and I felt very uncomfortable from them.

By now I was feeling very miserable indeed and on seeing an aircraft approaching head-on thought it must be a Hun coming to finish me off; so I hung my head and pretended to be out. Nothing happened and after a few seconds I looked out and it was a Hurricane doing a few circuits of me.

I felt a bit better after this and started to take stock a little. My boots had gone and my overalls were flying in tatters. I suppose the boots had stuck in the rudder pedals when I left.

My sleeves also were in ribbons and my hands still appeared to have a rather tattered pair of silk gloves on. However, this seeming queer, I took more careful stock and found that it was really all the skin which had come away. Curiously, my hands did not hurt awfully; the greatest discomfort being from my forehead and neck where I'd been burnt between the folds of my scarf.

I then had a look round to see where I was; but couldn't pin-point myself at all. I couldn't see the sea which was a comfort as I was rather afraid of coming down in the water.

I didn't seem to be dropping at all and except for an occasional flap from the brolly it all seemed very quiet. The Hurricane was still circling me and was soon joined by a Spitfire, soon after the Hurricane left.

Very soon I got close to the ground and began to wonder where I should land. I soon saw I should land in a sort of small park with big trees in it and wondered if I should hit one. I was drifting quite fast now and facing up-wind, so I tried to turn to face the way I was going. I got hold of the straps over my head; but didn't seem to be able to do much, though I managed to get half-round before I got down. I landed quite safely and sat down and managed to undo my harness buckle. However, there was hardly any wind on the ground and the brolly collapsed quite quickly.

There were several soldiers about a hundred yards off coming towards me. They didn't look very fierce and, not being able to get my helmet off as it was all stiff from the heat, I called to them to come and help me off with my things. This they did and were very nice to me, doing up my head and neck and my hands which were not much good by now.

The Spitfire stayed and circled for a minute or two after I landed and then pushed off. Soon someone drove a car into the field and took me off to an army ambulance post after I'd got one of the men to promise to get on to Biggin to tell George I was OK.

The chaps that picked me up were a Troop Carrying Unit who seemed quite pleased to have some diversion from their exercise and told me that at least four machines had come down out of the dogfight.

At the first-aid post I was given some coffee and some Tannafax for my neck which was very sore by now and then was packed off by ambulance to the hospital.

At the 'Hundredth Hun' dinner, I had a talk with Tannoy [Bill Read] and it seems certain that he was the Spitfire, as he said he circled a brolly right down to the ground and described the field just as I saw it. He said he was flying at about 4,000' when he saw the brolly open some little way away so he went to investigate.

It never occurred to me that I had actually passed out leaving my machine; but I must have been out while I went from 21,000' to 4,000' which explains why it seemed such a comparatively short time till I got to the ground after opening the brolly.

With no recollection of his flying boots being caught in the rudder pedals it is most likely Black lost his boots after leaving the aircraft. As his unconscious body tumbled through the air, the speed, airflow and gravitational forces would have quickly conspired to fling his cumbersome flying boots from his feet into space but it could also have been the jerk sustained when the canopy opened. Black was wearing the same black flying overall, with the 603 badge on the left-hand pocket, that he had been wearing since the outbreak of war. He had not been wearing gloves. Rapid hospital treatment, in particular, intravenous and oral infusion of fluids to compensate for the dehydration which is symptomatic of burns, was vital. Tragically, such treatment was not always prescribed and a number of fine young men died as a consequence of severe shock, one example being the 601 Squadron American Hurricane pilot, Billy Fiske.

Ludwik Martel.

Black was admitted to the station hospital at Hornchurch where he remained as non-effective-sick until February 1941, when he was posted to the Manchester UAS as an instructor.*

During the same combat in which Black was shot down Ludwik Martel was credited with destroying a 109, Sgt Andy Darling claimed a 109 probable while Brian Carbury damaged another.

The third raid developed between 13.30-14.50 and began with an attempt to lure up the RAF fighters before the bombers arrived. A fighter sweep by about 25 enemy aircraft at 20,000 feet flew to Maidstone, Isle of Sheppey and over the coast at North Foreland. One hundred enemy bombers then followed escorted by fighters of which 50 reached central London but then turned south-east and rejoined the rest of the original formation which had remained over central Kent, before

*See Appendix 'Life After 603'.

heading back to France. Sixteen squadrons were sent up to intercept.

Between 13.40-14.35 hours 80 enemy aircraft crossed the coast by St Albans Head and bombed Poole. This attack was clearly synchronised with that over Kent. At 15.30 hours two formations of about 50 aircraft crossed the coast between Dungeness and Hastings and attacked targets in Kent, East Sussex and East Surrey. Thirteen squadrons were ordered to intercept. The raiders retreated on a reciprocal course around 16.30. The final daylight attack occurred between 17.15-17.40 when 60 enemy aircraft crossed the coast at Selsey Bill in two formations. Although they initially headed inland, they turned and made for Tangmere and Southampton. Eleven squadrons were ordered to intercept but 603 were not one of those sent up.

Sunday 6 October 1940

The morning saw a few isolated bombing raids by single aircraft. At 12.25 about 60 enemy aircraft approached Dover and Manston but did not penetrate inland. Twenty-two squadrons were ordered to intercept. Enemy activity continued to increase throughout the afternoon with a multitude of single raids which finally ended by around 18.00 hours. That same afternoon Filton and the Bristol Aircraft factory was bombed.

Tannoy Read and Brian Macnamara had an unnerving experience when they were scrambled together and took off into low cloud which the meteorology ('met') office assured them would break at 5,000 feet. They climbed as a pair until their instruments froze in the wet and then freezing temperatures in the cloud. At 28,000 feet they were still in cloud and hoping that the visibility would clear enough for them to turn and descend without colliding. When they did eventually try to descend they lost each other in the cloud but, by some miracle, met again and stayed in touch until they broke out of the cloud over Eastchurch. The cloud was so low that the tops of the tall wireless masts were hidden. They landed on the airstrip only to find it virtually deserted. A skeleton staff of old Polish servants rustled up something to eat and showed them a disused hut where they could sleep. It had previously been occupied by a Polish contingent and was full of empty gin and scent bottles.

Monday 7 October 1940

The squadrons of 11 Group attempted to repel three major raids over Kent and London. The first was between 09.30-11.00, a second between 13.00-14.00 and a third between 15.30-17.00 hours.

At 09.35 hours 603 were ordered into the air. Having been preceded by a fighter sweep of about 30 Bf109s an estimated force of 150 enemy aircraft, the greater number being fighters, flew inland – the fighters at 20,000-30,000 feet, the bombers at 15,000-20,000 feet. 603 were vectored towards an incoming staffel of 109E-4s of JG26 over Kent. Led by Adolf Galland, JG26 were carrying out the first of three escorts of Jabos against London that day from their bases at Audembert, Marquise and Caffiers in northern France. There were experienced pilots in JG26, and 603 and Sgt John Strawson, just four days after arriving at Hornchurch, never saw the 109 which shot him down. His Spitfire was hit in the radiator and the hoses carrying the engine coolant and he was aware that it would be a matter of time before the engine would overheat and seize as a result. Losing height rapidly he managed to put his aircraft down on the surface of the Thames, in the estuary. On impact with the water he was flung forward sustaining a severe cut to his forehead in the process as well as other facial injuries. As he attempted to struggle free of the cockpit the sea water came rushing in, pinning him to his seat and forcing copious quantities into his nasal airways and down his throat. When the aircraft began to sink, so the sunlight began to disappear and Strawson was by now panicking as he attempted to escape from what was fast becoming his tomb. On leaving the surface the Spitfire inverted before continuing to plunge towards the seabed. As it turned turtle Strawson found that the pressure from the water lessened and he was able to free himself. With lungs at bursting point, he struggled out and swam hard for the daylight above which seemed so far off. He lost control and gulped water before breaking free of the surface and gasping the fresh air. Strawson was picked up by a RN launch, rushed to dry land and taken to hospital, where he remained for 11 days. The injury to his head was stitched but by far the most serious reaction was due to the amount of seawater he had ingested. His brother, Bill, reflects on the last time he saw his brother:

What John told me at the time was that he had been shot down by a German fighter while in combat and explained that the German fighter came out of the sun which, I suppose, is a classic error to make. He was hit in the radiator… He also said, I remember very clearly, that he thought the Spitfire would slow down sufficiently on the surface to enable him to get out, but this wasn't the case and he had great difficulty getting out of the cockpit. I believe this is when his facial injuries occurred.

He also remembers the ghastly reaction his brother's body had to the salt water: 'The reason he was home on sick leave after being discharged from the hospital was as a result of swallowing so much Thames estuary water. I remember the top half of his body was covered with huge boils.'

During the same patrol in which Strawson was downed, the Squadron lost P/O Henry Matthews who was shot down at 10.45 and killed by Feldwebel Roth of 4/JG26, as AHB records show:

> 40551 Flying Officer H.K.F Matthews was lost on 7 October 1940 whilst flying Spitfire K9807 of 603 Squadron. The aircraft crashed at Godmersham Park, 5 miles NE of Maidstone.
>
> 741453 Sergeant J.M. Strawson sustained injuries whilst flying Spitfire N3109 of 603 Squadron on 7 October 1940. The aircraft crashed into the sea after sustaining damage in a flying battle. Sgt Strawson was admitted to the Royal Navy Hospital at Chatham with minor injuries.

Sgt John Strawson (taken later in the war as a squadron leader).

Spitfire K9807, in which Matthews was purported to have been lost, was actually shot down on 5 October with Black Morton at the controls. As the wreckage of Matthews' Spitfire has since been unearthed there is little doubt that the aircraft he was flying was N3109. Scant information was recorded in the 603 ORB but successive 11 Group composite reports provide all the details.

Following Combat report received from Hornchurch 7.10.40.

Preliminary Combat Report.

A. Dover area.
B. 11 A/C Squadron 603 left Hornchurch at 0935 hours.
C. 9 A/C returned to Hornchurch at 1110 hours.
D. Our losses 2 pilots and A/C missing.
E. Enemy losses NIL.

Composite Combat Report 603 Squadron 7.10.40.

11 A/C left Hornchurch at 0935 and climbed to 29,000. They were meant to rendezvous with 92 Sqdn. B. over Maidstone but did not see them. Detailed to raid 27, when south of Dover saw 20 yellow nosed Me.109's approaching from the east at 31,000. Me.109's went to one side and turned attacking 603 from rear out of the sun. Dogfights ensued after 603 Sqdn. had formed a protective circle.

Cloud 4/10. 6,000.

No assistance from A.A.

Our Casualties: P/O Matthews missing. Sgt Strawson slightly wounded landed on sea off Southend.
1 A/C missing. 1 A/C Cat.3.
Enemy casualties....NIL.
9 A/C landed at Hornchurch 1110 hours.

The day's action continued for 603 Squadron when they were sent up in response to a second attack by the Luftwaffe. This consisted of three waves of fighters flying over the coast at Dover and Hastings at ten-minute intervals. Of the 70 fighters reported, some carried bombs. Two raids reached the IAZ the third machine gunned the Dover barrage balloons. Fourteen squadrons were sent to intercept. HQ Fighter Command subsequently received the following composite combat report from 11 Group:

F/L David Scott-Malden, 'Scottie'.

> 603 Squadron 7.10.40 9 A/C left Hornchurch – 1250 and climbed to 28,000 ft. 20 miles south of Biggin Hill saw 40 Me.109's at 27,000 ft. which passed under them on the beam. Sqdn turned starboard and went into sections line astern diving after E/A which were in a large cluster in no special formation and they dived. 603 Sqdn were unable to catch them though they chased them nearly to France. Only two pilots fired but at long range and did not observe any results. No assistance from A.A. Cloud 4/10 at 3,000. Our casualties NIL.
>
> Enemy casualties NIL.
>
> 9 A/C landed at Hornchurch 1420.

Later that afternoon a third attack developed between 15.36-17.10 hours and consisted of a total of 80 aircraft, all fighters. It arrived in two phases, the first continued until 16.30, the second until 17.10 hours. Thirteen RAF squadrons were despatched. According to the 603 ORB, the following pilots were in action again: S/L Denholm (X4490), F/O Carbury (X4164), F/O Pinckney (R6836), F/O Macnamara (P9499), P/O Berry (R6626), P/O Goldsmith (X4259), P/O Stapleton (X4248), P/O Read (P9440), P/O Scott-Malden (X4347), Sgt Darling (N3099) and Sgt Burt (N3100).The 11 Group composite report for the patrol states:

> 603 Sqdn. 7.10.40. 11 A/C 603 Sqdn took off from Hornchurch 1544 and climbed to 2500 ft. over base, vectored to Biggin Hill area and then east of Maidstone where they saw about 30 yellow nosed Me.109's in ragged formation between 20 to 25 ft. Sqdn went into line astern formation and dived to attack. P/O Scott-Malden got separated from the Sqdn and saw 3 bombers escorted by Me.109's but they were too far away over the Channel going towards France for him to attack. Cloud 3/10ths 1500, No A.A. Assistance 11 A/C landed at Hornchurch 1645. Our casualties Nil, enemy casualties 1 Me.109 destroyed (crashed nr Ashford).

Brian Carbury destroyed the 109 over Maidstone. The effectiveness of the attack by the 603 aircraft was hampered by the presence of a number of Hurricanes which the pilots claimed showed as much aggression towards them as to the German fighters. This was Pilot Officer David 'Scottie' Scott-Malden's first patrol with the Squadron, and it marked the beginning of a successful career as a fighter pilot. Scottie had been at Winchester with Black and the two remained friends until Black's death in 1982.* The frantic air fighting continued with the pilots flying two or three sorties a day.

---

*Although the exact date is not known, during a later patrol Scottie's aircraft was hit by return fire as he broke away from an attack and he headed back to the aerodrome with his left arm hanging uselessly by his side. With great difficulty he managed to land by juggling the control column and throttle with his right arm only. The ambulance and fire tender dashed out to meet him, at which point feeling began to return to his arm. Although he dared not look down to see what damage had been caused when he did eventually take a glance he was surprised that there was a distinct lack of blood. Resting on the fuse box under his left elbow was the core of an armour piercing bullet, which had had just enough force to penetrate the armour plate and strike the funny-bone in his left elbow without even breaking the skin! Relieved, Scottie called up control and said he could taxi to dispersal under his own steam.

Tuesday 8 October 1940

Between 08.30-09.45 a raid by bomb-carrying fighters crossed the coast in the Winchelsea Bay area and dropped bombs in central London. A second raid consisting predominantly of fighters, crossed the coast in the Dungeness area and also headed for the capital. Sixteen squadrons were ordered up. Between 10.30-11.00 hours a force of about 30 fighters flew inland over Dymchurch and on to London while a larger force followed.

At 11.35 Uncle George (X4490) led the Squadron to intercept: F/O Carbury (X4164), F/O Macnamara (P9499), P/O Stapleton (X4348), P/O Berry (R7020), P/O Martel (R6626), P/O Scott-Malden (K9795), P/O Goldsmith (N3099), Sgt Burt (N3100) and Sgt Darling (X4019).

Ras Berry claimed a 109 probable. The Squadron landed at 12.15. Between 11.20-12.50 and 11.30-11.50 attacks were carried out by 24 and 20 aircraft which came inland and headed for London and Chatham respectively. Three squadrons were ordered to intercept.

From his hospital bed, Strawson recounted his experiences of the previous day in a letter home:

> Ward C1
> Royal Naval Hospital
> Chatham
> Kent
> Tuesday 8th/10/40

Dear Mum,

My pride has received a severe blow and so have I. On my first sortie (fight) I have been shot down by an ME109.

This is very aggravating as I didn't get the chance to fire a single shot, the blighter surprising me when I thought we had sent them back and had the sky to ourselves. However, I won't bother you with details (which I will save for Bill).

Incidentally, I did not get hit, only the engine, so I made a forced landing on the sea in the Thames estuary near some ships. Unfortunately, I wasn't quick enough getting out and went down to a fair depth in the plane.

Fighting myself out of the cockpit, which was almost upside down, was the toughest part and I wasn't at all happy just then. That is when I got my odd superficial injuries I think. These are not a bit serious, a gash in the forehead, 9 stitches (without anaesthetic either!!) and a couple of smaller ones on the left cheek with of course a black eye.

The funniest of the lot and which I hardly believe, is the doctors say my nose is broken, I have tried to explain that it is always bent but they won't have that.

'Doc' says it will look like Ramon Navanno's when he's done with it. It looks just the same as ever to me.

I was awful cold and shivery at first, shock I suppose but feel as fit as a fiddle now. I am in this big naval hospital which is the most marvellously comfortable place imaginable, right in the heart of Kent. I was lucky the torpedo boat that picked me up brought me to the south side as I'm sure this beats anything the RAF have got.

The ward is big and pleasant with real fires in the middle and only a very few of us in it. I am sure the nurses and sisters are the sweetest women God ever made. Nothing is too much trouble for them and their care is almost embarrassing when there is really so little the matter with me. The doctor, a Naval Officer, won't let me sit up yet for some reason or other, although I expect to get up tomorrow and was hoping to be home in a day or two. I suppose it may be a bit longer, it depends on the nose.

The professional pride of these people is terrific, for instance they skilfully bandaged up a small sore on my left heel which had been made by a boot and was already half better before the accident.

Very luckily I had decided not to wear my best suit and left it off yesterday morning. Incidentally, we were getting up at 5.30am to get on readiness by dawn, 'how's that'. The affair occurred about 10.30am yesterday, Monday morning.

The ride in the fast motor torpedo boat was terrific – about 40 mph on the water.

Do not have any silly ideas about coming to see me. I am sure to get a bit of leave (can fix the car).

You cannot see me here anyway, but I should be most unforgivingly cross if you tried. Not because I don't like seeing you, but you're better at Marnham.

This should be a lesson to Harry to stick to farming. I've had a lot more training than he would get and his luck is never as good as mine in accidents.

Love to all
John

The following report was sent from 11 Group to Headquarters Fighter Command:

'PLEASE AMEND CASUALTY STATE FOR 7.10.40 AS FOLLOWS. SQDN 603 SORTIE 0935 TO 1110 P/O MATTHEWS KILLED.'

Keith Lawrence's time with 603 came to an end when he, along with a number of other experienced pilots, was posted to 421 Flight, then forming at Hawkinge with the Spitfires of 66 Squadron. During a four-week period with the Edinburgh Squadron Keith had flown 18 patrols in 15 days – what he modestly describes as '…a rather eventful time'!

Keith has retained fond memories of a number of his fellow 603 pilots, including George Denholm:

He was a quiet, likeable chap who was in the air a lot. Everybody respected him. I renewed my acquaintance with George in 1990 at London's Guildhall as guests of the Lord Mayor of London on the 50th anniversary of the Battle of Britain.

My only written reminder [of WWII] is my log book but like many pilots' log books it was not so much a diary as just a record of flying hours required by the CO at the end of each month and consequently little in it to refresh my thoughts on times long past. However... we flew on operations most days; not even a 'sector recce' on arrival and only two non-operational trips in fifteen days. This of course meant a good deal of daylight hours were spent at one of the states of 'readiness' down at the flight office which I think for A Flight was on the east or south-east side of the field. 54 Squadron with its illustrious names was on the north side. I seem to recall 'one hour's readiness' meant mealtimes at the mess. This fact sticks in the memory because I had an aversion to being 'scrambled' on an empty stomach.

Whether in the mess or at dispersal a constant interruption of normal life at Hornchurch was the air raid alerts, sometimes followed by bombs. Flying also tended to be a bit fraught and sometimes even disconcerting.

Following days when there was flying, with the possibility of being shot at, off-duty relaxation for aircrew seemed to be somewhat of a necessity and 603 pilots being no exception were not slow in taking advantage of the fact that Hornchurch was on the District Line and only forty-five minutes from the West End and its attractions. Peter Dexter used to take us to the Wellington Club in Knightsbridge, which he frequented. We would drink all night and return early the next morning to go on readiness. It wasn't something we did *that* regularly but as young men we *did* live it up. Typically, once airborne, we relied on Air Ministry oxygen to sober us up. I think quite a few must have sampled this nightlife, with the added experience of the night bombing of London thrown in.

Not being a raconteur, or even having a good memory, I regret I cannot recount any gripping or graphic accounts of 603's exploits in the air, not even a 'there I was, upside down, with nothing on the clock but the maker's name...' story, but just my fading impressions of life in September 1940 on Group Captain Bouchier's station at Hornchurch.*

Thursday 10 October 1940

The previous day had featured two, three-phase attacks on the south-east and London but 603 were not involved. There were a number of operations by the Luftwaffe during the 10th, however. East Kent, the Thames estuary and Hornchurch (08.30-09.20), east Kent and the estuary (09.53-10.30), Weymouth area (12.00-12.35) and east Kent (15.00-16.00).

---

*See Appendix 'Life After 603'.

At 09.45, in response to a second incursion which consisted of two large formations which crossed the coast between Dover and Dungeness, 12 Spitfires of 603 took off from Rochford through thick cloud with orders to patrol Hornchurch at 30,000 feet: S/L Denholm (X4490), F/O Carbury (X4164), F/O Pinckney (X4594), F/O Macnamara (P9499), P/O Read (P9440), P/O Goldsmith (X4019), P/O Martel (R6626), P/O Soden (X4593), P/O Dewey (R6752), Sgt Bailey (X4347) and Sgt Burt (R7020).

At 25,000 feet they joined forces with 41 Squadron which led the formation as they climbed to 32,000 feet over Dover, flew back to Sheppey before heading south-east. Successive waves of German aircraft flew inland over Hythe towards Faversham, some of which eventually appeared over the estuary. About 85 enemy aircraft were engaged by eight squadrons of RAF fighters in what was apparently a series of fighter sweeps. 603 were vectored over the Channel between Canterbury and Dover where they saw 15-20 109s heading for France just above the cloud 3,000 feet below them 'in wide pairs at 5 to 10 span intervals'. The Squadron made an astern attack and the leading 109s were seen to climb slightly while the rear aircraft turned for battle.

A dogfight ensued. Interestingly, a further 12 109s were seen mid-Channel which the 603 pilots reported seeing with British top camouflage with red and blue roundels 'sides and bottom of nose were yellow or white. Undersurfaces was silver grey, with black crosses.'

Brian Carbury led his section in an attack on a group of 20 109s and destroyed two. One crashed into the sea, the other on the beach at Dunkirk. Soden destroyed another 109 and Pinckney damaged a fourth. The dense cloud made flying conditions very difficult and whilst six aircraft landed back at Rochford at 11.20, three others landed at Coltishall with two more at Martlesham Heath.

Brian Carbury's award of a Bar to his DFC was announced in 11 Group I.B. No.80. This was probably Bill Bailey's last patrol with the Squadron. By the end of the month Bailey was sent to 7 FTS at Peterborough as an instructor and on 7 January 1941 he was posted to 31 SFTS at Kingston, Ontario, where he taught FAA pilots advanced flying skills, formation flying and dive-bombing.*

Saturday 12 October 1940

On Friday 11 October, 603 were not involved in the action. The next day, however, from 09.00-16.30 hours enemy activity was almost continuous and consisted of six phases. As one attack ended so another developed. All were directed against London. In the afternoon there were two consecutive attacks against the capital following which activity was limited to three raids which approached the coast.

603 didn't achieve success until the second afternoon phase of enemy operations (15.30-16.30). Three raids totalling about 80 aircraft, reported as mainly fighters, crossed the coast at 20,000 feet between Dover and Dungeness. All three raids targeted London but all approached taking different routes. Eleven squadrons were ordered to intercept. 603 consisted of F/L Boulter (R6626), F/L Haig (R6752), F/O Carbury (X9164), F/O Pinckney (N3099), F/O Macnamara (R7027), P/O Stapleton (X4348), P/O Scott-Malden (X4347), F/O Martel (X4593), P/O Soden (P9499), P/O Goldsmith (X4019) and P/O Dewey (X4265).

At 14.45 they saw a large formation 3,000 feet below and as they approached P/O Scott-Malden picked one out, turned inside it and fired a deflection shot developing into a stern chase. Black and white smoke soon appeared and the 109 lost height. By the time Scottie broke off his attack the German fighter was at 5,000 feet and still losing height with smoke coming from the engine. Another 109 circled over him as he went down. Scottie later reflected on this being the most vivid aerial combat of the Battle of Britain and which has remained in his mind. It occurred soon after he joined 603:

---

*On 27 May 1941 he was commissioned and promoted to Flying Officer on 27 May the following year and Flight Lieutenant 27 May 1943. Bailey returned to Britain in October 1943 and on 7 December was posted to 15(P) AFU as an instructor. Bailey left Training Command on 2 May 1944 and went to 105 OTU (Transport), Bramcote, before moving to 107 OTU at Leicester East. His last posting was to 271 Squadron at Down Ampney. Bailey left the RAF on 25 November 1945 as a Flight Lieutenant and died in 2001.

The Squadron was depleted by losses and eight aircraft were directed into a large 'gaggle' of Me109s. The squadron split up individually and passed head-on through the enemy formation. There was a sense of shock, as a distant series of silhouettes suddenly became rough metal with grey-green paint and yellow noses, passing head-on each side. At the far end I had a few minutes' dog-fight with the last 109, scoring hits which produced a tail of black smoke. Then we were alone at 20,000 feet, the German gliding down with an engine which coughed and barely turned over, I with no ammunition and very little petrol. He glided hopefully towards the Channel: I looked for an airfield before the last of my petrol ran out. Strangely, I felt inclined to wave to him as I left. But then, I was only twenty years old.

F/L David Scott-Malden, Flight Commander of 603.

He landed at Rochford at 16.30. The Messerschmitt 109, (1966) with a black '11' on the fuselage, crashed high on the Kent Downs at Deans Hill, Hollingbourne scattering the wings and the DB601 engine down the steep slope. The pilot, Staffelführer Oberleutnant Buesgen of 1/JG52 had been engaged on a freelance fighter sweep. He was slightly injured but managed to bale out and became a PoW. In addition to what was Scottie's first claim for an enemy aircraft destroyed, Boulter and Soden also claimed 109s destroyed. In the 603 ORB all three pilots were only credited with probables. It is clear that John Boulter's experience had prompted George Denholm to select him as his new deputy since the death of Ken Macdonald when he couldn't lead the Squadron. Jack Haig was another option and by the end of the battle he had led three patrols.

Sunday 13 and Monday 14 October 1940
On the 13th it would seem that poor weather deterred any large-scale attacks until late morning as only a number of armed reconnaissance raids were carried out by single aircraft. Three attacks then developed between 12.30-16.10 hours, the first two following one after the other. All targeted London and consisted of 109s.

Due to the continuing bad weather, enemy activity the following day consisted of tip and run raids by single armed reconnaissance aircraft operating almost exclusively over the south-east and south Midlands. One raid was reported to have bombed Hawkinge and sprayed the streets of Folkestone with machine-gun fire. Only one formation attack was carried out by the Luftwaffe during the day and took place after the weather had improved in the late afternoon.

At 12.30 Jack Haig and Brian Carbury took off in Spitfires X4259 and X4164 respectively with orders to intercept armed reconnaissance raiders. They landed again at 13.15, Brian having damaged a Ju88.

Tuesday 15 October 1940
Six attacks were carried out during the hours of daylight. The first developed soon after 08.00 hours. The next four took place between 09.00-13.15, an attack on Southampton by 109s and 110s developed between 12.00-13.00 hours, and the last occurred between 15.50-16.30. There were no reports of bombers being used in these attacks, only bomb-carrying 109s.

Twelve 603 Spitfires took off at 15.15 led by George Denholm: F/L Boulter (R6626), F/O Pinckney (R6836), F/O Macnamara (X4274), P/O Goldsmith (X4259), P/O Read (P9440), P/O Stapleton (X4348), P/O Martel (X4593), P/O Soden (P9499), P/O Scott-Malden (X4347), P/O Dewey (X4594) and Sgt Burt (R7020).

During the patrol at 15,000 feet, Bill Read was bounced by 109s and his radiator was shot through with cannon fire. The engine quickly overheated and seized and Tannoy managed to put his aircraft down safely in a field of terrified cows adjacent to East Horsley railway station. The station master's wife made him a cup of tea and the porter tipped him a shilling to buy some cigarettes –

gestures which Tannoy recalled with gratitude right up until his death. Stapme destroyed a 109 which crashed in the sea. Fog, mist and cloud the next day meant no mass raids.

Thursday 17 October 1940
John Strawson underwent a medical whilst in Chatham which he failed. With only a At Bt rating by the medical board he was discharged the following day and sent on sick leave. Meanwhile 603 Squadron took delivery of two of the first Mk II Spitfires with Rotol airscrews and a better rate of climb (an additional 18lbs of boost). Ras and Scottie managed to grab these before any of the other pilots and flew them for the first time on the 17th.

Four attacks by 109 fighter-bombers with escort were carried out on targets in London and Kent. The second attack developed between 13.30-14.10 hours and involved 603 Squadron.

A force of 50 enemy aircraft crossed the coast at Folkestone and headed towards Maidstone where the formation split in two. The smaller of the units flew west of Biggin Hill to the IAZ as far as Hornchurch before returning over Sheppey and back over the coastline at Deal. The larger of the 'split' flew to Dartford where it divided again and 40 aircraft flew back over north and east Kent and out over South Foreland. The remaining aircraft flew over Biggin Hill, Canterbury and South Foreland. Meanwhile a formation of ten enemy aircraft crossed the coast over Dymchurch at 15,000 feet and on reaching Hawkhurst split. One section flew back over Winchelsea, the other circled back over Folkestone before flying inland to Maidstone and leaving the coast at Dymchurch. Seven squadrons were ordered to intercept.

Stapme claimed a 109 probable during a patrol which, according to the ORB, took off at 17.10 and was back on the ground again by 17.40. (According to the 11 Group I.B. No.86, the time of the patrol was 13.20-14.36, which is likely to be correct.) The pilots were: F/L Boulter (P7327), P/O Stapleton (P7324), P/O Scott-Malden (P7286), P/O Berry (P7309), P/O Soden (P7315), F/O Pinckney (P7350), P/O Dewey (P7328), F/O Carbury (P7365), P/O Read (P7287), F/O Macnamara (P7325) and P/O Martel (P7285).

The following day enemy activity was restricted by adverse weather conditions and consisted of a few reconnaissance missions over East Anglia and the Thames estuary. A number of single armed reconnaissance aircraft flew over the group area during the afternoon. Bombs were dropped sporadically over Kent. On the 19th the weather again prohibited any large-scale attacks during the morning and armed reconnaissance flights were the only activity. The afternoon was busier with an attack carried out against London.

Sunday 20 October 1940
From mid-morning until late afternoon the Luftwaffe carried out what appeared to be almost continuous attacks but were actually five daytime incursions between 09.45-15.40. Eight squadrons were sent up for the first two raids, five for the third, seven for the fourth and fifth respectively.

Uncle George led the Squadron on another patrol at 12.55 in P7365 with: F/L Boulter (R7327), F/O Carbury (X7325), F/O Pinckney (P7295), P/O Stapleton (P7324), P/O Dewey (P7297) and Sgt Darling (P7287).

Whilst on the Maidstone patrol line they were ordered north of the river and joined forces with 41 Squadron who warned that there were about 50 Bf109s ahead. The two squadrons eventually caught sight of the enemy formations over Hornchurch and pursued them to the coast of Dungeness. Colin Pinckney and Dewey each claimed a 109 destroyed. Stapme and Andy Darling were each credited with a probable while Denholm and Dewey each claimed to have damaged a 109. The Squadron was back on the ground at 14.05.

On this day Pilot Officers Harry Prowse and Archie Winskill joined 603. Prowse came from 266 at Wittering:

> On my very first day, at the end of our second patrol, my engine developed a bad glycol leak and packed up altogether as the Squadron prepared to land on Hornchurch. I did my best to make a text book landing down wind and unable to see a thing through a thick cloud of glycol smoke. It was not very successful, although I did walk away from it. An inglorious start to what proved to be a most enjoyable stay with 603. I was 19 years old at the time, with 405 flying hours behind me.

Archie Winskill (later Air Commodore Sir Archie L. Winskill, KCVO, CBE, DFC*, AE) was sent to the Squadron to 'fill dead men's shoes.' He reflects on a few of his colleagues during the Battle of Britain and his close association with 603 in the years after the war:

> I flew mostly as number two to 'Sheep' Gilroy. He was a very impressive fighter pilot who could spot the enemy before anyone else. I put this down to his career as a sheep farmer with eyes trained to search for lost animals, particularly in the winter time, on the fells of Scotland. Razz Berry was always clocking up a healthy score of kills. Stapme Stapleton was a definite character.*

Monday 21 October 1940

Due to low cloud, rain and drizzle resulting in poor visibility the Luftwaffe made no large-scale attacks during daylight hours with only attacks by singleton raiders which occurred more frequently between 11.00-13.30 hours with as many as 20 plotted over the 11 Group area at 12.00 hours. Several patrols were despatched with two interceptions. 603 remained on the ground.

Stapme was promoted to Flying Officer.

Tuesday 22 October 1940

The foggy conditions which blanketed southern England throughout the day curtailed any significant enemy activity apart from two small attacks between 14.20-14.55 and 16.20-17.05 hours when targets in Kent and a convoy were attacked by a force of 50 aircraft. Other activity consisted of reconnaissance missions.

The award of the DFC to S/L George Denholm was particularly fitting and described by Marshal of the Royal Air Force Sir Arthur (later Lord) Tedder as '…an outstanding Distinguished Flying Cross'. Due to poor weather, enemy activity was limited the next day.

Thursday 24 October 1940

Throughout the morning there was a certain amount of activity over the Channel when a number of raids approached the coastline but veered away, out to sea again. Of the raiders that crossed the coast, two Do17s were shot down. During the afternoon very few aircraft crossed the coast, although two raids did reach London and bombed Willesden, Brentford and Hayes.

Keen to be involved in the action, Pilot Officer Peter Olver was posted to 603 from 611 at his own request. He received an unexpected welcome from Uncle George which was probably as a result of the loss of so many of his Squadron:

> I wasn't particularly a German hater but at that time I was worried that the war would be won before I could assist in causing them to eat their words about us all being so decadent. George Denholm was the CO and he didn't seem overjoyed at my arrival saying that I was too inexperienced in flying hours and would just lose another aircraft for him, but consented to give me a trial flying as his No.2 whilst dropping some pilot's ashes in the Channel. This attitude was galling to me and particularly so as he proved to be approximately right, as I got shot down next day by a Messerschmitt along with my No.1, Sowden [Soden] and also a Pole called Ludwig [Ludwik] Martel. I thought he would send me packing but by chance I landed in the same field near Hastings where George himself had been caught by his parachute in a tree some days before, and picked up by the same Army unit.

Peter Olver later wrote: '…one may assume that it was a very good Squadron and I was very fortunate to have served with it.'

---

*Archie maintained his close connections with 603 when he later commanded RAF Turnhouse 1955/56 and the same time was ex-officio the Wing Leader of the Scottish auxiliary squadrons – Glasgow, Aberdeen and Edinburgh. He often led the wing around Scotland much to the delight of the Scots. Of the period he recollects:

Mike Hobson was a first class CO of 603 and popular with both officers and ground crew. Being on the doorstep I often flew with them. Gibraltar (summer camp) was an example. Post war a few of the Auxiliaries (George Denholm, Shag Wallace etc) started a scheme for erecting a war memorial to those pilots who had lost their lives during the conflict whilst serving in 603. This came to nought. I therefore rescued a Spitfire from the breakers yard, erected it at the entrance to the airfield and had it properly consecrated by the local padre circa 1955. An inscribed stone was provided by one of the pilots on the Squadron at that time. Today the Spitfire Memorial and plaque is situated outside Edinburgh (Turnhouse) Airport.

Friday 25 October 1940

In contrast to the previous lull in fighting due to poor weather, the 25th saw much action. The first raid of the day consisted of three waves and occurred continuously between 08.45-10.30 but for a short gap at 09.30. Of an estimated 140 enemy aircraft, 10-12 were Dorniers spotted in the first wave, the rest were Bf109s. Most of the enemy aircraft were confined to Kent although some made it to London where they dropped their bomb loads.

The Squadron lost three aircraft in quick succession during dogfights with Bf109s. Firstly, P/O Ludwik Martel was shot down in combat with 109s over Hastings at 10.10. A cannon shell struck his aircaft exploding in close proximity to Ludwik who received shrapnel wounds in his left leg and body but managed to land his Spitfire Mk II (P7350 now BBMF), which although damaged was repairable. He spent ten days in hospital being treated for his injuries.

At 10.15, following combat with 109s over the Sussex coast, P/O John Soden baled out over Brede, injuring his right leg on landing at 'Perryfields'. He was admitted to the East Sussex Hospital, Hastings. His Spitfire, P7325, XT-W, was written off when it crashed at Stonelink Farm, Brede.

Having only arrived the previous day, as noted previously, at 10.20 P/O Peter Olver was shot down by 109s over Hastings. Despite his injuries he baled out of Spitfire P7309 and landed at Westfield. His aircraft crashed at Pickdick Farm, Brede, Sussex, and was written-off.* On the same day Ras Berry was awarded the DFC and Brian Carbury received a Bar to his DFC (promulgated in the *London Gazette* on 25 October 1940), one of the 'few' to be awarded DFC and Bar both during this period. The citation reads:

Peter Olver.

> Flying Officer Carbury has displayed outstanding gallantry and skill in engagements against the enemy. Previous to the 8th September 1940, this officer shot down eight enemy aircraft and shared in the destruction of two others. Since that date he has destroyed two Messerschmitt 109's and two Heinkel 113's and, in company with other pilots in his Squadron, also assisted in the destruction of yet another two enemy aircraft. His cool courage in the face of the enemy has been a splendid example to other pilots of his Squadron.

The second attack consisted of a succession of raids in two main formations of 50 and 30 enemy aircraft and occurred between 11.50-12.45 and crossed the coast between Dover and Dungeness. Ten squadrons were sent up to intercept and a wing of three squadrons from 12 Group. The raiders reached as far as Hornchurch and Chatham.

That afternoon there were three further large-scale attacks but the interceptors did not include 603.

Saturday 26 October 1940

Plotters had at least one raid on the table throughout the day and much of the time a good many more. There were three attacks over Kent between 10.15-11.00, 11.30-12.25 and 13.30-18.00 hours. 603 Squadron neither achieved success nor lost pilots.

Jack Stokoe was at 25,000 feet over the Channel when the engine of his Spitfire seized during the return flight to Hornchurch. Having weighed up the odds he decided he had enough altitude to glide back. As he crossed the coast he chose a field in which to land and, using the manual pump, he lowered the flaps and undercarriage and carried out a successful landing. Examination of the Merlin engine revealed an oil gallery blockage which had caused the oil to pump over in a non-return fashion and this had resulted in a seizure. Several aircraft and pilots had been lost recently by mysterious engine failure. By being able to land the Spitfire intact Jack allowed the problem to be revealed and rectified.

---

*In 1972, P7309 was the subject of a major archaeological dig by the Wealden Aviation Archaeological Group.

Sunday 27 October 1940

11 Group composite report states:

> The day was one of tremendous activity. From 07.30 hours until lunchtime squadron after squadron of enemy aircraft, mostly fighters, were operating in the Channel and over land. Individual attacks were not large. Reports were also received of enemy naval activity in the Straits and some of the patrols may have been to cover this. After an afternoon of small patrols in the Channel a large scale attack covering the whole Group area, of a scale not experienced for some time developed about 16.30 hours. The end of the day phase was marked by intensive activity over the 12 Group area, presumably enemy attacks directed against our bomber aerodromes.

At 12.50 the Squadron were ordered into the air: S/L Denholm (P7315), F/L Haig (P7311), F/O Gilroy (P7356), F/O Goldsmith (P7439), P/O Prowse (P7295), P/O Olver (P7324), P/O Scott-Malden (P7327), P/O Maxwell (P7286), P/O Dewey (P7365), P/O Berry (P7309), Sgt Darling (P7289) and Sgt Terry (P7324).

There was scattered cloud over the Weald to the south of Maidstone when 603 were bounced by a superior force of Bf109s of III/JG27 late into the patrol at 14.05. Yet again the Squadron paid a high price for being caught at a disadvantage. South African, F/O Claude Goldsmith was shot down over the Kentish Weald, south of Maidstone. He attempted a forced landing but his Spitfire crashed near Waltham, Kent. He initially survived the impact but was terribly injured. His shattered body was gingerly removed from the wreckage and rushed to hospital. Sadly, he died the next day from shock and multiple injuries. He was 23 years old and is buried in Hornchurch Cemetery.

Two other pilots recently arrived from 611 Squadron were shot down in this same combat. It is believed P/O Robert Dewey was also killed whilst trying to carry out a forced landing. His aircraft crashed into a tree at Apple Tree Corner, Chartham Hatch at 14.05 killing him instantly. His Spitfire was written off. Bob Dewey was buried in Hornchurch Cemetery. He was 19. P/O David Maxwell's Spitfire was badly damaged but he managed to force-land at Bethel Row, Throwley at 14.10. He was unhurt and the aircraft repairable.

Monday 28 October 1940

There was little enemy activity during the morning and it consisted of incursions by singletons. A small raid occurred at 14.30 hours followed by another on a larger scale between 16.20-17.15 which flew over Kent towards London.

After the previous day's tragic losses some retribution was inflicted on the enemy when, between 13.10 and 14.55, the following Spitfires led by F/L Jack Haig in Spitfire P7529, encountered 16 109s: F/O Gilroy (P7496), F/O Macnamara (P7324), P/O Berry (P7528), P/O Scott-Malden (P7327), P/O Read (P7289), Sgt Stokoe (P7295) and Sgt Terry (P7285).

Sheep Gilroy, Jack Haig and Tannoy Read used their altitude advantage to bounce the German fighters. Sheep destroyed a 109 while Haig and Read each claimed a 109 damaged. As the 603 Squadron confirmed score was nearing the hundred mark the Bf109 that fell to Sheep's guns that day was the last to fall to the Edinburgh Squadron in the official Battle of Britain. Although a few of their pilots and many others besides would continue to fight, yet more would lose their lives before the end of WWII. It should not be forgotten that this aerial battle continued into 1941, when many, including the German pilots, believed the Battle of Britain truly ended.

Following the second patrol, which took place between 16.11 and 17.30 hours, Archie Winskill was credited with a Bf109 probable while Andy Darling claimed another 109 probable and a damaged. During the patrol Scottie climbed head-on through a large gaggle of 109s over Surrey firing as he went. With inconclusive results he found himself out of ammunition and almost out of fuel. He recognised Croydon airfield below and landed down-wind, hitting a Chance light in the overshoot area and cutting his head on the gun-sight during the initial impact. The injury was not serious and his aircraft was only slightly damaged.

During late October P/O Hartas left 603 with Keith Lawrence to join 421 Flight when it was formed at Hawkinge. It is noticeable that while the pilots in the Squadron were being rotated,

Hartas had not flown with 603 for some time. Whether the move was as a consequence of this is not known.*

On the 29th the Luftwaffe carried out five large-scale attacks during the day, three over Kent towards London, one against Southampton and the last against airfields in Kent and Essex. Records show 603 were not involved in the action. Following several reconnaissance missions flown by the Germans during the following morning, other activity consisted of two attacks over south-east England. One between 11.40-12.40 hours comprised three waves of 50, 20 and 45 aircraft; the second between 15.30-17.00 came in two waves of 130 and 30 enemy aircraft. Ten squadrons were sent up and destroyed five with seven probable and one damaged – all 109s.

Thursday 31 October 1940

Poor weather conditions hindered activity by the Luftwaffe. Nevertheless, between 08.05-16.30 hours Ju87s, Ju88s, Bf109s and an appearance by the Regia Aeronautica (Italian Air Force) carried out a total of seven raids on various targets in Kent as well as London, Portsmouth, Dover and shipping in the estuary. This was the first use of Ju87 en-masse since 18 August.

Whilst the fighting continued, this day was later chosen as the official end to the Battle of Britain. During October the Squadron added a further 25 enemy aircraft destroyed and 20 damaged to their tally giving an initial total of 103½ destroyed with 45 probable. Over the years the figures have been, and continue to be, reassessed. All invariably show that over-claiming was on a massive scale on both sides with the RAF claiming at a rate of 2:1. Nevertheless, the Edinburgh Squadron was the top-scoring day-fighter unit in Fighter Command in the Battle of Britain with 85.8 enemy aircraft claimed destroyed. Of those, 57.5 were confirmed which is more than double the average of other fighter squadrons operating the Spitfire, giving 603 Squadron an impressive 67% accuracy of claims rate. With 47 of their 57.5 confirmed kills being Bf109s they also shot down more of the Luftwaffe's top fighter than any other squadron. Of the 64 days 603 were with 11 Group in the Battle of Britain (out of a total of 113, including their time in Scotland), they were actually engaged on 32 of those during their time in the south and acquired a credited victory/loss ratio of 1.9 enemy aircraft destroyed to one 603 Spitfire. In contrast, 603 paid a high price for their success losing 30 aircraft with many casualties. The fact that 603 was an auxiliary unit is almost irrelevant, as many non-auxiliary pilots had joined before and during the battle and been responsible for much of its success in combat (Carbury, Stapleton and Berry were credited with more than half of the Squadron's victories). This number continued to increase as the new pilots arrived to replace those lost. It was therefore an auxiliary squadron by name only. It is interesting to note that the next highest scoring squadron was 609, another auxiliary unit.

The 603 pilots believed by this time that they had won the particular air battle they had been fighting but they continued to fly fighting patrols throughout November as well as practice flying which enabled the inexperienced pilots the opportunity to hone their skills and the veterans to assist as well as keep their own ability as keen as possible.

---

*On 1 December he claimed a Bf109 destroyed over the Channel and a share of a probable Do17 off Dover on the 18th. On 11 January 1941, 421 Flight was renumbered 91 Squadron. Hartas was killed on 10 February, as a Flying Officer with the squadron. He was 21 and is buried in Folkestone New Cemetery.

CHAPTER 13

AFTER THE BATTLE

1 November saw early morning reconnaissance flights which were later followed by two attacks on London, two on Portsmouth, one on Dover and one on shipping in the Thames estuary. Between 08.25 and 11.45 on the 2nd there were three further 'fair sized' attacks against London and Manston followed by a number of individual sorties by enemy aircraft in the afternoon. The rain and low cloud on the 4th negated enemy activity during the morning. During the afternoon a number of single raiders were active over the estuary. One Do 215 was shot down. The bad weather continued the following day and enemy raiders consisted of a few single aircraft.

The 5th saw the resumption of larger attacks with four main incursions between 09.45-16.45 hours. The third raid of the day occurred at 14.35-15.30 hours and consisted of 60 109s directed towards the Thames estuary, not penetrating further west than Gravesend.

Between 14.45-15.55 hours 603 were airborne on a defensive patrol: S/L Denholm (P7315), F/L Boulter (P7528), Sgt Terry (P7509), P/O Olver (P7288), P/O Berry (P7449), P/O Stapleton (P7436), ------ (P7387).

After patrolling Maidstone they carried out a sweep over Kent when they spotted a number of Bf109s. Sgt Patrick Terry was shot down by Bf109s in combat over Canterbury and, as a result of wounds received, was admitted to Charlton Hospital, Canterbury. His aircraft was assessed as Cat.2. Archie Winskill opened fire on an enemy fighter, without result.

Sergeant Ron Plant was posted to 603 from 611 Squadron. He was to play a short but poignant part in the Squadron's history.

Stapme's award of the DFC was announced in the day's 11 Group bulletin. It was sometime later when he received his medal from the King:

> I travelled down from Drem with Razz Berry and we were presented with our awards by the King at Buckingham Palace. There was a queue of award recipients and the event was memorable when an Indian wearing a turban was presented to the King and saluted so briskly, he lost his balance and toppled slightly! After the ceremony we travelled back to Scotland.

Following a quiet morning enemy activity on 6 November consisted of attacks on Southampton and Kent. Ludwik Martel returned to ops after being shot down on 25 October.

After another quiet morning on the 7th the Luftwaffe carried out two attacks on the Southampton area and one on shipping in the estuary. In response eleven 603 Spitfires took off from Hornchurch at 13.55: F/L Boulter (P7436), F/L Haig (P7295), P/O Gilroy (P7496), F/O Kirkwood (P7285), P/O Berry (P7449), P/O Stapleton (P7528), P/O Prowse (P7543), P/O Winskill (P7529), P/O Read (P7389), Sgt Stokoe (P7387) and Sgt Darling (P7297).

Ten miles east of Rochford they encountered a single Messerschmitt Bf110 at 10,000 feet and eight of the pilots attacked in turn. Return fire from the rear gunner was quickly silenced and the unfortunate crew were killed either by gunfire or when the aircraft eventually plunged into the sea. All aircraft landed again at 15.15 and Boulter, Sheep, Archie, Stapme, Harry Prowse, Ras, Jack Stokoe and Andy Darling were each credited with a share.

On 8 November the Luftwaffe carried out three main attacks between 10.00-17.05 hours against targets in Kent, Sussex and shipping in the estuary.

At 15.50 the Squadron took off and joined forces with 74 Squadron over Biggin Hill, climbed to 20,000 feet and were sent to convoy 'Booty' at the mouth of the Thames. 603 comprised: F/L Boulter (P7436), F/L Haig (P7543), F/O Pinckney (P7529), P/O Gilroy (P7496), F/L Kirkwood

(P7285), P/O Berry (P7449), P/O Read (P7389), P/O Stapleton (P7528), P/O Prowse (P7295), P/O Maxwell (P7297), Sgt Stokoe (P7589) and Sgt Darling (P7387).

There were no enemy aircraft attacking the shipping when the pilots saw it and they continued to fly beyond. Due to the considerable enemy activity over the estuary and out to sea, 603 split up. When 15-20 miles east of Deal Jack Stokoe spotted two 109s which he pursued to the French coast firing without success. On returning he came across five more 109s of which three made off while Jack engaged the other two. Opening fire at 250 closing to 150 yards he damaged one and left it with glycol streaming from the engine at which time he broke off to engage the second which he shot down with one long burst and saw it crash into the sea. Jack landed at Manston to refuel.

Ras Berry was flying guard and was alone with Colin Pinckney at 25,000 feet when he saw and pursued two lone 'He113s' [109s]. He damaged one breaking off his attack when he saw black smoke pouring from it.

Sheep Gilroy saw 50 109s ten miles out to sea off Margate. He attacked a 109 head-on and managed to get in a short burst. A bullet went through his canopy and he was forced to break off his attack and return to base with slight wounds caused by splinters of perspex. On landing he reported seeing 20 Ju87s making their way home after bombing a single ship off the Naze.

Stapme pursued three Ju87s flying very low ten miles east of Ramsgate, heading east, but lost them in the haze.

Flight Lieutenant Mark Kirkwood (RAF No.39287) was reported 'missing' following combat with Ju87s and Bf109s east of Deal, later confirmed killed.* The remaining 603 pilots landed at 17.10.

Brian Macnamara was promoted to Flight Lieutenant.

On the 9th the whole day's enemy activity consisted of single aircraft patrolling the Channel, Straits of Dover and the North Sea. A few crossed the coast and a number of interceptions were made.

Sergeant Joey Sarre was posted to Central Flying School, Upavon, as a flying instructor.**

Enemy activity on the 10th consisted of armed reconnaissance raids by individual Do17s, Ju88s and 109s which bombed various targets.

The following day saw an escalation in attacks with London and shipping off the Essex coast and estuary being the main targets. The Italian Air Force (fighters, CR42s, and bombers, BR20s) were used for the first time in large numbers, unescorted by German fighters, and suffered a mauling by the RAF fighters.

At 11.45 the Squadron were ordered up to intercept the raiders attacking shipping in the Thames estuary. Joining forces with 64 Squadron, 603 led the formation out over the estuary at 20,000 feet where they saw the convoy off North Foreland being bombed and AA fire bursts from the convoy. The 603 pilots also spotted various formations of 109s spread over a wide area and

---

*Having joined the RAF on a short service commission in October 1936, he was given the rank of acting Pilot Officer on 21.12.36 and sent to 10 FTS, Ternhill on 16 January 1937. His rank of Pilot Officer was confirmed on 12.10.37 and on 4 May the following year he joined the staff at 3 Armament Training Station, Sutton Bridge. He was promoted to Flying Officer on 12.7.39. During 1940 he was with 4 Ferry Flight and on 3 September he was promoted to Flight Lieutenant and on the 6th he was posted to 7 OTU at Hawarden where he converted to Spitfires. On the 22nd he was posted to 610 Squadron at Acklington. Keen to fight with a front-line fighter squadron, sometime in the interim he opted for a move to 603 from 610 Squadron. He is remembered on Panel 4 of the Runnymede Memorial.

**Joey had initially been involved in the thick of the fighting. Following combat on 30 August, he returned to Hornchurch with damage to his tail, and that same afternoon he managed to shoot down a 109 but the tail of his own aircraft was hit by cannon fire causing the entire section to break off. He managed to bale out. On 4 September he made a forced landing at Elstead, near Ashford and on the 7th he was shot down again over the Thames and baled out with wounds to his hand which initially kept him off flying. Although he had survived he suffered great trauma and it was most likely this which led to his being kept on the ground until he was posted. Uncle George was clearly sympathetic and instrumental in his move to a training unit. In February 1945 he was commissioned, the rank of Pilot Officer being promulgated on 25 February. He was promoted to Flying Officer on 25 August and released from the RAF in 1946 as a Flying Officer. The strain of combat took its toll on Joey. Jack Stokoe said of his friend: '…he became an instructor after losing his nerve during the 'blitz'. He never flew in combat again.' Sadly, Joey Sarre took his own life in 1980.

heading towards them. Those airborne were: S/L Denholm (P9550), F/L Boulter (P7329), F/O Macnamara (P7388), F/O Pinckney (P7311), P/O Prowse (P7543), P/O Read (P7389), P/O Stapleton (P7528), P/O Martel (P7359), P/O Olver (P7288), P/O Winskill (P7389), Sgt Stokoe (P7295) and Sgt Darling (P7387). They intercepted and attacked 109s escorting Ju87s.

Peter Olver spotted a number of Junkers Ju87s in ragged formation and engaged one. The formations took evasive action and dived to low level '…about 20 feet above the water.' When the rest of the Squadron followed, the Junkers were seen to ditch their bombs. The escort of 109s dived from superior altitude to attack. Stapme, Harry Prowse, and Uncle George each claimed 109s destroyed whilst Colin Pinckney claimed a 109 probable and Peter Olver a Ju87 probable. Without loss to the Squadron 11 pilots landed at Hornchurch at 12.50 while the other landed at Manston.

Due to the wintry weather conditions enemy activity on the 12th consisted of only armed reconnaissance raids. 603 remained on the ground. On the 13th, George Denholm passed on the news to the rest of his pilots that the death of Peter Pease had been confirmed. This came as no surprise to the veterans of 603. During the day the Luftwaffe carried out three attacks over Kent consisting of 200 aircraft. Raids by singletons and shipping reconnaissance missions took place over the Straits, Channel and East Anglian coast.

On 14 November there were two large attacks, one in the morning the other in the afternoon. Both against shipping in the estuary. From Rochford the Squadron took off on patrol and were bounced by 109s. As the German fighters dived through them Sergeant Alf Burt was wounded. On landing he was taken to hospital.

Although he had already returned to the fighting with 603, on this day Sheep Gilroy was officially listed as having been posted back to the Squadron from RAF Hornchurch on 'ceasing to be non-effective sick.'

The next day saw further shipping and reconnaissance raids by the Luftwaffe. Two main attacks by a total of 175 aircraft occurred between 09.00-16.30 hours, when south-east England, Southampton, Selsey Bill and the Isle of Wight were the targets. 603 carried out two 'fighting patrols' without incident.

On 16 November the poor weather kept enemy activity to a minimum with almost all incursions by reconnaissance aircraft. A small fighter offensive occurred over Kent in the morning and shipping was attacked off Orfordness in the afternoon.

The next day there were three main attacks between 09.45-16.10 when the targets were in Kent, estuary convoys and the Beachy Head/Mayfield area.

At 08.00 the Squadron were ordered into the air on a defensive patrol: F/L Boulter (P7359), F/L Haig (P7311), P/O Gilroy (P7297), F/O Pinckney (P7529), F/O Macnamara (P7556), P/O Read (P7289), P/O Berry (P7489), P/O Stapleton (P7315), P/O Olver (P7288) and Sgt Stokoe (P7287).

Having joined forces with 41 Squadron at the north end of the Maidstone patrol line they spotted approximately 30 109s and 603 dived to attack. Ras, Bolster and Jack Stokoe each destroyed 109s, Colin Pinckney was credited with a probable, landing again at 09.40 without loss to themselves.

Bolster's destruction of a Bf109E over the Thames estuary brought with it unofficial 'ace' status.

For Monday 18 November 1940 the ORB reads: 'Nil Flying' due to inclement weather. Although the bad weather continued some operational flying took place the following day. The Luftwaffe still carried out a number of small raids. On the 20th enemy activity was on a much reduced scale due to the inclement weather. Only one raid was reported to have dropped bombs (Margate) and three other raids on Southampton were the only ones plotted over the coast. 603 remained on the ground again due mainly to the bad weather. Sgt Alf Burt was discharged from hospital.

The Squadron's 100th kill

On 21 November enemy activity continued on a small scale, the majority of aircraft being involved in shipping reconnaissance. A convoy was bombed off Harwich and various towns were targeted. At Wickham Market and Worthing civilians and soldiers in the streets were machine-gunned.

A section of three aircraft of 603 were sent up at 11.55 hours to intercept raiders: Sgt Plant (P7378), F/O Gilroy (P7496) and P/O Winskill (P7543). The outcome of the sortie was that Ron

Plant destroyed 603's 100th confirmed victory. His is yet another sad story of a young man who died for what he believed, however.*

On 24 October whilst with 611 Squadron at Ternhill, Plant had delivered Spitfire Mk II P7281 to Hornchurch. This trip may have motivated him to ask for a move south, as he was posted to 603 on 5 November and first flew with them on the 13th, a 'sector recco, Thames estuary' in P7449. By this time he had accumulated a total of 240 hours 5 minutes flying time in his log book, very few on Spitfires, however.

On 21 November he was killed during what was only his second sortie with the Squadron when his Spitfire P7387 collided with He111 A1+GM of 4/KG53 which he was attacking. The bomber, flown by Gefreiter Arthur Hagspiel, crashed in flames at Bucklands Cross, near Teynham, Kent. Two of his crew managed to bale out but were killed, two other bodies were later recovered from the wreckage, one being the pilot. Sadly, two of the local firemen who attempted to put out the flames were killed when the bomb-load exploded. Plant's attack had saved lives however, in that the aircraft was brought down before unleashing its lethal load on the civilian populace. Although there are a large and varied number of explanations for the accident it is possible his windscreen had been crazed by return fire rendering him unable to see, or more possibly he had actually been hit as George Denholm later surmised. The pilots of 603 and Plant's family believed he committed himself to bringing down the Heinkel by ramming before Gefreiter Hagspiel could reach the cloud in which he was intending to seek refuge. It was common knowledge that with his friends and family Plant felt great bitterness towards the German bombing of Coventry on 14 November. Perhaps today his cause would be questionable but Ron Plant believed and fully understood what he was fighting for.

---

*Ronald Eric Plant, RAF No.748027, was born Ronald Eric Davies in Coventry. His mother suffered from placenta previa at Ron's birth and struggled to bring up her three other children (she had already lost two children who died in infancy). She decided to 'farm-out' Ron to her sister and brother in-law, Flo and Bob Plant, who did a fine job in bringing him up. Bob Plant was from the Preston area and moved to Coventry to work for Lea Francis but ended up buying Everards, the city pork butchers. The business made his fortune and it was alleged that this came about because the butchers was the biggest source of black market pork in the city! Ron's transition to a wealthier environment meant he moved in completely different social circles to that of his immediate family and his friends were most probably not the friends of his brother although it was left to him to go to Coventry station to meet the escort bringing Ron's remains home following his death.

Ron was very close to his aunt and uncle and actually referred to his aunt as 'Mother'. When he attended The King Henry VIII Grammar School in Coventry he was enrolled as Ronald Plant. He kept the name for the rest of his life and following his death any information was sent to the Plant family and not to the Davies'. This point rankled with the Davies side of the family and caused something of a family rift. With the family in a secure financial position Ron drove a new Morris Coup which he bought from the County Garage Stratford. His brother recalls: '...he used to drive at break neck speeds, very much a dare devil and risk taker.' This trait continued unabated and on more than one occasion resulted in the removal of foliage from the trees surrounding the family farm in Stratford.

Ron first flew on 5 March 1939 in Tiger Moth N5464 with Flying Officer Hudson as pilot. He joined the RAFVR on 28 April 1939 as an airman u/t pilot and on his Form 1866, RAF Volunteer Reserve notice paper, he records his profession as 'Gents Outfitter.' His personal details describe him as 5' 7" tall. He was 20 years and 63 days old on signing up and having enlisted on 28 April was promoted to Sergeant the following day. He was remustered on 11 May and from mid June until 17 August he flew almost every day (totalling 33.10 hours dual and 31.30 hours solo) by which time he was flying Harts at 9 F&RFTS at Ansty, just outside Coventry. He didn't fly again until 12 December. He was called up on 1 September and sent to ITW, Bexhill, from 30 October until 10 December 1939, followed by flying training at 8 FTS at Montrose where he saw the Spitfire for the first time. Coincidentally, it was aircraft of detached units of 602 and 603 Squadrons which were at Montrose at that time. In a letter home Plant wrote: 'We now have 'Spitfires' and we have a number of notches on our guns, casualties none.' Plant is referring to B Flight 603 Squadron. Six months later Plant joined them at Hornchurch. He completed his FTS course on 15 May 1940 and the following day was posted to 72 Squadron at Acklington, which had been withdrawn from front-line fighter operations in the south of England. On the 31st he flew a Spitfire for the first time for a 15-minute flight, but following this brief experience his early days were spent undergoing further training. He also flew Harvards at Acklington, in particular P5866 which Bubble Waterston had damaged at Prestwick in December 1939. He eventually progressed to flying the Spitfires of 72 Squadron and his next flight was on 26 June. In early August he was sent to 5 OTU at Aston Down for full conversion training on the Spitfire by which time he had accumulated a total of 11 hours 50 mins on Spits and a total flying time of 60 hours dual, 120.30 solo, 1.45 night dual and 2.45 night solo. It was at Aston Down that Plant came under the instruction of Flying Officer K.I. 'Killy' Kilmartin who had also been Richard Hillary's instructor during his time there. On 10 October he was posted to 611 Squadron at Ternhill where he flew Spitfires on six separate sorties.

Left: Sergeant Ronald Eric Plant.
Right: Ron Plant was credited with bringing down 603 Squadron's 100th victory, a He111. Sadly, in doing so he collided with the bomber. Both aircraft crashed killing Plant and the crew of the Heinkel.

It is possible he just misjudged when to break away. Sadly, Ron lacked experience for even a first successful attack from astern but what he lacked in experience he made up for with courage. His Spitfire crashed and burned out at Buckland Farm, Widdenham. It has been said that Plant managed to bale out but fell dead when in fact his body was recovered from the wreckage. His body was taken with its escort by train to Coventry to be buried.

The Fighter Command combat report Form 'F' compiled on 1 December by the 603 Squadron IO provides further information about the incident:

> Yellow Section, 3 aircraft of 603 Squadron took off from Hornchurch at 11.55 hours to investigate a raid in the Mouth of the Thames. After orbiting at Sheppey they were vectored by Controller into a raid approaching from the Manston direction, and were brought round to approach the raid out of the sun. When at 5,000 feet about 4 miles S.E. of Faversham they were warned of the presence of a bandit to the N.E., and sighted an He111 through a gap in the cloud, flying N.W. at about 2,000 feet. Cloud was 2,000 to 3,000 feet 7/10ths. P/O Gilroy attacked from above, developing into an astern attack, firing 1520 rounds, and breaking away to starboard. The He111 which was doing about 120 m.p.h., started to turn west and then south towards a cloud.
>
> P/O Winskill then made an attack from the port quarter, firing 240 rounds and breaking away over the starboard side of the He111. Neither of these two attacks seemed to have much effect on the He111.
>
> Sgt Plant was then seen to close in from astern at a high overtaking speed, and collided with the E/A. He did not appear to attempt to break away, and both machines broke up in the air with the force of the collision. Both aircraft crashed at Buckland [Bucklands Cross] near Faversham.
>
> P/O Gilroy noticed return fire from rear gun of He111. Two aircraft landed at Hornchurch at 1300 hours. <u>Our Casualties</u>. Sgt Plant – killed. Aircraft Cat.3. <u>Enemy Casualties</u>. 1 He111 – destroyed (by Plant).

Also on the same patrol were two more Spitfire IIs of 603: P7324 flown by S/L George Denholm and P7315 flown by P/O Maxwell. As Plant's Spitfire dived towards the Heinkel it was noted that the closing speed had been particularly fast, with no attempt to break off his attack, even at the last second. Sheep wrote in his log book 'He111 crashed into by No.3!!'

It is possible the 603 pilots had actually encountered *two* Heinkels. Another He111, A1+GP of 6/KG53, flown by Leutnant Hugo Seefried was attacked and crashed into the sea. The body of Seefried was recovered but the other three crew were listed as 'missing'. So what was initially perceived by the 603 pilots as being a single Heinkel dodging in and out of the cloud may have actually been two.

On the 22nd bad weather kept enemy activity to a minimum which comprised raids by singletons very few of which crossed the coast. 11 Group bulletin No.114 announced F/L John Boulter's award of the DFC.

Back home at 72 Beaconsfield Road, Coventry, Ron Plant's father, Mr R.J. Plant, received the official telegram notifying him of his son's death. That same day George Denholm drafted a letter of condolence to him in which he described events which led up to the death of 21-year-old Plant. After it was typed instead of it being returned to the CO for signing, a poor forgery of George's signature was attempted before it was sent and an 'e' was added to his surname. Nevertheless, the letter provides an example of many such letters he felt obliged and duty-bound to write:

> I write to offer you and your family my most sincere sympathy on the loss of Ronald. He met his end nobly fighting to defend our country from the enemy.
>
> As a member of a section which had been detailed to intercept a German Heinkel 111 he was the third man to attack and coming straight behind it he failed to break away but crashed into it very fast. Both aircraft fell together in flames. From the force of the crash I think he must have been killed at once.
>
> We will never know of course exactly why it happened but the bomber's crew had been firing at all of them and I suspect Ronald was either hit or had his windscreen smashed and was unable to see properly. His attack, however you look at it, killed four German airmen and destroyed a much more valuable machine, and incidentally it was the 100th enemy aircraft destroyed by members of this Squadron.
>
> He was a very likeable lad who I had expected to become a very valuable member of 603 and personally I deeply regret his most untimely death.
>
> Yours with deep sympathy.
> George Denholm (signed)
> Squadron Leader Commanding
> 603 City of Edinburgh Squadron
> Auxiliary Air Force*

CR42s, 603's opponents on 23 November.

---

*Plant's family never received this letter and George wrote another similar letter from RAF Drem in January 1941.

On 23 November Sergeants R.B. Price and Stone joined the Squadron from 222 and 611 respectively.

The Luftwaffe and Italtian Air Force, operating out of Belgium since October, carried out three fighter sweeps over the south-east between 09.00 and 16.40 hours.

At 11.40, 12 603 Squadron Spitfires took off from Rochford: S/L Denholm (P7550), F/L Boulter (P7597), F/L Haig (P7311), F/O Gilroy (P7496), F/O Pinckney (P7529), F/O Macnamara (P7388), P/O Scott-Malden (P7289), P/O Prowse (P7543), P/O Winskill (P7389), P/O Berry (P7449), F/O Stapleton (P7528) and Sgt Darling (P7324). They were patrolling the airspace above their aerodrome when they were diverted to intercept a raid on shipping in the Channel and came up against 29 CR42 biplanes of 18° Gruppo, Corpo Aereo Italiano.

Led by Maggiore F. Vosilla with Sottotenente Franco Bordoni-Bisleri as his wingman they were on a fighter sweep which was intended to take them over the Channel at Dunkirk and on to Margate, Eastchurch, Folkestone and Calais. They were covered by 24 Fiat G.50s of 20° Gruppo operating a little further inland.

41 Squadron were also vectored to the area. Ten miles south-west of Dover 603 sighted the CR42s. According to the RAF pilots the Italian fighters were flying in two separate groups in line astern. In the first group there were four aircraft flying wing tip to wing tip, a single aircraft to starboard and several to port. The second formation consisted of 'vics' and pairs in no particular order. Behind and approximately 300 feet above could be seen two enemy aircraft flying straight, not weaving. Richard Hillary later recalled Colin Pinckney's version of events during one of his hospital visits. Uncle George called out:

'Wops ahead.'
'Where are they?' asked 41 Squadron.
'Shan't tell you,' came back the answer. 'We're only outnumbered three to one.'
Colin told me that it was the most unsporting thing he had ever had to do, rather like shooting sitting birds, as he so typically put it.

The CR42 was a slow (max speed 267 mph) but highly manoeuvrable biplane, single-seat fighter. Its armament consisted of two 12.7mm machine guns mounted on top of the fuselage. They had white spinners, yellow engine cowling and green and black camouflage resembling a mackerel. One of the 603 pilots remarked that they were so pretty it seemed a shame to shoot them down. They were flying at about 200 mph when 603 Squadron dived on the rear formation from 28,000 feet and from astern. The CR42s were badly mauled in the ensuing combat and lost Tenente Guido Mazza of 83ª Squadriglia flying MM5694 and Sergente Maggiore G. Grillo of 95ª Squadriglia flying MM5665 who were both shot down into the sea and posted missing. On returning to base Sergente Maggiore F. Campanile and Sergente P. Melano of 83ª Squadriglia had to force-land. Both were slightly injured. It was later discovered that Campanile had been extremely fortunate. With a lack of armour in the aircraft, his parachute had stopped several .303 rounds and probably saved his life. During the combat Tenente Giulio Cesare Giuntella's CR42 was hit several times but he managed to fly back to base and even claimed to have hit a Spitfire. Maresciallo Felice Sozzi of 83ª Squadriglia (83-15) reported having attacked and chased off a Spitfire from the tail of Sergente Maggiore Luigi Gorrini's aircraft which was in the process of attacking another Spitfire. Sozzi was pursued and hit from behind by two other Spitfires leaving him to fly his damaged aircraft back to base with three bullets in his lungs. Despite agonising pain and blood loss he successfully carried out a forced landing on a Belgian beach. He survived and was later awarded the Medaglia d'argento al valore militare 'in the field.'

The outcome was inevitable and seven of the Regia Aeronautica fighters were claimed destroyed, with two probables and two damaged. Only two were actually destroyed but nevertheless it was a morale booster for the Squadron. The claims were: Archie Winskill 2 destroyed (his first two claims); Andy Darling 2 destroyed; Brian Macnamara 1 destroyed; Colin Pinckney 1 destroyed (his third claim); Ras 1 destroyed (his ninth claim) and 1 probable; John Boulter 1 probable (his last claim) and Scott-Malden 2 damaged. No 603 aircraft were lost although Archie's aircraft was hit by a number of rounds from Giuntella's CR42, shattering his canopy. The 603 pilots were impressed at the morale and willingness to fight of the Italian pilots compared with the 109 pilots at that time. It was noted that none of the Italians baled out when shot down and it appeared as if each pilot had been killed.

Years later, during an interview Ras recalled the Italian fighters being more difficult to shoot down than initially anticipated. The greater speed of the Spitfires had been a hindrance as the much slower CR42s could out turn the Spitfires causing them to overshoot. On two occasions he found himself in a flat spin, and having regained control he found that on each occasion an Italian had latched onto his tail! 'I was sick of spinning! They didn't get me, and it was very exciting, that fight'.

As 603 engaged the CR42s, further RAF units were alerted to the presence of other enemy units. At 12.25, 92 Squadron together with 74 took off from Biggin Hill and later identified enemy aircraft some miles south of Dover as Bf109s. They were probably the Italian Fiat G.50s of 20° Gruppo.

The 24th saw little enemy activity apart from three fighter sweeps over Kent between 09.00 and 16.40 hours. The next day widespread fog put paid to anything other than small-scale enemy activity.

On the 26th Luftwaffe activity consisted mainly of reconnaissance flights over the south-east coast. Two Bf109s and a He 60 were destroyed. Pilot Officer Rafter returned to 603 from RAF Station Hornchurch on ceasing to be 'non-effective sick' following the serious injuries received on 5 September. On that day another name was added to the casualty list when AC1 A. Reynolds was killed in a motor accident at RAF Hornchurch.

Apart from a large number of reconnaissance flights the Luftwaffe activity on the 27th was confined to a fighter sweep of 70-80 Bf109s over Kent between 15.15-16.45 hours.

The 28th saw a similar pattern to previous days. Between 10.30 and 15.00 hours the Luftwaffe carried out a number of fighter sweeps over Kent and the Channel. Meantime 603 continued to patrol. Sergeants R. Thomson and R.D. Jury joined the Squadron from 616.

Having failed his second medical board on the 18th a further board passed John Strawson A1b on the 28th. Although still not authorised to fly he was eager to get back in action and immediately returned to 603 Squadron where he continued his recovery. Unfortunately, bad luck continued to stalk him.

On Friday 29 November 1940 the tragic story of Pilot Officer William 'Robin' Rafter reached a conclusion.

Apart from a small fighter sweep over Kent between 13.40-14.40 hours, the Luftwaffe were restricted to small-scale formations or singletons. At 09.50 hours George Denholm led 12 Spitfires away from Hornchurch with instructions to patrol the airspace over Ramsgate. By this time the updated Spitfire Mark II with its increased boost (all 'P' series aircraft) was in Squadron use: S/L Denholm (P7528), F/O Carbury (P7597), F/O Gilroy (P7496), F/O Pinckney (P7529), P/O Scott-Malden (P7289), P/O Maxwell (P7311), P/O Winskill (P7299), P/O Read (P7389), P/O Rafter (P7449), P/O Olver (P7288), F/O Macnamara (P7388), and Sgt Stokoe (P7295).

Robin Rafter now had the chance to fulfil his intentions as expressed to his mother: '…to get my own back on the Jerries'. However, while the pilots were climbing to intercept, his Spitfire inexplicably dived out of formation and plunged into a meadow at Cherry Tree Farm, near Kingswood, Kent. It had been only his second operational flight. The cause was recorded as 'unknown' but as the Squadron had not made contact with the enemy his having been hit by return fire was ruled out. Oxygen starvation (hypoxia) with the onset of unconsciousness (due to anoxia) is a probable cause. Although some pilots opted for a moderate flow of oxygen from take-off, which they increased to full as they climbed, the actual height at which oxygen is required is 14,000 feet and over. However, the reported height of 13,000 feet from which Robin broke formation was only a rough estimate, he could have been higher and his supply could have failed. Another likely possibility, and one his sister believed to be the cause, is that he blacked out, a legacy of the serious head injury he had received on 5 September. He was 19-years old. A RAF recovery team spent three days at the site recovering Robin's body and most of the wreckage of his aircraft. Tragedy had already struck the Rafter family while Robin was in hospital. On 11 October his brother, Pilot Officer Charles Rafter, was killed along with three of his crew in a flying accident at RAF Stradishall while serving as a pilot with

Robin Rafter's memorial.

214 Squadron. During take-off the Wellington he was flying developed swing, he lost control and the aircraft crashed into a hangar. Although badly injured, three of the crew survived. The brothers were buried with their father at St Peter's churchyard, Harborne, Birmingham, close to the family home. On 29 November 2002 a memorial was unveiled on the crash-site by the Shoreham Aircraft Museum following a dig which yielded the bullet-proof windscreen, airscrew boss and a variety of cockpit parts of Rafter's Spitfire.

Following Robin's death, the rest of the Squadron made visual contact with a lone Bf110 'A5+AA' of Stab/StG.1, and nine of the 11 Spitfires attacked and shot it down over the sea. Both pilot, Oberleutnant R. Pytlik, and gunner/radio operator, Oberleutnant T. Fryer were killed. According to the Squadron ORB, the pilots were 'frustrated as being in search of bigger game', as a consequence this combat was described as something of a 'turkey shoot' with the pilots taking full advantage of the situation. The nine 603 pilots solemnly claimed a share and later all signed a copy of the intelligence patrol report. Sheep landed at Rochester before returning to Hornchurch.

That evening the Squadron celebrated their 100th confirmed victory at The Dorchester with a grand night out. The menu was impressive for wartime London:

MENU

Huitres Natives
Sauman d'Ecosse Fume

———

Coupe de Tortue Verte
Brindilles Diablees
Creme Ambassadeur

———

Flan aux Fruits de Mer a la Mode de Paimpol

———

Faisan Roti a l'Anglaise
Coeur de Celeri au Jus
Pomme Fondantes

———

Poire Roxane
Biscuits Secs

———

Cafe

———

The Dorchester   Friday
Park Lane, W.1.   29th November, 1940

Scribbled in the top right hand corner of this copy of a surviving menu are the words: '100 Huns. 603 Squadron.' Organised by George Denholm, Group Captain 'Boy' Bouchier was the guest of the Squadron.

Such a function would have been very expensive and although there were members of the Squadron who were quite wealthy and with peacetime occupations that attracted a good salary, it was not they who paid the bill. The kind donor approached Uncle George and offered to pay for the function on the condition that he remain anonymous. For many years it has been a well-kept secret as to his identity but recently it has come to light that it was the Squadron padre, James Rossie Brown, who had paid the bill.

The next day 603 remained on the ground although the enemy incursions continued with a number of large-scale fighter sweeps over the south-east and south coast between 09.45-16.00 hours. The only other activity comprised a number of shipping reconnaissance flights.

December 1940

On 1 December 1940 the Luftwaffe continued with fighter sweeps over Kent and reconnaissance flights over Dover, the Straits and the Channel. 603 were not involved. On the morning of the 2nd the enemy carried out one fighter sweep consisting of about 70 Bf109s in two main waves over Kent and East Sussex with patrols throughout the afternoon.

On the 3rd bad weather restricted enemy activity to singletons on armed reconnaissance flights over land and shipping in the Channel. The next day was much the same but if anything the weather had deteriorated. Not a single enemy aircraft flew into the Group area during the morning. One or two raids were carried out as well as a number of tip-and-run missions. 603 did not fly. With orders to move to RAF Station Southend (Rochford), until then their forward airfield, the Squadron began to ferry stores and equipment to their new location.

Next day (5 December) saw an improvement in the weather and the Squadron aircraft were flown to Rochford from where they carried out two patrols. Between 11.00 and 15.40 hours there were two attacks on east Kent by fighters, some carrying bombs. Otherwise, enemy activity consisted of aircraft on shipping reconnaissance patrols.

Gale force winds on the 6th were problematic although there was still some activity by the Luftwaffe in the form of shipping reconnaissance flights and singleton raiders. 603 continued to patrol.

According to the 603 ORB, F/L John Boulter was awarded a well deserved DFC; the citation credited him with five enemy aircraft destroyed. He had by this time also been credited with one shared destroyed and three and one shared probable.

For 7 December 1940 the 11 Group resume of enemy activity reads: 'Apart from the usual morning fighter sweep over Kent and Sussex, bad weather on the Continent restricted enemy activity to not more than ten aircraft on reconnaissance flights.' According to the log book of Sheep Gilroy he was involved in a dog fight without result during a 20 minute patrol.

Activity for the 603 pilots on the 8th was limited to a 1 hour 40 minute patrol. Many of the new pilots within the fighter squadrons were becoming increasingly frustrated with the lack of activity. Having arrived towards the end of, or after the intense fighting of the Battle of Britain, they were afraid they would miss out on the opportunity to prove themselves.

On 9 December the low cloud and intermittent rain restricted enemy activity to a few reconnaissance flights. Only two enemy aircraft were plotted over 11 Group all day. Later, Sheep carried out a night-flying test. Enemy activity was on a similar scale the next day and 603 were sent up on patrol without incident. On the 11th, apart from one fighter sweep by 50 mainly 109s over Kent, enemy activity continued on a small scale and the 603 pilots continued to patrol and carry out practice flights.

Overnight an estimated 400 bombers operated over the country with Birmingham as the main objective.

On 12 December, apart from a fighter sweep over Kent by 40 109s between 10.50 and 12.30, enemy activity was minimal. The Squadron continued with operational and practice flying with two patrols and an 'offensive sweep' as recorded in Sheep's log book. On this day a new initiative began when five squadrons joined in an offensive sweep over the Pas de Calais. Although nothing was seen it was significant in that it was one of the first operations of its kind. It marked decisively the end of the threat of invasion and the beginning of a period during which operations would be over enemy-occupied territory.

Due to very poor weather on 13 December the 603 ORB recorded no flying. Enemy activity was minimal. F/L Jack Haig left the station and travelled to Ipswich where he married his long-term girlfriend, Diana Mary Folt, the next day. Despite being away from the dangers of combat John Strawson's bad luck continued when he and Sgt Stone were injured when their motorcycle, on which Strawson was riding pillion, was in collision with a bus. Both men were hospitalised at the Southern General, Stone with serious injuries.

On this day the Squadron began its preparations for its return from RAF Southend to RAF Drem in Scotland after the long hard battle in the south. Whilst 603 was destined to return to the fight the make-up of the Squadron would have changed significantly by then.

CHAPTER 14

BACK TO SCOTLAND

Following the announcement that AVM Keith Park AOC 11 Group was relinquishing command, on 17 December 1940 the following letter was included in 11 Group bulletin No.131:

In handing over Command of 11 Fighter Group, I wish to express sincere appreciation for the loyal support of all ranks of Fighter Squadrons, Sector Stations and forward aerodromes during the past eight months hard fighting.

The Squadrons operating under the control of 11 Fighter Group have soundly beaten the German Air Force in the Spring, Summer and, finally, Autumn of 1940. The following enemy aircraft have been accounted for in combat against heavy odds:

Destroyed	2,424
Probably destroyed and damaged	2,161
	<u>4,585</u>

The outstanding successes were due to the courage and skill of our fighter Pilots, who have been so ably supported by the operational and ground staffs at all Aerodromes, in spite of casualties and severe damage caused by enemy bombing attacks by day.

The German Air Force may again launch heavy attacks by day against England in 1941, and I feel confident that the Units of 11 Group will again defeat the enemy bombers and fighters, however numerous.

I am proud to have commanded 11 Fighter Group throughout the heavy fighting of 1940, and wish all ranks good luck in 1941.

RAF Drem

On 17 December the 603 pilots departed Rochford for Drem leaving the other squadrons of 11 Group to carry on with their duties on what was another fairly quiet day in the south due to inclement weather over northern France.

En route their Spitfires were refuelled at Catterick. Having taken the precaution of arranging lunch in advance of their arrival at Drem on landing they discovered that 602 Squadron had beaten them to it and eaten everything!

The arrival at Drem, with its notorious slope, was marred by an unfortunate accident. Sheep Gilroy – now with 357 hours flying time in his log book – Scottie Scott-Malden and Sgt Price landed together. Price's Spitfire struck the tail of Sheep's, bounced into the air and crashed down on top of the fuselage. Scottie took evasive action to avoid worsening the situation and made an emergency stop. Leaping from his cockpit he ran to Sheep's Spitfire, jumped onto the wing and dragged his colleague clear of the aircraft just as the flames started to lick around his boots in the leg-well of the cockpit. The fire did not catch hold and the rapid arrival of a fire tender made doubly sure. Sheep was taken to hospital with severe but not life-threatening injuries and was out of action until the second week in February 1941. His logbook reads: 'Rochford – Catterick, Catterick – Drem – Crash!'

Earlier in the day Sgt Alf Burt left 603.*

On 19 December the newcomers to the unit from OTUs were kept busy with intensive practice flying – much as George Denholm had insisted in the run-up to the Battle of Britain – until such times as their flight commanders thought them ready to become operational. Once operational, as we have seen, inexperienced pilots were part of a section with experienced pilots whose duty it was to hone their skills.

On the 20th Sergeant Pilots Hurst, Raw, Squire, Webber and Wilson were posted to 603 from 72 Squadron and were soon undergoing practice flying.

During a practice flight on the 21st Sgts Jack Stokoe and John Strawson both crashed on landing at Drem. Their aircraft undercarriage was severely damaged in the process. Both pilots had yet to familiarise themselves with the airfield and the problems continued. The next day George Denholm crashed whilst landing at the airfield but for different reasons. Following a night-flying exercise his Spitfire collided with an 'unlighted obstruction'.

On Christmas Day (the enemy were no respecters of holidays) at 12.55 Blue Section, F/O Brian Carbury and Sgts Squire and Wilson, where ordered up to intercept an intruder. They spotted a Ju88 at 1,000 feet 12 miles NE off St Abbs Head and Brian carried out two attacks during which the undercarriage of the enemy aircraft dropped down. The aircraft was left trailing black smoke from its starboard engine which eventually stopped. Brian was later credited with a damaged and the three Spitfires landed again at 13.50 with the newcomers having benefited from seeing the master at work. It was to be Brian's final combat experience.

P/O David Maxwell was posted to 66 Squadron at Biggin Hill where, on 14 February 1941, aged 24, he was killed. His body was not found and he is remembered on Panel 33 of the Runnymede Memorial.

Having requested a move back to 11 Group, Peter Olver departed for 66 Squadron at Biggin Hill on 25 December.

According to the ORB, from 26-29 December the Squadron carried out 'operational and practice flying' without incident. Despite the strain of combat flying many of the experienced pilots in the Squadron were becoming bored with the lack of aerial activity and incessant training flights. Although the latter was vital to help integrate the newcomers into the Squadron and increase the overall level of competency, for many of the battle-weary fighter pilots it was a hard adjustment to make. After six months with 603, Colin Pinckney left to join 243 Squadron 'going to Near East'.**

Tuesday 30 December 1940
603 lost two more of its veteran pilots when Jack Haig and Brian Carbury were posted to 58 OTU at Grangemouth where their experience proved vital in the training of new pilots.*** Brian Carbury's achievements in particular had been outstanding. By December his total claims stood at 15 enemy aircraft destroyed, two shared destroyed, three probable and four damaged between 7 December 1939 and 25 December 1940. His Battle of Britain credited claims stand at 15 destroyed, two probables and two damaged – a truly outstanding achievement which placed him among the top-scoring pilots of Fighter Command and consigned his name to the history books as one of the greatest fighter pilots.

---

*He was sent to CFS, Upavon for an instructor's course after which he went to 15 FTS Kidlington, Oxford. Commissioned on 24 August 1942, on 24 February the following year Burt was promoted to Flying Officer and on 24 August 1944 to Flight Lieutenant. On 28 February 1945, Burt was posted to 512 Squadron. His award of the AFC was gazetted on 4 June 1945. A year later he was posted to 271 Squadron as a pilot and Squadron Training Officer. At the end of 1946, 271 Squadron was disbanded and re-numbered 77 Squadron. On 27 January 1948 Burt was sent to 241 OCU, North Luffenham and later took part in the Berlin Air Lift. He was promoted to Squadron Leader on 1 January 1951. On 1 January 1955 his award of a Bar to his AFC was gazetted. Burt held a number of staff appointments until his retirement as a Squadron Leader on 27 July 1958 after 26 years in the service. He died in 1980 aged 64.
** See Appendix 'Life After 603.'
***See Appendix 'Life After 603.'

Lieutenant Iain Horne of the Scots Guards had been in the operations room at Turnhouse during October/November 1939 when the Squadron saw its first action. Later in the war he transferred to army co-operation and it was at Grangemouth whilst he was undergoing flying training that he met Brian who was his instructor. At a spritely 89 he reflects on his many memories of the period:

> Brian was a really terrific chap, so easy to get on with – everybody did – he was a first-class pilot and flying instructor. I recall many of my lessons with him in particular instrument flying. I got to know him quite well. He was very tall, slim, warm, charismatic, a genuine character, no false airs and graces.

Another regular serviceman wrote:

> I would have been closer to Brian, but for the accursed stupid gulf, which kept the Gentlemen (Officers) apart from the Peasants (Other ranks – e.g.. Sgt Pilots) which still strongly existed in 1938 and until much later. However, being a New Zealander, Brian had no time for such senseless class-distinction and he fraternised with the NCO's and other ranks, probably to the consternation of his seniors – it most certainly surprised me as a long serving regular in the RAF.

John Mackenzie, one of the 603 ground crew who knew Brian Carbury throughout the Battle of Britain, described the awe in which they held him and his combat ability:

> The 'Carbury Trick' was the expression we gave to his tactic of getting in very close to the enemy before firing. He didn't mess around firing from distance. He could also push the Spitfire to its limits if the enemy fighters got on his own tail, thus shaking off all but the most experienced German pilots. We needed his combat experience after the Battle of Britain, he could have risen in the ranks and flown again operationally. What a waste.

The surviving ground crew personnel expressed great pride in having served with Brian. He displayed a great strength of character and independence as a young man; but was an important member of a dedicated and tenacious team of pilots. In 1940, Brian recorded:

> ...once in contact with the enemy, there were frequently so many of them, it was a matter of fighting your way out and knowing when to break off – 'He who turns and flies away, lives to fight another day'. It was often a case of flying full tilt through the formations and shooting at anything in range.

In 1945, Brian was to write that he had not expected to live through the Battle of Britain and that every attack was tantamount to a suicide mission.

The Battle of Britain drew to a close, the autumn days shortened and the weather gradually turned with the approach of winter. The weary pilots and ground crew of Fighter Command – particularly those who had served in 11 and 12 Groups – had a chance to draw breath and the command as a whole was able to re-build and recover from the summer's exertions and losses. Although the lengthening nights brought with them the German Blitz on London and the other major cities it would reduce the unrelenting pressure on the day squadrons. It was not lost on the airmen that despite all of their worst fears, the expected German invasion had not materialised.

After 15 September, there was no sudden cessation of the daylight attacks by the Luftwaffe but rather a gradual reduction in their intensity as attention switched to the night raids. But Fighter Command did not know what lay ahead of it in 1941. For all they knew, this might be only a temporary switch for the winter and they could be thrown into another summer of intense daylight attacks on the south coast of England as a prelude to another invasion attempt. They had successfully prevented the invasion in 1940 – but it might yet come in 1941.

The summer of 1940 had indeed been critical to the survival of Britain in the Second World War. It is easy with the benefit of hindsight to assess and re-assess the importance and criticality of the Battle of Britain and it is now clear that Hitler had his own reasons for not executing the invasion of Britain as aggressively and single-mindedly as he might have. What is undeniable is that the exertions and sacrifices of the airmen – both in the air and on the ground – in Fighter Command preventing the Luftwaffe achieve air superiority (or supremacy) over southern England in the summer of 1940 also prevented the German forces achieve suitable conditions to launch the invasion across the English Channel. But the Germans contributed to their failure making strategic errors that helped the British; notably their failure to destroy the British Expeditionary Force (BEF) encircled at Dunkerque and their decision to switch their bombing campaign away from Fighter Command's airfields to London at the moment when it was becoming almost impossible for Fighter Command to continue operations from airfields south of the Thames, and the need for a withdrawal to the airfields further north was becoming a certainty. They unwittingly helped to give Britain and Fighter Command the breathing space they needed to hold their own so that the conditions necessary to mount a successful invasion were not achieved.

In 1940, Fighter Command had adopted a defensive posture but this was to change in 1941 as more offensive activities were undertaken with 603 playing as full a part as possible.

As Christmas came and went, newcomers joined the Squadron where they were taught by veterans who were tired and in need of rest. Some preferred a return to combat rather than the mundane daily flying exercises and uneventful patrols. As the first full year of war drew to a close no one was sure what lay ahead but all were aware the fight was far from over. The Squadron had already lost many pilots and ground crew killed or wounded and many more would make the ultimate sacrifice. Despite everything the spirit was still good and with a nucleus of experienced men and a reputation as an outstanding fighting unit already established, they faced the future with enthusiasm and professional fervour.

THE CONCEPTION OF THE AUXILIARY AIR FORCE

Trenchard's Vision

The Royal Auxiliary Air Force celebrated its 75th Anniversary on 9 October 1999. The integral part played by the Auxiliaries, past and present, in widely different roles in support of the Royal Air Force was recognised in 1984, in its Diamond Jubilee Year by the award of its own badge. The words of the motto are 'COMITAMUR AD ASTRA – We go with them to the stars'. The badge forms the basic motif of the Sovereign's Colour, which was presented on 12 June 1989 by Her Majesty the Queen, the Air Commodore in Chief at RAF Benson.

Conception

The conception of the Territorial and Auxiliary Forces dates back to the year 1907, when the Territorial and Reserve Forces Act was passed. In 1917 General Jan Christian Smuts was appointed by Lloyd George to examine the organisation of the air services and he recommended the establishment of an air ministry and the amalgamation of the Royal Flying Corps and Royal Naval Air Service to create the Royal Air Force on 1 April 1918.

In November 1917 the Air Force (Constitution) Act was passed and Section 6 of the act, following upon the experience gained with the old volunteers and the territorial army, made provision for the creation of an auxiliary air force.

Such a formation was first suggested by Air Marshal Sir Hugh 'Boom' Trenchard (who later became Chief of the Air Staff and Marshal of the Royal Air Force, the Lord Trenchard) in a memorandum dated 27 November 1919 at the instigation of Winston Churchill, the then Secretary of State for Air. The memorandum was entitled 'An Outline of the Scheme for the Permanent Organisation of the Royal Air Force'.

On 11 December 1919, Winston Churchill, then Secretary of State for Air, presented to Parliament a White Paper prepared by Lord Trenchard on the permanent organisation of the Royal Air Force. Winston Churchill and Major General Sir Frederick Sykes CMG, Trenchard's successor as Chief of the Air Staff in April 1918, opposed the concept of part-time service. Major General Sir Hugh Trenchard became Chief of the Air Staff again on 1 November 1919 and was therefore able to see through his proposal for an auxiliary air force. Lord Trenchard realised that a fighting service must possess a non-regular branch with its roots firmly set in the civil life of the country.

By 1922, Trenchard had laid down his proposals for the formation of reserve squadrons in the form of a draft bill. Subsequently, in 1923, the Salisbury Committee (a sub-Committee of the Committee of Imperial Defence) recommended that the 'Home Defence Air Force' should consist of 52 squadrons and be organised in part on a regular and in part on a territorial or reserve basis, which would have the effect of increasing the strength of the Royal Air Force by 34 squadrons. The Committee's proposals were accepted by the Government and announced to Parliament on 26 June 1923. An Act of Parliament followed, dated 14 July 1924, which extended to the Auxiliary Air Force the provisions of the Territorial and Reserve Forces Act 1907 and made 'provision as to the organisation and conditions of service of the Auxiliary Air Force'. The act also provided for the formation of County Joint Associations and Auxiliary Air Force Associations. The actual establishment of these associations under whose auspices the first squadrons started to form in 1925 was authorised by an Order in Council dated 9 October 1924.

Sir Samuel Hoare (later Viscount Templewood) was the Air Minister responsible for authorising the first squadrons. Referring to '...the first experiment with non-regular units in military aviation,' he said in the House of Commons on 26 February 1925:

We are in the ensuing year starting the experiment of introducing into our programme two types of non-regular unit… During the next 12 months we hope to see formed a number of Special Reserve squadrons… Then there are four Auxiliary Air Force squadrons also to be formed this year. The Special Reserve squadrons are formed on a Militia basis, that is, on a cadre basis, with the greater part of a squadron liable to embodiment in time of emergency. One of the two Special Reserve squadrons will probably be formed in the neighbourhood of London, and the other in the neighbourhood of Belfast. The Auxiliary Air Force squadrons will be formed more nearly upon a territorial basis. They will have a nucleus of regular officers and men, but, apart from that, will be recruited speaking generally upon a territorial basis. I have already decided to locate two of these squadrons in the neighbourhood of London, one in the neighbourhood of Edinburgh and the fourth in the neighbourhood of Glasgow.

Later, in his autobiographical book *Empire of the Air – The Advent of the Air Age 1922 – 1929,* Viscount Templewood wrote:

The first step was to interest the local authorities in the centres where we planned to form the first units, and particularly to gain the support of the Territorial Associations, with which the squadrons were to be affiliated. The complete plan was for twenty squadrons, but we wisely decided to proceed by cautious stages, and to begin with five. The City and County of London were to have one each, Warwickshire one in the industrial Midlands, and two in Scotland based on Edinburgh and Glasgow. In addition, there were to be one or two Special Reserve Squadrons, composed half of regular and half of non-regular personnel, the first of which was to be stationed at Waddington, near Lincoln.

Under the provisions of the Auxiliary Air Force and Air Force Reserves Act 1924, there were to be seven special reserve squadrons (allocated 500 series numbers) and six auxiliary squadrons (allocated 600 series numbers), with 20 auxiliary squadrons as the long-term target. The primary difference between reserve and auxiliary squadrons was in the composition of squadron personnel and the way in which the units were administered; special reserve squadrons comprised a nucleus of one third of their strength who were regulars, including offices, airmen and the officer commanding and were administered directly by the Royal Air Force. In contrast, the auxiliary squadrons had a very much higher proportion of locally raised volunteers, including the officer commanding, who were administered by the County Territorial Associations.

Both the special reserve and auxiliary squadrons were raised around centres of population with a suitable RAF airfield in the vicinity. A town headquarters in the city centre provided the focus for recruiting, training and social activity, whilst operational training was carried out at the airfield which would become their war station in time of national emergency.

On 15 May 1925, 502 (Ulster) Squadron made history when it began forming at Aldergrove as the first Special Reserve Squadron.

In June 1925, the Air Ministry published Air Ministry Pamphlet 1. This document outlined Auxiliary Air Force regulations. In peacetime each auxiliary squadron was to be located at an aerodrome near an urban centre from which it would recruit. It would also be associated for the reasons of Home Defence, with a regular Royal Air Force aerodrome. In the event of hostilities or crisis, the auxiliary squadron would be called out to take its place alongside frontline squadrons of the Royal Air Force. The auxiliary squadrons would be commanded by an Auxiliary Air Force officer, who would be selected by the local County Joint Association and approved by the Air Ministry. The adjutant and other key officers would be regular RAF officers. In addition, between 20 and 30 regular airmen would be attached to the squadron to assist in the training of auxiliary personnel.

As per Air Ministry Instruction No.583321/25/0.Z. Headquarters Special Reserve(SR) and Auxiliary Air Force(AAF) was established at 145 Sloane Street, Sloane Square, London on 14 May 1925 under the command of Air Commodore Newell CMG CBE AM Air Officer Commanding Special Reserve Units. This was followed on 15 September 1925 by the formation of the first auxiliary squadron, 602 (City of Glasgow). During 1925, a further three auxiliary squadrons were formed: 600 (City of London) at Northolt, 601 (County of London) at Northolt and 603 (City of Edinburgh) at Turnhouse, all formed on 14 October as light bomber squadrons.

Command and Control

All military organisations are highly structured and have a chain of command. The 1923 Salisbury Committee proposed a re-organisation of the structure of the Royal Air Force to create a more effective and appropriate chain of command. The major element of this was the formation of the Air Defence of Great Britain (ADGB) on 1 January 1925, under the command of Air Marshal Sir John Salmond KCB CMG CVO DSO, to control all home bomber and fighter squadrons not attached to the Coastal Area (which was formed on 15 September 1919, under the command of Air Commodore A.V. Vyvyan CB DSO, to control all aerial units operating in home waters with the Royal Navy).

These ADGB units were organised into Wessex Bombing Area and Fighting Area (to control bombers and fighters respectively); also included was Air Defence Group (ADG) with its, mainly, special reserve cadre and auxiliary squadrons.

The auxiliary squadrons were formed within the ADGB under the Special Reserve and Auxiliary Air Force Group which was constituted on 14 May 1925. On 18 July 1927 it was renamed Air Defence Group and further renamed No.1 Air Defence Group on 25 August 1927. This became 6 (Auxiliary) Group on 1 April 1936 followed by 6 (Bomber) Group on 1 January 1939. From the period of its formation on 14 October 1925 until 27 October 1938, 603 Squadron was under this structure until it became part of Fighter Command, along with other auxiliary squadrons, following the 1936 command re-organisation which brought auxiliary squadrons into regular groups during the period 1936-1938.

Conditions of Service

To be eligible to join a squadron, an early auxiliary pilot had to hold a Private Pilots Licence and be prepared to make time from his employment and private life to attend courses and flying training to RAF standards in order to gain his wings. Most of the original auxiliary pilots had already qualified on DH Moths, Avro Avions and Blackburn Bluebirds at local civilian flying clubs. To assist their conversion and instruct raw recruits, a nucleus of RAF flying instructors was posted to each squadron. Avro 504Ns, followed by Avro Tudors, were the basic trainers from which the pilots progressed to the more powerful DH9As, Westland Wapitis and Wallaces and, eventually, Hawker Harts and Hinds.

On enlistment, other rank recruits were assured that they would never be called upon to serve further than five miles from their home airfield (an assurance that must have sounded somewhat hollow in later years as the auxiliaries found themselves serving in all theatres of war from Europe to the Far East). Both members of the RAFVR and AAF were expected to reach and maintain a high standard of efficiency by regular attendance at evening and weekend training sessions and exercises and, in order to provide a period of more intensive training and to assess operational standards, an annual summer camp was held at an RAF station away from the squadrons' normal areas.

Both officers and airmen were engaged for a minimum of four years and had to attend for a minimum number of parades and lectures at their town headquarters or airfield. Provided an auxiliary had fulfilled the required number of attendances and training, he qualified for an annual tax-free bounty of no less than £3, rising to £5 in later years. In due course, and grudgingly, travelling expenses were also granted to auxiliaries and volunteers (similar conditions apply to today's Royal Auxiliary Air Force). Then, as now, most auxiliaries regard any financial return as a bonus. Being a member of the Auxiliary Air Force and being in support of the Royal Air Force was reward enough. Conditions of service and rules and regulations were governed by Air Publication 968.

AIR FORCE LIST FOR AUGUST 1938

The List is reproduced exactly as it was printed:

552a
A.A.F. Squadrons
No.603 (City of Edinburgh) (Bomber) Squadron
No.6 (Auxiliary) Group.

Aerodrome – Turnhouse, Edinburgh 12.
Town H.Q. – 25 Learmonth Terrace, Edinburgh.

Hon. Air Commodore.

The Rt. Hon. The Earl of Stair, K.T., D.S.O., D.L., J.P	5 Aug.30

Sqdn. Ldr.

Ernest H. Stevens	4 Jan.37

Flight Lieuts.

F.H. Tyson	4 Jan.37
E.L. Colbeck-Welch	6 Dec.37
Thomas M. McNeil (Admin Duties)	23 July.29
Ivone Kirkpatrick	7 Jan.31
James L. Jack, M.B.E., M.C. (a)	25 Jan.27
George A. Reid	17 Mar.31
Patrick Gifford	30 June.31

Flg. Offs.

Iain D. Shields	23 Mar.31
John G.E. Haig	11 June.32
George L. Denholm	27 June.33
J.M. Showell	1 Nov.35
F.W. Rushmer	19 Oct.34
Harold K. Macdonald	4 Mar.35
John L.G. Cunningham	6 May.35
Geoffrey T. Wynne-Powell	19 June.35

Pilot Offs.

J.A.B. Somerville	14 Jan.37
R. McG. Waterston	3 Feb.37
I.S. Ritchie	15 Feb.38
C.D. Peel	25 Feb.38

EQUIPMENT BRANCH
Flight Lieut.

Harry F. Webb	1 Feb.33
Accountant Branch	

Flg.Off.

Thomas C. Garden	13 Jan.35
Medical Branch	

Flight Lieut.

A.G.L. Dick, M.D., F.R.C.S	15 June.35

CHAPLAINS BRANCH

Rev. James R. Brown, MA	17 Jan.31

EDUCATION OFFICER

Grade III

H. Priestley, B.Sc., Ph.D., A. Inst. P	25 Apr.38

WARRANT OFFICER

J.G. Dalziel	3 May.38

APPENDIX 3

603 CITY OF EDINBURGH (FIGHTER) SQUADRON, AUXILIARY AIR FORCE

NOMINAL ROLL OF OFFICERS AS AT 3 SEPTEMBER 1939

Rank (Sept. 1939)	Name	Rank (Dec. 1942)	Civil Occupation
S/Leader	E.H. Stevens	G/Capt	Writer to the Signet
S/Leader	Rev. J. Rossie Brown	W.Com	Chaplain
F/Lieut.	J.L. Jack	W.Com	Bank Agent
F/Lieut.	I. Kirkpatrick	W.Com	Writer to the Signet
F/Lieut.	P. Gifford	Killed	Solicitor
F/Lieut.	G.L Denholm	W.Com	Timber Merchant
F/Lieut.	I.A.G.L. Dick	W.Com	Surgeon
F/Lieut.	T.C. Garden	S/Leader	Chartered Accountant
F/Officer	F.W. Rushmer	Killed	Electrical Engineer
F/Officer	H.K. Macdonald	Killed	Writer to the Signet
F/Officer	J.L.G. Cunningham	Killed	Grain Merchant
F/Officer	G.T. Wynne-Powell	S/Leader	App. Chart. Accountant
F/Officer	R. McG. Waterston	Killed	Engineering Student
F/Officer	J.G.E. Haig	S/Leader	Paper Maker
F/Officer	I.S. Ritchie	S/Leader	Writer to the Signet
F/Officer	J.A.B. Somerville	Killed	Bank Clerk
F/Officer	C.D. Peel	Killed	App. Chart. Accountant
P/Officer	G.C. Hunter	S/Leader	App. Chart. Accountant
P/Officer	G.K. Gilroy	W.Com.	Sheep Farmer
P/Officer	J.S. Morton	S/Leader	Mining Engineer
P/Officer	D.K.A. Mackenzie	Killed	App. Chart. Accountant
P/Officer	W.A. Douglas	F/Lieut.	Student
A/P/O	C.E. Hamilton	Killed	Student
Pupil Pilot	R. Mackay	F/Lieut.	Travel Agent

NOMINAL ROLL AS AT 3 SEPTEMBER 1939

Reproduced as per official list quoted in 603 Squadron Benevolent Fund Booklet.

No.	Rank	Name
803149	W/O.	Dalziel, J.
803364	F/Sgt	Mackie, R.
803093	F/Sgt	Prentice, J.
803303	F/Sgt	Scott, J.
803313	Sgt	Davidson, D.
803177	Sgt	Erskine, C.
803287	Sgt	Gillies, A.
803415	Sgt	MacKenzie, D.
803314	Sgt	Mann, J.
803386	A/C/U	Campbell, I.
803474	Cpl.	Cairns, R.
803459	Cpl.	Charles, R.
803370	Cpl.	Downie, D.
803420	Cpl.	Murray, J.
803333	Cpl.	Reilly, P.
803404	Cpl.	Robertson, A.
803237	Cpl.	Shepherd, W.
803391	Cpl.	Struthers, J.
803407	A/C/U	Wright, T.
803567	A.C.2	Adams, R.
803631	A.C.2	Alcock, D.
803380	A.C.2	Allan, A.
803503	A.C.2	Anderson, J.
803621	A.C.2	Anderson, J.B.
803473	A.C.1	Archer, S.
803515	L.A.C.	Aspey, J.
803548	A.C.2	Atherton, J.
803518	A.C.1	Bain, R.
803374	A/C/U	Baldie, A.
803619	A.C.2	Baldie, W.
803170	L.A.C.	Barnes, J.
803520	A.C.2	Bell, S.
803441	A.C.1	Bennett, J.
803607	A.C.2	Berry, J.
803596	A.C.2	Black, W.
803490	A.C.2	Blaikie, J.
803500	A.C.2	Blainey, J.
803626	A.C.2	Blake, W.
803491	A.C.2	Brown, H.

No.	Rank	Name
803604	A.C.1	Brown, J.
803568	A.C.1	Brand, G.
803017	L.A.C.	Brydon, A.
803492	A.C.2	Bryden, D.
803433	L.A.C.	Bull, G.
803598	A.C.2	Burgess, J.
803638	A.C.2	Burt, T.S.
803552	A.C.2	Campbell, D.
803569	L.A.C.	Campbell, A.
803610	A.C.2	Carroll, A.
803611	A.C.2	Carroll, W.
803599	A.C.2	Cassidy, A.
803508	A.C.1	Cessford, C.
803590	L.A.C.	Clark, J.
803627	A.C.2	Clater, D.
803342	L.A.C.	Cockell, A.
803542	A.C.1	Cockell. R.
803622	A.C.2	Cook, G.
803529	L.A.C.	Corbett, M.
803612	A.C.2	Cornwall, A.
803498	A.C.2	Crean, J.
803450	L.A.C.	Crooks, J.
803523	A.C.1	Cridland, J.
803570	L.A.C.	Cuthbertson, T.
803351	L.A.C.	Davidson, T.
803437	L.A.C.	Day, H.
803476	A.C.1	Day, A.
803628	A.C.2	Devlin, T.
803241	L.A.C.	Dickson, H.
803583	A.C.2	Dickson, J.
803428	L.A.C.	Dorward, C.
803632	A.C.2	Duff, D.
803571	L.A.C.	Erskine, L.
803544	A.C.1	Farquhar, D.
803435	L.A.C.	Feeney, F.
803468	A.C.2	Fergus, W.
803460	L.A.C.	Ferguson, D.
803507	L.A.C.	Ferguson, D.
803363	L.A.C.	Forrest, J.

No.	Rank	Name	No.	Rank	Name
803605	A.C.2	Forrest, T.	803558	A.C.2	McFarlane, D.
803629	A.C.2	Forrest, T.I.	803623	A.C.2	McKechnie, A.
803482	A/C/U	Gibson, A.	803617	A.C.2	Mackenzie, V.
803461	A/C/U	Gilchrist, G.	803639	A.C.2	Mackenzie, J.
803603	A.C.2	Gillies, J.	803648	A.C.2	Mackenzie, J.
803468	A.C.2	Gordon, R.	803593	A.C.2	MacLachlan, J.
803543	A.C.1	Goulding, J.	803049	A.C.2	Maclean, J.
803405	A/C/U	Gray, R.	803562	A.C.2	Macleod, D.
803592	A.C.1	Greig, J.	803576	L.A.C.	McLaren, G.
803452	A/C/U	Hall, R.	803071	L.A.C.	Maclaggan, R.
803580	A.C.2	Hamilton, W.	803643	A.C.2	McMichael, T.
803516	A.C.2	Harris, A.	803527	A.C.1	McVie, G.
803533	A.C.1	Haston, H.	803597	L.A.C.	Noble, O.
803630	A.C.2	Hay, J.	803463	L.A.C.	Oldershaw, C.
803613	A.C.1	Highley, O.	803554	A.C.2	Paterson, W.
803584	A.C.2	Hill, A.	803514	L.A.C.	Penny, R.
803346	L.A.C.	Hogg, J.	803484	A/C/U	Piggott, T.
803633	A.C.2	Hood, M.	803595	A.C.2	Prentice, T.
803545	A.C.2	Hoy, J.	803488	L.A.C.	Pritchard, E.
803556	L.A.C.	Howieson, G.	803546	A.C.2	Pringle, H.
803637	A.C.2	Inglis, R.	803549	A.C.2	Payne, R.
803208	A.C.1	James, A.	803609	A.C.1	Pyper, A.
803614	A.C.2	Jarvis, T.	803505	L.A.C.	Rendall, J.
803600	A.C.2	Johanson, D.	803352	L.A.C.	Rennie, J.
803502	A.C.2	Hunter, J.	803577	A.C.1	Rennie, W.
803480	L.A.C.	Kerr, W.	803485	A.C.2	Rennie, J.
803388	L.A.C.	Kidd, W.	803594	A.C.2	Rennie, J.
803534	A.C.1	Knox, G.	803547	A.C.2	Ritchie, T.
803453	L.A.C.	Laurie, T.	803522	A.C.2	Robb, B.
803557	A.C.2	Law, J.	803379	L.A.C.	Robertson, A.
803634	A.C.2	Law, A.	803640	A.C.2	Robson, J.
803573	A.C.2	Ledgerwood, M.	803644	A.C.1	Ritchie, J.
803635	A.C.2	Lee, J.	803438	A.C.1	Scanlon, T.
803606	A.C.2	Leitch, A.	803618	A.C.2	Scott, G.
803298	L.A.C.	Liddle, A.	803581	L.A.C.	Shepherd, J.
803504	L.A.C.	Marshall, J.	803479	A.C.1	Sinclair, J.
803574	A.C.1	Marsland, F.	803509	L.A.C.	Sim, J.
803645	A.C.2	Melrose, J.	803495	A.C.2	Simpson, J.
803559	A.C.2	Methven, O.	803615	A.C.2	Skinner, J.
803458	L.A.C.	Miller, J.	803550	A.C.2	Skinner, D.
803538	L.A.C.	Miller, J.	803477	L.A.C.	Smith, S.
803451	L.A.C.	Moffat, C.	803555	A.C.2	Smith, W.
803532	A.C.1	Muir, G.	803564	A.C.2	Smith, H.
803649	A.C.2	Mullay, G.	803496	L.A.C.	Somerville, H.
803519	A.C.2	Murray, T.	803620	A.C.1	Spanswick, J.
803575	A.C.1	Murray, W.	803449	A.C.2	Speirs, J.
803483	A.C.1	Munro, R.	803328	A.C.2	Stenhouse, J.
803059	A.C.2	Munro, A.	803585	A.C.1	Stewart, G.
803472	L.A.C.	Myddleton, C.	803591	A.C.2	Struthers, C.
803553	A.C.2	Munro, A.	803646	A.C.1	Swanson, W.
803245	L.A.C.	McBain, J.	803465	A.C.1	Swanston, J.
803467	A.C.1	McClean, J.	803565	A.C.2	Tait, W.
803487	L.A.C.	McFarlane, J.	803525	L.A.C.	Thomson, J.

No.	Rank	Name	No.	Rank	Name
803579	L.A.C.	Thomson, W.	803566	A.C.2	Wickstead, J
803624	A.C.2	Thorburn, J.	803531	L.A.C.	Wisdom, L
803466	L.A.C.	Towsey, J.	803647	A.C.2	Wilson, R
803513	A.C.1	Turbayne, V.	803540	A.C.2	Willox, G.
803641	A.C.2	Wallace, W.	803551	A.C.2	Whitecross, A.
803528	A.C.1	Walshe, T.	803588	L.A.C.	Wishart, A.
803521	A.C.1	Ward, W.	803601	A.C.2	Worthington, J.
803537	L.A.C.	Watt, E.	803608	A.C.2	Watson, W.
803625	A.C.2	White, J.	803169	L.A.C.	Watson, W.A.
803444	A.C.1	Wilson, A.	803642	A.C.2	Vaughan, E.

Auxiliary Air Force Reserve

No.	Rank	Name	No.	Rank	Name
803162	F/Sgt	Gunn, J.G.	803280	Cpl.	Marwick, G.W.
803122	F/Sgt	Steedman, W.	803358	L.A.C.	Cantley, A.
803316	Cpl.	Gardiner.	803207	L.A.C.	Craik, R.
803285	Cpl.	Gunn, D.	803309	L.A.C.	Dickson, T.
803376	Cpl.	Ross, H.	803238	L.A.C.	Riley, J.
803257	Cpl.	Sanderson, F.			

APPENDIX 5

SQUADRON BADGE

The Squadron had three badges during its career, of which two were unofficial . These were :

603 (City of Edinburgh) Bomber Squadron: October 14 1925 – October 26 1938 (unofficial)
603 (City of Edinburgh) Fighter Squadron: October 27 1938 – March 1940 (unofficial)
603 (City of Edinburgh) (F) Squadron: March 1940 (official)

Badge: On a rock a triple towered castle (David's Tower) flying there from a pennon.
Motto: Gin ye daur (Doric) 'If you dare.'
Authority: King George VI, March 1940.

NO 603 (CITY OF EDINBURGH) RAUXAF
BATTLE HONOURS 1939-40

Home Defence 1940-42
Battle of Britain 1940*

* 58 enemy aircraft destroyed (RAF Hornchurch), 14 pilots lost.

HONOURS AND AWARDS

Year	Name		Award /*London Gazette* Entry
Pre-War			
1936	Flight Lieutenant J.L. Jack MC	AAF	MBE
1938	Squadron Leader G.N. Douglas-Hamilton	AAF	AFC
1939-1940			
1939	Flight Lieutenant P. Gifford	AAF	DFC 28.11.1939. 7961.
1940	Pilot Officer C. Robertson	RAF	DFC 31.5.40. 3256.
1940	Pilot Officer G.K Gilroy	AAF	DFC 13.9.40. 5488.
1940	Sergeant J.R. Caister	AAF	DFM 13.9.40
1940	Flying Officer B.J.G Carbury (NZ)	RAF	DFC 24.9.40. 5654.
1940	Flying Officer B.J.G Carbury (NZ)	RAF	Bar to DFC 25.10.40.
1940	Acting Squadron Leader G.L. Denholm	AAF	DFC 22.10.40. 6134
1940	Pilot Officer R. Berry	RAFVR	DFC 25.10.40. 6194.
1940	Pilot Officer B.G. Stapleton (SA)	RAF	DFC 15.11.40. 6570
1940	Flight Lieutenant J.C. Boulter	RAF	DFC 6.11.40. 6938.

ROLL OF HONOUR 1928-1940

On 2 July 1989, Her Majesty Queen Elizabeth II unveiled a Scroll of Honour in the Canongate Kirk, (the Kirk of Holyrood House) Edinburgh commemorating those members of the Squadron who lost their lives whilst serving with the Squadron in peace and war.

1928	7 Jul	P/O	J.T.L Shiells	AAF
1930	3 Aug	F/O	A. Miller	AAF
1938	26 Mar	F/O	C.A.G Thomson	AAF
	26 Mar	AC2	R.H. Starrett	AAF
1939	18 Feb	P/O	I.E. Pease	AAF
	1 Oct	F/O	J.A.B. Somerville	AAF
1940	19 Mar	P/O	G.I. Thomson	RAF
	12 Jun	P/O	D.K.A. Mackenzie	RAF
	17 Jul	F/O	C.D. Peel	AAF
	28 Aug	F/L	J.L.G. Cunningham	AAF
	28 Aug	P/O	D.K. Macdonald	RAFVR
	28 Aug	P/O	N.J.V. Benson	RAF
	31 Aug	F/O	R. McG. Waterston	AAF
	31 Aug	LAC	W.J. Baldie	RAF
	31 Aug	LAC	J.E. Dickson	AAF
	1 Sep	AC1	J. Worthington	AAF
	5 Sep	F/L	F.W. Rushmer	AAF
	15 Sep	F/O	A.P. Pease	RAFVR
	18 Sep	P/O	P. Howes	RAFVR
	27 Sep	P/O	P.M. Cardell	RAFVR
	28 Sep	F/L	H.K. Macdonald	AAF
	7 Oct	F/O	H.K.F. Matthews	RAF
	27 Oct	P/O	R.B. Dewey	RAF
	28 Oct	F/O	C.W. Goldsmith	RAFVR
	8 Nov	F/L	M.T. Kirkwood	RAF
	21 Nov	Sgt	R.E. Plant	RAFVR
	26 Nov	AC1	A. Reynolds	RAFVR
	29 Nov	P/O	W.P.H. Rafter	RAF
	31 Dec	Sgt	B.C. Webber	RAFVR

This list includes all members of 603 (City of Edinburgh) Squadron who died while serving with the Squadron in peace and war. Confirmed by Air Historical Branch (RAF) and the Commonwealth War Graves Commission.

NO 603 (CITY OF EDINBURGH) SQUADRON CHRONOLOGY

Date/Year	Event
14 Oct 1925	Formed at Turnhouse with DH9A within Bomber Command under the Command of S/L J.A. McKelvie AFC
1926	Town Headquarters at 25 Learmonth Terrace, Edinburgh
Mar 1930	Re-equip with Wapiti aircraft
5 Aug 1930	The Rt Hon The Earl of Stair Kt DSO appointed Honorary Air Commodore
Feb 1934	Re-equip with Hawker Harts
Feb 1938	Re-equip with Hawker Hind
1938	To Fighter Command
Mar 1939	Re-equip with Gloster Gladiator Mk I, becomes part of Fighter Command
Sep 1939	Re-equip with Supermarine Spitfire Mk I
1 Oct 1939	First wartime casualty; Flying Officer J.A.B. Somerville killed in an air accident at Grangemouth
16 Oct 1939	Squadron Spitfires shoot down first German aircraft to fall on British territory since 1919
16 Dec 1939	To Prestwick
17 Jan 1940	To Dyce det Montrose
Mar 1940	Sqn badge approved by King George VI. Motto 'Gin Ye Daur'
14 Apr 1940	To Drem
5 May 1940	To Turnhouse det Montrose, Dyce
28 Aug 1940	To Hornchurch, Battle of Britain, highest scoring squadron with 58.5 kills, under the Command of S/L George Denholm
Oct 1940	Re-equip with Spitfire IIA
3 Dec 1940	To Southend
17 Dec 1940	To Drem

THE ESHER TROPHY

The Esher Trophy – a bronze figure of Perseus by Sir Alfred Gilbert, was presented by the Late Viscount Esher. It was awarded every year to the premier AuxAF flying squadron of that year. It was first awarded in 1926 (601 Sqn) and last awarded in 1955 (500 Sqn): The Squadron was awarded the Esher Trophy in 1938 and 1950. For the latter award 603 achieved 458.2 points out of a possible 475.0 and was presented the trophy the following year.

DISTINGUISHED FLYING CROSS (DFC)
1939-1940 – *LONDON GAZETTE* ENTRIES

BERRY, Ronald, Pilot Officer (78538) RAFVR. 603 Sqn.
London Gazette: **25/10/1940: 6194.**
Pilot Officer Berry has personally destroyed six enemy aircraft, and assisted in the destruction of several others. Through innumerable engagements with the enemy he has shown the greatest gallantry and determination in pressing home his attacks at close range. The skill and dash with which this officer has led his section have done much to assure their success.

BOULTER, John Clifford. Flight Lieutenant (37757) RAF. 603 Sqn.
London Gazette: **6/12/1940: 6938.**
This officer has continuously been engaged on active operations since October, 1940. He is an excellent and determined leader, and his coolness and initiative have enabled him to destroy at least five enemy aircraft and share in the destruction of others.

CARBURY, Brian John George, Flying Officer (40288) RAF. 603 Sqn.
London Gazette: **24/9/1940: 5654.**
During operations on the North East coast Flying Officer Carbury led his section in an attack on two enemy aircraft. Both were destroyed. From 28th August 1940, to 2nd September 1940 he has, with his squadron, been almost continuously engaged against large enemy raids over Kent, and has destroyed eight enemy aircraft. Five of these were shot down during three successive engagements in one day.

CARBURY, Brian John George, Flying Officer (40288) RAF. 603 Sqn
Bar to Distinguished Flying Cross.
London Gazette: **25/10//1940: 6193.**
Flying Officer Carbury has displayed outstanding gallantry and skill in engagements against the enemy. Previous to the 8th September, 1940, this officer shot down eight enemy aircraft, and shared in the destruction of two others. Since that date he has destroyed two Messerschmitt 109's and two Heinkel 113's and, in company with other pilots of his squadron, also assisted in the destruction of yet another two enemy aircraft. His cool courage in the face of the enemy has been a splendid example to other pilots of his squadron.

DENHOLM, George Lovell, Acting Squadron Leader (90190) AAF. 603 Sqn
London Gazette: **22/10/1940: 6134.**
Since the commencement of hostilities, Squadron Leader Denholm has led his squadron, flight or section in innumerable operational patrols against the enemy. His magnificent leadership has contributed largely to the success of the squadron, which has destroyed fifty-four enemy aircraft in about six weeks; four of these aircraft were destroyed by Squadron Leader Denholm himself.

GIFFORD, Patrick. Flight Lieutenant (90188) AAF. 603 Sqn.
London Gazette: **28/11/1939: 7961.**
During October, 1939, this officer, leading a section of his squadron, sighted an enemy bomber over the mainland heading towards the sea at high speed. Flight Lieutenant Gifford led the attack with skill, daring and determination, and as the result of a final burst of firing from his own guns the enemy aircraft crashed into the sea. Later in October 1939, this officer's section intercepted a bomber apparently engaged in

reconnoitring a British convoy. The enemy aircraft attempted to take cover in the clouds but Flight Lieutenant Gifford led his section after it, firing short bursts as opportunity offered. The pursuit continued some eleven miles out to sea where the raider, showing signs of having been hit, turned and crashed into the sea.

GILROY, George Kemp. Pilot Officer (90481) AAF. 603 Sqn.
London Gazette: **13/9/1940: 5488.**

ROBERTSON, Colin. Pilot Officer (33412) RAF. 603 Sqn.
London Gazette: **31/5/1940: 3256.**

STAPLETON, Basil Gerald, Pilot Officer (41879) RAF. 603 Sqn.
*London Gazette:***15/11/1940:6570.**
Pilot Officer Stapleton has flown with his squadron in active operations since the war began. He has personally destroyed at least six enemy aircraft and has shared in the destruction of two others. Pilot Officer Stapleton has displayed great skill and courage in the face of superior numbers of the enemy.

DFM

CAISTER, James Russell. Sergeant (358860) AAF. 603 Sqn.
London Gazette: **13/9/40.**
His Majesty has been graciously pleased to award the Distinguished Flying Medal to Sergeant J.R. Caister.

APPENDIX 11

HONORARY AIR COMMODORES
1930-Present

The Rt. Hon. The Earl of Stair Kt DSO, JP, DL, MP   : 5 Aug 1930 – 5Aug 1938
The Rt. Hon. Sir William Y. Darling CBE, MC, DL, JP, FRSE, MP : 23 Feb 1943 – 1951*
HRH The Princess Elizabeth   : 16 June 1951 – 31 May 1957
(HRH The Princess Elizabeth who, at her own express wish, continued as Honorary Air Commodore when she ascended the Throne on 6 February 1952.)
The Rt. Hon. Lord Selkirk of Douglas QC, LLB, MA   : 1 October 1999 – December 2000
Her Majesty Queen Elizabeth II   : December 2000 – Present.

*Sir William Darling originally took over as Honorary Air Commodore for five years but in 1948 he extended his term in office for a further five years but resigned in June 1951 to allow HRH The Princess Elizabeth to take over as Honorary Air Commodore of 603 Squadron.

COMMANDING OFFICERS
1925-The Present

Sqn Ldr J.A. McKelvie AFC, AAF	1 Aug 25 – 14 Apr 31
Sqn Ldr H. Murray-Philipson MP, AAF	14 Apr 31 – 1 Apr 34
Sqn Ldr G.N. Douglas-Hamilton AFC, AAF	1 Apr 34 – 1 Apr 38
Sqn Ldr E.H. Stevens, AAF	1 Apr 38 – 4 Jun 40
Sqn Ldr G.L. Denholm DFC, AAF	4 Jun 40 – 1 Apr 41
Sqn Ldr F.M. Smith RAF	1 Apr 41 – 25 Jul 41
Sqn Ldr M.J. Loudon RAF	25 Jul 41 – 17 Oct 41
Sqn Ldr R.G. Forshaw RAF	17 Oct 41 – 18 Dec 41
Sqn Ldr Lord D. Douglas-Hamilton RAFVR	18 Dec 41 – 20 Jul 42
Sqn Ldr W.A. Douglas RAF*	20 July 42 – 3 Aug 42
Sqn Ldr P. Illingworth RAF**	10 April 42 – 4 June 42
Sqn Ldr F.W. Marshall RAFVR***	3 Aug 42 – 28 Jan 43
W/C H.A. Chater RAF	28 Jan 43 – 1 Dec 43
W/C J.R.H. Lewis DFC, RAF	1 Dec 43 – 15 Jun 44
W/C J.T.D. Revell, RAF	15 Jun 44 – 2 Aug 44
S/L C.D. Paine (Acting) RAFVR	2 Aug 44 – 23 Sept 44
W/C C.N. Foxley-Norris RAF	23 Sept 44 – 26 Dec 44
S/L E.H.M. Patterson DFC, RAFVR****	10 Jan 45 – 26 Jan 45
S/L T.C. Rigler DFC, DFM, RAFVR	26 Jan 45 – 1 Apr 45
S/L H.R.P. Pertwee DFC, RAFVR	1 Apr 45 – 15 Aug 45

Squadron disbanded 15 August 1945
Squadron reformed 11 June 1946

S/L G.K. Gilroy DSO, DFC, AAF	11 Jun 46 – 23 Sept 49
S/L J.M.E. Holmes DFC, AFC, RAF	23 Sept 49 – 1 Dec 50
S/L P.J. Anson DFC, RAF	1 Dec 50 – 22 Mar 53
S/L R. Lloyd-Davies DFC, RAF	22 Mar 53 – 25 Aug 53
S/L R. Schofield, RAF	25 Aug 53 – 9 May 56
S/L M.E. Hobson AFC, RAF	9 May 56 – 10 Mar 57

Squadron disbanded 10 March 1957
Squadron reformed 1 October 1999

W/C A.J. Beaton RAuxAF	1 Oct 99 – Present

*	Posting Notice 92/05/42 dated July 1942, then to reconstituted 229 Squadron. PMC, RAF Records Innsworth.
**	Officer Commanding Ground Party.
***	Administrative Officer Commanding Ground Party.
****	Ex-229 Squadron. Non-effective sick throughout period of command.

SQUADRON BASES

Turnhouse	14 Oct 1925
Prestwick	16 Dec 1939
Dyce/Det. Montrose	17 Jan 1940
Drem	14 Apr 1940
Turnhouse/Det. Montrose & Dyce	5 May 1950
Hornchurch	27 Aug 1940
Rochford (Southend)	3 Dec 1940
Drem	13 Dec 1940

SUMMER CAMPS 1926-1938

The annual summer camps were held in the first two weeks of July during the Edinburgh Trade Fare Fortnight.

Pre- War 1926 to 1938

1926	Leuchars
1927	Leuchars
1928	Leuchars
1929	Leuchars
1930	Manston
1931	Turnhouse
1932	Manston
1933	Manston
1934	Manston
1935	Tangmere
1936	Leuchars
1937	Hawkinge
1938	Ramsgate

MARKINGS AND CODES

Before April 1939, squadron aircraft featured their identity on the fuselage, i.e. '603' together with the unofficial squadron badge in black on the silver tailfins. Following the Munich Crisis of late 1938, Air Ministry Order (AMO) A.154/39, dated 27 April 1939, allocated two letter combinations to all the then existing squadrons; 603 was allocated the code letters 'RL' which appeared on its Gloster Gladiators Mk I aircraft. This code was changed to 'XT' upon the outbreak of war in September 1939, and this was retained whilst the Squadron was based in the United Kingdom.

APPENDIX 16

AIRCRAFT FLOWN 1925-1940

Training Aircraft:
In December 1926, one Avro 504K was replaced by the 'Lynx' engine type 504N. By the end of 1927, the old 'Mono Avros' had all been replaced by the Lynx.

Avro 504K – October 1925 – December 1927:
H2528, H2975, H2979, E3333.

Avro 504N – December 1927 – 1937:
J8501, J8507, J8557, J8570, J8690, J8694, J8742, J8752, J9253, J9255, K1798, K1822, K1975, J2349, K2417.

DH Moth 60M – 1931-1938:
K1108, K1901.

Avro Tutor – March 1937 – December 1939:
K3254, K3454, K3455, K3456.

DH Tiger Moth II – November 1938 – July 1939:
N6931.

Miles Magister I – 1939 – 1940:
L5934, N3918, N3934, N5410.

North American Harvard I – December 1939 – June 1940:
P5866.

Operational Aircraft 1925-40:

De Havilland DH 9A – October 1925-May 1930:
J7020, J7023, J7070, J7120, J7123, J7127, J8129, J8136, J8144, J8145, J8160, J8166, J8168, J8209, J8211, J8472.

Westland Wapiti IIA – March 1930-March 1934:
J9608, J9858, J9859, J9862, K1135, K1136, K1137, K1138, K1139, K1140, K1144, K1145, K1151, K1319, K1377, K2240, K2259, K2262.

Hawker Hart I – February 1934-February 1938:
K2447, K2475, K2996, K3039, K3045, K3052, K3730, K3750 (Trainer), K3847, K3848 (Trainer), K3859, K3860, K3861, K3863, K3864, K3867, K3868, K3871, K3872, K3876, K3879, K3880, K3895, K3898, K3903, K3969, K3972, K4459, K4642, K5895 (Trainer), K6809.

Hawker Hind – February 1938-March 1939:
K4642, K5392, K5498, K5499, K6627, K6629, K6755, K6809, K6811, K6814, K6815, K6816, K6817, K6819, K6843, K6844, K6845, K6847.

Gloster Gladiator Mk I – March 1939 – October 1939:
K7894, K7917, K7918, K7920, K7921, K7924, K7925, K7926, K7927, K7928, K7929, K7931, K7932, K7935, K7936, K7938, K7972, K7990.

Spitfires flown by 603 Squadron
Mk I September 1939 – December 1940.
Mk II December 1940 – June 1941.

Supermarine Spitfire F37/34, F16/36 Mk I & II

K-Series:
Spitfire Mk Is up to serial number K9960 had Rolls-Royce Merlin II engines, the rest had Merlin IIIs. Up to K9963 had a mahogony two-blade, fixed-pitch propeller, all were retro-fitted with the constant speed three-blade de Havilland propeller. The remainder had three-blade, two-speed, de Havilland props which were also replaced in June 1940 with a constant speed unit.

Dates of arrival with unit does not always correspond with ORB and not all details are available. In some cases there is doubt as to whether a particular aircraft did or did not fly with 603 Squadron.

K9795 To 19 Sqn. 27.9.38. 64 Sqn. 18.4.40 – shot down by AA fire over Dover, landed Hawkinge, 13.7.40. 49 Maintenance Unit (MU) 15.7.40. General Aircraft Ltd. 603 Sqn. 29.9.40, XT-G. 222 Sqn. 14.10.40 – engine failed, crashed Terling P/O Edridge safe, Cat.2, 15.10.40. Struck off charge (SOC) 12.1.41. Operational Training Unit (OTU) 26.2.41. To 4867 M6, School of Technical Training (SoTT) 1.1.42.

K9803 66 Sqn. 28.10.38. 616 Sqn. 30.10.39. 19 Sqn. 3.5.40. 603 Sqn. 13.9.40 – Damaged by Bf109 near Ashford, Kent. Sgt Bailey safe. Cat.2. 45MU 23.2.41. Heston Aircraft Ltd. (HAL) 30.3.41. Armstrong Whitworth (ArmW) 8.11.41. 61 OTU 19.3.43 – Flying accident, Cat.B, 8.1.44. OTU 21.5.44. 33 MU 13.8.44. SOC 21.6.47.

K9807 12 First Flew (FF) George Pickering 10.10.38. 19 Sqn. 11.10.38. 616 Sqn., 7.8.40, Cat.2 ops 15.8.40. 603 Sqn., 29.9.40, shot down by Bf109, P/O Morton abandoned a/c 5.10.40.

K9833 47 FF George Pickering 29.12.38. 41 Sqn. 3.1.39. 602 Sqn. 20.1.40. 603 Sqn. 5.7.40. 602 Sqn. 4.8.40 – FA 28.8.40. 58 OTU 2.1.41 – force-landed, Dunblane, Perthshire, Cat.E, 18.4.41. To 2574M.

K9890 67 FF George Pickering 28.1.39. 41 Sqn. 4.2.39. 294 Sqn. 4.6.40. 602 Sqn. 13.7.40. 41 Sqn. 21.7 40. 603 Sqn. 20.9.40 – C.2, 23.9.40. Air Service Training (AST) out of fuel, landed near Hooton Park in River Mersey 1.2.41.

K9916 127 FF, George Pickering, 28.3.39. 65 Sqn. 1.4.39. 603 Sqn. 14.12.39 – Failed to return from patrol, F/O Peel assumed dead, 17.7.40.

K9926 137 FF 6.4.39. 72 Sqn. 14.4.39. 603 Sqn. – Cat.E. Aircraft collided with Avro Anson whilst taking off at Dyce. P/O Gilroy unhurt, 25.3.40. SOC 31.5.40.

K9956 170 FF 1.5.39. 65 Sqn. 6.5.39. 603 Sqn. 4.12.39 – crashed on landing, overturned, Drem 17.4.40. P/O W.A. Douglas unhurt. AST. SOC 13.5.40.

K9995 209 MIII. FF 26.5.39. 504 Sqn. 2.11.39. 603 Sqn. 6.11.39 – C2 operations 19.7.40. 1 Contractors (Civilian) Repair Unit (CRU). 602 Sqn. 19.8.40. 65 Sqn. 27.8.40. Flying Accident 27.8.40. Cunliffe Owen Aircraft (COAL). 57 OTU hit ground while flying low off Dee estuary 8.6.41. Repaired on-site (ROS), 57 OTU 6.9.41. Flying accident, Cat.E, aircraft total wreck 21.9.41. SOC 14.10.41.

All Spitfires from K9961 fitted with de Havilland three-blade, two-speed propeller:

K9963 176 FF 4.5.39. 602 Sqn. 8.5.39. AST 27.11.39. 611 Sqn. 4.6.40. 234 Sqn. 1.9.40. 603 Sqn. 6.9.40 – Cat.3 operations 5.10.40. SOC.

K9995 209 MIII. FF 26.5.39. 504 Sqn., 2.11.39. 603 Sqn., 6.11.39, Cat.2 ops 19.7.40. 1 Contractors (Civilian) Repair Unit. 602 Sqn., 19.8.40. 65 Sqn., 27.8.40. FA 27.8.40. Cunliffe Owen Aircraft Ltd. 57 OTU, hit ground flying low off River Dee estuary 8.6.40. Repaired on-site. 57 OTU 6.9.40 Flying Accident Cat.E, total wreck 21.9.40. SOC 14.10.40.

K9996 210 MIII. FF George Pickering 26.5.39. 504 Sqn. 2.11.39. 603 Sqn. 6.11.39. Air Services Training 15.11.39. 266 Sqn. 17.8.40. 616 Sqn. 7.9.40. 57 OTU 4.4.41. Flying accident 26.4.41. Cat.B. Crashed on take-off from Hawarden after engine failed. 30.7.41. Cat.E. SOC 9.8.41.

K9997 211 MIII. FF 1.6.39. 504 Sqn. 2.11.39. 603 Sqn. 6.11.39. AST 6.1.40. Flying accident. Cat.B 17.4.40. 609 Sqn. 4.6.40. Damaged due to enemy action 12.8.40. 7 OTU 5.10.40. Scottish Aviation Ltd. 22.4.41. 53 OTU 17.7.41. repaired on-site 20.9.41. Crashed Cat.E 24.1.42.

K9998 212 MIII. FF 1.6.39. 504 Sqn. 2.11.39. 603 Sqn. 6.11.39. AST 24.2.40. 92 Sqn. 2.7.40. 7 OTU 1.11.40. Westland Aircraft Ltd (WAL) 4.11.40. 57 OTU – Flying accident, Cat.B 16.8.41. Crash-landed at Hawarden 26.8.41. 1 Contractors (Civilian) Repair Unit. To 2822 M6. SoTT 27.12 41. SOC 4.12.41.

L-Series which were all FMk IA, with Merlin III engines unless otherwise stated:

L1007 230 FF 15.6.39. AMDP 21.6.39. 2x20mm installed VA Boscombe Down 21.6.39, handling and performance trials. 603 Sqn. XT-K. AFDU October '39. 65 Sqn. 5.11.39. 609 Sqn. 18.4.40 as prototype Mk IB. 72 Sqn. Drem, shot down Heinkel over Scotland, January 1940. SOC Cat.E., 28.5.40.

L1017 230 FF 15.6.39. 5 MU 19.6.39. 610 Sqn. 4.10.39. Air Service Training 31.5.40. 603 Sqn. 1.9.40. AST 6.9.40. 7 OTU 28.9.40 FAC2 10.10.40. AST to 3206M 4 School of Technical Training 11.3.41. Cat.E 23.9.44.

L1020 234. FF 16.6.39. 20 MU 26.6.39. 603 Sqn. 15.9.39, XT-L, Cat.E operations 6.9.40. SOC 21.9.40.

L1021 235. FF 16.6.39. 20 MU 26.6.39. 603 Sqn. 15.9.39, XT-M – 'Sredni Vashtar' – shot down, forced landed near Lympne, P/O Richard Hillary safe, 29.8.40. 57 OTU 4.4.43. 57 OTU 18.11.43. Cat.E. SOC 6.3.45.

L1022 236. FF 19.6.39. 20 MU 26.6.39. 603 Sqn. 15.9.39 – Collision with Oxford whilst taxiing at Montrose, F/O Boulter safe, 20.3.40. SOC April 1940.

L1023 237. FF 17.6.39. 20 MU 26.6.39. 603 Sqn 15.9.39 – stalled/crashed in finals turn at Turnhouse, 7.10.39, total wreck, P/O Graham Hunter injured. SOC.

L1024 238. FF 17.6.39. 20 MU 26.6.39. 603 Sqn. 15.9.39, XT-R, damaged on operation from Montrose, P/O D.K. Macdonald safe, 1.9.40. 57 OTU 23.10.40. Flying accident, Cat.C, 9.5.41. 52 OTU 16.5.42. Allied Expeditionary Air Force (AEAF) Communication Flight 20.1.44. SOC 2.6.47.

L1025 239. FF 20.6.39. 20 MU 26.6.39. 603 Sqn. 15.9.39 – undercarriage jammed after heavy touch and on landing, aircraft abandoned, Cat.E, P/O Stapleton safe. SOC 5.5.40.

L1026 240. FF 20.6.39. 20 MU 20.6.39. 603 Sqn. 15.9.39 – lost in fog, flew into ground, Slains, Aberdeen, P/O G.I. Thomson killed, 19.3.40.

L1046 261. FF, George Pickering, 5.7.39. 603 Sqn. 20.9.39, XT-K, *Ard Choille* – Failed to return (missing), operations, P/O D.K. Macdonald missing. 28.8.40.

L1047 262. FF, George Pickering, 5.7.39. 603 Sqn. 18.9.39 – L1059 landed on L1047 whilst it was taxiing at Grangemouth, F/O Somerville killed, 1.10.39. SOC.

L1048 263. FF 7.7.39. 19 MU 11.7.39. 603 Sqn. 18.9.39 – FA 13.6.40. 152 Sqn. 28.9.40. 609 Sqn. 28.9.40, 152 Sqn. 3.10.40 – crash landed near Torquay 3.10.40. Director General of Research and Development (DGRD), Vickers Armstrong (VA) 20.12.40. RAF Northolt 23.12.40. To 3248M. 7 SoTT 14.3.41. Squadron Leader Training Command 4.5.44. Reduced to produce (rtp) 18.5.44.

L1049 264. FF 6.7.39. 19 MU 11.7.39. 603 Sqn. 18.9.39 – damaged on operations 18.7.40. 602 Sqn. 23.9.40. 57 OTU 24.10.40. Flying accident, Cat.2, 16.12.40. Crash landed at Speke. To 3876M 1 SoTT 26.3.41. Air Service Training, Hamble, 22.7.44. Cat.E 3.8.44.

L1050 265. FF, George Pickering, 7.9.39. 9 MU 12.7.39. 603 Sqn. 19.9.39 – Flying Area. Crashed, Balerno, Midlothian, Cat.E, P/O Mackenzie killed, 12.6.40. SOC 19.6.40.

L1057 272. FF, George Pickering, 13.7.39. 603 Sqn. 16.9.39, XT-X. Scottish Aviation Ltd. 22.9.40. SOC 5.4.41 to 2644M, 12 SoTT 13.7.42. SOC 12.4.45.

L1058 273. FF 14.7.39. 27 MU 22.7.39. 603 Sqn. 6.9.39. Failed to return, operations, 1.6.40. SOC 8.6.40.

L1059 274. FF 14.7.39. 27 MU 22.7.39. 603 Sqn. 16.9.39 – crashed on to L1047 whilst landing at Grangemouth, 1.10.39. AST 30.11.39. 266 Sqn. 4.6.40 – struck building whilst landing at Wittering, Cat.2, Sgt Eade safe, 9.8.40. 1 Contractors (Civilian) Repair Unit 19.10.40. 58 OTU 29.1.41 – dived into ground, Slamannan, Stirling, destroyed by fire 14.2.41. SOC 21.2.41.

L1061 276. FF 15.7.39. 27 MU 22.7.39. 603 Sqn. 16.9.39, XT-B. Air Service Training, Hamble. 7 OTU 26.10.40. 1 Contractors (Civilian) Repair Unit 21.4.40. 53 OTU 23.7.40. AST 29.9.42 converted to F.VA M45, 9.2.43. 61 OTU 8.5.43. Cat.E 30.6.44.

L1062 277. FF 17.7.39. & MU 27.7.39. 603 Sqn. 16.6.39. 610 Sqn. 30.9.39 – Failed to return from operation 29.5.40. Flying hours (FH) 97.40.

L1067 282. FF 20.7.39. 27 MU 26.7.39. 603 Sqn. 16.9.39, XT-D – 'Blue Peter' – Shot down by Bf110s. S/L Denholm abandoned aircraft, safe, 30.8.40.

L1070 285. FF 24.7.39. 27 MU 26.7.39. 603 Sqn. 16.9.39, XT-A, 'Stickleback/Excaliber' – turned over after having undershot on landing at Prestwick in low visibility, Sgt W.W. Thomson unhurt, 13.1.40. Cat.2 operations 1.9.40. 57 OTU 25.10.40 – Flying accident Cat.C 23.7.41. General Aircraft Ltd. 7.10.41. SOC 29.12.41.

L1075 289. FF 10.8.39. 24 MU 14.8.39. 610 Sqn. 5.10.39. 603 Sqn. 17.10.39. Failed to return, operations 9.7.40.

L1076 290. FF 11.8.39. 24 MU 14.8.39. 610 Sqn. 5.10.39. AST 7.7.40. 603 Sqn. 1.9.40 – Shot down by Bf109, F/L H.K. Macdonald killed 28.9.40.

Of the 96 L-Series Spitfire Mk I As built, 50% were damaged by enemy action with a further 40 involved in accidents.

N-Series:

N3026 315. FF 9.9.39. 72 Sqn. 11.9.39. 603 Sqn. 21.2.40 – crash landed at Montrose, S/L Denholm safe, 23.7.40. 303 Sqn. 10.9.41. 61 OTU 2.10.41. 52 OTU 9.6.42 – dived into ground near Nailsworth, Glos, aircraft destroyed by fire, Sgt Booth killed. SOC, Cat.E, 8.11.42.

N3056 345. FF, George Pickering, 2.10.39. 24 MU 5.10.39. 611 Sqn. 25.1.40 – damaged on operations 2.6.40. 603 Sqn. 20.7.40, XT-B, shot down by Bf109 near Maidstone, Sgt Stokoe abandoned aircraft injured, 2.9.40. Flying hours 151.25.

N3099 370. FF 17.10.39. 8 MU 19.10.39. 611 Sqn. 21.1.40. 41 Sqn. 21.1.40 – Flying Accident 30.7.40. 603 Sqn. 29.9.40. 266 Sqn. 17.10.40. 111 Sqn. 8.4.41. 58 OTU 29.5.41 – Flying Accident, Cat.E, aircraft destroyed by fire 10.8.41. SOC.

N3100 371. FF, George Pickering, 18.10.39. 9 MU 19.10.39. 41 Sqn. 19.3.40 – Cat.2 operations 21.7.40. 603 Sqn. 18.9.40. 266 Sqn. 17.10.40. 111 Sqn. 8.4.41. 58 OTU 29.5.41 – collision (air) with P9545, crashed near Abernethy, Perthshire, 21.4.42. Royal Naval Air Station 19.5.43 aircraft damaged (deteriorated) beyond recovery. SOC 26.1.45.

N3105 375. FF 20.10.39. 9 MU 23.10.39. 603 Sqn. 11.4.40, XT-P, shot down by Bf109, crashed, P/O Benson killed, Cat.3, 28.8.40.

N3109 379. FF 23.10.39. 24 MU 25.10.39. 602 Sqn. 24.12.39. 603 Sqn. 5.10.40 – shot down by Bf109 near Godmersham Park, F/O Matthews killed, 7.10.40. Flying hours 195.30.

N3196 437. FF 27.11.39. 27 MU 2.1.40. 41 Sqn. 14.4.40. Air service training, Hamble, 5.5.40. 603 Sqn. 3.9.40 – Shot down by Bf109, force landed, P/O Stapleton safe, 7.9.40. AST. 57 OTU 7.8.41 – dived into ground at Shotley Bridge, Northumberland, Cat.E, 9.4.43. SOC 25.4.43.

N3229 454. FF 7.12.39. 9 MU 12.12.39 – damaged ops 25.3.40. 603 Sqn. 11.4.40 – Cat.2, operations, 23.7.40. 72 Sqn. 2.9.40 – Cat.2, operations, 4.9.40. 92 Sqn. 3.11.40 – Cat.3, operations, 17.11.40. AST. 308 Sqn. 18.5.41 – for defence of Vickers Armstrong Works, crash landing, Aston Down 5.12.41. 52 OTU 12.11.44. Flying accident, Cat.B 5.12.44. SOC 6.12.44.

N3236 460. FF 11.12.39. 24 MU 21.12.39. 603 Sqn. 3.5.40 – Flying Accident, crash landed at Turnhouse, P/O Stapleton safe, 5.6.40. 122 Sqn. 2.6.41 – Flying Accident, Cat.B, 13.9.41. Westland Aircraft Ltd., SOC 4.12.41 to 2826M.

N3244 469. FF 16.12.39. 24 MU 29.12.39. 266 Sqn. 16.2.40 – Flying accident, Cat.2, 18.7.40. 603 Sqn. 21.9.40 – shot down by Bf109, crashed into sea off Folkestone, P/O Cardell killed, 27.9.40.

N3267 480. FF 29.12.39. 9 MU 16.1.40. 603 Sqn. 11.4.40, XT-S, Cat.2, operations, F/O Boulter injured, 29.8.40. 41 Sqn. 19.9.40 – shot down by Do17 near Folkestone, P/O Adams abandoned aircraft, 7.10.40.

N3268 479. FF, George Pickering, 29.12.39. 9 MU 10.1.40. 603 Sqn. 11.4.40. Farnborough June 1940. 92 Sqn. 13.8.40 – damaged by Do17 off St Gowans Head, force landed, F/L Stanford Tuck injured, 25.8.40. Cunliffe Owen Aircraft. SOC 21.9.40.

N3288 499. FF 13.1.40. 27 MU 19.1.40. 603 Sqn. 31.5.40, XT-H, damaged on landing at Dyce, P/O Gilroy safe, 26.7.40. AST. Damaged on operations 1.9.40. 609 Sqn. 18.9.40, Cat.2, operations 26.9.40. AST. 65 Sqn. 20.10.40. 145 Sqn. 23.1.41. 178 Sqn. 8.3.41 – Flying accident, Cat.C, 20.3.41. 123 Sqn. 11.10.41. 58 OTU 6.11.41. 61 OTU 13.8.42. Westland Aircraft Ltd. 8.1.43 to 3545M 12SoTT 3.2.43. SOC 5.5.45.

P-Series:

P9394 577. FF 7.3.40. 24 MU 11.3.40. 212 Sqn. 7.4.40. Rolls-Royce, Hucknall, June 1940. 603 Sqn. 30.8.40. 41 Sqn. 13.9.40 – damaged by Bf109 near Hornchurch, Cat.2, 30.9.40. 57 OTU 23.12.40 – Cat.2, operations, 30.9.41. Philips Powis 27.3.42 new engine. 52 OTU 15.7.42. 53 OTU 13.12.43. SOC 16.8.44.

P9440 603. FF, George Pickering, 30.3.40. 6 MU 1.4.40. 152 Sqn. 11.5.40 – damaged by Bf109, P/O Baynes safe, Cat.2, 18.7.40. AST. 603 Sqn. 3.9.40 – damaged on operations 15.10.40. AST. 61 OTU 28.6.41. 19 Sqn. 7.9.41. 331 Sqn. 17.11.41. 61 OTU 29.10.42. 39 MU, Non Effective Aircraft, 21.11.44. SOC 3.5.45.

P9459 622. FF 9.4.40. 9 MU 11.4.40. 603 Sqn. 6.5.40, XT-N, damaged by Bf109, force landed, F/L Rushmer injured, 29.8.40. Cunliffe Owen Aircraft. 53 OTU 3.9.41 – air collision with X4823, crashed into sea off Nash Point, Glam., 29.10.41.

P9467 630. FF 12.4.40. 24 MU 15.4.40. 609 Sqn. 4.6.40 – Cat.2, operations, 12.7.40. 1 Contractors (Civilian) Repair Unit. 603 Sqn., shot down on operations 7.9.40, Sgt Sarre abandoned aircraft injured.

P9499 642. FF, George Pickering, 17.4.40. 8 MU 20.4.40. OTU 3.5.40. 603 Sqn. 6.9.40. 266 Sqn. 30.10.40. 111Sqn. 3.4.41 – Flying Accident, Cat.C, 28.4.41. 58 OTU 16.6.41 – spun into ground at Bannockburn, 2.10.41. 52 OTU 23.11.41. 61 OTU 30.1.43 – crashed, following forced landing, Rednal, Cat.B, 5.8.43.

P9553 738. FF 29.5.40. 6 MU 10.4.40. 603 Sqn. 8.9.40 – shot down over Thames estuary by Bf109, P/O Dexter abandoned aircraft injured, aircraft destroyed by fire 2.10.40. (Aircraft originally for Turkey)

R-Series:

R6619 708. FF 21.5.40. 12 MU 24.5.40. 65 Sqn. 1.6.40. 603 Sqn. 10.9.40. 41 Sqn. 10.9.40 – damaged by Bf109 near Hornchurch, Cat.2, 28.9.40. Scottish Aviation Ltd. 111 Sqn. 3.5.41 – Flying Accident, Cat.E, 8.5.41. SOC 22.5.41.

R6626 FF, George Pickering, 23.5.40. 12 MU 25.5.40. 603 Sqn. 20.7.40, XT-V. 266 Sqn. 20.10.40. 111 Sqn. 11.4.41 – Cat.AC, operations, 16.4.41. 58 OTU 17.6.41. Scottish Aviation Ltd. 4.6.42. Photographic Reconnaissance Unit, Benson, 24.9.42. 222 MU 10.8.43. Empire Rhodes, 14.8.43. Portugal 29.8.43.

R6717 771, FF 11.6.40. 12 MU 13.6.40. 603 Sqn. 29.6.40 – crashed, Inkhorn, Aberdeen, Sgt Arber safe, Cat.3, 2.8.40.

R6721 775. FF 12.6.40. 12 MU 13.6.40. 603 Sqn. 14.7.40. 92 Sqn. 24.9.40 – force landed near Effingham, Sgt Kingaby safe, 27.10.40. Flying Hours 67.20.

R6751 777. FF 13.6.40. 12 MU 14.6.40. 12 MU 14.6.40. 603 Sqn. 14.7.40, XT-U, shot down, Cat.3, 28.8.40, F/L Cunningham missing. Flying hours 21.30.

R6752 778. FF 13.6.40. 12 MU 14.6.40 – crashed on delivery flight to 603 Sqn., P/O Manlove safe, 20.7.40. 603 Sqn. – wheels-up landing at Hornchurch after combat, F/O Haig safe, 2.9.40. 1 Contractors (Civilian) Repair Unit. 266 Sqn. 17.10.40 – Cat.2, operations, 15.11.40. 72 Sqn. 27.3.41. 57 OTU 2.5.41. 58 OTU 23.8.41. 61 OTU 17.6.42. 57 OTU 8.8.43 – Cat.AC 22.10.43.

R6753 779. FF 13.6.40. 12 MU 14.6.40. 603 Sqn. 14.7.40, XT-G, shot down by Bf109 which badly damaged R6753, F/O Pinckney abandoned aircraft, injured by fire, 29.8.40.

R6754 784. FF, George Pickering, 12.6.40. 12 MU 18.6.40. 603 Sqn. 20.7.40, XT-F, aircraft damaged in combat with Bf110 over Deal, Sgt Sarre safe, 30.8.40. 66 Sqn. 24.9.40. 57 OTU 1.11.40 – Flying Accident 11.11.40 to 2419M.

R6755 785. FF 14.6.40. 24 MU 19.4.40. 603 Sqn. 5.7.40 – damaged by He111, force landed at Old Meldrum, P/O Gilroy safe, 18.7.40. Scottish Aviation Ltd. 41 Sqn. 20.9.40 – shot down by Bf109, near West Malling, F/L Ryder abandoned aircraft which was destroyed by fire, 27.9.40.

R6808 812. FF, George Pickering, 24.6.40. 6 MU 25.6.40. 603 Sqn. 28.7.40, XT-Z, Flying Accident, Cat.C3, 1.9.40. SOC 11.9.40.

R6835 829. FF, George Pickering, 28.6.40. 12 MU 1.7.40. 603 Sqn. 14.7.40, XT-W, Cat.2, operations, 31.8.40. 1 Contractors (Civilian) Repair Unit 11.9.40. 457 Sqn. 22.6.41. 53 OTU 20.10.41. Station Flight, Atcham, 13.6.42 – Flying Accident, Cat.C, 24.6.42. 61 OTU 14.8.42. Royal Naval Air Station 17.5.43.

R6989 923. FF, George Pickering, 20.7.40. 8 MU 21.7.40. 603 Sqn. 8.8.40, XT-X, shot down, Cat.2, F/O Ritchie injured, 28.8.40. Cunliffe Owen Aircraft. 61 OTU 2.9.41 – Flying Accident, Cat.CB, 1.12.41. Repaired on site. 57 OTU 28.7.41 – engine failed, crashed near Holywell, Flintshire, Cat.E, 15.8.42.

R7019 933. FF 23.7.40. 12 MU 25.7.40. 54 Sqn. 28.7.40. 603 Sqn. Cat.2 ops 15.9.40, S/L George Denholm baled out safe. A/c crashed on Warren Farm, Fairlight near Hastings. AST. SOC 27.9.40.

R7020 934. FF 24.7.40. 12 MU 25.7.40. 609 Sqn. 13.8.40 – Flying Accident, Cat.2, 13.8.40. 1 Contractors (Civilian) Repair Unit. 603 Sqn. 6.10.40. 266 Sqn. 17.10.40 – Flying Accident, Cat.B, 11.2.41. Air Service Training, converted to PRIII Type C. 8 OTU 24.5.42 – Flying Accident, Cat.AC, 1.9.42. Repaired on site. 57 OTU 3.7.43 – hit H/T cables, over-turned during forced landing, near Netherwitton, Northumberland, 14.3.44.

R7021 935. FF, George Pickering, 24.7.40. 12 MU 25.7.40. 603 Sqn. 28.7.40, XT-X, shot down by Bf109, crashed near West Malling, aircraft abandoned, Sgt Sarre safe, 30.8.40. Aircraft total wreck.

X-Series:

X4019 597. FF George Pickering, 26.7.40. 6 MU 28.7.40. 54 Sqn. 1.8.40, damaged by enemy aircraft P/O Campbell safe, 24.8.40. 603 Sqn. 7.10.40. 266 Sqn., 17.10.40. 111 Sqn. 11.4.41. 58 OTU 29.5.41. Castle Bromwich Aero Factory 24.12.41. 82 MU 6.11.42. *Peter Mearsk* 8.11.42, lost at sea 8.1.43.

X4163 1002. FF 8.8.40. 9 MU 9.8.40. 603 Sqn. XT-O, damaged by 109 over Canterbury 30.8.40, F/O R. McG. Waterston safe. 54 Sqn. 13.8.40. 41 Sqn. 22.2.41. 452 Sqn. 24.4.41. 313 Sqn. 1.6.41. 53 OTU 20.10.41, Flying Accident Cat.B 5.12.41. Westland Aircraft Ltd. 57 OTU 16.4.44. SOC 24.5.45.

X4164 1003. FF 8.8.40. 9 MU 10.8.40. 152 Sqn. 19.8.40. 603 Sqn. 20.8.40. 266 Sqn. 13.10.40 – landing accident, Sgt Ody safe, 17.10.40. 111 Sqn. 11.11.40. 58 OTU 28.5.41. Scottish Aviation Ltd. 111 Sqn. – air collision with K9863 near Sealand, Cat.E, 26.1.42.

X4185 1025. FF, George Pickering, 13.8.40. 12 MU 12.8.40. 603 Sqn. 1.9.40 – Shot down by Bf109 over Thames estuary, P/O Stewart-Clark abandoned aircraft injured, 3.9.40.

X4250 1049. FF 20.8.40. 38 MU 21.8.40. 603 Sqn. 30.8.40 – damaged by Bf109, force landed at Hornchurch, S/L Denholm safe, 7.9.40. Flying Accident, Cat.2, 27.9.40, force landed on Folkestone beach, P/O Dexter safe but wounded.

X4259 1057. FF 22.8.40. 12 MU 24.8.40. 603 Sqn. 1.9.40. 266 Sqn. 17.10.40 – Flying Accident, Cat.2, 5.11.40. SOC 12.1.41.

X4260 1058. FF 22.8.40. 12 MU 23.8.40. 603 Sqn. 1.9.40 – shot down over France, P/O Caister PoW, 6.9.40. SOC 2.11.40. Flying hours 9.55. X4260 captured by the Germans and taken to Rechlin Research Centre for evaluation.

X4261 1059. FF 22.8.40. 12 MU 24.8.40. 603 Sqn. 1.9.40 – shot down by Bf109, F/L Rushmer killed, 5.9.40. SOC 1.12.40. Flying hours 8.60.

X4263 1061. FF 23.8.40. 38 MU 24.8.40. 603 Sqn. 30.8.40 – engine failed, crash landed, Sgt Sarre safe, 3.3.41. Dived into sea off Llan. SOC 26.8.41.

X4264 1062. FF 23.8.40. 38 MU 25.8.40. 222 Sqn. 3.9.40 – Shot down by Bf110, forced landing at Detling, Sgt Hutchinson injured, 14.9.40. 603 Sqn. 14.10.40. 266 Sqn. – crashed at Stradishall, P/O Williams killed, 21.10.40. SOC 25.10.40. Flying Hours 17.40.

X4265 Limited information available. FF 24.8.40. Possibly 266 Sqn., 17.10.40.

X4271 1070. FF 25.8.40. 6 MU 27.8.40. 603 Sqn. 30.8.40, XT-N, shot down by Bf109, crashed at Wanstead, P/O Gilroy abandoned aircraft, 31.8.40. Flying Hours 3.50.

X4273 1072. FF 26.8.40. 6 MU 27.8.40. 603 Sqn. 30.8.40, XT-K, shot down by Bf109, crashed on Repository Road, Woolwich, F/O Waterston killed, 31.8.40.

X4274 1073. FF 26.8.40. 6 MU 27.8.40. 603 Sqn. 30.8.40, XT-F. 266 Sqn. 17.10.40 – Flying Accident, Cat.E, aircraft destroyed by fire 19.1.41. SOC 27.1.41 – cancelled. Air Service Training 25.2.41. 57 OTU 3.6.41. 215 MU 29.10.42. Tarantia 20.11.42. Port Sudan 27.1.43. Middle East 28.2.43. SOC 27.7.44.

X4277 1076. FF 27.8.40. 6 MU 28.8.40. 603 Sqn. 30.8.40, XT-M, shot down in flames off N. Foreland, P/O Hillary abandoned aircraft, severely injured, 3.9.40. Flying hours 7.45.

X4323 1087. FF 29.8.40. 9 MU 31.8.40. 603 Sqn. 3.9.40 – Shot down by Bf109, crashed near Fennington, P/O Howes killed, 18.9.40.

X4324 1088. FF 29.8.40. 9 MU 31.8.40. 603 Sqn. 3.9.40 – Shot down by Bf109 over Kent, aircraft crashed at Kingswood, destroyed by fire, F/O Pease killed, 15.9.40. SOC 21.9.40.

X4327 1091. FF 30.8.40. 9 MU 2.9.40. 603 Sqn. 5.9.40. 66 Sqn. – Shot down by Bf109 near Ashford, P/O Robbins injured, 14.9.40. SOC 31.9.40.

X4347 1108. FF 4.9.40. 9 MU 7.9.40. 603 Sqn. 8.9.40. 266 Sqn. 17.10.40. Flying Accident, aircraft destroyed by fire 8.3.41. SOC 17.3.41.

X4348 1109. FF 5.9.40. 9 MU 7.9.40. 603 Sqn. 8.9.40. 266 Sqn. 17.10.40. 111 Sqn. 8.4.41. 58 OTU 29.5.41 – Flying Accident, Cat.B, 30.7.40, aircraft repaired on-site. Flying Accident, Cat.E. SOC 1.9.40.

X4349 1110. FF 5.9.40. 9 MU 6.9.40. 603 Sqn. 8.9.40 – Cat.3, operations, 23.9.40. SOC 2.10.40.

X4415 1131. FF 11.9.40. 6 MU 12.9.40. 603 Sqn. 14.9.40 – Flying Accident, Cat.2, 23.9.40. Scottish Aviation Ltd. 53 OTU 9.5.41 – Flying Accident, Cat.C, 12.9.41. Air Service Training, Marwell. SOC October 1941.

X4489 1166. FF 20.9.40. 8 MU 21.9.40. 603 Sqn. 24.9.40 – Cat.2, operations, 5.10.40. 122 Sqn. 8.7.41. 76 MU 22.9.42. 'City of Evansville' 21.10.42. Port Sudan 23.12.42. Middle East 31.1.42. SOC 27.7.44.

X4490 1167. FF, George Pickering, 20.9.40. 8 MU 21.9.40. 603 Sqn. 24.9.40. 266 Sqn. 17.10.40. 111 Sqn. 23.4.41. 58 OTU 30.5.41. 57 OTU 1.8.41. AST 21.12.40, converted to PRIII, 1 Photographic Reconnaissance Unit 7.3.42. 8 OTU 17.6.42. Merchant Ship Fighter Unit, Speke, 23.4.42. 53 OTU 27.2.43 – struck by X4659, waiting to take off, Hilbald, Cat.AC, 10.8.44, recat E.

X4593 1201, 'Kerala'. FF, George Pickering, 1.10.40. 8 MU 2.10.40. 603 Sqn. 8.10.40. 266 Sqn. 17.10.40 – Flying Accident, Cat.3, total wreck, 22.11.40. SOC 1.12.40. Flying hours 85.05.

X4594 1202, 'Andhradesa', FF 1.10.40. 8 MU 2.10.40. 603 Sqn, 8.10.40. 266 Sqn. 17.10.40. Failed to return after combat with Ju88, 8.3.41. Flying hours 183.40.

X4613 1233. FF 13.10.40. 6 MU 13.10.40. 603 Sqn. 17.10.40. 266 Sqn. 24.10.40 – Cat.E, operations, 2.3.41. SOC 20.3.41.

P-Series Supermarine Spitfire F37/34 Mk II:

P7285 Morris. 8 MU 1.7.40. 266 Sqn. 5.9.40. 603 Sqn. 17.10.40 – Failed to return, operations, 8.10.40, F/L Kirkwood missing.

P7286 Morris. 9 MU 13.7.40. 152 Sqn. 17.7.40. 603 Sqn. 17.10.40, XT-C, shot down by Bf109, P/O Maxwell unhurt, 27.10.40, aircraft severely damaged. AST Boscombe Down 16.1.41, trials with Rotol constant-speed propeller, Morris radiator and Inertia weight. 234 Sqn. 12.5.41. Vickers Armstrong 3.7.41. 66 Sqn. 31.7.41. 152 Sqn. 3.9.41 – Cat.AC, operations, 16.9.41. Air Service Training, Exeter. SOC 10.11.41.

P7287 Morris. 9 MU 13.7.40. 266 Sqn. 6.9.40. 603 Sqn. 17.10.40. 65 Sqn. 29.6.41. 122 Sqn. 31.9.41 – Flying Accident, Cat.E, 24.10.41. Air Service Training, Marwell, converted to FVA M45, 28.1.42. 2 USA 6.8.42. Cunliffe Owen Aircraft 17.3.44 for conversion.

P7288 Morris. 9 MU 15.7.40. 266 Sqn. 6.9.40. 603 Sqn. 29.10.40 – Flying Accident, Cat.B, 10.1.41. 111 Sqn. 24.5.41. 610 Sqn. 8.9.41. 340 Sqn. 28.11.41. 58 OTU 30.4.42 to 4409M 14 SoTT 30.11.43.

P7289 First Spitfire built in Castle Bromwich Aeroplane Factory under Vickers management. 6 MU 17.7.40. 266 Sqn. 6.9.40. 603 Sqn. 20.10.40, XT-D. 19 Sqn. 7.9.41. 33 Sqn. 30.10.41. 331 Sqn. 20.2.42. Central Gunnery School 8.12.42 – Wing struck ground, aircraft crashed at Redhouse Farm, near Long Sutton, Lincs, 9.9.43. SOC 30.9.43. Flying hours 422.80.

P7294 37 MU 21.6.40. 266 Sqn. 6.9.40. 603 Sqn. 24.10.40. 41 Sqn. 6.4.41. 145 Sqn. 28.7.41. 417 Sqn. 8.1.42. 266 Sqn. 6.9.42. 52 OTU 24.10.42. 53 OTU 26.9.43 – Over shot on landing, hit wall at Kirton-in-Lindsey, Cat.B, 26.6.44. Cat.E 16.8.44.

P7295 37 MU 25.7.40. 266 Sqn. 6.9.40. 603 Sqn. 17.10.40, XT-F. 65 Sqn. 12.8.41. 61 OTU 31.10.42 – hit mountain Cadair Bronwen, Denbighs., Cat.E, 14.12.42.

P7297 37 MU 27.7.40. 266 Sqn. 6.9.40. 603 Sqn. 17.10.40, XT-H. 602 Sqn. 6.7.41. 41 Sqn. 6.8.41. 33 MU 18.11.41 – converted to FV M45. 350 Sqn. 17.12.41. Northolt Station Flt., 23.3.42. 61 OTU 2.6.44. SOC 21.11.44.

P7307 24 MU 30.7.40. 266 Sqn. 7.10.40. 603 Sqn. 20.10.40 – Cat.2, operations, 26.10.40. Westland Aircraft Ltd, 421 Flight, 30.12.40. 65 Sqn. 19.4.41. 308 Sqn. 21.7.41. 154 Sqn. 23.11.41. 61 OTU 8.3.42 – air collision with BM140, crashed Hayes, Middlesex, Cat.E, 15.3.42. SOC 1.9.42. Flying hours 117.15.

P7309 24 MU 3.8.40. 260 Sqn. 5.9.40. 603 Sqn. 17.10.40 – Shot down by Bf109 over Hastings, crashed on Pickdick Farm, Brede, Sussex, P/O Olver baled out wounded, 25.10.40. SOC 11.11.40.

P7311 24 MU 1.8.40. 266 Sqn. 6.9.40. 603 Sqn. 17.10.40 – Flying Accident, Cat.3, 17.12.40. SOC 27.12.40.

P7315 12 MU 6.8.40. 266 Sqn. 19.9.40. 603 Sqn. 17.10.40 – Flying Accident, Cat.B, 17.12.40. Air Service Training. 41 Sqn. 8.5.41. 145 Sqn. 28.7.41. 417 Sqn. 5.12.41. 53 OTU 22.2.43. Middle East or Mediterranean Air Forces 6.11.44.

P7324 8 MU 16.8.40. 266 Sqn. 5.9.40. 603 Sqn. 17.10.40. 111 Sqn. 25.5.41. Air Service Training 23.8.41, converted to FVA M45. 81 Sqn. 4.1.42. 165 Sqn. 12.4.42. 167 Sqn. 29.5.42. 521 Meteorological S, 16.8.42. 61 OTU 18.5.44. Recat. E, 22.8.44.

P7325 9 MU 14.8.40. 266 Sqn. 6.9.40. 603 Sqn. 17.10.40 – Cat.3, operations, Spitfire crashed, Stonelink Farm, following combat with Bf109s over Sussex coast, P/O Soden baled out, injured leg in landing at 'Perryfields', 25.10.40. General Aircraft Ltd. 41 Sqn. 30.3.41. 145 Sqn. 28.7.41. 19 Sqn. 21.9.41. 331 Sqn. 6.11.41 – Flying Accident, Cat.B, 16.11.41. Scottish Aviation Ltd, converted to Air-Sea Rescue (IIc). 57 OTU 22.6.43. 277 Sqn. 31.12.43. Cat.E, 25.7.44.

P7327 8 MU 15.8.40. 266 Sqn. 5.9.40. 603 Sqn. 17.10.40, XT-S, Cat.2, operations, 28.10.40. 616 Sqn. 19.5.41 – Failed to return, operations, 25.6.41. Flying hours 113.55.

P7328 8 MU 16.8.40. 603 Sqn. 17.10.40, XT-R, Flying Accident, Cat.2, 24.10.40. Air Service Training, Exeter. 74 Sqn. 11.3.41 – Failed to return, operations, 27.3.41. Flying hours 88.55.

P7350 Taken on charge. 6 MU 13.8.40. 266 Sqn. 603 Sqn.17.10.40 – Shot down by Bf109 near Hastings, Cat.B, P/O L.A. Martel wounded, 25.10.40. 1 CRU. 616 Sqn. 10.4.41. Scottish Aviation Ltd 5.8.41. Central Gunnery School 27.4.42. Air Service Training, sold J.Dale donated to RAF Colerne. As G-AWIJ, used in film Battle of Britain. Extant with Battle of Britain Memorial Flight, RAF Coningsby (See separate history of P7350).

P7359 6 MU 27.8.40. 603 Sqn. 7.11.40. 64 Sqn. 13.8.41. 66 Sqn. 3.9.41. 19 Sqn. 6.9.41. 331 Sqn. 2.11.41. 58 OTU 4.5.42 – Flying Accident, Cat.C, 26.10.42. Scottish Aviation Ltd 23.3.43, converted to Air-Sea Rescue (IIc). 377 Sqn. 4.5.43. Air Service Training, Exeter, Recat. B, 28.5.44.

P7365 8 MU 30.8.40. 266 Sqn. 6.9.40. 603 Sqn. 17.10.40 – Shot down by Bf109, P/O Dewey killed, 27.10.40.

P7387 39 MU 14.9.40. 603 Sqn. 28.10.40, XT-E, collided with He111, both aircraft destroyed, Sgt Plant killed, 21.11.40.

P7388 39 MU 14.9.40. 603 Sqn. 28.10.40, XT-P. 111 Sqn. 24.5.41. 123 Sqn. 22.11.40. 331 Sqn. 5.2.42. 58 OTU 17.4.42. Central Gunnery School 2.9.44. SPA Fighter Unit 5.1.45. SOC 28.6.45.

P7389 39 MU 15.9.40. 603 Sqn. 28.10.40, XT-B. 64 Sqn. 24.7.41. 611 Sqn. 12.11.41. 340 Sqn. 28.12.41. 53 OTU 17.4.42. Central Gunnery School 8.12.42. Heston Aircraft Ltd 22.2.44.

P7436 37 MU 29.9.40. 603 Sqn. 27.10.40. 609 Sqn. 15.5.41 – Failed to return, operations, 21.5.41. Flying hours 39.15.

P7439 37 MU 29.9.40. 603 Sqn. 25.10.40 – Shot down by Bf109, aircraft crashed near Waltham, F/O Goldsmith severely injured (died 28.10.40), Cat.E, 27.10.40. SOC 14.11.40.

P7449 'Bidar.' 9 MU 2.10.40. 603 Sqn. 24.10.40, XT-R, crashed on operations, P/O Rafter killed 29.11.40. 57 OTU 25.1.42. Cat.C, 24.3.42.

P7496 38 MU 5.10.40. 603 Sqn. 25.10.40, XT-G, damaged in combat 8.11.40. 64 Sqn. 13.8.41. Central Gunnery School 27.4.42. Flying Accident, Cat.C, 24.6.42. SOC 24.6.44. Flying hours 822.0

P7509 9 MU 12.10.40. 603 Sqn. – Damaged on operations 5.11.40. Air Service Training. 19 Sqn. 17.1.41. 234 Sqn. 21.8.40. 350 Sqn. 18.12.40. 52 OTU 24.3.42 – crashed into River Severn, Cat.E, 23.7.42.

P7528 8 MU 15.10.40. 603 Sqn. 27.10.40. 111 Sqn. 25.5.41 – Failed to return, operations over France, 19.8.41.

P7529 8 MU 15.10.40. 603 Sqn. 27.10.40, XT-J. 111 Sqn. 25.5.41. 403 Sqn. 3.9.41. 457 Sqn. 4.10.41. 57 OTU 24.5.42 – Flying Accident, Cat.B, 3.12.42. Westland Aircraft Ltd – Crash landing, Cat.B, Esk, 11.12.42. Recat.E, 24.12.42.

P7543 8 MU 21.10.40. 603 Sqn. Arrival date unknown, XT-K. 234 Sqn. 52 OTU – crashed near Babdown Farm, Cat.E, 17.10.42.

P7546 8 MU 24.10.40. 603 Sqn. 22.11.40, XT-E, Cat.2, operations, 12.1.41. 1 Contractors (Civilian) Repair Unit 21.1.41. 303 Sqn. 4.3.41. Cat.B, operations, 20.4.41. No.1 Flight 7.9.41 – Dived into ground at East Wretham, Cat.E, 26.2.42. SOC.

P7549 9 MU 24.10.40. 603 Sqn. Exact date of arrival unknown. 57 OTU – Air collision with P7598, crashed near High Kinnoton, Flint., Cat.E, 16.7.42.

P7550 9 MU 25.10.40. 603 Sqn. 5.11.40 Crashed, Cat.E, Grantshouse, Berwickshire, 31.12.40. SOC 9.1.41.

P7564 9 MU 29.10.40. 603 Sqn. 11.12.40, XT-Y. 111 Sqn. 25.5.41, Cat.C, operations, 27.6.41. 401 Sqn. 12.9.41. 57 OTU 5.5.42 – Engine failed, crash landed at Beeches Farm, near Maw, Cat.E, 21.8.42.

P7597 12 MU 1.11.40. 603 Sqn. 17.11.40 – Flying Accident, Cat. E, 16.2.41. SOC 28.2.41. Flying hours 65.30.

P7683 'Londonderry.' 12 MU 24.11.40. 603 Sqn. 22.12.40, XT-H. 111 Sqn. 24.5.41. 123 Sqn. 25.11.41. 58 OTU 12.3.42. 53 OTU 24.9.42. 58 OTU 7.7.43 – Air collision with P8387, crashed near Hammering Mere Farm, Cat.E, 19.8.43. SOC 19.8.43. Flying hours 744.05.

P7686 24 MU 24.11.40. 19 Sqn. 11.12.40. 603 Sqn. 6.12.40 – Flying Accident, Cat.2, 21.12.40. Air Service Training. 152 Sqn. 3.3.41. 266 Sqn. 5.7.41. 1 Contractors (Civilian) Repair Unit 9.9.41, converted to FVA M45. 2 USA 22.5.42. 332 Sqn. 8.11.41.61 OTU 7.12.44. SOC 19.7.45.

P7749 'City of Bradford IV'. 12 MU 8.12.40. 603 Sqn. 22.12.40. 111 Sqn. 24.5.41. 306 Sqn. 28.10.41 – Crashed in circuit, in bad weather near 'S' Gate, aircraft destroyed by fire, Cat.E, 5.12.41. SOC 13.12.41.

P7750 'City of Bradford V'. 12 MU 7.12.40. 603 Sqn. 31.12.40. 111 Sqn. 24.5.41 – Air collision with P7848, crashed, Cat.E, 23.7.41. SOC 1.8.41.

APPENDIX 17

GIFTED SPITFIRES

Each Spitfire gifted to the nation bore a name suggested by the donor and this was marked, according to official instructions, in four-inch yellow characters on the engine cowling, but this ruling was not rigidly applied. Some limiting factor was necessary in order that camouflage was not compromised.

Most of the names are indicative of the donor, but where this is not clear and the sponsor is known, additional information is given in the remarks column. Some names were originally chosen by 603 pilots who had christened their aircraft at the start of the war with the same name being subsequently reassigned by donor or fund committee:

Name	Mark	Aircraft No.	Remarks
Bidar	IIA	P7449	Hyderabad War Purpose Fund
City of Bradford V	IIA	P7750	Bradford Fund.
City of Bradford IV	IIA	P7749	Bradford Fund.
City of Liverpool IV	IIA	R7210	Lord Mayor City of Liverpool Fund (£20,000).
Leyland Leeds City	IIA	P8161	Leeds Fund (£15,000, W.F. Leyland £5,000).
N.E.M.	IIA	P7742	National Employers Insurance Ltd (£5,000).
New Zealand High Commission	IIA	P8428	
Londonderry	IIA	P7683	Bedford Telegraph Fund (£85,000).
Sialkot II	IIA	P8239	

BATTLE OF BRITAIN SURVIVOR
VICKERS ARMSTRONG SUPERMARINE
SPITFIRE MK IIA P7350

Powered by a Rolls-Royce Merlin XII liquid-cooled in-line engine, the Mark IIa has a maximum speed of 370 mph. Its armament consists of eight .303 machine guns. P7350 is the oldest surviving example of an airworthy Spitfire. It is also the oldest aircraft currently operated by the RAF and is the sole surviving airworthy Spitfire which fought in the Battle of Britain.

P7350 was completed on 18 August 1940 at Castle Bromwich, near Birmingham, and is possibly the 14th Mark II Spitfire off the production line at the Midlands works. The aircraft was sent to 6 Maintenance Unit at Brize Norton on 13 August 1940 and on 6 September was sent to 266 Squadron at RAF Wittering. It briefly saw combat in the Battle of Britain. On 17 October it was sent to 603 Squadron at Hornchurch and flew with the Squadron the same day between 17.10-17.40 hours, flown by F/O Colin Pinckney. On 25 October it was shot down in combat with Bf109s near Hastings, East Sussex, receiving Category B damage. P/O Ludwik A. Martel was struck in the leg and body by cannon shell splinters. P7350 was sent to No.1 Contractors (Civilian) Repair Unit, Cowley, Oxon, for repair following battle damage on 31 October, the repaired bullet holes can be seen today. On 7 December it was issued to 37 Maintenance Unit at Burtonwood, Cheshire for return to service. It joined 616 (South Yorkshire) Squadron at Tangmere on 18 March 1941, but on 10 April it was moved to 64 Squadron at Hornchurch. On 5 August it was moved again to Scottish Aviation Ltd, Prestwick, Scotland for an overhaul and on 29 January 1942 it was sent to 37 MU, Burtonwood, Cheshire, for return to service. Its days as a combat aircraft at an end, it was sent to Central Gunnery School, newly established at Sutton Bridge, Lincs, on 27 April 1942. On 2 February 1943 it was sent to Air Service Training (AST), Hamble, Hants, for unspecified work. On 20 March it was still awaiting collection from Hamble. On March 23 it was issued to 6 MU, Brize Norton. On 31 March P7350 was on charge with 57 Operational Training Unit, Hawarden, North Wales. On 22 April 1944, another Spitfire taxied into P7350 as it lined up on the end of the runway at Eshott (satellite to Brunton), Northumberland. On 30 April it was returned to AST, Hamble for repairs. By 13 July the repairs were complete and the Spitfire awaited collection. On 24 July it was issued to 39 MU, Colerne, Wiltshire, for allocation to duties where it remained in store. In July 1948, P7350 was declared a 'non-effective' airframe and sold along with a number of other Spitfires to John Dale & Co Ltd, a local scrap merchant, but it never left the hangarage at Colerne. Unlike so many that were cut up for scrap during the post-war years, P7350 was one of the lucky few. The historical significance of the Spitfire was realised when John Dale perused the log book and he subsequently decided not to cut up the aircraft and turn it into ingots but to donate it to Colerne where it was restored for static display in the Station museum. It remained there until 1967, when it came to the attention of Spitfire Productions Ltd and surveyed by Group Captain T.G. 'Hamish' Mahaddie and his team of RAF technicians who were looking for aircraft to take part in the forthcoming film *The Battle of Britain*. The early war configuration of P7350 made it perfect for the part when so many other later mark Spitfires had to be 'disguised'. In fact, P7350 was found to be in such good condition a rebuild/refurbishment to air-worthiness was initiated at RAF Henlow, Bedfordshire, where work was underway on other Spitfires which had been acquired for the film. It was moved to Henlow by road on 3 March 1967. Ultimately it was restored to flying condition and used in the production. Although it was still the property of the Ministry of Defence, on 25 April 1968, P7350 was civilian registered as G-AWIJ to Spitfire Productions Ltd., for the purpose of operation by a civilian company. On 8 November, following completion of filming, P7350 was presented to the Battle of Britain Flight at Coltishall, Norfolk, where it became known as 'P7' or, more affectionately, 'Baby Spit'. On 1 January 1969 the Flight was renamed Battle of Britain Memorial Flight (BBMF). On 1 March the BBMF relocated to RAF Coningsby. Interestingly, on 29 February 1984 the registration G-AWIJ was cancelled, this despite the fact that P7350 only became a civilian aircraft for the duration of the filming of *The Battle of Britain*. For some reason the civilian registration had remained active for 16 years!

Each year (when serviceable) Baby Spit has thrilled millions of spectators at airshows, ceremonial flypasts and other events at which the BBMF participates. The pilots and technicians with the BBMF are well aware of the historical significance of P7350. Described by Officer Commanding, BBMF, Squadron Leader Paul Day, OBE, AFC, as 'superbly balanced and responsive in the air' and 'a much more pleasant aircraft to fly compared with the Mark IX and PR XIX in the Flight', Mark II, P7350, is a lighter aircraft than the other Spitfires displayed by the BBMF, therefore the pilots operate an imposed crosswind limit of 10 knots on the aircraft as Baby Spit (Mark II and Vs in general) has a predilection to hang on the wind when landing. This is not a particular problem for Squadron Leader Day, who has accumulated many hours flying time on P7350 since he joined the Flight in 1980. He recalls:

> The aircraft behaves itself very well. On a very hot day it is prudent to get airborne as soon as possible after engine start otherwise the Merlin will boil over. We operate our aircraft at relatively low power settings, compared to wartime usage, so we can get 400 nautical miles range out of the Mk II cruising at between 150 and 180 knots. This includes a display routine during which we use higher power settings.

During its time with the Flight P7350 has worn a number of different squadron markings. These changes are normally initiated at the same time a major service takes place. The trend has been to represent the units which took part in the Battle of Britain. The squadron codes worn by P7350 are:

Duration	Codes	Squadron
1968-1971	ZH-T	266
1972-1977	UO-T	266
1978-1981	QV-B	19
1982-1984	SH-D	64
1985-1988	EB-Z	41
1989-1990	UO-T	266
1991-1993	YT-F	65
1994-1996	RN-S	72
1997-1998	BA-Y	277
1999-	XT-D	603

In 1999, the code was changed to represent XT-D, L1067, 'Blue Peter', as flown by Squadron Leader George Denholm on many occasions during the time it arrived at Turnhouse in September 1939 until it was shot down on 30 August 1940 with Uncle George at the controls. During 1940, 603 Squadron lettering was the minimum height of 24". The wording Blue Peter was in gold with red (highlighting) enamel paint on the fuel tank cowling. During the period following the delivery of the first Spitfires to the Squadron many of the pilots claimed and named their own aircraft. As time went on and things became hectic they were less likely to hang on to one specific aircraft for long, it was either damaged or lost or used by others when they were taken off flying for whatever reason. Nevertheless, at Turnhouse, Montrose or Dyce, they got their ground crews to paint their chosen name on their aircraft, usually in white as it was readily available but some were more ambitious and with the help of their ground crew they used a variety of colours. F/O Waterston had 'Ard Choille' painted in gold and red lettering on the fuel tank cowling of XT-K, L1046, F/L Laurie Cunningham had 'Auld Reekie' in the same colours on and style on XT-M, L1021, as did George Denholm with Blue Peter. It is likely that George Knox did the artwork as he acquired the paints from Woolworth in Edinburgh.

APPENDIX 19

THE AUXILIARY AIR FORCE IN THE BATTLE OF BRITAIN

The following is a table showing the pilots who flew with AAF squadrons during the Battle of Britain:

Name	Service	Squadron	Credited Victories	Shared
F/L R.F. Boyd	AAF	601	11	1
F/O B.J.G. Carbury RAF (SSC)		603	15	0
F/O J.C. Dundas	AAF	609	11	2
F/O C.R. Davis	AAF	601	10	1
Sgt R.F. Hamlyn	RAF (DEAP)	610	10	0
Sgt J.H. Lacey	RAFVR	501	19	1
F/L A.A. McKellar	AAF	605	19	1
Sgt A. McDowell	RAFVR	602	11	0

The contribution by AAF pilots (by Squadron):

Squadron	AAF Pilots	Credited Victories	Shared
501 (County of Gloucester)	4	2	0
504 (County of Nottingham)	8	5	4
600 (City of London)	11	1	0
601 (County of London)	18	31	11
602 (City of Glasgow)	10	27	3
603 (City of Edinburgh)	10	14	9
604 (County of Middlesex)	16	0	0
605 (County of Warwick)	5	19	1
607 (County of Durham)	11	3	2
609 (West Riding)	10	21	4
610 (County of Chester)	13	15	0
611 (West Lancashire)	13	6	7
615 (County of Surrey)	14	14	7
616 (South Yorkshire)	11	6	1
Total AAF Pilots	154	164	49

(Four pilots flew with two different AAF Squadrons giving an actual total of 150).

GROUND CREW MOVEMENTS

Date	From	Date	To	Remarks
23.8.39	232 Easter Road	23.8.39	Turnhouse	Mobilised
15.12.39	Turnhouse	–.12.39	Prestwick	Convoy Squadron
18.1.40	Prestwick	19.1.40	Dyce	Convoy Squadron. Blizzard
3.3.40	Dyce	3.3.40	Montrose	B Flight. By train.
11.3.40	Montrose	11.3.40	Dyce	Squadron. By train
13.3.40	Dyce	23.3.40	Montrose	Motor. B Flight
4.4.40	Montrose	14.4.40	Drem	Squadron. By train.
4.5.40	Drem	4.5.40	Turnhouse	Convoy Squadron
–.6.40	Turnhouse	– .6.40	Mamby	Bomb Course. By train.
–.6.40	Mamby	– .6.40	Turnhouse	Squadron. By train.
–.7.40	Turnhouse	–. 7.40	Dyce	Convoy. Raid!
–.7.40	Dyce	– .7.40	Turnhouse	Motor.
2.9.40	Turnhouse	3.9.40	Hornchurch	Squadron. By train. 'B of B'.
–.10.40	Hornchurch	–.10.40	Rochford	Motor. Flights!
–.11.40	Rochford	–.11.40	Hornchurch	Convoy. Squadron.
–.12.40	Hornchurch	–.12.40	Rochford	Squadron. Convoy.
–.12.40	Rochford	–.12.40	Drem	Squadron. By train.

SELECTED PEN-PORTRAITS OF COMMANDING OFFICERS

Squadron Leader J.A. McKelvie AFC

Squadron Leader McKelvie was the first Commanding Officer of 603 (City of Edinburgh) Bomber Squadron, as was then, and was appointed on 1 August 1925. He was an experienced pilot who, as a Major, had commanded 22 Squadron in the First World War, flying Bristol Fighters. He was Gazetted on 1 August 1925. His full-time adjutant was Flight Lieutenant C.R. Keary, a Regular RAF Officer who was responsible for flying training, general administration and discipline. Squadron Leader McKelvie left the post on 14 April 1931.

Hylton Ralph Murray-Philipson, MP

Hylton Ralph Murray-Philipson was born in 1902, the eldest son of Hylton Philipson and the Hon. Nina Charlotte Murray – fourth daughter of the 10th Lord (1st Viscount) Elibank who had married in 1896. The couple had two sons and a daughter and lived at the Red House, Cruden Bay, Aberdeenshire. Hylton Philipson DL, was born in 1866 and was the third son of Hilton Philipson and Jane Dorothy, daughter of John Dalglish. He was an outstanding sportsman; captaining Eton and then the Oxford Cricket XIs (he won four Blues at Oxford); he later kept wicket for England in the 1894/95 Test Series in Australia and, on several occasions, played with W.G. Grace. He was always known as 'Punch' Philipson because of his prominent nose! Hylton was educated at Eton and it was when he decided on a career in politics that he added the 'Murray' in order to differentiate himself from the Hylton Philipson cousins. In 1923 he married Monica, the only daughter of Mr W.C. Beasley-Robinson. They had one son and a daughter and lived at Stobo Castle, Peebleshire.

He was the Chairman of the North-Eastern Engineering Company, Wallsend-on-Tyne; he was also Director of Manvers Main Collieries and travelled extensively in the Empire. He went to the Ottawa Conference as Personal Assistant to the Chairmen of the Federation of Chambers of Commerce of the British Empire.

He contested the Peebleshire and South Midlothian seat in 1929 as a Unionist Candidate, but was beaten by the Socialist Candidate Mr J. Westwood. He was elected MP for Twickenham from 1932-34 with a majority of 4,807, following the death of Sir John Ferguson. In due course the untimely death of Murray-Philipson created another bye-election.

He was a Member of the Royal Company of Archers Kings' Bodyguard for Scotland; he was a County Councillor 1925-33 and JP for the County of Peebles; Assistant County Commissioner for the Boy Scouts; he was a member of the Carlton, Royal Air Force, Northern Counties and the New Edinburgh Clubs.

He regularly piloted his aircraft on long and short business trips in Scotland and England and regularly flew between Stobo, Turnhouse and Heston. In June 1930, an aircraft piloted by him crossed the Channel, struck the water in fog and sank. He and his two companions were rescued by a French trawler. He joined 603 (City of Edinburgh) Bomber Squadron, Auxiliary Air Force on 14 April 1931 as Commanding Officer with the rank of Squadron Leader and his own private aircraft (a Moth) became a regular sight at Turnhouse which he used to fly to the airfield from Stobo.

He brought his tireless energy, vision and enthusiasm to 603 Squadron and, although a firm disciplinarian, quickly won the admiration, support and affection of all officers and ground staff.

In May 1932, Mr Paton, the owner of the Squadron's bombing range at Belstane, suddenly died. He had been a good friend to 603 and had always been keenly interested in its activities. It was necessary to find a new range and the Commanding Officer made one available on his estate at Stobo. However, little practice was possible due to bad weather and in 1934 a young Flying Officer Stevens offered a site near West Calder which was accepted.

Weather conditions at Stobo were not always favourable for bombing and the Squadron made increasing use of the 'Camera Obscura' which had recently been installed at Turnhouse. This consisted of a lens set in the roof of a small darkened building near one of the hangars. When an aeroplane flew high over the aerodrome, its image was projected by the lens on to a chart of the locality. The bomb aimer used the Camera Obscura building as his target. When he thought he was in the correct position to make a direct hit he pressed the key of his wireless transmitter. The signal was picked up on a receiver in the building and the exact position of the aeroplane was noted on the chart. The probable impact of the bomb was then calculated using the known height and speed of the aeroplane and the estimated wind speed and direction.

One of Murray-Philipson's last actions as CO was to institute an annual squadron magazine. In the introduction to the first issue in December 1933, he wrote:

> It was felt that the activities of the Squadron were becoming so numerous and the keenness of all concerned so real, that some permanent record of Squadron events should be made which would be a source of interest and encouragement to everyone in the Squadron as well as those who will join in the future.

Ill health finally forced him to resign and on 1 April 1934, his place was taken by Squadron Leader Lord George Nigel 'Geordie' Douglas-Hamilton, Commander of A Flight.

Hyltie died at home at 43 Portland Place, London, W1, on 24 May 1934. A Memorial Service was held at St Cyprians, Clarence Gate on 28 May and attended by the Mayor of Twickenham (Alderman D.A. Farrar) and representatives of the three political parties as well as members of the Royal Air Force and Auxiliary Air Force.

A funeral service was held on 29 May at Stobo, Midlothian, and the remains of the Laird of Stobo were interred at Stobo churchyard. The pallbearers were officers of 603 Squadron. During the service in the Castle, and while the cortege made the journey to the place of burial, a Hawker Hart of 603 Squadron circled overhead.

Following her husband's death, Mrs Murray-Philipson maintained her close ties with 603 Squadron and presented the band with a pipe-major's banner. This rests in the National War Museum of Scotland, Edinburgh Castle.

Group Captain Lord George Nigel Douglas-Hamilton

As one of the Chief Intelligence Officers at Headquarters Fighter Command and the C-in-C's (Air Marshal Sir Hugh Dowding) close confidant, Lord 'Geordie' Douglas-Hamilton (The Earl of Selkirk), one of the four Douglas-Hamilton brothers, all of whom were at one time squadron commanders in the RAF, experienced the security put in place in the Home Counties during the Battle of Britain and the public's own kind of enthusiastic support of the official line in the form of 'free enterprise surveillance.' In 1984 he recounted his experiences during one of his many visits, during which he flew by himself, to the various battle stations:

> I was returning from Hornchurch to Hendon and had been delayed by an air raid. By that time the evening was turning to nightfall and the visibility murky, so without night-flying equipment I decided that land was on the whole a more satisfactory location. I settled on a playing field in Cricklewood, in spite of goal posts and other obstructions which were obligatory at that time.
>
> Rather satisfied with myself, I was surprised to see a sturdy young man advancing menacingly towards me waving a cricket stump. He was quickly followed by an officer of

the police who politely but firmly required my presence at the police station. He was not impressed by my uniform nor by the papers which I carried, so I rang my office at Fighter Command where my voice was recognised. This made no impression on the officer so strict were the instructions issued to the police.

He then asked did I know anyone at Hendon, to which I could only say that I had no reason to believe that I did. However we proceeded to Hendon and there my luck changed; by pure chance I met Squadron Leader Urie whom I had known in Glasgow with 602 squadron, formerly commanded by my brother, Douglo [Group Captain The Duke of Hamilton]. At last the diligent police officer was content.

If anyone doubts the value of such strict policies, their views would I believe change following even a cursory glance at the book *Double Cross*, by the late Sir John Masterman. Therein is very convincing evidence of how valuable these policies were.

The Earl of Selkirk, Wimborne, Dorset, 1984

Group Captain Ernest Hildebrand Stevens OBE

Stevens, known as 'Count' but also as 'Steve' by some of his closest friends in 603 Squadron was born on 2 June 1909 to Mr and Mrs E. G. C. Stevens of Kuala Lumpur, FMS, and Hermand, West Calder. His father, Ernest John Carwithin Stevens of Bedford, was an accountant in Malaya and his mother came from a family which had gained its wealth from the coal mines of West Lothian; hence their residence there. Ernest, junior, was educated at Merchiston Castle School and Edinburgh University where he gained his LL.B in 1935, and his 'blue' as a member of the University Rowing Club. Stevens took a lively interest in field natural history, was an accomplished shot and fencer and was a member of the Scottish Amateur Fencing Union. Before the war he competed in winter sports competitions in Switzerland with some success. On leaving university he was apprenticed as a Writer to His Majesties Signet to W.J. Guild, WS, from 1935-37, the sole partner of Mssrs Guild and Guild WS at 5 Rutland Square. Stuart Guild, the brother of W.J. Guild, did his apprenticeship at the same time as Stevens. In 1937 the two visited W.J. Guild and his family at their farm holiday house at Pitlochry in Stevens' SS Jaguar open top sports car. He became a family friend of the Guild's. He was eventually admitted to the Society of Writers to His Majesties Signet on 20 December 1937 after three years as an apprentice and remained with the firm as a qualified legal assistant in the office of W.J. Guild until he was called up in 1939. Stevens was well-known in service and civil flying circles. He was chairman of Edinburgh Flying Club and as a founder member of that organisation did a great deal to develop interest in flying in the Edinburgh area. Before the war he flew up to Pitlochry in an Avro Tutor and landed in a field near the Guild's farm after having driven the sheep to one corner by taxiing towards them. He stayed a couple of days before flying back in the same aircraft. The Tutor was clearly visible from the Main Street and became the talk of the town. Stuart Guild (son of W.J. Guild, not to be confused with W.J. Guild's brother) recalled:

> He [Stevens] was an extremely nice chap. He had trouble with his shoulder 'coming out' but could force it back in. In 1936, when I was 12, my uncle bought me a *Daily Mail* glider made of plywood, which I was unable to make. Stevens took it away and had the fitters at Turnhouse make it up. Instead of covering it with tissue paper, they covered it in aeroplane fabric. I was told that before they returned it to me, they flew it off from the roof of the hangar several times. I flew it for a few years afterwards as it was extremely strong. That was the sort of fellow he was; very kind.

Stevens had a number of close friends including the Squadron padre James Rossie Brown and Ivone Kirkpatrick. All three spoke fluent German. Neither 'Kirk' nor 'Count' flew operationally against the Luftwaffe. Another good friend of Stevens was Lord Geordie Douglas-Hamilton, former CO and someone who recommended Stevens to succeed him as officer commanding 603 Squadron in April 1938. Stevens was also good friends with Sergeant Angus 'Angy' Gillies, who was badly injured during the bombing of Hornchurch on 31 August 1940. Before the war, on any occasion when Stevens was due to fly to another base, Gillies would drive Stevens' car from Turnhouse in order to keep him mobile in-situ. During the summer camp of 1938 almost the entire compliment of 603 Squadron's airmen crossed the Channel for a day trip to Calais. Angy Gillies had joined the Auxiliary Air Force in order to enjoy such events. For the officers Count Stevens organised a trip to the Prince of Wales Theatre in London, booking the front two rows, and inviting officers and wives.

Following his call-up, Stevens commanded the Squadron as a squadron leader and it was on 16 October 1939 that the Squadron shot down the first German aircraft to fall since WWI. After leaving 603, he was responsible for the direction of the huge number of aircraft which were used as fighter escort for the daylight raids over Germany and the escort for the invasion of Normandy on 6 June 1944. In July 1945, as Deputy Commander, Allied Forces in Norway, he had attained the rank of Group Captain, was awarded the OBE (Mil.) for his two years work at Fighter Command directing operational flying at RAF (Fighter) Command HQ, and was in line for promotion to Air Commodore. For his work in Norway he was awarded the Norway Freedom Cross.

On 11 May 1945, when 603 Squadron was at Drem, two white Ju52 transport planes landed with a number of high-ranking German Luftwaffe officers onboard. They had come to sign the capitulation of Nazi-occupied Norway. 'Uncle' George Denholm had overseen the procedures in Norway and Group Captain Stevens was the senior British officer present in Scotland. A table from one of the billets was used for the signing which took place in the middle of the airfield with a number of 603 Squadron pilots looking on. Following the signing, the German officers were put onboard an SMT bus and taken to Turnhouse via the streets of Edinburgh where they suffered further indignation under the gaze of the people of the Scottish capital.

Stevens appeared briefly in an RAF Control Room scene in the film *First of the Few*, the story of the life of Reginald J. Mitchell, starring Leslie Howard and David Niven.

Although a fighter pilot at the beginning of the war his shoulder injury had curtailed any hope of seeing action. He was a very proud, if overly possessive, commanding officer of 603. Reunited later in the war and also after the conflict he found that he had grown distant from the now battle-hardened veterans of the Edinburgh Squadron he had known prior to the war and did not rejoin the unit.

On his return to civilian life in 1946 he became an active partner with W.J. Guild. He continued to live with his parents at Hermand, West Calder. On his return from service in the Far East in 1947, W.J. Guild's son, Stuart, became apprenticed to Stevens and his father. By then, Stevens owned a Jeep which Stuart occasionally used on office business. Stevens was responsible for Guild's court work and had some wealthy clients whom he looked after. In 1947 there was an important document which required a signature prior to a marriage. Stevens flew up to Fortingall in a monoplane, described as similar to the Piper Cub, and landed in a harvest field nearby. Stevens had the deed signed by W.J. Guild and took off again. The company stock with the locals increased. What had impressed them most was the fact that Stevens had climbed out of the cockpit dressed in a suit clutching his briefcase!

Stevens and a number of other lawyers were flown out from Drem with Stevens assigned to the trial of Nikolaus von Falkenhorst formerly Generaloberst in the German Army who, as leader of the Wehrmacht during the invasion of Norway, remained in situ for the duration of the war. Von Falkenhorst was tried for the executions of 14 Norwegian saboteurs in October 1942 (in compliance with orders from Adolf Hitler on 18 October 1942) who had been caught following operations 'Freshman' and 'Checkmate'. One of these operations involved a raid on the Glamfjord Power Station. Falkenhorst had decreed the deaths of these Allied fighting men who were taken prisoner by the German forces in Norway 'contrary to the law and usages of war.' They had been taken to an isolated wood where they were shot and their bodies buried. Under the supervision of the Allied forces they were later exhumed by those responsible for the atrocity .

Following his work in Nuremburg Stevens returned to Edinburgh and edited Volume VI of a series of 42 volumes published on the war crimes trials entitled: 'Trial of Major War Criminals by the International Tribunal Sitting at Nuremberg, Germany (1947-49). Volume VI by Stevens was entitled: 'The Trial of Nikolaus von Falkenhorst'. It was subsequently published in 1949, after his death. The Rt. Hon. Sir Norman Birkett PC, Member of the Military Tribunal at Nuremberg wrote the foreword in which he recalled of Stevens:

> His equals for the task are plainly to be seen in the nature and quality of his work. Stevens possessed one great advantage in that he was Second-in-Command of the RAF Occupational Forces in Norway at the time of the happening of the events he discusses with so much knowledge and insight.

During the latter stages of the war Stevens had been seeing Olga Blakelock, the daughter of a doctor in Dirleton. Her previous boyfriend was Logan John Beveridge of 1 Murrayfield Avenue, Edinburgh, a 31-year-old, six-foot, six-inch Captain in the Royal Scots who was from a farming background. During WWII he served in Italy and was taken prisoner and incarcerated for the remainder of hostilities. After his release Beveridge returned from captivity and became an apprenticed chartered accountant. He also resumed his relationship with his former girlfriend, much to the distress of Stevens. With the couple's engagement came tragedy. The following article appeared in the *Daily Mail* on Monday 24 January:

TWO SHOTS END A
3 am PARTY AT VILLA

Two shots in a bedroom at 3 a.m. yesterday ended a week-end party at an Edinburgh villa. One killed Ernest Hildebrand Stevens, aged 39, well-known lawyer and former Group Captain. The other wounded Logan John Beveridge, 31-year-old apprenticed chartered accountant. Beveridge, 6ft 6in tall, was once a captain in the Royal Scots. Police medical experts said last night they are convinced Stevens shot himself and that Beveridge was wounded while trying to intervene. Beveridge is in the Royal Infirmary with a wound in the left arm; it is not serious. Stevens is said to have left the party – at Cumin Place – in the early hours and to have returned after driving round the city in his car. Guests said that he seemed considerably upset and was morose. A woman was mentioned. When Stevens came back the party had broken up and only a few people were having coffee. The shooting occurred in one of the top-floor bedrooms. Stevens died in hospital.

It has been said that Stevens left the party on the evening of 23 January to get his gun. On returning to the villa at 19 Cumin Place in the Grange District of Edinburgh, owned at that time by Archibald Watt, he confronted the couple in an upstairs bedroom shortly after 3.00 a.m., and opened fire with his automatic pistol. The couple fell to the floor and Stevens, perhaps due to his desperate emotional state and/or realising the enormity of his crime raised the gun to his own head and shot himself. Beveridge had been hit in the left upper arm, fracturing the left shoulder. Medical opinion later confirmed that Stevens' wound 'a shot to the head' was 'self inflicted by an automatic pistol.' No other fatal shots had been fired by Stevens who was rushed to hospital but was pronounced dead half an hour after the incident. The couple had instinctively taken evasive action in falling to the floor. Perhaps Stevens had decided to deny his former love of both he and her husband to be. The tragedy was felt by all who knew him, including his family, close friends and colleagues at Guild and Guild. Stuart Guild recalls: 'It was a great shock to us at the time, especially to my father who was grooming him to succeed him. He made him a sleeping partner in 1944 in case I did not come back.'

Possibly as a consequence of the tragedy, Olga never married Beveridge who is remembered by his regimental colleague, Second Lieutenant Iain Parks, as being very well built but not particularly intelligent or charismatic, '…many thought Olga had been wrong to choose Logan over Stevens, which led to the tragedy. She is remembered as someone who played the field a bit.'

Stevens had been well-known and highly respected as a lawyer in the city.

COMBAT CLAIMS DURING THE BATTLE OF BRITAIN
(Total by the end of WWII in brackets)

Arber – 1 (2) shared destroyed

Bailey – 2 (2) destroyed, 1 (1) shared destroyed

Benson –

Berry – 7 (14) destroyed, 4 (10) shared destroyed, 6 (17) damaged, 6 (9) probably destroyed, (7 destroyed on ground)

Boulter – 3 (4) destroyed, 1 (1) shared destroyed, 2 (2) damaged, (3 probably destroyed)

Burt – (2 shared destroyed)

Caister – 2 (2) destroyed, 1 (4) shared destroyed

Carbury – 15 (15) destroyed, 2 (2) shared destroyed, 4 (5) damaged, 2 (2) probably destroyed

Cardell – 1 (1) destroyed

Cunningham – 1 (1) shared destroyed, (1 damaged)

Darling – 2 (2) shared destroyed, 1 (1) probably destroyed

Denholm – 2 (3) destroyed, 1 (3) shared destroyed, 5 (6) damaged, 2 (3) probably destroyed, 1 (1) unconfirmed destroyed, 1 (1) shared probably destroyed

Dewey – 2 (2) destroyed

Dexter – 2 (5) destroyed, 1 (2) probably destroyed

Gilroy – 3 (14) destroyed, 1 (10) shared destroyed, (5 damaged), 1 (4) shared damaged, 2 shared probables, (3 shared destroyed on ground)

Goldsmith –

Haig – 1 (1) destroyed

Hartas – 1 (2) destroyed, (1 shared probable)

Hillary – 5 (5) destroyed, 1 (1) damaged, 2 (2) probably destroyed

Howes -

Lawrence – 2 (4) destroyed, (2 shared destroyed), 4 (9) damaged, 1 (1) shared damaged

HK Macdonald – 4 (5) destroyed, (3 shared destroyed), 2 (2) probably destroyed

DK Macdonald –

MacPhail – 2 (2) destroyed

Macnamara – 1 (1) destroyed, 1 (1) shared destroyed

Martel – 1 (2) destroyed, (2 damaged)

Matthews – 2 (2) destroyed, 1 (1) shared destroyed

Maxwell -

Morton – 4 (6) destroyed, 3 (4) shared destroyed, 6 (6) damaged, 5 (5) probably destroyed, (1 unconfirmed destroyed)

Olver – (4 destroyed, 2 shared destroyed, 4 damaged, 3 probably destroyed, 2 shared damaged, 1 shared probable, 3 destroyed on ground)

Pease – 1 (1) destroyed, 1 (1) shared destroyed

Peel –

Pinckney – 2 (7) destroyed, 1 (3) damaged, 1 (3) probably destroyed, (1 destroyed on ground)

Prowse – (2 destroyed, 1 probably destroyed)

Rafter -

Read – 1 (1) shared destroyed

Ritchie – 1 (2) shared destroyed

Rushmer – 1 (1) shared destroyed

Sarre – 1 (1) destroyed

Scott-Malden – 1 (5) probably destroyed, (3 destroyed, 2 shared destroyed, 12 damaged, 1 shared damaged)

Soden – 2 (2) destroyed, 1 (1) shared destroyed

Stapleton – 5 (6) destroyed, 1 (2) shared destroyed, 2 (2) damaged, 8 (8) probably destroyed

Stewart-Clark – 2 (4) shared destroyed

Stokoe – 2 (7) destroyed, (1 shared destroyed), 2 (4) damaged, 1 (2) probably destroyed, (1 shared probably destroyed)

Terry –

Waterston – 1 (1) destroyed, 1 (1) shared destroyed

Winskill – 1 (1) destroyed, 1 (1) shared destroyed

LIFE AFTER 603

The story of some of 603's men of the Battle of Britain after they left the Squadron, in alphabetical order.

Flight Lieutenant Brian Carbury DFC and Bar

Brian Carbury was posted to 58 OTU in December 1940. His promotion to Flight Lieutenant was gazetted on 27 April 1941. Formed on 2 December 1940 at Grangemouth they were disbanded on 5 October 1943 to become 2 Combat Training Wing in which Brian continued to instruct to a very high standard. 58 OTU eventually reformed on 12 March 1945 at Poulton by redesignating an element of 41 OTU. It was finally disbanded on 20 July 1945 at Hawarden.

In 1944, it is believed Brian was dismissed from the RAF. As a consequence the service lost an outstanding fighter pilot and the fact that he remained an instructor for more than three years after the Battle of Britain and never returned to operational flying, leads one to consider that there were underlying problems. Brian's 603 colleagues, Ras Berry and David Scott-Malden, along with former members of the ground crew who had known him, including his own rigger and fitter, stated that he faced court martial for bouncing cheques. Today, Brian Carbury's case would certainly not be a serious misdemeanour but back in those days and, in accordance with RAF law, it was and carried a lengthy prison sentence if convicted. Wages were paid by two civilian companies. For the purpose of paying salaries, personnel were listed in alphabetical order with each company given responsibility for half of the list. Issuing a cheque for an account which did not hold sufficient funds constituted fraud (obtaining by false pretences). As he was accused of having committed the offence on between nine and 17 occasions he was therefore in a great deal of trouble. It has also been said that he also refused to serve overseas (he was not prepared to leave his wife). There is much anecdotal information which alleges that while the couple were staying in a hotel local to RAF Grangemouth, she regularly ran-up bills which Brian found increasingly difficult to pay. If the number of offences are anything to go by it would seem that his superiors had actually been quite tolerant of the misdemeanours and, as an officer, in accordance with RAF law, resigning his commission to avoid a court martial was not an automatic right and therefore not an option he could take. Even if he had resigned his commission there is no record of further service after his leaving date. The Air Officer Commanding (AOC) would have also been aware not only of his achievements but also the problems he was having, thus suggesting a degree of tolerance on the part of authority until matters became serious.

Brian's first marriage eventually broke down. His wife, described by members of his family as 'a disaster for him', subsequently deserted her husband. It is possible they were divorced in the 1940s. In 1948 Brian had his British pilot's licence suspended for ferrying aircraft to Israel, which was not permitted at that time.

Brian eventually found employment as a sales representative for a heating and ventilation engineering company. He married again during the early 1950s to a woman who has been described as the antithesis of his first wife. Happily married, the couple settled in Telston Close, Bourne End, Wooburn, near High Wycombe. He had just completed the redecoration of the home they had named 'Haeremai' when he was taken ill. Tragically, terminal acute monocytic leukaemia was diagnosed and Brian died soon after on 31 July 1961, in The War Memorial Hospital, High Wycombe, aged only 43 years. His wife was at his bedside. He left a son, also called Brian, who has two sons.

Brian Carbury's premature death was a very sad end of a great and highly respected combat pilot who had done so much to help win the Battle of Britain. Brian's body was cremated at Breakspear Crematorium in Ruislip. In Wellington, New Zealand, the town of Brian's birth, a memorial was erected in his memory.

Flight Lieutenant Peter Dexter DFC

In April 1941, Peter Dexter returned to 603 Squadron, back in Scotland at that time, and on 26 June was posted to 611 Squadron at Hornchurch where he took part in numerous 'Circus' operations – escorting bombers during daylight sweeps over occupied Europe. Flying Spitfire W3309, Dexter made his first operational flight with the Squadron in Circus 35 on 5 July which was an attack by Stirling bombers with a large fighter escort on the marshalling yards at Abbeville and the Fives-Lille steel and electrical works at Lille. Although the Squadron was attacked by fighters over the target area, no losses were sustained. At 14.30 on 8 July 1941 Dexter (flying Spitfire W3247) took part in what was the second circus of the day Circus 40, this time the target was the Kuhlmann's chemical factory at Loos, south-west of Lille. At 15.45 he was involved in combat and later submitted the following report:

> I was Charlie 3 and dived with the rest of the section when we were jumped just before reaching the target. I lost the section and joined another squadron over Lille. On my way back I saw Charlie 1 diving in pursuit of an Me109 and followed him down. On the way I was attacked from behind, but evaded them by diving. Climbing up to rejoin the bombers I saw an Me109 and chased him. I got in one burst of about half a second. He dived vertically and I followed him a short distance behind. When I pulled out of the dive he was within 500 feet of the ground still diving vertically. I did not see him hit the ground, but at the speed he was travelling there was very little probability of him being able to pull out. Climbing up again I was attacked by three Me109s and forced down to ground level. These pursued me to the coast but I was able to get away from them in the mist on the water. I turned back and saw four Me109s circling about 500 feet up over the beach south of Gravelines. I shot at these and saw one Me109 spin into the ground with glycol pouring out. Once more I was chased and beat it back home. They did not follow me very far.

The 611 Squadron ORB reads: 'Dexter and Sergeant Fair continued to do well with 1 Destroyed and 1 Probable; and 1 Destroyed respectively, which brings the day's bag to 6 Destroyed, 2 Probable – what a Squadron!' On 14 July 1941, Peter Dexter, flying Spitfire V, P8581, made his last flight. The 611 Squadron ORB reads:

> HORNCHURCH 14.7.41. A lovely cool morning after thundery rain for the last thirty-six hours which enabled 54 and 611 Squadrons to be released for the whole of yesterday. We had an early conference at 09.00 hours and took off as part of an escort cover wing for Circus 48 on Marshalling yards at Hazebrouck at 09.45 hours. We were still short as poor old Gilmour had tummy pains and were one shorter still when the squadron returned minus Dexter who seems to have collided with Sgt Panter of 54 Squadron over Boulogne – one parachute was seen to come out of the mess so his chances are 50-50 – rather hard luck.

Dexter was reported 'missing' and later 'missing believed killed'. The Squadron later heard through the Red Cross that he had been found dead in his parachute. F/O Peter Dexter DFC was buried in the Samer Communal Cemetery, France. The Commonwealth War Graves Commission record that Dexter's remains were repatriated after the war. Dexter's room-mate and close friend was P/O Wilfred G.G. Duncan Smith (later Group Captain Duncan Smith DSO and Bar, DFC and two Bars, father of Iain Duncan Smith) who recalled:

> He was a great friend and dear companion and I was cut up about his death in 1941 while we were together in 611 Squadron at Hornchurch. I knew his fiancée too for we often met and had a party in London when we could get away from the camp. I often wondered what became of his girl but... keeping in touch with people during war-time is not only difficult but also tiresome, even depressing.

Duncan Smith was so deeply moved by the death of Dexter that he asked the mess secretary to allow him to have a room of his own and maintained the arrangement until he left the squadron in 1942. A survivor of Dunkirk and the Battle of Britain Dexter was one of only a small number of pilots who had actually shot down a Bf109 whilst flying a Lysander. Dexter was handsome, charismatic, courageous and an excellent pilot and 23 years old when he died.

Squadron Leader Jack Haig

On 1 December 1941 Jack was promoted to Squadron Leader and by 1944 was at Clayton, S.Yorks. Released from the RAF in 1945 he retained the rank of Squadron Leader and continued to attend 603 functions until it was disbanded in 1957.

Post-war the Guardbridge Paper Company took him back and sent him on a refresher course to Manchester: 'I had been in papermaking all my life and in no time I was selling again.' A short while later he applied for the post of assistant to the managing director at John Galloway, Balerno, Midlothian. He was chosen for the job and promotion quickly followed:

'The transition back to peacetime work was fairly easy. For a while prior to the end of the war I was in Bahrain, doing no ops at all and that period made it easier for me to get back to the quiet of civilian life... My work in this business engages all my attention. It's far from humdrum and I have a lot of responsibility... I've flown a great deal since the war but for about ten years after I wasn't too keen on flying – as a passenger. I had done no personal flying, that was out, and I didn't fly as a passenger until the commercial aircraft had four engines!'

Jack blamed a memory blur on his unwillingness to talk about the Battle of Britain and often had to consult his log books to confirm specific details. 'It's very difficult to recapture authentically what happened in those days.' he said. 'It's best not to say anything. All I can say is I'm proud to have led a squadron on at least three successful missions... very successful do's.' Jack's claims amounted to three destroyed with others probable and damaged. He was too modest to admit to any more: 'Probably because I wasn't a very good shot,' he concluded with frank honesty. Jack died during the 1980s.

Flight Lieutenant Keith Lawrence DFC

According to Keith 421 Flight flew 'Jim Crows' from Hawkinge, Gravesend and Biggin Hill and provided up-to-date information on incoming raids in an attempt to endorse the depleted RDF curtain which had suffered during the bombing: 'Park and Dowding knew the raids were coming in and our Spits were sent up in pairs or solo to flank them... at high altitude and report in plain language on the R/T on the raids, knowing the Germans were listening.' For a brief period 421 Flight were re-equipped with the Hurricane II. This was not a popular move with the pilots and CO, prompting the rapid return of Spitfires to the unit. On 23 November Keith damaged a Bf110 and during a weather reconnaissance over Ramsgate on the 26th he was shot down by Bf109Es. He believes a cannon shell struck the wing root on his Spitfire which subsequently blew up at an altitude of 8,000 feet. In that instant he was blown through the side of his disintegrating aircraft, and he found himself falling free. He managed to pull the ripcord to release his parachute and landed in the Channel. Once he was free of his parachute he released his dye sachet into the water to indicate his position. Fortunately, he was picked up by a minesweeper, landed at Deal and taken to Ramsgate where he was admitted to hospital with extensive injuries which included a dislocated and broken right shoulder, a severely broken right leg with both tibia and fibula fractured half way up the shin, and the calf muscle on his left leg practically blown off. He was taken to Queen Mary's RAF Hospital, Halton, where his left calf was sewn back on and his broken bones set. It was while he was at Halton that he met his wife to-be who was a VAD nurse at the Buckinghamshire hospital.

During June or July 1941, Keith was sent to the officers convalescent facility in The Grande Hotel, Torquay for a lengthy period of recuperation. His future wife was also sent there and during her work she came to know, amongst others, the 'Guinea Pigs' Bill Simpson whom she went out with, and Richard Hillary.

Keith left Torquay on 4 December 1941, by which time he had been promoted to Flight Lieutenant, and rejoined his unit, which had by that time been re-numbered 91 Squadron. He was sent on a short refresher course on Spitfires to 52 OTU, Aston Down, rejoining his Squadron on 10 January 1942. Soon after he was posted to HQ RAF Mediterranean at Valetta, Malta. On 17 February Keith joined 185 Squadron at Hal Far flying Hurricanes. During the spring the unit was involved in heavy fighting in a period he likened to: '...another Battle of Britain' and remembers that the air echelon of 603, by then 229 Squadron, was on the opposite side of the airfield. Further combat claims followed: on 23 March he shared a He111, on 9 April he damaged a Ju88, on the 24th he damaged a Bf109 and on 9 May he claimed a probable Ju87 and a damaged Bf109. On the 10th he claimed another probable Ju88 and on the 19th a damaged Mc202 when his own aircraft was also damaged. On 28 May 1942, he was promoted to Squadron Leader and took command of 229, recently re-equipped with Spitfires, which he led until he returned to the UK in early August. He was initially posted to 52 OTU, Aston Down but on 4 September was moved to 57 OTU, Hawarden. His award of the DFC was gazetted on 12 September 1942, the citation crediting him with four destroyed, two probable and seven damaged.

During the early part of 1943, Keith was sent to RAF Duxford for liaison duties with the USAAF. On 26 October he was posted to 56 OTU, Sutton Bridge, on the Pilot Gunnery Instructors Training Wing. On 15 March 1944 whilst on a flight from Leaconfield, the DH Dominie Mk I in which he was passenger suffered engine failure and the pilot (Mason) managed to carry out a 'heavy landing' at the home of 54 OTU at RAF Charterhall in the Borders, having clipped a hedge during the approach to the airfield. This was later listed along with the other 321 accidents which occurred during the time it was open and the reason behind the ominous nickname it earned during the war years of RAF 'Slaughter 'all'. These accidents claimed 84 lives.

During late May 1944, Keith was sent to 28 OTU, Wymeswold, where he flew Hurricanes by both day and night against Wellingtons to aid the training of air gunners. He then moved to 18 OTU, Worksop, on similar duties.

On 5 February 1945, he returned to operational flying as CO of 124 Squadron at Manston flying Spitfire Mk IXs. He led the unit on dive-bombing attacks on the V2 launch sites in Holland, and on bomber escort duties. On 15 July 1945, he transferred to the RNZAF and in August 124 Squadron were re-equipped with Gloucester Meteors. Keith finished the war credited with four destroyed, two shared destroyed, nine and one shared damaged.

In late May 1946 Keith returned to New Zealand where he opened a shop in Christchurch. In September he went onto the reserve and for the next seven or eight years he served as a Flying Officer air traffic controller with the Territorial Air Force before returning to England where he and his wife ran a general store and post office in Sussex. He later became involved in various commercial enterprises including a dry cleaning business from which he eventually retired. He lives in Exeter, Devon at the time of writing.

Squadron Leader J.S. Morton DFC*

In March 1941 Black moved to Sheffield UAS where he also instructed. He was awarded the DFC (24.4.41) and on 3 September he was promoted to Flight Lieutenant. In August he made a brief return to 603 to train as a controller and by October he had started a second tour as a flight commander with 54 Squadron at Hornchurch under his friend and former 603 colleague David Scott-Malden. In January 1942 he was posted to 51 OTU, RAF Cranfield, Bedfordshire, for a night-fighter course and in February 1942, was reunited with his old colleague, George Denholm, when he was posted to 1460 (Turbinlite Havocs) Flight at Acklington, which George was commanding at the time. Black took over command on 1 March. The unit became 539 Squadron in September 1942. Black remained there until it was disbanded on 25 January 1943, when he was posted to 219 Squadron, UK.9BNAF, at Scorton as a flight commander.

The contents of Black Morton's log book and combat diary provides a valuable insight into the experiences of a fighter pilot during the Battle of Britain and feature in this book. The following is the final entry made when he was shot down on the night of 14/15 March 1943, for the second time during the war, after shooting down a Do 215:

> 14.3.43. Half moon, no cloud, much haze low down, wind 10/15 SW. 22.40-23.55.

> Took off 22.40 on flaps from Ops – Huns E. of Flamborough flying NW – V8609 with Charles Strange as Operator. Went out to patrol N & E of Whitby under Goldsborough CHL [Chain Home Low] 10,000 feet. Goldsboro seemed rather confused and we were sent here and there to little purpose mostly at about 7,000. Got first contact well below, went down hard but it was too far below and lost it. It was probably right down, as, just as we lost it, saw bright green tracer from a ship right under us. Shortly after, had a contact right above at 2,000 feet. Climbed flat out to 11,500 but still above us and unable to keep contact any longer.

> Shortly after this Goldsboro put us on to another at 4,000 feet. During this we got contact on something else and told Goldsboro who said to investigate it. Went up to 7,000 feet and started to overhaul quite well. It was jinking very violently – we were turning through more than 90 degrees at a time – but was making its way in the general direction

SW to Hartlepool. It seemed to be changing height quite a lot, up and down constantly.

We closed gradually, however, and eventually I had a visual on exhaust flames at about 3,000 feet. It was nicely above us and weaving about like mad. Got a true visual at about 2,000 feet and identified at about 1,500 feet as Do217. As well as weaving and going up and down he seemed to be changing speed a lot as we almost overshot once. After this we went in cautiously to attack and were just about to shoot when we hit his slip stream slightly. He didn't seem to have noticed us, so didn't shoot but tried to steady up. Suddenly a shower of red sparks came out of him and ripped beneath us. They all appeared to miss below and I immediately opened fire as, not only had he obviously seen us, but we were now very close indeed – less than 100 – as the ring sight didn't cover the engines.

We were dead astern and there were a good few strikes on the starboard side and top of the fuselage and the starboard centre section out to the engine, including a very bright flash from the engine.

The Hun had started a steep turn and pull-off to port immediately after he fired at me, so my strikes went out to starboard and I was unable to follow due to the slip stream.

As I ceased fire a number of balls of fire – far too bright and white for petrol – came out of the Hun's belly and shot past my port wing. I thought at first he'd loosed a flare to blind me, but they continued in an intermittent stream and I think must have been his incendiary bombs. By the time I had got my sights on again he was going down in a very steep pull-off to port and I was about to take a nice 20 degree shot from his port quarter when there was a terrific scream from the starboard motor as the revs went right off the clock. I was going to take a shot, but Charles started to shout to throttle back and also we began to swing violently. Then we hit his slip stream again – fully this time, and shooting was hopeless. One of the balls of fire then came between us and that was the last I saw of him – going down hard and trailing lights but still apparently flying OK.

By the time I'd recovered from the slip stream and got the engine throttles back we were just about 5,000 feet.

The starboard engine was still going very fast, it seemed to be in fully fine and the vibration was terrific. There was a good deal of smoke coming back from the dead engine so I switched off the petrol and ignition and it then seemed to slow down a little. The port engine seemed quite happy, so I headed for home and transmitted to say I had one engine gone and wanted an emergency homing. Control gave me a bearing and we reckoned we were about 12-15 miles NE of Hartlepool.

We carried on quite happily for a minute or two, although the vibration was still very bad, especially I think in the back as Charles kept asking if we were all right. I was checking the gyro with the compass when I noticed the starboard propeller seemed to be stopping. It then came off altogether and seemed to sidle round the near edge of the engine cowling towards me. I suppose it was very quick but it seemed to take ages. Then there was a loud bank from the front and a terrific draught. I could see a big gash from the instrument panel aft to about the level of the back of the seat. I told Charles what had happened and also that, although the vibration had now stopped the machine was getting more difficult to control. He seemed quite happy and continued to make encouraging remarks. Suddenly the port engine faded out altogether. I fiddled with the knobs, but got no response at all and so, as we were now beginning to lose height very fast, told Charles to bale out. He wasn't very keen but I told him I couldn't fix the engine and we were going down fast, so he said OK. I then transmitted for emergency fix as I was baling out. In the middle of this transmission the RT faded out altogether and I could get nothing from any of the electrics system. I now undid my Sutton harness, collapsed the seat and opened the escape door; fortunately it opened by itself, as I couldn't find the ring to pull it open.

I kept on looking round to see if I could see how Charles was getting on, but there was still a light in the back and I thought I'd better hang on a bit as he might be having difficulty with his door which could have been bashed by the propeller. We were now below 3,000' and I was getting very worried as I didn't want to ditch, with the door open and the gash in the nose and it would soon be too late to bale out.

Suddenly the port engine came on with a bang. I opened it up pretty fully and tried to wind on more bias, I then noticed the bias control had been removed by the propeller which had also taken the compass off its mounting.

The engine kept hesitating, but was giving a fair amount of power and we were now only losing height very slowly. The light was still on in the back so I kept going for a bit. I then thought that the fires on the land were getting quite close and perhaps if I hung on we might get over land. We were down below 2,000 feet now and still losing height, but they seemed quite close.

The light was still on in the back, but I now noticed that it was always in the same place and seemed to be on the floor, so I took it that Charles had got away after all and this light was his spare torch which he kept in his boot and which had fallen out in the excitement.

I kept a good lookout for the coast but couldn't see it as it was very hazy.

However, we were now almost between two lots of fires and I felt fairly confident we were over land. Then a searchlight came up from quite close on the starboard side. It groped about a bit quite close to us and then doused without any flak coming up to join it. This decided me and as we were now below 1500', I leant back and pulled myself over the hatch. I hesitated for a moment thinking to put my hand on the ripcord ring before letting go so I dropped out. I found the ripcord immediately and gave it a good pull. The brolly seemed to take a bit to open and I wondered if it would then it did with a jerk and swung me right way up. As it did so there was a terrific flash, seemingly from above, (though this must have been a reflection off the canopy) and the whole place was beautifully floodlit. I saw I was about 100 feet over a ploughed field with the machine burning just over the hedge. There was very little time to get settled and I landed rather heavily getting a face full of ploughed field and making my nose bleed. However, nothing more seemed to be wrong, so I let go the brolly and went back to the prang which was just 150 feet away. It was spread over a big area and burning furiously with all the ammo going off. I went and sat on a little hill overlooking it and watched for about 10 minutes until I thought someone might be coming and then started to shout. I got an answer almost immediately and went towards it. It turned out to be a policeman and an air raid warden – both very suspicious until they'd undressed me and found my wings and then totally disappointed I wasn't a Hun.

I got them to take me to the station and we rang Ops to say I was OK and Charles was in the sea and where we thought he was. They hadn't got any message to say I was baling out, but had feared the worst and sent the boats out already.

I then had a very large whisky and washed my face and felt better.

At about 2.30 transport came and we got back about 4.30. I couldn't sleep much so got up about 8.30 but the weather was far too thick to fly and when it did clear they wouldn't let me go. About lunch time we heard they'd got Charles, but that he'd not managed to get into his dinghy and was dead.

I claimed a very shaky 'damaged' on the Hun but apparently he was seen to go straight in flames, so we got a 'confirmed' after all.

The squadron went to North Africa in May 1943 where, on the night of the 16/17 August, Black and his R/O claimed a He111 destroyed off Bone. By October he had finished his tour and returned to the UK suffering from ill health.

From 10 November 1943, as an instructor based at 54 OTU, Winfield, the satellite to RAF Charterhall, he commenced a tour of RAF training units demonstrating flying skills, air/sea rescue, air-to-air firing and aircraft tests on the Beaufighter Mk VI. The venues included: Acklington, Leuchars, Cranfield, Twinwoods Farm, Drem, Turnhouse, Thornaby, Wittering, Honiley, Bradwell Bay and Melton Mowbray. Black received a Bar to his DFC, gazetted on 30 November 1943; the citation credited him with 12 victories – six and four shared destroyed, one unconfirmed destroyed (16 October 1939), five probables and six damaged. He was promoted to Squadron Leader on 8 March 1944 and left Winfield in August 1944 to attend the Army Staff College (ADGB), Camberley. In December he joined the staff of HQ, Fighter Command, where he remained until 8 November 1945, when he was released from the RAF as a Wing Commander. With the rank of Squadron Leader (AuxAFRO) Black re-joined the AuxAF on 1

August 1946 and commanded 613 'Manchester' Squadron from its reformation on 1 November 1946 until 15 March 1951.

After initial trouble in adjusting to life after the war, he started a successful engineering business. Having achieved what he believed to be a pinnacle in his life, when he and his family moved into Woodcote Manor, a large manor house in Hampshire with 100 acres of farmland, he gradually made the transition from engineering to farming, which he enjoyed enormously.

Black married Marguerite (Mardi) on 8 December 1941 and they had five children. Over the years the Mortons remained very close friends with their former 603 colleagues and their families and Black attended 603 functions at the Old Town HQ.

Jim 'Black' Morton died suddenly in 1982 from a heart attack in the driveway to his Hampshire home. His health had suffered a rapid decline during the final years of his life. He was 65.

Wing Commander Peter Olver DFC

On 27 May 1941, he shared in the destruction of a He111 and damaged another and on 20 August he claimed a Bf109 probably destroyed and damaged another. In October, Olver was made a flight commander and, tour-expired, was posted to Warmwell to formulate the 10 Group Towing Flight, flying Lysanders. He volunteered for the Middle East and on 8 June 1942, he arrived at Gambut where he was attached to 213 Squadron, operating as supernumary Flight Lieutenant. On 30 June he was posted to 238 Squadron in the Western Desert, as a flight commander. On 15 July, Olver damaged a Ju88, on the 16th he claimed a Ju87 probable and on 7 August he damaged a Bf109. Olver was given command of 213 Squadron on 13 October 1942. On 2 November he destroyed a Ju87, claimed a second probably destroyed and a third damaged. On the 14th he destroyed three CR42s on the ground at Agedabia. On 1 January 1943, Olver took command of 1 (SAAF) Squadron. He was awarded the DFC, promulgated on 5 January 1943. On the 21st he destroyed a Mc202 and was appointed Squadron Leader Flying 244 Wing on 5 February. On 16 April, Olver took temporary command of the Wing when the CO, Wing Commander Ian 'Widge' Gleed, was killed in action. On the 17th, Olver shared in the destruction of an Mc205 and damaged a Bf109. On 5 May, he was promoted to Wing Commander and his appointment as Wing Commander Flying 244 Wing, was confirmed. He also damaged a Bf109. On 11 June 1943, while leading a patrol over the American landings in Sicily, Olver destroyed two Bf109s and pursued a number of Ju88s. During the combat his fuel tank was hit and set alight by return fire from the German dive bombers. Despite a valiant attempt to put his burning Spitfire IX down in the sea, he was unable to make the distance and baled out low over Caltagirone. Burned and wounded, Olver was captured and initially hospitalised in Sicily and Naples where he remained for some time before being well enough to be moved to a PoW camp at Hammerstein, Kassel, before finally ending up in Stalag Luft III at Sagan (PoW No.2006). On 8 May 1945, VE Day, Olver was flown home from Diepholtz. After a refresher course on Harvards at Coleby Grange, he went to Technical Training Command where he was put in charge of 3 Wing at RAF Wilmslow. He was later posted to RAF Chivenor on Spitfre XVIs. In 1947, as a squadron leader, Olver left the RAF at his own request. In September 1947, he took his family to Kenya where he became a farmer. In 1963, he returned to England and bought a farm at Nettleton, near Chippenham, Wiltshire, which he worked until he retired.

Flight Lieutenant Colin Pinckney DFC

At the end of December 1940 Pinckney left 603 and joined 67 Squadron at its conception. After a 'boring voyage' during which he spent the time trying to learn Malay, Colin arrived in Singapore on 16 January 1941. Whilst with 67 Squadron in Malaya he was responsible for the training of pilots during the build-up of the air force in preparation for war against the Japanese. By March 1941, he was a Flying Officer, acting commanding officer. In September 1941 he moved with the unit when they were sent to Mingalodon airfield in Burma and continued as A Flight commander. At that time the unit were equipped with the American Brewster F2A-2 Buffalo. A short, stubby fighter with a top speed of 330 miles per hour. Due to its instability it was, to some, an unpopular aircraft to fly. Three months later the war against Japan broke out and early the next year Colin and his fellow pilots went into combat against the Japanese bombers. He saw action during the initial attack on Rangoon, by the Japanese, in December 1941, where records show he flew aircraft W8190 and W8191. It was thought that he made two claims for enemy aircraft destroyed during this time, but this now appears not to be the case. Colin wrote home after his first engagement with the enemy:

The Jap Air Force is competent and inefficient at the same time. If we have the strength we can easily deal with them. I was not very lucky myself, as the Japanese fighters picked me as their target and chased me down and round the paddy fields and pagodas for what seemed like half an hour. Fortunately they were damned bad shots. I was not able to be particularly offensive myself. The squadron is doing well, though we don't get the publicity given to the Americans.

Army Liaison Officer, O.D. Gallagher, described Colin during the Rangoon air battles:

We came across two lonely figures shrouded in blankets; two RAF boys, Flight Lieutenants Pinckney and Bingham-Wallace. Both had fought in the Battle of Britain [Wallace had not]. They were doing some night-fighting between them. No one else was there, just the two of them. Bingham-Wallace was going to do the flying and Pinckney was going to give him directions from the ground with the help of a portable radio-transmitter. He was going to spot for Bingham-Wallace...

They went into action as a team that night, but did not shoot anything down. I called at their dispersal hut on the airfield the next day. It had a sign up saying 'Pinker's Kiwis – Tokyo or Bust – The Dinkum Oil'. Colin was the senior officer of this unit, and all his fellow pilots, except Bingham-Wallace, were New Zealanders – hence the Kiwis painted on each of their aircraft. Pinckney said: 'Come and look at this. I should have had that hippo last night, not Bingham-Wallace." We looked at a trench. 'I was in there with the radio – and there – three feet away! – was the bomb!' Pinckney was a hero. He was a twenty-three-year-old Wiltshire man.

For his part in these actions Colin was awarded the DFC (8.5.42), and the official citation reads:

...as a flight leader this officer has displayed great skill and determination in his attacks on the enemy. In the Far East, he completed numerous sorties and destroyed several aircraft on the ground by machine-gun fire. He also destroyed two locomotives. He participated in the Battle of Britain, during which he destroyed at least four hostile aircraft.

After nine months in Malaya, and after the novelty of life on the Equator had worn off, his letters home frequently complain of boredom. After the state of readiness to which he had grown accustomed during the Battle of Britain, he found the easy-going attitude and comparative inactivity of routine administration, very irritating in the heat. He consoled himself with off-duty pastimes of sailing and visiting family friends in New Zealand (while in Malaya, Colin had contact with the New Zealand branch of the Pinckney family, and at one time toyed with the idea of going down to see them. His cousin Nonie Pinckney replied, and sent him a box of chocolates). Among the more outstanding events in this rather uneventful period was a visit to the Sultan of Johore, who threw a party for about 30 guests, which included: 'Arabs, Persians, Malays, Javanese, Englishmen, Eurasians, a Free-Frenchman, a White Russian and a Chinese.'

On 23 January 1942 Colin was shot down and killed by 50th Sentai Ki27s while flying Buffalo W8239. In the company of a wing man in another Buffalo they had been engaged by a large number of enemy fighters. In order to avoid combat with such a superior force both pilots dived through the cloud, but on pulling out of the dive Colin's wing man had lost sight of Colin's aircraft and the enemy. A few minutes later he saw something burning on the ground. Reports from eyewitnesses on the ground state that an aircraft was seen to crash in that locality, but it was so far away that it was impossible to identify it. The only other detail of relevance was a report that a nurse in a Pegu hospital had seen his body brought in. This report was unconfirmed and Colin's body was never recovered. O.D. Gallagher wrote to Colin's father: 'The New Zealanders in his flight had a great respect and liking for him. You no doubt know of the aptitude Dominion men have to criticise Englishmen (I am South African). Well, I can tell you that the New Zealanders' dealings with 'Pinker' gave them a new idea about the Englishman.' Mr Perrett, a lecturer from Colin's time at Cambridge offered this tribute:

You must have realised that the boy was very exceptional. He was gifted with so many and such diverse qualities and with all he was so very attractive to me... he was full of adventure and yet he had a perfectly balanced view of life. He knew more ways of getting out of Trinity after hours than any old resident.... He never bothered to get proctorial permission for his car.... He was frequently right out in the depths of the Fens after duck at dawn. He once failed me. He was to have been here for lunch, but round about 5 p.m. a dirty, very much begrimed Colin turned up complete with silk hat on the back of his head – his old car had conked out and he had spent half the day trying to get it going again. But Colin never allowed himself to be beaten. He had got the car going by himself, and a wash and mug of beer put him on his feet and he got to Knebworth in time for dinner. If he had been under the necessity of getting a First Class in the Tripos I am sure he would have got it. When, after baling out in the Battle of Britain, he could not use a 12-bore gun, he came down here and stayed with me, desperate to get a tramp through the fen with some sort of gun. He had a 4.10 and with that he managed to get several pheasants, though he could not use one arm.

The award of the DFC was gazetted on 8 May 1942 and the citation credits him with four victories. He actually destroyed four with three probable, two damaged and one destroyed on the ground. Mrs Bingham-Wallace, wife of his fellow pilot, said of him:

Colin was at our house in Rangoon the day before he was killed, the first rest he had had for weeks, and I recall now how Mummie and I tried to persuade him to take a rest for a few days; he looked so tired, and I feel if only he hadn't been so overworked he would have been here with us today. However, he was greatly admired for his devotion to duty, and I know from experience how greatly he was loved and respected by all his men. All I can say is I hope my small son Colin will grow up as charming as his namesake.

Squadron Leader Brandt, DFC, wrote of Colin:

I served with Colin in Malaya and Burma and was 'B' Flight commander of 67 Squadron at the time he was commanding 'A' Flight, and as I had the greatest admiration for him, I would like if I may to pay a small tribute. The beginning of the war with Japan found us pretty well unprepared, and I don't think I exaggerate when I say that we all had a pretty rough time. Our role was varied, and we operated frequently from jungle air strips, and it was on these trips that I think I got to know Colin pretty well. I admired above all else his complete sang-froid, and his wonderful self-control even after the most nerve-wracking events. I remember so well his casual accounts of the many times he spent fighting off enemy fighters who at the time were so much more manoeuvrable than we were, and of the time when a bomb landed not two feet away from his slit trench.

On one occasion I know that he and probably only one other could have been so successful in fighting off the number of fighters that were attacking him at the time. It was a great blow to us all when he failed to return from an interception, particularly as we were able to get so few details of his last sortie. He was a fine leader, and I don't think I can put it better than to say that although I was some years his senior in the RAF, I fully expected him to eventually assume command of the squadron, and I would have been proud to have served under him.

There are memorials to Colin at St Neots, Eton, Trinity College, Cambridge, Hungerford, Charlton-cum-Rushnall, and together with the other Battle of Britain pilots in Westminster Abbey.

By the end of WWII the Pinckney family had lost both sons. Brian had joined the SAS and was parachuted into Sicily on a clandestine mission whilst suffering from a broken back. He was quickly captured and executed by the Carabinieri. Both Brian and Colin are remembered on the memorial in the Trinity College chapel. Years later the nieces and nephews of both sides of the family, Pinckney and Gresham-Cooke, were to learn that four of their uncles had perished in action during WWI and II. One uncle was killed while serving aboard HMS *Vanguard* with the navy in WWI. Brian was killed while serving with the army and Colin and Nicholas Gresham-Cooke were killed with the RAF – Nicholas was serving with 264 Squadron, equipped with Defiants, when on May 31 1940, while in action over Dunkirk, he was reported 'missing' over the North Sea. As an ex-Trinity student he is also remembered on the same memorial as Brian and Colin.

By that time Richard Hillary was the sole survivor of 603's 'Triangle of Friendship.'

Reflections of a Life

Robbie Robertson DFC

After a lengthy recovery from his injuries, Robertson was sent to Canada as a navigational instructor on the Empire Training Scheme (ETS). Famous as one of the pilots responsible for downing the first German aircraft of WWII, he returned to Britain with another 'first performance' when he was the first pilot to fly a Hudson across the Atlantic. Following his return he became a staff officer at Fighter Command and was awarded the DFC. He travelled to Buckingham Palace accompanied by his 'Ma' and sister (left) to receive the award from the King. On 10 October 1942, as a Flight Lieutenant, he married Agnes McAndrew Black in Middle Church, Perth. Robertson's final posting was to 25 Squadron flying night fighters. Details of the accident which claimed the life of Robbie Robertson at the age of 27 make interesting reading.

On 12 December 1943, 25 Squadron was briefed at short notice on an operation which entailed flying at dawn to meet the returning bombers from the raid on Peenemunde on the Baltic coast, the development establishment for the V1 flying bomb; the harsh logic of wartime being that if the twin-engine, two-man fighters could distract the German fighters, perhaps a few more four-engine bombers with a six or seven man crew, might reach home. Robbie Robertson was at that time commanding B Flight and passed on the benefit of his experience as a daytime fighter pilot, as the squadron experience consisted of only night fighting with no formation flying. To try to compensate for this short-coming in some small way Robbie gave a briefing on the tactics to be adopted by his fellow pilots when confronted by the nimble single-engine fighters of the Luftwaffe. He advised: '...fly straight at them – they'll get out of the way'.

That afternoon he took his flight up to practice formation flying when the incident occurred. His Mosquito was seen to break away very fiercely causing vapour trails to stream from both wing tips. Considering the weather conditions of that day this was seen as an extremely vigorous manoeuvre. Not only did Robertson lose his life, but so did his navigator Bartholomew. The tragedy was compounded by the fact that, at equally short notice, the operation was cancelled.

At the time of his death Robertson's wife, Agnes, was four months pregnant with their first child. Lynette (Lyn) was born five months after her father's death and his widow subsequently remarried.

Wing Commander John Young AFC was appointed chairman of the Board of Enquiry following the accident in which Robertson lost his life. He later reflected on what was a sad episode:

> Robbie Robertson was in 41 Squadron with me, although he was in the other flight. He had just returned from doing a navigation course – to my surprise because in fact my understanding was that Robertson was a top man at his job. He had been an Armament 1., at Halton. He'd come to 41 Squadron as a fighter pilot and then went to 603 Squadron with me, although I went up there with Carbury on 6 October, a week or so later than Robertson. When I arrived there Robertson was with George Denholm's flight as the navigation instructor in the Squadron, despite the fact that Waterston had a navigation instructor qualification. He didn't do any navigation instruction while I was there. Shortly after I left 603 Squadron, I was posted to 249 Squadron, Robertson had a riding accident in which he hit his head on a low branch whilst belting along. He was debonair and daring you might say and a very nice man. As a result of the accident he was judged unfit to fly and this remained the case for quite some time. He came back a Flight Lieutenant and by early November 1943, he was a Squadron Leader Flight Commander in 25 Squadron and was leading the Squadron in some Balbo in preparation for a mission. The idea was to get the whole Squadron flying as a formation – at that time the unit was a night-fighter Squadron and therefore familiar only with singleton operational flying. The exercise was being watched by the Station Commander at Church Fenton. Suddenly from behind the formation a Spitfire came into position piloted by Pilot Officer Diamond, who had been my air frame fitter in 41 Squadron at the beginning of the war. He was taking camera gun shots as part of his OTU course on Spitfires. As he carried on Robertson suddenly opened his throttles fully, pulled up vertically and over and as he rolled out to do an attack on Diamond at the rear of the

formation, Robertson's aircraft flipped over and went into the Yorkshire Dales.

I was called to be the Chairman of the Court of Enquiry. I was at that time a Flight Commander of the Intruder Flight of 264 Squadron. I arrived at Church Fenton in appalling weather conditions to take charge of the Court of Enquiry and conditions were clearly too bad to go onto the moors that night so I stayed in the mess and went up first thing in the morning, only to find that the airman who had been posted to guard the wreck had burnt most of the Mosquito fragments in order to keep warm!

I took a lot of evidence on Robertson, having first compiled evidence of my own as an acquaintance of his. I came to the conclusion that his medical category hadn't taken into account the fact that Robertson had suffered personality changes since his accident – from debonair to foolhardy – and that his last action as a pilot had indeed been foolhardy. Fighter Command did not agree with my findings because of course they were ipso-facto, critical of the medical people. Paul Richey came down to see me at my own Station to ask me to change my findings but I told him I wouldn't. I gave him an example of his personality change: there was a time when Robertson would go into a railway station, buy a first-class ticket and then leave the station to go and have a cup of tea somewhere. He then returned to the station and hid somewhere outside and as the train pulled in he would vault the fence and dive into a first-class carriage. As he did so he was inevitably nabbed by the guard but he then promptly showed his ticket. This was the debonair Robertson I had known.

It has been mentioned that Robertson was not used to flying with another crew member. The action he took in December 1943 was something he may well have taken had he still been flying Spitfires, but in a Mosquito he unfortunately had a navigator by his side.

Robin Waterston

Bubble Waterston's sister, Jean, hadn't had many opportunities to think of her brother as he prepared for war. In fact she was of the belief that he would come back safely. When they did meet it was usually back home with the rest of the family. As far as she was concerned he was doing what he loved most, flying, and in the company of those that meant most to him. She later trained as an occupational therapist at Stracathro Hospital, just outside Brechin. In 1941, Jean was invited to the officers mess at Montrose where she was immediately surrounded by the young pilots eager to get to know the pretty young sister of one of 603's most popular characters: 'Very soon there was a line of glasses on the bar containing gin and lime, but I was going to have none of that, despite being very young, and didn't drink them!' The event remains a special memory to Jean. The CO had asked his officers to take special care of the sister of one of the Squadron's Battle of Britain heroes. Jean remembers that she became aware of this as the pilots trying *too* hard to make her feel at home.

On hearing the news of Bubble's death Angus Davidson's mother wrote to Mabel Waterston to express her sorrow at the loss of her son. Mrs Davidson received a moving reply dated 19 September 1940, written while the grieving parents were taking a few days holiday at the Lighanloan Hotel, at Fearman, Loch Lay, Perthshire, thanking her for her kind words of support and confirming the devastating effect his death had had on the rest of what was a large family:

> Dear Mrs Davidson,
>
> My husband and I send our warm thanks for your kind letter of sympathy. Robin was so happy playing with the children in those all too few carefree 'leaves' they had at Invermark. He was the second youngest in a family of eight and they were all happy together. It is hard to bear, but these kind letters all help.
>
> Yours sincerely
>
> Mabel Waterston   (signed)

The letter has remained in the Davidson family for over 60 years as a poignant reminder of his brief but memorable presence in their lives. They have also kept a small wooden boat that Bubble had carved for the children during one of his visits to Glen Esk. They never forgot his sacrifice. Bubble's younger sister Jean recalls:

My memories of Robin are all of very happy times until the terrible news came of his death. I couldn't believe it, as to me he was the hero of heroes and invincible.

We were born and brought up in Edinburgh. My father was chairman of George Waterston and Sons, master printers and stationers. My mother had trained as a Norland nurse in London in 1898 and married in 1899 when she was 20 and my father 24. It was not surprising therefore with her love of children that they had a family of eight, Robin being the seventh child and fourth son (b.1917), and I was the eighth and fourth daughter (b.1921).

Robin went straight from school into insurance, much against his will but the job was waiting for him. He did everything he could to get off work, his main trick being to look out for accidents and to be the first on the scene hoping to be called to court as a witness! After one year he realised his first ambition and started at Edinburgh University to study engineering. His first car was bought for £4.00 – a two-seater Wolsey with a dickey seat. I think he learned more about engines in the six months he managed to keep that car on the road than he did at Varsity. Motor bikes and fast driving were his joys. He taught me to drive when I was still 16 so that as soon as possible I would be responsible for driving the family around and leave him free for his various girlfriends! But the main joy of all was flying.

The University gave him the opportunity to join 603 Squadron. He loved every moment of his flying experience and all the fun and joy and companionship. At school his pink and white complexion had led him to having to play female parts in the school productions – singing and acting. Rugby he enjoyed; golf and fishing came next. Evening activities included attending all-in wrestling matches with a cousin who lived with us and were followed up by mock wrestling at home – hilarious. Climbing, camping and cycling were his recreations.

He was therefore very appreciative of the opportunities given to the Squadron when they were stationed at Montrose and the Earl of Dalhousie gave them the freedom of Glen Esk – stalking and fishing.

He was overjoyed when flying Spitfires became a reality – and I think now looking back that he realised only too well that the realities of war were becoming very obvious. But not to me. I was nursing at the Astley Ainslie Hospital in the middle of training as an occupational therapist and had never anticipated anything happening to Robin. All his friends were indestructible – alas! My only warning was on Robin's last visit to our home by this time at Haughead, near Pathead, 12 miles from the city. When Robin was leaving he unexpectedly gave me an extra hug – very unusual.

His biggest disappointment I think had been to have had a day off on the day when the Heinkel was brought down in the Lammermuirs – very bad luck.

We always wondered how any of the boys would ever settle down to peacetime, but they were not to be given the chance. The war for me finished on 31st August 1940 when Robin was killed – aged 23. I was 19; my parents never really got over it.

I hope this brief note is not too sentimental but... I have tried my best. Robin is as much alive to me today as all those years ago – all youth's problems are what he and his friends had to face. All our memories are of fun and excitement. Richard Hillary's book was a great source of comfort.

Pip Cardell

That Friday evening on 27 September 1940, Pip's fiancée Joan was returning from her place of work with the Air Ministry in Cambridge. She remembers knowing little of what was happening with the war:

The period from when Philip had first joined the RAFVR, undergone training in various parts of the country and been posted to his first squadron had passed so very quickly. We didn't even have time to write to each other! I lodged in town during the week and returned by bus to St Neots each Friday night where I was met by my mother and driven home to Great Paxton. It was one such night that she greeted me with the news that Philip had been killed. Details of his death were very limited but we were told that he had baled out too low over the sea and that his parachute had failed to open. He had died of multiple injuries. I was absolutely devastated and could not be consoled even by the close-knit family around me.

Due to wartime conditions it took some time for Pip's body to be returned to Great Paxton churchyard for burial and not without further problems. As the local funeral party waited at St Neots railway station the expected time of arrival came and went. A telephone call was made enquiring as to the whereabouts of the body of Pilot Officer Cardell and the family and helpers were told that it was being sent to Scotland! This mistake can only be explained by the fact that Philip was flying with 603 and they had assumed he was Scottish. Fortunately, they managed to intercept Pip's body en route and it was taken off at Peterborough and brought back to St Neots and finally Great Paxton, under escort from his family and the villagers that had watched him growing up. A rather unusual grave marker was chosen in place of the standard RAF headstone. During the summer of 1939, Pip had renovated the farmhouse pond by reconstructing and edging it with broken paving slabs. He also constructed an ornamental sundial from old roof tiles. This he placed on a plinth in the middle of the pond. After the death of his son, Harold Cardell took the slabs and repositioned them over the grave, minus the pond, and filled in the centre with other similar slabs forming an oval patio. He then placed the sundial in the middle. As the family farm house was only

separated from the churchyard by a stone wall and a row of bushes he also inserted a gate in the wall providing easy access for members of the family.

At that time, Teddy, Philip's younger brother who was also an RAF pilot, became enraged and determined to avenge his brother's death but was subsequently withdrawn from active service at his father's request, he being afraid he might lose his remaining son. Teddy returned to his career in the family business as a farmer. However, his father had wrongly taken it for granted that he would follow in his footsteps when farming was not something that he was good at and he believed he had no future in. Of the two brothers Philip had been the gifted one with great aptitude as a farmer and had inherited some of his father's business habits. He had looked forward to his future at the farm. Teddy, however, did not.

Joan was to experience the grief of losing a loved one on no less than three more occasions by the end of the war. Two pilots, one of whom was Pip, and two soldiers, one of which died at the hands of the Japanese.

In 1967 further tragedy struck the Cardell family when Margaret, Philip's sister, died of cancer of the womb at only 43 years of age after quite considerable suffering. She is buried next to Philip and both share similar markers above their graves, ornamental paving slabs that were originally part of the farmhouse garden decoration.

Teddy went from one job to another before he emigrated to California in 1980. Evidence of his religious faith – Baha 'U' Llah – appears on the gravestone of his parents. When Elsie Cardell died on 18 October 1981 (the father having already predeceased her on 30 October 1974) Teddy returned from America and changed the father's existing headstone and the burial service to include the words of his faith: 'The soul after its separation from the body, will continue to progress until it attaineth the presence of God. Baha 'U' Llah.' Teddy also claimed that his new faith allowed him to make contact with Philip's spirit, and this he had done. Today Pip is in the company of his sister, father and mother and grandparents. The family graves of the Cardell family are maintained by local residents, who believe that Pip and the like should never be forgotten. The village of Great Paxton is devoid of any remaining members of the Cardell family.

THE SAGA OF RUSTY'S GRAVE

The 20-year investigation to confirm that the grave marked 'unknown' is that of F/L Fred Rushmer

In 1970 during an aviation archaeology dig led by Tony Graves and John Tinkner of the London Air Museum, the wreckage of a Spitfire was recovered from a crash-site in a hop garden at Buckmans Green Farm, Smarden owned by the Batt family. Tony and John had already concluded that the aircraft must have been X4261. The excavation revealed a number of items, with the heaviest objects at the greatest depth: a shattered Rolls-Royce Merlin engine, two propeller blades – one still attached to the propeller boss, remains of the instrument panel, and one undercarriage leg. The team also recovered items confirming the pilot had died with the aircraft: a silver half-Hunter pocket watch, a box of Swan Vestas matches, fragments of RAF uniform, the remains of scorched parachute silk and a map which Rusty kept in the top of his flying boot. All these items would have been in close proximity to the body of the pilot and it is almost inconceivable that small fragments of skeletal remains would not have also been discovered at this time. However, nothing tangible to establish beyond a doubt the identity of the aircraft (airframe number) and the pilot in order to satisfy the requirements of officialdom was found anyway.

It was with the publication of *The Battle of Britain – Then & Now* in 1980 that historian Peter Cornwell first publicly made the link between the crash site, excavated by the London Air Museum, and the grave at Staplehurst and F/L Fred 'Rusty' Rushmer. Also that year further progress was made when the artefacts recovered by Tony and John were acquired by Andy Saunders and the Tangmere Memorial Museum. Andy had been keen to solve a number of mysteries involving missing aircrew from the Battle of Britain and this was yet another, but he was unaware at the time it was a quest which was to take him 18 years.

In most cases the CWGC Registers hold no details regarding next-of-kin, home address or age of wartime casualties. At the early stage therefore details were not forthcoming and the trail which would lead Andy to the family seemed 'cold'. During 1986 a search in the Indexes of Registered Births at St Katherines House in the 1900 to 1920 period revealed a F.W. Rushmer registered at Loddon in the County of Norfolk during 1910. Andy then acquired a copy certificate revealing further details; the birth had been Frederick William Rushmer on 12 May, 1910, it had taken place at Lodge Farm, Sisland. Andy reasoned this had to be the same person.

The next stage was to check in the telephone directory and a tentative enquiry to a Miss Muriel Rushmer living near Beccles, Suffolk, revealed that she was Rusty's sister. Andy subsequently sent her his research material and in a letter written in 1987 Muriel told how she had put these findings to her two sisters Agnes and Margarete. All three agreed that it was entirely possible that the grave at Staplehurst might be the last resting place of their brother. From then on Andy with the three sisters in support campaigned for the grave at Staplehurst to be recognised and marked as that of Flight Lieutenant F.W. Rushmer. Andy's rationale for this was straight forward: there were only two 'missing' RAF casualties that had been flying Spitfires on 5 September: Squadron Leader H.R.L. 'Robin' Hood and Fred Rushmer. But both had gone down at distinctly different geographical locations and at different times. 603 had been involved in a huge mêlée with Bf109s in the Maidstone area at approximately 10.00 hours. It was from this battle that Rusty, the highly respected and very likeable B Flight commander, failed to return. As far as officialdom was concerned no trace of him was ever found. It wasn't until 15.00 hours that Squadron Leader Hood led the Spitfires of 41 Squadron into battle over Billericay, Essex. In 1987, Squadron Leader 'Ben' Bennions wrote to Andy and recalled:

On 5th September 1940, 'Robin' Hood was leading the Squadron – both in the morning and the afternoon. During the afternoon both Hood and Terry Webster (our 'B' Flight Commander) were killed. Norman Ryder ('A' Flight Commander) thought they may have collided whilst trying to avoid an attack by Me109s [there were other reports of this]. I'm afraid I did not see what happened. We were in line astern. I was about 10th in line and we carried out a head-on attack on a formation of Messerschmitt 109's and Heinkel 111's. It was chaotic! I think we were just north of the Thames estuary at the time, and it would have been approximately 3.00 – 3.30 p.m.

This testament by Ben confirms that Hood was still alive until at least 15.00 and it is known from ARP records that the Buckmans Green casualty was killed around 10.00 a.m. This had been the approximate time Rusty had disappeared. In 1987 the silver half-Hunter watch uncovered during the 1970 dig was cleaned and only then was it discovered that the hands (since lost) had stopped at 10.10. Andy had also learnt from Rusty's sisters that their brother had been given an identical watch by his father on his 21st birthday. However, despite the evidence, in 1987 the MOD remained unconvinced stating that there had been two Spitfires lost that day with both pilots recorded as missing with no known graves. This was compounded by an inaccurate casualty record card at RAF Historical Branch which gave Hood's time of death as 09.40 which, despite the 41 Squadron ORB and Ben Bennions' confirmation of the time of Hood's loss, was the cause of further delay. Repeated attempts to resolve the situation went unheeded for many years. Finally, in August 1997 Barry Murphy, Information Officer at the CWGC, stated that the MOD and CWGC were near to accepting evidence previously published in *The Battle of Britain – Then & Now*, but were seeking any further evidence that the crash was that of Rusty Rushmer and not Hood. In response Andy provided all the written correspondence, official and otherwise, which he had accumulated over the years and highlighted the obvious conclusion that the grave at Staplehurst must be that of Rusty. Official interest had been earlier raised by a newspaper article by John Crossland, a military aviation enthusiast and friend of Andy Saunders. Enthusiastic to find an answer to the mystery, John was keen to do a follow-up article for the *Sunday Telegraph*.

Within weeks the MOD and CWGC announced they were to accept the evidence and provide a named headstone for the grave at Staplehurst to replace that of the 'Unknown Airman'. It was John Crossland's article in the *Sunday Telegraph* on 14 September 1997, which provided the first public release of this information. Fittingly, it was Battle of Britain Sunday. On Friday 27 March 1998 a new headstone was erected over Rusty's grave, almost 18 years since the campaign had been triggered. During the interim period Andy Saunders had regularly sought to have the record set straight.

Meanwhile, there were others who believed the grave at Staplehurst was that of Fred Rushmer and were keen to see it recognised as such. For some years Ted Sergison, a local historian and native of the village of Staplehurst, had been keen to confirm the identity of the unknown pilot in his local cemetery, and thus began his own quest. Ted accumulated the testimony of witnesses who had seen a Spitfire (with canopy shut) dive vertically into the ground and burst into flames in a hop garden with many of the 'pickers' in fairly close proximity. A number of those present in the adjacent fields confirmed that they had been first on the scene and noticed that as the flames subsided, some of their dogs were attracted to the site by what was discovered to be some scattered fragments of Rusty's remains including a leg complete with flying boot. The dogs were taken away from the area before the workers collected up the gruesome remains, placing them in a sack as they went. The rest of the wreck-site is believed to have been left untouched until the arrival of the crash recovery team some time later.* Witnesses stated that a number of foxes had visited the site, with some evidence to support this when the burnt-out wreckage was approached in daylight hours. On arrival the crash recovery team took charge and carried out a surface clearance – removing any remnants of the incinerated wings and fuselage that had been left on the surface after impact. In a rather poignant exchange, the farm workers handed over the sack containing Rusty's remains. As they met the official requirements for a burial it was those remains which were subsequently interred.** In the main, bodies of Battle of Britain pilots were usually taken to local

---

*Some witnesses recall the team arrived days later which is possible. The remains were not interred until 11 September, six days after the crash, although the authorities did attempt to confirm the identity of the victim.
**Only seven pounds of human remains were required to constitute a funeral and burial but must include at least one recognisable vital organ.

mortuaries before being collected by Frank Rivett and Sons of Hornchurch who then transported them to RAF Hornchurch for return to the families for burial. In certain circumstances they would have been buried in St Andrews churchyard, Hornchurch. If Rusty's remains had been identifiable they would probably have been collected and interred there, close to the airfield from where he had taken off that fateful morning. As it was, he was taken to the more local undertakers of Fred Harris prior to burial at All Saints churchyard, Staplehurst. What remained would not have been identifiable by anyone who had known Rusty.

Ted Sergison's investigation took him to Fred Harris, of the Harris family firm of undertakers, the nearest business at the time of Rusty's death. In Fred Harris' care was the Parish Burial Register which recorded on page 192, entry 1534, details of grave 1F11: 'Fragmentary remains of an unidentified airman (RAF) who died as a result of enemy action on Thursday 5th September 1940. Plane crashed in the Parish of Smarden, Kent.' These remains were buried on 11 September, four days after another Battle of Britain fighter pilot had been buried nearby, the identity of that pilot confirmed. The Smarden churchyard, closest to the crash-site, was not a working cemetery and therefore did not carry out burials. Staplehurst cemetery, situated nine miles away, did, which explained the reason for Rusty's burial at Staplehurst. Official records show that no coroner's report or death certificate was ever produced perhaps indicating that only a local undertaker was used. A grim and sad end to a fine and much loved man.

Both Rushmer and Hood flew Spitfires and were stationed at RAF Hornchurch. The exact cause of the loss of Hood's Spitfire, P9428, during a head-on attack on Dornier Do17s over the Thames estuary at 15.25 hours is unknown, other than that B Flight was attacked by Bf109 fighters of JG/54 during the combat. Tragically, Hood baled out of his Spitfire but his parachute became snagged on his aircraft and he was dragged to his death. He was reported missing.

During the patrol in which Rusty went missing Tannoy Read of 603 Squadron remembers seeing a Spitfire dive into the ground near the railway line between Redhill and Ashford. The line runs through the parish of Smarden and it is known that the crash at Buckmans Green Farm occurred in the morning. By the mid 1990s the Ministry of Defence had been contacted and a request was made that the grave at Staplehurst be officially recognised as that of Fred Rushmer and for a new headstone with his name on to be authorised.

In 1990 Jean Liddicoat had moved into the village of Staplehurst, her home being next to the churchyard. One day she discovered the overgrown and neglected grave of an 'unknown' pilot and began caring for the plot. The inscription read: 'An Airman of the 1939-45 War, Royal Air Force, September 1940 – Known unto God.' By 1995, Ted Sergison and Jean Liddicoat were united in their effort to have the grave site confirmed as that of Fred Rushmer with Andy Saunders working independently of them.

By that time, Jean had also made contact with Rusty's two sisters, Agnes and Margarete and assured them the grave was being lovingly cared for. Agnes had been working in India as a nurse with the Indian Army when she received the terrible news that her young brother had been killed. In 1943 she had travelled from India to Egypt to work before returning to England. Agnes was informed about the campaign to have the crash site re-excavated, with permission from Mr Batt, the owner of Buckmans Green Farm, having already been granted. An application was also made to the MOD for a licence to re-excavate the site. In June 1996 Ted was informed by the MOD that the procedures for acquiring such a licence had recently been amended and that he should reapply under the new guidelines. This he duly did. In August 1996 Ted was told that his licence had been refused. In response, he collated all his research and sent it to the MOD. This information included: a copy of the entry on page 192 of the Burial Register, copy of a photograph of the half-Hunter watch found at the crash site, copies of relevant pages from 603 Squadron's ORB and copies of various letters from Agnes, in one of which she identified the watch as being that of her brother: 'It was his! I remember father giving it to him as a 21st birthday present,' she proclaimed when she saw it. The possession of such a watch by Battle of Britain fighter pilots was not common. On Ted's suggestion Agnes also wrote to the MOD requesting that the site be re-excavated. Agnes and Margarete were two very old ladies and time was not on their side if the grave was to be recognised in their lifetime, and so it proved when, on 9 November 1996, Agnes passed away at the age of 97. Margarete vowed to continue the fight and wrote again and again to the MOD. She too confirmed that the half-Hunter watch had been given to Fred on his 21st birthday and that she recognised that watch from the photograph. John Crossland's article in the *Sunday Telegraph* on 14 September 1997 told how the Rushmer family had persuaded the MOD to recognise the grave as that of Fred Rushmer. Neither Ted nor Margarete knew anything about such a decision and when they contacted the MOD they said that the story was premature and had been leaked by the Commonwealth War Graves Commission (CWGC). In any case the story said that the new headstone would read 'believed to be', which, for the Rushmer family, was not enough. By now Rusty's nephew, John Rushmer, a solicitor, had also taken up the torch on behalf of the family and journalist, Peter Birkett, wrote a number of articles for *The Times* and *Telegraph* reporting on events as they unfolded. Together, Ted and the Rushmer family expressed their dissatisfaction over the handling of the matter. Margarete wrote to the MOD and informed them that she was hoping to get the Royal Family involved if an excavation was not authorised and both Margarete and John Rushmer also wrote informing them that the proposed alteration on the headstone was not acceptable. Within days John Rushmer received a reply stating that the MOD now recognised the remains in the 'unknown' airman's grave as those of Flight Lieutenant Fred Rushmer and that the CWGC would be authorised to replace the existing headstone with one that bears his full name and details without the words 'believed to be'. They also offered to provide a chaplain and a bugler if required and stated that the family could choose the words they wished to have inscribed on the headstone.

Since the grave has now been recognised the Rushmer family have written to the MOD to express their concern over the failure to have the site re-excavated by the RAF Crash Recovery Team. Using official records, along with the information forwarded to the MOD, they would, by process of elimination, have been able to establish beyond any doubt that it was Fred Rushmer's Spitfire.

And so it was in October 1997, during the Battle of Britain commemorative weekend, that the MOD finally announced after such persuasion from the family of Rushmer, bolstered by the campaign of historians and enthusiasts, to authorise the Commonwealth War Graves Commission to replace the headstone. The CWGC also stated that the decision was made through: '....a deductive rather than a physical discovery.' Initially they had considered that until S/L Hood's fate could be determined the grave would not be named. But the evidence, which was subsequently reviewed by the MOD, now allowed them to confirm matters. When Margarete received news of the MOD's decision she stated:

> This is wonderful news, so unexpected after all this time. I am only sorry that Agnes didn't live to see it. Fred was the baby of the family. He was a flight commander and the strain caused the RAF to urge him to take a rest, but he wouldn't. He had shot down one German plane and had crash-landed himself before he was killed.

Air Chief Marshal Hugh Dowding C-in-C Fighter Command wrote an interesting and relevant piece on the subject of exhaustion among his 'chicks':

> Many of the pilots were getting very tired. An order was in existence that all pilots should have 24 hours leave every week, during which they should be encouraged to leave their station and get some exercise and change of atmosphere: this was issued as an order so that the pilots should be compelled to avail themselves of the opportunity to get the necessary rest and relaxation. I think it was generally obeyed, but I fear that the instinct of duty sometimes over-rode the sense of discipline...'

Rusty disobeyed in order to continue to support those he felt responsible for.

The death of his close friend Bubble Waterston on 31 August had hit Rusty very hard. On 1 September he wrote a letter to Helen, his older sister, in which he asked her to follow specific instructions when informing their mother in the event of his death. Having witnessed the loss of some of his close colleagues he was only too aware that his own demise was likely and he wished to be prepared. Of his girlfriend, Mary, he wrote of his concern that he should perhaps have married her by then but that something deep inside had compelled him to wait; perhaps the imminence of war and the possibility of being killed. Of Mary he wrote: 'She had no money, was not pretty, but she was a wonderful person.' Tragically, Mary also died young.

On Sunday 6 September 1998 a dedication service was held at All Saints Parish Church, Staplehurst. The awful weather forecast failed to materialise and the day was warm and bright for the 402 dignitaries and guests that filled the small parish church. The media were there in abundance and this particular subject became the main item on BBC News for the day, with Jean Liddicoat and Stapme Stapleton claiming centre stage in front of the cameras. People had travelled from all over the country including Group Captain the Reverend Eric Alsop who, at a sprightly 87, conducted the service; Wing Commander Alasdair Beaton,

Officer Commanding, No.2 (City of Edinburgh) Maritime Headquarters Unit, Royal Auxiliary Air Force; and his predecessor Wing Commander Bob Kemp (on 1 October 1999, 2 [City of Edinburgh] Maritime HQ Unit was renumbered 603 [City of Edinburgh] Squadron RAuxAF). There was also a large contingent from the Rushmer family. Old 603 Squadron Association members, John Rendall, Jim Renwick, Chic Cessford and John Renwick travelled down for the occasion. John and Chic had known each other since they were boys and had known Rusty from when he first joined the Squadron. Chic said of him:

> Rusty gave me my first flight in an aircraft, it was a Hawker Hart. He threw me a helmet
> and goggles and off we went. It was a thrill I have never forgotten. He was a lovely man
> and we thought very highly of him.

They were also re-united with Stapme for the first time since 1940. Although memories were fading many recollections were exchanged between the now elderly pilot and his ground crew. At the graveside the 603 men moved forward to place their wreath against the headstone, amongst so many others, including one from Mardi Morton, representing the families of George Gilroy and George Denholm. Chic Cessford had climbed out of his wheelchair in order to be with his lifelong friends in the placing of the wreath. Words were said and they turned solemnly and walked away. Chic was the last to move away. As he did, with tears running down his face, he uttered the words: 'I've been waiting to do that for a very, very, long time my friend... and now it's done. I am so pleased to have had the opportunity.' When Stapme was interviewed for his chief memories of the occasion he replied: 'The interest shown by the public; the attendance of 402; and being reunited with the old ground crew boys again.'

A meadow with cows grazing in September 1940, the crash site of Rusty Rushmer is today a hop garden. Point of impact was centre right, a few yards from track. Trees on left were not there.

APPENDIX 25

THE MYSTERY OF THE THIRD JU88 LOST
ON 16 OCTOBER 1939

One of the myths that developed over the years following the raid by the Germans on 16 October 1939, is that one of Hauptmann Helmut Pohle's crew was Frederich Gustav Hanson, a Scottish national and native of Newstead near Melrose in the Scottish Borders whose bomber crashed in the Borders following the raid. However, it isn't too far from the truth.

Friedrich 'Sonny' Hansen, as he was affectionately nicknamed was born on 9 January 1913, to Herman Hansen, a German national who had a successful hairdressing business in Abbey Street, Melrose, and local girl Jessie Hansen, (née Wilson). The family lived in Claymires Cottage before moving to Mill Cottage, Newstead. The eldest son, Wilhelm Wilson Hansen was born on 1 November 1911. The births of both sons are recorded in the Melrose Parish Church. During WWI there was considerable prejudice shown towards Germans in Britain and even in Newstead and Melrose certain individuals were vociferous in their condemnation of Herman that he often walked to his shop in Melrose escorted by his friends in the village. Nevertheless, he was badly treated and eventually interned. After the war he was bitter and resentful at this treatment and in 1920, returned to Germany with his family and were largely forgotten until 1936 when the mother of Jim Forrest, a former class-mate of Sonny's who had been the school caretaker and a friend of the Hansen family, heard that Friedrich had joined the Luftwaffe. The source of this information is not known but it is most likely that, after leaving the country, the Hansens remained in touch with their friends and relatives in Melrose. At that time the Great War was over and, for Britain, WWII was still three years away, so the news from the Hansens was of no particular interest to anyone other than those who had been close to the family. Many years later, Sonny Hansen's former school colleague, Jim Gordon, recalled:

> On Sunday 3 September 1939, at about 11.30 a.m. I was walking near the Trimontium Memorial at Newstead when a man passed by on a bicycle. 'The war's on,' he said. 'I've just heard it on the wireless.' As I returned homeward, little did I realise that, at an air base in northern Germany, my old Newstead school-mate, Sonny, was making preparations to attack the land of his birth.

On 16 October 1939, many of the Luftwaffe Ju88s of KG30 were badly mauled by the Spitfires of 602 and 603 Squadrons. Pohle and Storp, the two most senior pilots in the unit were shot down. Other aircraft were hit, some severely, and until recently all but Pohle and Storp's aircraft were believed to have made it back to Sylt. Two of the surviving Ju88s limped back to base on just one engine. With a number of the German dive bombers having been so badly damaged it was always considered surprising that the long journey home across the North Sea hadn't claimed more victims (Interestingly, German sources state that *four* Ju88s were lost on this raid). Many local folk were incensed at the audacity of the Germans in carrying out such a raid on their country. Certainly, the villagers of Newstead would have been further angered had they known that in one of the bombers was a former member of their community, Sonny Hansen. What they were not to learn for many years was the entry in German records which states: 'Friedrich Gustav Hansen 1913, *gefallen am* 16.10.1939.' The Ju88 in which Sonny Hansen had been a crew member did not make it back to Sylt after all.

The Second World War came to an end and the Scottish Borders settled after the conflict. However, whilst opening a garden fete at Darnick, Miss Judy Heiton, who resided in Darnick Tower, started the myth by telling the story of a German aircraft which crashed in the Scottish Borders. She recalled how the incident had brought back memories of the German boy born beside the Mill House in Newstead before WWI, who left Scotland between the wars and who died in WWII, a member of the Luftwaffe. She also recalled some of the details: She had been living at Darnick Tower during WWII when it was reported that an enemy aircraft had got into difficulty and crashed in the Borders. Curiously, when approached, the pilot had asked for locals by name, including the parish minister the Reverend R.J. Thompson. Miss Heiton was unable to recall the names of those involved at the time, however, her aunt could. She told her neice that there had been a family in Melrose called Hansen and that the father had run a hairdressing business in Abbey Street, Melrose, and that their son had been born in the town and christened in the church. Her aunt recalled:

> I believed the aeroplane got into difficulties during a raid on the Forth Rail Bridge and came down about Eyemouth. The pilot was severely injured and asked for Mr Thompson and after his death it was he who buried him.

Another clue came from the Reverend Bob Henderson, the minister of St Cuthberts Church, Melrose, who checked through the rolls for the parish church, which dated back to 1904, and found the birth dates and family details of Wilhelm Wilson Hansen and Friedrich Gustav Hansen. This became the subject of an article in *Southern Reporter* under the heading: 'Melrose, The Birthplace of German War Pilot Who Crashed in the Borders' (It has not been established whether Sonny Hansen had been the pilot of his Ju88 or just a member of the crew). The article came as a surprise to the Newstead villagers and led to further conjecture. From elsewhere another myth developed which had Sonny Hansen as a member of Pohle's crew, that he had been seriously injured and pulled from the Ju88 in the Forth on 16 October. With his dying breath Sonny had asked to see the Reverend Robert Thompson of Melrose parish. When Thompson arrived he was astonished to discover the German was Sonny Hansen whom he had christened at Newstead. Sonny died and the Reverend Thompson conducted the burial service at which Pohle's other crew members, Kurt Seydel and August Schleicher, were also interred. P.C. Ormiston, a resident of Newstead, was one of the police officers which provided the overnight guard in St Philips's Church, Portobello (this part of the story is actually true). Jim Forrest and Jim Gordon had both known Sonny Hansen at school and had both initially believed the rumours but, intrigued by the story, checked the records of German dead at Cannock Chase and discovered two graves which bore the name of Hansen. Neither was of Friedrich Hansen. In an attempt to find out where Sonny had been buried the two friends spent many fruitless years searching, without success. Through Squadron Leader Bruce Blanche, at that time serving with 603 Squadron, they got in touch with the *Deusche Dienststelle* in Berlin and the German War Graves Commission at Kassel. At last they located the grave of their old school chum. The news came as a revelation and set the story straight. Sonny had indeed been with KG30 on 16 October and had flown on the raid. His aircraft didn't make it home again, crashing west of Etten, near Breda in Holland. Most likely, his was one of the badly damaged aircraft which were attacked but not downed by the Spitfires of 602 or 603. Perhaps the compass had been shot away or by flying conditions were so poor they were unable to navigate effectively. The aircraft made landfall but then crashed killing all onboard who were not already dead. Sonny Hansen is buried at Ijsselstein Cemetery, in the parish of Venray, Holland, grave No.33 in the second row of the third field. The death was recorded in the register of Wahrenholz district of Gifhorn. Despite uncovering the truth, Jim Gordon and Jim Forrest were disappointed at the discovery but, nevertheless, the myths were scotched and the story itself is a fascinating one.

The German authorities also confirmed that Sonny's older brother, Wilhelm, died on 3 May 1945, from war wounds received whilst serving as a member of the 2nd Unit (War) Correspondents Department 352 in Prien Hospital, Bavaria. Burial place is Travenstein Cemetery, grave No.8-33. The death is recorded in 1945 in the Register of Prien, Bavaria, under the number 62/45.

Whilst persecuted in Scotland, we can only speculate at how Herman's wife Jessie and two Scottish-born sons were treated in Germany, although by the time war was declared the boys were in their mid-late twenties. Whether dedicated Nazis or not we will never know but Sonny may have felt compelled to fight the war with the Luftwaffe, possibly knowing he would be called-up, as it was the most acceptable way for him to fight. His old friend Jim Gordon said: 'I cannot accept that my school-mate Sonny Hansen could ever have been a Newstead Nazi!'

THE BATTLE OF BRITAIN CLASS (No. 34077)
603 SQUADRON LOCOMOTIVE

British Railway (BR) Number 34077, the *603 Squadron*, Battle of Britain Class Locomotive was built at the Brighton works and completed in July 1948 (the BR number applied to all locomotives after nationalisation in 1948). It was named after the squadron in recognition of its distinguished role in the Battle of Britain and proudly wore the squadron's brass badge and nameplate on its boiler. Its streamlined casing was painted malachite green, with horizontal yellow bands running from the front of the engine to the rear of the tender. The engine and tender weighed 135 tons 13 cwt, were 67ft 6ins long and cost £22,108. It entered service in July 1948 based at Ramsgate, Kent, and was used for working express passenger trains to London via Dover, Ashford and Tonbridge. In December 1948 during the course of a visit to Brighton Works, the words 'British Railways' were painted on the tender and a cast-iron smokebox number plate 34077 was fitted. At the same time the gunmetal nameplate, in the shape of a wing with a blue background, an oval squadron badge in full colour vitreous enamel were attached. The engine was sent to Stewarts Lane shed, Battersea, to work express trains from Victoria to Margate and Ramsgate, and boat trains to Folkestone and Dover. In December 1949 it returned to Ramsgate depot where a 74B shedplate was fitted and in August 1951 it visited Eastleigh Works for repainting into standard BR locomotive dark green livery with orange and black lining. In 1952 the nameplate background was painted black. In 1954, *603 Squadron* went on loan to Brighton depot, but in January 1958 returned to Stewarts Lane.

In July 1960, *603 Squadron* entered Eastleigh Works to be rebuilt at a cost of £12,864 whereupon it returned to Stewarts Lane looking more like a conventional steam locomotive. It was still in BR dark green livery but the nameplates were fitted onto a backplate with the badge set above. The nameplate background reverted to the earlier blue in the 1960s. *603 Squadron* hauled the last steam 9.30 a.m. boat train from Dover to Victoria on 25 March 1961. In May 1961 it moved to Nine Elms shed to work passenger trains from Waterloo to Salisbury, Exeter, Bournemouth and Weymouth, including the Ocean Liner Express to Southampton Docks.

Early in 1964 it moved briefly to Feltham depot and in September to Eastleigh where the nameplates, badges and smokebox numberplate were removed for safekeeping. In March 1967 the locomotive was withdrawn from service, stored at Eastleigh shed and sold for scrap to Messr. John Cashmore, Newport, Monmouthshire, in July 1967. The *603 Squadron* had run a total of 745,642 miles in service.

The Recovery of the *603 Squadron* Nameplate and Badge

In 1963, Joe McCulloch, an ex-member of 603 travelling on holiday to Bournemouth with his family noticed that the Battle of Britain class locomotive heading the train from Waterloo bore the 603 Squadron nameplate and badge. A civil engineer with British Railways by trade, he returned to Glasgow and set in motion an attempt to acquire the nameplate and badge for his former Squadron.

With its withdrawal from service in 1967, Southern Region promised to allocate the engine's nameplate and the official badge to the Squadron association when the engine was scrapped. However, in 1968 the association were informed that although the solid brass nameplates had been carefully cut off, they had then disappeared 'missing – presumably stolen' as recorded by BR. Wing Commander Bob Kemp (now Group Captain) the then CO of 2 (City of Edinburgh) Maritime HQ Unit, RAuxAF (603 Squadron as of 1 October 1999), recalled: 'BR promised that 603 Squadron could have it, but it was thought to have been stolen and down through the years, ex-squadron personnel kept hoping.'

Twenty-nine years later a notice was spotted in the magazine *Steam Railway* in an advertisement for an auction of 'railwayana' in Sheffield, featuring a 603 Squadron nameplate and badge. Original correspondence with BR about the panels was dug out and copies of the significant letters were sent to the Chairman of British Railways Board, the Auctioneer and British Transport Police. It seemed that if no evidence existed of title, the nameplate and crest should revert to BRB and thus be available to the Squadron.

During the week before the auction there ensued a burst of activity in which Detective Constable Mushet of the British Transport Police, Sheffield, ultimately played a pivotal role in the final outcome. He had been allocated the case in the knowledge that it could prove problematical. As a collector of 'railwayana' and a native of Edinburgh, he was interested in the history of the City of Edinburgh Squadron and recognised the significance of their successors obtaining the crest and nameplates. He acted as a link man with the various parties who became involved and it emerged that:

- the seller could not prove title. He had bought the nameplate openly from BR in the late 60s. Any receipt he had was destroyed when his business premises went on fire.
- BRB solicitors intimated that because of the lack of evidence of theft, and the time elapsed, they were unable to pursue the matter further.
- a suggestion that a nameplate and crest were already in the former Town Headquarters of the Squadron was refuted by the CO of the incumbent RAuxAF unit, 2 Maritime Headquarters Unit, who expressed interest in acquiring these historical tems.

In short, following DC Meshet's examination of the 30-year-old files he could not prove that any foul-play had been involved and that therefore the nameplate had been purchased legally from a scrap dealer (Messr. John Cashmore of Newport South Wales) who had possibly been unaware of the promise made by Southern Region BR to 603 Squadron.

At this time the Inspector Royal Auxiliary Air Force, alerted by the CO of 2 MHU, entered the fray. He established that nameplates of other squadrons were held by the RAF Museum, Hendon, and perhaps a swap could be arranged:

- a commission bid of £19,000 had already been received from a potential purchaser but when the historical interest in the 603 crest etc was explained to him he agreed to accept an alternative nameplate if his bid was successful.
- regretfully, under the terms of its constitution, Hendon was unable to part with any nameplate, but offered to contribute £5,000 if a bid were to be made on behalf of the RAuxAF.
- influenced to some extent by the history of the Squadron, a benefactor emerged who offered to donate to the potential buyer a suitable nameplate etc available to the RAuxAF.
- the danger was recognised that the commissioned bid might be exceeded at auction on the day. However, the RAF Museum's offer of £5,000 plus a sum promised on behalf of ex-members of the Squadron provided a contingency fund.

As the auction day dawned the worst fears were realised. The bidding went to a world record nameplate price of £25,000. However, the combined efforts of the benefactor and the contingency fund just managed to rescue the plate.

When Mr Wright, the auctioneer, learnt of the plight of the 603 Association members he had decided to act. He recalled: 'Group Captain Richard Mighall, put the case very movingly and I felt that the nameplate and the badge belonged with the museum and the 603 Squadron Association.' Mr Wright persuaded the buyer to take other rare items from his own collection in part exchange, and then made up the difference. The nameplate and crest were refurbished and handed over to the RAF Museum whence they have been loaned for display to 2 MHU – the RAuxAF unit in Edinburgh (renamed 603 Squadron on 1 October 1999). It was unveiled by Honorary Air Commodore Lord James Douglas-Hamilton on Saturday 24 May 1997, at a special ceremony at the Squadron Town HQ at Learmonth Terrace where Mr Wright was applauded as the major benefactor when the full story of how the nameplate was acquired was told to an invited audience. Group Captain George Denholm was present and in the company of many of the ground crew personnel who had served with him in the summer of 1940, said: 'It is the end of a long search. A very happy ending for all of us.'

To commemorate the event the CO, Wing Commander Bob Kemp commissioned a print of the Battle of Britain Class Locomotive '603 Squadron' by aviation and locomotive artist Group Captain Stuart Black. Today the nameplate hangs on display in the stair-well of the Squadron Town Headquarters at Learmonth Terrace. The end of a 33-year quest.

BULLEID PACIFICS 4-6-2
BATTLE OF BRITAIN CLASS LOCOMOTIVES
Named after (Royal) Auxiliary Air Force Squadrons

Squadron	BR No.	Built	Rebuilt	Withdrawn
501 (County of Gloucester)	34085	1948	1960	1965
601 (County of London)	34071	1948	1960	1967
602 (City of Glasgow)	34089	1948	1960	1967
603 (City of Edinburgh)	34077	1948	1960	1967
605 (County of Warwick)	34083	1948	–	1964
615 (County of Surrey)	34082	1948	1960	1966

READINESS AT DAWN

An excerpt from a fictionalised account of the Battle of Britain written in 1940 by 'Blake', the pseudonym of Squadron Leader Ronald Adam, Controller in the Operations Room at RAF Hornchurch during the height of the battle who left a lasting impression on the pilots of 603 Squadron:

One of the new squadrons from the north was [codenamed] Amber. Its Squadron Leader was a neat figure with a quiet, diffident manner, shy eyes and a soft voice. Amber had been released from readiness to available and were at lunch. From over the entrance door to the dining room came the crackle of the loudspeaker as Operations Room switched on. 'Operations calling Amber. Operations calling Amber. Readiness. Readiness. Switching off.' They dropped their knives and forks. They ran to the entrance where their cars were waiting for them. The last out of the mess galloped down between the cars, jumping on them as they gathered speed. As they reached their dispersal point, the loudspeaker was issuing its next message. 'Operations calling. Amber Squadron scramble. Amber Squadron scramble. Patrol base. Patrol base. 10,000 feet.'

They ran for their Mae Wests, their helmets and goggles and gloves and their parachute harness, and so to their aircraft. 'Amber Squadron taxiing into position,' lookout's voice said in the Operations Room. 'Amber Squadron A-Flight taken off. Amber Squadron B-Flight taken off.'

'Hallo, Tartan. Hallo, Tartan. Amber Leader calling. Are you receiving me? Amber Leader to Tartan. Over.'

'Hallo Amber Leader. Hallo Amber Leader. Tartan answering. Receiving you loud and clear. Are you receiving me? Tartan over to Amber Leader. Over.'

'Hallo, Tartan. Amber Leader answering. Receiving you loud and clear. Have you any instructions?'

'Hallo Amber Leader. Tartan answering. Patrol base 10,000 feet. Possible attack developing. Will keep you informed. Listen out.'

'Close up B-Flight,' Amber Leader could be heard saying to one of his flight commanders.

'OK, OK. Just behind you.'

[The Controller] watched the plots. It was the old business, or what in those full and hurried days now seemed old. From the south-east they marched, the steady long line of them as each observer centre gave its message. Fifty plotted, then a hundred, then another hundred just behind, with diversionary attacks north and south of the main road.

Cricket and the other new squadron, Falcon, had engaged the fighters far away, towards the coast. The bombers came on.

'Hallo, Amber Leader. Tartan calling. What is your height?' 'Amber Leader answering. 10,000. 10,000.'

'Hallo, Amber Leader. Many enemy bombers south of you now turning north. Height reported 13.'

'Hallo Tartan. Shall I turn away and gain height?'

[The Controller] paused for a moment. Height was everything. But the bombers had now left no doubt of their objective. It was to be the aerodrome.

'Hallo, Amber Leader. Base is likely to be attacked. Bombers very near. Leave it to your discretion.'

The quiet voice of the Squadron Leader answered. 'Hallo, tartan. Will try and gain height here.' Another voice broke in.

'Hallo Amber Leader. Ack ack fire due south of us. Ack ack fire. Twelve o'clock from you. Twelve o'clock.'

And then another voice. 'There they are – tally-ho! Twelve o'clock above us, coming towards us.'

Amber Leader's same quiet, unhurried voice spoke: 'Line astern. Amber Squadron, line astern. Going in. Head-on attack.'

From the rampart of the Operations Room the anti-aircraft puffs, woolly in the distance, crisp in the foreground, poised their snowballs in the sky. The crack of the guns and the woompf of the bursting shells were more and more audible. The group captain was at his vantage point, tin hat at the same angle, hands on hips, sturdy little figure, erect and gazing upwards. The anti-aircraft fire swelled to a roar. In that roar, the crackle of machine-gun and cannon fire was lost, and then suddenly the roar ceased and the crackle came through clear.

'They're turning away,' the group captain called back through the window. 'By Jove, they're turning away!' Amber Squadron had gone in. Climbing with every ounce of help their engines could give them, they had met the bombers as these had steadied their course for the aerodrome. There was no time for tactical manoeuvering. In a minute or two the bombs would be falling on their base. They went in, firing at the great obscene objects that were carrying destruction to their station. One voice after another spoke: 'returning to base for more ammunition.' The anti-aircraft fire broke out again. But this time its noise was more distant and the puffs nearby became woolly while those far away were crisp. The enemy was retreating.

'Hallo, Amber Leader. Hallo, Amber Leader. Tartan calling. Are you receiving? Over.'

But Amber Leader had gone. No one found him or his machine ever again. He had led the squadron into the bombers as the anti-aircraft fire was at its densest. A shell had burst and a puff of billowing smoke marked the position Amber Leader had once been.

A BRIEF HISTORY AND WAR SERVICE OF THE EDINBURGH ROYAL AIR FORCE VOLUNTEER RESERVE CENTRE

Prior to mid 1936 the resources of the RAF had consisted of the regular squadrons and their ancillary organisations, the Royal Air Force Reserve of Officers (RAFRO), various classes of reservist, and a limited number of auxiliary squadrons. These latter squadrons consisted of a rather special class of aircrew – those with the finances and leisure time available to fly at the weekends.

The Air Ministry came to realise that there were large resources of suitable and, as yet, untapped manpower available and the RAFVR seemed to provide the means to take advantage of these sources.

The formation of the RAFVR was announced by the Secretary of State for Air in July 1936 and the first Town Centre was opened in June 1937 at Bristol. During the following two and a half years centres were opened all over England, Scotland and Northern Ireland.

Following the ephemeral Munich agreement, and with war looming ever nearer, the Air Ministry desperately increased its efforts to strengthen the RAF. From the headquarters of Reserve Command at Hendon, effort was increased to take all trades, especially aircrew, into the RAFVR and new VR Town Centres opened in conjunction with an increase in the establishment of existing old centres. Initially only pilots were enlisted but by early 1939 instructions were issued for the enlistment of observers, wireless operator/air gunners and, where training facilities were available, ground personnel. Great difficulty was encountered when trying to recruit suitable Commandants and Assistant Commandants for the new Town Centres but by employing ex-Army and, to a lesser degree, ex-Navy, officers, these posts were eventually filled. By the end of September 1939, 39 Town Centres were in operation, including three in the London area.

In Scotland, the Perth Town Centre was opened in early 1937, and Glasgow, with its aerodrome at Prestwick, was opened in March 1938. These two units made rapid progress in recruiting high quality personnel. Edinburgh was due to open next with Aberdeen, with its airfield at Dyce, and Inverness to follow.

Towards the end of March 1939, whilst ground training was in the process of being organised, Flight Lieutenant W.C.F. Wilson OBE, Assistant Commandant of Perth Town Centre, was appointed Commandant of the Edinburgh VR Centre with the honorary rank of Wing Commander. He arrived in the Scottish capital to take up the post on 10 April. His first duty was to acquire a property in Coates Place in which he and his skeleton staff could commence a recruitment campaign. Edinburgh, with its many banks, large insurance businesses and important printing interests contained a large number of youngsters whose education and training made them potential candidates for enlistment in the RAFVR, especially as aircrew. The Selection Board under the chairmanship of W/C Wilson was established with representatives of both flying and ground duties and set a very high standard in the acceptance of candidates. From the outset the call for volunteers had been well organised and within a few hours of opening the Town Centre was besieged with callers keen to acquire the necessary forms for enlistment. Among the applicants were a number of women who would later be considered for recruitment into the WAAF at Turnhouse which began a short while after. The Selection Board met for the first time at the end of April 1939 with a Medical Board from Reserve Command in attendance to assess candidates adjudged suitable for aircrew. Twenty-three were passed fit during the first occasion. Interestingly, the period of enlistment revealed two facts which stood out during the medical examination: the number of cases of colour blindness and the shocking condition of the teeth of a large number of the entries. Those suffering from the former were rejected, the latter were advised to seek dental treatment which had to be completed before final acceptance into the RAFVR. The Medical Boards put a strain on staff as it was often difficult to persuade some candidates that for one reason or another they were unsuitable for aircrew. Eventually several RAFVR doctors were posted to the Town Centre where, in conjunction with the fortnightly Medical Boards, they were also authorised to complete the medicals of observers and air gunners. In addition to their working day, these volunteers gave a great many hours during their evenings to candidates already accepted by the Selection Board.

In the case of candidates under the age of 21, the parent's or guardian's consent, in writing, to their enlistment, was necessary. It was due to the refusal of a parent to agree to his son joining the RAFVR that a candidate, who ultimately had the supreme honour of winning the Victoria Cross as a flying-boat pilot, was not included in the ranks of the Town Centre.

The unit was dependant on having a suitable aerodrome and the time it took in acquiring such a facility meant a lengthy delay in the centre being able to take advantage of the considerable human resources that became available. Turnhouse and Macmerry were in the area but Turnhouse was occupied by 603 Squadron with the airfield itself undergoing extensive alterations, and Macmerry, a small airfield, was being used for training of the civil air-guard. Fortunately, a large site at Grangemouth was made available and in early 1939, following consultation with Scottish Aviation Ltd, the company responsible for the provision of flying instruction and training, work commenced in preparing the site.

By May the work was sufficiently advanced for the first pupil pilots to use the aerodrome. In the meantime the Commandant appointed an Assistant Commander in Flight Lieutenant (Rear Admiral) Sir K.E.L. Creighton, KBE, MVO*, an Inspecting Officer (Chief Inspector in Scotland of Reserve Command), Wing Commander W.M. Graham (Bill Graham was killed in action with Bomber Command in May 1941) and made contact with the Chief Flying Instructor appointed by Scottish Aviation Ltd, Flight Lieutenant Chalmers Watson, a former veteran of 603 Squadron who had transferred to the RAFVR. He and his chief assistants, F/L George Reid, another pre-war veteran of 603 Squadron, and F/L David Young lost no time in throwing themselves enthusiastically into their task, despite being seriously hindered by the fact that the Air Ministry would not release from service any other officers suitable for instructional duties and competent instructors were hard to find. Nevertheless, they worked tirelessly at Grangemouth and when mobilisation came a large number of pilots had gone solo. Although some had fallen by the way they were remustered to observer with a high number showing enthusiasm and considerable promise. Ansons were used for the training of observers and wireless operator/air gunners. The requirement for instructors however, became vital and the Reserve Command eventually provided several Class E Reservists and one serving NCO (armament), and 603 Squadron showed willing to assist in the tutelage of its small brother the Volunteer Reserve and provided three keen and competent officers to instruct in airmanship and navigation: Flying Officers Fred Rushmer, Laurie Cunningham and Robin Waterston. All three were subsequently killed during the Battle of Britain and their loss deeply felt by those whom had benefited from their dedication in passing on flying instruction.

The newly enlisted aircrew showed tremendous enthusiasm both when attending air training at Grangemouth but also at the more mundane lectures at the Town Centre which candidates were required to attend twice weekly for two hours a night. Attendance at lectures remained consistently high and exceeded 98 per cent throughout the pre-war period. By June 1940, the Air Ministry urged the enlistment and training of fitters and riggers but by the outbreak of war the 20 riggers and 20 fitters enlisted and trained in accordance with Air Ministry instructions had received no instruction in their trades due to the failure of the acquisition of a suitable training venue. Turnhouse and Drem were the only active RAF Stations within reach of Edinburgh. Neither were in a position to carry out the training of the RAFVR ground personnel and no enlistment into ground trades was made until a few weeks before the start of the war, when a few members of the Civilian Wireless Reserve were transferred to the RAFVR. Later a number of other ground tradesmen employed by Scottish Aviation at Grangemouth were enlisted, in addition to the aforementioned fitters and riggers.

---

*Rear Admiral Creighton later rejoined the Navy and served for over three years as a Commodore of ocean convoys. In 1941, during a gale, his ship was torpedoed and sank within 30 seconds. As he was thrown into the water he was struck a glancing blow to the head by the mast of the ship. Despite going down about 50 feet he eventually resurfaced and was later picked up by ten members of his crew who had scrambled aboard a raft. Three hours later they were taken onboard a corvette. His next appointment was as Commodore of Combined Operations, Portsmouth Command, a post he held for a year following which he was sent to Egypt where he took up the appointment of Director General of Ports and Lights. En route, accompanied by his wife on the journey, the ship was hit by a torpedo. With the vessel listing badly, the launching of lifeboats proved very dangerous but they were eventually lowered, some dangerously over-laden, and all were saved. Creighton held his appointment until the end of the war and was made a Knight of the British Empire and Mentioned in Despatches.

With the Conscription Act came additional duties for the staff at the Edinburgh Centre. The Commandant was appointed Chairman of the Conscript Selection Board for the RAF and all applications, totalling 1,300 for conscript service in the RAF, were submitted to the Town Centre. Having been sorted and vetted 120 were selected for interview by the Board to fill approximately 70 vacancies in all trades, including air and ground duties.

With war came the mobilisation of the personnel at the Town Centre. All training came to a halt and in most cases the trainees left their full-time employment and were paid at the full Air Force rates of their ranks. Their sole duty was to report at intervals to the Town Centre and then go off to spend their emoluments. The Class E Reservists on the staff also received their calling up papers and their long discarded uniforms which had been put into store at depots. These uniforms were of obsolete styles, tight pantaloons, puttees and tunics with high-hooked collars. Some of these reservists were shocked to discover that the garments which had fitted them as youngsters, could not be persuaded to stretch around more fulsome figures! Then, to their relief, new uniforms arrived and there was a great deal of hustle as each person was fitted.

During the period of waiting an idle existence on full pay was hardly adequate preparation for the strict training and the stresses and strains of war so the Watsonian authorities were contacted and were willing to put their playing fields at the disposal of the Town Centre. Daily parades with co-ordinated physical exercise routines followed by a 'punt-about' were instituted and eventually, after a great deal of struggle by the less fit individuals, the majority came to appreciate the hardening process and a certain *esprit de corps* was acquired. Heart of Midlothian Football Club provided a football and soccer and rugby teams were formed and golf matches organised to reduce the tedium whilst awaiting posting. Whilst the rugger team showed promise a large number of its members suffered injuries. In the golf team were a number of low handicappers, including McKinna who had represented Scotland. While working at Town Centre he won a tournament – playing one round in the morning at Gullane and a second in the afternoon at Turnhouse, he topped off his day with a couple of hours flying at Grangemouth in the evening! McKinna was lost over Germany having already received a DFC and Bar.

One of the highlights whilst waiting was the pilots' and observers' dance at which the Commandant distinguished himself in the 'Dashing White Sergeant' which happened to be the regimental march past of the Royal Berks Regiment, the first regiment in which the Commandant had served.

The removal of personnel into wartime training establishments was deficient and the absorbing of the Town Centre personnel was particularly slow. During training a number of wireless operator/air gunners had required some knowledge of machine guns during their all too brief training and were subsequently drafted to Drem, Montrose and Leuchars for airfield defence duties. Many months later these men were discovered by the Commandant who was by then a staff officer at an Operational Group of Coastal Command. Fortunately, he was in a position to be able to bring to the attention of the authorities the plight of these 'forgotten men' and they were absorbed into training schools shortly after.

As the numbers at Town Centre gradually dwindled as personnel were dispersed to training units, those who remained continued to draw pay and, as had become the custom, continued to book seats for Friday nights at the Kings Theatre. As a finale prior to a large group of pilots leaving for training a farewell party was literally staged. RAF Volunteer reservists joined the company on stage and comedian, Dave Willis, cut a large, substantial and pre-austerity cake following which the reservists danced with the 'Half-Past Eight' girls before an admiring audience.

By mid-October the majority of the personnel had left Edinburgh and the Commandant's honorary commission was terminated. The command of the Town Centre then devolved to Flight Lieutenant Bradley who remained until the ultimate liquidation in February 1940. Despite a short-sighted financial policy on the part of the Treasury which greatly hampered the operation at the Town Centre its brief record was one of concentrated effort with success achieved and brilliantly illustrated by the war records of the Edinburgh Town Centre personnel.

***

In 1947, former Commandant, W/C Wilson, produced a booklet, published by the RAF Benevolent Fund, in tribute to the activities of the unit during 1939. On 12 March 1947, Lord Selkirk wrote the foreword:

I am so glad to have the honour of writing a short foreword to the record of the RAFVR Unit, whose headquarters were in Edinburgh and whose flying training was carried out at Grangemouth.

The men of the pre-war VR were drafted individually into operational squadrons, so that their achievements cannot be measured in terms of individual units but rather as a leavening of the whole body of the Royal Air Force. These were the men who came forward eagerly in time of peace to fit themselves, both in mind and body, for the exacting tasks which the Royal Air Force demanded. As the RAF expanded they were found in every sphere of organisation and operations, carrying with them those qualities of leadership which personal character and longer service enabled them to display.

But their most signal service was given in that desperate battle in which all had the will but few the skill to play their part. That battle which, as surely as the Battle of Trafalgar, was the decisive turning point of the war. It may well be said that the VR personnel, trained before the war, just turned the balance of the conflict. This was their great moment. Of them it can truly be said:

> The great need no advertisement,
> Their deeds seek no applause;
> The noble spirits' aim is the event,
> Its triumph is the cause.

Wing Commander Wilson has done a valuable service, which I know has involved much application, in assembling the records of this Unit, not only because it is typical of what the pre-war VR stood for throughout the length and breadth of this country, but because their contribution has been merged, and to some extent forgotten, amidst the bigger numbers of volunteers and conscripts who joined the RAF after the outbreak of war.

Wilson's contribution included :

Before the war I was Commandant of the Edinburgh Town Centre RAFVR and had indeed the honour of starting it. Since the war ended I have felt that while the regular RAF and the Auxiliary Air Force have received unstinted and well-merited praise, insufficient recognition has been accorded to the pre-war RAFVR.

The personnel of the RAFVR who joined before the war gave their spare time and energy to preparing themselves for the great ordeals they were to undergo. A high percentage achieved aircrew status.

The record of the members of the Edinburgh Town Centre is second to none. Their casualties were certainly as heavy as those of any Town Centre in Britain. No less than 116 were killed out of a total of 244 who enlisted at aircrew. As, however, forty-nine of the latter failed to qualify as pilots, observers, or wireless operator/air gunners, aircrew losses amounted to 58 per cent. Ten also became prisoners of war. Of forty-three ground personnel enlisted, one died on active service. A total of well over fifty honours was won by the staff and members. It is, therefore, with deep pride in their achievements and grief for their losses, that I dedicate this book to all ranks of the Town Centre.*

---

*Flight Lieutenant John Alexander 'Jock' Cruickshank was awarded the VC at Holyrood Palace by King George VI following action whilst serving in Coastal Command on 17 July 1944 when he and his crew attacked a U-Boat in their Catalina. The aircraft was hit by return fire resulting in Cruickshank receiving an astonishing 72 individual wounds. Post war he resumed his career in banking.

APPENDIX 30

DOWDING AND GUN HARMONISATION

Following the Battle of Britain Dowding wrote a report on the harmonisation of the guns and type of ammunition used:

A great deal of discussion took place before and after the early stages of the war as to the best method of 'harmonisation' of the guns of an 8-gun Fighter: that is to say the direction, in relation to the longitudinal axis of the aircraft, in which each gun should be pointed in order to get the best results. There were three schools of thought:

One maintained that the lines of fire should be dispersed so that the largest possible 'beaten zone' might be formed and one gun (but not more than one) would always be on the target.

The second held that the guns should be left parallel and so would always cover an elongated zone corresponding with the vulnerable parts of a bomber (engines, tanks and fuselage).

The third demanded the concentration of the fire of all guns at a point.

Arguments were produced in favour of all three methods of harmonisation, but in practice it was found that concentration of fire gave the best results. Guns were harmonised so that their lines of fire converged on a point 250 yards distant: fire was therefore effective up to about 500 yards, where the lines of fire had opened out again to their original intervals after crossing at the point of concentration.

It was very desirable to get data as to the actual ranges at which fire effect had been obtained. The reflector sight contained a rough range-finder by which the range of an aircraft of known span could be determined if it was approached from astern, but, in spite of this, pilots, in the heat of the action, generally underestimated the ranges at which they fired.

Cinema guns, invaluable for training purposes, were used in combat also; and many striking pictures were obtained, from which valuable lessons were learned.

The types of ammunition used in the guns varied during the course of the Battle. It was necessary to include some incendiary ammunition, but the type originally available gave a distinct smoke-tracer effect. Now tracer ammunition in fixed guns at any but very short range gives very misleading indications, and I wished pilots to use their sights properly and not to rely on tracer indications. (The above remarks do not apply at night, nor to free guns, where tracer is essential for one of the methods taught for aiming.)

During the Battle 'de Wilde' ammunition became available in increasing quantities. This was an incendiary ammunition without any flame or smoke trace, and it was extremely popular with pilots, who attributed to it almost magical properties. 8-gun Fighters, of course, were always liable to be sent up at night, and it was therefore desirable to retain some of the older types of incendiary bullets. These were preferred to the 'tracer' proper, which gave too bright a flame at night. A typical arrangement, therefore, was: Old-type incendiary in the two outer guns, de Wilde in one gun while supplies were limited, armour piercing in 2 guns, and ball in the other 3.

NOTES

[1] During 1938/39 Theodore Rowehl had carried out the first German aerial reconnaissance of Scotland for military use. Using a civilian Heinkel He111 fitted with concealed Rb30 cameras he was able to clandestinely photograph the North Sea coast of Scotland and England as well as the Channel coastlines of England and France. The photographs were scrutinised by German intelligence and information was subsequently added to the photos, where known. Military intelligence photographs were, and still are, used to select bombing targets, determine bombing accuracy, assess bombing damage, determine enemy orders-of-battle, analyse equipment capability, pin-point defence positions and serve as a basis for maps and to search for indications of enemy initiatives or intentions. Interestingly, the German photo-reconnaissance effort was divided between the various Luftflotten (air forces) of the Luftwaffe and was mainly tactical in nature, with no centralised intelligence gathering organisation to inform high-level strategic decisions. Each Luftwaffe reconnaissance squadron had its own photographic laboratory where film was developed and printed.

[2] The Luftwaffe's Intelligence Branch lacked independence and was not held in very high regard. Unlike the RAF intelligence officers, a German intelligence officer (IO) may have the burden of further duties such as censorship and propaganda. Additionally, no IO was stationed at any unit below a Fliegerkorps. Competition between the various Intelligence agencies resulted in no sharing of material. This aspect was particularly evident between the 5th Abteilung, the Intelligence Department of the Luftwaffe General Staff under 'Beppo' Schmid, and the 3rd Abteilung, the Luftwaffe Signals and Cypher Service led by General Wolfgang Martini. The German Intelligence agencies were victims of the political system where knowledge brought power which was retained and withheld from opponents within the same system. On matters relating to the air force, intelligence was gathered by eight information agencies while radar was gathered by ten. Those in intelligence told their superiors what they wanted to hear. 'Beppo' Schmid gave reports during and after the Battle of Britain that were rarely without embellishment. Ultimately, the intelligence branches were inefficient in three vital areas which proved critical during the Battle of Britain: The first was ignorance of the wide use of Radio Directional Finding (RDF) by the British. On 16 July the 5th Abteilung produced a summary of the RAF, with no mention of RDF, although General Martini's 3rd Abteilung was aware of its existence and before the war had tried to determine the frequencies used. This oversight, due to ignorance or rivalry, was to later prove costly to the Luftwaffe. The second point was ignorance of the 'Dowding System' of fighter interception – a sophisticated system of communication, allowing pilots to be directed to targets – with Schmid believing the RAF fighters were confined to defending their 'home bases' and were unable to defend a mass attack. The reality probably came as the greatest surprise to the Luftwaffe and that operations were controlled by officers no longer accustomed to flying. Had the German leaders been passed more accurate intelligence on the power and potential of the RAF it is likely their strategy would have been different.

[3] A good example of a German reconnaissance photograph is held in the photographic archive of the National Monuments Record of Scotland showing North and South Queensferry. Taken in mid 1939, with intelligence added on 2 October, it clearly shows the naval shipping in the Firth of Forth which ultimately became targets for the Luftwaffe on 16 October.

[4] While the Luftwaffe had more aircraft available than the British, the advantage was considerably offset by the quality of the British defensive system (referred to as the 'Dowding System') and the German ignorance of it. The British defensive system consisted of a network of anti-aircraft guns and barrage balloons as well as RAF fighters. Using RDF and the Observer Corps, Fighter Command was more effective in defending Britain than the Luftwaffe was in attacking it. The Chief Operations Officer of Luftflotte III stated: 'Radar at least doubled the efficacy of their fighter force.' At that time Britain had the best system of aerial defence in the world and whilst the RAF knew they had to defend Britain the Luftwaffe had less clear objectives and failed to maintain a specific aim. During the Battle of Britain RAF Fighter Command fought an effective strategic battle using RDF and radio control, whilst the Luftflotten carried out heavy-weight attacks with little strategy. The superior numbers gave the Germans little advantage.

[5] The effectiveness of the Luftwaffe bomber force was reduced considerably by the abandonment of the development of the Heinkel He 177 early in 1937, brought about primarily by the intervention of Germany

in the Spanish Civil War where the effectiveness of tactical co-operation between air and ground forces had come to the fore. Had the Luftwaffe not opted to pursue development of the Ju88 dive bomber, the He177, a long-range four-engine heavy bomber, would have been able to deliver a far more devastating bomb load on targets well beyond the boundaries of Germany. The Luftwaffe never had such an aircraft during WWII, a significant point, preferring that all their bombers have a dive-bombing capability. As with the Junkers Ju87 'Stuka' the Ju88 was most effective whilst supporting ground forces as a dive bomber, but its effectiveness would have terminated when the German forces reached the Channel in 1940. When the Germans decided to attack our vulnerable trade routes the heaviest bomber they possessed was the He 111k, which was only a medium bomber. Had the He 177 been used on 16 October or during subsequent raids on Edinburgh it would not be unreasonable to assume the damage inflicted would have been far greater.

[6] The total number of bombs carried by all 12 bombers was only 24. At least one of which was to drop their lethal load on another target, further east in the estuary, to far greater effect than anything else achieved that day.

[7] It is has previously been thought that Richard's great, great, great, uncle was Lieutenant Colonel Sir William Hillary who, while living in the Isle of Man, founded the RNLI 116 years previously. He himself had been awarded the institution's Gold Medal for gallantry in saving more than 300 lives from shipwrecks off Douglas on the Isle of Man. Richard's father, Michael Hillary, later wrote to the RNLI to thank them for saving the life of his son. The letter was dated 10 September 1940:

> Dear Sir,
>
> I am told by my son Pilot Offier R. H. Hillary, who is now an inmate of the Margate Hospital, that he was rescued by the Margate Lifeboat and I want to express the heartfelt thanks of my wife and myself, to the coxswain and his crew for returning him to us.
>
> It would surely have afforded my ancestor, who founded the service, the liveliest satisfaction to know that his own kith and kin were numbered amongst those who have benefited by its wonderful work.
>
> Yours very truly
>
> Michael Hillary

In response the RNLI wrote back requesting more information about the Hillary family connection with the founder of the service, Sir William Hillary, and two months after receiving the letter Michael Hillary wrote to them once again:

13th December 1940

> Dear Sir,
>
> With further reference to your letter of the 13th September, I have made some enquiries but, owing to people having evacuated their homes and not having access to their papers, I have not been able to find out anything very definite.
>
> As far as I have been able to discover, my father is a descendant of Richard, a brother of Sir William Hillary, who was one of the three sons of William Hillary of Wensleydale, Yorkshire, so that Sir William Hillary would be my father's great-great-uncle. I hope this will be sufficient for your purpose.
>
> Thank you very much for sending me the literature of the RNLI. I enclose my cheque for a guinea and shall be glad if you will enrol me as an annual subscriber for that amount.
>
> Yours faithfully
>
> Michael Hillary
>
> PS. The name of my son who was rescued is Richard also.

Michael Hillary travelled to Margate to meet the crew, but as he arrived the boat was launched in response to an SOS call and they never met. He remained a member of the RNLI but had no further contact.

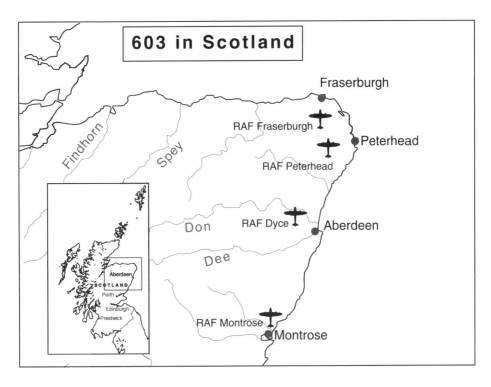

603 in Scotland

Fraserburgh

RAF Fraserburgh

Peterhead

RAF Peterhead

Findhorn

Spey

Don

RAF Dyce

Aberdeen

Dee

Aberdeen

SCOTLAND

Perth

Edinburgh

Prestwick

RAF Montrose

Montrose

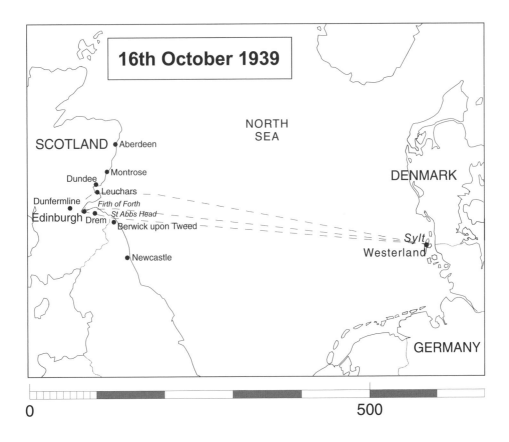

16th October 1939

NORTH
SEA

SCOTLAND ● Aberdeen

DENMARK

Dundee ● Montrose

● Leuchars

Dunfermline *Firth of Forth*

Edinburgh Drem *St Abbs Head*

Berwick upon Tweed

Sylt

Westerland

● Newcastle

GERMANY

0   500

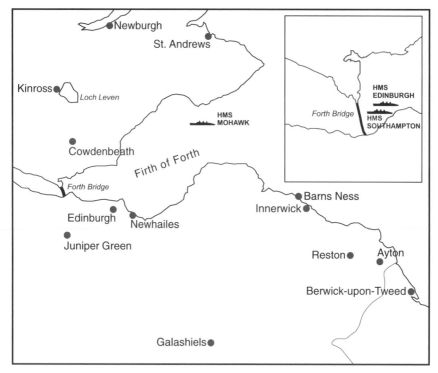

16th October 1939 - 13 Group Fighter Command

BIBLIOGRAPHY

NB: The following is not intended as a comprehensive bibliography of 603 Squadron which would occupy an excessive number of pages. It is intended to show the primary works on which the authors have drawn in their research and to acknowledge their debt to their authors as well as provide suggestions for further reading:

Anon. *Auxiliary Air Force*, Flight February 1922.

Anon. *Auxiliary Air Force Organisation*, Flight October 1924.

Anon. *Auxiliary Air Force*, *Air Estimates Etc*, Flight March 1924.

Anon. *Auxiliary Air Force* and *Air Force Reserve Bill*, Flight May 1924.

Anon. *Non-Regular Air Squadrons The Special Reserve and Auxiliary Air Force*, Flight January 1925.

John Alcorn, *Top Guns of the Battle of Britain*, Aeroplane September 1996.

Bruce Blanche, *The Auxiliaries of Auld Reekie*, RAF Yearbook 1999.

Bruce Blanche, *Edinburgh's Own – A History of 603 Squadron*, Flypast March 1987.

Bruce Blanche, *The Week-end Flyers*, Aeroplane August 1999.

Bruce Blanche, *Royal Air Force Turnhouse – A Brief History*, Unpublished manuscript 1995.

J.F. Bowyer, *Royal Auxiliary Air Force*. Scale Aircraft Modelling, Vol. 7 No.1, 1984.

A. Boyle, *Trenchard – Man of Vision*, Collins London 1962.

Henry Buckton, *The Birth of the Few*, Airlife 1998.

K Burrell, *603 Squadron Royal Auxiliary Air Force – Behind Closed Doors*. Houses and Interiors, Scotland. Issue 20, November 2001.

N & C Carter, *The DFC and How it was Won – 1918-1995*, Vols 1 & 2. Savannah Publications London 1998.

Winston Churchill, *History of World War II 'Their Finest Hour'*, Cassell.

Peter V. Clegg, *Flying Against the Elements*.

Brian Cull, Bruce Lander, Heinrich Weiss, *Twelve Days in May*, Grub Street 1995.

Sir Morris Dean, *The RAF and Two World Wars*, Cassell 1979.

K Delve, *The Source Book of the RAF*, Airlife 1994

James D. Ferguson, *The Story of Aberdeen Airport*, Scottish Airports. Glasgow 1984.

Norman Franks and Paul Richey *Fighter Pilot's Summer*, Grub Street 1993.

Norman Franks *Royal Air Force Fighter Command Losses of the Second World War, Volume 1 1939-1941*, Midland Publishing Ltd 1997.

J.J. Halley, *The Squadrons of the RAF and Commonwealth*, Air Britain 1980.

Richard Hillary, *The Last Enemy*, Macmillan 1942.

L. Hunt, *The Story of 603 Squadron*. Edinburgh Evening News and Dispatch, Series of three articles 5-8 April 1965.

L. Hunt, *Royal Auxiliary Air Force*. Airfix Magazine, March 1969.

L. Hunt, *Twenty-One Squadrons – A History of the Royal Auxiliary Air Force 1925-57*. Garnstone Press, London 1972.

L. Hunt, *Trenchard's Mechanical Yeomanry*, RAF Yearbook 1973.

J. L. Jack, *The Record of Service and Achievements of No. 603 (City of Edinburgh) Squadron, RAuxAF*. Private publication. 1979.

C.G. Jefford, *RAF Squadrons*, Airlife 1988.

Andrew Jeffrey, *This Present Emergency*, Mainstream Publishing 1992.

Andrew Jeffrey, *Who Drew First Blood*, Scots Magazine Vl 141 Oct 1994.

AVM Sandy Johnstone with Roderick Grant, *Where No Angels Dwell*, Jarrold 1969.

A. Scott Kennedy, *'Gin Ye Daur' – Edinburgh's Fighter Squadron in Peace and War in 603 City Of Edinburgh Fighter Squadron – A Record of some of its Achievements*, Scotsman 1943.

A. Lake, *Flying Units of the RAF*, Airlife 1999.

Eric Morgan and Edward Shacklady, *Spitfire, The History*, Key Books Ltd 1987.

P. Moyes, *Bomber Squadrons of the RAF and their Aircraft*, MacDonald Janes London 1976.

R.A. Nicholls, *The RAF's Auxiliaries*, Aircraft Illustrated 1980, Ian Allen.

D. Nimmo & G. Wake, *A History of RAF Turnhouse and Edinburgh Airport*, Airfield Review 1998.

Mick J. Prodger, *Luftwaffe vs RAF Flying Equipment of the Air War, 1939-45*, Schiffer 1998.

Mick J. Prodger, *Luftwaffe vs RAF Flying Clothing of the Air War, 1939-45*, Schiffer 1997.

RAF Benevolent Fund. *The History and War Service of the Pre-War Edinburgh Town Centre RAFVR.*

Winston G. Ramsey, *The Battle of Britain Then and Now,* After the Battle 1980.

Winston G. Ramsey, *The Blitz Then and Now*, After the Battle 1987.

J.D.R. Rawlings, *Fighter Squadrons of the RAF and their Aircraft*, Janes, London 1969.

B Robertson, *Spitfire – The Story of a Famous Fighter*, Harleyford Publications Ltd. 1960.

F.A. de V. Robertson, *No.603 (City of Edinburgh) Bomber Squadron AuxAF*, Flight September 1932.

A E Ross (Ed). *Through the Eyes of Blue – Personal Memories of the RAF from 1918,* Airlife 2002.

F.A. de V. Robertson, *Gauntlers Vs Harts*, Flight May 1935.

A.E. Ross, *75 Eventful Years – A Tribute to the RAF 1918-1993,* Wingham 1989.

A.E. Ross, *The Queen's Squadron*, Private 1989.

David Ross, *Richard Hillary*, Grub Street 2000.

David Ross, *Stapme*, Grub Street 2002.

Saga Magazine, January 2000.

Edward Shacklady *Hawker Hurricane*, Tempus 2000.

Chris Shores and Clive Williams, *Aces High*, Grub Street 1994.

D. J. Smith, *Military Airfields Scotland and North East and Northern Ireland. Action Stations No 7,* Patrick Stephens Ltd, Cambridge 1983.

I.G. Stott, *Edinburgh's Own – A History of No.603 Squadron, RAuxAF*, Air Pictorial August 1977.

C.R. Sutherland, *The Week-end Flyers*, The RAF Yearbook 1974.

Templewood, (Sir Samel Hoare), Viscount, *Empire of the Air – The Advent of the Air Age 1922-29,* Collins 1957.

O.G. Thetford, *No.603 (City of Edinburgh) Squadron – A Short History*, Air Reserve Gazette April 1948.

Sir H. Trenchard, *The Air Defence of Great Britain – Sir Hugh Trenchard's Adddress at Cambridge University*, Flight May 1925.

E.A.C. Wren, *The Part-Timers*, The RAF Yearbook 1977.

Ken Wynn, *The Men of the Battle of Britain*, CCB 2000.

J. Yoxal, *The Queens Squadron – A History of No.603 (City of Edinburgh) Squadron, RAuxAF*, Flight April/May 1954.

Other Sources

Air Historical Branch (RAF), Ministry of Defence – records of honours and awards, squadron histories, records of casualty records, Air Narrative Vol.II The Battle of Britain July-Oct 1940.

Public Record Office, Kew – RAF Fm 540 Operational Record Books – 603 (City of Edinburgh) Squadron 1925-1945.

RAF Museum, Hendon – Air 27/2079 – 2081 I-E and AIR 50/167 I-E (combat reports), 11 Group composite intelligence reports, flying log books, official documentation/legislation.

Commonwealth War Graves Commission, Maidenhead. War graves details.

National Library of Scotland – photographs, press cuttings, documents.

Edinburgh Central Library – press archives and reading room files: *Edinburgh Evening News, The Scotsman.*

Robert Vacha, articles in *Edinburgh Evening Despatch* 15, 16, 17 August 1960.

Times – obituaries

Daily Telegraph – obituaries

The recorded memories of:
Air Commodore R. Berry DSO, OBE, DFC*; Air Commodore C.A. Bouchier CBE, DFC; W.A.A. Read AFC; Air Commodore Brian Macnamara CBE, DSO; Air Vice Marshal F. David Scott-Malden CB, DSO, DFC.*

The flying log books of:
Group Captains Ivone Kirkpatrick and George Gilroy; Wing Commander Bill Douglas; Squadron Leaders Hyltie Murray-Philipson, Jim Morton, Jack Stokoe and Pat Gifford; Flight Lieutenant Keith Lawrence; Warrant Officer Allan Otto, Sergeant Ronald Plant and LAC T.E. Dickson.

Roger and Anne Gresham Cooke, *Your Uncles*, Private.

Horst Von Riesen, First Encounter, the story of 16 October 1939. Private. Translated from German.

603 (City of Edinburgh) Squadron: Historical archives – 603 Squadron Magazines 1933-1938, press cuttings – *Scotsman, Edinburgh Evening News*, Squadron photographs, flying log books, personal diaries/papers, press cuttings 1928- present.

The private collections (photographic and documentary) of David Ross and Bruce Blanche.

603 (City of Edinburgh) Squadron Association: Personal diaries/papers, Squadron photographs.

INDEX OF PERSONNEL

(Photo refs in italics. Refs apply to body of book only, not appendices.)

A

Adams, AC1 163, 220
Adams, S/L J.S.T. 33, 100
Adams, Ronald G.H. 181, 212
Albert, Prince 84
Allen, W/C 'Dizzy' 233
Allt, Dr 162
Arber, Sgt Ivor K. 133, 138, 164, 173, 182
Arnold, Feldwebel Ernst 203
Atcherley, AM Sir Richard 122

B

Bailey, Sgt George J. 'Bill' 138, *138*, 245, 252, 256, 257, 258, 259, 266, 270, 271, 273, 274, 278, 286
Baldero, F/O C.H.W. 11
Baldie, LAC *52, 57*, 163, 220, 221
Bamber, P/O L.L.W. 'Bambi' 34, 39
Bar, Feldwebel Heinz 225
Barkla, Hugh 63
Barnes, LAC J.H. 44, 93, *132*
Barthrop, W/C 'Paddy' 106
Barton, P/O J.E.A. 'Albert' 53, 107, 111, 114, 119, 120, 123, 124, 126
Barton, Mrs Monique 53
Bauer, Oberleutnant 223
Bean, P/O C.O. 101, 103
Beaverbrook, Lord 176, 244
Beer, Unteroffizier 166
Belford, Edward 6
Benson, P/O 82
Benson, Brian J.N. 138, 139, *139*, 140
Benson, Dr Joseph 138, 139, 192
Benson, Margaret 138, 139, *139*, 193
Benson, P/O Noel J.V. 'Broody' 82, 107, 109, *125, 132, 135,* 138, *138*, 139, *139*, 169, *169*, *171*, 174, 179, 186, 187, 190, 191, *192*, 193, 194, 203, 222, 267
Benson, Olive 'Daisy' 138, 139, 192
Berry, Mrs Nancy 178, 181, 239
Berry, A/C Ronald 'Razz' or 'Ras' 53, 91, 95, 99, *101*, 103, 106, 107, 109, 112, 114, 123, *125*, 132, *132*, 133, 140, *140*, 141, *141*, 142, 167, 169, 170, 172, 174, 178, 181, 182, 183, 186, *186*, 187, *187*, 188, 190, 194, 201, 203, 206, 207, 208, 212, 218, 219, *221*, 224, 225, 226, 227, 228, 233, 235, 239, 247, 251, 253, 256, 258, 259, 262, 265, 270, 271, 272, 273, 278, 283, 284, 288, 289, 290, 291, 292, 293, 294, 295, 299
Berry, Mr W. 140
Berry, Mrs W. 140
Binder, Leutnant Walter 214, 216, 219
Black, Dr. 73
Blackadder, F/L 126
Blackbourn, P/O W.L. 134, *186*, 224, 263, 264
Bode, Hauptmann Erich 231
Bolitho, S/L Hector 204
Bordoni-Bisleri, Sottotenente Franco 299
Bouchier, G/C Cecil A. 'Boy' 179, 212, 245, 285, 301

Boulter, F/O John C. 'Bolster' 51, 81, 85, *93*, 109, 119, 124, 126, *132*, 141, *141*, 172, 174, 186, 187, *191*, 195, 196, 201, 202, 205, 207, 212, *221*, 223, 224, 225, 233, 235, 239, 242, 247, 249, 255, 256, 258, 259, 260, 266, 270, 271, 273, 274, 278, 286, 287, 288, 293, 295, 298, 299, 302
Bowhill, Sir Frederick 82
Boyle, S/L D.A. 24
Boyle, Ella 65
Brand, AVM Sir Quintin 46
Braun, Leutnant 225
Brayton, Lily 122
Broadhurst, G/C Harry 126
Brooke-Popham, Air Marshal Sir Robert 14
Brown, S/L the Rev James Rossie 7, 10, *10*, 14, 23, 28, 33, *36,* 44, 50, 78, 86, 87, 92, 123, 124, 301
Brownlie, F/L 3, 4
Bruce, P/O A.H. *9*
Brucksch, Leutnant Heinrich 102
Buchanan, S/L the Rev W.B.C. 5, 10, *10*
Buesgen, Oberleutnant 287
Buffer, Petty Officer 78, 83
Burt, Sgt Alfred D. 142, *142*, 283, 284, 286, 287, 295, 304
Burt, Tom *52*
Burton, Mr 5

C

Caister, Sgt James R. 'Bill' *93*, 98, 99, 103, *105*, 107, 109, 111, 114, *115*, 117, *119*, 133, 134, 135, 142, 164, 168, 170, 173, 174, 178, *179*, 182, 185, 221, 224, 227, 230, 235, 239, 245, 259
Cameron, P/O Sorel *9*
Campanile, Sergente Maggiore F. 299
Campbell, Ian 'Micky' *29*
Cantley, Corp *132*
Carbury, P/O Brian J.G. 51, 52, 53, 84, 95, 103, 106, 109, 118, 132, *135*, 142, *142*, 143, *143*, 170, 171, 172, 183, 186, 187, 188, 195, 196, 197, 203, 205, 206, 207, 208, 209, 212, 214, 217, 218, 219, 220, 222, 224, 225, 227, 233, 235, 240, 243, 246, 249, 253, 259, 260, *263*, 274, 278, 280, 283, 284, 286, 287, 288, 290, 292, 300, 304, 305
Cardell, Elsie 143
Cardell, Harold 143, *144*
Cardell, Margaret 143, *144*
Cardell, P/O Philip M. 'Pip' 132, 143, *143*, 144, *144*, 156, 157, 158, 159, 160, 179, *183*, 210, 211, 222, 223, 227, 230, 247, 255, 258, 259, 262, 263, 264, 270, 274
Cardell, Teddy 143, *144*
Carey, F/L G.V. 14
Carnegie, G/C 118
Carroll, AC1 Arthur 'Artie' 52, *57*, 142, 163, 220
Carter, Mr 68
Cavalcanti, Alberto 90
Cescotti, Leutnant Roderich 254
Cessford, James 'Chic' 163

Chalmers Watson, W/C I.E. 28
Chamberlain, W/C 118
Chamberlain, Neville 89, 90
Champion, F/Sgt 23
Christie, Mr 14
Churchill, F/L Walter 102, 103
Churchill, Sir Winston 176, 188, 194, 244, 251, 265
Clark, James 69
Clydesdale, Marquis of 23
Cockell, Reg 163
Colbeck-Welch, AVM 'Ted' 28, 30, 33
Collins, Sir Edward 55
Colquhoun, P/O A.G.C. 131, 134, 164
Cozens, S/L H.I. 143
Craig, Alec 73
Crawshaw, Joe 212
Crespigny, AVM H.V. Champion de 134
Crooks, Jackie 163
Cross, Bombardier John 214, *214*, 215, 216
Cunningham, F/O J.Laurie G. 21, 25, *27*, 28, 44, 68, 84, 100, 101, 103, 106, 107, 109, 114, 116, 123, 134, 144, 145, 165, 169, *171*, 172, 182, 186, 187, 188, 193, 194, *198*, 200, 222
Cunningham, Mrs 68, 189

D
Dagenham, Mayor of 218
Dahmer, Unteroffizer Hugo 216
Dalhousie, Earl of 171, 172
Dalziel, W/O J.G. 53, *119*
Darling, Sgt Andrew S. 145, 270, 271, 273, 274, *275*, 278, 280, 283, 284, 288, 291, 293, 294, 295, 299
Darling, Lord Provost Will 79
Davie, Mrs 172
Davie, Betty 173
Davie, Rhoda 145
Davis, Sgt 210
Day, Albert *37*
Deere, S/L A. 'Al' 209, 210, 257
de Havilland, Olivia 79
Delg, F/O 203
Deller, Sgt Alan 241
Denholm, Mrs Betty (née Toombs) 39, 40, 103, 127, 137, *137*, 178
Denholm, Christine
Denholm, S/L George L. 'Uncle George' 18, *19*, 21, 23, *27*, 28, 30, *33, 35, 36*, 39, 40, 41, 43, 44, *44*, 47, 53, 54, *56*, 69, 70, 84, 85, 88, 95, 98, 99, 101, *101, 102*, 103, *104*, 108, 109, *111*, 111, 112, *115*, 119, *119*, 123, *126*, 127, 133, 134, 137, *137*, 146, 151, 156, 169, 173, 174, 179, 182, 186, 187, 189, 190, 191, *191*, 193, 194, 195, 197, 201, 202, 203, 204, 209, 222, 223, 224, 225, 226, 227, 230, 233, 240, 243, 245, 249, 250, 251, 253, 254, 256, 257, 258, 261, 262, 264, 265, 266, 270, 271, 273, 274, 275, 276, 278, 280, 283, 284, 285, 286, 287, 289, 291, 293, 295, 297, 298, 299, 300, 301, 304
Denholm, Jimmy 137
Denholm, Michael 137
Denholm, Minnie Scott (née Lovell) 137
Denholm, William Andrew 137
Devlin, 'Tommy' 163, *182*
Dewey, P/O Robert B. 145, 265, 270, 271, 272, 273, 286, 287, 288, 291
Dexter, P/O Peter G. 'Lizzie' 145, 146, 231, 245, 256, 258, 259, 262, 263, 264, 273, 274, *274*, 285
Dick, F/L Iain G.L. 21, 25, 28, *33*, 112

Dick, James 79
Dickinson, AC1 163, 220
Dickson, John E. 'Ernie' LAC 163, 220, *220*
Dickson, John 72, 90, 91
Dickson, John (Jnr) 72, 91
Dickson, Cpl Thomas F. 8
Dickson, William 72
Doensch, Major Fritz 168
Donaldson, John 72
Dorward, Charles 22, 23
F/O Douglas, William A. 'Bill' 39, 44, 45, 51, *111, 115*, 118, 119, 123, *123*, 124, 125
Douglas and Clydesdale, S/L The Marquis of 2
Douglas-Hamilton, S/L Lord David *16*, 107, 127
Douglas-Hamilton, G/C Lord Geordie 12, *13*, 16, *16*, 17, *20*, 22, 23, 24, *24*, 27, 28, 29, 174
Douglas-Hamilton, P/O Lord Malcolm 10, 12, *13, 16*
Dowding, ACM Sir Hugh 39, 47, 63, 64, 77, 82, 90, 100, 176, 178, 190, 195, 200, 201, 222, 223, 227, 251
Drummond, David 89

E
Eade, Sid 191
Ebeling, Oberleutnant Heinz 240
Eckersley-Maslin, S/L 30
Edsall, P/O 210
Edward VIII, H.M. The King 11, 12, 13, 21, 23, 164, 293
Elgin, Earl of 78
Elizabeth, H.M. The Queen Mother 25, 251
Elizabeth II, H.M. The Queen 189
Ellington, Air Chief Marshal Sir Edward 9, 14
Engledue, Lt Ralph 76
Esher, Viscount 12
Ettler, Feldwebel 249
Evers, Feldwebel Walter *209*

F
Farish, Alex 68
Farish, Brian 68
Farquhar, S/L Douglas 22, 58, 59, 77, 78, 83, 86
Ferguson, F/O Ian 58, 62, 78
Fielden, 'Mouse' 12
Fiske, P/O William M.L. 'Billy' 280
Fison, Sgt K. Wilfrid Y. 233
Fleming, W/C D.M. 'Don' 69, 103, 114
Fletcher, Captain 120
Fletcher, Cpl 5
Flynn, Errol 79
Flynn, Frank 80
Folt, Diana Mary 302
Ford, Sgt Maj 13
Forrest, AC1 163, 220
French, Dereck 142
Friendship, Sgt Basil 102
Fry, F/O L.J. 51
Fryer, Oberleutnant T. 301

G
Galland, Hauptmann Adolf 102, 216, 281
Gandar Dower, Eric 110
Garbo, Greta 118
Garden, F/L Thomas C. 21, 28, *33*, 43
Garvey, Sgt Leonard A. 276, 277
Gatheral, P/O G.H. 11, *13*
George V, H.M. King 7, 21
George VI, H.M. King 24, *24*, 25, 26, 27

Gibson, Cecil 68
Gifford, F/L Patrick 11, *13*, 26, *27*, 28, 29, *29*, 30, *33*, 34, *36, 38*, 44, *44, 51*, 53, 62, 69, 70, 71, 72, 73, *73*, 76, 77, 84, 86, 87, 88, 93, 95, 96, *96*, 98, *100*, 101, *101*, 102, 103, *129, 179*, 182
Gilbert, Sir Alfred 12
Gillam, F/L Denys 206
Gillies, Sgt Angus 'Angy' 30, 92, 98, *132*, 163, 179, 182, *182*, 220, 235
Gilroy, P/O George K. 'Sheep' *36*, 43, 44, 53, 69, 70, 71, 73, *83*, 84, 88, 95, 98, *105, 107*, 109, 111, *111*, 114, *115*, 116, 117, 119, *119*, 124, *126*, 127, *127, 128*, 133, 134, 135, 137, 145, *145, 146*, 164, 168, 170, 174, 178, *179*, 182, 186, 187, 189, 197, 199, 203, 206, 207, 212, 218, 222, 233, 245, 250, 257, 260, 270, 289, 291, 293, 294, 295, 297, 299, 300, 302, 303
Giuntella, Tenente Giulio Cesare 299
Gleave, S/L T .P. 'Tom' 203
Glenny, F/O J.E. *9*
Goertz, Feldwebel von 253
Goldsmith, P/O Claude W. 146, 231, 235, 270, 271, 273, 274, 283, 284, 286, 287, 291
Goodman, Sgt Geoffrey 220
Göring, Herman 60, 62, 244, 255
Gray, F/O Colin F. 181
Greenhouse-Allt, Patricia *128*, 162, 178, 217
Greenhouse-Allt, Vera 217
Gribble, Pilot Officer 225
Grillo, Sergente Maggiore G. 299

H
Hafer, Oberleutnant 209
Hagspiel, Gefreiter Arthur 296
Haig, F/O John G.E. 'Jack' 28, 40, 44, 48, 53, 107, 108, 109, 111, *111, 115*, 119, *119*, 121, *126*, 130, 146, *146*, 170, 178, 186, 190, 203, 205, 207, 212, 224, 225, 226, 235, 250, 256, 257, 258, 262, 270, 271, 273, 274, 278, 286, 287, 291, 293, 295, 299, 302, 304
Hall-Livingstone, J. 79
Hamilton, A/P/O/ C.E. 44, 93
Hamilton, Duke of 7, *16*
Hancock, F/L C.R. 13
Hanks, F/L 'Prosser' 160
Hansen, Sonny 61, 82, 83
Harkness, Andrew 72
Harkness, Sandy 72
Hartas, P/O Peter M. 146, 260, 270, 273, 274, 291
Harting, Feldwebel Wilhelm 235
Hehringlehner, Unteroffizier R. 132
Heidinger, Feldwebel O. 132
Heimbach, Gefreiter 166
Henderson, PC 57 James 71
Hesslewood, Cpl F.E. 267
Heur, Leutnant 169
Hielscher, Feldwebel Hans Georg 69, 72, 74
Higginson, Sgt F.W. 'Taffy' 220
Hillary, Michael 198

Hillary, P/O Richard H. 54, 90, 134, *134*, 140, 141, 143, 144, 145, 147, *147*, 153, 154, 155, 156, 158, 162, 163, 170, *171*, 172, 173, 174, 179, 186, 187, 190, 191, 195, 197, 198, 202, 203, 204, 205, 206, 207, 209, 210, 211, 212, 214, 221, 222, 223, 224, 225, 226, 227, 228, 230, 231, 232, *232*, 233, 255, 257, 258, 267, 270, 275, 299
Hirst, Geoffrey 217
Hitler, Adolf 67, 117, 147, 255, 256, 257, 261, 305

Hodge, F/L 96
Hodnett, John 215
Hoffmann, Feldwebel 231
Hollmann, Oberleutnant Ottmar 165
Holt, Diana 178
Hood, Mrs Jane 89
Horne, 2nd Lt Iain 46, 97, 305
Howes, P/O Peter 134, *147*, 147, 186, 203, 231, 245, 256, 257, 258
Huck, Leutnant 164
Hunter, P/O Graham C. *33*, 44, 51, 66, 78, 86, 100, 107, 112, 129, 132
Hurst, Sgt J. 'Johnnie' 304

J
Jack, P/O 3
S/L Jack, James L. *5, 9, 11*, 22, *27*, 44, *46*, 50, 51, 86, 87
Johnson, Sapper Albert B. 266, 267
Johnston, Tom 92
Johnstone, S/L Robert 'Bob ' 46, 58, 69
Johnstone, AVM 'Sandy' 22, 23, 58, 62
Jolly, Commander Richard 78
Jones-Williams, S/L 9
Joppien, Ben 197
Jury, Sgt R.D. 300

K
Kageneck, Oberleutnant von 93
Keary, G/C Charles R. 2, 121, 122, 124
Kennedy, A. Scott 2, 42, 87, 88
Kent, Duke of 8, 21
Kent, Marina Duchess of 8
Kerkhoff, Unteroffizier 164
Kerr, John 77, 83
Kesselring, Albert 200, 206, 222, 223, 226
Kipling, Rudyard 136
Kirkpatrick, G/C Ivone *8*, 10, *11, 13*, 23, *27*, 28, *36*, 44, 91, 101, 103, 109, 112
Kirkpatrick, Rev James 23
Kirkwood, F/L Mark 293, 294
Knox, George 162, 163
Kowalke, Unteroffizier Gottlieb 97
Kramer, Obergefreiter 69, 70, 73
Kunze, Oberleutnant Herbert 253

L
Lamb, Captain 77
Landry, Leutnant 187
Lawrence, P/O Keith A. 147, *147*, 228, *228*, 244, 245, 252, *252*, 256, 257, 258, 259, 270, 285, 291
Leathart, S/L James 225
Legg, F/L R.J. 11, *13*
Lehmkuhl, Kurt 97
Leigh-Mallory, AVM Trafford 46
Liedtke, Unteroffizier 166
Loidolt, Oberleutnant Johann 220
Lorenz, Oberleutnant 166
Londonderry, Marquis of 24
Lossberg, Major Victor von 166

M
Macdonald, F/O Donald K A. *11, 13*, 33, 39, 41, 42, *42*, 44, 127, 129, *148*, 148, 149, 150, *150*, 164, 165, 167, 168, 170, 187, *188*, 188, 189, 193, 194, 199, 200, 222, 249, 261, 268
Macdonald, F/O D.M.T. 12

Macdonald, Ewen *26*, 130, 149, 249, 250
Macdonald, Harold 148, 149, 189, 199
Macdonald, F/O Harold K 'Ken' 21, 25, 26, *26, 27,* 28, *35, 36,* 39, 40, *42,* 42, 43, 44, 62, 70, 71, 72, 76, 84, 87, *99, 100,* 101, 103, *104, 105, 107,* 109, 111, *111, 115,* 116, 118, *119, 127,* 129, *129,* 130, 137, 148, *148,* 149, *149,* 150, 164, 165, 168, 170, *179, 181,* 182, 186, 187, 189, 190, 193, 194, 197, 199, 202, 205, 206, 207, 209, 211, 212, 222, 223, 228, 230, 233, 235, 242, 248, 249, 250, 256, 257, 258, 259, 260, 262, 265, 266, 267, 268, *269,* 270, 272, 275, 287
Macdonald, Mrs May 148, 149, 200
Mackie, F/Sgt *132*
Mackay, Pupil Pilot R. 44, 93
Mackenzie, AC1 Alec 109, 142, 163
Mackenzie, AC1 John B.S. 'Tails' 163, 189, 305
Maclaren, George *29*
MacLean, Lt A.C.H. 120
MacLean, F/O Hector 120, 121, 124, 175
Macnamara, F/O Brian R. 150, *150,* 151, 155, 205, 212, *221,* 240, 247, 248, 249, 253, 258, 259, 262, 265, 278, 281, 283, 284, 286, 287, 288, 291, 294, 295, 299, 300
MacNeece-Foster, A/C 15, 18
MacPhail, P/O James F. J. 151, *151,* 155, 205, 246, *246,* 251, 252, 259, 260
Macpherson, F/L George 17
McFarlane, James 'Spanky' 163
McGowan, Peter 89
McIndoe, Sir Archibald 232
McIntyre, F/L D.F. 2
McKellar, F/O Archie 56, 57, 59, 62, 74, 75, 76, 86, 96, 98
McKelvie, S/L J.A. 2, 3, 5, 6, 7, *9,* 10
McKelvie, P/O Kenneth J. 2
McKenzie, P/O D.K.A. 'Ching' 51, *101,* 118, 119, 125, 127, *127, 128,* 182
McKerrow, Mary 145
McLaren, LAC G. 44, 93
McLean, P/O Hector 78
McLuskie, Joseph 80
McMahon, Adam 65
McMillan, Alexander 79
McNeil, F/L Thomas M. *6, 9, 11,* 14, 28
Maltby, G/C P.C. 14
Manlove, P/O R.G. 169
Marshall, Jim 66
Marsland, Freddy 163
Martel, Ludwik 151, *151,* 212, *221,* 231, 270, 273, 274, 278, 280, *280,* 284, 286, 287, 288, 289, 290, 293, 295
Matthews, P/O Henry K. F. *151,* 151, 271, 273, 274, 282, 291
Maxwell, Bill 65
Maxwell, P/O David A. 151, *151,* 294, 297, 300, 304
Maxwell-Woosnam, Denise 153, 178, 179, 255
Mazza, Tenente Guido 299
Melano, Sergente P. 299
Menzie, W/C 114
Mevlin, 'Olly' *29*
Middlehurst, 'Ben' *29*
Milch, Erhard 255
Millais, Sir John 162
Millar, Ian 19
Miller, F/L A.R.H 10
Milne, A.A. 168
Mitchell, F/O A. 11, *11*
Mollison, Jim 19
Money, F/L 3, 4

More, Herbert 71
Moreton Pinfold, F/L H. 34, 40, 44, 45, 48, 53, 82, 103
Morrison, Andrew 217
Morton, Anthony S.M. 151
Morton, Mrs Donna 151
Morton, Hannah 151
Morton, Dr Harold 151
Morton, P/O James S. 'Black' *33, 36, 38,* 39, 43, 44, *44,* 50, 52, 69, 70, 71, 73, 77, 78, 79, 80, 84, 88, 93, *94,* 95, 100, 109, 117, 118, *119,* 124, 150, 151, *151,* 152, *152,* 157, 165, 166, 167, 174, 179, *179,* 182, 186, 187, 193, 194, 197, 201, 203, 205, 206, 207, 211, 212, 214, 223, 224, 225, 226, 227, 233, 235, 240, 242, 244, 245, 250, 256, 257, 258, 259, 262, 265, 266, 271, 272, 275, 276, 278, 280, 282, 283
Morton, Jay 152
Morton, John R.C.M. 151
Morton, Marguerite 'Mardi' 39, 40, 41, 43, 109, 116, 118, 149, *149,* 150, 152, 164, 178, 248, 250, 275, 276
Mount, Robert 149
Mullay, George 163, *182, 208*
Muller, Oberfeldwebel Alfred 251
Muller, Oberfeldwebel Wilhelm 197
Müncheberg, Hauptmann Joachim 240
Murray, Cpl 132
Murray-Philipson, S/L Hylton *9,* 10, 11, *11,* 13, 15, 16, *46*
Murray-Philipson, Mrs 11, 16

N
Neilson, Mr A. 67
Neilson, Mrs A. 67
Newall, Sir Cyril 82
Newhall, AC James 3, *3*
Newman, P/O C.A.
Nicholson, Jack 90
Nicholson, F/O R.S. 125
Niehoff, Leutnant Rolf 96, 97, 98

O
Olver, P/O Peter 152, *152,* 289, 290, *290,* 291, 293, 295, 300
Orde, Cuthbert 141

P
Palmer, Joan 143
Park, AVM Keith 46, 176, 177, 178, 184, 185, 200, 206, 222, 227, 229, 251, 273, 303
Paton, Mr 9, 12
Pattullo, Pilot Officer B. 252
Pease, F/O A. Peter 42, 134, *134,* 150, 153, *153,* 154, 158, 170, *171,* 172, 174, 178, 179, 182, 187, 195, *195,* 197, 201, *201,* 203, 224, 227, 230, 240, 242, 243, 254, 255, 257, 274
Pease, P/O I.E. 34
Pease, Lady 153
Pease, Sir Richard 153
Peel, P/O Charles D 27, *35,* 44, 84, *93, 108,* 109, 114, 116, 121, 125, 126, 129, 153, *153,* 167, *167,* 182
Peel, Lt Col W.E. 153, 167
Pendergast, G.E. 216
Pfeifer, Unteroffizier 196
Pinckney, Brian 154, *154*
Pinckney, F/O Colin 42, 134, *134,* 150, 153, 154, *154,* 155, 158, *171,* 172, 174, 179, 190, 197, 198, 222, 255, 258, 262, 265, 266, 270, 283, 286, 287, 288, 293, 294, 295, 299, 300, 304
Pinckney, J.R. Hugh *154*

Pinkerton, F/L George 56, 57, 59, 62, 63, 74, 75, 76, 83, 84, 86, 101
Plant, Sgt Ronald E. 'Ron' 293, 295, 296, 297, *297*
Plant, Mr R.J. 298
Plischke, Unteroffizier 164
Pohle, Hauptmann Helmut 60, *60*, 61, 62, 63, 64, 65, 66, 67, 68, 69, 72, 74, 75, 76, 77, 83, 84, 91
Prefzger, Obegefreiter 165
Prentice, Chris 79
Prentice, W/O 'Snuffy' 17, *29*
Prentice, Mr 127
Price, Sgt R.B. 298, 303
Priebe, Oberleutnant Eckhart 206
Pringle, Bert 126, 163
Pritchard, LAC E.W. 44, 93
Probst, Obegefreiter 165
Prowse, P/O Harry A. R. 155, *155*, 288, 291, 293, 294, 295, 299
Pytlik, Oberleutnant R 301

Q
Quinnell, AC J.C. 27, 32

R
Rabe, Unteroffizier F. 132
Radcliffe, Lt General Sir P de B 13
Rafter, Sir Charles 155
Rafter, P/O Charles 300, 301
Rafter, Lady 155
Rafter, P/O William P. H. 'Robin' 151, 155, *155*, 205, 236, 237, 249, 300, 301
Rau, Oberleutnant Helmut 218, 219
Raw, Sgt 304
Read, Mrs Mary (nee Hellyer)
Read, P/O William A.A.'Bill' or 'Tannoy' 7, 132, 144, 155, 156, 157, 158, 159, 160, 167, 168, 170, *183*, 187, 195, 196, 197, 203, 206, 207, 214, 223, 224, 225, 242, 247, 251, 256, 257, 258, 259, 262, 265, 266, 270, 278, 280, 281, 283, 286, 287, 288, 291, 293, 294, 295, 300
Reid, F/O Colper 8, 17
Reid, F/L George A. *9, 11*, 14, *27, 47*, 116, *179*
Reilly, LAC Johnny 211
Reilly, Philip 8, 22
Reimann, Gefreiter Bruno 97
Reinhardt, F. 165
Rendall, John 22, 40, 131
Rennie, 'Pud' 52
Reynolds, AC1 A. 163
Ribbentrop, Joachim von 24
Richards, Mrs 143
Richthofen, Manfred von 181
Riesen, Leutnant Horst von 61, 69, 81
Rintoul, P/O A. *13*
Ritchie, AC1 163, 220
Ritchie, F/O Ian S. 'Woolly Bear' 27, *37,40*, 44, *44*, 50, 53, 66, *104*, 108, 109, *111, 112, 115, 119*, 124, *126*, 133, 134, 156, 166, 167, 168, 178, *179*, 182, 186, 187, 189, 190, 194, 222, 237, 250
Robertson, P/O Colin 'Robbie' *49*, 51, 52, 53, 54, 62, 70, 71, 72, 76, 77, 78, 79, 80, 84, 93, 95, 98, 101, 108, 109, 111, 114, *115*, 116, 117, 119, 131, 142, 162, 182
Robertson, George (father) 131
Robertson, George (brother) 131
Robertson, H. 79
Robertson, Maisie 131
Robertson, Richard 131

Robins, Lt 76
Roch, Leutnant Eckardt 230
Roebuck, Ordinary Seaman Bernard 91
Rohnke, Feldwebel Hugo 69
Rosier, ACM Sir Frederick 233
Ross, S/L 116
Ross, Sgt Harry 210, 211
Ross, LAC Harry 17, 40, 163
Roth, Feldwebel 282
Roth, Gefreiter Heinz-Werner 102
Rowlatt, C.J. 153
Rushmer, F/L Frederick W 'Rusty' 23, *27*, 28, 44, 81, 85, 99, 100, 106, 107, 109, 112, 116, 121, 123, *132*, 134, *135*, 145, 156, 156, 157, *157*, 159, 165, 169, *169*, 170, *171*, 174, 176, *176*, 178, 186, 190, 195, 197, *197, 213*, 214, 222, 223, 225, 226, 227, 236
Ruttkowski, Leutnant Gunther 225

S
Salmond, Air Marshal Sir John 13
Sanderson, Arthur 2, *132*
Sarre, Sgt Alfred R. 'Joey' 132, 144, 156, 157, *157*, 158, 159, 160, *183*, 190, 195, 201, 202, 203, 222, 235, 240, 241, 243, 248, 294
Satchell, S/L W.A. 'Jack' 126, 127
Satchell, Mrs 126, 127
Saul, AVM Richard 46, 58, 77, 82, 92, 118, 126
Scarlett, F/O 6
Scarret, AC2 R.H. 28
Schersand, Unteroffizer 252
Schild, Gefreiter 253
Schleicher, Gefreiter August 91, 92, *92*
Schmid, Major Beppo 62
Schneider, Oberleutnant Walter, 266
Schoepfel, Hauptmann Gerhard 241
Schottle, Feldwebel Otto 191
Scott, S/L 116
Scott-Malden, Francis D. S. 'Scottie' 157, *157*, 158, 212, *221*, 283, *283*, 284, 286, 287, *287*, 288, 291, 299, 300, 303
Seefried, Leutnant Hugo 298
Seydel, Unteroffizier Kurt 91, 92, *92*
Shephard, Earnest 190
Shepherd, LAC J.D. 44, 93
Shewell, F/O J.M. 28
Shields, F/O Iain D. 7, 10, *11*, 17, 28, 137
Shiells, P/O J.T.L. 5, 6
Sholto Douglas, AM 233
Simpson, James 2
Simpson, John 204
Skinner, Jim 22, 163, 235
Skokan, Unteroffizier 164
Slocombe, Arthur *143*
Smith, Bill 163
Smith, F/L Cairns 63
Smith, S/L Forgrave M. 'Hiram' 123
Smith, P/O J. 44
Smith, G/C W.G.G. Duncan 233
Soden, P/O John F. 158, 249, 256, 257, 258, 266, 270, 271, 273, 278, 286, 287, 288, 289, 290
Somerville, P/O J.A.B.'Hamish' 7, 25, 26, *27*, 28, *33, 35, 36*, 41, 44, 50, *51*, 52, 99, 182
Somerville, LAC James 4
Sozzi, Maresciallo Felice 299
Squire, Sgt 304, 304
Stair, Right Honourable The Earl of 10, 12, 28, 32

Stapleton, AVM Deryck C. 158, *158*, 241
Stapleton, S/L B Gerald, 'Stapme' 53, 83, 107, 108, 109, 112, 114, 124, *125,* 126, 132, 141, 146, 151, 158, *158,* 159, 169, *171*, 172, 181, 182, 190, 195, 196, 197, 199, 206, 207, 210, 212, 214, 219, 220, *221*, 224, 225, 230, 231, 235, 236, 237, 239, 240, 241, 242, 243, 246, 247, 252, 253, 255, 256, 257, 258, 259, 260, 265, 266, 270, 271, 273, 274, 283, 284, 286, 287, 288, 289, 292, 293, 294, 295, 299
Stapleton, Joan (née Cox) 158, 178, 181, 239
Stapleton, John Rouse 158
Steele, Lord Provost Sir Henry 79, 88, 90, 92
Stevens, G/C Ernest H. 'Count' *9*, 10, *11*, 14, *18, 20, 27,* 28, 29, 32, 33, 35, 38, 44, *44*, 46, 52, 76, 99, 100, 103, 109, *111*, 114, 117, 118, *119*, 124, 126, 127, 129, 134, 137, 169, 235, 271
Stevenson, Barbara 73
Stevenson, P.C. Henry 'Harry' 73
Stewart-Clark, P/O Dudley 124, 133, 135, 159, *159*, 165, 166, 170, 182, 221, 223, 225, 227, 230, 231, 250
Stokoe, Evelyn 178
Stokoe, Sgt 'Jack' 'Doggie' 132, 144, 156, 157, 158, 159, *159,* 160, *160*, 170, 178, 179, *183*, 197, 198, 203, 206, 207, 209, 210, 211, 212, 214, 216, 219, 223, 224, 225, 227, 228, 239, 290, 291, 293, 294, 295, 300, 304
Stone, Sgt 302
Strawson, Sgt John M. 161, 275, *275*, 276, 278, 281, 282, *282*, 284, 285, 288, 300, 302, 304
Strawson, Lois Elizabeth 161, 284
Strawson, William Henry 161, 281
Struthers, 'Jock' *29*
Stone, P/O Norman 298
Storp, Leutnant Hans Sigmund 60, *60*, 61, 62, 63, 64, 66, 67, 69, 70, 71, 72, 73, 74, 83, 85, 90, 91
Stumpff, Generaloberst Hans-Jurgen 167

T
Tedder, Marshal of the Royal Air Force Sir Arthur 289
Terry, P/O Patrick H. R. R. 161, 291, 293
Thompson, P/O G.I. 108, 119
Thompson, F/O K.T. 33
Thompson, Sgt W.W. 107, 109, 117, 118
Thomson, F/O G.A.G. *27*, 28, 109, 182
Thomson, Joseph 71
Thomson, Sgt R. 300
Thorl, Leutnant Helmut 225
Tidd, S/L 116
Townsend, S/L Peter 206, 207
Townson, W/C S.E. 13
Trenchard, Marshal of the Royal Air Force Lord 3, 9, 42, 45, *46*
Tyson, S/L Frank H. 26, 28, 34

U
Udet, Ernst 255
Urie, F/L Dunlop 77
Usher, P/O 6

V
Victoria, H.M. Queen 84
Vosilla, Maggiore F. 299

W
Waitt, F/L Tommy 'Tiger' 58, 62
Wallace, P/O Alen 'Shag' 7, *9, 11, 13,* 52, 53, 99, 103, 109, 114, *119*, 120, 248

Wallace, Eltider 178
Walmsley, Air Marshal Sir Hugh P. 7, *9,* 10, 11, 13
Walz, Unteroffizier 165
Waterston, James S. 161
Waterston, Jean 92, 162
Waterston John L. 161
Waterston, Mabel 161
Waterston, Phillip B. 161
Waterston, P/O Robin McG. 'Bubble' 25, *25*, 26, *27*, 28, *33*, 44, *47,* 53, 92, *105,* 108, *108*, 114, 116, 124, *125, 128,* 134, 159, 161, *161*, 162, *162*, 163, 169, 170, 172, 176, *176,* 182, 186, 188, 190, 191, *191*, 203, 205, 207, 210, 211, 212, 214, 215, 216, 217, 221, 222
Watson, Dr. Chalmers 122
Watson, David 63
Watson, F/L. I.E.Chalmers *9*, 116, 122
Watson, F/L W. *11*
Watt, Watson *59*
Watts, F/O *7, 27*
Webb, AC 145
Webb, P/O Paul 56, 57, 74
Webber, Sgt 304
Wells, H.G. 88
Werra, Oberleutnant Franz von 83, 236, *236*, 237
Weymar, Gefreiter 253
Wieczoreck, Unteroffizier P. 132
Wien, Unteroffizier 253
Wilkinson, Sgt 'Wilkie' 102
Wilson, Sgt 304
Wilson, Bob 163, 182, *182*
Wilson, 'Tug' 163
Winkler, F/L 3, 4
Winskill, A/C Sir Archie L. 163, *163*, 288, 289, 293, 295, 297, 299, 300
Wood, S/L 114, 118
Woosnam, Max 153
Worthington, J. AC1 163, 220
Wright, Jack 211
Wynne-Powell, F/O G.T. 'Wimpy' *27*, 28, *33*, 44, 81, 85, 101, *101*, 103, 106, 112, 123, 124, *125*, 132

Y
York, Duke of 21
York, Duchess of 21
Young, F/L David 116
Young, W/C John R.C. 52, 53, 98, 99, 100, 106, 107, 108, 110, 112, *112*, 119, 122, 123, 124, 142, 167
Young, Cpl R.B. 8
Young, William H. 7